Sourcebook on
the New Immigration

Sourcebook on The New Immigration

Inplications For The United States and The International Community

Edited by
ROY SIMÓN BRYCE-LAPORTE

Assisted by
Delores M. Mortimer
Stephen R. Couch

Transaction Books
New Brunswick, New Jersey

Library of Congress Catalog Number: 78-64477
ISBN: 0-87855-305-3 (cloth)
Printed in the United States of America

Library of Congress Cataloging in Publication Data

Main entry under title:

Sourcebook on the new immigration.

   Includes bibliographical references and index.
    1. Minorities—United States.   2. United States—Emigration and immigration.   3. Emigration and immigration. I. Bryce-Laporte, Roy S. II. Mortimer, Delores M. III. Couch, Stephen R.
E184.A1S68   301.32'973   78-64477
ISBN 0-87855-305-3

CONTENTS

DEDICATION

To Camila Roxanne, Robertino, and René Bryce-Laporte, Nathan Franklin Couch, Jeri Anice Dyson, Dominique Filostrat, and their generation, with hopes that theirs will be a better, more equal, and enjoyable world, where people will be better able to migrate and resettle, or do neither, based on freedom of choice rather than constraints of economics and politics. Obviously, for that kind of world they will have to be prepared to struggle, to share, and to make sacrifices.

FOREWORD[1]

S. Dillon Ripley

This volume, in a sense, is the culmination of ten years' activities preparing for the year 1976, a symbolic moment in our history. The future of this institution and of the country during the next hundred years is really what is presaged by this book. The future is what we look forward to with continued dedication to the aspirations, the moral and ethical hopes on which this country was founded. We must have the conviction that humankind will continue to find in this country some of the dreams and aspirations which those who preceded us expected two hundred years ago. If we do not—if we as people do not find it—then we have only ourselves to blame. And, it will not be because of a lack of honest inquiry and convinced idealism on the part of many, many people in the United States.

I continue to find surcease, myself, in the feeling that this country is the greatest country in the world and that it has the most promise for the future. I continue to find myself upheld in my own conviction by things that happen almost every day, and by people whom I meet almost every day—they give me a sense of renewal and of renewed faith.

We must have a sense of rededication in this country and we do and will express it in our plans and aspirations for the future. And, in doing so we will be no more than living out our natural heritage and our expectations for this great country of ours.

The Smithsonian is seen in the public image as a museum and, therefore, a treasure house of the dead. It is by no means a sepulcher. In the National Gallery we have had a recent celebration of mortuary rites; for example, the King Tutankhamun Exhibit which, once again, demonstrated the inordinate human fascination with the problems, attitudes, aspects, and artifacts of death. We have this in this country but no more than in many other parts of the world. We have our Forest Lawns everywhere in this country. But, the point is that the Smithsonian is not a mortuary. Indeed, we have celebrated these past ten seasons with extraordinary activity in our folk festivals on the mall, in which RIIES played an active advisory role. These festivals have been a triumph for presentation and rediscovery. I am delighted to be able to join with you in expressing my hopes for the Smithsonian of the future and that there will be more and more consideration of the kinds of issues that are presented together in this volume.

Certainly it is fitting that the Smithsonian is involved in fostering consideration and reflection on immigration, a process which continues, and thus alive and ongoing. As in the past, people still come to this land in search of a better life, bringing with them their skills, aspirations, hopes and fears, and presenting this country with new challenges and contributions. United as a breed of people motivated by the natural desire to find the ''good life,'' and willing to sacrifice primary allegiance to their land of birth, many have stopped their wanderings here. I am very pleased that the Smithsonian is actively engaged in working to understand this phenomenon and to spread that understanding to as many people as possible.

I congratulate Dr. Bryce-Laporte, the staff of the Research Institute on Immigration and Ethnic Studies, and the contributors to this groundbreaking collection on the new immigration.

NOTE

[1]This Foreword has been extracted and modified from a transcript of remarks made by Secretary Ripley at the opening of the conference on ''The New Immigration,'' which was the first major conference on this subject, sponsored by the Research Institute on Immigration and Ethnic Studies, Smithsonian Institution, November 15–17, 1976, in Washington, D.C.

I invite you to become more engaged in the understanding of this increasingly important phenomenon which now has been escalated to become one of the critical issues of the day. I hope that you may find within the pages of this scholarly collection, those insights and information which would enhance that understanding as well as facilitate decisions on the problems and prospects which the new immigrants present.

PREFACE

Beginning with de Toqueville's early impressions of this country and terminating with his own, John F. Kennedy characterized the United States as a nation of nations, more specifically a nation of immigrants. Himself a second generation American of Irish descent, he observed, even after granting some exception to the Amerindian population, that all other resident groups of this country are in themselves immigrants or descendants of immigrants. But, it may be added, since the origin of the Amerindian, or Native American, population is indeed Asian, no matter how long ago, technically all residents of this country are immigrants or descendants of immigrants.

It is quite befitting then that the themes of immigration and ethnicity were ubiquitous in the activities conducted by the Smithsonian Institution in its observance of the Bicentennial of the American Revolution. The prominence of the themes not only reminds us that the Institution itself owes its beginning to the donation of wealth of an Englishman, but that this country as well, because it is still young and growing, also owes its continued formation, economic development, ethnic and cultural cosmopolitization, and its international status to the labor and lives of peoples from other parts of the world.

Within this context the worldwide success and impact of Alex Haley's *Roots* is much more than the consequence of ingenious promotional salesmanship or racial idiosyncrasies of the work and its author. *Roots* is not simply the story of the origin, emergence, and experience of one black family in its saga from Africa to America and the struggles of its race from slavery to citizenship. Rather, it is the story of the people of the United States most of whose origin begin outside the country. Moreover, it is the story of peoples from many parts of the world whose relatives have followed and continued to follow various routes into the United States, or to other countries or parts of countries similarly situated or perceived.

To paraphrase Oscar Handlin, the history of the United States is a history of immigration and even though immigration is directed to many other countries in the world, particularly of this hemisphere, perhaps no other nation has absorbed so many immigrants in its space as this one. Though often conceived as massive, discrete waves of foreigners entering into the country, it is also true of immigration into the United States that it has never really ceased to occur. The condition, magnitude, characteristics, and origin of immigrants in each wave, however, tend to be different. Such differences are generally neither capricious, mechanistic, or inconsequential even though there are times when immigration is ignored as a public issue.

Today we are witnessing the newest wave of immigrants. The characterization of this wave as new is appropriate for reasons beyond its discretion and its recency into the United States. The new immigrants do not comprise a simple extension of those who preceded them, though some may have had family ties or bonds of friendship and familiarity with persons in the United States. Usually, they are not from the same countries or continents as the immigrants of older waves, but even if they are they tend to represent a decrease either in proportion or number compared with those who preceded them from the old country. Although in some cases some continuity is visible and operative, the new immigrants represent a distinctive configuration of nationalities or ethnic types, legal statuses, and even occupations, and sex or age ratios. And the circumstances of their departure from their homeland, their arrival, and reception in this country are also different, even though there are perhaps some underlying linkages and some likely processes which they will share with other immigrant groups of previous movements.

More specifically, the new immigration is marked by a significant number of so-called illegals, refugees, and women. It has a large non-European (for example, Asian, Caribbean, and Latin American) component and, therefore, is extremely visible. These alien newcomers share greater akinness with the traditional American minorities than the older immigrant groups or the old stock

American majority. Their presence is felt in significant ways in the continental United States as well as the outlying states and territories. Some of the latter themselves contribute massive outflows of native emigrants or serve as conduits for substantial numbers of legal and illegal foreign immigrants en route to the mainland. Finally, compared with its predecessors, this new wave of immigrants is not a simple response of foreign people to the attractiveness, opportunity, or refuge represented by the United States. There is strong suggestion that it also responds to needs of the present stage of certain developments in the American economy and to dominant political roles and aggressive economic policies of the United States in these particular areas of origin.

The mark-off date for all these changes was circa 1965—the year of the passing of the latest and most comprehensive immigration bill since the McCarran-Walter Act of 1952. The new bill is a radical departure from its predecessors which were explicitly exclusionary, selective, and racist in fashion. It was evidently an outgrowth of the thought and influence—a legislative legacy—of the late President Kennedy. But the period of the 1960s was marked by many other efforts to redress inequality, internationally and nationally: the emergence of many new independent nations; intense revolutionary struggles within the Third World; the felt insufficiency of the first significant civil rights victories followed by urban and ethnic revolts; mobilization of the poor; radical student movement and anti-Vietnam protest; and massive but ambivalent reactions by the U.S. government and reactionary white backlash to the demands by minorities for change in the *status quo*.

The new American law expressed some of the egalitarian demands of the period, and the new immigration pattern soon indicated that it was to become as much an adjustment to meet new political-economic needs of the U.S. and similarly situated countries as it was to be a safety valve for immigrants hard-pressed by limited opportunity in their home economies. In some ways, then, while the new bill as advertently intended as a sympathetic effort toward equalization of opportunity for individual aliens and to open doors to emigrés from all countries, the overwhelming response, including the volumes of illegals and non-immigrants, indicated the extent to which structural inequality existed among and within nations. Hence the new immigration suggests new levels of international problems to be resolved, but on the domestic level it reminds us that there are basic economic practices, structural arrangements, and deeply entrenched fears and prejudices toward visible strangers which have not been overcome.

Even during the 1960s, immigration was treated as a subject of the past and, thus, the pasttime for historians. Despite the early rootings which the social sciences may have had in the study of immigrants, the cities in which they settled, the cultural changes they contributed, and the adjustments which they underwent, the concern with immigration among these fields of study had been, for most purposes, abdicated (even within the field of human demography). One consequence of this is the absence of reliable quantitative data or sophisticated methodology and tools for analyzing the earlier stages of present immigration. It is now apparent, however, to all concerned that the United States is gathering new roots and branches and the world is experiencing a new immigration. An alert, creative, modern social science can still try to help us discern from where, with what, and why the new immigrants are coming, where and why do they settle (when they do), and how well (or badly) they are doing. There is no reason for us to stare in shock or in wishful hope that we could live to read the historians of the next century tell how deep the roots have gone, how far the branches have stretched, or how well (badly) their fruits have done.

Already the new immigration has become the latest issue, only second to the Vietnam War, in depicting the intimate ties between domestic and foreign policy. It is unfortunate, in the absence of a sophisticated theory, methodology, and set of data, that the determination of such policies are left in the hands of special interest groups and pressured public officials. Neither debate nor demand, neither chauvinism nor charity contains the fuller answer to the challenges of the new immigration. It presents a clear need for serious, grounded academic input and a clear challenge for a new and broader perspective to deal with phenomena that go beyond national interests to become worldwide issues, and to appreciate the interlink between structural conditions and individual motives and behavior of the new immigrants.

In addition to its foreword, preface and afterword, this volume contains forty-three essays plus two appendixes. The principal contributors are almost totally comprised of academic scholars; the commentators include public officials as well. The main essays are modified versions of a conference held by the Research Institute on Immigration and Ethnic Studies (RIIES) as one of the Smithsonian Institution's observances of the Bicentennial of the American Revolution. Intended to be the first major scholarly conference on the subject of the new immigration, a purposeful effort was made to obtain the thoughts of scholars from across and outside the country who had attained expertise and experience in the study of new immigrants or clearly related problems. Committed to a view of immigration as an international phenomenon, as well as a social process, RIIES organized sessions to accommodate not only theoretical, methodological, and contextual problems, but allowed for concentration on the implications of scholarly findings for recipient societies, host societies, and the immigrants themselves, and also provided some opportunity therein for comparison by including essays on non-U.S. and also noncontinental U.S. situations.

For purposes of this volume, the order of presentation of the essays begins with a section which attempts to put U.S. immigration patterns and policy into a historical context and ends with a chapter on theoretical and methodological considerations. The intervening chapters move from development implications for sending countries to various levels of implications for host societies and the immigrants themselves. Within the latter groupings there are more specified subdivisions such as diplomatic, political, occupational, and public service concerns of the established segments or sectors of the host society as distinguished from the concerns which relate to the native minorities. Again, in the case of adjustment implications for the immigrants themselves, papers are grouped to deal with various reports on adaptations as distinct from examples of inter- and intra-ethnic conflicts among the immigrants.

In the Afterword, two efforts are made by RIIES personnel to review and reflect on the contents and message of the formal papers. The set of appendices which follow include proceedings of two public panels held at the conference and a background commentary by another member of our staff. In addition, the Institute has prepared for separate distribution a Supplement which includes transcripts of commentaries, discussions and presentations not included in this Sourcebook, and a statement on background information. Readers are urged to give special attention to the Supplement—where many novel, spontaneous critical and useful points are contained. The background commentary summarizes the development of the conference and activities which led to this volume. We think such information provide basis for our felt pleasure regarding most of the activities and the final outcome of the original idea, especially given the limitations with which we at the Research Institute on Immigration and Ethnic Studies have been called upon to operate since our recent inception in 1974.

We think the aforementioned provide support for our felt pleasure regarding most of the activities and the final outcome of the original idea, especially given the limitations with which we at the Research Institute on Immigration and Ethnic Studies have been called upon to operate since our recent inception in 1973.

It is pointless to presume our product to be errorless. The dynamic nature of social phenomena and the concomitant subjectivity which influences its study negate such possibilities. This is particularly true in cases, such as the new immigration, which are characterized by their contemporaneity, complexity, and saliency. We are even more aware that there are areas of omission or, more precisely, insufficient commission among the topics which could have been covered in this volume.

We acknowledge the limitations of the volume, many of which are inherent in the compiling of any compendium of this scale. However, we hasten to point out that many of these areas require a rededication of interest on the part of scholars, and the availability of avenues through which their works can receive the attention of their colleagues, public officials, and an interested readership, such as we have attempted to provide via this work.

Roy Simón Bryce-Laporte, Ph.D.

ACKNOWLEDGEMENTS

Given the dedication of the Research Institute on Immigration and Ethnic Studies to research, dissemination, stimulation, and facilitation of multidisciplinary study, and consultation services on the broad range of knowledge of contemporary immigration to the United States, its limited size and resources, and the recency of its founding, RIIES has found it necessary to utilize the assistance of individuals and institutions beyond its confines in order to achieve its goals. This has been particularly true with reference to its complex of bicentennial activities. (See Supplement.)

While the Institute reiterates, at this point, our deep appreciation to all those who may have assisted us in any way in the pursuit of the bicentennial activities, including the conference from which this volume was born, there are particular institutions, units within the Smithsonian Institution, and individuals whom I would like to acknowledge personally for their direct or indirect contributions to the completion of this volume. In this regard we thank Susan Hamilton, who, in her capacity as coordinator of the Smithsonian Institution's bicentennial projects, exercised the discretion that facilitated the initial outlay of funds to finance the project and the employment of a staff to help us execute it.

Further, we express special appreciation to the Ford Foundation, the Rockefeller Foundation, the German Marshall Fund, the Offices of the Secretary and the Treasurer of the Smithsonian Institution, particularly Jon Yellin and Andy McCoy, for the provision of supplementary funds to carry out the project.

Similarly, we appreciate the interventions in our behalf by the Offices of the Assistant Secretary for Science and the Director of the Museum of Natural History, including Catherine Kerby and Sherrill Berger of the staff of the Center for the Study of "Man." A special acknowledgement is merited by the Supply Division for their assistance in matters having to do with contracts and duplication services, and the American Folklife Program for the use of their recording equipment without which our progress would have been seriously impaired. We extend our special gratitude to Blanchard White, who provided us with personal assistance and advice, and to Carmen Hilda Allende, Joyce Justus, and Elizabeth Payne, who volunteered their services in different stages of the project.

I must acknowledge a very special and deep-felt appreciation to the staff of RIIES, more specifically to Delores M. Mortimer into whose hands fell the Spartan task of primary responsibility for coordinating the conference and the editing of this manuscript; Stephen Couch for his crucial support, demonstrated discipline, and editorial assistance; Betty Dyson for her consistent patience, continual loyalty, and various levels of contributions; Mary Jane E. Kubler for her versatile assistance and spontaneous injection of urgency and relaxation when needed and last, but most definitely not least, to Constance Trombley, whose tact, patience, ingenuity, and dedication have been the critical factors in making this volume the reality that it finally has become. My utmost appreciation goes out as well to David Harris (a former staff member of RIIES), Georgia Moen, Sonya Reed, Vera Wells, and Katherine Williams for the specific and valuable technical contributions each made in the final stages of preparing the volume for publication.

Dorotea Lowe Bryce and Simon J. Bryce deserve special mention here, insofar as they are the two surviving persons with whom I have shared the most significant periods of my life to date. As fellow immigrants and family, I hope they can identify particularly with this book.

And, finally, I would like to acknowledge those friends and relatives who cannot be enumerated here but to whom I am grateful for their explicit and tacit support. Special thanks go to the contributors of this volume for their patience, cooperation, and substantive input to its realization.

I hope that all the aforementioned find adequate reasons to be proud of this work. However, with the contributors, I assume primary responsibility for any shortcomings or controversies therein contained.

Accordingly, the positions expressed in the forthcoming pages in no way represent the official position of the Smithsonian Institution or the staff of RIIES, and should not be regarded as such.

Sourcebook On The New Immigration

Part 1

Contextual Considerations: United States Immigration and Policy

VOLUME AND COMPOSITION OF UNITED STATES
IMMIGRATION AND EMIGRATION

Robert Warren

INTRODUCTION

The present immigration policy of the United States is directed toward reuniting the families of immigrants, continuing the tradition of accepting refugees from troubled areas of the world, and providing the opportunity for limited numbers of people from all countries to migrate to the United States. During the past fifteen years, important changes have occurred in national immigration trends. In addition, issues concerning illegal immigration, emigration of citizens and aliens, the admission of Cuban and Vietnamese refugees, and the contribution of immigration to U.S. population growth have focused increased attention on the flow of migrants to and from the United States. At the same time, it has become increasingly evident that serious gaps exist in our information about the volume of immigration and emigration and the social and economic characteristics of the migrants. The purpose of this paper is to give an overview of recent trends in immigration and emigration and to examine some major deficiencies in the underlying data.

Most of the information about immigration to the United States comes from the annual reports of the Immigration and Naturalization Service and the decennial census of population.[1] The annual report of the Immigration and Naturalization Service provides data on alien immigration, including age, sex, country of origin, and state of intended residence. Statistics are shown for aliens living in the United States (who are required to register each year) and for aliens who become citizens each year. The decennial census provides data on the social and economic characteristics of the foreign-born population by year of immigration and country of birth. The following discussion is based on data from these two sources.

ALIENS ADMITTED FOR PERMANENT RESIDENCE

Millions of persons enter and leave the United States each year. Most of these are visitors from other countries or tourists going abroad for short periods of time; many are U.S. citizens not subject to our immigration laws.[2] Since national immigration policy does not affect U.S. citizens or temporary visitors, the discussion of immigration in this paper will be largely concerned with alien immigration and emigration. Aliens entering the United States illegally are not included in this analysis because no reliable data are available on the size, rate of growth, or demographic characteristics of the illegal alien population. This methodological problem is discussed in a later section of this paper.

Immigrants admitted, 1960 to 1975

The total number of aliens admitted annually for permanent residence in the United States has increased gradually from under 300,000 during the 1960–65 period to about 400,000 during the past four years. The numbers are shown in Table 1.

1974 - 1975	386,194
1973 - 1974	394,861
1972 - 1973	400,063
1971 - 1972	384,685
1970 - 1971	370,478
1969 - 1970	373,326
1968 - 1969	358,579 [3]
1967 - 1968	454,448
1966 - 1967	361,972
1965 - 1966	323,040
1964 - 1965	296,697
1963 - 1964	292,248
1962 - 1963	306,260
1961 - 1962	283,763
1960 - 1961	271,344
1959 - 1960	265,398

TABLE 1
Aliens Admitted for Permanent Residence,
July-June 30, 1960-75

The increase in the level of alien immigration during the past fifteen years has not been due to increased quotas but rather to increases in the immigration of aliens not subject to numerical limitations. Before the Immigration Act of 1965 went into effect, the quota for countries outside the Western Hemisphere was about 150,000 per year, but only about 100,000 quota immigrants were admitted annually from 1960 to 1965.[4] The number of immigrants in categories exempt from numerical limitations (for example, natives of Western Hemisphere countries and immediate relatives of U.S. citizens) increased gradually during the period.

After all of the provisions of the Act of 1965 went into effect, the worldwide numerical limit on U.S. immigration was 290,000, excluding immediate relatives of U.S. citizens, who continued to be exempt from numerical limitation.[5] The latter group increased from 60,000 in 1969 to 105,000 in fiscal year 1974, accounting for all of the growth in alien immigration during the past five years.

Immigration Act of 1965

The Immigration Act of 1965 represented a major change in national immigration policy. The national origins system, established by the Act of 1924, assigned to each country outside the Western Hemisphere an annual quota based on the national origins of the United States population in 1890. As a result, large quotas were assigned to countries of Northern and Western Europe, which had contributed most heavily to immigration during the earlier years of the settlement of the United States. The Act of 1965 abolished this system and substituted a limitation of 20,000 immigrants per country, with an overall limitation of 170,000 immigrants for countries outside the Western Hemisphere. At the same time, a stronger preference was given to close relatives of United States citizens and to immediate relatives of resident aliens. Under the old law, 50 percent of the quota was reserved for close relatives; under the new law, 74 percent of the available numbers are so reserved. Another important change was the imposition of a limitation on immigration from the Western Hemisphere.

The most substantial change brought about by the Act of 1965 was a pronounced shift in the geographic origin of immigrants. Of the 43 million immigrants admitted during the century and a half between 1820 and 1965, about 81 percent or 35 million were from Europe, with Germany (6.8 million), Italy (5.0 million), Ireland (4.7 million), Great Britain (4.7 million), Austria and Hungary (4.3 million), and the U.S.S.R. (3.3 million) contributing the largest numbers of immigrants.[6] Before the establishment of the national origins quota system in the 1920s, millions of Europeans immigrated to the United States, while immigration of Asians was severely restricted. By reserving about 94 percent of the immigrant visas for European countries, the national origins quota system assured that most of the immigrants after 1925 would also be from Europe. Western Hemisphere immigration before 1965 represented a small part (15 percent) of total immigration, and about 60 percent of the Western Hemisphere immigrants before 1965 were from Canada. After the Act of 1965 went into effect, immigration from Europe and Canada fell sharply while immigration from Asia and Mexico increased substantially.

The sharp changes in the countries of origin of recent immigrants can be shown by comparing the number of immigrants admitted during the 1960 to 1964 and 1970 to 1974 periods (see Table 2). The share of total immigration from Europe dropped from 45 to 25 percent while immigration from Asia increased from 8 to 30 percent. The rapid decline in annual immigration from Germany, Canada and the United Kingdom during the period is illustrated in Figure 1. Figure 2 shows the dramatic rise in immigration from Asia after 1965 and the large increases from Mexico, the West Indies and Central America, and Southern Europe.

Migration between the United States and Canada

An interesting facet of recent immigration is the flow of migrants between the United States and Canada. The trends in the number of Americans moving to Canada and the number of Canadians moving to the United States have been in opposite directions since 1965, with fewer Canadians com-

TABLE 2
Alien Immigration by Country of Birth, 1960-74

Country or Region of Birth	Annual average		
	1960-1964	1965-1969	1970-1974
All countries	284	359	385
Europe, total	127	126	95
Germany	28	17	7
Greece	4	11	13
Italy	17	22	21
Portugal	4	11	11
United Kingdom	25	23	11
Balance of Europe	49	42	31
Asia, total	22	52	115
China & Taiwan	4	13	16
India	1	4	13
Japan	4	4	5
Korea	2	4	19
Philippines	3	12	30
Balance of Asia	9	16	31
Africa	2	4	7
North & Central America	110	151	144
Canada	33	27	11
Mexico	44	43	60
Cuba	13	37	20
Dominican Republic	5	11	13
Haiti	1	5	6
Jamaica	2	10	13
Other North & Central America	12	18	21
South America	20	24	21

Source: 1974 and 1969 Reports of the Immigration and Naturalization Service, Table 14.

Note: Data are for periods beginning July 1 and ending June 30.

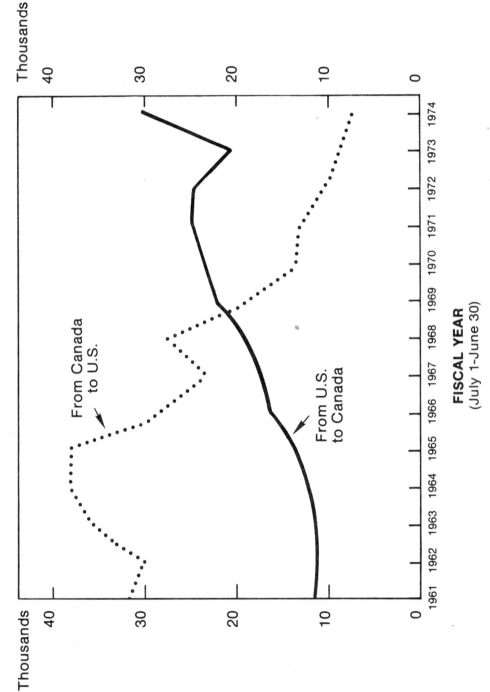

FISCAL YEAR
(July 1–June 30)

Source: 1974 and 1969 Reports of the U.S. Immigration and Naturalization Service, Table 14; Immigration from U.S. to Canada — Annual Immigration Statistics published by Department of Manpower and Immigration, Canada.

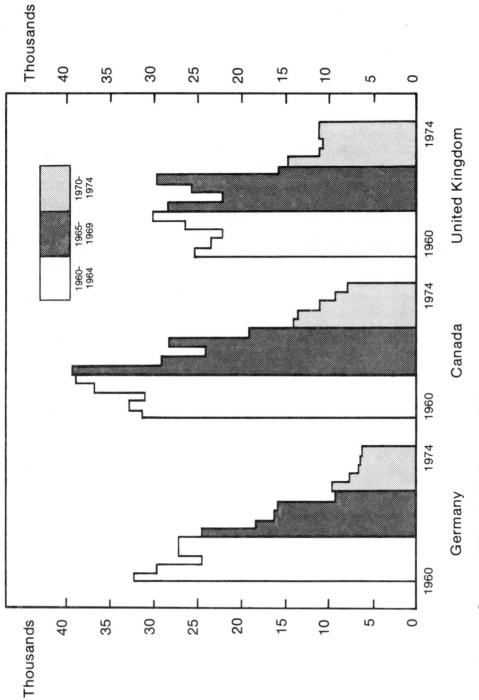

Source: 1974 and 1969 Reports of the Immigration and Naturalization Service, Table 14.

ing to the United States and an increasing number of Americans moving to Canada (Figure 3). Between 1961 and 1965 more than 30,000 Canadians moved to the United States annually, but the number dropped steadily after 1965 and has been below 10,000 in each year since 1972. The annual number of Americans moving to Canada increased from about 11,000 during the early 1960s to 30,000 in 1974. Although these figures represent persons intending to reside permanently in the respective countries, there is evidence of a considerable return flow. For example, between 1946 and 1955 about 91,000 U.S. citizens moved to Canada and 42,000 U.S. citizens (former residents of Canada) returned to the United States.

TABLE 3
Parolees Entering U.S., July 1-June 30, 1960-75

Year July 1 - June 30	Entering Parolees
1974 - 1975	108,000
1973 - 1974	12,000
1972 - 1973	9,000
1971 - 1972	21,000
1970 - 1971	46,000
1969 - 1970	46,000
1968 - 1969	42,000
1967 - 1968	45,000
1966 - 1967	46,000
1965 - 1966	34,000
1964 - 1965	5,000
1963 - 1964	19,000
1962 - 1963	16,000
1961 - 1962	75,000
1960 - 1961	64,000
Total	588,000

Parolees

Refugees from Cuba, Vietnam, Hong Kong, and communist-dominated countries of Eastern Europe totaled nearly 600,000 between 1960 and 1975. These immigrants, termed parolees by the Immigration and Naturalization Service, are aliens who are not admitted for permanent residence when they first arrive in the United States but are permitted to enter at the discretion of the Attorney General. Parolees are not counted against hemispheric quotas or included in the annual alien immigration statistics until their status is adjusted to that of permanent

resident. For example, about 89,000 Cuban refugees (who had been in the United States for as many as eight years) were adjusted to permanent resident status in 1968 in order to be admitted on a permanent basis before the Western Hemisphere limitation of 120,000 went into effect on July 1, 1968.

Cubans fleeing the Castro regime after 1959 accounted for about 466,000 of the estimated 588,000 parolees who entered the United States between 1960 and 1975. Chinese refugees from Hong Kong and refugees from communist countries of Eastern Europe added about 15,000 to the total. Approximately 100,000 Vietnamese refugees entered the United States as parolees during May and June of 1975. Annual figures from parolees admitted to the United States are given in Table 3.

Commuters

Alien immigration is usually restricted to aliens who intend to establish permanent residence in the United States. However, one sizable group of alien immigrants obtains visas with no intention of residing in the United States. This group is comprised of residents of Canada and Mexico who have been admitted for permanent residence in the United States, but who reside in Canada or Mexico and commute each day to places of employment in the United States.[7] To become a commuter, an alien must first obtain lawful immigrant status as prescribed by the Immigration and Nationality Act. Upon admission, the alien receives an alien registration receipt card, Form I–151, which is renewable each year and can be used for admission into the United States for work each day. The alien must continue to be permanently employed in the United States in order to retain his commuter status. The difference between commuters and other alien immigrants is that commuters are not required to establish permanent residence in the United States. The number of daily commuters from Mexico is about 45,000 and the number from Canada is about 9,000.

State of intended residence of immigrants

California and New York, the states with the

largest alien populations, continue to attract the largest numbers of new immigrants (see Table 4). About one-fourth of the alien population resided in California in January 1974, and 22 percent of the 395,000 immigrants admitted during fiscal year 1974 intended to reside in California. As Table 4 shows, 80.2 percent of all aliens live in ten states with the largest number of aliens (42.1 percent live in California and New York), and 78.5 percent of the immigrants admitted during 1974 intended to reside in the same ten states (44.3 percent in California and New York).

Aliens naturalized

During the past ten years over one million aliens have become United States citizens. The annual number of persons naturalized averaged approximately 125,000 between 1960 and 1964, dropped to about 105,000 between 1965 and 1971, and increased gradually to almost 132,000 during 1974.

Although the annual number of aliens becoming citizens has been relatively stable for two decades, the geographic distribution (by country of birth) of new citizens shifted considerably following passage of the Immigration Act of 1965. The proportion from Europe fell from two-thirds in 1964 to one-third in 1974, while the proportion from Asia, especially from China, the Philippines, and Korea, increased rapidly. Table 5 summarizes the changes between 1964 and 1975.

More than one-third of the 131,655 aliens naturalized during 1974 live in New York (26,359) and California (23,460). Other states with large numbers of persons naturalized during 1974 include Florida (11,323), New Jersey (9,011), and Illinois (8,801). Five cities—New York, Chicago, Miami, San Francisco, and Los Angeles—had nearly one-third of the new citizens during 1974, while about 51,000, or 39 percent, live in cities with populations less than 100,000.

SOCIAL AND ECONOMIC DATA ON RECENT IMMIGRANTS

The volume of immigration to the United States should be determined only in part by the capacity of the United States to absorb new immigrants into the social and economic systems. The possible contributions of immigrants as well as the possible problems created by the presence of additional immigrants should be taken into account. If the optimum level of immigration is to be determined, considerably more information on the social and economic characteristics of immigrants and emigrants is needed than is available. At present the primary source of information on the social and economic characteristics of immigrants is the census count of the foreign-born population. The following description of the characteristics of recent immigrants[8] is based on 1970 census data on the foreign-born population who entered the United States between 1960 and 1970.[9]

Age composition

Although the median age of the 1960–70 immigrants was close to the median age of the U.S. population (28.7 compared with 28.1), a smaller proportion of recent immigrants were over 64 or under 15. Only 3 percent of 1960–70 immigrants were 65 and over compared with 10 percent of the total population, and about 20 percent were under 15 in contrast to 29 percent for the total population.

Marital status

The distribution by marital status of 1960–70 immigrants (14 years and over) was similar to that of the total population, although a much smaller proportion of recent immigrants were widowed (3.6 percent) than in the total population (7.8 percent) because of the smaller proportion of immigrants in the older ages.

Economic status

Relative to the total U.S. population, a larger proportion of the 1960–70 immigrants are in the labor force (64 percent compared with 58 percent). Unemployment for recent immigrants is 4.8 percent of those in the labor force, a slightly higher proportion than the 4.4 percent for the total population. Recent immigrants are less likely to be managers

TABLE 4
State of Residence of the Alien Population, January
1974, and State of Intended Residence of Alien
Immigrants Admitted During Fiscal Year 1974

State	Alien Population – January 1974		State of Intended Residence	
	Permanent Residents	Percent of Total	Admitted during FY 1974	Percent of Total
U.S. total	4,100,300	100.0	394,861	100.0
California	1,015,379	24.8	86,861	22.0
New York	709,972	17.3	88,068	22.3
Texas	305,991	7.5	28,976	7.3
Florida	278,262	6.8	19,409	4.9
New Jersey	247,895	6.0	24,679	6.3
Illinois	243,190	5.9	24,814	6.3
Massachusetts	163,595	4.0	12,417	3.1
Michigan	129,710	3.2	10,072	2.6
Pennsylvania	97,565	2.4	8,721	2.2
Connecticut	95,750	2.3	5,855	1.5
All others	812,991	19.8	84,989	21.5

Source: 1974 Report of the Immigration and Naturalization Service,
          Tables 35 and 12A.

and administrators, sales workers, or clerical workers than the total population. The occupational distribution of the total population and of recent immigrants in 1970 is shown in Table 7.

The median income of families who entered the
United States during the 1960–70 period was
$9,157 in 1969, compared with $9,590 for all families in the United States. About 13 percent of recent
immigrant families were below the poverty line in
1970, contrasted with about 11 percent of all families in the United States. Although median *family*
income of recent immigrants was lower than the

TABLE 5
Sources of Citizens Naturalized, 1964 and 1975

Persons naturalized

Area	1964			1974	
	Number	Percent			Percent
All Areas	112,234	100.0		131,655	100.0
Europe	71,636	63.8		48,014	36.5
Asia	15,724	14.0		37,780	28.7
North America	19,782	17.6		36.050	27.4
Canada	9,479	8.4		4,084	3.1
Mexico	5,213	4.6		5,206	4.0
Cuba	2,683	2.4		18,394	14.0
Other N. A.	2,407	2.1		8,366	6.4
Other Areas	5,092	4.5		9,811	7.5

Source: 1974 and 1964 Report of the Immigration and Naturalization Service, Table 39.

TABLE 6
Percent of Total Population of U.S. and Total
Immigrant Population, 1960-75, by Marital Status

Percent of total population
14 years and over

Marital Status	Total U.S. Population	1960-1970 Immigrants
Total	100.0	100.0
Single	25.4	27.1
Married	63.4	67.1
Widowed	7.8	3.6
Divorced	3.4	2.2

---

median family income of all families in the United States, the opposite was true for unrelated individuals (that is, persons who are not related to any person with whom they reside). Median income of recent immigrants who were unrelated individuals was $3,134, while median income for unrelated individuals in the total population was $2,489.

Nearly three-fourths of all unrelated individuals lived alone in 1970.

MAJOR DEFICIENCIES IN
IMMIGRATION DATA

A first step in measuring the impact of immigra-

TABLE 7
Occupations of U.S. Population and 1960-70
Immigrants

	Percent in each occupation	
	U.S. Population	1960-1970 Immigrants
All Occupations	100.0	100.0
Prof., Tech., & Kindred	14.8	18.4
Managers & Administrators	8.3	4.5
Sales Workers	7.1	3.9
Clerical & Kindred Workers	18.0	14.2
Craftsmen & Kindred Workers	13.9	12.2
Operatives, except Transport.	13.7	22.6
Transport Equipment Operatives	3.9	1.5
Laborers, except Farm	4.5	4.4
Farmers & Farm Managers	1.9	0.1
Farm Laborers & Farm Foremen	1.2	2.2
Service Workers, except Private Household	11.3	13.6
Private Household Workers	1.5	2.4

tion on population growth in the United States is to determine the precise number of persons establishing residence in the United States and the number of persons leaving to establish permanent residence abroad. At present, the only category of net immigration for which direct data are available is alien immigrants admitted for permanent residence. Few or no data are available for two major categories—illegal immigration (aliens) to the United States and emigration (aliens and citizens) from the United States.

Illegal immigration

The number of illegal aliens in this country has been of increasing concern as "estimates" of the number of illegal aliens have risen dramatically. A *Washington Post* editorial on September 22, 1975, asserted that over a million illegal aliens become U.S. residents each year, with an estimated payroll amounting to $10.4 billion. It went on to state that while nobody knows exactly how many illegal aliens live in the United States, Immigration and Naturalization Service Commissioner, Leonard F. Chapman, says the estimate of 10 million may be close. The reader might conclude that reasonably accurate statistics on the annual number of illegal aliens are available. Unfortunately, this is not the case; the estimates given in the editorial were conjectures which lack any verifiable statistical basis.

The large and increasing number of illegal aliens apprehended each year by the Immigration and Naturalization Service suggests that illegal immigration is increasing, but the number and rate of increase of illegal aliens in the United States has not been determined. The lack of reliable information about the size and impact of the illegal alien population, along with the increasing urgency of the problem, make it difficult to formulate effective policies in a rational atmosphere. Decisions about the resources to be allocated and the measures to be taken to deal with the issue of illegal immigration could have important consequences for the United States at home and abroad.

Emigration

Emigration is often ignored in discussions of immigration policy because no current information is available and because the movement out of the United States is generally believed to be small.[10] Published data on alien emigration for 1908 to 1957 and recent research on the volume of emigration during the 1960s suggest that the flow of persons out of the United States is large and should be an important consideration in analyzing past trends and in formulating immigration policies.

The arrival of immigrants into the United States has always been accompanied by the departure of former immigrants to other countries. For example, between 1908 and 1957, 15.7 million immigrants came to the United States, and 4.8 million aliens emigrated (see Table 8).[11]

TABLE 8
Recorded Numbers of Alien Immigrants and Emigrants, 1908-57

Period	Alien Immigrants Admitted	Alien Emigrants
1948-1957	2,344,204	254,036
1938-1947	648,614	156,662
1928-1937	1,137,415	583,737
1918-1927	3,960,327	1,354,177
1908-1917	7,630,286	2,463,883
1908-1957	15,718,846	4,812,495

Since the Immigration and Naturalization Service stopped collecting data on alien emigration in 1957, *no* statistics have been collected on the number of persons who permanently move out of the United States. Because of the many problems involved in collecting adequate data on emigration, it is likely that future statistics on foreign-born emigration will be derived from demographic analysis of census data rather than from statistics collected at departure points.

By analyzing 1960 to 1970 census data on the foreign-born population, it was estimated that 1.1 million foreign-born persons emigrated from the United States between 1960 and 1970 (see Table 9).[12]

TABLE 9
Estimates of Foreign-Born Emigration from the United States, by Age and Sex: 1960-70

Age in 1970	Foreign-born emigration, 1960-1970		
	Total	Male	Female
All ages	1,065	431	634
Under 25	228	102	126
25-44	443	182	261
45-64	227	102	125
65+	166	45	121

The finding that nearly 25 percent of the foreign-born emigrants during the decade were women 25 to 44 years of age in 1970 suggests the possibility that large numbers of children who were born in the United States (and are therefore native) emigrated with their parents. The estimate of 166,000 emigrants 65 years and over during the decade is supported by data on Social Security beneficiaries abroad which showed an increase from 101,000 in 1960 to 232,000 in 1970.

The overall estimate of 1.1 million foreign-born emigrants during the decade was generally consistent with an independent estimate of alien emigration derived by using annual alien registration data for 1962 to 1970. The independent estimate was nearly 900,000. If the two figures are accepted as accurate, they suggest that a large proportion of the foreign-born emigrants during the decade were aliens and not naturalized citizens.

A disadvantage of estimating foreign-born emigration by analysis of census data is that the figures are not available until years after the intercensal period. For example, the level of emigration during the 1970s cannot be determined by this method until the early 1980s. New demographic methods are needed in order to make current estimates of the number of aliens leaving the United States.

During the 1960s, the emigration of aliens was considerably larger than the emigration of American citizens. However, the available data indicate that emigration of citizens more than doubled between 1960 and 1970. By compiling data on im-

TABLE 10
Emigration of United States Citizens, by Country of Destination, 1960-70

(Data from sources in countries listed.)

Country	Total, 1960 to 1970	Calendar Year										
		1960	1961	1962	1963	1964	1965	1966	1967	1968	1969	1970
All Countries	385,468	21,840	23,281	25,062	26,148	29,211	33,789	37,498	41,669	43,264	47,663	56,043
Canada	164,310	10,060	10,395	10,452	10,313	11,350	13,857	16,154	18,013	19,059	21,474	23,183
Australia	63,474	2,386	2,867	3,432	3,591	4,777	5,663	6,089	6,684	7,203	9,041	11,741
New Zealand	7,388	439	514	625	663	763	688	762	782	501	659	992
United Kingdom	16,920	889	932	1,189	1,221	1,286	1,440	1,536	1,823	1,963	2,075	2,566
South Africa	3,410	134	225	215	376	344	365	401	349	364	322	315
Belgium	31,123	1,245	1,274	1,637	2,092	2,203	2,509	2,820	4,532	3,881	4,187	4,743
Denmark	12,837	902	1,000	939	994	1,010	1,321	1,264	1,374	1,224	1,409	1,400[1]
France	7,736	N.A.	291	350	670	682	731	722	874	1,009	1,141	1,266
Netherlands	22,353	1,361	1,465	1,746	1,639	2,109	2,227	2,389	1,891	2,327	2,370	2,829
Norway	13,859	1,257	1,006	1,158	1,193	1,209	1,228	1,209	1,296	1,430	1,284	1,589
Portugal	17,593	947	1,030	1,126	1,287	1,359	1,695	2,079	2,032	2,199	1,163	2,676
Sweden	19,190	1,699	1,902	1,859	1,844	1,894	1,779	1,736	1,451	1,406	1,820	1,800[1]
Argentina	3,769	511	380	292	187	162	222	292	319	424	391	589
Other Countries	1,506	10	0	42	78	63	64	45	249	274	327	354

1/ Estimate based on previous year. Not shown on original table.

Source: Ada Finifter, "Emigration from the United States, an Exploratory Analysis," prepared for the Conference on Public Support for the Political System at the University of Wisconsin – Madison, Aug. 13-17, 1973.

migration of U.S. citizens obtained from various foreign countries, Finifter estimated that 385,000 American citizens moved out of the United States between 1960 and 1970.[13] The countries receiving the largest numbers of Americans were Canada (164,000), Australia (63,000), and Belgium (31,000). Table 10 shows annual estimates of emigration of citizens from the United States for 1960 to 1970 by country of destination. The level of emigration of citizens increased gradually from 22,000 in 1960 to 56,000 in 1970, with Canada receiving more than 40 percent of the total.

Although the estimates of emigration of citizens and aliens during the 1960s are approximations, the figures show clearly that the flow of emigrants was substantial. Additional research is needed in order to determine whether emigration has continued at or above the level estimated for the 1960s or whether the rate of emigration was unusually large during the period. Estimates of the number and characteristics of recent emigrants are essential for determining the true volume of net immigration and hence the real impact of immigration on the population of the United States.

SUMMARY

The annual number of aliens admitted for permanent residence increased gradually from less than 300,000 in the early 1960s to nearly 400,000 after 1970. In addition, almost 500,000 Cuban refugees were admitted between 1960 and 1975, and about 100,000 Vietnamese refugees arrived in the United States during May and June, 1975.

The Immigration Act of 1965 represented a major change in United States immigration policy. The Act eliminated the discriminatory national origins quota system and established a limit on Western Hemisphere immigration for the first time. By eliminating the severe restrictions on immigration from Asia, lowering the large quotas for European countries and restricting Western Hemisphere immigration to 120,000 per year, the new law sharply altered the geographic distribution of the new immigrants' countries of origin. After 1968 immigration from Asia and Mexico increased considerably, while immigration from Europe and Canada dropped. The proportion of U.S. immigration from

Europe fell from two-thirds in 1964 to one-third in 1974, while the proportion from Asia increased rapidly.

The 1970 census enumerated about 2.9 million immigrants who entered the United States between 1960 and 1970. Their median age in 1970 was similar to that of the total population, but a larger proportion were in the labor-force age span. The proportions of immigrants who were married, single, or divorced were similar to those of the total U.S. population. Compared with the U.S. population, a slightly higher proportion of these immigrants were in the labor force, and a slightly higher proportion were listed as unemployed. About 13 percent of recent immigrant families were below the poverty line in 1970 in contrast to about 11 percent of all families in the United States.

Because of major deficiencies in the present system of collecting immigration data, it is impossible to determine precisely the number of aliens moving to and from the United States each year. No defensible method has been developed to measure the size of the illegal alien population, although the large and increasing number of illegal aliens apprehended each year suggests that illegal immigration is increasing. No statistics on alien emigration have been collected since 1957, but demographic analysis employing the 1960 and 1970 census data indicates that roughly one million foreign-born persons left the United States during the 1960s. A comprehensive review of our entire system of collecting immigration data is urgently needed if we are to measure the impact of immigration on the population of the United States.

NOTES

1. Additional data are provided by the Department of Defense, the Puerto Rico Planning Board, the Social Security Administration, and the Civil Service Commission.
2. These include U.S. military personnel, federal civilian employees and their dependents, private citizens working for companies abroad, and migrants between the United States and Puerto Rico. There is no limitation on movement between the United States and Puerto Rico because persons born in Puerto Rico are citizens.
3. Includes 88,555 Cubans who entered the United States before 1968 but whose status was adjusted to permanent residence status during 1968.
4. 1965 Report of the Immigration and Naturalization Service, Table 7.

5. The following persons are exempt from numerical limitation: parents of U.S. citizens over twenty-one years of age, spouses, minor unmarried children of U.S. citizens, and permanent resident aliens returning from abroad. All other relatives, including alien brothers and sisters of U.S. citizens and immediate relatives of resident aliens, are subject to numerical limitations.

6. 1965 Report of the Immigration and Naturalization Service, Table 13.

7. For a detailed discussion of commuters, see "Commuters: Historical Background, Legal Challenges, and Issues," *Report of the Select Commission on Western Hemisphere Immigration* (Washington, D.C.: U.S. Government Printing Office, 1968), p.101.

8. More precisely, the survivors of 1960–70 immigrants still residing in the United States in 1970.

9. U.S. Bureau of the Census, Census of Population: 1970, Subject Reports Final Report PC(2)-1A, *National Origin and Language* (Washington, D.C.: U.S. Government Printing Office, 1972).

10. See Bernard Axelrod, "Historical Studies of Emigration from the United States," *International Migration Review,* 6, No.1, (Spring 1972), 32-49.

11. Robert Warren and Jennifer Peck, "Emigration from the United States: 1960 to 1970," paper presented at the annual meeting of the Population Association of America, Seattle, Washington, April 17–19, 1975.

12. Ibid.

13. Ada Finifter, "Emigration from the United States, an Exploratory Analysis," prepared for the Conference on Public Support for the Political System at the University of Wisconsin-Madison, August 13–17, 1973.

IMMIGRATION POLICY AND THE
NEW IMMIGRANTS, 1965–76

Charles B. Keely

The United States has not adhered to a consistent immigration philosophy during the almost ninety years of federal legislation on the matter. Even today, U.S. immigration law does not represent the legislative embodiment of an integrated immigration policy. Rather, the policy is a patchwork. The complication and inconsistencies of the resulting legislation, and the bureaucratic complexity involved in administering it, are monumental.

I will outline current immigration law and review some of its effects on the composition of immigration. In addition, I will comment on some of the implications of and dilemmas posed by current legislation and the composition of recent immigrant streams, including population growth, the foreign-born population, undocumented migrants, and the future of ethnic pluralism in the United States.

POLICY REVIEW

The 1965 Immigration and Nationality Act, which amended the basic immigration statute of 1952 (the McCarran-Walter Act), represented a major break with the past. First embodied in legislation of 1921, the basic assumptions of the national origins quota system were clearly racist. Although the retention of the quota system in the 1952 Act was justified by a less strident form of ethnic and religious discrimination, the Asian-Pacific Triangle provisions of 1952 clearly were a continuation of racist ideas. So, too, was the maintenance of sub-quotas for colonies, still a feature of current legislation.

The 1965 Immigration Act discarded most, but not all, of the provisions introduced or justified by theories of racial superiority or cultural unassimilability. It introduced four basic policy changes: the abolition of the national origins quota system, a new preference system, labor certification procedures, and a limit on Western Hemisphere immigration. To discuss these changes, one must realize that for immigration purposes the law divides the world into two hemispheres: the Western Hemisphere (South and North America and the Caribbean), and the Eastern Hemisphere (all other continents and islands).

The 1965 Act abolished the national origins quota system which applied to Eastern Hemisphere nations.[1] This was accomplished over a thirty-one-month period (December 1965–June 1968) during which the quota system remained in effect. However, unused visa numbers from undersubscribed countries were put into a visa pool for use by preference immigrants from nations with a waiting list. The Asia-Pacific Triangle provisions, which discriminated against those of Asian ancestry, were immediately abolished. Beginning with fiscal year 1969, immigrant visas were distributed without regard to country of birth in the Eastern Hemisphere (except for colonies, of which more will be written below). However, natives of an Eastern Hemisphere country could not receive more than 20,000 visas a year, and total Eastern Hemisphere visas were limited to 170,000 per year.

A second important change in immigration policy contained in the 1965 Act was the placing of greater emphasis on family relationships as a basis for selection of immigrants.[2] This change was accomplished in two ways. First, parents of United States citizens over the age of twenty-one were added to the list of immigrants not subject to numerical limitations of any sort. Second, the order and size-of-preference categories were altered so that family reunification was emphasized. The preference system applied only to the Eastern Hemisphere countries.

The Appendix lists the preference systems contained in the McCarran-Walter Act of 1952 and in the Immigration Act of 1965. The McCarran-Walter system was applied to each country's quota. Under the 1965 Act, the new preference system was to be applied during the transition period to the quota of each country and to the visa pool for those immigrants from oversubscribed countries. After July 1, 1968, this new preference system was to be applied to the 170,000 numerical ceiling for the natives of the Eastern Hemisphere, regardless of the immigrants' country of origin. Comparison of the preference limitations of the two systems indicates the recent law's intent to facilitate the reunion of families. Another difference between the two systems is that the more recent system distinguishes between levels of skill, giving preference to the professional and higher skill levels.

The third major policy change effected by the 1965 legislation was that employment clearances were required of certain persons intending to immigrate. Under Section 212(a) (14) of the MacCarran-Walter Act, aliens seeking entry into the United States for the purpose of performing skilled or unskilled labor could not enter *if* the Secretary of Labor certified that there were sufficient able and qualified United States workers to fill the job category, or that the alien would adversely affect the wages and working conditions of the United States work force. The 1965 Act reversed this procedure. It specifies that no worker shall enter the United States *unless* the Secretary of Labor certifies that there are *not* sufficient able and qualified workers in the United States, and that the alien would *not* adversely affect wages and working conditions. It places the burden of proving no adverse effect upon the applying alien. Elaborate administrative procedures were introduced in the Department of Labor for making these clearances.

This requirement for labor certification applied to the third and sixth preferences (the occupational preferences), to the nonpreference category, and to all natives of the Western Hemisphere except the parents, spouses, and children of United States citizens and resident aliens.

The fourth alteration found in the 1965 Act was a series of changes concerning control of Western Hemisphere immigration. The basic regulators were an annual ceiling of 120,000 visas, and the labor certification requirement for all except the

immediate relatives of United States citizens and permanent resident aliens. Both the House and the Senate wanted to change the policy of unlimited immigration from this hemisphere for all who met the personal requirements about health, criminal record, and self-support. The House sought to do this by the labor certification requirements alone, without resorting to an overall ceiling, without which there would be no need for a preference system. The purpose was to avoid foreign policy implications of imposing a ceiling. The Senate wanted the ceiling and the Senate conferees were adamant on this point in the House-Senate conference. The final version of the bill called for a ceiling of 120,000 with no per country limit after 1968, labor certification except for the close relatives of citizens and resident aliens as already cited, and no provision for any preferences. The law did call for a commission to further study the matter and make recommendations. The commission made its report but no action was taken on it; hence the law went into effect as written.

A final important difference in treatment of this hemisphere in the 1965 Act was the question of "adjustment of status." This process allows someone in the United States with certain types of temporary visas to apply for and receive an immigrant visa without applying at a consulate overseas (assuming all other requirements are met and a visa number is available). This obviously gives advantages to aliens who do this, such as in securing a job. The 1965 Act prohibited adjustment of status to natives of the Western Hemisphere. For the Eastern Hemisphere, this process was eased in 1970 when requirements for exchange of visitors and temporary workers were relaxed.

A special note should be made on the status of colonies. Under the 1965 Act, all colonies were permitted 200 visas, which were counted against the country's ceiling of 20,000 and the hemispheric ceiling of the mother country. The impact of this has been to check the demand of colonies in the Caribbean and high-demand places like Hong Kong.

But much of this is now history. For on October 20, 1976, President Ford signed PL94-571 into law. Under this new bill, a slightly revised preference system, individual labor certification and adjustment of status provisions will apply to both hemispheres. Each hemisphere retains its quota of 170,000 for the Eastern and 120,000 for the Western Hemisphere. All countries now have a 20,000 per country limit. Colonies now can use up to 600 visas, but these will now be counted against the hemisphere ceiling of the colony's location. Table 1 summarizes these changes in the law. People are still speculating about the effects of the new changes. I should add parenthetically that the law requires what a recent administrative rule had proposed, namely no longer to count Cuban refugees who adjust status against the Western Hemisphere's 120,000 limit. The extra visas this will make available, the effect of the 20,000 immigrant limit on Mexico, the impact of the preference system on a brain drain, and the effects of permitting adjustment of status are all open questions. I should also add that the administrative mechanisms and personnel used to adapt to these changes will play a large part in determining the results of the new provisions. The topic of administration of United States immigration law is a vast area of unexplored territory in need of study. We know little in a systematic way of the effect of administration on de facto policy and its results.

TABLE 1
Percent Immigrants Admitted by Country and Continent of Origin: 1961-65, 1966-68, 1969-73

PREFERENCE SYSTEMS

Immigration and Nationality Act of 1952
(McCarran-Walter Act)

1. First preference: Highly skilled immigrants whose services are urgently needed in the United States and the spouse and children of such immigrants.

    50 percent plus any not required for second and third preferences.
2. Second preference: Parents of United States citizens over the age of twenty-one and unmarried sons and daughters of United States citizens.

    30 percent plus any not required for first and third preferences.
3. Third preference: Spouse and unmarried sons

and daughters of an alien lawfully admitted for permanent residence.

    20 percent plus any not required for first or second preference.
4. Fourth preference: Brothers, sisters, married sons and daughters of United States citizens, and an accompanying spouse and children.

    50 percent of numbers not required for first three preferences.
5. Nonpreference: Applicants not entitled to one of the above preferences.

    50 percent of numbers not required for first three preferences, plus any not required for fourth preference.

Immigration Act of 1965

1. First preference: Unmarried sons and daughters of United States citizens.

    Not more than 20 percent.
2. Second preference: Spouse and unmarried sons and daughters of an alien lawfully admitted for permanent residence.

    20 percent plus any not required for first preference.
3. Third preference: Members of the professions, and scientists and artists of exceptional ability.

    Not more than 10 percent.
4. Fourth preference: Married sons and daughters of United States citizens.

    10 percent plus any not required for first three preferences.
5. Fifth preference: Brothers and sisters of United States citizens.

    24 percent plus any not required for first four preferences.
6. Sixth preference: Skilled and unskilled workers in occupations for which labor is in short supply in the United States.

    Not more than 10 percent.
7. Seventh preference: Refugees to whom conditional entry or adjustment of status may be granted.

    Not more than 6 percent.
8. Nonpreference: Any applicant not entitled to one of the above preferences.

    Any numbers not required for preference applicants.

Immigration Act of 1976

Same as 1965 with the following changes:

Third, sixth and nonpreference all require a job offer—no blanket certifications.

Fifth preference: The petitioning United States citizen brother or sister must be over twenty-one years of age.

EFFECTS ON THE IMMIGRANTS' CHARACTERISTICS

Although the legislative summary presented here only highlights current law and passes over a great deal of detail that affects individual decisions about visas, it is only to be expected that tremendous changes would be wrought by the 1965 Act in the composition of the immigrant stream. I will now attempt to highlight the effects of the 1965 Act.[3] To do this I will compare the last five years of the McCarran-Walter Act (1961–65) with the first five years under the full provisions of the 1965 Act (1969–73).

First, the volume of immigration in the second period was increased about 30 percent over that of the first period. Secondly, the geographic origins of immigrants shifted. The Eastern Hemisphere contributed a greater share in 1969–73 than in the 1961–65 period (57.3 percent vs. 50.8 percent). Also, there were important shifts within the Eastern Hemisphere. The European share of total immigration dropped from 41.9 percent to 27.3 percent, and

tions of less-skilled workers. The converse was true for Asia, Africa and Oceania (especially significant is Asia due to the numbers involved). Their proportional contributions to the work force were greater, and they were of a higher occupational level.[5]

Asia overtook Europe as the chief source of Eastern Hemisphere immigration, moving from 7.6 percent to 27.4 percent. Within Europe, southern and eastern countries took the lead as the share of northern countries declined, since they no longer had the advantage of large quotas. The natives of many Asian countries benefitted greatly under the new law (notably India, the Philippines, and China).

The Western Hemisphere declined in its share of total immigration. A decided shift took place away from Canada. Caribbean countries increased in their proportions, while Latin countries from Mexico to South America generally declined.

Table 2 presents a summary of the composition of immigration for all countries, with 2,500 or more immigrants coming to the United States between 1961–72. The data are presented for three periods: the last five years of the McCarran-Walter Act, the transition to the new act's provisions (phasing out the quota system), and the first five years under the new act.

The labor force data taken from immigration statistics present many problems of accuracy and interpretation.[4] Nevertheless, it is apparent that some of the shifts are dramatic. Between 1961–65 and 1969–73, the proportion of immigrants stating an occupation declined from 45.6 percent to 41.3 percent. However, of all immigrants giving an occupation, the proportion who listed a professional occupation increased from 19.8 percent to 28.9 percent. For Asia and Africa, the proportion was over 60 percent. The proportion of professionals actually declined for North and South America. Table 3 summarizes these data by continent.

The point of these data is to highlight that the 1965 Act had different effects for various countries and regions. What had been nontraditional sources of immigration during the quota period have jumped into the limelight. Secondly, the brain drain has been increased, but not universally so. Of particular note are the regions of this hemisphere where the drain has not been notably exacerbated. Concerning the overall labor force characteristics, I repeat what I have stated elsewhere (however, using data only to 1972):

The proportionally smaller contributions to the work force of Europe and the Americas were also contribu-

There are other characteristics which I could compare and analyze as I and others have done elsewhere. Such analyses can give us insight into the effects of legislation on population characteristics and serve as rough guidelines to the effects of the new law and further revisions which may come along. However, what such data and analyses do not tell us is very important. They do not tell us of

TABLE 2
Proportion of Immigrants with a Stated Occupation, Professionals Among Those with a Stated Occupation,
Continental Origin of Professional Immigrants, Area of Origin, by Continent: 1961-65, 1966-68, 1969-73

Area	1961-65	1966-68	1969-73
Europe	41.9	35.3	27.3
Czechoslovakia	.6	.4	.7
France	1.4	.9	.5
Germany	9.0	4.4	2.1
Greece	1.4	3.2	3.8
Ireland	2.1	.8	.5
Italy	5.7	6.6	6.1
Netherlands	1.3	.6	.3
Poland	3.0	1.9	1.1
Portugal	1.0	3.1	3.3
Spain	.7	1.0	1.1
United Kingdom	8.7	6.6	3.2
Yugoslavia	.8	1.4	2.0
Other Europe	6.1	4.5	2.7
Asia	7.6	13.9	27.4
Hong Kong	.2	1.1	1.1
India	.2	1.0	3.2
Iran	.2	.3	.6
Japan	1.3	1.0	1.2
Jordan	.2	.4	.6
Korea	.7	.9	3.8
Philippines	1.1	3.0	7.4
Thailand	--	.1	.8
Vietnam	--	.1	.7
China	1.4	4.1	4.2
Other Asia	2.1	1.9	3.7
Africa	.9	1.1	1.8
UAR	.3	.4	.9
Other Africa	.6	.7	.9
Oceania	.4	.6	.8
North America	41.0	43.5	37.0
Canada	12.0	7.0	3.5
Mexico	15.4	11.5	14.5
Jamaica	.6	2.7	3.7
Trinidad & Tobago	.1	.7	1.8
Cuba	5.3	13.1	5.1
Dominican Republic	2.4	3.3	3.1
Haiti	.7	1.2	1.7
Costa Rica	.7	.4	.3
Other North America	3.7	3.5	3.3
South America	8.1	5.6	5.6
Argentina	1.7	.9	.7
Brazil	.7	.6	.4
Colombia	2.4	1.8	1.6
Ecuador	1.2	.9	1.2
Peru	.8	.4	.3
Other South America	1.3	1.0	1.3

[*]N for 1961-65 = 1,450,314: N for 1966-68 = 1,139,460: N for 1969-73 = 1,887,131

TABLE 3
Projections of U.S. Total Population, 1975-2050
(in thousands)

	Persons with Stated Occupation (1)	Professionals as Proportion of Col. (1) (2)	Proportion of all Professionals from Geographic Region (3)	Proportion of Total Immigration from Geographic Region (4)
Total*				
1961–65	45.6	19.8	100.0	100.0
1966–68	43.0	24.6	100.0	100.0
1969–73	41.3	28.9	100.0	100.0
Europe				
1961–65	50.5	19.5	45.9	41.9
1966–68	46.1	22.8	35.2	35.3
1969–73	45.2	18.7	19.4	27.3
Asia				
1961–65	29.6	39.5	9.7	7.6
1966–68	41.4	51.5	27.7	13.9
1969–73	41.1	60.5	56.7	27.4
Africa				
1961–65	43.7	36.0	1.6	.9
1966–68	47.3	45.6	2.3	1.1
1969–73	51.7	61.2	4.8	1.8
Oceania				
1961–65	36.8	41.1	.8	.5
1966–68	37.1	48.6	1.0	.6
1969–73	39.9	42.4	1.2	.8
North America				
1961–65	44.4	16.1	32.4	41.0
1966–68	41.3	16.4	27.9	43.5
1969–73	38.4	11.8	14.1	37.0
South America				
1961–65	41.7	25.8	9.7	8.1
1966–68	40.7	27.3	5.9	5.6
1969–73	40.0	20.7	3.9	5.6

*
N for 1961–65 = 1,450,314; 1966–68 = 1,139,460; 1969–73 = 1,887,131.
Annual averages volume for the three periods respectively are: 290,063; 379,820; 377,426
Source: U.S. Department of Justice, Annual Report of the Immigration and
          Naturalization Service, 1961–1973.

family separations, coping mechanisms for adjustment, and the contributions immigrants continue to make. Mostly, we hear criticism of immigrants these days. It is to some of those criticisms that I will now address myself and emphasize some dimensions which I think have generally gone unnoticed.

DILEMMAS AND CONTROVERSIES

Population growth

The role of immigration in the population dynamics of the United States has been the object of recent demographic analysis and policy debate. Immigration has obviously been historically important in population growth, but its role has not been as great as we might expect. Gibson estimates that slightly less than half (48 percent) of the 1970 population is accounted for by the estimated net immigration between 1790 and 1970.[6] But contemporary interest focuses on future growth. In this context, recent fertility-rate declines and increased immigration following the 1965 Act have led to the conclusions of a relatively greater, although possibly misleading, importance of net immigration.[7] Given this apparently larger role of immigration, some have wondered about the effect of stopping all immigration. Discussion has focused on two topics: the impact of immigration on future growth, and the effects of immigration on the path to, and characteristics of, a stationary population (zero population growth.)[8]

Most projections of the effect of immigration assume net immigration to be at a level of 400,000. However, Warren and Peck have estimated the emigration of the foreign-born from the United States between 1960 and 1970 to have been over one million.[9] Native-born emigration has been running over 50,000 per year, judging from the immigration statistics of other countries. Further, the 400,000 figure often cited and used in projections includes others than alien immigrants, such as United States citizens born abroad and net Puerto Rican movement.

To estimate the effects of recent net alien immigration, a colleague and I have made projections of population growth using Series II assumptions from the Census Bureau. Instead of assuming 400,000 immigrants with the age-sex structure used by the Census Bureau, we substituted a net alien immigration and age-sex structure, which results from using the average alien immigration of 1969–73 minus estimates of alien emigration based on Warren and Peck.[10] These estimates put net alien migration to the United States in recent years at about 264,000 rather than 400,000.

Table 4 presents some of the results of our analyses. To highlight the table, the lower estimate would result in almost 700,000 fewer people between 1975 and 1980; 3.8 million fewer within twenty-five years, or by the year 2000; and 13.6

million fewer over seventy-five years.[11]

The second question related to the population issue is what adjustment in native fertility would be necessary if the United States were to achieve a zero population growth rate and continue immigration. Coale analyzed this question in a paper for the Population Commission. We replicated Coale's methodology, except that we used our estimate of recent net alien immigration's volume and age-sex structure rather than the 400,000 figure and the age-sex structure Coale used. Coale's results estimated that the net reproduction rate and total fertility rate necessary to accommodate immigration at the 400,000 level would have to decline from 1.0 and 2.11 to .934 and 1.971 respectively. Our estimates are .948 and 2.0. The ultimate size of such a stationary (no growth) population would be about 8.4 percent larger for having accommodated immigration, according to Coale's estimates, and 5.8 percent larger by our estimate. Coale concluded that the necessary accommodations should not lead to reducing immigration from current levels.[12] Our lower estimates would lead us to concur (see Table 5).

It should be underscored that these estimates and projections are not predictions but are benchmarks that are only as reasonable as the assumptions about mortality, fertility, migration, and population structure on which they are based. Their purpose is to provide guidelines and to point out the effects of the size of or changes in population processes on future populations. They can give us insights into the relative impact of various changes. In the present case, they reveal that an immediate cessation of immigration would not provide a particularly large boost to achieving zero population growth.

The foreign-born population

Despite the increase in immigration after the 1965 Act, the foreign-born population declined by about 122,000 people between 1960 and 1970. The 24.3 million foreign born in 1960 represented about 5.4 percent of the population, while the 23.9 million foreign born in 1970 accounted for 4.7 percent of the 1970 population.[13] The residents of the United States included in the census are overwhelmingly native-born. Nor do I think the situation will change

TABLE 4
Comparison of Estimates of the Implications of
Female Immigration for a U.S. Stationary
Population

Year	Series II*	Revised**
1975	213,448	213,448
1980	222,495	221,797
1985	233,793	232,357
1990	244,887	242,673
1995	254,557	251,528
2000	262,815	258,934
2005	270,688	265,914
2010	279,071	273,367
2015	287,522	280,863
2020	294,898	287,268
2025	300,613	292,002
2030	304,929	295,331
2035	308,537	297,943
2040	311,949	300,351
2045	315,571	302,961
2050	319,673	306,044

*Basic data from U.S. Bureau of the Census, *Current Population Reports*, Series 25, No. 601, "Projections of the Population of the United States: 1957 to 2050." Oct. 1975. The Series II projections assume the "most realistic" trends in fertility which are intermediate to other projected fertility trends. Series II assumes an annual level of 400,000 net immigration and the age distributions by sex shown on p. 134. These total population figures are those resulting from the replication of U.S. Bureau of the Census projections. These figures do not equal equivalent published totals due to slight differences in mortality assumptions. Percentage differences between the displayed population figures and published totals for each year are generally less than 0.5 percent.

**Revised projections include estimated levels of annual net alien immigration of 264,357 and the age distribution by sex, from our net immigration estimates.

Adapted from: C. B. Keely and E. P. Kraly, 1977.

to a degree to foster any concern, much less xenophobia. Again referring to our projections using Coale's methodology on the relationship of immigration with zero growth, the size of the foreign born in such a population would be about 5.8 percent. The foreign-born population in 1970 contained many older persons. If continued, current immigration rates would not appreciably increase the proportion of foreign born in the population. Similarly, native born with one or both parents who

Table 5
Comparison of Estimates of the Implications of Female Immigration for a U.S. Stationary Population

Parameters and Results of Analyses	Coale, 1972	Revised
Level of Female Immigration (000's)	223.3	134.7
Fertility of Foreign Born Females	2.11	2.11
Native Fertility Required for U.S. Stationary Population		
Net Reproduction Rate	.934	.948
Total Fertility Rate	1.971	2.000
Percent Difference between Size of Stationary Population without and with Assumed Immigration	8.4	5.8

Source: See Table 3.

---

were foreign born declined by 356,000 persons, or from 13.6 percent of the 1960 population to 11.8 percent in 1970.

Hopefully, discussions of immigration policy will not center on nativist arguments as in the past. The effect of current size and age structure of immigration on the future population ought to blunt the arguments used in the past which play on fears about foreigners, and which raise specters of "foreign influence," "unassimilability," and "racial pollution." Blatant forms of these arguments will probably not rear their heads or will be dismissed if they do. But more subtle forms of the arguments may appear, especially given the change in the countries of origin of recent immigrants.

Clandestine migration

So much has been said recently about clandestine migration to the United States that I hesitate to add to the verbal deluge. I think there is broad and growing agreement on the concept of amnesty of some sort for clandestine migrants who have resided in the United States for three to five years. Agreement is also broad-based about the probability of continued clandestine migration to the world's stronger economies and growth poles. Only a more equitable distribution of economic wealth and opportunity will ultimately lead to the end of these movements. Creativity is needed in devising policies which can lead to that goal.

The real question is what to do between amnesty and a more equitable economic order. Those who oppose amnesty now frequently do so because they believe there will be the repeated need of future amnesties. A larger border patrol may lead to some reductions, but it is too costly on a number of counts. Prohibiting employers from hiring undocumented workers is a widely accepted alternative, but enforcing such a policy without discrimination against citizens and resident aliens, or without requiring universal identification cards, presents very important civil rights questions.

Despite all the rhetoric, we are only beginning to address the problem. If such migration has economic roots, and is inspired by the desire for and availability of jobs, we must go beyond policies of securing borders and turning employers into arms of the law. We must look beyond the role of the Immigration and Naturalization Service and include the Departments of Labor and State. We must examine the structure of our productive system which requires intensive labor inputs. We have to address the roles of business and unions and the incentives needed to have them face the problem.

I think we are just beginning to do these things. Hopefully, we are moving beyond arguments about estimates of the amount of illegal migration and its social costs and benefits, as well as beyond simplistic solutions which rely on the border patrol and immigration investigations. Argument and even agreement on the size, costs, and benefits of this phenomenon have not taken us very far. Agreement that improved enforcement is a first and even necessary step is quickly followed by the caveat from the enforcers themselves that it will not solve the problem.

My point in raising the question here is that we have not really addressed the question of clandestine migration in this country. We have only raised it to the level of consciousness and given a knee-jerk reaction to it of more law enforcement. It deserves more than that. It involves the lives of people here and abroad. And it goes to the heart of immigration policy. What role should immigration have in meeting labor needs? What are to be the priorities among family reunion, asylum for refugees, labor needs, avoiding brain drain, and so on? Are we to continue a policy of settlement migration or return to wide-scale temporary labor, and under what conditions? Too often our immigration legislation and the administration of the law have dictated policy. I suggest the opposite for a change. Address these questions and formulate policy. Then let our law and its administration reflect that policy.

Pluralism

The topic of immigration policy and the future of pluralism covers a broad range of interesting and important areas. Are we moving toward Spanish-English bilingualism, perhaps even at an official level? What will the patterns of adjustment by and to the new ethnics be?

Among other things, I think that the new immigration is fostering another round of discussion on pluralism. Some foreign analysts of the United States such as Renel and Servan-Schreiber have emphasized this social system's flexibility, and its ability to absorb profound change which is rooted in the personal and collective crises of diverse and often contradictory cultural systems.

One need not be sanguine about the United States' ability to absorb change or even to be in the state of constant revolution within the institutional structure of society. However, I think it is clear that, in the area of ethnic relations, ideology has and is shifting, and there is continuing effort at redefining the ideology of ethnic relations. Even though pluralism is generally accepted as the norm, there are both profound opponents of the idea and a great deal of disagreement about what it means. I see this as a continuing process with no ultimate resolution. Many who defend pluralism would oppose official bilingualism. There is a clear clash between pluralism and the values of individualism and universalistic criteria. The debate on pluralism represents another level of the contest of ethnic group interests and relations.

However, I do not think the debate can be dismissed as just another ideological squabble having no impact on events. Whether or not we are a pluralistic society and what that means influences the lives of many Americans from birth to death. Ethnic institutional structures, political socialization of school children, career patterns, and even birth, death, and migration rates are but a few examples of areas where pluralism (what we mean by it and do about it) affects us.

Obviously, immigration policy is directly tied into the image of the United States as a pluralistic society. Do we want a continual infusion of persons of foreign culture? Is the recent declining proportion of foreign born and foreign stock a portent for the future? Does the citizenry still hold to a fear of non-Western cultures which may be exacerbated by the current national origin composition? How does one react to the generally agreed upon need for opportunity for United States minorities and women, and the high proportion of professionals among immigrants? The questions and the conflicts go on. They influence and in turn are influenced by our understanding of pluralism.

As I stated, I do not think the question of pluralism will be resolved in a final and fixed way. However, I do think that the debate on the issue is ignored at one's peril. Whatever the social sources of group positions on the subject, and the dominant definition at any given moment, the debate both affects and reflects ethnic relations.

NOTES

1. U.S. Congress, House, *Amending the Immigration and Nationality Act and for Other Purposes*, Report No. 745, Eighty-Ninth Congress, first session, August 6, 1965, p.8, and U.S. Congress, Senate, *Amending the Immigration and Nationality Act and for Other Purposes*, Report No. 748, Eighty-ninth Congress, first session, September 15, 1965, p.10.
2. House Report, ibid., p.12, and Senate Report, ibid., p.13.
3. See also the following articles by Charles B. Keely: "Effects of the Immigration Act of 1965 on Selected Population Characteristics of Immigrants to the United States," *Demography* 8 (1971), pp.157–69; "Immigration Composition and Population Policy," *Science* 185 (1974), pp.587–93; and "Effects of U.S. Immigration Law on Manpower Characteristics of Immigrants," *Demography* 12 (1975), pp.179–91.
4. S. M. Tomasi and Charles B. Keely, *Whom Have We Welcomed? The Adequacy and Quality of United States Immigration Data for Policy Analysis and Evaluation* (New York: Center for Migration Studies, 1975), Chapter 6.
5. Keely, *Effects on Manpower Characteristics*, op. cit., p.188.
6. Campbell Gibson, "The Contribution of Immigration to the United States Population Growth: 1790–1970," *International Migration Review* 9 (1975), pp.157–77.
7. U.S. Commission on Population Growth and the American Future, *Population and the American Future* (Washington, D.C., 1972), p.114.
8. Ansley J. Coale, "Alternate Paths to a Stationary Population," in Charles F. Westoff and Robert E. Parke, Jr., eds., *Demographic and Social Aspects of Population Growth*, U.S. Commission on Population Growth Research Reports, 1 (Washington, D.C., 1972).
9. Robert Warren and Jennifer Peck, "Emigration from the United States: 1960–1970," paper presented at the Annual Meeting of the Population Association of America, Seattle, Washington, 1975. (Mimeographed.)
10. Warren and Peck, ibid.
11. Charles B. Keely and Ellen Percy Kraly, "Recent Net Immigration to the U.S.: Its Impact on Population Growth and Native Fertility," paper presented at the Population Association of America, St. Louis, Missouri, April 21, 1977.
12. Coale, op. cit.
13. U.S. Department of Commerce, Bureau of the Census, *Census of Population: 1970 General Social and Economic Characteristics, Final Report, United States Summary*, pp.1–361.

IMMIGRATION LAW AND ITS ENFORCEMENT: REFLECTIONS OF AMERICAN IMMIGRATION

Franklin Abrams

INTRODUCTION

As an example of United States public law, the Immigration and Nationality Act presents a good opportunity for comparison of the relationship between the intention of the draftsmen of a statute and the results of their handiwork.

The 1965 reform of the Immigration and Nationality Act made radical changes in U.S. Immigration Policy. It abolished the "national origins quota system" which had so heavily favored Northern and Western Europeans. This reform was proclaimed as both the most humanitarian and the most sensible immigration policy in the nation's history, for it asked of the alien not what was the place of his birth, but what family ties he had to the United States or what skills he possessed. The reuniting of families and the admission of needed workers were the keystones of the new policy.

After 1965, the attention devoted to the immigration issue declined almost immediately, and has been revived only recently with the current concern over the illegal alien problem. Therefore, it will come as a surprise to many to learn that a number of the actual effects of the 1965 legislation were simply unexpected, while others were directly contrary to the intent of its authors.

It was probably not foreseen, for example, that the population gain from immigration would come to equal a figure one-third as high as natural population growth (excess of births over deaths). It was probably not foreseen (though it should have been) that immigration from Asia would rise 500 percent. Nor was it foreseen that so many Asian professionals would enter the country that, today, there are more Filipino doctors in the U.S. than there are black doctors. Since the 1965 Act assumes there will be great difficulty in choosing among Eastern Hemisphere applicants, while all Western Hemisphere applicants will be accommodated, it was clearly not understood that the reverse would be true: today, the supply of visas meets the total demand from Europe, Asia and Africa, while the demand far exceeds the supply for North and South America. Intent on reuniting families, the supporters of the bill would undoubtedly be surprised to learn that a two and one-half year backlog in Western Hemisphere visas means a husband and wife may be separated for that long period by the workings of the present system. Least of all would supporters of the bill have expected their handiwork to have given impetus to an unprecedented wave of illegal immigration. The 1976 amendments to the act, just signed into law in October 1976, are intended to remedy some of these unintended results; their likely effects will be discussed later.

IMMIGRATION AND POPULATION GROWTH

For any country trying to establish or to reform an immigration policy, the very first question to ask is how many immigrants should be admitted. Prior to 1921, no overall numerical limitation was placed on immigration to the United States, and the statistics reflect this "open door" policy: between 1881 and 1921 alone, almost 25 million immigrants entered the U.S.

The 1965 legislation, like the Acts of 1921, 1924, and 1952 which preceded it, set an overall limit on immigration. In 1965, the total was set at 290,000: 170,000 for the Eastern Hemisphere and 120,000 for the Western Hemisphere. These totals are not changed by the 1976 amendments. However, immediate relatives of American citizens (minor children and spouses of citizens, and parents of citizens over twenty-one) are exempt from the numerical limitation, of whom more and more arrive each year (last year about 100,000). Thus, total legal immigration per year reached about 400,000.

Apparently, the concentration of the authors of the 1965 Act on abolishing the discriminatory manner in which immigrants had been chosen was so great that little attention was paid to the question of setting a numerical ceiling. In fact, the 170,000 and 120,000 figures are derived from none of these theories, nor from any other. They are simply pulled from the air, and bear no relationship to any theory or principle at all. A Senate report notes that the 170,000 figure "is believed to be the present absorptive capacity of this country."[1] How our "present absorptive capacity" was determined is nowhere explained.

The link between immigration and population growth has been repeatedly stressed by zero population growth advocates. Without going into great detail over the arguments on both sides, it should be pointed out that the proportion of population growth that is accounted for by immigration is indeed rising. But the number of immigrants admitted each year has been virtually constant. That is, the rise in the proportion is accounted for almost entirely by the falling birth rate.

One more point should be made. The Census Bureau calculates that if the current birth and immigration rates continue, the U.S. population in the year 2000 would be 266 million, only 6 percent of whom would be composed of immigrants from 1969 to 2000 and their descendents. Demographic studies indicate that the total U.S. population will vary only slightly whether immigration is moderately increased or moderately decreased. The simple fact is that there is no scientific or objective way to determine how many immigrants should be admitted or can be "absorbed" by the United States. In view of this fact, and in view of the evidence that immigration has but a marginal effect on total population figures, Congress was correct in deciding in 1965 that humanitarian, economic, and political considerations, and not dubious Malthusian presumptions, should determine U.S. immigration policy.

Though the numerical totals in the 1965 Act are arbitrary, the need to set some limit is, for the United States today, incontrovertible. The United States' wealth, political freedom, and economic opportunities would probably attract more immigrants than even the most hospitable citizen is likely to welcome. Accordingly, the next question faced by the reformers in 1965 was how to choose among the would-be immigrants.

U.S. PREFERENCE SYSTEMS AND THEIR RESULTS

From the time immigration was greatly limited in 1921, until 1965, the "national origins quota system" was in effect. Based on a melange of bigotry and pseudoscientific racial theories, the policy had been to admit Northern and Western Europeans and to exclude all but a few immigrants from any other region outside our hemisphere.

While the 1921, 1924 and 1952 quota laws had most effectively implemented the policies which produced them, support for those policies eroded steadily after the Second World War. The desire for increased population and for admission of workers with needed skills, compassion for the plight of European refugees, and narrowing support for the view that our "basic strain" had to be protected combined to produce a tangle of public laws, new regulations, and private bills designed to create paths through and around the national origins quota laws. In the end, it took the irresistible pressure of the 1964-65 Great Society tide to bring about a change.

The broad outlines of the new policy were a matter of general agreement. "Reunification of families is to be the foremost consideration," the Senate report states,[2] meaning that close relatives of American citizens and aliens admitted for permanent residence will be given priority. In addition, needed workers are to be admitted: "aliens who are members of the professions, arts, or sciences, and . . . skilled or unskilled laborers who are needed in the United States." Finally, provision is to be made, continuing the United States' tradition, for the admission of "certain refugees."

Once it is decided to give priority to relatives and to workers needed by our economy, the next question is how much priority to give to each. The 1965 law gives special treatment to the very closest relatives of American citizens: parents of citizens over twenty-one, and spouses and unmarried minor children of citizens, are admitted without numerical limitation. This priority is difficult to criticize, but beyond it, the choices are less clear.

It may well be asked why the occupational preferences receive only 20 percent of the available visas, plus any kept for the non-preference category. Are relatives, with 80 percent, four times as valuable as skilled workers? No "scientific" judgment can be made here, and therefore, while it is worthwhile to note that Congress has made choices and that these are purely judgmental, it is difficult to criticize the decisions made.

As to the priority given to third preference workers (professionals, often doctors, and scientists and artists of exceptional ability) over sixth (skilled and unskilled workers), this judgment seems obvious but has, indirectly, come under considerable attack. The advantage of the present system is clear: it provides the U.S. with highly trained new workers in areas in which their presence is needed. Further, it does so at relatively little cost to us, since most of these individuals will have been trained elsewhere. There is an obvious logic to the desire to admit, among workers, the more intelligent over the less intelligent, the skilled over the unskilled, those with the most to contribute over those with less.

Whatever the mechanics of the selection system, the preference given to professional workers needed in the U.S. contributes in some degree to a "brain drain" and to some extent injures many Americans by lessening the incentive to develop the skills of our own manpower.

The "brain drain" is a separate subject requiring full-scale treatment on its own. It is important to note here, however, that the selection of the best-trained applicants, an obvious goal for an immigration system, is often said to clash directly with other domestic policy goals or to harm relations with the countries from which the skilled immigrants are coming.

In September 1976, Congress passed a medical education law which contained a section greatly favored by the American Medical Association. This section virtually stops the entry into the U.S. of all foreign doctors. Whether this law is well-advised at this time is certainly open to dispute. Whatever the hopes of the AMA regarding medical manpower in the future, at the present time many of the hospitals in our large cities are staffed largely by foreign doctors. In my mind, the cutting off of this supply can only exacerbate these hospitals' staffing problems and reduce the quality of medical care.

Under the McCarran-Walter Act, immigration from Northern and Western Europe was greatly favored. With the introduction of the preference system, the countries sending the most immigrants changed entirely, as the following lists show.

WESTERN HEMISPHERE
1965

Canada	38,327
Mexico	37,969
Cuba	19,760
Dominican Republic	9,504
Argentina	6,124
Ecuador	4,392
Haiti	3,609

1975

Mexico	62,205
Cuba	25,955
Dominican Republic	14,066
Jamaica	11,076
Canada	7,308
Colombia	6,434
Trinidad & Tobago	5,982
Haiti	5,145

EASTERN HEMISPHERE
1965

United Kingdom	27,538
Germany	24,045
Italy	10,821
Poland	8,465
Ireland	5,463
China	4,057
France	4,039
Japan	3,180
Philippines	3,130
Netherlands	3,085

1975

Philippines	31,751
Korea	28,362
China	18,536
India	15,773

EASTERN HEMISPHERE (CONT.)

Portugal	11,845
Italy	11,552
United Kingdom	10,807
Greece	9,984
Germany	5,154
U.S.S.R.	5,118

In 1965, one-fourteenth of all immigrants were Asians; in 1975, just under one-third were. The top four source countries are now the Philippines, Korea, China and India. The reason is, of course, that the national origins quota system has been replaced by the preference system, bringing to the U.S. individuals who, due to family ties to the United States or to special skills needed here, are believed to be the most worthy of the limited number of visas available.

As striking as the changes in the national origins of Eastern Hemisphere immigrants are the changes in the patterns of their occupational skills. Eastern Hemisphere immigrants, and especially Asians, are much more likely to be highly trained or professional workers than are immigrants from any other area.

Finally, no discussion of our immigration laws should fail to deal with U.S. policy towards refugees. The seventh preference, which is accorded 6 percent of the 170,000 Eastern Hemisphere visas, is available to refugees who "because of persecution or fear of persecution on account of race, religion, or political opinion . . . have fled from any Communist or Communist-dominated country or from any country in the general area of the Middle East," or to "persons uprooted by catastrophic natural calamity as defined by the President." No president has ever admitted refugees under the "natural calamity" provision despite many calamities since 1965, although the few thousand available visas would probably not have been of much help. The seventh preference has almost never been oversubscribed; apparently, fewer than 10,200 refugees per year are able to prove the legitimacy of their cases to the satisfaction of the Immigration and Naturalization Service.

THE SPECIAL CASE OF THE WESTERN HEMISPHERE

Meanwhile, in the Western Hemisphere, where demand for visas far exceeds the supply, there was, until now, no preference system available for choosing among applicants. It was thought in 1965 that such choices could be avoided. Historically, there had been no limitation placed on Western Hemisphere immigration, and the national origins quota had not applied. Continuation of this treatment was included in the early proposals for reform in 1965 and the Administration backed this position as being part of our "Good Neighbor" policy. The assumption was that no numerical limitation was necessary. Available statistics showed that immigration from the Western Hemisphere had averaged about 160,000 per year in the years 1961–65, and the high birth rates and comparatively low economic opportunities prevailing in much of this hemisphere are not state secrets. Congressmen and senators were sufficiently worried to tack on the numerical ceiling of 120,000, effective after a three-year transition period, before passing the bill.

Since the original reform proposals had been drawn up with no numerical limit for Western Hemisphere immigration and since, in any case, the supply of visas was expected to exceed the demand, no attempt was made in the 1965 Act to give relatives preference over workers, or to distinguish between closer and more distant relatives or among workers of varying levels of skills. Applicants were simply granted visas on a first-come, first-served basis. However, in order "to protect the U.S. economy from job competition and from adverse working standards as a consequence of immigrant workers entering the labor market," the labor certification previously mentioned was required of all immigrants entering the labor market, except for parents, children under twenty-one, or spouses of citizens or permanent resident aliens.

If only 120,000 people each year applied for visas from Western Hemisphere countries, the system established by the 1965 Act would have worked. The alien would apply for a visa, and after some paperwork (obtaining a labor certification or an exemption therefrom based on family relationship), would be admitted a few months later. In fact, however, the delay in getting a visa is now two and one-half years, meaning that 300,000 more people have applied for visas than the State Department, doling them out at the mandatory rate of 120,000 per year, has been able to process.

While the cause for the delay is obvious—more applicants than visas—the great leap in the number of applications is not really understood. The explanation is unknown but, although information is in short supply, some reasons may be advanced. For example, increasing educational levels and urbanization mean that more people become familiar with the U.S. and its standard of living. A somewhat higher standard of living abroad means that many more people can afford the trip to the U.S., especially since air fares recently have been declining. High birth rates have led to explosive population growth, with concomitant un- and under-employment. All of these are incentives to emigrate to the U.S., where the large number of Spanish-speaking residents (among them Cubans, Puerto Ricans, and Mexican-Americans) permits the new arrival to make his way without knowing English. All these trends have accelerated and fed upon each other in the last ten years. The end result is that many more people from the Western Hemisphere wish to come here than the law at present is willing to admit.

The delay in obtaining a visa distorts and to some extent defeats the key goals of our new immigration law. It is obvious that a two and one-half year delay in the reuniting of a family is contrary to the central policy behind the 1965 Act. Until now, the situation in which, for example, a permanent resident may be forced to wait two and one-half years for permission for his spouse to join him is precisely what the Congress thought it was legislating against. It is equally clear that a two and one-half year delay in permitting the entry of needed workers destroys the responsiveness of the Act to the conditions of our economy. Some less apparent effects are equally significant. First, no distinctions whatsoever are drawn among applicants, an acceptable policy when all are admitted, but a foolish one when all are not, Thus, close relatives receive no preference over workers, and highly skilled or professional workers are admitted no sooner than are the unskilled, with doctors getting no preference over maids so long as

there is some degree of shortage of both. One fine example of inequity in the system, certainly unintended by Congress, results from the section of the law providing, for the Western Hemisphere, that parents of U.S. citizens are exempt from the labor certification requirement. Thus, a woman, whether married or not and without any skills, establishes her right to a visa if she gives birth while physically in the U.S. She is then the parent of an "American citizen," exempt from the labor certification requirement and thus entitled to a visa. These cases, called "baby cases" by immigration lawyers, have now come to take up a significant proportion of the 120,000 visas available in the Western Hemisphere. (As mentioned earlier, this type of case was discontinued after January 1, 1977.)

A second and related point is that a two and one-half year wait between job offer and ultimate admission is most likely to discourage potential immigrants who are doing best at home due to their ability and training, or whose home country offers a substantial amount of opportunity, and for whom the move to the United States is not a matter of intense commitment.

Third, the backlog gives rise to a substantial amount of illegal immigration. In order to obtain a labor certification, the alien must have a specific job offer from a prospective employer. The alien's qualifications for his particular job, the lack of Americans in that job category who are "able, willing, qualified, and available," and the effect of the alien's proposed terms and conditions of employment must all be approved. Obviously, it is not easy for an alien to learn of a job opening and to obtain an offer for it while abroad. Still less likely is it that the prospective employer will be willing to file a set of papers with the Labor Department and possibly haggle with them over job requirements and wages, on behalf of an alien whom he has never met, for a job to be taken two or three years later when the alien is finally admitted. As a result, Western Hemisphere aliens by the thousands enter the U.S. with visitors' visas forbidding them to work, and then seek and obtain job offers and illegally fill those jobs while awaiting their visas. When the visa is available, they return home briefly to receive it from the Consul and are back at work here in the U.S. soon after.

While introducing delays and disorders in the handling of Western Hemisphere immigration, the 1965 reforms have had only slight impact on the patterns of either national origin or occupational skill of the immigrants as the above lists show.

As to the occupational mix, statistics show very few changes of great magnitude, especially when compared with the changes brought about in the Eastern Hemisphere by the preference system. The only noticeable changes appear to be a drop in professionals and a rise in laborers and service workers—that is, a *downgrading* of the skills of arriving aliens. The lack of a preference system and the long backlog are almost certainly the culprits here.

In short, the "reforms" for the Western Hemispheric immigration introduced in 1965 managed to defeat many of the basic purposes of the 1965 Act, to increase illegal immigration, to downgrade slightly the average skill of arriving immigrants, and to create a two and one-half year backlog of would-be immigrants.

THE "WESTERN HEMISPHERE BILL" OF 1976

To remedy many of these problems, Congress passed H.R. 14535 in September 1976. The so-called "Western Hemisphere Bill" was to equalize the treatment of Eastern and Western Hemisphere immigrants. Basically, the law does the following (insofar as Western Hemisphere immigration is concerned):

(1) The Western Hemisphere numerical limitation remains at 120,000, exclusive of immediate relatives of U.S. citizens.

(2) The quota for any individual colony or dependency is raised from 200 to 600. This will greatly ameliorate the situation in the British colonies in the West Indies, whose quotas had previously been only 200.

(3) The limitation of 20,000 per country per year is imported from the Eastern Hemisphere. The imposition of the 20,000 per year limitation means that the waiting list from Mexico will increase. The exact effects of the limitation will be discussed later.

(4) The adjustment to permanent resident status of a Cuban refugee will no longer count against the 120,000 Western Hemisphere limitation.

(5) The preference system which obtains in the Eastern Hemiphere is applied to the Western Hemisphere. The effects of this change are impossible to calculate at this time because the Western Hemisphere waiting lists make no mention of the method by which applicants become registered. In any case, several new categories of possible immigrants are added.

The probable results of the 1976 Amendments on the Western Hemisphere may now be computed. First, assume that the Western Hemisphere waiting list is 300,000, of whom 100,000 are Mexicans. Second, subtract the 65,000 Cubans from the 200,000 non-Mexicans, to be called hereafter simply non-Mexicans.

The first preference, unmarried sons and daughters (over twenty-one) of U.S. citizens, is allowed 24,000 visas per year. There is no way to assess the number of applicants in this class, but it will not exceed a few thousand per year (the Eastern Hemisphere currently uses about 1,000 per year) even for the first few years.

The second preference will absorb all the people currently registered as spouses or minor children of legal residents, assuming the resident files a petition, plus many new applicants who are unmarried sons and daughters over twenty-one of legal residents. We must first figure the period from January 1, 1977 to September 30, 1977. The Immigration Service will be receiving, but not yet approving, petitions for all preferences because of clerical backlog, so this period is apt to proceed as before. Thus, because of the removal of Cubans from the waiting list, the list could well be down to eighteen months, or 180,000, by October 1, 1977. Of this number, about 60,000 would be eligible for the second preference category (about 35,000 non-Mexicans plus 25,000 Mexicans). About 50 percent more for new petitions from previously ineligible adult children can be added, arriving at 52,500 non-Mexicans and 37,500 Mexicans on the waiting list as of October 1, 1977. This preference is allowed 24,000 per year, plus spilldown from unused first-preference visas—we can estimate almost 48,000 for the first year. After October 1, 1977, the triggering provision for Mexico comes into effect, and Mexico will be limited to an absolute maximum of 8,000 second-preference visas per year (20 percent of 20,000, plus almost 20 percent spilldown from first preference), making the wait for Mexicans in this category another four and one-half years. Congress specifically refused to make an exception for Mexico in the 1976 Amendments, and thus the result that a bill designed to reduce backlogs greatly increases them for Mexicans. For the non-Mexicans, the lmost 40,000 visas available per year should quickly liquidate the backlog.

The third and fourth preferences are apt to be quite undersubscribed, with visas readily available. The fifth preference, brothers and sisters of U.S. citizens over twenty-one, may well be backlogged for some time since one U.S. citizen may well have many brothers and sisters. This is especially so because this category never existed before in this hemisphere. But there will be 28,800 visas per year, plus probably 10,000 spilldowns from third and fourth preferences, making 40,000 visas per year. Again, the wait for Mexico is apt to be longer than for the rest of the hemisphere.

The sixth preference, nonprofessional workers, is another problem area. If, as we assumed above, the waiting list is down to 180,000 persons by October 1, 1977, there would be 60,000 eligible for sixthpreference, 35,000 non-Mexicans and 25,000 Mexicans. This category is allowed only 12,000 visas per year (2,000 Mexicans and 10,000 others), and thus the wait could easily be three years for non-Mexicans and ten years for Mexicans.

As for nonpreference, this category will have on its list all the present "baby cases" (parents of U.S. citizen children), plus parents of legal permanent residents. On October 1, 1977, there will be about 35,000 of these non-Mexicans, plus about 25,000 Mexicans. The nonpreference category will receive the spilldown of unused visa numbers (if any) from the preferences. There should be several thousand of these visas available per year, since seventh preference (refugees) will hardly be used at all (7,200 per year) and fifth preference may not use all the available visas. Again, Mexico will only get 1,200 of these, making the wait for Mexicans almost interminable. For non-Mexicans as well, the wait could well be a long one.

IMMIGRATION AND LABOR

One of the major reforms of the 1965 Act was the new labor certification program, designed to protect the U.S. economy from unemployment and adverse effects on wages and working conditions. The program is largely a failure since it does not, and cannot, limit the immigration of workers to job categories in which there is a shortage. There are two reasons for this. First, the vast majority of immigrants do not require a labor certification because they arrive as relatives exempt from the certification requirements. In 1972, it is estimated that only 11.7 percent of all immigrants were required to get labor certifications. Even if, as has been estimated, only half of all immigrants join the labor force (the rest may be too old, or too young, or not work for some other reason), this percentage may be doubled and, thus, only one-quarter of all immigrants joining the labor force need a labor certification before doing so.[3]

Second, immigrants have absolutely no obligation to stay on the particular job, or even in the field of work, for which they were certified. Indeed, it has been variously estimated that within two years of entry, 57 to 66 percent of immigrants in the labor force change occupations.[4]

An explanation of how the program works will indicate that it is less than innocuous. For tens of thousands of applications for certification, the Manpower Administration, usually working through state employment services, must investigate and determine whether the job requirements listed are valid ones, whether the alien's qualifications are sufficient, whether there is a shortage of workers in that job in that locale, and then whether the terms of employment are average or better. The program obviously consumes great numbers of man-hours for a procedure that does not touch over 85 percent of incoming aliens.

The alternative proposed most often is for a list of occupations and regions in which a shortage of workers exists. If the job he seeks is on the list, the alien is admitted; if it is not, he is not. No specific job offer would be required. This reform, while it would shortcut bureaucratic delays, would prejudice the alien in one way: the current system allows the employer to list his specific requirements and the alien his specialized skills, while the proposed alternative would enable the Labor Department to bar entire categories of applicants. In any case, the proposed reform would not overcome a basic contradiction in our immigration policy: the great emphasis we place on the admission of relatives makes it impossible to exercise much control over the effects of immigration on the U.S. labor market.

The 1976 Amendments make several changes in the labor certification requirements, evidencing some Congressional dissatisfaction with the implementation of the section by the Department of Labor. Originally, the labor certification provision said that the Secretary of Labor must certify that there are not sufficient workers "in the United States" available for the alien's job. The Department of Labor sometimes took this comment literally, denying an application because of a nationwide oversupply of engineers without first determining the local job market and whether any of the distantly-located engineers wanted to relocate. The 1976 version simply leaves out the phrase "in the United States." Second, colleges and universities had complained that they had difficulty hiring specialist scholars, since the Labor Department usually indicated that there were "qualified" Americans available in the field. The 1976 version adds the words "(or equally qualified in the case of aliens who are members of the teaching profession or who have exceptional ability in the sciences or the arts)," thus mandating approval unless the U.S. worker is *equally* qualified.

ILLEGAL IMMIGRATION

It is often argued that the real threat to employment and to working conditions is *illegal* immigration. To begin with, the magnitude of the problem is unknown. Furthermore, discussion of the subject is distorted unless the Mexican border problem is treated separately. Each year, approximately 90 percent of all located deportable aliens are Mexicans, and most are found in the border area. Therefore, gross figures about aliens located, deported, or required to depart are often misleading. For example, most Mexican "illegals" are here without any

papers whatsoever—the proverbial "wetbacks" who cross the Rio Grande. By contrast, in New York City, 90 percent of aliens deported came here legally with temporary visas which have run out.

Still, some of the explanations for increased illegal immigration from Mexico apply to the increase in illegal immigration in general. As has been noted, the labor certification program requires a specific job offer, and many prospective immigrants believe, probably with good reason, that they will not be able to procure one unless they are here to seek it out. For Eastern Hemisphere aliens (and after January 1, 1977, for Western Hemisphere aliens too), "adjustment of status" (from, for example, visitor) to permanent resident is permitted while the alien remains in the U.S. It is estimated that in 1972 a full 40 percent of all labor certification beneficiaries were adjustees.[5] The alien often finds himself here with a job offer, and with the assurance that his status will be changed and that he will be allowed to stay permanently. Very often, he simply starts to work before his labor certification comes through. More likely, the alien must start work to prove his qualifications to his employer. It is the rare employer who will sponsor an alien without thorough testing, and thus the labor certification requirement almost requires illegal work. It is for this reason that one study concluded that "the adjustment process . . . legalizes the presence of a substantial number of previously illegal workers."[6]

Now the adjustment will be available to Western Hemisphere applicants, the lure will be even greater. On the other hand, this year Congress attempted to penalize the illegal worker. Adjustment of status will no longer be available to an applicant from *either* hemisphere who is or becomes illegally employed after January 1, 1977, and who has not yet filed his application for adjustment. To my mind, this will to some extent increase the amount of "off the books" work by illegal aliens, but will have little other effect because the alien will still be eligible for an immigrant visa at the United States Consulate in his home country.

The 1965 reforms have created a good deal of illegality: the requirement that the alien get a specific job offer, and the backlog in visa availability in the Western Hemisphere combine to produce a tremendous incentive for aliens to work here illegally. Second, another reason for the great number of illegal aliens here is that there is no penalty for this violation of the immigration laws except expulsion from the U.S., and due to the lack of enforcement officers, the illegal alien is correct in assuming that he is likely never to be caught.

I have previously expressed my opinion, based on current evidence and research, that, on the whole, illegal aliens do not either depress U.S. working conditions or take jobs from Americans, and I shall not repeat the arguments here. Rather than making it a crime to hire illegal aliens, the Federal Government should simply spend more money on the enforcement of the immigration laws already on the books. The Government, if it criminalized the hiring of illegal aliens, would be inviting a judicial and administrative nightmare. Aside from the touchy question of when an employer "knows" that his employee is illegal (that is, what is the employer's duty), the probability is that employers would flee to the other extreme, refusing to hire anyone who looked or sounded foreign.

PUTTING OUR CHOICES IN PERSPECTIVE

Many of the problems resulting from the new immigration law are soluble and, with the 1976 Amendments, Congress has at least attacked the problem. It remains to be seen what the actual results of the reform will be, but legislation cannot, of course, resolve the irreconcilable conflicts built into our immigration policy: as has been noted, if we emphasize the economic role of immigration and admit more and more skilled workers, we sacrifice the goal of reuniting families; if we stress (as is now the case) the admission of relatives, we lose control of the affect of immigration on our labor market. If we admit highly skilled immigrants, we may be hurting their home countries and our own less privileged citizens; if we fail to admit the highly skilled applicants, we deprive our country of their badly needed talents. At the same time, we face these difficult choices because our country remains immensely attractive to enormous numbers of aliens, and because we are willing to admit a substantial number of these. It is in this context that the successes and failures of the Immigration and Nationality Act must be evaluated.

POSTSCRIPT

Since the presentation of this article, there have been several developments worthy of mention.

First, settlement of the matter involving visa numbers for Cuban refugees has made about 150,000 more visas available for Western Hemisphere applicants. Any applicant whose case was begun before January 1, 1977 can receive a visa. In addition, the demand has not exceeded the supply since January 1, 1977, and all new cases can also be accommodated with the exception of the second preference for Mexico, which is a few months behind. On the whole, the selection system in the Western Hemisphere is working quite well with no delays. In the Eastern Hemisphere, the demand has exceeded the supply in the nonpreference category, and that category is oversubscribed by almost two years.

In addition, those countries which exceeded the 20,000 per year limit, China, Korea, and the Philippines, now have delays in several preference categories. The worst situation is in the Philippines where third preference, fifth preference, and nonpreference are all more than seven years behind.

Another development is the adoption by the U.S. Department of Labor of new regulations requiring advertising and other efforts to attract a U.S. worker before an alien can be certified. On the whole, the system seems to be working, except that the amount of paperwork involved has doubled or tripled and there are delays of many months in processing.

It appears that the new regulations will be more sensitive to the individual characteristics of the job involved and, therefore, fairer to the alien, but the delays are unfortunate.

NOTES

1. Senate Report 748, Report of the Judiciary Committee U.S. Code Congressional & Administrative News, Eighty-ninth Congress, First Session (1965), p. 3, 332.
2. Ibid.
3. Immigrants and the American Labor Market," Manpower Research Monograph #31, U.S. Department of Labor Manpower Administration (Washington, D.C., 1974), p.49.
4. Testimony of Robert Brown, Associate Manpower Administrator, to House Hearings, No. 17, *supra,* p.25.
5. "Immigrants and the American Labor Market," No. 3, *supra,* p.42.
6. Ibid., p.32.

POLARITY IN THE MAKEUP OF CHINESE IMMIGRANTS[1]

Betty Lee Sung

CHINESE IMMIGRATION TO THE UNITED STATES

Chinese have been on United States soil for more than a century and a quarter. They were among the "Forty-niners" who flocked to California during the Gold Rush. These Chinese came from the southern China province of Kwangtung, near the mouth of the Pearl River. They left their homes, braving the unknown, pulling up firmly embedded roots, risking the executioner's axe, and journeying 7,000 miles across the Pacific in sail-driven vessels to seek their fortunes in a new land they called the "Mountain of Gold" (referring to the hills of San Francisco during the days of the Gold Rush). The pull was the prospect of gold, but the push was the impoverished soil that would not yield even a marginal livelihood and which was made poorer by civil strife and political unrest.

Hardly two years after the first cry of gold went up, 25,000 stalwarts from Cathay were found in California. The virgin lands and undeveloped country needed hands, and the Chinese willingly provided the manpower to work the mines, drain the ditches, till the soil, harvest the seas, and build the network of railroads that bound the nation together. When their work was done, their ungrateful beneficiaries said, "The United States is for whites. Go back to where you came from." Thus was set in motion a racist campaign that resulted in a continuing series of legislative maneuvers designed to keep the Chinese out and to make life intolerable for those who remained.

CHINESE EXCLUSION

Chinese immigrants dropped from 40,000 in 1882 to 10 persons in the year 1887. During the next sixty-one years, fourteen separate pieces of legislation were enacted by Congress which virtually sealed the doors of the United States against Chinese immigrants. These laws were repealed in 1943 when a gesture of good will was made toward China, but repeal was little more than just that—a gesture.

Beginning in 1943, the Chinese were given a quota of 105 per year, and this quota took in anyone of Chinese blood regardless of his country of birth, residence or allegiance. For the next twenty-two years, until 1965, a mere 6,055 Chinese persons were admitted to the United States under the quota. This figure included persons admitted under a number of refugee relief acts, and averaged about 275 per year. At that rate of admission it is a wonder that there were any Chinese at all extant in the United States.

To preserve themselves against complete extinction, the Chinese resorted to inconspicuous circumvention of the immigration laws so that, for half a century before repeal, the Chinese population for the entire country hovered around 60,000 to 80,000 and was almost all adult male. If they were all to attend a football game at the same time one afternoon in the Orange Bowl in Miami, they would fit comfortably into the stadium. Dispersed throughout the country, they were hardly noticeable and politically impotent. It was the express intent of the United States Government to keep it that way.

Not only was governmental policy directed against the Chinese, it was aimed also against people of darker shades of skin coloring. This was spelled out in the immigration laws in the national origins quotas, so that countries like Great Britain, Germany, Ireland, and the Scandinavian countries had claim to about 120,000 quota slots out of the 150,000 available annually. By 1965, this racist viewpoint was no longer in vogue and absolutely indefensible. The national origins quotas were amended and an entirely different premise substituted for American immigration policy.

The Chinese and most other Asiatic countries were prime beneficiaries of this change in the immigration laws. Formerly, with the exception of Japan with a quota of 185, and China with 105, no other

TABLE 1
Chinese Immigrant Aliens by Sex, 1944-75

Years	Male	%	Female	%	Annual Total
1944	10	29	24	71	34
1945	20	41	64	59	109
1946	71	31	162	69	233
1947	142	13	986	87	1,128
1948	257	8	3,317	92	3,574
1949	242	10	2,248	90	2,490
1950	110	8	1,179	92	1,289
1951	126	11	957	89	1,083
1952	118	10	1,034	90	1,152
1953	203	19	890	81	1,093
1954	1,511	55	1,236	45	2,747
1955	1,261	48	1,367	52	2,628
1956	2,007	45	2,443	55	4,450
1957	2,487	49	2,636	51	5,123
1958	1,396	44	1,799	56	3,195
1959	2,846	47	3,185	53	6,031
1960	1,873	51	1,799	49	3,672
1961	1,565	41	2,273	59	3,838
1962	1,916	42	2,753	58	4,669
1963	2,297	43	3,073	57	5,370
1964	2,597	46	3,051	54	5,648
1965	2,242	47	2,527	53	4,769
1966	8,613	49	8,995	51	17,608
1967	12,811	51	12,285	49	25,096
1968	7,862	48	8,572	52	16,434
1969	10,001	48	10,892	52	20,893
1970	8,586	48	9,370	52	17,956
1971	8,287	47	9,335	53	17,622
1972	10,437	48	11,293	52	21,730
1973	9,937	46	11,719	54	21,656
1974	10,724	47	11,961	53	22,685
1975	11,179	48	12,248	52	23,427

Source: U.S. Bureau of Immigration and Naturalization, *Annual Reports*

Asian country had more than 100, which was the minimum. The Immigration Act of 1965 extended the upper limit of any one country to 20,000. Consequently, it was inevitable that a spurt in Asian immigration would result.

Chinese immigration has been particularly spectacular. The number of Chinese aliens admitted to the United States by sex for the thirty-two years following the repeal of the Exclusion Acts is shown in Table 1. The fact that the numbers exceed the quota of 105 allotted the Chinese was due to several relief measures. In 1946, an amendment was passed permitting Chinese male citizens to bring their wives and children into the country without charge to the national quota. The same year the War Brides Act was passed allowing GI wives to join their husbands in the States, again without charge to the quotas. Consequently, Chinese immigration slowly climbed to six thousand until, by executive order, President John F. Kennedy permitted the admission of a number of refugees. This took Chinese immigration onto a higher plateau, but when the full force of the 1965 Immigration Act took effect, Chinese immigration shot upward, increasing as much as 400 to 500 percent.

This increase in immigration has made a tremendous impact upon the Chinese communities in the United States and has completely altered the demographic characteristics of this ethnic group. The immigrants of yesteryears were able-bodied males whose purpose in coming was to earn and save enough money to go back to China. They brought no family and they lived the lives of rootless transients. They filled the gap in the lower occupational strata, working at jobs that others disdained. They clustered in Chinatowns for familiarity and security in numbers. They were poorly educated and made little or no attempt to learn the English language.

Before 1943, Chinese immigrants were not permitted to become citizens, no matter how long they had resided in this country. They had no political backing and little use for American customs. They were made scapegoats for the ills of the times, and they were used as a political football to be booted and booed at even when their numbers had dwindled to the point of insignificance. They were forbidden by the Alien Land Acts to own land. Denied a normal family life by a court ruling which stated that all Asians were aliens ineligible for citizenship and hence not permitted the benefits of the family reunification aims under the immigration laws, they were also denied the right to intermarry in many western states.

Cowed and oppressed by the weight of institutionalized discrimination, the Chinese worked hard within their circumscribed confines, looking only to the day when they could be free to return to their homeland. Therefore, by true definition, the Chinese were not immigrants but transients—sojourners. Each generation departed these shores, leaving no roots that reached into American soil. In spite of the long history of the Chinese in this country, each successive generation had to start anew without the benefit of a foundation built by those before them.

The picture began to change after World War II. The impetus was not the repeal of the entire body of Chinese exclusion acts in 1943—the 105 person quota was tantamount to exclusion and was so intended. It was the War Brides Act of 1946 that wedged open the door for wives of Chinese who had served in the Armed Forces of the United States. The spurt in Chinese immigration after 1946 reveals that almost 90 percent of the immigrants were females, taking the first opportunity they could to join their husbands in this country.

Almost every year since that time, female immigrants have exceeded males. The tremendous disparity of the sexes seemed to exert a magnetic pull that is still evident among Chinese immigrants today. The ratio of females to males hovered around nine to one for many years. It has declined, but as late as 1975, females still made up 52 percent of total Chinese immigrants (see Tables 2 and 3).

The preponderance of females in the Chinese immigration pattern has great implications for the Chinese population in this country. For one, the genocidal policy of cutting off future native-born generations of Chinese was arrested. Children born of the reunions made possible by the War Brides Act are the emerging leaders of their people, and their outlook is entirely different from that of past generations. The communities are better balanced by the presence of women and children, young and old,

TABLE 2
Chinese Immigrants Admitted by Sex and Age Group, 1966-75

IMMIGRANTS	1966 M	1966 F	1967 M	1967 F	1968 M	1968 F	1969 M	1969 F	1970 M	1970 F
TOTAL	17,608		25,096		16,434		20,893		17,956	
	8,613	8,995	12,811	12,285	7,862	8,572	10,001	10,892	8,586	9,370
Under 5 Yrs.	548	520	734	646	399	450	686	622	437	438
5-9 Yrs.	953	828	1,125	1,006	639	518	989	891	685	636
10-19 Yrs.	1,888	1,739	2,309	2,187	1,412	1,523	1,964	2,037	1,427	1,428
20-29 Yrs.	1,376	1,649	2,221	2,913	1,436	2,409	1,588	2,756	1,776	3,249
30-39 Yrs.	1,817	1,480	3,310	2,329	1,996	1,478	2,337	1,823	2,258	1,602
40-49 Yrs.	998	912	1,528	1,223	904	789	1,277	1,182	1,028	862
50-59 Yrs.	532	904	879	955	530	645	709	744	551	557
60-69 Yrs.	355	630	514	683	379	478	311	545	285	374
70-79 Yrs.	130	289	160	288	151	223	117	239	117	177
80 Yrs. +	16	44	31	55	16	59	23	53	22	47

IMMIGRANTS	1971 M	1971 F	1972 M	1972 F	1973 M	1973 F	1974 M	1974 F	1975 M	1975 F
TOTAL	17,622		21,730		21,656		22,685		23,427	
	8,287	9,335	10,437	11,293	9,937	11,719	10,724	11,961	11,179	12,248
Under 5 Yrs.	396	390	617	531	571	539	599	582	611	562
5-9 Yrs.	561	509	755	734	750	660	769	741	749	653
10-19 Yrs.	1,153	1,245	1,506	1,548	1,445	1,583	1,602	1,737	1,862	1,771
20-29 Yrs.	2,106	3,679	2,610	4,264	2,537	4,058	3,091	4,209	3,381	4,295
30-39 Yrs.	2,345	1,606	2,622	1,797	1,981	1,630	1,905	1,641	1,866	1,621
40-49 Yrs.	901	767	1,234	965	1,164	1,045	1,189	1,064	1,180	1,184
50-59 Yrs.	484	556	629	688	765	1,119	818	1,013	807	1,103
60-69 Yrs.	246	367	323	467	526	743	532	680	548	734
70-79 Yrs.	87	171	112	239	174	277	196	238	147	259
80 Yrs. +	8	45	29	60	24	65	23	56	28	66

Source: U.S. Immigration and Naturalization Service, *Annual Reports* (Washington, D.C.: 1966-1975), Table 9.

TABLE 3

Percentage of Chinese Immigrants Admitted, by Sex and Age Group, 1966-75

AGE GROUP	1966 M	1966 F	1967 M	1967 F	1968 M	1968 F	1969 M	1969 F	1970 M	1970 F
Total (100%)										
Under 5 Yrs.	6.4	5.8	5.7	5.3	5.1	5.2	6.9	5.7	5.1	4.7
5-9 Yrs.	11.1	9.2	8.8	8.2	8.1	6.0	9.9	8.2	8.0	6.8
10-19 Yrs.	21.9	19.3	18.0	17.8	18.0	17.5	19.6	18.7	16.6	15.2
20-29 Yrs.	16.0	18.3	17.3	23.7	18.3	28.1	15.9	25.3	20.7	34.7
30-39 Yrs.	21.1	16.5	25.8	19.0	25.4	17.2	23.4	16.7	26.3	17.1
40-49 Yrs.	11.6	10.1	11.9	10.0	11.5	9.2	12.8	10.9	12.0	9.2
50-59 Yrs.	6.2	10.1	6.9	7.8	6.7	7.5	7.1	6.8	6.4	5.9
60-69 Yrs.	4.1	7.0	4.0	5.6	4.8	5.6	3.1	5.0	3.3	4.0
70-79 Yrs.	1.5	3.2	1.2	2.3	1.9	2.6	1.2	2.2	1.4	1.9
80 Yrs. +	0.2	0.5	0.2	0.4	0.2	0.7	0.2	0.5	0.3	0.5

AGE GROUP	1971 M	1971 F	1972 M	1972 F	1973 M	1973 F	1974 M	1974 F	1975 M	1975 F
Total (100%)										
Under 5 Yrs.	4.8	4.2	5.9	4.7	5.8	4.6	5.6	4.9	5.5	4.6
5-9 Yrs.	6.8	5.5	7.2	6.5	7.6	5.6	7.2	6.2	6.7	5.3
10-19 Yrs.	13.9	13.3	14.4	13.7	14.5	13.5	14.9	14.5	16.7	14.5
20-29 Yrs.	25.4	39.4	25.0	37.8	25.5	34.6	28.8	35.2	30.2	35.1
30-39 Yrs.	28.3	17.2	25.1	15.9	19.9	13.9	17.8	13.7	16.7	13.2
40-49 Yrs.	10.9	8.2	11.8	8.5	11.7	8.9	11.1	8.9	10.6	9.7
50-59 Yrs.	5.8	6.0	6.0	6.1	7.7	9.6	7.6	8.5	7.2	9.0
60-69 Yrs.	3.0	3.9	3.1	4.1	5.3	6.3	5.0	5.7	4.9	6.0
70-79 Yrs.	1.0	1.8	1.1	2.1	1.8	2.4	1.8	2.0	1.3	2.1
80 Yrs. +	0.1	0.5	0.3	0.5	0.2	0.6	0.2	0.5	0.3	0.5

Source: Table 2A

thus bringing about a restructuring of Chinese-American society into families rather than bachelor groups held together by communal affiliations.

SOURCE AND DESTINATION OF CHINESE IMMIGRANTS

In the past, Chinese immigrants generally originated from the area within a small radius of the mouth of the Pearl River near the city of Canton. To be specific, the county or district of Toishan and four or five districts adjoining it are the fountainhead. To ascertain whether Chinese immigrants are more diverse in their place of origin now, or whether these places are still the main sources of immigration to the United States, a count was taken from the data of a study by the China Institute. Of those indicating their hometown, 48 percent of those surveyed in 1972 were from Sze Yup or the four districts, and 30 percent from Toishan itself. Twelve percent were from the city of Canton. These data seem to indicate that Chinese immigrants are still predominatly Toishanese, but those from other areas and provinces are increasing.

The immigrants hail from the above-mentioned districts in mainland China, but they embark from Hong Kong because an exit visa is difficult to obtain from the Chinese government. An exit visa is also required to leave Taiwan, and immigrants to the United States from this island constitute a growing proportion, though not as great as those from the Pearl River Delta. These two groups speak a different dialect, and their backgrounds are quite dissimilar.

More and more, Chinese immigrants are coming into the United States from places other than Hong Kong and Taiwan. In the wake of Castro's takeover in Cuba, a sizeable group of Chinese fled Havana and have resettled in Miami and New York. Unrest in Trinidad and Jamaica brought others from the Caribbean area. Southeast Asia has sent its share of Chinese to the United States. They come from the Philippines, Indonesia, Malaysia, and Singapore. Some who had fled the Mainland some years ago and gone to places like Japan, Canada, and Brazil are now relocating to this country. And, the most conspicuous group of Chinese from a non-Chinese country are those from Vietnam. Though they are considered Vietnamese refugees, in culture and blood many are Chinese. Upon their arrival in the United States, they attached themselves to the Chinese community, thereby diluting its homogenity.

In 1960, the census showed that three states contained almost three-fourths of all the Chinese in the United States. California held the lead with 40 percent. New York and Hawaii trailed with 16 percent each. By 1970, a shift had taken place. California maintained its position, but New York pulled ahead of Hawaii by more than doubling its Chinese population. By looking at Table 4 one can readily see why. Immigrants heading for New York outnumbered by a wide margin those who indicated that their future home would be in San Francisco/Oakland, Honolulu, Los Angeles, or Chicago. California's population increase comes from births, but New York's increase comes from immigration. Consequently, the native-born/foreign-born ratio for the three states varies widely, as shown below:

	Native-born	Foreign-born
California	54.4%	45.6%
New York	35.6%	64.4%
Hawaii	88.9%	11.1%

What significance do these figures have? A trans-Pacific leap means major readjustment and adaptation for the new immigrants, who must deal with a new environment, new culture, new language, new job, and new social alignments all at once. And the experience at times is overwhelming and bewildering. The Chinese community of New York, therefore, will experience greater difficulties than that of Hawaii or California because of its large percentage of newcomers.

CHARACTERISTICS OF CHINESE IMMIGRANTS

Chinese immigrants tend to be adults in their prime. Through the years, one-third of the females were consistently between 20 to 29 years of age. Until 1973, Chinese males were older—more within the 30 to 39 year age bracket—when they came to this country. Now their largest single age bracket is also 20 to 29 years.

TABLE 4
Intended City of Residence of Chinese Immigrants
(years ended June 30, 1966-75)

	1966	1967	1968	1969	1970	1971	1972	1973	1974	1975
San Francisco and Oakland	3,621	3,233	1,827	2,502	1,845	968	1,696	1,683	1,657	1,896
New York City and New Jersey	3,336	4,624	3,029	3,304	2,776	3.263	4,839	4,738	4,583	4,649
Honolulu	303	294	220	369	385	242	334	410	362	486
Los Angeles and Long Beach	865	1,300	772	938	743	802	930	914	1,286	1,107
Sacramento	402	353	146	223	163	107	146	146	126	129
Seattle	207	301	224	251	158	150	199	198	210	252
Chicago	306	754	386	407	367	402	661	432	391	388
Boston and Cambridge	337	418	308	252	206	223	241	244	262	217
Philadelphia	82	167	119	136	99	135	184	168	148	148
Houston	124	175	121	155	184	106	177	212	157	158

Source: Immigration & Naturalization Service, *Annual Reports* (Washington, D.C.: 1966-1975), Table 12A.

Immigration of those less than ten years old is insignificant. The future young of the Chinese-American population will be born of the heavy influx of young women and will be born in the United States. At the same time, it is surprising to see men and women in their eighties immigrating to the United States. This is a definite departure from the past when the old invariably returned to China to enjoy their later years, to die and be buried in the motherland, whereas now traffic seems to be heading the other way.

The fact that Chinese immigrants consist overwhelmingly of grown adults has its implications. First, these people are already set in their ways and outlook. In other words, adjustment takes longer than for younger immigrants and most likely there will be a gravitation toward, and hence expansion of, Chinatowns. Second, they will need a livelihood immediately. Third, they are producers rather than dependents. Instead of adding to the taxpayers' expense for schooling, they will join the labor force directly.

OCCUPATIONS

How much will they add to the labor force or, viewed negatively, how many jobs might they take away from people already here? Using the number of immigrants for 1975 as an example, there were 8,203 females and 7,234 males between the ages of 20 and 60. Assuming a labor force participation rate of 50 percent for the females and 75 percent for the males, the total comes to an approximate number of 9,500.

Not only is this number in itself insignificant, but the Chinese tend to create jobs for themselves. Approximately one out of every six Chinese persons employed is connected with eating and drinking places which, broadly interpreted, means Chinese restaurants. Many others make their livelihood by providing goods and services to their own growing communities.

Because of past immigration barriers to this country, such as exclusion and detention in quasi-prisons like Ellis Island or Angels Island, only the laboring classes would subject themselves to the indignities of trying to gain admission to the United States. What Chinese of any wealth, position,

background, or educational attainment would come to the United States? Hardly any. Not until the 1950s was there any shift in the emphasis from brawn to brains.

The very early immigrants were miners, farmers, and railroad laborers. Then followed the service workers and operatives, who perpetuated themselves in the laundry and restaurant business until recent times. Today, of those who indicate their occupation in their application for immigration, the largest percentage are professionals and technicians. This fact was verified by the figures put out by the Immigration and Naturalization Service, by a direct tabulation of applications from the Hong Kong Consulate, and by a special tabulation of the 1970 Census.

Between 1967 and 1971, the professional and technical category exceeded the other occupational groups by a wide margin (see Tables 5 and 6). Note that for the year 1971, 24 percent fell into the professional and technical category. The percentages for the other named occupations were inconsequential. There remains the catchall category of "Housewives, Children, No Occupation, or Occupation Not Reported," which always makes up a substantial proportion of the immigrants. In all likelihood, these people are dependents of the ones who reported occupations.

To a large measure, the preponderance of professionals is dictated by the preference system of the Immigration and Naturalization Act that gives priority to those with needed skills and training. However, it is also a reflection of the flight of the intelligentsia and monied classes from China, Taiwan, and Hong Kong following the overthrow of the Nationalist government and the takeover by Mao Tse-Tung in China in 1949. A highly elite corps of former officials and personnel experienced in business, technology, and education sought political refuge in this country, and this group has contributed immeasurably to the advancement of science, medicine, and art, as well as our understanding of China. Thousands of these refugees now teach in U.S. colleges and universities, and thousands more are in private industry. Since 1949, over 20,000 Chinese have entered the country under the various refugee relief acts.

From the American point of view, the high cali-

TABLE 5
Immigrant Aliens Admitted from China and Hong Kong as Region of Birth, by Major Occupation Group 1966-75

	1966	1967	1968	1969	1970	1971	1972	1973	1974	1975
Number Admitted	17,608	25,096	16,434	20,893	17,956	17,622	21,730	21,656	22,685	23,427
OCCUPATION										
Professional, Technical & Kindred Workers	1,281	4,327	2,880	2,882	3,924	4,292	4,263	2,952	2,796	2,915
Farmers & Farm Managers	30	26	19	15	18	5	1	5	17	11
Managers, Officials & Proprietors	588	909	608	617	580	482	718	1,042	1,273	1,535
Clerical & Kindred Workers	627	880	584	722	700	647	863	828	1,005	1,137
Sales Workers	226	217	133	216	155	155	217	204	243	250
Craftsmen, Foremen & Kindred Workers	260	365	240	464	347	361	480	467	465	541
Operatives & Kindred Workers	1,415	1,350	631	735	619	672	1,065	967	743	822
Private Household Workers	137	266	358	542	223	129	233	141	242	127
Service Workers except Private Household	1,921	2,107	1,139	1,290	1,027	1,189	1,578	1,572	1,571	1,414
Farm Laborers & Foremen	34	30	27	18	16	16	22	13	307	145
Laborers, except Farm & Mine	89	162	110	316	179	57	151	242	319	631
Housewives, children, & Others with No Occupation or Occupation Not Reported	11,000	14,457	9,705	13,076	10,168	9,617	12,139	13,223	13,704	13,899

Source: Immigration & Naturalization Service, *Annual Reports* (Washington, D.C.: 1966-1975), Table 8.

*Figures reflect immigration from China (including Taiwan) and Hong Kong.

TABLE 6
Immigrant Aliens Admitted from China and Hong Kong as Region of Birth, by Major Occupation Group and Percent, 1966-75

	1966	1967	1968	1969	1970	1971	1972	1973	1974	1975
Total Admitted	100	100	100	100	100	100	100	100	100	100
Professional, Technical & Kindred Workers	7	17	18	14	22	24	20	14	12	12
Farmers & Farm Managers	•	•	•	•	•	•	•	•	•	•
Mgrs., Officials & Proprietors	3	4	4	3	3	3	3	5	6	7
Clerical & Kindred Workers	4	4	4	3	4	4	4	4	4	5
Sales Workers	1	1	1	1	1	1	1	1	1	1
Craftsmen, Foremen & Kindred Workers	1	1	1	2	2	2	2	2	2	2
Operatives & Kindred Workers	8	5	4	4	3	4	5	4	3	4
Private Household Workers	1	1	2	3	1	1	1	1	1	1
Service Workers, except Private Household	11	8	7	6	6	7	7	7	7	6
Farm Laborers & Foremen	•	•	•	•	•	•	•	•	1	1
Laborers, except Farm & Mine	1	1	1	1	2	•	1	1	1	3
Housewives, Children & Others with No Occupation or Occupation Not Reported	62	58	59	63	57	55	56	61	60	59

*Figures reflect immigration from China (including Taiwan) and Hong Kong.

•Less than one-half of one percent

Source: Table 4A.

ber of recent Chinese immigrants is a positive factor because the human resources of a nation are its most valuable asset. But, from the point of view of the emigrating nation, it is an incalculable loss and is popularly termed a "brain drain."

The anomaly of the situation is that the brain drain is not always reflected in the official immigration figures. Many Chinese are admitted under the nonimmigrant classifications as officials, students, or visitors. Afterwards, their status is adjusted to permit them to remain in this country.

Table 7 shows the number of students from China and Hong Kong admitted to this country over the past thirteen years. The number rose from 2,045 in 1963 to 11,263 in 1975. Students from Taiwan are included in the figures. These students must be college graduates over twenty-two years old and, if male, have completed their military service. Most must qualify by highly competitive examinations before they are permitted to go abroad for further study. To use a cliche, these students are the cream of the crop. Their family circumstances must also be above average to enable them to support their sons and and daughters abroad. This is no mean feat considering the unfavorable rate of exchange between Hong Kong or Taiwan dollars and United States currency. The students are more inclined to be males because of the traditional emphasis placed upon giving males in the family better educational opportunities than females.

To swell the numbers further, students of Chinese descent, originating from Southeast Asia, Canada, or Latin America, are tabulated separately under their country of origin. In the United States, these students tend to identify more closely with the Chinese population rather than with the country that issued them a passport, but they are not counted in the totals of Chinese students.

Of those who leave Hong Kong, mainland China, and Taiwan, how many remain in this country? Estimates are taken from two studies: "A New Estimate of the Student Brain Drain from Asia" by Tai K. Oh[2] and "China or Taiwan: The Political Crisis of the Chinese Intellectual," by Shu Yuan Chang.[3] Mr. Oh based his deductions on a survey of Asian students on the campuses of the Universities of Wisconsin and Minnesota. His estimates of those who did not plan to leave the United States immedi-

TABLE 7
Students Admitted to the United States from Hong Kong and China, 1963-75

Year	Hong Kong	China*	Total
1963	831	1,214	2,045
1964	854	1,674	2,528
1965	895	1,995	2,890
1966	1,202	2,713	3,915
1967	1,287	2,127	3,414
1968	1,673	2,306	3,979
1969	2,412	3,082	5,494
1970	3,336	3,400	6,736
1971	3,954	3,014	6,968
1972	4,633	3,561	8,194
1973	4,161	3,645	7,806
1974	4,639	4,550	9,189
1975	3,772	4,126	7,898

Source: Immigration & Naturalization Service *Annual Reports*, 1963-1975.

* Includes Taiwan

ately upon completion of their studies was approximately 80 percent at the highest and 46 percent at the lowest. Ms. Chang's study included intellectuals as well as students. When queried about whether they would like to remain permanently in the United States, only half said yes. Ten percent were undecided and 40 percent said no. Yet Ms. Chang found that only 2 to 6 percent of the Chinese students from Taiwan actually went back during the years 1962 to 1969.

This discrepancy is quite revealing. Many do not intend or desire to remain, but they stay on anyway, hoping that political conditions in their homeland will improve so that they can go home. In many ways, this ambivalence creates a great deal of uncertainty in their lives.

In the last few years, a reversal in the trend toward professionals and technicians among Chinese immigrants is evident. From a high of 24 percent in 1971, the proportion is down to 12 percent for 1975. The phenomenon is somewhat puzzling, except that a notable increase, from 3 to 7 percent, is seen in the "Managers, Officials, and Proprietors" category. Perhaps these Chinese are involved in business and trade. If so, they may bring a whole new dimension to the occupational pursuits of the Chinese in the United States.

TABLE 6
Quota & Nonquota Immigrants From China &
Hong Kong 1963-1975

Year	Quota		Nonquota	
	No.	%	No.	%
1963	367	6.8	5,003	93.2
1964	333	5.9	5,315	94.1
1965	1,152	24.2	3,617	75.8
1966	12,900	73.3	4,708	26.7
1967	19,712	78.5	5,384	21.5
1968	12,386	75.4	4,048	24.7
1969	17,258	82.6	3,635	17.4
1970	14,699	81.9	3,257	18.1
1971	14,598	82.8	3,024	17.2
1972	16,546	85.2	2,881	14.8
1973	17,405	80.4	4,251	19.6
1974	18,367	81.0	4,318	19.0
1975	17,727	81.5	4,021	18.5

Source: Immigration & Naturalization Service
          Annual Reports, 1963-1975

Glancing back at Tables 5 and 6, one sees that the last category, "Housewives, Children, and Others with No Occupation, or Occupation Not Reported" is consistently the largest group. Almost 60 percent of the immigrants fall within this category. Breaking down this figure for a closer look, generally more than half of these are children or the elderly. Of the remainder, no doubt most are women—wives and mothers who keep a home for their families. From these figures, it is obvious that over half of the immigrants from China and Hong Kong are not immediate contenders in the labor market. They come to lend stability to the Chinese community by immigrating as a family unit or to be reunited with family members already in the United States. Immediate family members such as spouse and children are entitled to enter the country without charge to the quota. Table 8 shows Chinese immigration by quota and nonquota. One can see a steady and consistent decline in the nonquota column, indicating that the objective of family reunification may soon be achieved, and that most Chinese immigrants will be coming in under the numerical limitations and preference categories of the quota.

In essence, then, Chinese immigration consists of two major groups, both of which directly reflect the immigration policy of the United States government. At one extreme, we have highly qualified professionals screened under the third preference, who in all probability are somewhat conversant in English. The other extreme mirrors the family reunification goal. The members of the latter group are relatives of former immigrants. In general, they have a lower educational and socioeconomic background. By and large, they do not speak English, and will have greater difficulty accommodating themselves to life in the United States.

Among the conditions upon which a visa is issued to an immigrant are those stating that he have a sponsor and can demonstrate that he will not be a public charge. In other words, he must have an offer of employment from an employer and certification from the Department of Labor that his line of work does not compete unduly with jobs of American citizens. The Department of Labor also requires that his skill or training be in short supply or in demand in this country. Consequently, most immigrants will not be unemployed. Their primary problem is underemployment. For instance, a former official in the Chinese government with years of technical experience accepted a job as a draftsman primarily because that firm offered to sponsor him. There are innumerable other instances of former doctors, teachers, accountants, and engineers who have taken jobs as janitors and waiters when they first arrive. Some stay in the rut because of language problems or because they are afraid to venture out and compete vigorously in the job market. For others, it is a matter of time before they can utilize their knowledge and skills in the profession in which they were educated.

In his study of "Immigrants and the American Labor Market," David S. North found that upper occupational level immigrants generally move lower and the lower occupational level immigrants generally move upward right after arrival in this country. The crucial variable of job success was command of the English language.[4]

HERE TO STAY

Unlike the Chinese immigrant in years past, today's immigrant is here to stay. This fact can be ascertained by the increasing numbers who apply for citizenship. The reason why the numbers are not greater than they are is that there is a waiting period of five years before citizenship can be conferred. Large-scale Chinese immigration was not possible before 1965. The bureaucratic process and red tape add to the interval between setting foot on American soil and issuance of that prized piece of naturalization paper. The jump from 2,800 Chinese naturalized in 1971 to 8,434 in 1972 attests to the eagerness with which the Chinese immigrants are becoming citizens as soon as they fulfill the requirements (see Table 9).

SUMMARY: POLARITY IN THE MAKEUP

Chinese immigrants will continue to fully utilize the maximum annual quota allotted any one country. In many ways, the makeup of today's immigrants tends toward the extremes. At one end, they are highly educated professionals or managers given priority under the third preference, or they are political or economic refugees from unrest or unstable conditions in their former homeland. At the other extreme, they are the beneficiaries of the nonquota provisions of the immigration law. Under this category, most are wives and children of former immigrants who came to this country as service workers or laborers. Females continue to outnumber males. Many of these women are uneducated and may even be illiterate. They are the people who gravitate to the Chinatowns of New York and San Francisco. Their socioeconomic background limits their occupational horizon and mobility. Their needs, their lifestyles, their outlooks, and their abilities are markedly different from their compatriots at the other end of the occupational or

TABLE 7
Chinese Who Became Naturalized Citizens
1963-1975

Year	Number
1963	4,268
1964	4,045
1965	3,692
1966	3,111
1967	2,924
1968	3,186
1969	3,399
1970	3,099
1971	2,880
1972	9,434
1973	9,056
1974	8,692
1975	9,683
Total 1963-75	67,469

Source: Immigration & Naturalization Service, *Annual Reports*, Tables 39.

educational scale. In essence, therefore, today's Chinese immigrants are two widely disparate groups.

NOTES

1. Excerpts from this paper are taken from my book, *A Survey of Chinese American Manpower and Employment* (New York: Praeger Special Studies, 1976).
2. *International Migration Review* No. 7 (1972): 449-56.
3. *Amerasia*, No. 2 (Fall 1973), 47-81.
4. U.S. Department of Labor, *Manpower Research Monograph* No. 31 (1974).

U.S. IMMIGRATION NOW AND IN PROSPECT: SOME POPULATION AND POLICY ASPECTS

George J. Stolnitz

Although our upsurging attention to immigration policy has numerous origins, demographic aspects are clearly central in direct and indirect ways. The numbers involved have significance not only on their own, but also for our main nondemographic causes of concern. Alien amnesty questions, immigrants and the unemployment rate, employment identification card proposals, the fiscal costs and benefits of foreign-born who have recently entered the country—none of these issues would be remotely as prominent politically, and some quite possibly would not even exist, were it not for their population-related dimensions.

On direct demographic grounds as well, our recent immigration trends have taken on momentous proportions, in some ways uniquely so. Meriting emphasis in particular are the implications of such trends for total population growth and the size of the labor force, as will be discussed in the first part of this paper. Two major types of obstacles to adequate policy formulation are then considered; though relevant in principle to all migration, internal as well as international, they apply with special force to the subject at hand. A final section considers some prospective effects of in-migrant movements on future population size both in this country and in Mexico.

Since migration data in the U.S. (as almost everywhere) are so poor, it is best to essay only a few rough orders of magnitude; though not good enough to pass close statistical review, they are sufficient for covering several main initial questions.

TWO MAIN QUESTIONS

A first question concerns the relative current importance or contribution of immigration to our total growth of population. To begin with, even with all due recognition of the uncertain data and trends under review, it seems safe to generalize that something like 300,000 to 400,000 legal alien immigrants per year are likely to enter in the near foreseeable future, much as has been the case for over a decade. Allowing for return emigration and for some recent ballooning of in-movements because of special refugee situations, perhaps 300,000 is an adequate, if conservative, order of magnitude to adopt for the legal part of total net immigration. Illegals are much more problematic, of course, but to use the most recent of the fickle estimates one encounters, perhaps one-half million is a not unduly high stab at numbers. In all, therefore, something like three-fourths of a million seems indicated as a bottom estimate of recent or prospective net actual immigration; perhaps a million would be a more reasonable "guesstimate."[1]

These figures should be juxtaposed with our published figures on current total population increase (including legal immigration only), which has been at the 1.5 million level very nearly at mid-decade, after trending downward since 1970; natural increase (births minus deaths) has been about 1.2 million and moving similarly downward. Approximately, therefore, our estimated—or at least widely bruited—net immigration in actual (legal plus illegal) terms comes to about one-half of our total growth as published. With illegal immigration added to published growth, the ratio comes to one-third.

Such ratios have rarely, if ever, been experienced in our history (even during the 1880-1910 periods of peak immigration). Moreover, those periods essentially involved only legal entries and gave way to a long period of substantial restrictionism. In comparing our turn-of-the-century migration experience with today's, it is also important that the earlier era was one of high rates of natural increase. In contrast, the current rates have been dwindling rapidly, to the point where even absolute increases are likely to diminish steadily over major parts of the next several decades.

The last seems indicated by the fact that since about 1960 our birth cohorts have been diminishing in absolute size almost every year and will soon be occupying the 20 to 30 age interval, the main years of childbearing. Unless fertility rates move sharply upward (which is contrary to strong present and prospective indications), numbers of births are likely to be even lower a decade from now than they are today. Indeed, such declines would seem far more probable over the next decade than the post–1960 decreases would have appeared a decade or so ago. The decline in births from about 4 million to 3 million during the 1960–75 period has not only been marked, but has occurred in the face of an enormous increase—now at its peak—in the number of women in the main childbearing ages. Meanwhile little, if any, countervailing effects can be expected on the side of mortality, since annual numbers of deaths appear as likely to rise because of the "aging" of the population as to fall because of declining death rates. If it increased rapidly enough, immigration could, in principle, cause birth numbers to rise, but this seems most improbable; for several decades at least, national numbers of births in the U.S. will surely be dominated by the size and fertility behavior of its native-born population.

It follows, therefore, that our immigrants-to-growth ratio could rise well beyond its current high levels, rather than tend to fall, under existing policy and trend conditions.

In considering the break between our current and past migration patterns, equally significant are the facts that so large a part of our "new" immigrant groups has been coming from a single country, that the country is a bordering one, and that its natural increase exceeds our own. The first two of these elements may command more immediate attention, being political in nature, but the third is likely to prove as important from long-run viewpoints. With less than a third of our population, Mexico is growing by some four to five times the U.S. rate, and has a current absolute size of natural increase which is some 50 percent higher than our own. The last could be subject to rapid change if recent, apparently sharp declines in Mexican fertility were to become sustained. However, it seems fair to say that nothing

distantly resembling this threefold combination of factors, each a potentially key element in its own right, has ever previously presented itself in our national history. Indeed, it may well be that no comparable situation has ever arisen anywhere in the modern era between a less developed country and a neighboring highly developed one.

Therefore, to an extent and in ways without precedent in our experience, the U.S. can expect to have to confront the following related questions: (1) are its main sources of future population growth (or nongrowth) to come from home or abroad; (2) in the latter case, is this growth to come through legal or illegal entry; and (3) in the latter event still again, is it to come from Mexico or other areas?

With respect to economic absorption, and quite apart from questions of legality of entry, ethnic identity, or national origins, two points of special interest stand out. First, the recent upsurge of actual immigration has coincided with the great rise of postwar "baby boom" numbers now within or still entering the younger labor force ages. These are the ages where unemployment has been relatively high, and continuously so, over the past decade. Not improbably, the recent upsurge of immigration—with its concentration of young adult job seekers, especially among those who enter illegally—has been acting to restrict employment opportunities (or exacerbate unemployment tendencies) for the younger labor force. And second, should immigration continue in anything like its present size and composition, in a decade or so it would become associated with diminishing native numbers in the younger labor force ages, as the declining birth cohorts since about 1960 become the workers of 1985 and beyond. A less competitive situation, one giving greater scope for complementary forms of employment, would seem likely under these conditions.

Debate surrounding these possibly divergent effects is already well underway. Pointing to an increasing need for relatively unskilled labor to take jobs that "Americans won't accept," some claim mainly positive effects from the viewpoint of domestic employment. Others judge harmful competition to be the more prevalent or important outcome, with special injury to native ethnic minorities. Conceivably, over time, the changing demographic contexts of the debate could change the nature of its conclusions.

In dealing with these particular questions (as with practically all major ones surrounding our current immigration patterns), a far more solid and ramified data base than now exists will be needed if adequately enlightened national decision making is to be achieved. Even with such a data base at hand, the social and humanitarian complexities are such that sound judgment will be especially difficult, perhaps among the most difficult we will face as a nation in the remaining decades of this century.

As is sometimes pointed out, it is true that our recent rates of net legal immigration have been in line with the rates during most of this century when expressed relative to population size rather than population growth; such rates have averaged not far from 2 percent decennially (.2 percent per annum), with the 1930s—a period of net emigration—being the main exception. During 1860-1910, moreover, the corresponding rates were some three to four times higher than the current level.

However, the relevance of these comparisons for purposes of gaining perspectives about the future seems dubious. For one thing, the 1860–1910 half century experience was in relation to a largely unsettled and primarily agricultural country, hence, one much more labor intensive in its productive structure than today. But quite apart from this, and going directly to the demographic facts alone, adding current numbers of illegal or undocumented entries to legal entries would raise the migrants-to-population ratio by a factor of two to three. And allowance for gross numbers of in-movements, including apprehensions, would raise the ratio by a further doubling to tripling. Unlike return migration from the U.S. historically, which was primarily or almost entirely voluntary, our policies with respect to today's apprehended are themselves very much of an issue. What, if anything, do we want to do about abating or enhancing our apprehension efforts, and what would be the effects of increased attempts if we undertook them? Although we have no way of knowing what proportions of the apprehended would return on their own if allowed to cross the U.S. borders freely, looking at net figures alone—which, whatever they are, are not small— would obscure our policy dilemmas rather than clarify matters. In short, that the gross numbers of in-movements involved are without parallel in our past history has direct and major policy relevance.

It is also pointed out and true that the current gross numbers of legally-entered, foreign-born persons constitute only a small fraction of our annual births (some 10 to 15 percent before netting out deaths). But, once again, the observation obscures rather than clarifies. To begin with, the migrants-to-births ratio is much higher than appears in the official U.S. series, which exclude the illegally entered foreign born (whether apprehended or unapprehended). And, obviously, births and immigrants (whether legal, or even more, illegal) are wholly different policy and analytic entities, not only on sociopolitical terms but also in narrow demographic respects, as well as, for example, in geographic location, sex composition, or in a host of vital characteristics directly associated with age.

MIGRATION POLICY

Migration policy has numerous aspects which distinguish it in theory and practice from other population policies, but two in particular may be singled out here. Both stem from obvious points of departure, either can greatly complicate political decisions, each is likely to be basic for adequate socio economic assessment of policy consequences, and both are all too often overlooked in actual formulation of policy.

A first aspect of special interest starts from the simple observation that one country's migration policies affect other countries. In contrast, a nation's policy options and their effects with respect to mortality or fertility are largely or exclusively domestic. Moreover, the larger the scale of migration, the greater are likely to be its outer-directed implications; the greater the probable impact of policy on birth and death rates, the stronger will be its inner-directed tendencies.[2]

Whether in the recent past or in prospect, it follows that full evaluation of our gross and net movements is likely to require a two-sided perspective, particularly with respect to large numbers of illegally entered immigrants. Whether the socioeconomic effects of such movements are positive or negative in both origin and destination areas, or operate in opposite directions, can be central to political relations and, hence, to policy. For obvious reasons, this is especially the case with Mexico, as becomes increasingly evident from our daily newspaper reports.

Migration history provides a diverse display of multiarea effects, sometimes simultaneous and sometimes lagged. Nineteenth-century out-migration from Europe, then a region of high natural increase and major resource inadequacies, to the largely unsettled lands of North America, must almost surely have been a striking case of movements with mutually reinforcing positive impacts. In contrast, recent "brain drain" phenomena, especially those involving movements from lesser developed to developed countries, have clearly involved significant offsetting impacts on origin and destination areas. And in the case of the remarkable south-to-north movements in Europe during much of the postwar period, the full history of the main effects is still being written, as the current adverse impacts of return migration on areas of origin become netted out with previously favorable impacts in both origin and destination areas.

A second main aspect of migration policy complexities is that the costs and benefits of migration to the individual person or family may differ substantially from those to society. Migration can entail major "externalities" in the area of origin, the area of destination, or both, since neither individuals nor families have reason to take large social consequences into account when deciding whether or not to move. Yet many such decisions, made individually, can have major effects on social infrastructure, job markets, and needs for public services.

A direct corollary of this point is that, however well executed and however much needed, micro-level or interview surveys are almost sure to miss important parts of the picture. Also needed are macroanalytic approaches to dealing with social level issues.

A further corollary is that an adequately ambitious research paradigm would encompass both individual, *cum,* social and multiarea aspects: individual and social consequences need to be examined for areas of origin and for areas of destination. Safely, one can predict that most of our ongoing debates and swings of opinion surrounding U.S. immigration policy will stem from inadequate attention, whether intentional or unintentional, to major parts of this paradigm.

IMMIGRATION EFFECTS ON FUTURE POPULATION: A COMPARISON OF THE U.S. AND MEXICO

A general, if unassessable, estimate has it that the U.S. includes something like a tenth of Mexico's 60 to 65 million native-born population. For this ratio to be maintained over time through allowed entry, approximately 150,000 to 200,000 Mexicans would have to migrate here annually on a net basis, thereby implying a one-third to one-half rise in our total net legal immigration. These orders of magnitude could be expected to prevail for between one to several decades, even if Mexican fertility were to continue along its apparently downward path. Or, to take another crude indicator of possible U.S. policy impacts on Mexican population growth, an attempt to equalize U.S. and Mexican growth by absorbing the surplus of Mexico's natural increase over our own (currently some 600,000) would leave that country's rate of growth at about triple ours, would double our annual net numbers of legal in-movers, and would raise our growth rate by over a third. Clearly, therefore, orders of magnitude which could impinge significantly on Mexico's population and development prospects would need to entail major demographic and related social reorientations of our own.[3] Such reorientations would obviously be increased by perceptible degrees if additional major, less developed areas of origin, such as the Philippines, and Colombia, were taken into similar account.

A fuller discussion of the demographic impacts of Mexican–U.S. migration trends, recent and potential, would delve into later-generation effects. Once migrant reproduction comes into play, Mexico's population would be further reduced below what it would otherwise be and, again, the U.S. numbers of native born would be simultaneously increased in analogous manner. Details are not possible here, but a few crude and highly speculative indications may be useful.

On the basis of the latest U.S. projections, using

replacement-level mortality and fertility assumptions throughout and letting net migration be either zero or 400,000 per year, one can infer a U.S. population size difference of some 10 to 15 million by the end of this century, and one of about 30 million by the year 2025.[4] These figures may well be too low because not only is current actual gross immigration from Mexico perhaps at least double the 400,000 figure, but also net reproduction among migrants will almost surely be well above replacement for a considerable time to come. With all due account for the possibility of rapid change on either score in the decades ahead, it would nevertheless appear that the U.S.–Mexican population size effects used in deciding upon our coming migration policies should come to over twice the above magnitudes, at a rough overall guess. Conceivably, well over half of such magnitudes (say 15 to 20 million as of 2000, and 40 million by 2025) could be attributable to net rather than gross in-migration. For the year 2000, projections for Mexico suggest that 15 to 20 million could amount to a one-fourth or one-third reduction of population growth on the sending side of the assumed migration movements.

Although their status as illustrations should be emphasized, these crude numerical outlines point to a final and much better confirmed set of general conclusions. United States' migration policy dilemmas with respect to Mexico form part of an essentially worldwide chain of analogous issues. It is safe to say that the discrepancy between the global numbers ready and willing to emigrate voluntarily if permitted, and the numbers that nations of potential destination are willing to accept, is at its highest point in modern times if not in all history. The reasons, which involve in significant measure both the "supply" and "demand" sides of the imbalance, are too lengthy to discuss here. But, if only because of the great changes ongoing in world transportation and communications, it would be well to anticipate that the imbalance will rise rather than fall throughout the rest of this century and well into the next one. Almost imperceptibly, but no longer doubtfully, U.S. migration patterns and policies have become an important part of our still emerging interrelations with the development destinies of the world's underprivileged areas.

NOTES

1. A recent officially used version of the number of illegal aliens in the U.S. puts it as some 6 to 8 million as of 1976. Other sources range from 4 to 12 million. Reported annual apprehensions of illegals have ranged from about three-fourths of a million to a million; of these, perhaps two-thirds to three-fourths represent different individuals, the remainder consisting of "repeaters." Whatever the actual value in either case, each is reported to be increasing.

2. The same, almost generic, types of contrast hold at subnational levels in considering internal migration, and tend similarly to be overlooked by policy and research analysts.

3. A closer analytic view than is being attempted here would also have to focus on the uneven subnational impacts of national Mexican–U.S. migration movements. Northern Mexico and the Southwest U.S., for example, would be far more affected in all main categories—demographic, social, political and economic—than would be true of their respective national impacts. Similar comments apply to questions of nongeographic or sectorial impacts.

4. U.S. Bureau of the Census, *Population Estimates and Projections*, Series P–25, No.601, October 1975, p.28. The differences being cited are between the Series II and II–X series.

Part 2

Development Implications of the New Immigration for the Sending Countries

INTERNATIONAL FLOWS OF TALENT

William A. Glaser

Recently, international movements by the more educated and more skilled have become leading questions in policy debates and in social science because retaining the educated is believed essential to a country's development, while losing them is unfairly profitable to another.

International flows of the talented take several forms. Students from one country study abroad as undergraduate students, graduate students, or postgraduate fellows. The college educated may be employed in other countries, either permanently or temporarily. These professional workers might have been educated in part abroad or might have studied entirely at home. Natural and social scientists settle in other countries temporarily for research projects, with results that may benefit the hosts as well as their home countries. Another form of movement abroad is international technical assistance: a substantial number of college-educated persons give advice or perform services in developing countries under special projects donated by their home governments or by international organizations.

STUDY ABROAD
Recent distribution

Throughout history, particular countries, universities, and institutes have been leaders in various fields of learning and science, and they have attracted many overseas students. Often they have been virtually international centers under national auspices, with faculty members from many countries. The flows of foreign students shift to different places, as existing fields change in style or as new specialties become important.[1]

World War II was followed by changes in the sites and organization of international education. Many more persons were needed to staff the bureaucracies, schools, and laboratories of developing countries and, therefore, enrollments from Asia, Africa, and Latin America greatly increased. As science, engineering, and modern management became the most prized careers and the fields most essential to development, foreign students shifted from the traditional European universities to centers in the United States. Larger proportions came for graduate training in these specialties, after completing undergraduate work at home.

By the late 1960s, nearly half a million persons were studying outside their home countries in universities or in equivalent institutions of higher learning. For the 1968–69 academic year, UNESCO estimated 440,556 students from 124 home countries.[2] The total had doubled during the 1960s.

The principal countries of study and numbers of foreign students around 1968 were the following: United States, 121,362; France, 35,753; Federal Republic of Germany, 26,783; United Kingdom, 21,750; Lebanon, 18,811; Canada, 17,424; U.S.S.R., 16,100. The "traditional" countries of foreign study—particularly Great Britian, Germany, Austria, and Switzerland have maintained the same levels for some time. Increases have been concentrated primarily in "newer" countries of foreign study, particularly the United States.

The home countries of foreign students are a mixture of developed and developing. The largest numbers around 1968 were from the following: Republic of China (Taiwan), 21,733; Jordan (largely Palestinian Arabs), 21,205; United States, 20,178; Canada, 15,094; India, 14,025; Syria, 12,584; Iran, 11,681; United Kingdom, 10,142. Some nationalities concentrated in one or a few developed countries. For example, Filipinos cluster at American universities; Koreans prefer the United States and Germany. But some nationalities, such as Iranians, attend universities in a wider range of developed countries.

The principal fields of foreign study and their respective percentages around 1968 were the following: arts, 22; engineering, 19; social sciences,

16; medicine, 13; science, 12; law, 5; education, 5; all others, 8.

Within the United States—by far the largest country of overseas study—slightly over half the foreigners were undergraduates and most others were graduate students.[3] Those from the Far East have steadily increased: now they are 37 percent of all foreign students in the United States, while the next groups in size are Latin Americans, Middle Easterners, and Europeans. The most common fields of foreign study in the United States are engineering (22 percent), humanities (16 percent), and physical and life sciences (14 percent).

The planning of educational exchanges

So long as education (whether domestic or foreign) was considered a consumption good, students were free to go abroad if their families could pay. Private foundations or government agencies gave scholarships to a few persons, particularly from Asia. Young persons from developing countries became more eager to study overseas.

Eventually policy makers became anxious about the consequences for manpower: an unregulated flow uses up scarce foreign exchange; students might learn things inappropriate to the home country; some might be tempted to stay abroad, depriving the home country of the investment in raising and educating them, and shifting the benefits of their future work to a richer country. Therefore, in recent decades many governments have tried to limit wasteful foreign study and direct students into the most productive ends. Many regimes and donors of technical assistance offer fellowships for foreign study to persons of proven competence and with a commitment to return. A few governments of developing countries forbid use of foreign exchange for private study abroad. Each country tries to create, expand, and perfect its own universities and special institutes.

The structuring and control over international education have increased but are far from complete. Governments write more elaborate development plans, indicating the fields of highest priority, and students can see the areas that will be most highly rewarded in the future. But few countries have developed good manpower planning as part of such programs, with specification of the skills that will be needed through overseas training. Few governments forbid students to go abroad when their families can find the resources, since the persons most ambitious to help their childrens' careers are the government officials themselves and the elites with political influence. Therefore, many students still go overseas on their families' money and study what they think best. Once in universities abroad, students are rarely contacted by their home governments; their choices of subject are influenced more often by faculty members in the countries of study. Many are helped by scholarships and jobs from the foreign university, which thereby further weakens their commitment to manpower policy at home.

WORK ABROAD

Recent distribution

Centers of leadership in science and learning have always attracted professional workers as well as overseas students. Rich and powerful countries that have not yet trained enough citizens with essential skills often catch up by offering higher pay and better working conditions. Certain professions in great demand, such as medicine, have a long history of work abroad.[4]

It is widely believed that very large numbers of the talented have worked in foreign countries for substantial periods since the end of World War II. It is difficult to state the exact magnitudes and to generalize accurately about countries of origin, host countries, and specialties.[5]

Since World War II, the flows from Europe have been overshadowed in public consciousness by rising migration of the talented from developing countries. At first, they followed the imperial flag: citizens of the British Commonwealth went to the United Kingdom; persons from the Francophone countries went to France; Filipinos gravitated to the United States. The booming economy and the expanding universities of the United States soon became magnets for everyone; increasing numbers of Indians, Chinese, Koreans, Latin Americans, and others studied and migrated there rather than to Europe. The United States liberalized its immigration laws in 1965, relaxing national quotas and specifically easing restrictions on professionals, and the result was a great increase in the entry of professionals from non-European nations for several years. American economic recession and tightened requirements for immigration visas—now the professional should have a job waiting for him—reduced the entry of most nationalities in most specialties after 1971.

A peak year was 1970, with 3,264 natural scientists and 9,305 engineers entering the United States on "immigrant" visas or (if they already resided there) changing their visas from "nonimmigrant" to "immigrant." Within engineering, the principal groups have been mechanical and civil engineers. Within the sciences, by far the largest group has been chemists. Entering physicians, surgeons, and nurses have steadily increased, and by 1973 the annual figure had reached 7,119 for doctors and 6,335 for professional nurses. Several other specialties are quite numerous: 3,457 accountants and 3,860 elementary and secondary school teachers were admitted during 1973. Persons in various other specialties—social scientists, humanists, architects, managers, and so on—enter in smaller numbers each year. In total, 400,063 professional, technical, and kindred workers were admitted during the fiscal year ending June 1973. In this combined total for 1973, the largest nationalities were Filipinos (16 percent), Indians (14 percent), Koreans (6 percent), Chinese (6 percent), and Britons (5 percent).[6]

In the migration of the talented into other developed countries, particularly into Europe, doctors are a larger proportion. In addition, Great Britain accepts many nurses each year, particularly from the West Indies. A few countries have flows of professionals in both directions.[7]

Length of stay

Recent reexamination of past data about migration reveals a greater return flow at that time and, therefore, migration is no longer definable as a single permanent act. Current research shows that many migrants work abroad temporarily, plan to return home eventually, and (in some cases) hope to move back and forth.[8] Therefore, not all foreign professionals will stay indefinitely. Some nationalities include a substantial proportion who view employment as part of their graduate training and expect to return home within a few years. A quarter or more of the foreign-trained professionals in some developing countries have obtained on-the-job experience as well as education abroad. The United States is the favorite site for such temporary employment; other developed countries attract higher proportions of persons planning to immigrate permanently. Length of stay varies by specialty: many engineers and scientists work abroad as a form of postgraduate training; doctors more often plan to stay permanently.[9]

Relation to study abroad

A widespread fear about educational exchanges is that many students take the opportunity to remain away permanently. It is true that foreign students are more likely to emigrate than persons who have never studied abroad; the former learn about opportunities and have acquired skills appropriate to foreign employers. But, most foreign students return home. In the mid-1960s in the United States, the proportions who returned home after (or shortly after) foreign study were between 75 percent and 85 percent. The proportion may be higher today, because of the reduction of European students in the United States and because of the tighter American job market.[10] The proportion of foreign students planning to immigrate may be higher in a few other developed countries, such as Canada, than in the United States. Many arrived in Canada with immigrant visas and always intended to stay.[11]

Half the immigrants in the United States had previously studied there or in another developed country.[12]

Fewer doctors start work abroad with prior degrees or formal education in developed countries, that is, most arrive after education entirely at home. Most foreign doctors arrive nominally as postgraduate students to work as hospital house staff under the tutelage of senior specialists, but actually they perform services with maximum autonomy and soon become integrated as full members of the medical profession.

RESEARCH ABROAD

Just as many persons have traveled abroad for extended periods to study or work, many have gone to conduct scientific research and then return home. The goal has been to advance knowledge in their fields for the advantage of everyone.

Because it spends so much for research, has developed large research installations, and combines research with other functions (such as teaching and development of techniques), the United States sends and receives the largest number of research persons in the natural sciences, social sciences, humanities, and other fields. During 1973, 6,589 American university faculty members were reported working abroad, and 10,848 foreign scholars were in the United States.[13]

But these figures probably were poor estimates of the true numbers: many of these Americans and some of the foreigners were teaching rather than performing research; many more Americans were conducting overseas research while employed by American organizations and, therefore, did not appear in censuses of those located overseas; an unknown number were doing research outside academia and, therefore, were not counted in exchanges of scholars. In recent years, serious questions (possibly for the first time) have challenged the traditionally permissive manner of conducting overseas research, particularly in the social sciences.[14]

EXPERTS IN TECHNICAL ASSISTANCE

Since World War II, many developed countries, international organizations, and private associations assist in the development of the less affluent countries. Besides capital grants, an important contribution has been their talent: they provide many experts to give advice, teach, manage, or demonstrate. Technical assistance has resulted in a large new migration of talent for varying periods.

In 1970, 100,490 experts were employed by the governments of developed countries on long-term assignments in developing societies. In addition, 11,241 were employed by the United Nations, and a few thousand more by other bilateral donors, private associations, and other international organi-

zations. The largest employers were France, 38,122; the United States, 22,417; and Great Britain, 17,354. The programs of the Great Powers peaked during the early 1960s and declined thereafter, but the number of experts from the United Nations has steadily increased. Besides these employed experts, 22,881 persons worked as volunteers in the technical assistance programs of governments, churches, and private organizations.[15]

Two-thirds of all bilateral experts work in Africa, particularly as teachers in French and British programs. Most others work in Asia. Nearly half the volunteers work in Africa. The United Nations' experts are spread more widely throughout the world.

Forty percent of all experts and volunteers are teachers. The next largest categories work in agriculture, health, power, transport, and communications.

REASONS FOR STUDYING ABROAD

Many questionnaire surveys have been conducted among foreign students, to learn their motives, adjustment problems, experiences, and career plans. Most have sampled foreign students in the United States, but a few covered other countries.[16]

Motives for going abroad

The most common reasons given by students are academic. By going to major universities in developed countries, students can learn the newest subjects in well-equipped facilities. Some have good universities at home, but they say that foreign degrees have prestige that will give them a competitive advantage after they return home. Other students are curious to see the outside world. Foreign study is also for persons who are looking for a more free social or political setting.

Some persons study abroad involuntarily. Their countries have small but select universities, and they were not admitted. Others study abroad either as part of a prearranged plan to emigrate or in order to learn whether a foreign society is better than home. While such emigrating students may total several thousand each year, the *proportion* among all the many foreign students in the world is small.

Barriers against study abroad

To go overseas, a student must be willing to ignore certain prospective disadvantages. For many, these remain serious adjustment problems after their arrival, cause an interruption in their studies before completion, or ensure their prompt return home after graduation.

Many are apprehensive about the costs of tuition and living abroad before they arrive. Money continues to be a big problem.

While persons in some home countries have attended secondary schools, or undergraduate college with curricula matching those in developed countries (for example, French *lycees* in several developing countries), many have been educated in ways that do not fit the foreign country of study easily. Having to study and live constantly in a foreign language bothers many students from Latin America and from developing countries that use only vernacular tongues.

Many foreign students (particularly from Asia and the Middle East) are bothered by the unfamiliar cultures and impersonal social relationships of North America and Europe. Usually they have strong family ties at home, and they miss their relatives. Complaints about racial discrimination are common. These social discomforts are relieved somewhat where the individual finds clusters of his countrymen at the same campus or in the foreign city.

REASONS FOR WORKING ABROAD

The literature contains lists of the possible reasons for the migration of talent.[17] Only a few systematic questionnaire surveys have been conducted about the motives inducing some to emigrate and others to return home after foreign study.[18]

Reasons for working abroad temporarily

Very few policy makers and social scientists have noticed the magnitude of temporary employment by the talented abroad as a stage in careers, and, therefore, hardly any surveys have asked persons' motives. The strongest reasons are educational: in several fields, such as engineering and physical science, practical experience is at least as important as formal education, and the foreign student can obtain this only by finding a job after getting his degree. Many hope to benefit by earning higher salaries in stronger currencies than they can obtain at home, and then by returning with their gains. Some stay abroad until the job market or the government improves at home.[19]

Reasons for emigrating or returning for an extended time.

The most general and strongest motives for extended migration are the perception of where one's children are best off, where the greatest contributions can be made to one's profession, adequacy of income, quality of jobs, and number of jobs. If a foreign country seems better than home, the professional will emigrate. If the home country has an excess of professionals, a limited job hierarchy with promotion by seniority, and uncertain prospects for improvement, the talented will consider it a poor risk for themselves and for their children. Societies with flexible structures, expanding organizations, and vigorous leadership can retain their talented persons.

Members of minority groups belong to the professions in large numbers throughout the world. The nationalistic and homogenizing policies of many governments worry them, and they are an important part of the brain drain, particularly to North America.

Income differences are associated with the migration of the talented, but not as strongly as is widely assumed. Many persons return to countries with low pay rates because of powerful family and cultural ties. Others emigrate from countries with satisfactory pay for nonmonetary reasons. Doctors are unusual: they are by far the highest paid group of immigrants, and they may be unusually responsive to the lure of money. But many other foreign professionals may not gain very much in real income by migrating to North America and Europe.

Avoidance of distasteful governments induces a few to emigrate, particularly in journalism, the arts, and sociology. Other professionals migrate in objection to unstable rather than to repressive political conditions.

CONTROVERSIES OVER STUDY ABROAD

Whether a country's students should gain their education abroad, in whole or in part, or whether they should study entirely at home, has inspired serious and sometimes angry debates. A worldwide community of specialists in international education has sprung up which has collected information about programs and the flows of students. They have discussed the issues, but as yet no international policy or world structure has been adopted in educational exchanges. For the moment, a variety of actions by individuals, governments, and universities continues, with a resulting melange of benefits and costs to the countries that send and educate the student. If any serious problems exist, they are not solved multilaterally, but each government is left to take whatever remedies it wishes.

From the standpoint of the sending country

In the literature over educational exchange, the principal cost or loss is the possibility that some or many students will stay abroad and thus become a permanent loss to a society needing them. If they had studied completely at home, they would not have acquired skills so readily marketable abroad, and they would not have learned about job opportunities. While traveling and living abroad, the students use up the home country's scarce hard currency. Another disadvantage of foreign study is that returnees might have learned techniques abroad fitting the West, but wasteful and too technical for home. They may demand that poor countries spend much to create special facilities for themselves; if they have political influence, they can distort the planned development of their countries. They may return with expensive tastes, political ideas, and other aspirations that disturb society.

On the other hand, study abroad can greatly benefit the country sending the students. New techniques are learned. While conservatives deplore the political and personal ideas the students learn abroad, others applaud them. A small country may not be able to support an expensive graduate program for only a few students, and they can obtain a better education at a lower total cost abroad. The students overseas may earn good will for the home country.

From the standpoint of the receiving country

The country providing education to foreigners may incur losses or experience disadvantages. It pays for some educational costs of persons who will not stay and work. Academic standards may drop because of the difficulty in teaching classes that include persons handicapped by language and by preparatory education. Facilities may alternate between overcrowding and underutilization, as the flow of foreign students fluctuates.

On the other hand, the receiving country may gain much. A more cosmopolitan environment prevails in the schools. Large numbers of foreign students may stay and work, thereby relieving shortages of manpower and postponing the creation of expensive new schools. In particular, short-run skilled jobs can be filled without the danger of training too many persons in these transitory fields. Many persons may return to their home countries with favorable images of the country of study, thereby creating long-term political and cultural alliances.

CONTROVERSIES OVER WORK ABROAD

Newspaper articles, books, and resolutions by international organizations generally deplore the permanent emigration of talented persons from developing to developed countries. However, a few dissenting voices argue that, if a country cannot muster the facilities and remuneration to motivate a professional to stay, he will likely be far more productive elsewhere, and, therefore, everyone—including his countrymen—will benefit from his move.[20]

Migration among the richer countries evokes less bitterness, since losers are still left with many professionals. However, when some were moving to the United States during the American economic boom of the late 1950s and 1960s, when some European organizations were left understaffed, and when it seemed as if American economic strength would continue to draw even more, the brain drain aroused many warnings and demands for remedies. Increasing opportunities in Europe and economic slowdowns in the United States ended the fears of a mass exodus across the North Atlantic, although many developing countries still worry about their own losses.

It has long been taken for granted that experts from developed countries provide indispensable help to developing countries. They explain and install the newest equipment and techniques of organization. They demonstrate manual skills and work habits that are integral parts of industrialization but that may be unfamiliar in the host country. They teach students and senior counterparts.[21]

Do the gains of developing countries from the work of experts offset their temporary or permanent brain drain to the developed countries? Some skeptics believe the net gain from technical assistance itself is not as great as was heretofore believed, In numbers of personnel, only France sends more experts than it receives in foreign professional workers. While the United States and Great Britain send substantial numbers of experts, their intake of foreign professionals is even larger. The developing countries losing personnel by brain drain (for example, the Republic of China, India, the Philippines, and the Republic of Korea) receive only limited technical assistance. The countries with many foreign experts (for example, Africa and Nepal) recover most of their foreign-trained professionals. Experts usually work in certain fields (such as agriculture and public health) that do not suffer great losses in the brain drain; emigration occurs in several fields (engineering, direct care of patients, elementary school teaching) that are not made up through technical assistance. Some governments now are trying to solve their manpower needs by reducing dependence on foreign experts, encouraging their citizens to learn skills of practical value according to manpower projections, and attracting back the talented persons now working abroad.

From the standpoint of the sending country

The principal loss from prolonged work abroad is the fact that the professional is not contributing to the development of his own country. Instead, he is helping the rich become richer, thereby accentuating the inequality among societies. The home country loses its investment in his upbringing and education before he left.

The country sending the professional might benefit. It might have an excessive number of persons in that specialty; the emigration of some relieves unemployment and increases the security and pay of those who remain. Some professionals may remit money home, as do less skilled overseas workers, and the country gains foreign exchange. If the professional ultimately returns, he comes back with the technical and managerial skills essential to development.

From the standpoint of the receiving country

The brain drain of professionals is supposed to be an immense benefit to the recipient, which obtains skilled manpower without having paid the costs of their upbringing and education before their arrival. The newcomers may relieve shortages of professional labor, as in medicine, without the receiving country incurring the expense of expanded curricula. Some foreign professionals may be unusually innovative; immigrants have had notable achievements in the sciences and humanities. The cultural stature and international standing of the country may increase greatly from the foreign infusions, as in the American experience described by Fleming and Hughes.[22]

On the other hand, the receiving country may experience some disadvantages. It will be attacked for "stealing" other countries' talent, and will be the target of critical resolutions in international forums. The immigrants may not be as well trained as local professionals and may not relate well to the public; services may expand in size but decline in quality.[23] If the receiving country previously was homogeneous, ethnic and racial tensions may arise.

Resolving the conflict of interests

Some governments now are trying to solve their manpower needs by reducing dependence on foreign experts, encouraging their citizens to learn skills of practical value according to manpower projections, and attracting back the talented persons now working abroad. Also, some have urged international organizations, such as the General Assembly of the United Nations, to recommend compensation of the losers by the recipients. Inspired by this controversy, a new trend in migration research searches for techniques to calculate the costs incurred by the losers in the upbringing and education of the migrants, the production it foregoes when professionals leave, and the value of the work gained by the receiving country. The aggregate consequences vary according to each country's economy: some losing countries are harmed more than others, particularly if their talent is scarce; the same personnel represent only a small total gain to the typical receiving country, which likely has a booming economy and many professionals of its own.[24]

So far, the research generalizes about the aggregate gains for a rich country's entire economy. The benefits for particular sectors attracting many immigrants appear to be greater. For example, many hospitals in American and British cities depend on foreign house staff. The rapid expansion of the American aerospace industry and the survival of small American colleges during the 1960s might have been impossible without foreign professionals.

NOTES

1. G. S. Métraux, *Exchange of Persons: The Evolution of Cross-Cultural Education* (New York: Social Science Research Council, 1952), and W. Adams, ed., *The Brain Drain* (New York: The Macmillan Company, 1968), Chapter 2.

2. This and the following estimates appear in UNESCO, *Study Abroad* (Paris: United Nations Educational, Scientific, and Cultural Organization, 1972), pp.20–24.

3. *Open Doors 1973* (New York: Institute of International Education, 1973).

4. Adams. op. cit.

5. Committee on the International Migration of Talent, *The International Migration of High-Level Manpower: Its Impact on the Development Process* (New York: Praeger Publishers, 1970); G. Henderson, *Emigration of Highly-Skilled Manpower from the Developing Countries* (New York: United Nations Institute for Training and Research, 1970); and J. G. Whelan, *Brain Drain: A Study of the Persistent Issue of International Scientific Mobility* (Washington: U.S. Government Printing Office, 1974).

6. U.S. Department of Justice, Immigration, and Naturalization Service, *1973 Annual Report: Immigration and Naturalization Service* (Washington, D.C.: 1974).

7. Compare B. Abel-Smith and K. Gales, *British Doctors at Home and Abroad* (Welwyn: The Codicote Press, 1964) with O. Gish, *Doctor Migration and World Health* (London: G. Bell and Sons, 1971) and L. Parai, *Immigration and Emigration of Professional and Skilled Manpower during the Post-War Period* (Ottawa: Economic Council of Canada, Queen's Printer, 1965).

8. F. Wilder-Okladek, "Research on Return Migration and the Concept of 'Intention of Permanence' in Migratory Theory," paper presented at the Conference on Policy and Research on Migration: Canadian and World Perspectives, International Sociological Association, Research Committee on Migration, University of Waterloo, Canada, 1973.

9. W. A. Glaser, *The Brain Drain: Emigration and Return* (Oxford: Pergamon Press, 1978).

10. R. G. Meyers, *Education and Emigration: Study Abroad and the Migration of Human Resources* (New York: David McKay Company, 1972), Chapters 3 and 4; and S. Spaulding et. al., *The World's Students in the United States* (New York: Praeger Publishers, 1976), Chapter 5.

11. Glaser, op. cit., yet unpublished tabulations from the multinational survey of students and professionals by the United Nations Institute for Training and Research.

12. National Science Foundation, *Immigrant Scientists and Engineers in the United States: A Study of Characteristics and Attitudes,* Survey of Science Resources Series (Washington, D.C.: National Science Foundation, 1973), p.3.

13. *Open Doors 1973,* op. cit.

14. I. L. Horowitz, ed., *The Rise and Fall of Project Camelot* (Cambridge: M.I.T. Press, 1967) and A. Szalai et. al., eds., *Cross-National Comparative Survey Research: Theory and Practice* (Oxford: Pergamon Press, 1977).

15. These and the following figures are from E. M. Martin, *Development Cooperation: Efforts and Policies of the Members of the Development Assistance Committee* (Paris: Organization for Economic Cooperation and Development, 1972), pp.170–71 and 230–31.

16. Spaulding, op. cit., and M. Kendall, *Overseas Students in Britain* (London: Research Unit for Student Problems, University of London, 1968). Among the larger surveys are M. S. Das, *Brain Drain Controversy and International Students* (Lucknow: Lucknow Publishing House, 1972); S. E. Deutsch, *International Education and Exchange* (Cleveland: The Press of Case Western Reserve University, 1970); Glaser, op. cit.,; and K. D. Sharma, *Indian Students in the United States* (Bombay: Academic Journals of India, 1970).

17. Whelan, op. cit., Chapter IV; and S. Watanabe, "The Brain Drain from Developing to Developed Countries," *International Labour Review,* 99, No. 4 (1969), pp. 401–33.

18. Meyers, op. cit.; J. R. Niland, *The Asian Engineering Brain Drain* (Lexington: Heath Lexington Books, 1970); Glaser, op. cit.; and a few others.

19. Glaser, op. cit., pp. 196-203.

20. Adams, op cit.; Committee on the International Migration of Talent, op. cit.; Whelan, op. cit., Chapters IV and V; and many other sources.

21. M. Domergue, *Technical Assistance: Theory, Practice and Policies* (New York: Frederick A. Praeger, 1968), and S. C. Sufrin, *Technical Assistance: Theory and Guidelines* (Syracuse: Syracuse University Press, 1966).

22. D. Fleming and B. Bailyn, eds., *The Intellectual Migration* (Cambridge: Harvard University Press, 1969), and H. S. Hughes, *The Sea Change: The Migration of Social Thought 1930–1965* (New York: Harper and Row, 1974).

23. Whelan, op. cit., pp. 180-93.

24. E. P. Reubens, "The New Brain Drain from Developing Countries: Cost and Benefits, 1960–1972," in R. D. Leiter, ed., *Costs and Benefits of Education* (New York: Twayne Publishers, 1975), and UNCTAD, *The Reverse Transfer of Technology: Its Dimensions, Economic Effects and Policy Implications* (New York: United Nations Conference on Trade and Development, 1975).

MEXICAN IMMIGRATION: CAUSES AND CONSEQUENCES FOR MEXICO[1]

Wayne A. Cornelius

INTRODUCTION

The scenario is a familiar one in twentieth century U.S. history: Americans beset with rising unemployment (sometimes combined with high inflation), high taxes, and other problems over which they feel they have little control begin searching for scapegoats. The search, feeding upon residual racial prejudice as well as economic woes, leads quickly to the foreign migrant, especially the Mexican, who is not only the most numerous among the foreign-born population but also the most visible. Politicians, journalists, organized labor, and other interest groups rush to blame the migrant for every imaginable problem afflicting American society, from high unemployment to depressed wages, poor working conditions, lack of union organization among wage earners, high social service costs, international balance-of-payments deficits, rising crime rates, drug abuse, infectious disease, insect infestation, overpopulation, environmental pollution, energy shortages, and even Communist subversion.[2] Citizens demand that their elected officials take action to solve these problems by deporting the migrants and restricting future entries. Never mind that just a short time before, the migrants' labor was considered essential either to a national war effort, to economic growth, or both; now, the Mexican migrant is viewed as an economic threat, an intolerable burden upon the U.S. taxpayer and a cultural-racial contaminant. The presence of large numbers of Mexicans in the country is attributed either to a monstrous conspiracy of big business and its allies in Congress against the American workers, or to the Mexican government which prefers to export its problems rather than solve them.

Most U.S. officials find such explanations convenient, since they divert public attention from their own failures of policy and performance. Responding to "popular demand," they proceed to deal with the "Mexican problem" through mass roundups and deportation (repatriation) campaigns. This general scenario has been played out no fewer than four times in the past fifty eight years: 1920–21, 1930–35, 1953–54, and 1973 to the present. The most recent episode has not yet culminated in mass roundups and deportations, although polls show that a majority of Americans would approve—once again—of this kind of solution.[3]

This paper represents an attempt to identify some of the basic factors underlying Mexican migration to the United States and U.S. responses to this migratory movement, primarily during the period since 1917. Particular attention is devoted to the role of the U.S. itself—including both public and private sector actors—in stimulating and institutionalizing migration from Mexico. The available evidence concerning the magnitude, characteristics, and socioeconomic impacts of the migration upon the United States and Mexico is summarized, and policy options for reducing or regulating the flow are discussed briefly.[4] These policy options are evaluated primarily with respect to their appropriateness to the *Mexican* component of the flow of illegal migrants, since Mexicans constitute at least 60–65 percent of the total flow and a much higher proportion of migrants to the U.S. Southwest.

CAUSAL FACTORS: THE U.S. ROLE IN PROMOTING MEXICAN MIGRATION

Special consideration for the Mexican component of the illegal migrant flow is also appropriate in light of the unique contribution of past U.S. government policies and private sector inducements to the creation and maintenance of a constant stream of Mexican migrants to this country during most of the last ninety years. Those with short memories find it easy to blame Mexico for the current state of affairs, and contend that the "illegal alien problem" exists mainly because Mexico has failed both to limit its population growth and to create enough jobs.[5] Even a superficial examination of the facts reveals this to be a gross oversimplification of the historical record.

Most Mexican and Chicano historians would begin a discussion of this topic with the U.S. annexation of Texas in 1845 and the Mexican war of 1846–48. Undoubtedly the most sordid war of aggression in U.S. history (Ulysses S. Grant later called it "America's great unjust war"), the war enabled the U.S. to seize half of Mexico's national territory—disputed land in Texas, all of California, most of New Mexico and Arizona, Nevada, and Utah, and part of Colorado and Wyoming. I shall begin the story some forty years' later, when the U.S. made its first serious efforts to recruit Mexican workers to meet the labor shortages being created by American economic expansion.

As early as the 1880s and 1890s, small groups of U.S. farmers were dispatching labor recruiters into northern Mexico. By 1911 or 1913, recruiting agents for U.S. railroads and mining companies had penetrated deep into central Mexico, spreading the word that high wages were being offered and even providing free transportation to the U.S.[6] They were soon followed by recruiters for Texas cotton growers, Colorado sugar beet growers, and even industrial employers in midwestern cities connected to Mexico by the railroads. Sometimes, rather than directly recruiting workers in the Mexican interior, hiring agents working under contract to a variety of U.S. companies would simply advertise the merits and location of their employment offices in the border cities and provide instructions on crossing the border.[7]

The efforts of private U.S. firms to recruit large numbers of Mexican workers were facilitated by a series of legislative and administrative actions, or deliberate inactions, which themselves served as powerful inducements to migration to the U.S. Mexicans were specifically exempted from the four dollar head tax imposed on each immigrant by the Immigration Act of 1907. In sharp contrast to their practice in east-coast ports of entry, U.S. immigration officials along the southern border did not enforce the clause of the 1907 act which prohibited the

entry of penniless aliens who would be "likely to become public charges."[8] The Contract Labor Law of 1885, which prohibited the entry of laborers who had been induced to come to the U.S. by specific job offers or promises of contracts, also went unenforced along the U.S.–Mexico border. Congressional passage of the Immigration Act of 1917 proved to be an indirect but powerful stimulant to Mexican migration to the U.S. By sharply restricting the entry of southern and eastern Europeans, the law automatically increased U.S. employer demand for Mexican labor. The 1917 law cut the supply of European laborers by almost 50 percent, and the immigration laws enacted in 1921 and 1924 reduced it still further. Meanwhile, the U.S. was maintaining an open-door policy for economic and political refugees from the Mexican Revolution, exempting them from most of the restrictions specified in the immigration laws. After U.S. entry into World War I, the U.S. Secretary of Labor, acting under a proviso of the 1917 Immigration Act permitting him to suspend any parts of the law in the event of a labor shortage, specifically exempted Mexican agricultural workers from all restrictions imposed by the 1917 Act and the 1885 Contract Labor Law; specifically, the eight dollar head tax, the literacy test, and the prohibition on entry of contract laborers. Under the terms of this waiver over 72,000 Mexican farm workers were formally admitted to the U.S. between 1917 and March 1921. In July 1918, the Secretary of Labor extended the waiver to include nonagricultural workers from Mexico (mostly contract laborers for the railroads, mines, and construction companies). This waiver remained in effect until March 1921,[9] with the result that direct recruitment of workers in the Mexican interior was stepped up.[10]

After a brief interlude (the repatriation of 1920–21) U.S. business and its allies in the Harding and Coolidge administrations resumed the courtship of the Mexican migrant. Seeking to promote U.S. economic growth through foreign investment and trade, Secretary of Commerce Herbert Hoover won approval of a new U.S. policy toward Mexico designed to create the best possible climate for expansion of U.S. trade and investments in Mexico.[11] A central element of the "new relationship" with

Mexico was nonenforcement of a racial exclusion clause of the 1924 Immigration Act which prohibited the entry of persons having "more than 50 percent Indian blood." Since enforcement of this clause would have had the effect of excluding a large proportion of Mexican workers, the vast majority of whom were mixed-blood *mestizos*, border officials were ordered to get around it by classifying all incoming Mexicans as "white."

The provision of the 1924 Immigration Act requiring all entrants to obtain visas also went unenforced along the U.S.–Mexico border until 1929. The newly established Border Patrol busied itself enforcing the customs and alcohol prohibition laws. Even on those rare occasions when Mexican illegals were apprehended by immigration officials, they were not deported. Instead, their U.S. employers were required to pay the visa and head tax charges for the worker (a total of eighteen dollars); "then the worker was brought to the nearest border point and allowed to re-enter the U.S."[12]

With the coming of the Great Depression, it was no longer profitable or necessary to attract a large supply of Mexican workers. The door was slammed shut, and mass roundups and less obvious forms of coercion were employed to rid the U.S. of "the intolerable burden" of Mexican workers who did not leave of their own volition. But twelve years later, with the labor shortages created by U.S. entry into World War II, the Mexican worker suddenly became a highly valuable commodity once again. In 1942, the *bracero* program was launched by passage of Public Law 45, which enabled U.S. employers to recruit Mexican contract laborers for short-term work in agriculture; the duration of the contracts ranged from forty-five days to six months. Extended under a series of U.S. statutes and binational agreements from 1942 to December 1964, the *bracero* program brought more than four million Mexican workers (including many "repeaters") to the United States.

Extensive publicity about the hiring centers established in Mexico City, Guadalajara, Irapuato, Aguascalientes, Monterrey, and other cities was beamed by radio into the smallest villages, many of which had not previously contributed many migrants to the U.S.–bound flow. In the village of

Tzintzuntzan, Michoacán, for example, 53 percent of all household heads and an additional unknown number of single men had been to the U.S. as *braceros* by the time the program was terminated in 1964.[13]

The *bracero* program was also a milestone in the history of several of the communities included in the present study. Before 1942, the volume of emigration from these communities to the U.S. had been relatively low. However, especially during the heyday of the *bracero* program, in the late 1950s "just about everyone went," as one informant recalls.[14] By the time the program ended in 1964, migration to the U.S. as a strategy of income maintenance or improvement had been thoroughly institutionalized in thousands of Mexican villages and towns with the active encouragement of the U.S. government and U.S. agribusiness.

The interlocking of the U.S. and Mexican economies has promoted Mexican migration in other ways. The U.S. has powerfully influenced the kind of economic development which has occurred in Mexico since the 1920s through direct private investment.[15] In Mexico, as in other Latin American countries, the technologies introduced by U.S. firms and U.S.–based multinational corporations have tended to be highly capital-intensive—certainly more capital-intensive than the technologies used by most Mexican enterprises. Over the years, many local firms, increasingly unable to compete with the more efficient subsidiaries of U.S.–based multinationals, have been absorbed by them. The result has been a higher rate of labor displacement—or a lower rate of job creation—than would otherwise have occurred in some sectors of the Mexican economy.[16]

This is also true of the agricultural sector, particularly in the irrigated farming areas of northwestern and central Mexico. There, the system of "contract farming," introduced by U.S.–based food processing corporations such as Del Monte, Campbell, and General Foods, has served the interests of larger growers at the expense of smaller, more marginal farmers. The companies' preference for working with larger growers (favoring them with credit, use of machinery, and advantageous marketing arrangements) has left the smaller producers in an increasingly uncompetitive position.[17] Eventually, many of the small landowners rent or sell their land to the larger growers, and then either work as wage laborers for the larger growers or migrate.

The economies of the U.S. and Mexico are now so closely intertwined that we invariably export our recessions and inflationary spirals to Mexico, thus increasing the volume of illegal migration. This can hardly be avoided with a trade relationship in which 69 percent of all Mexican exports go to the U.S., and about 61 percent of the goods imported by Mexico come from the U.S. It should come as no surprise that the serious economic problems experienced by Mexico since 1969 (to be discussed further below) have coincided, albeit with a time lag, with the U.S. recession-inflation cycles of the 1970s.

Finally, while the U.S. Federal Government continues to do battle against illegal migrants from Mexico and elsewhere, state and local government officials in many parts of the country either welcome their presence or acquiesce in it. Among other things, state and local governments issue licenses and permits for all sorts of economic activity, from retail commerce to roof repair, with no proof of U.S. citizenship or legal resident status required. Such practices enable the illegal migrant who manages to accumulate some capital to go into business for himself. Since it is virtually impossible to make the issuance of such permits "secure" (even if proof of legal resident status is required, the birth certificates or other credentials used to demonstrate such status can easily be purchased or fraudulently obtained), illegal migrants will continue to receive them. Many local school districts actively recruit Mexican migrants (regardless of legal status) into their adult education programs. Especially in border areas, there seems to be a plethora of groups and organizations—church groups, private social service agencies, legal defense organizations, and so forth—which provide assistance to illegal migrants.[18]

The point is not that such assistance should be denied to the illegal migrant; it is simply to call attention to another facet of the U.S. role in initiating and perpetuating this migratory movement. Through extensive labor recruiting, manipulation of the immigration laws, investment practices of U.S.

firms within Mexico, activities of a wide variety of public and private entities on our side of the border, and through many other ways, the U.S. has done much to "push" and "pull" Mexican migrants into this country. "In these forms Mexican aliens have been told that their labor is welcomed in the United States, and they have responded accordingly. The 'illegal alien' problem is, therefore, one whose seed has been planted time and time again by the United States."[19]

The point of departure for illegal alien policy making should be a recognition that the U.S. bears a heavy share of responsibility for the present situation. Yet, while we continue to welcome with open arms the Indochinese "refugees from communism" to whose condition we contributed, the refugees from poverty streaming across our southern border—to whose condition and behavior we have also contributed—are shunned.

THE MEXICAN SIDE: SHORT-TERM ECONOMIC PUSH FACTORS

During most of the period from 1900 to the mid-1960s, the most potent factor stimulating as well as constraining Mexican migration to the U.S. was undoubtedly the fluctuating demand for Mexican labor in the United States.[20] Since the late 1960s, however, "push" factors on the Mexican side seem to have been more important. Indeed, there is no other way to explain the large increases in illegal migration from Mexico to the U.S. in recent years, since these increases come at a time when the demand for Mexican labor in U.S. agriculture is dropping rapidly due to mechanization, when living costs in the U.S. are elevated, and when the difficulty and expense of illegal entry is rising due to increased INS enforcement activities along the border. While basic "background" factors, such as natural population growth and low rates of job creation in Mexico, are crucial to an explanation of Mexican migration in the long run, Mexican migration can also be highly sensitive to short-term economic fluctuations.

The post-1968 wave of illegal migration has coincided with Mexico's most serious economic crisis since the late 1930s. From 1950 to 1974, Mexico's

TABLE 1
Inflation in Mexico, 1950-77

Period	Wholesale Price Index* (Compound annual growth rate)	Year	Consumer Price Index** (1968 = 100)
1950-60	6.4%	1969	103.5
		1970	108.7
1960-65	2.0	1971	114.6
		1972	120.3
1965-70	2.8	1973	134.8
		1974	166.8
1970-75	10.3	1975	191.8
		1976	222.1
		1977	298.3

*Source: Reynolds (1977: Table 1, p. 45).

**Source: Banco de México, *Indicadores Económicos*, 1977.   The index for the year 1977 is preliminary, based on data compiled through September

gross national product increased, in real terms, at an average annual rate of 6.4 percent, while the per capita growth rate averaged 3.0 percent per year. In 1976, the growth rate plummeted to 2 percent, and in 1977 it was only 2.5 percent—not enough to stay ahead of population growth. Unemployment has risen sharply, and real incomes have been eroded by inflation at a rate two to three times higher than the average inflation rate prevailing during the 1950–70 period (see Table 1). At the same time, the Mexican government has been required by the International Monetary Fund to implement austerity measures as a condition of a $960 million loan made to Mexico in late 1976; these include a 10 percent ceiling on wage increases in 1977 (a year when inflation was running at 20–25 percent), and a 12 percent ceiling in 1978. As usual, those who have suffered most from the inflation and austerity measures are the poor, both rural and urban.

But the recent economic development which has undoubtedly had the greatest impact on migration to the U.S. was the devaluation of the Mexican peso in September 1976—the first such devaluation in twenty-two years. Flotation of the peso on international money markets induced, in part, by a massive increase in public expenditures, and financed largely through external borrowing under President Luis Echeverría, caused its value in U.S. currency to decline by nearly half. Before September 1, 1976, if a migrant working in the U.S. sent one U.S. dollar to his family in Mexico it brought 12.50 pesos. Today, if he sends one dollar, it brings 22.95 pesos. With U.S. dollars yielding nearly twice as much as before, rapid inflation, and with a high unemployment rate in Mexico, a large increase in illegal migration during 1977 was inevitable.

LONG-TERM STRUCTURAL PROBLEMS

Unemployment and underemployment

For many years, Mexico's economy has not generated enough jobs to keep pace with the number of new entrants to the labor force. In recent years there have been an estimated 700,000 new job seekers annually, but even when the economy is expanding at an annual rate of 6–7 percent (nearly three times the 1976–77 growth rate), no more than 300,000 jobs are created each year. The result is unemployment and underemployment on a massive scale which are the most important factors fueling migration to the U.S. Most estimates of the proportion of the total working-age population affected by unemployment and underemployment are in the 45–55 percent range.[21] Of these seriously affected workers, about two-thirds are in rural areas.[22]

Within the rural sector, underemployment is a much more pervasive problem than open unemployment. Due to natural population increase and mechanization of commercial agriculture, landless laborers in the countryside find fewer days of work each year. From 1950 to 1960 alone, the average number of days worked per year by agricultural wage workers fell from 190 to 100.[23] In regions which lack irrigation facilities, even peasants who own land have little or nothing to do from December until late May or early June each year except wait for the rains to come.

Among the most recent group of illegal migrants included in the current study, over 31 percent cited lack of work as the principal reason for making their first trip to the United States (see Table 2). As might be expected, given population growth and Mexico's economic difficulties in the 1970s, the relative importance of joblessness or underemployment as a motive for migration seems to have increased in the period since 1969. My interview data also show that underemployment is a more important factor promoting migration to the U.S. than open unemployment. Only 6 percent of the most recent illegal migrants had been unemployed in their home community just before they went to the U.S. for the first time, but another 18.5 percent lacked remunerated work; they were simply helping their father on the

family farm plot or in the family business without salary. Nearly half of the agricultural workers in my sample had only six or fewer months of work per year, mostly during the rainy season. Even among those employed in commerce and services, underemployment was a problem for more than one out of five workers.

Low wage scales

For many Mexican migrants to the U.S., it is not just a lack of work, but lack of reasonably stable and adequately *paid* work which impels them to go. Among the most recent illegal migrants interviewed in my study, low income from their jobs in Mexico was given as the main reason for their first trip to the U.S. by as large a proportion as those who mentioned lack of work (see Table 2). Not only are Mexican wage scales low in an absolute sense; they seem much lower by comparison with U.S. earnings. For example, the average landless agricultural worker represented in the present study earned about 35 pesos ($1.53 US) per *day*, or 840 pesos ($36.62 US) per month in 1976.[24] The average illegal migrant from my research communities working in the U.S. in that same year was earning $2.50 (US) per *hour*, or $480.12 per month—an income differential of 13 to 1. Even when travel, *coyote* fees, and other expenses are subtracted, the average illegal migrant from this region can usually net more income from three months or less of work in the United States than he could from an entire year of labor in his home community. Nor has the U.S.–Mexico gap in earnings been narrowed in recent decades, despite Mexico's impressive economic development, in aggregate, GNP terms, during most of the period since 1940. In fact, the same 13 to 1 differential between migrant earnings in the U.S. and average agricultural wage rates in the region of Mexico where my research was done has apparently prevailed since the first decade of this century.[25]

Maldistribution of income

Perhaps the most striking aspect of Mexico's pattern of development since 1940 is its uneven-

TABLE 2
Reasons for Initial Migration to the U.S.

Question: "The first time you went to work in the U.S. -- why did you decide to go, that time?"

Reason	Pre-1969 illegal migrants	Post-1969 illegal migrants
Lack of work (unemployment or underemployment)	22.4%	31.4%
To increase income (needed more money to subsist or to improve standard of living; attracted by higher wages paid in the U.S.; etc.)	27.1	31.4
Had to go because of "hard times" in home community (owing to drought, flooding, some other temporary condition)*	9.4	6.1
Wanted to help out parents financially	1.2	0.9
To repay debts incurred in home community	4.7	3.9
To live more comfortably (to be able to have more "conveniences," acquire other non-essential consumer goods)	2.4	0.4
Just wanted to travel, get to know another place ..	20.0	10.9
They were hiring people for the *bracero* program ...	2.4	4.4
Family reasons (went with his parents; had family problems in home community; to join relatives who were already in the U.S., etc.) .	7.1	3.5
Other	3.3	7.1

Source: Author's sample survey in Jalisco, 1976. *Pre-1976 illegals* are persons whose most recent work experience in the U.S. was as an illegal migrant during the period before 1969. *Post-1969 illegals* are persons whose most recent work experience in the U.S. was as an illegal migrant during the period since 1969.

*There is probably some overlapping in responses between this category and the two categories preceding it. For example, a respondent who gave "lack of work" or need to increase income" as his reason for initial migration may, in fact, have been responding to a temporary local condition (e.g., crop failure, but only if specific mention was made of such "hard times" would the response have been coded into that category.

ness. This is clearly reflected in the national distribution of income, which is one of the most unequal in the world. The post-1940 period of rapid economic growth was also one of income concentration; in fact, the share of income going to the poorest 20 percent of the Mexican population declined from 6.1 percent in 1950 to 4 percent in 1969. Expressed another way, "if the per capita income of Mexico today is about $1,000, the poorest six million people receive only about $400 per year . . . [while] the upper six million receive $3,700."[26] According to one calculation, by the 1960s, the degree of income inequality in Mexico was about as high as it was in 1910 *before* the outbreak of the Mexican Revolution.[27] It is probable that the income distribution has become even more unequal during the 1970s due to high inflation rates, the expansion of capital-intensive agriculture, and other trends.

While living standards improved, in absolute terms, for a large proportion of the population,[28] there was probably no real income gain for the poorest 40 percent of Mexicans during the 1940–75 period. In fact, one study found that, among landless agricultural workers, average annual income actually declined from 700 pesos to 499 pesos during the 1960–69 period.[29] The last three decades of uneven development have also brought steadily widening income gaps between rural and urban areas and, within the rural sector, between the northern (irrigated commercial agriculture) and central-southern ("dry" subsistence farming) regions.

Inequalities of this type are deeply rooted in the kinds of development policies which have been pursued, particularly with regard to the rural sector, by Mexican governments during most of the period since 1940. The basic strategy during this period was to use public investments, especially in irrigation projects, to stimulate the development of large-scale, mechanized, export-oriented agriculture, particularly in the cotton and wheat-growing regions of northern and northwestern Mexico. As Cynthia Hewitt de Alcántara has noted: "The policy of concentrating government investment in infrastructure, credit, and technical assistance within irrigated oases during the past thirty years has consid-

erably widened the gap between the productivity of farms in these oases and the rest of the agricultural holdings of the country."[30] Government-financed irrigation permitted the larger landowners to introduce "Green Revolution" technologies (high-yield seeds, fertilizers, pesticides, and so forth), and the profits resulting from increased productivity made it possible for the larger farmers to invest heavily in labor-saving machinery. The result was increased exports of primary products, but also accelerated mechanization, increased income inequalities, more concentration of landownership (as small farmers, undercapitalized and unable to compete, sold off or leased their land to the large-scale producers), more unemployment and underemployment. The proportion of adult rural dwellers owning land fell from 42 percent in 1940 to 33 percent in 1970. By the early 1970s, despite a land reform program in which more than 75 million hectares of land had been expropriated and transferred to about three million peasant recipients, there were an estimated 3.2 to 3.6 million landless agricultural laborers in Mexico—more than in 1930, before land reform had even been undertaken on a large scale.[31]

While the Mexican government under President Luis Echeverría (1970–76) increased both the level of investment benefiting the subsistence sector of agriculture and the overall share of federal funds allocated to the rural sector,[32] the basic imbalance between large- and small-scale farmers has not been redressed in terms of access to irrigation, credit, and other necessary inputs. Small-holding agriculture continues to be viewed by most officials as inherently inefficient and unproductive; government investment patterns continue to reflect the notion that export and domestic consumption needs can only be met by concentrating most of the inputs in the hands of a relatively small group of large-scale farmers.

Population growth

Many of the problems discussed in the preceding pages have been exacerbated by (though not necessarily the result of) Mexico's extraordinarily high rate of natural population increase since the 1940s. In most rural communities, an excess population—relative to the amount of cultivable land and the number of nonagricultural employment opportunities—is one of the most important factors promoting migration to the United States as well as to cities within Mexico. Mortality rates have fallen sharply in Mexico since 1940, due to improved health care, sanitation, and nutrition, while fertility rates have remained quite high.[33] A great deal of future population growth is already assured. Approximately 46 percent of Mexico's total population of 64 million are under fifteen years of age. While the proportion of Mexicans living in rural areas has probably dropped to about 38 percent today, due to natural population increase the economically active population in the agricultural sector is not likely to begin declining, in absolute terms until after 1985.[34]

When the Mexican government launched its family planning program in 1974, the national population was growing at a rate of 3.5 percent per year, doubling every twenty years. The rate of natural increase in rural areas was even higher (3.7 percent per year in my research communities as of 1975). Studies by demographers at El Colegio de México indicate that during the last three years the national population growth rate has declined from 3.5 percent per year to 3.2 percent. It is still too early to tell whether this decrease represents the beginning of a long-term decline, a temporary condition, or a statistical artifact. While the Mexican government appears to be firmly committed to the expansion of its family planning program, it will take longer to reduce growth rates in the countryside than in the cities, if only because of the extreme geographic dispersion of the rural population (more than 90,000 separate localities must be reached). As of late 1976, most residents of the research communities were aware of the government's family planning campaign (mainly as a result of extensive radio publicity), but specific birth control information and services remained conspicuously unavailable in most communities.

THE "OIL BONANZA": WHAT DIFFERENCE WILL IT MAKE?

In recent years, very large deposits of oil and natural gas have been discovered along Mexico's Gulf coast. As of late 1977, according to the Mexican government's figures, proven reserves of 16 billion barrels of oil had been discovered; probable reserves were set at 29.2 barrels, and possible reserves were estimated from geological data at 120 billion barrels. (If the 120 billion barrel figure proves accurate, Mexico would be second only to Saudi Arabia in total reserves.) Estimates of Mexico's foreign exchange earnings from oil and gas exports range from four to eight billion dollars per year by 1982, "if all goes well."[35] Amid such predictions of future wealth, it has become fashionable to expect that Mexico's oil and gas earnings will provide a quick way out of most of the country's developmental problems, thus greatly reducing the pressures for migration to the U.S.[36]

It is unlikely, however, that oil and gas revenues per se will eliminate the basic push factors underlying illegal migration, at least in the short-to-medium run. In the first place, the new "investable" revenues generated by hydrocarbon exports will be substantially less than the export earnings themselves. To realize the projected export earnings, the Mexican government will have to invest about twenty billion dollars between 1977 and 1982 to extract the oil and gas, continue exploration, and install processing plants;[37] at least half of that investment will probably have to be obtained through external borrowing. Debt service alone will eat up a sizable portion of the anticipated export earnings.[38] There are other sources of difficulty which could also affect the amount of new revenues to become available (for example, completion of a huge pipeline for exporting gas to the U.S. which is now being held up by the controversy over U.S. energy policy). The greatest uncertainties from the standpoint of migration to the United States, however, are not those relating to the total amount of revenues which may or may not flow from Mexico's hydrocarbon deposits; rather they concern the rate at which the oil wealth can be translated into concrete improvements in jobs, incomes, and welfare for the Mexican poor. The experiences of other oil-rich, less-developed countries (for example, Venezuela, Iran, and Algeria) in converting income from petroleum exports into benefits for the masses are not very encouraging. The case of Venezuela since

1973 is particularly instructive: over 17 billion *bolivares* have been invested by the government in the agricultural sector since 1976, yet agricultural production has declined; the land reform program is years behind schedule; and the flow of credit to small farmers has not been improved appreciably. Observers attribute these outcomes to such problems as corruption, mismanagement, resistance from local elites, and market forces at work within Venezuela's mixed economy.[39]

Given the same kinds of constraints operating on most rural development programs in Mexico, it would be unrealistic to expect a dramatically different kind of outcome, at least in the short run. It is also possible, as Fagen and Nau have suggested, that very fundamental structural changes would be needed in both the public and private sectors in Mexico before oil wealth could be translated into the kinds of programs that would have maximum impact on rural employment and incomes in Mexico.[40]

But what of job opportunities within the nonagricultural sector? Here again, there is little cause for excessive optimism. The technology used in the oil and petrochemical industries is notoriously capital-intensive. Gordon has pointed out that while 5,000 construction workers are being employed in building a huge $500 million natural gas processing complex in the state of Chiapas, only 2,000 workers will be needed to operate the twelve plants in the complex. This fact translates into an investment of $250,000 for each job created![41] Not only will few jobs be created within the oil and oil-related industries themselves, but also a large-scale shift of public and private investment capital into this sector may actually have a negative impact on total job creation by diverting capital from more labor-intensive sectors of the Mexican economy.[42]

In summary, the recent oil discoveries may have altered the parameters of the development process in Mexico in a variety of ways. Certainly, oil revenues will remove much of the foreign-exchange constraint on economic development. Nevertheless, prudence dictates that neither U.S. nor Mexican policy be based on the assumption that the "oil bonanza" will miraculously remove the pressures for migration to the U.S. from Mexico's rural communities.

ILLEGAL MIGRATION: THE ECONOMIC IMPACT ON MEXICO

The impact of migration to the U.S. on the economies of migrant households, their communities of origin, and Mexico as a whole is difficult to overstate. It can be seen perhaps most vividly in the lines of wives and children queuing up in front of rural post offices each day during the high season of migration to the U.S., anxiously awaiting their monthly or fortnightly money order from the breadwinner abroad. Mexican illegals typically remit a third or more of their U.S. earnings to relatives in Mexico: 30 percent of monthly U.S. earnings in the North and Houstoun study; 37 percent in the Villalpando study; 35 percent in my study.[43] Among the most recent illegals interviewed in my study, 79 percent reported that they sent money regularly (usually by money order or check) to their relatives in Mexico during their most recent work experience in the United States. Among those who sent money, the average remittance was $169.65 US per month. As might be expected, married men with dependents remit substantially more than young single men send to their parents. For more than 70 percent of the migrants' families represented in this study, these remittances were their sole source of income while the family head was working in the United States. The illegal migrants in my study were supporting an average of 5.8 dependents in Mexico during their last period of U.S. employment.

Apart from the money which is remitted periodically by the migrants while they are working in the U.S., most of them (65 percent in my study) are able to save and bring money back with them when they return to Mexico. Among my interviewees, the average sum brought back after their most recent trip to the U.S. was $301, not including the value of gifts, household appliances, or other goods purchased in the U.S. which the migrant brought back. The total amount returned to Mexico in the form of remittances and accumulated savings by illegal migrants, both temporary and permanent, is quite large, probably in excess of $2 billion per year (see Appendix 1 for derivation of estimate). These funds are a crucial (if generally unacknowledged) factor in the Mexican balance of payments; they are considerably more important than income from tourism which has generated about $500 million in net foreign exchange earnings in recent years.

In most cases, income from U.S. employment is crucial to the maintenance of the migrant's family, not only while he is in the U.S. but after he returns to Mexico. While the migrant is away, virtually all of the money he remits is typically used for family maintenance. Among the illegals interviewed for the present study, 37 percent also used the lump sums brought back from the U.S. after their most recent trip for family maintenance. Another 16 percent invested most of their U.S. earnings in capital goods (land, livestock, small businesses); 9 percent used the money to buy or improve their house; 8 percent used it to pay previously accumulated debts; and 6 percent used the money to pay medical expenses. Another 12 percent used most of their accumulated earnings to purchase clothing; while only 8 percent of the migrants spent most of the money brought back from the U.S. on nonessential consumer goods (kitchen appliances, television sets, stereos, and so forth) or recreation.

The capital returned by migrants working in the U.S. is dispersed throughout their home communities. Local commerce often depends heavily on the spending generated by migrant remittances. Some new jobs are created by the capital investments made by returned migrants; and, while they are in the U.S., there are more local employment opportunities for those who remain. The scarcity of new land for cultivation has driven up land prices in many rural Mexican communities, but earnings from employment in the U.S. permit some formerly landless people to break into the tight local land market, despite their inability to raise the purchase price by borrowing within the community. More generally, migration to the U.S. has improved possibilities for social and economic mobility in small towns and villages where most wealth, especially in the form of land, had formerly been acquired only through inheritance.[44] Thus, social stratification is less rigid and the local distribution of wealth is more equitable than would otherwise be the case. As one anthropologist has observed, on the basis of fieldwork in rural Michoacán:

I can state unequivocally from domestic group his-

tories that nearly all of the households involved in migration to the U.S. had incomes well below the median (of the community) before sending members to the U.S., and that some now above the median would be well below it if they were no longer permitted to work in the United States.[45]

Community development may benefit from migration to the U.S. in a variety of ways. Some community facilities and infrastructure improvements are installed that would otherwise be beyond the means of the community because residents have more money to contribute toward the cost of such improvements, because permanent emigrants living in the U.S. sometimes contribute additional money, and because the local leadership necessary for such projects is more likely to be available. As Dinerman has noted, one effect of migration to the U.S. is to "encourage hardworking men in prosperous households to expend time, effort, and cash on behalf of the community by rendering 'voluntary' administrative services. Such men, often the most capable in the community, are willing to bear the cost of [such service] because 'one can always go North.' "[46]

Some social scientists have been concerned about the potentially negative consequences of human capital loss for the rural sector and the Mexican economy generally. It is feared that, because migrants to the U.S. tend to be the "best and the brightest" (youngest, best educated, most highly motivated, and so forth) in their home community. the migration may contribute to rural stagnation, or even permanently stunt the development of some sending communities. This, of course, assumes that the skills and aptitudes of those who now migrate to the U.S. could be utilized productively within the local economic opportunity structure, but this is seldom the case. Data gathered for this study indicate that a substantial proportion (from about 20 to 50 percent, depending on the occupational category) of those who migrate to the U.S. would have been unemployed or severely underemployed had they remained in their home community—hardly a productive use of human resources.

The argument also assumes that the human resource loss to the sending community is a permanent one, whereas in fact, the vast majority of those who go to the U.S. *do* return to their home communities, and not just as "burnt-out" older men. Apart from a handful of "professional migrants" who return to the U.S. year after year for most of their productive lives, few residents of the research communities make more than four or five trips to the U.S. during their lifetime; in fact, the average for migrants lacking papers is two or three trips.

Others have been concerned about the impact of migration to the U.S. on agricultural production in Mexico. Preliminary findings from a study of one village in the state of Zacatecas indicate that local corn production does tend to fall during periods of high migration to the U.S., as the amount of land under cultivation decreases.[47] Among the communities included in the present study, however, this phenomenon could be detected in only one community, one which had a significantly higher per capita rate of migration to the U.S. than any of the other eight communities. Among the total sample of recent illegal migrants interviewed in my study, only 19 percent of those who farmed their own land (*ejidatarios* and small private holders) left it idle during their stay in the U.S. Nearly two-thirds of the interviewees left their land in the care of relatives; another 8 percent leased the land to sharecroppers; and 9 percent made some other arrangement to keep the land in production. The amount of land left idle during migration to the U.S. would be even smaller if farmers had more incentives to keep it in production: access to irrigation, credit, fertilizers, more favorable marketing arrangements, and so forth. It is the scarcity or absence of these inputs, much more than migration to the U.S., which depresses agricultural production in most rural Mexican communities.

Under present conditions, were the U.S. suddenly to close its borders to Mexican migrants, it would inflict severe economic hardship upon those Mexican families and communities which have come to depend on this source of income. For others, an end to the migration would probably mean a decline in living standards or more limited prospects for socioeconomic mobility. Given the present trends in rural unemployment, underemployment, inflation, and population growth, it is highly unlikely that alternatives to migrating to the U.S. as a vehicle of economic improvement, or simply a mechanism of survival during lean years, will be-

come available to the bulk of Mexico's rural population in the near future.

If most of the men who would otherwise have sought employment in the U.S. were prevented from doing so, labor markets in some regions of Mexico would be completely overwhelmed. Unemployment and underemployment would rise sharply. Confronted with a greatly expanded labor supply, local elites in rural areas and small towns might respond by freezing or even lowering wage scales. And in provincial Mexico, unlike the United States, there is no welfare, no unemployment compensation system, and no enforced legal minimum wage to keep a "floor" under incomes.

Lower wage scales and greater competition for the few job opportunities available in rural communities would force some of those who might otherwise have remained in the countryside to migrate to a Mexican city. In fact, the most certain consequence of a closure of U.S. employment opportunities would be a major increase in permanent outmigration to Mexico's principal urban centers. Rural-to-urban migration has been heavy in Mexico since the 1940s, but the rate is substantially lower than it would have been in the absence of temporary migration to the United States. Most of those leaving rural areas have settled in the Mexico City metropolitan area which, with about thirteen million inhabitants, is the third largest urban agglomeration in the world after Shanghai and Tokyo. The diseconomies of further growth of Mexico City are already quite evident, and these costs are ultimately borne by the rest of Mexican society. Already, a very large share of total Mexican government revenues is being used to provide basic services and infrastructure for the inhabitants of Mexico City.[48] A strong case could be made that the economic and social-equity costs of a huge new influx of rural migrants into Mexico City and the country's other principal metropolitan centers are prohibitively high, yet a more restrictive U.S. immigration policy would make that influx unavoidable. With labor markets in Mexico City and other major cities already nearing saturation, accelerated inmigration from the countryside would soon create new pressures for migration to the United States.

The social and political tensions which would be generated within Mexico by a sharp reduction in migration to the U.S. are difficult to estimate, but the fact that such migration has served to ameliorate hardship and injustice in the past cannot be ignored. Among other things, an increase in peasant demands for land redistribution could be expected, followed by an increase in the incidence of land invasions when these demands go unmet. Adaptation, rather than rebellion, has been the traditional response of the Mexican peasant to economic hardship, but, as one student of rural Mexico recently observed, "until the immigration ends, one can never be sure."[49] INS Commissioner Leonel Castillo has sounded a similar cautionary note, while drawing an interesting parallel: "You've got to remember that when we return undocumented aliens to Mexico, we're dumping a lot of unemployed and even homeless people on an economy that already is having trouble. What would happen if we unloaded thousands of jobless people in Cleveland?"[50]

Yet, viewed from another perspective, the very magnitude of economic dislocations which could result from fewer employment opportunities for Mexicans in the United States constitutes the best argument for reducing gradually illegal migration and with adequate compensatory opportunities being created within Mexico. If two million Mexican illegals work for some period of time in the U.S. each year, these workers represent more than 13 percent of the Mexican labor force. And if (as my research indicates) each illegal supports an average of 5.8 dependents, that would mean that some 13.6 million Mexicans, or 21.3 percent of the present total population of Mexico, depend to some extent upon U.S. earnings in any given year. The dependence of such a large segment of the Mexican population upon cash income earned in the U.S. is clearly undesirable as well as risky to those involved in this dependency relationship.

It should be recalled that three times during the past fifty-eight years the U.S. has attempted to cut off employment opportunities for Mexicans in this country. We are now witnessing another concerted effort to restrict Mexican access to the U.S. labor market. In the past, U.S. recessions and mass deportation campaigns aimed against Mexicans have caused considerable hardship in those areas of Mexico which contribute most of the illegal mi-

grants to the U.S.; the potential for human suffering as a consequence of U.S. efforts to restrict the flow is much greater today. It is true that, even without the migration, Mexico would be economically dependent on the United States, if only by virtue of geographic proximity. But it is equally clear that a massive flow of migrants heightens that dependence.

CONCLUSION:
SOME POLICY CONSIDERATIONS

If the United States and Mexico should seek to reduce illegal migration gradually over the next two decades, what are the most appropriate policy instruments? The United States might simply opt to wait for Mexico's oil earnings to be converted into jobs and higher living standards for the Mexican poor; but a more prudent course would be to assist the Mexicans now to finance programs of job creation and income improvement in the migrants' places of origin. This is by far the most cost-effective approach to reducing the flow of migrants to the United States, since it is the only approach that would help to reduce the push factors which compel migration. Only when the low-income Mexican has viable alternatives to seeking employment in the U.S. as a strategy of income maintenance or improvement will he cease to migrate. Moreover, the United States has a clear responsibility to assist in financing job creation/income improvement efforts in Mexico—preferably through contributions to international development programs—in light of its central role in the creation and maintenance of the flow of migrants from Mexico.

Under the general rubric of job creation/income improvement measures, there are a variety of policy instruments which merit consideration. Trade and tourism preferences for Mexico would stimulate overall economic growth in Mexico, but would probably not create enough jobs, in the right places, to have a significant impact on the flow (though they would clearly help in some regions). More promising are programs of *direct* job creation in rural areas and small-to-medium towns, through labor intensive public works projects, construction of small-scale irrigation works to permit double-cropping and increase employment opportunities, development of small-scale, labor-intensive rural industries, and provision of incentives (credit, tax concessions, and so forth) to migrants returning from the U.S. to encourage them to invest their U.S. earnings in small businesses or other productive enterprises.

It must be emphasized, however, that even with the best possible rural development programs in Mexico, with optimal utilization of oil and gas revenues (from the standpoint of jobs, income, and welfare), and with overall economic growth rates of 7, 8, or 9 percent per year, it will be virtually impossible for Mexico to absorb all of the expected additions to its labor force over the next fifteen years into productive employment. These future entrants to the labor force have already been born; family planning programs will not diminish their numbers. Thus, unless it opts to close the southern border by military force or a Berlin-type wåll, the United States will undoubtedly have a sizeable Mexican migrant presence in its labor force for at least another fifteen years. Given this situation, the principal policy objectives should be to *regulate* the flow of migrants and to reduce the size of the *illegal* component. The number of opportunities to migrate legally to the U.S. could be increased by raising the legal immigration quota for Mexico to a realistic level (that is, more closely approximating the actual Mexican demand for immigrant visas), by administering the existing "H–2" temporary worker visa system in a less restrictive way,[51] or by instituting a new type of temporary worker program not modeled on either the H-2 system or the former "bracero" program, with greater protections for the worker. Such measures would create meaningful alternatives to illegal migration for those who must continue to seek employment in the United States.

APPENDIX ON REMITTANCES

By way of comparison, it is estimated that, in 1974, the Mediterranean countries (Greece, Turkey, Yugoslavia, Spain, Portugal, and Algeria) received at least $7 billion (U.S.) in remittances from migrants (legal and illegal) working in Western Europe.[52]

My figure for migrant remittances from the U.S. to Mexico is, admittedly, a rough estimate. It is based on the following assumptions: (1) that 70 percent of illegal Mexican immigrants working in the U.S. remit money regularly to their relatives in Mexico; (2) that those migrants who *do* send money remit an average of $169.65 per month; (3) that the average duration of employment in the U.S. among Mexican illegals is 5.5 months per year; (4) that 65 percent of illegal Mexican migrants bring money back with them to their home communities at the end of a period of employment in the U.S.; (5) that the average amount brought back by these migrants is $301; (6) that a total of 2,000,000 illegal Mexican migrants work in the U.S. for some period of time and return to Mexico in the course of a given year.

Assumptions 1–5 are based on data from my study of Jalisco migrants, which are consistent with the findings of other recent studies of illegal migrants originating in many different parts of Mexico. For example, among the Mexican illegals interviewed in the North and Houstoun study, the average amount remitted to relatives in Mexico (among those making such payments) was also $169, and 89 percent of the illegal Mexicans interviewed remitted money. Assumption 6 is based on INS apprehension statistics for Fiscal Year 1977, and data from my study which permit estimation of the ratio of illegal migrants *apprehended* to illegal migrants *unapprehended*, and the proportion of illegals who return to Mexico each year after being employed in the U.S. Accordingly, I estimate the total amount "returned" to Mexico—either in the form of monthly remittances or accumulated savings brought back after U.S. employment—at $1.9 billion per year. This compares with an estimate of $1.5 billion per year, made by North and Houstoun on the basis of their study.[53]

But, to gauge the *total* flow of funds from the U.S. to Mexico resulting from illegal migration, we must add the monies remitted by Mexican illegals who are permanently based in the U.S. to their relatives in Mexico. Field studies have found that about 4 to 7 percent of the households in rural Mexican communities receive remittances from relatives who have settled more or less permanently in the United States, but the available data do not show what proportion of these permanent emigrants are illegal and what proportion have legal immigration status.[54]

NOTES

1. This paper draws upon research conducted for a large-scale study of Mexican migration scheduled for completion in 1979. The research is currently supported by the Center for Population Research, National Institute of Child Health and Human Development, National Institutes of Health. Previous sources of financial support include the SSRC–ACLS Joint Committee on Latin American Studies and the Smithsonian Institution. Data have been gathered during nearly two years of fieldwork in Mexico (the northeastern region of Jalisco state) and nine months of interviewing Jalisco migrants living in California and Illinois. A variety of data collection techniques have been used including complete population censuses, sample surveys, archival research, unstructured interviewing in both the migrants' communities of origin and their U.S. places of residence, and participant-observation. The research sites in Mexico were nine carefully selected rural communities located in the Los Altos region, which has traditionally been one of the most important source regions for Mexican migrants to the United States. This paper reports findings from a sample survey conducted in the Jalisco research communities in July-August 1976. A total of 994 interviews (all with a random probability sample of adult male residents) were completed, including 230 with men who had worked in the United States as illegal migrants at least once during the 1969–76 period. Findings from the Jalisco survey reported in this paper refer to this most recent group of illegal migrants unless otherwise noted.

2. American GI Forum of Texas and Texas State Federation of Labor, AFL-CIO, "What Price Wetbacks?" in *Mexican Migration to the United States* (New York: Arno Press, 1976), p.30 ff., and Robert J. Lipshultz, *American Attitudes Toward Mexican Immigration* (San Francisco and Palo Alto, California: R & E Research Associates, 1971), reprint of Ph.D. dissertation, 1962.

3. Gallup Organization, Inc., "The Gallup Study of Attitudes toward Illegal Aliens," Survey for the Immigration and Naturalization Service, June 1976, p.18.

4. For a more detailed discussion, see Wayne A. Cornelius, "Undocumented Immigration: A Critique of the Carter Administration's Policy Proposals," *Migration Today*, 5, No. 4 (October 1977), pp.5–8, 16–20.

5. See, for example, Donald Mann, "Immigration Should not be Allowed to Further U.S. Population Growth," letter to the editor, *The New York Times* (26 August 1977), p.A20.

6. Paul S. Taylor, *A Spanish-Mexican Peasant Community: Arandas in Jalisco, Mexico,* Ibero-Americana Series, No. 4 (Berkeley, Calif.: University of California Press, 1933), p.55; Victor S. Clark, "Mexican Labor in the United States," *U.S. Bureau of Labor Bulletin* 78 (September, 1908), p.471; and Mark Reisler, *By the Sweat of Their Brow: Mexican Immigrant Labor in the United States, 1900–1940* (Westport, Connecticut: Greenwood Press,

1976), pp.5, 9–11.

7. Reisler, ibid., p.10.

8. Reisler, ibid., p.12.

9. Lawrence A. Cardoso, "Mexican Emigration to the United States, 1900–1930: An Analysis of Socio-Economic Causes" (Ph.D. dissertation, University of Connecticut, 1974), pp.76–79.

10. Carey McWilliams, *North from Mexico: The Spanish-Speaking People of the United States* (New York: Greenwood Press, 1968), p.178.

11. Joan Wilson, *American Business and Foreign Policy, 1920–1933* (Lexington, Kentucky: University of Kentucky Press, 1971), pp. 161–66.

12. Cardoso, op. cit., pp.172, 174.

13. Robert Van Kemper, "Migration and Adaptation of Tzintzuntzan Peasants in Mexico City" (Ph.D. dissertation, University of California at Berkeley, 1971), p.34.

14. The data from the family migration histories in these communities bear him out. Not until 1974 did emigration to the U.S. once again reach the level attained in 1959 when virtually all of the migrants went as *braceros*.

15. Richard S. Newfarmer and William F. Mueller, "Multinational Corporations in Brazil and Mexico: Structural Sources of Economic and Noneconomic Power," report to the Subcommittee on Multinational Corporations of the Committee on Foreign Relations, U.S. Senate, Ninety-Fourth Congress, first session (Washington, D.C.: 1975).

16. By 1968, at least 625 subsidiaries of U.S.-based corporations were operating in Mexico. Fifty-eight percent of these enterprises were in the manufacturing sector, and of these 365 subsidiaries, 43 percent had been established by acquisition of Mexican-owned firms. See Salvador H. Cordero documents this absorption in *Concentración industrial y poder económico en México,* Cuadernos del Centro de Estudios Sociológicos, No. 18 (Mexico City, D.C.: El Colegio de México, 1977), pp. 30–32.

17. See two articles by the North American Congress on Latin America (NACLA) in *NACLA Latin America and Empire Report*, "Harvest of Anger: Agro-Imperialism in Mexico's Northwest," 10, No. 6 (July-August 1976), and "Mexico: Canned Imperialism," 10, No. 7 (September 1976), pp.12–15.

18. See Ellwyn R. Stoddard, "Illegal Mexican Labor in the Borderlands: Institutionalized Support of an Unlawful Practice," *Pacific Sociological Review*, 19, No. 2 (April 1976), pp.175–210.

19. Gilbert Cárdenas, "United States Immigration Policy Toward Mexico: An Historical Perspective," *Chicano Law Review*, 2 (Summer 1975), p.89.

20. Compare with Taylor, op. cit., p.40.

21. Saul Trejo Reyes, "El desempleo en México," *Commercio Exterior*, 24 No. 7 (July 1974), pp.730–38; Manuel Gollás, "El desempleo en Mexico: soluciones posibles," *Ciencia y desarrollo* (May-June 1978) p.74; Donald B. Keesing, "Employment and Lack of Employment in Mexico, 1900–70," in James W. Wilkie and Kenneth Ruddle, eds., *Quantitative Latin American Studies: Methods and Findings*, Statistical Abstract of Latin America, Supplement No. 6 (Los Angeles, California: Latin American Center, University of California at Los Angeles, 1977), pp.3–22; and Redvers Opie, "The Mexican Economic System: Prepared Statement," in U.S. Congress, Joint Economic

Committee, *Recent Developments in Mexico and Their Economic Implications for the United States, Hearings of the Subcommittee on Inter-American Economic Relationships*, Ninety-Fifth Congress, first session, 1977, p.35.

22. David Felix, "Income Inequality in Mexico," *Current History* 72, No. 425 (March 1977), p.113.
23. Sergio Reyes Osorio, et al., *Estructura agraria y desarrollo agricola en México* (México, D.F.: Fondo de Cultura Economica, 1974), p.343. See also Gloria Gonzales, *Problemas de la mano de obra en Mexico* (Mexico, D.F.: Instituto de Investigaciones Economicas, 1971), pp.47–48.
24. The rate of conversion applied here is 22.95 Mexican pesos to the U.S. dollar, the rate prevailing in early April 1978. From 1954 to August 31, 1976, the exchange rate was constant at 12.50 pesos to the dollar. Since the currency devaluation ("flotation") announced by former President Echeverría on September 1, 1976, the exchange rate has oscillated from 20 to 28 pesos to the dollar.
25. Calculated from data in Taylor, op. cit., pp.35–36.
26. Clark Reynolds, "Why Mexico's 'Stabilizing Development' Was Actually Destabilizing," in U.S. Congress, Joint Economic Committee, *Recent Developments in Mexico and Their Economic Implications for the United States, Hearings of the Subcommittee on Inter-American Economic Relationships*, Ninety-Fifth Congress, first session, 1977, p.71.
27. Felix, op. cit., p.112.
28. James W. Wilkie, "Conflicting National Interests Between and Within Mexico and the United States," in U.S. Congress, Joint Economic Committee, *Recent Developments in Mexico and Their Economic Implications for the United States: Hearings of the Subcommittee on Inter-American Economic Relationships*, Ninety-Fifth Congress, first session, 1977, Table 1, p.11.
29. Cynthia Hewitt de Alcántara, *Modernizing Mexican Agriculture: Socioeconomic Implications of Technological Change: 1940–1970* (Geneva: United Nations Research Institute for Social Development, 1976), p.133.
30. Ibid.
31. Ibid., pp.119 and 130.
32. Merilee S. Grindle, "Policy Change in an Authoritarian Regime: Mexico under Echeverria," *Journal of Inter-American Studies and World Affairs* 19, No. 4 (November 1977), p.253.
33. In 1975, fertility was, if anything, a bit higher than it had been twenty years before. See Ansley J. Coale, "Population Growth and Economic Development: The Case of Mexico," *Foreign Affairs* 56, No. 2 (January 1978), p.423, and Francisco Alba, *La población de México: evolución y dilemas* (México, D.F.: El Colegio de México, 1977).
34. See Reyes Osorio, et. al., op. cit., pp.322–23.
35. Opie, op. cit., p.33, and David Gordon, "Mexico: A Survey," *The Economist* (London) 267, No. 7025 (April 22, 1978), p.23.
36. See, for example, George W. Grayson, "Mexico's Opportunity: The Oil Boom," *Foreign Policy* 29 (Winter 1977–78), pp.82-86.
37. See Gordon, op. cit., p.23.
38. Richard R. Fagen and Henry R. Nau estimate some $19 billion will be needed during the 1977–81 period just to service the external public debt accumulated by Mexico

through 1976. See "Mexican Gas: The Northern Connection," paper presented at the Conference on the United States, U.S. Foreign Policy, and Latin American and Caribbean Regimes, hosted by SSRC-ACLS Joint Committee on Latin American Studies, Washington, D.C., March 1978, p.14.

39. "Special Supplement on Venezuela," *Latin America Economic Report* (London, January 1978). Compare with M. R. Redclift, *Agrarian Reform and Peasant Organization on the Ecuadorian Coast*, Institute of Latin American Studies Monographs, No. 8 (London: Athlone Press for the University of London, 1978).
40. Fagen and Nau, op. cit., p.54.
41. Gordon, op. cit., p.26.
42. John S. Evans and Dilmus D. James, "Conditions of Employment and Income Distribution in Mexico as Incentives for Mexican Migration to the United States: Prospects to the End of the Century," *International Migration Review*, forthcoming, 1979.
43. David S. North and Marion F. Houstoun, *The Characteristics and Role of Illegal Aliens in the U.S. Labor Market: An Exploratory Study* (Washington, D.C.: Linton & Co., Inc., 1976); M. Vic. Villalpando, et al., *A Study of the Socioeconomic Impact of Illegal Aliens on the County of San Diego* (San Diego, Calif.: Human Resources Agency, County of San Diego, January, 1977).
44. Laura H. Zarrugh, "Gente de mi tierra: Mexican Village Migrants in a California Community" (Ph.D. dissertation, University of California at Berkeley, 1974), p.67, and Richard Mines, "The Workers of Las Animas: A Case Study of Village Migration to California," essay for the Department of Agriculture and Resource Economics, University of California, Berkeley, May 1978, p.38.
45. Raymond E. Wiest, "Wage-Labor Migration and the Household in a Mexican Town," *Journal of Anthropological Research* Vol. 29, No. 4 (Autumn, 1973), p.197.
46. Ina R. Dinerman, "Patterns of Adaptation among Households of U.S.-bound Migrants from Michoacán, Mexico," paper presented at the Joint National Meeting of the Latin American Studies Association and the African Studies Association, Houston, Texas, November 1977, pp.27–28.
47. Mines, op. cit., p.40.
48. See Gustavo Garza and Martha Schteingart, "Mexico City: The Emerging Megalopolis," in Wayne A. Cornelius and Robert V. Kemper, eds., *Metropolitan Latin America* (Beverly Hills, Calif.: Sage Publications, 1978), p.51–86.
49. Dinerman, op. cit., p.29.
50. The U.S. Department of Labor currently allows fewer than 1,000 Mexican workers to enter the U.S. on H–2 visas each year. In fact, more H–2 visas are granted to Canadians and workers from the British West Indies than to Mexicans.
51. Leonel J. Castillo, "Why the Tide of Illegal Aliens Keeps Rising: Interview with Leonel J. Castillo, Commissioner, Immigration and Naturalization Service," *US News and World Report* (20 February 1978), p.35.
52. International Labour Office (ILO), *Employment, Growth and Basic Needs: A One-World Problem* (New York: Praeger, 1977), p.132.
53. North and Houston, op. cit., p.81.
54. Wiest, op. cit., Table 1, p.187.

THE MIGRATION PROCESS IN COLOMBIA: SOME CONSIDERATIONS ABOUT ITS CAUSES AND CONSEQUENCES

Carmenines Cruz

FROM PROMOTION OF IMMIGRATION TO ITS RESTRICTION AND CONCERN WITH EMIGRATION

Beginning in mid–1957, even though Colombian officials did not explicitly adopt a position against the immigration of foreigners to Colombia, there is no mention of the advisability of promoting immigration, as had been done for more than a century. Several of the laws which had been passed to foster immigration were repealed, probably due to the generalized tendency twoard greater selectivity on the part of the receiving countries in choosing immigrants admitted to their respective territories. In 1954, during the World Population Conference held in Rome, demographers had aired their concern about the danger of the so-called "population explosion" and the "overpopulation" of the Third World countries. Both sets of ideas were debated on an international level, and they began to slowly penetrate into Latin American countries, where most of the countries were experiencing excessive natural population growth—Colombia included.

For those who accepted that Colombia was "overpopulated" and affected by the "population explosion," statutes that aimed at encouraging unlimited immigration of foreigners proved to be incongruous, to say the least. But if it was not advisable to propose birth control measures, then they could turn to another source of population growth, namely, the immigration of foreigners. In Colombia, this recourse aroused very little or no resistance. Moreover, the measure proved to be quite harmless due to the minimal importance that immigration had had in the settlement of the territory.

While all this was happening, the country was undergoing two very important processes: industrialization and modernization. The two progressed at different speeds, producing important changes in the country's social and economic structure and

altering its outer appearance. The changes entailed in these processes produced noticeable increases in the natural population growth and an intense migratory process. Initially it was made up only of rural-urban domestic migration, but later it also included immigration to foreign territories. The creation of factories in urban centers, the mechanization of agriculture, and access to modern technology imported from more advanced countries brought about a deep-set change in the attitudes, values, and behavior of the people both in rural and urban areas. Thus, they became participants in a rapid process of modernization, urbanization, and population growth.

In order to understand emigration and the flow of Colombians to the United States, we need the framework of the total migratory phenomenon seen within Colombian society. International migration is basically a similar type of process to internal migration except that the former includes the requirement of crossing a border and selecting one country or another as a destination. Migration seems to depend greatly on the individual's status within the social stratification system and his or her geographic location in regard to other countries' borders.

Along with the country's modernization and industrialization process, and as a result of the pattern thereof, at least two other phenomena arose that altered the country's features and are particularly important for this study. They are (1) the rapid urbanization process of the population (concentration in urban centers), and (2) a meaningful increase in natural population growth.[1]

It has also been observed that not only do peasants migrate to small towns, intermediate cities, or large metropolitan areas, but the inhabitants of towns and cities do likewise, moving to larger cities. Thus, fill-in migration seems to be the prevailing migration pattern in Colombia.[2]

Violence as a push factor

Colombia in the 1950s and early 1960s experienced a protracted period of social unrest in the countryside.

"Violence" as a cause of migration can operate in two ways: as a sense of insecurity prevalent in the countryside, and the destructive effect on agriculture which reduced production and limited the job market for rural population.

At present, a controversy exists over the influence the "violent era" had on rural migration to the larger cities, and it tends to refute the idea that violence was one of the most important factors that helped originate this kind of migration. Having observed results of studies on people who have migrated to Bogotá, Cardona states that "almost none of the family heads admitted having migrated to the city for safety reasons."[3]

Modernization

Mechanization (the introduction of advanced technology and the way of life in urban centers) also caused changes in the mental outlook of the populace, as new social and economic perspectives loomed ahead, within society's modernization plan chosen as the guideline for the process of change. That is, there is a tendency to accept and adjust to the standard preexisting and prevailing in more advanced societies. Consequently, modern instrumental aspirations tend to guide the individual's acts, particularly of those who dwell in urban centers as they are more frequently and intensely exposed to the demonstration effect of modern societies.

Simultaneously, education, or rather schooling within the structure of the formal educational system, acquired great prestige and almost mythical value, especially in the most deprived and middle social classes for whom schooling has been traditionally denied. Now it acquires instrumental importance because it is presented as a significant element for the country's development, while also being considered a selective factor and channel for social mobility. Both of these characteristics attributed to education are strongly imbued in the people. Thus, a stereotype on the value of education is created, supported by society's higher strata for whom the system reserves the highest educational levels and which explain and justify the majority's limited participation in society's main institutions, precisely because of their lack of education.

Also, because the political and administrative system is essentially centralized and urban oriented, the large cities get more attention and hold most of the industrial, political, commercial, financial, and cultural activities. The city is especially attractive because the services therein, now highly esteemed, are virtually nonexistent or poorer in quality in the less urbanized or rural areas.

A problem arises, however. In the developed nations the urbanization process goes hand in hand with the industrialization process. In Colombia, as in other Latin American countries, there is a gap between the rate of advancement of both processes, so that while thousands of migrants arrive in the cities, industrial development does not advance at the same rate. Therefore, in Colombia as in other underdeveloped countries, urbanization is not a synonym for industrialization. That is why Colombian cities are unable to provide not only for such a large migrant population, but also for many of those who were born and raised in them.[4] The possibility of taking part in society's central institutions depends mostly on one's position in the social and economic structure and not on the person's migrant or native condition in an urban center, or how long one has lived there.

Urban inhabitants' participation in the labor force

Undoubtedly, participation or exclusion of urban inhabitants from the labor force operating in the cities is an important indicator of synchronization (or non-synchronization) with which industrialization and urbanization processes are developed. We have already mentioned that in Colombia these processes are not synchronized, and this is confirmed by the high unemployment rates observed in the population.

The exclusion also reveals the social system's incapacity for helping its members reach goals which have been imposed as culturally desirable, such as a job in which economic success might be achieved. Computations suggest that a rate of five percent unemployment would be the "maximum acceptable."[5] If this were to be accepted, we find that, during the last twelve years (for which estimates exist), the open unemployment level in the four largest cities has been kept at a rate double the acceptable maximum; if we add disguised unemployment, we find that in Bogotá the total unemployment rate for those years would frequently not only have doubled, but also would have tripled the acceptable maximum. It is necessary to consider visible and invisible subemployment, the measurement of which presents serious difficulties, but reaches important levels and has serious effects as a population-expelling agent.

EMIGRATION OF COLOMBIANS

While thousands of Colombians have responded to the "expelling" pressures exerted upon them in their native towns by migrating to middle-size urban areas, or to the big cities, or simply to other places within the national boundaries, others have decided to leave Colombia and settle in foreign countries. Like the first group of internal migrants, this second group leaves Colombia with the hope of being able to satisfy certain needs which they feel cannot be satisfied while they remain in Colombia. This "exit," which started to become significant at the end of the 1950s, has received little attention.

Emigratory flows

At the present time Venezuela, the United States, Ecuador, and Panama are the countries that have the largest numbers of Colombian emigrants. These countries, then, become the main receiving societies for the migratory flows leaving Colombia. Some evidence indicates that an important amount of such emigrants enter without legal permission to remain within the receiving country's borders. For this reason, this type of migration is often referred to as "illegal," "tourist," or "indocumentados."

According to some observers, the oldest of these migratory flows is perhaps the one to Panama. Vil-

legas places the beginning of this flow at the end of the 1920s, increasing in volume at the end of the 1940s.[6] The migratory flows into Venezuela and the United States possibly date from the end of the 1940s as well. And lastly, the most recent flow into Ecuador began during the 1970s.

The migratory flows into Venezuela and Ecuador are reversed ones. Years ago, it was Colombia that received Venezuelan and Ecuadorian immigrants, "because of the better economic conditions in Colombia compared to the economic situations in those countries during that period the migratory flow went in the other direction."[7]

Regarding the number of Colombian immigrants in each of the receiving countries, there are only estimates and approximations that widely fluctuate. The United States 1970 Census registers a total of 63,538 residents born in Colombia. Subsequently, in January 1975, a total of 69,614 Colombians reported their addresses in compliance with the requirement to do so by the U.S. Justice Department's Immigration and Naturalization Service. Meanwhile, several observers believe that "with and without papers" approximately 350,000 Colombians currently live in the United States. Others think this number too high and place it around 250,000. In Ecuador, an estimate done in 1973 showed 22,560 Colombians living there. Today, some observers suggest that "with or without papers, there are 60,000 Colombians living in Ecuador."[8]

As we can see from the observations made above, the migratory flow to the United States, the one we are concerned with here, appears to be the second most important one in terms of numbers, with the Venezuelan flow ranking first. However, observers think that the flow to the United States is particularly important because those who make up this group seem to be more qualified and better trained.

COLOMBIAN IMMIGRATION TO THE UNITED STATES

A comparison of Colombians with other nationals immigrating to the United States

Of the twenty countries which have had the largest number of immigrant visas granted to their nationals by the U.S. during the last ten years (1965–74), Colombia occupies positions that fluctuate between number seven and number eighteen. In other words, even when all countries from both hemispheres are taken into consideration, Colombia has always been among the eighteen countries having the largest number of citizens allowed to immigrate to the U.S. When only Western Hemisphere countries are considered, Colombia always appears among the eight countries receiving the largest number of immigrant visas granted (1965–74).[9] Finally, when only the citizens of South American countries are taken into consideration, and now referring specifically to those admitted to the United States as immigrants, a broader view of the past can be seen. Beginning with 1951, we can see that in the last twenty-five years Colombia has always been the South American country which has had the greatest number of its nationals admitted to the U.S. as immigrants.

The U.S. Immigration Act of 1965

The adoption of the 1965 act signified very drastic changes for immigration from the Western Hemisphere. This is so because the act means a change from a situation in which immigration was numerically unlimited, and only restricted by a minimum number of requirements, to a new situation in which there is a conscious effort to reduce and select the numbers and types of immigrants coming from the Western Hemisphere. Two basic changes were introduced by the act. The first was the establishment of an annual ceiling of 120,000 visas. However, the distribution of this overall quota among the independent countries of the Western Hemisphere is not prescribed in any way, nor is there any explicit recommendation indicating how many immigrants may be admitted from each country. The second was the requirement of a labor certification, which is the same for immigrants from the Eastern Hemisphere, excepting here too parents, spouses, and children of U.S. citizens and of legal foreign residents.

The effects of the enforcement of the act adopted in 1965 have been very diverse. The act of 1965 stimulated the immigration of professionals and highly trained workers from the Third World. Even before this law had been passed, it was easy to foresee that the advantages would act to attract highly qualified and professional foreigners to the United States from underdeveloped countries. Moreover, the exclusion of the immigrants of the Western Hemisphere from the preference system that is in effect for the Eastern Hemisphere has proved to be a considerable disadvantage for the first group. Representative Peter W. Rodino has observed that the ceiling limit of 120,000 has proved to be disastrously inadequate to people from this hemisphere. Close relatives of U.S. citizens and permanent residents in the U.S. must now wait a year and a half to obtain a visa. As a result, a marked increase in the number of illegal aliens in the United States has occurred.

When did Colombians begin to immigrate to the United States?

One can identify three periods in the history of Colombian immigration to the United States. The first period is brief, 1939–45, and consists only of records of admission of 1,825 Colombians as immigrants. However, some people who did not intend to stay in the U.S. also entered with immigrant visas, since they were easy to obtain. This would cause the real number of immigrants to be less than the figure given for the number of immigrants admitted.

The second period begins with the postwar period and ends when the Immigration Act was passed in 1965 (July 1, 1945, to June 30, 1965). During this period, 55,004 Colombians were admitted as immigrants. Colombians, like citizens of other American countries, could immigrate to the U.S. after complying with elementary requirements.

Lastly, as we have already mentioned, the *third phase* began when legislation was passed with a view to restricting immigration by imposing numerical ceilings and labor restrictions for natives of the Western Hemisphere. This gave rise to "illegal immigration" of those who cannot meet the requirements imposed by United States law. This period clearly begins on December 1, 1965, with the enforcement of some of the measures introduced by the Immigration Act passed on October 3 of the same year. We are especially referring to the labor certification required as of December 1, 1965, for immigrants from the Western Hemisphere. And, during the first decennial of the third period (1966–75), 64,427 Colombians were admitted to the United States as immigrants.

If the immigration during the past ten years were added to the unknown volume of illegal immigrants (which increased after 1968), we would probably find that they comprise approximately two-thirds of the total number of Colombians immigrating to the United States since 1936.

Obstacles to migration

From the point of view of the multiplicity and magnitude of the obstacles that must be overcome by the emigrant who makes up the Colombian flow, those who migrate to the United States seem to face the largest number of physical, legal, and psychocultural obstacles. They confront a different language, a long distance and costly transportation between the two countries, quantitative and qualitative legal restrictions to enter the receiving society as an immigrant, and different social and cultural patterns. Meanwhile, the other countries also receiving Colombian immigrants—Venezuela, Ecuador, and Panama—pose less difficulties since they are geographic neighbors. And further, those who immigrate to these nations seem to be inhabitants of the areas near the border. Therefore, distance and cost of transportation do not represent especially difficult obstacles. The nature of the border zones and their topographic features also facilitate migration of people who may not have the necessary legal authorization. Common language, race, and cultural similarity of these societies also make immigration less of a problem.

In view of all these considerations, we would expect that, since obstacles for immigration to the United States seem harder to overcome than those involved in migrating to Venezuela, Ecuador, and Panama, migration to the United States is thought to be more selective.

Sex distribution of Colombian immigrants admitted to the United States

During the period from 1960 through 1975, the percentage of women admitted was higher than the percentage of men, with women accounting for a bit more than one-half.[10] The predominance of women in this long-distance migration contrasts with the pattern observed in internal migratory movements both in Colombia and in other Latin American countries. When analyzing the results of five studies on migration in Colombia and another in Peru, McGreevey notices that men predominate in long-distance migration.[11]

This suggests differential action of the distance factor in composition by sex of Colombian migrants, whether dealing with internal or international migration. Nonetheless, it is obviously not possible to reach this conclusion after studying only the composition by sex of the immigrants admitted to the United States. Furthermore, we should not discard the possibility that U.S. immigration laws may influence the composition by making the visa easier to obtain for one sex or the other. Since it is not possible to compare the proportion of visas granted to men and women with the composition by sex of the total number of persons who apply for visas, we can only state that in all the years analyzed, the proportion of Colombian women admitted to the United States as immigrants was always higher than the proportion of men.

Age distribution

Without exception, during the seventeen years for which information has been collected, the 20 to 29 year old group shows the highest percentages. At the same time, the immigrants between the ages of 30 and 39 constitute the third largest group.[12] When these two age groups are looked at together, we find that close to half of the immigrants admitted are between 20 and 39 years old. This means that they fall within the economically active population group.

TABLE 1
Colombian Immigrants Admitted to the United
States According to Occupation, 1958, 1960-75

Occupational Group by Rank	Number	%
1. Housewives, children, others with no occupation or occupation not reported	64,492	61.2
2. Professionals, technical and kindred workers	8,488	8.1
3. Craftsmen and kindred workers	7,401	7.0
4. Clerical and kindred workers	7,043	6.7
5. Operatives	6,224	5.9
6. Private household workers	4,846	4.6
7. Service workers (except private household)	2,475	2.3
8. Managers, Administrators, proprietors	2,265	2.2
9. Sales workers	1,078	1.0
10. Laborers	732	0.6
11. Farm laborers and farm foremen	277	0.3
Total (1958, 1960-1975)	105,321	100.0%

SOURCE: 1958, 1960-1975, *Annual Report. Immigration and Naturalization Service.* U.S. Department of Justice, Washington, D.C.   Based on Table Number 8.

Distribution by occupation

It is widely believed that immigration to the United States is mainly done by highly qualified people (see Tables 1 and 2). Taking all of the immigrants admitted during this period together, 61.2 percent of the total is found to be a dependent category: housewives, children under fourteen, students, retired people, people with pensions, and other relatives who do not work outside of the home.

Those Colombian immigrants who engage in remunerative activities represent 38.8 percent of the immigrants admitted during the period referred to.

TABLE 2
Colombians Admitted to the United States as
Professionals, Technicals, and Kindred Workers,
1954-75

YEAR	HEALTH SCIENCES	TEACHERS[2]	ENGINEERS	TECHNICIANS	AUDITORS & ACCOUNTANTS	RELIGIOUS WORKERS[3]	OTHERS	TOTAL (100%)
1954	12	2	21	12	–	–	11	58
1955	23	2	22	16	–	–	9	72
1956	30	4	30	6	–	–	14	84
1957	38	8	46	17	–	–	16	125
1958	75	9	64	33	–	–	38	219
1959	73	8	52	15	–	–	26	174
1960	81 *	5	36	22	–	–	196	340
1961	77 *	67	30	46	43	35	57	355
1962	107	95	38	79	74	26	36	455
1963	132 *	124	48	118	100	52	57	631
1964	210 *	170	62	178	126	26	152	924
1965	140 *	180	70	180	89	29	111	799
1966	113	160	84	154	77	17	118	723
1967	137	53	74	46	16	10	56	392
1968	170 *	81	110	171	82	23	92	729
1969	117 *	11	103	153	93	20	150	647
1970	91	37	53	72	43	16	78	390
1971	121 *	12	71	43	34	33	120	434
1972	133 **	39	60	59	15	21	39	366
1973	120 **	45	38	37	14	30	16	300
1974	66 **	40	28	53	17	27	47	278
1975	91 **	47	24	49	16	21	63	311
Total	2,157 (24.5)	1,199 (13.6)	1,164 (13.2)	1,559 (17.7)	839 (9.5)	386 (4.4)	1,502 (17.1)	8,806 (100.0)

[1]Includes doctors from different specialties, 28 veterinarians, dentists, optometrists, pharmacists, and professional nurses.
[2]Includes professors and instructors from university, secondary, and primary levels, in different branches of teaching.
[3]Includes priests and other members of religious communities.
*Includes nursing students   **Includes therapists and dieticians
SOURCE:Tabulations taken from "Immigrants admitted to the United States as professionals, technicals, and kindred workers, students and other occupations according to country or place of last permanent residence and occupation" 1954–1975) Immigration and Naturalization Service. U.S. Department of Justice, Washington, D.C.

The second largest group consists of professional, technical, and kindred workers, followed by the craftsmen, clerical workers, operatives, and ending with "laborers" and "farm laborers and farm foremen" as the fourth largest category.

During the period observed, for every person with paid work admitted as an immigrant, 1.6 people entered the country who at the time of their entry were considered to be economic dependents. This means that they entered because of their family ties with immigrants who had been admitted because of their professional and job abilities, or because of their ties with other U.S. citizens.

Those who were admitted on the basis of their job qualifications (40,828) represent a very select group. Many were professionals and technicians, with 8,488 representing one-fifth of the total number admitted on the basis of job qualifications. If craftsmen, clerical, and skilled workers are added to the number of professionals and technicians, these four groups make up 71.1 percent (29,156) of those persons admitted to the U.S. on the basis of their job qualifications. Only one-fifth of those admitted could be considered as having very limited job qualifications, such as domestic employees, service workers, unskilled workers, agricultural workers.

Another factor in this emigration is how the individual identifies himself with the United States. This identification of frame of reference was possibly solidified during the individual's stay in the university, where not only subjects are studied and learned, but where methodology and the technology used in training are also transmitted to the student. He then is in direct contact with U.S. technology and becomes familiar with it, and learns to find the optimal conditions for practicing his profession and advancing in it in the United States.

It is well-known that people who have training in a certain job area which is in little demand on the United States labor market register themselves in other areas that will make obtaining the necessary labor certification easier. This is the case with secretaries and school teachers who immigrate as domestic employees.

However, even though the said selectivity is an observable characteristic during the entire period, it has tended to diminish in the first part of the 1970s. The same could be said for the number of professionals and technicals admitted, which is decreasing along with the number of clerical workers, administrators, and property owners. At the same time, the number of operators, craftsmen, and service workers has increased, which reflects the changes in U.S. labor market needs.

Composition of the professionals, technicals, and kindred workers group

We shall now analyze more thoroughly this particular group of immigrants, for it is the largest group of immigrants admitted to the United States within paying jobs categories during the last twenty-two years. This group represents highly qualified Colombians whose emigration is reason for special concern.

Professionals from the health sciences, teaching, and engineering fields were the ones admitted in the greatest numbers between 1954 and 1975. Professionals from the health sciences account for one-fourth of the total, while teachers make up 13.6 percent and engineers represent 13.2 percent. These three groups together represent a little more than half (51.3 percent) of the occupational category under discussion here.

Health science professionals make up 24.5 percent of the total number of Colombian professionals and technicals admitted to the United States over the last twenty-two years. They are then, in the professional fields, the group that provides the largest number of highly qualified immigrants. This group includes medical doctors, dentists, nurses, dieticians, nutritionists, and therapists (see Table 3).

It has been observed that a nation may gain from temporary emigration. For example, if doctors tend to return, they bring with them their increased knowledge and also, perhaps, their accumulated savings. Therefore, the real loss caused by the emigration of physicians would be reduced to the number of doctors who did not return to Colombia and to those doctors who returned to Colombia but who did not remain.

Nurses. In 1965, Colombia had a total of 1,968

TABLE 3
Colombian Physicians, Registered Nurses, and
Dentists Admitted to the United States as
Immigrants, 1954-75

Year	Physicians	Registered Nurses	Dentists
1954	12	-	4
1955	18	5	1
1956	15	15	2
1957	25	13	3
1958	51	24	6
1959	51	22	6
1960	47	32	6
1961	52	21	6
1962	75	32	7
1963	90	41	16
1964	158	51	14
1965	82	56	12
1966	80	33	10
1967	116	21	6
1968	116	50	17
1969	47	67	28
1970	36	34	12
1971	78	29	12
1972	82	21	2
1973	75	17	3
1974	37	18	3
1975	68	14	2
Total	1411	616	178
Yearly Average	64	28	8

Source: Tabulated from "Immigrants Admitted to the
         United States as Professionals, Technical
         and Kindred Worker, by Country or Region of
         Latest Permanent Residence and Occupation,"
         1954-1975. Immigration and Naturalization
         Service, U.S. Department of Justice,
         Washington, D.C.

nurses.[13] This means that for that year there was a ratio of 0.6 nurses per 10,000 residents. When compared with the twenty-one American countries, only the Dominican Republic had a smaller ratio (0.5), while the United States had a ratio of 33.5 nurses per 10,000 residents.

Information showing where nurses emigrate to is not available. However, reliable sources suggest that most of those nurses and physicians who do emigrate go to the United States.

It is the opinion of some nurses that, unlike doctors, to study or work in the United States does not necessarily result in the enjoyment of increased professional prestige and salary when they return to Colombia. This is possibly why those nurses who emigrate rarely return to Colombia.

Dentists. In 1970, according to the Ministry of Health Personnel Inventory (INPES), there were 2,743 dentists in Colombia, or one dentist for every 7,748 residents.[14] This works out to a ratio of 1.3 dentists per 10,000 residents. Some observers from the Ministry of Health have remarked that the exodus of dentists from Colombia is primarily directed towards the United States.

Information on dentists returning to Colombia is not available. However, due to the higher income received by dentists who manage to establish themselves, it may be assumed, according to some observers, that an established dentist in the U.S. would only rarely return to Colombia.

Engineers. Including all of the branches of engineering, there was a total of 1,164 engineers admitted between 1954 and 1975 (a yearly average of 53).

The engineer's situation seems to be the result of the country's inability to adequately absorb the growing number of engineers who graduate each year.

Priscilla Walton studied a sample of thirty Colombian professionals living in Chicago. She points out that, in general, the people interviewed immigrated to the United States in search of higher salaries and better working conditions. The engineers in the sample basically talked about the high rate of competition that there is in Colombia in their field. They also pointed out, however, that it is not easy to get involved in the labor market in the

United States as engineers, and that they often had to work their way in, beginning as intermediate technicians. In this study, physicians frequently mentioned their desire to work in a professional environment that had higher scientific and technological levels and that would also allow them to continue their studies and specialize. They also spoke of the importance of obtaining better salaries.

Teachers. Finally, professors, instructors, and teachers from different educational areas are also another kind of professional very much affected by emigration. This group makes up 13.6 percent of the total number of professionals admitted to the U.S. in the last twenty-two years. Possibly teachers (except for university professors who have a certain degree of prestige), as was mentioned before for nurses, find themselves confronted with a situation in which, even if unemployment were not a serious problem for them, the poor salary they are paid and their low social status are problems.[15]

When all of the information of Colombian professionals, technicals and kindred workers who have been admitted to the United States over the last twenty-two years is looked at together, some general features can be distinguished. Firstly, this immigration reached its peak for all professionals between 1963 and 1969. That is, it reached its peak during the time before the passage of the Immigration Act of 1965 and during the transition period which ended June 30, 1968. The peak figures of immigration continued on into 1969 possibly because, in that year, professionals who had obtained immigration visas the previous fiscal year were admitted.

Secondly, in 1970, when the Immigration Act of 1965 was in full force, the total number of professionals admitted fell 40 percent compared to the previous year. From that time on, there had been a decreasing trend. In 1971 and in 1975, there was a slight increase in immigration compared to the years immediately preceding them, but nevertheless, the main trend from 1970 on has been one of decrease.

SUMMARY OF PROFESSIONAL MIGRATION

(1) There are four professional areas most affected by immigration to the United States. They are the

following:

(a) Those fields with universally applicable knowledge, such as medicine, nursing, and dentistry, as opposed to other much more local fields, such as law, and political science.

(b) Highly technical fields and fields in which professional activity requires or allows for the use of complex and modern technology. Thus, we have such fields as engineering (chemical, electric, electronic systems, and metallurgical), surgery, optometry, and bacteriology, as opposed to other fields such as social work and psychology which usually do not require such sophisticated technology.

(c) Those fields that in Colombia only give the professional limited social recognition and which also have low salaries, like nursing and teaching.

(d) Those fields which, because of the prestige that goes along with them, attract more people into the professional market than can be absorbed. For example, engineering and architecture are two such fields.

(2) Medical doctors, professional nurses, and dentists are the health professionals who immigrate to the United States most. Dieticians, nutritionists, therapists, etc., also immigrate to the U.S. but their numbers are far fewer than the first group's.

(3) The period between 1964 and 1969 saw the greatest amount of emigration of these health professionals. However, from 1970 on, there has been a definite decreasing trend, which is more pronounced for dentists and nurses than for physicians.

(4) Important indications show that the return of these professionals to Colombia depends on which one of them is being discussed. Return seems notably higher among physicians than nurses and dentists, but more information is needed on this subject.

(5) Return tendencies of medical doctors could suggest that, rather than a loss to Colombia, their emigration for a period of time could really be benefiting the country. The emigration of nurses and dentists could, however, represent a loss of highly qualified health personnel because they tend not to return to Colombia.

(6) Finally, what seems to be most important in this emigration is that, although medical doctors, nurses, and dentists are three professions that are not affected or very little affected by unemployment in Colombia, they emigrate in significant numbers. In the opinion of several of the people interviewed, this emigration can be explained "because just having work or a job is not enough." There must also be professional, economic, and social gratification involved in the work. The opportunities for such gratification are insufficient in Colombia, unless the health professional comes from the upper class.

Location of Colombians in the United States

Figures on the spatial distribution of Colombians in the U.S. territory at arrival between 1966 and 1975 show a definite tendency of immigrants to concentrate in just a few states. However, it is interesting to note that all fifty-four states and territories show the presence of Colombians.[16] Only five of them (Hawaii, Montana, South Dakota, Wyoming, and Guam) show numbers of five or less for the period under consideration.

New York has consistently been the state which has attracted the greatest number of immigrants admitted. New York alone has 45.3 percent of the total number of Colombians admitted during the decennial, with only slight fluctuations each year.

Next, New Jersey, a neighboring state of the metropolitan New York City area, is number two in the order of preference. However, there is a great difference between the number of Colombians in New Jersey and in New York. New Jersey has 12.8 percent of the total which places it well behind New York. Then follow Florida, California, and Illinois to make up the five states which consistently attracted the greatest number of Colombians: 80 percent of the total number admitted during the period of time under consideration.

If the next five states are considered (Connecticut, Puerto Rico, Massachusetts, Pennsylvania, Rhode Island, and Texas), they then make the ten states and territories attracting the most Colombians. Thus, we have that these ten political and administrative divisions received around 90 percent of the total number of Colombians admitted to the United States between 1966 and 1975. Therefore, only 10 percent of the Colombians admitted were distributed in the other forty-four states and territories of the United States.

Colombians are concentrated in a small number of cities, especially the big cities: New York, Miami, Los Angeles, Chicago, and neighboring areas.[17]

The coastal zone of the Northeastern area received 70 percent of the total number of Colombians admitted between 1966 and 1975.

Several possible reasons that explain this tendency among immigrants in general and Colombians specifically to concentrate in the states and cities mentioned are the following:

(1) The location of the labor sources. Those states and cities that are traditionally identified as large industrial centers, and which, therefore, the immigrants consider as the most important work sources, have always been and continue to be the major point of attraction for them. They include New York, New Jersey, Illinois, and California.

(2) The attraction of the big cities. They seem to be more cosmopolitan with a more Latin atmosphere and much bilingual activity. Several Latins, when talking about New York, go on to say that the big cities provide different possibilities and resources which smaller cities do not always have. It is also important to remark that, as it was mentioned before, migratory movements in Colombia showed a definite urban tendency so that preference for big cities in the U.S. agrees with the tendency observed in Colombia. This also supports what we said before, that is, that Colombians emigrating to the United States basically come from intermediate and large urban centers in Colombia and not from rural areas or little towns.

(3) Regarding the states of California, Florida, and Texas, it must be mentioned that there is a third reason related to the sociocultural affinity which Colombians find in these states due to the Latin influence and the number of other Latins living in them (Mexicans, Cubans, and other Central and South Americans). These states do not have such severe climate changes as those in the Northeast, making them more attractive from this point of view.

(4) Furthermore, the "chain migration effect" we spoke of early in reference to migration could be operating in this question of choosing permanent residence by increasing these concentrations even more. This is because, in the places where most Colombians live, there would be more of a chance that other Colombians would immigrate to the same place as parents, spouses, or relatives, as well as friends and acquaintances who found out about the place from resident immigrants living there and who would use the resident alien's help in the migratory process.

NOTES

The text was taken from a much more developed research project of the Corporación Centro Regional de Población (CCRP) by a research team consisting of Ramiro Cardona, CarmenInés Cruz, and Juanita Castaño, and with collaboration of Elsa Chaney, John Macisco, and Mary G. Powers of Fordham University, and funded jointly by the Interdisciplinary Communications Program of the Smithsonian Institution and CCRP.

1. Bernal Segundo, "Algunos aspectos sociológicos de la migración en Colombia," in Ramiro Cardona, ed., *Las Migraciónes Internas* (Bogotá: Asociación Colombiana de Facultades de Medicina, 1972), pp.63–65, and several census reports by Colombia, including *Censos de población Colombiana 1938, 1951 and 1964*, and *XIV Censo nacional de población y III de Vivienda*, advance sample, provisional results, October 1973.
2. William P. McGreevey, "Causas de la migración interna en Colombia," in *Empleo y desempleo en Colombia* (Bogotá: Centro de Estudios Sobre Desarrollo Enconómico, Facultad de Economía, Universidad de los Andes, 1968), p.216.
3. Ramiro Cardona, "Migración, urbanización y marginalidad," in Antares-Tercer Mundo, ed., *Urbanización y marginalidad* (Bogotá: Asociación Colombiana de Facultades de Medicina, 1968), p.64.
4. Cardona, op. cit., p.76.
5. Hernando Gómez Buendía, "El desempleo urbano: raices, tendencias e implicaciones," *Revista* (March 1976), p.10.
6. Jorge Villegas, "Condiciones del trabajador migrante," Cumentos de Trabajo, No. 3, Bogotá. Organización Internacional de Trabajo. 1974. (Mimeographed.)
7. Villegas, ibid., p.11.
8. Jorge Villegas, "Migraciones fronterizas de mano de obra colombianas hacia los países del grupo andino," paper for the Ministerio de Trabajo, Bogotá, 1975, pp.2–3. (Mimeographed.)
9. U. S. Department of State, Visa Office, *Annual Reports* (Washington, D.C., 1967–74, inclusive).
10. U.S. Department of Justice, Immigration and Naturalization Service, *Annual Reports: Immigration and Naturalization Service, 1958, 1960–1975* (Washington, D.C., 1967–74 inclusive), Table 9.
11. McGreevey, op. cit., p.218.
12. Immigration and Naturalization Service, op. cit., 1958, 1960–75, Table 9.

13. Ricardo Galán, Charles Meyers, and Daniel Luecke, *Análisis y proyección de la demanda de servicio y de personal médico-odontológico en Colombia* (Bogotá: Ministry of Health, Harvard University, INPES-Ministry of Health Personnel Inventory, 1975).

14. Galán, Meyers, and Luecke, op. cit.

15. Carmen Angulo and Alvaro Betancourt, ''Estratificación social y universidad'' (tésis de grado, Departmento de Sociología. Universidad de Colombia, 1969).

16. U.S. Department of Justice, op. cit., 1966–75, Tables 12 and 12A.

17. U.S. Department of Justice, ibid., Table 12A.

THE PROCESS OF MIGRATION AND THE SOCIAL STRUCTURE OF PUERTO RICAN SOCIETY

Ricardo Campos

INTRODUCTION

Puerto Rico is a colony of the United States of North America. Since the 1830s, the United States has exercised a decisive influence on the development of the colony. Even under Spanish political domination the colonial contradiction in which Puerto Rico found itself (politically tied to one country but with strong economic links to another) allowed an expanding nation like the United States to determine the production and circulation of the island's principal agricultural product: sugar. Changes in the production of sugar and in the social division of labor and the geographical mobility of the peasant population were subject to the internal necessities of the North American market, the principal buyer of Puerto Rican sugar. Geopolitical factors, the need to establish a periphery to furnish the metropolis with raw materials, and to allow for the direct exploitation of labor, precipitated the Spanish American War.

In 1898, Puerto Rico became a direct colony of the United States. Since that year the relationship between the metropolis and the colony has incurred substantial transformations in models of development and the mode of production, such as the change from a plantation-based to an industry-based economy. To define the present-day colonial relationship is an extremely complex task. While the island continues to be a direct colony of the United States, this relationship has assumed new forms and thus eludes classical definitions.

At the present time, the process of absorption of the colonial society into the socioeconomic structures of the metropolis has reached an extremely high level, as is evident in the sheer magnitude of capital, commodities, and population set into motion by this process. The dynamic quality of investment (both direct and indirect), the structure of the commodity and labor markets, the level of monetary disbursements by the Federal Government, the political-administrative superstructure, together form a situation that can be examined here only in a preliminary fashion.

We should begin by recognizing one of the basic contradictions of the colonial relationship. On the one hand, to a certain extent, Puerto Rican society has developed as if the colony were, in fact, a *state* of the union. And, on the other hand, Puerto Rico continues to be a *nation*, politically and economically subjugated by the North American metropolis. This particular historical determination has provoked important alterations in the social structure, the mode of production, and the political life of the island, which have in turn engendered numerous and complex mechanisms serving to reinforce and reproduce this situation.

The study of any social process, including that of population movement, must be seen in this context. In other words, the above problematic forms our point of departure in treating the relationship between the migratory process and the Puerto Rican social structure. For this reason we have divided our study into two principal sections: I. Migration and the Capitalist Mode of Production, an attempt to define the movement of the working population as a function of the dominant relations of production, and II. Migration and the Puerto Rican Social Structure, an attempt to define the characteristics of the capitalist mode of production on the island and the dynamic created by the diversity of movements of the working population.

MIGRATION AND THE CAPITALIST MODE OF PRODUCTION

In order to understand the geographic movement of the population in a particular society, we must first situate this phenomenon within the context of the general structural transformations occurring within the society. Just as the concept of population becomes an abstraction if not seen in relation to the organization of production, allotment of resources, and distribution of means of employment and subsistance, the migratory process in itself does not explain changes in the social structure in a given country.

To understand the migratory process, we must first point to some basic assumptions: (1) the study of *particular modes of production* must be substituted for the concept of "economy" in general; (2) different migratory movements must be distinguished according to the historical moment in which they occur; and (3) the stages in the development of the mode of production must be ascertained both historically and geographically. In other words, the movement of the population, in general, and the type of socioeconomic development at work in the society, must be seen within the context of the sociohistoric evolution of the mode of production. In this case what we are attempting to define is the migratory process within the context of the capitalist mode of production.

In societies where capitalist relations of production predominate, the working population constitutes population available to capital. The social relation assumed by capital is based on the extraction and realization of surplus value generated by the social forces of labor. As the turnover of capital as a whole, and the reproduction of the mode of production, require that capital be constantly in motion, the absorption of the labor force by capital presumes the permanent mobility of labor. The movements of the labor force occur on different levels and in different directions, depending on the phase of development of the mode of production.

In general terms, we can distinguish four basic types of movement which characterize the labor force within the capitalist mode of production.

In direct relation to capital as a whole and in relation to the mode of production

The working population is subject to the total demand for employment in the different spheres of operation of capital. This first movement, then, determines the circulation of the population in and out of the active labor force, depending on the average necessary labor required by capital. This movement is both constant and permanent. The accumulation and concentration of capital along with periodic crises accelerate this circulation and increase the proportion of the population thrown out of the active labor force. The dual aspects of this movement are manifested as follows: (1) the *active-inactive* and (2) the *active-reserve* dynamic.

Active-inactive dynamic. In general, the average necessary labor required by capital and the decrease in the amount of socially necessary labor determine the creation of a latent relative surplus population which is set in motion when reclaimed by capital. The relative surplus population is a result of the capitalist mode of production and remains subject to the oscillations of capital and capital's dynamic of attraction and repulsion. Thus, the active or inactive condition of the labor force refers to the short term alterations of the diverse forms of relative overpopulation (latent, floating, and intermediate) in relation to the average needs of capital as a whole.

Active-reserve dynamic. In the long run, the inactive condition is institutionalized within the mode of production and comes to form a labor reserve at the service of capital. In other words, the inactivity of a part of the labor force is manifest in another form at the level of the mode of production, largely independent of the attraction and repulsion of workers at the level of capitals as a whole. In the last instance, however, the active-inactive-reserve conditions designate levels of differentiation and forms of manifestation of a basic relationship: the dynamic between the labor force and capital.

In relation to the social division of labor

Capital is concerned not only with the extraction but also with the realization of surplus value and the constant reproduction of the conditions of accumulation. Thus, capital, in its permanent relation, generates particular spheres of functioning based on the moment within its turnover in which it finds itself. In the same way, it institutionalizes those mechanisms which allow for the constant reproduction of the system as a whole. As the working population exists as labor for capital, capital determines the distribution of the labor force within the cycle of its turnover and reproduction according to the needs of production.

The movements of the working population which stem from this process occur according to the social division of labor, as broken down into three areas: production, circulation and reproduction. The distribution of the labor force into these areas depends on the level of development of the capitalist mode of production. The movement of the population by means of the social division of labor occurs over the long run, over large periods of time, depending on the accumulation and concentration of capital in the different branches of production. This type of movement not only has a decisive influence on the relationship between the labor force and capital (active-inactive-reserve), it also transforms the social composition of the working population. This occurs because of the tendency toward concentration and centralization of capital, which reduces the labor force within the sphere of the production of tangible material goods and enlarges the spheres of circulation and reproduction. This dynamic results in the movement of the active labor force through the different levels of the social division of labor, and the movement of the "reserve" in moments of the expansion of determined spheres of work. These movements—attraction, repulsion, and transference from one sphere to another—are difficult to measure, but they have enormous impact when they occur in a society over a short period of time.

Production. This sphere constitutes the basis of the capitalist mode of production. Whether in the production of material commodities or of services, the appropriation of exchange values by capital is directed toward the extraction of surplus labor from the labor force. On this level, the creation of surplus value determines the movement of the labor force. Higher levels of productivity and higher levels of extraction of relative surplus value correspond to a reduction in the average socially necessary labor, and a higher level of expulsion of workers from the productive spheres. Here, the dynamic between necessary labor and surplus labor (in relation to the labor force, and the dynamic between constant cap-

ital and variable capital (in relation to capital) become organically intertwined, circulating, absorbing, or repulsing the labor force within the sphere of production. The production of new-use values and the realizing of exchange value for old-use values contributes to the phenomenon. In this way, the absorption and the repulsion of workers within the sphere of production is accelerated. The general tendency, however, is toward a considerable reduction in the number of productive workers.

Circulation. Capital needs to redefine exchange values and to realize the surplus value contained in commodities. Thus, a part of the labor force is directed toward *unproductive* work, or the acceleration of the transformation of exchange values thrown into the market. As the time of capital circulation is the negation of its production time, capital seeks to shorten the former in order to accelerate the conversion of surplus value into money. Therefore, in times of production expansion, the circulation sphere absorbs more workers, and in periods of contraction, fewer workers. Nevertheless, the increasing mechanization of the means of exchange, and the decreasing level of specialization characterizing much of this work, reduces the average necessary labor in the diverse moments of the circulation process. Thus, in the long run, there is a tendency for labor in this sphere to leave the active component of the labor force.

Reproduction. The reproduction of capital on an expanded scale is a social imperative of the capitalist mode of production. The various mechanisms which legitimize and conserve the system require a considerable contingent of the labor force. Two tendencies are evident in respect to this sphere. On the one hand, the state, being the principal agent of the reproduction of the conditions of the capitalist mode of production, increasingly broadens its participation in the economy. This is a function of the need to impose some order on the anarchy of capitalist production, the need to operate enterprises characterized by a low rate of profit which are not attractive to private capitalists, and the need to absorb a portion of the "surplus" labor force. The state's participation transfers the mechanisms of attraction-repulsion and the active and inactive condition of the labor force into the reproduction sphere. In considering the absorption of productive economic activities by the state, the creation of surplus value ultimately determines the movement of the labor force, providing the basis upon which the average socially necessary labor time is determined and, thus, the index upon which the number of employees is defined. In these cases, the labor force directly confronts capital although the latter temporarily appears as revenue in the hands of the state. In the last instance, public corporations, capitalist enterprises, are located structurally within the sphere of production although they are under the tutelage of the principal agent of reproduction—the state—which in this form exists as a "manager" of capital. On the other hand, the increase in unproductive work within the reproductive sphere confronts the labor force with state revenues and not capital directly. Theoretically, the movement of this sector of the labor force would be determined by the demand for the average socially necessary labor. The present tendency, however, runs in contradiction to this general rule. The need to absorb part of the surplus labor force inflates the ranks of the bureaucracy whether labor is necessary or not. In this case the attraction-repulsion mechanisms are determined by the level reached in the productive spheres and the revenues available to the state. The contradiction inherent in this process is manifested in periods of fiscal crisis, leaving considerable contingents of workers inactive.

Reproduction of the labor force

The birth-death dynamic is perhaps the aspect of population change most independent of consistent turnover of capital. Because of the contradictory character of the reproduction of the labor force in the capitalist mode of production, this process is studied in great detail in order to regulate and adjust the general conditions of capital accumulation. This is so because the reproduction of the labor force includes both the active and "reserve" components. It is, perhaps, the reproduction of the "reserve" which most worries capital. This reproduction

amounts to an unproductive cost in the cost-benefit analysis, as the deterioration of this component neither produces surplus value nor contributes to the circulation and general reproduction of capital.

It is in the reproduction of the "surplus" labor force that the contradictions in production and circulation which generate a relative surplus population are most evident. But, while these contradictions may be temporarily regulated and adjusted to the needs of capital through other mechanisms of production and circulation, reproduction of the labor force remains beyond the influence of these mechanisms. In fact, reproduction of the "surplus" labor force posits the need for some regulating mechanism originating outside of the spheres of production and circulation. It is for this reason that the phenomenon of "marginal" population is usually debated as a product of disproportionate population growth, and not as a product of capitalist relations of production.

Geographic displacement of the working population

This type of movement is the result of the way in which the labor force confronts the means of employment under capitalist relations of production. In other words, the movement of the labor force in direct relation to the social division of labor generates the spatial displacements necessary to situate the labor force in those locations which correspond to the mode of production. These types of movement intersect and overdetermine each other constantly. Nevertheless, this process is not exempt from contradictions. The active part moves into the reserve and, vice versa, the productive component moves into the sphere of circulation, etc. And, once the mobile capacity of the labor force has been unleashed, it remains, in large part, beyond the control of capital. Migratory flows in multiple directions, agglomerations in areas unnecessary to the mode of production, unharnessed growth of labor reserves, the specialized reserves of the social division of labor that resist relocating out of a particular branch of production—these are the contradictory results of the setting in motion of the labor force by capital.

At the same time, as the capitalist mode of production is transformed into an international system of dominance and subordination among capitalist nations, and between capitalist and precapitalist nations, the labor force is also socialized on a worldwide scale. The active-reserve dynamic is internationalized, creating an international division of labor. As a result, the movements of the labor force necessarily occur by means of geographical displacements, principally from the periphery with its large labor reserve, to the metropolitan centers. National reserves are converted into international reserves, into the reserves of transnational monopoly capital. In the same way, the active labor force remains subject to the general movement of the international division of labor, which provokes migration, circulation, and return migrations.

MIGRATION AND THE SOCIAL STRUCTURE OF PUERTO RICO[1]

The last three decades of the nineteenth century constitute a period of transition to the capitalist mode of production on the island. This transition produced an array of migratory movements, all on a small scale but symptomatic of the changes in the economic order. These movements were rooted in the proletarianization of various rural groups, a process which freed more labor than could be absorbed by commercial agriculture and the almost nonexistent industry and urban employment. During this period, groups of Puerto Ricans left the island for the Dominican Republic, Cuba, Venezuela, and other neighboring countries. Both legal restrictions and industrialization programs were proposed to curb these migrations. Two additional currents also characterized the colonial situation: the flow of young people from the landed class toward Europe in search of professional training, and the movement of political dissidents from this same class to the United States where they formed revolutionary groups to struggle for the liberation of Cuba and Puerto Rico. A small contingent of artesans and skilled workers, particularly cigar makers, joined this northern current during the same period.

The U.S. invasion markedly accelerated the development of capitalist agriculture. Appropriation and concentration of the land, the proletarianization

of the labor force in tobacco production as well as home needle work, and total control of foreign trade and consumption proceeded at a dizzying pace. The massive implantation of capitalist relations of production also provoked the appearance of a "surplus" of laborers, cyclical economic crises which culminated in the collapse of the system in the thirties, and the intensification of migratory pressures. This last element began to manifest itself at the beginning of the century, when eleven expeditions left for Hawaii, but the surplus population, generated by the reorganization of the economy during the first decade of the North American occupation, also provoked migrations to Cuba, the Dominican Republic, Ecuador, and other countries. At the same time, a small outflow to the United States continued. With the expansion of wealth and the increases in productivity, widespread misery and the constant pressures of chronic and seasonal employment intensified. In the 1920s, several projects for sending workers to the United States as agricultural and railroad laborers were drawn up by the government. The Depression brought the first important instance of reverse migration (1930–34), but the flow toward the United States was resumed until World War II. Migration played a minor numerical role in terms of demographic changes during those years, although certain basic patterns and important nuclei in the United States were established. The late 1940s saw the consolidation of new political forces on the island with a new program for the next phase of capitalist development. In this project, massive emigration figured as a permanent necessity and as the basis for the strategy for agrarian reform and industrialization.

The principal structural changes which occurred in Puerto Rico after 1940 were seen as part of a practical design for the economic development and political restructuring of a small country, in "association" with specific political and economic sectors within the metropolis. The U.S. component within this power bloc maintained overall control and defined the limits within which reform and development policies could be realized. This project was altered and adjusted over time. After a brief developmentalist phase, supported by the direct participation of the State in the promotion of light industry through the attraction of small North American companies, the process finally arrived at the present stage of domination by transnational monopoly capital. Massive emigration was undoubtedly a key factor facilitating the level of economic expansion achieved, particularly since 1965.

The establishment of large North American corporations marked the almost complete control of the social and economic activities in the colony by the corresponding metropolitan structures. This process assumes the reproduction within the colony of the mechanisms of production and distribution, and of the class composition and relations which characterize the metropolis. It also assumes the reproduction of the contradictions brought on by these mechanisms and relations within the United States.

Several factors must be considered to understand this phenomenon: (1) the quantity of U.S. investment in Puerto Rico ($18 billion); (2) the conversion of the island into a vast consumer market for U.S. products (a population of three million people constitutes the fifth largest buyer of U.S. products in the world); (3) the extension of U.S. juridical-political legality to the island; (4) the amount of federal money in circulation within Puerto Rico; (5) the circulation of the Puerto Rican labor force between the United States and Puerto Rico.

The appropriation of the fundamental means of production in the colony by the U.S. bourgeoisie and the expansion of the Puerto Rican consumer market have generated new forms of geographic movement. Emigration, return, and circulation took on massive, unforeseen, and at times uncontrollable proportions. The Puerto Rican working population has been transformed into a mobile social force at the service of U.S. capital, whether in the United States or in Puerto Rico.

On the other hand, the industrialization and socioeconomic absorption of the colony has generated a new division of labor which in turn has altered the social composition of the working class. Thirty-five years of industrial development and migration have brought changes in occupational patterns that point to a new Puerto Rican social structure (see Table 1). The enlarged spheres of circulation and reproduction occupy an important position in the new division of labor. This is largely due to the expansion of the Puerto Rican market as a consumer of U.S. commodities. As time passes, the employment structure more and more resembles that of the metropolis. One can easily observe the social phenomena characteristic of this process: the reduction in the rural proletariat, the growth of the unproductive sectors of the working class, and the urbanization of the rural areas through their incorporation into the market. As a result, Puerto Rico is today an urban society with a large population concentrated in the metropolitan areas.

The most visible contradiction of capitalism in Puerto Rico today is its impact on the working population. This impact was initially evident in the process of mass emigration in the period 1940–65, and presently can be observed in the uncontrollable and systematic growth of the reserve industrial army, a growth of gigantic proportions. This phenomenon is perhaps the principal problem both for the colonial bureaucracy and for the U.S. federal government, to the extent that means and resources must be found to support an increasing sector of the working population which does not participate in the active labor force. The decreasing need for living labor in the production of material goods which accompanied the advance of capital accumulation and concentration is a fundamental law of the capitalist mode of production; as a U.S. colony, Puerto Rico has suffered excessively from the rigorous workings of this law.

In the last 35 years the rate of participation of the labor force has been declining, as has the proportion of the working population in absolute terms with respect to the total population.

	1940	1960	1975
Rate of Participation	52.1	45.4	41.0
Employment Rate for the Total Population	27.4	23.4	21.2

Sources: Junta de Plantificación, *Informe sobre los Recursos Humanos* (I, 1974); U.S. Dept. of Commerce, *Census of the Population* (1940, 1960); Departamiento del Trabajo, *Empleo Horas y Salarios en las Industrias Manufactureras* (1975).

Table 1
Percentages of Employment by Occupation in 1976

	Puerto Rico	United States of America
Professional and Technical	12.4	15.2
Manager, Administrators (except farm)	9.3	10.4
Salespeople and Clerical Workers	20.8	23.8
Craft and Kindred Workers	12.0	12.9
Operatives	19.9	15.3
Non-farm Laborers	6.3	4.9
Service Workers	13.8*	13.8
Farmworkers (salaried)	2.8	1.4
Government	30.1	17.0

*Only 0.8 are in domestic service.

Sources: *Monthly Labor Review*, U.S. Department of Labor, Bureau of Labor Statistics, September 1976. *Empleo y desempleo en Puerto Rico*, Depto. del Trabajo, Estado Libre Asociado de Puerto Rico, Septiembre 1976.

These percentages demonstrate that labor activity rests on an ever smaller proportion of workers within a steadily increasing population. In January of 1975, the total population was estimated at 3.074 million, of whom 2.060 million were classified as "civilian population of 14 years or less." The "working group" was formed by 872,000, and "outside the working group" were found another 1.189 million. Of the latter, 300,000 were in school; 99,000 incapacitated; 548,000 involved in household tasks; 76,000 retired, while 120,000 were classified as "idle." This last category refers to those unemployed persons who were not "actively" seeking work during the week of the survey. If we add the last figure to the 134,000 "officially"

unemployed (1974–75 average), we obtain a real rate of unemployment of 25.5 percent. And this group, together with the 165,000 underemployed, make up the 419,000 in the industrial reserve army (discounting the more than half a million performing household duties). In reality, 42.1 percent of the Puerto Rican labor force is either completely inactive (25.5 percent) or is underutilized (16.6 percent).

One of the principal characteristics of this inactive part of the population is its composition by age. Among the "officially" unemployed, 64 percent were persons between the ages of 14 and 34. Among the "idle," 51.6 percent were between the ages of 14 and 24. With regard to distribution by

Table 2
Rate of Unemployment by Level of Schooling

Level of Schooling	1973	1974	1975
0	12.2	11.2	13.6
1 - 3	12.5	13.2	15.5
4 - 6	13.8	14.2	17.6
7 - 9	15.7	16.3	20.7
10 - 11	17.3	19.4	22.3
12	10.8	11.2	14.3
13 y más	4.1	5.1	7.1

Source: *Informe económico al governador.* Junta de Planificación, Estado Libre Asociado de Puerto Rico, 1973.

Unemployment by Age (thousands)

	1970	1971	1972	1973	1974	1975	1976
14–19	16	18	20	19	22	24	29
20–24	21	23	26	28	30	34	38
25–34	17	19	23	25	27	36	50
35–44	11	13	14	14	15	20	35
45–54	8	8	9	9	9	12	15
55–64	5	6	6	5	6	7	--

Source: *Compendio de Estadísticas Sociales.* Junta de Planificación Estado Libre Asociado de Puerto Rico, 1975; *Empleo y desempleo en Puerto Rico.* Departamento del Trabajo, Estado Libre Asociado de Puerto Rico, 1976.

---

sex, women made up 25 percent of the "officially" unemployed and 40 percent of the so-called "idle." On the other hand, the industrial reserve army increasingly absorbs people who have attained a high education level (see Table 2).

It is important to recall that the gap between the population and its economically active portion tends to widen gradually; large contingents of the Puerto Rican working class tend progressively to be concentrated in the industrial "reserve." This has been the experience of the last thirty-five years, despite the massive emigration between 1940 and 1965 (the island lost around one million inhabitants) and the birth control programs. At the present time, one-third of all Puerto Rican women of fertile age have been sterilized, most of them already having borne children. If we add to this situation the fact that close to 60 percent of Puerto Rican families are below the poverty level, and that the food stamp program constitutes a major source of income for two-thirds of Puerto Rican families, we will have a true picture of socioeconomic development in the colony.[2]

On the one hand, the social configuration of the labor force is similar to that in the metropolis; there has been a fusion of certain sectors of the labor market; the urbanization of the society as a whole has accelerated; and the indices of per capita income have risen sharply. On the other hand, a growing sector of the working class has been pauperized and lives on food stamps and unemployment insurance or both. If we were to count Puerto Rico as a state in the union, the island would occupy first place in terms of population receiving food stamps and fourth place in terms of persons receiving unemployment payments that originated in another state. This last example is an index of the high level of mobility of the Puerto Rican labor force.

Attempts to represent the Puerto Rican migratory process as beneficial for the migrant are unacceptable. In the long run, the process has not alleviated social problems within the colony which were supposed to have been reduced by this process: that is, the explosion of relative overpopulation and the highly unequal distribution of wealth. As for the position of the migrant, the most recent studies are quite significant. Migrants who return do not demonstrate a higher level of training or skills than when they left,[3] while the socioeconomic conditions of Puerto Ricans in the United States have deteriorated relatively over the last several years.[4]

In the past decade, the colony has become a country receiving immigrants, principally Cubans and Dominicans. At the same time there has been a growing return immigration of Puerto Ricans from the United States. These movements toward the island coincide with periods of expansion of the market, the increasing circulation of money, and the liberalization of credit. The artificial stimulus provided by the government to certain industries, particularly construction, should also be noted. In the period 1969–75, we can demonstrate the increase in

money in circulation, a situation which gives the appearance of prosperity and economic stability. A few figures will serve to demonstrate this situation. Between 1969 and 1975, spending by the colonial government increased significantly, the government's share in net income rising from $507 million to $1,317 million. Employment generated by the government rose during the same period from 113,000 to 220,000 (presently this constitutes 30 percent of the active labor force). The expansion of personal credit has also been significant. Taking the use of credit cards as an index of personal debt, this debt rose from $300,000 to $62 million during the period in question. Singularly important are the federal government's disbursements. While in 1969, the gross disbursement was $630.7 million, in 1975 the figure was $1,966.7 million. In net terms, the figures are respectively $418.7 million and $1,361.7 million. This last figure is similar to the profits obtained by North American corporations on the island. That is to say, the federal government to a large extent maintains the reproduction of a part of the Puerto Rican population.[5]

Thus, it is clear that the colony partially reproduces the social structure in the metropolis, including the capacity to attract and absorb immigrants, and at the same time to locate an increasing sector of the labor force in "reserve," living from federal subsidy. In general terms, the maintenance of the colonial relationship is costly for the federal government, and it is difficult to predict how long such a contradictory situation can be maintained.

As for the Puerto Rican migrants, we turn to a passage in a recent study on European worker migration: "As a result, we may expect the migrants themselves to be left suspended between two lands indefinitely, for decades, perhaps for generations, in a position of extreme insecurity."[6]

CONCLUSION

In the first section of the present study, I pointed out that the working class in capitalist society constitutes human population at the service of capital. In a colony like Puerto Rico this means that the working class is directly subject to changes in the social division of labor, to alterations in the balance of active/inactive forces within the productive process, and to constant geographic displacement. All three conditioning factors result from the dominant impact of U.S. capital and assume acute contradictory qualities because of the colonial position of the society as a whole. This interchange between U.S. capital and the Puerto Rican labor force, customarily presented as the structural base for a supposed "model of national development," has culminated in the present-day social reality of Puerto Rico, which I described in the second part. Clearly, North American capital invested in the colony has generated greatly expanding profits, which serves as an excellent example of the diverse ways in which imperialism seeks to maintain its control and exploitation of economically less developed nations. At the same time it points to the impossibility of any genuine national development within the framework of a direct or indirect colonial relationship. I have attempted to define the social and economic contradictions which really characterize this would-be "model."

Neither the migration of Puerto Rican workers as a process with a high social and human cost, nor the particularly contradictory social structure on the island, can be resolved within the present context of metropolitan domination or within capitalist relations of production. Only a profound structural change in the organization of production based on adequate planning for the needs of the working population can begin to seriously confront these dislocations.

NOTES

1. For an extended analysis of these historical developments, see Centro de Estudios Puertorriquenos, *Labor Migration under Capitalism: The Puerto Rican Experience* (New York: Monthly Review Press, 1978).
2. *Committee to Study Puerto Rico's Finances*, 1975.
3. *A Comparative Study of Labor Market Characteristics of Return Migrants and Nonmigrants in Puerto Rico*, Planning Board, 1973.
4. *Puerto Ricans in the Continental United States: An Uncertain Future*, Report of the Civil Rights Commission, 1976.
5. *Boletin de Gerencia Adm.* Negociado del Presupuesto. Estado Libre Asociado de Puerto Rico, ano XXIV, No. 222 (1975).
6. Anthony Ward, "European Migratory Labor: A Myth of Development," *Monthly Review* 27, No. 7 (December 1975).

SPACIAL DIFFUSION OF NURSING SERVICES FROM THE COMMONWEALTH CARIBBEAN TO BRITAIN

Simon Jones-Hendrickson

INTRODUCTION

Early studies of migration of Caribbean labor out of the Caribbean to Britain were tangential encounters with the crux of the parameters underlying the movement of the labor. The studies identified, or rather catalogued, a set of so-called push and pull factors as the causal determinants of outward mobility, as well as regional mobility. These early studies, however, failed to come to grips with a broad set of methodological problems and, in many cases, shied away from ideological determinants in the movement of labor out of the Caribbean.

Implicit in the early works of G. W. Roberts, Ceri Peach, Bob Davidson and others, was a pure demographic perspective. Attention was not riveted on the stark realities of socioeconomic, sociocultural *cum* political forces which may have served as the initial catalyst in the movement of labor from the Caribbean to non-Caribbean regions.

The Caribbean is one of those regions in which it is popularly felt that more could be done for the region outside rather than inside. It is also a region which is characteristic of literally more people outside than inside. Many typifications have been given to the Caribbean in the search for the causal roots of the outward mobility. But in several respects the works were basically descriptive; no *meaningful* attempts were made to concretize the determinants of labor mobility.

While it is necessary to itemize the descriptive material pertaining to the movement of labor, it is not sufficient to remain at that level of analysis. With this point of departure in mind, our study seeks to give some rigor to the oft discussed, but inadequately identified and poorly specified, parameters of the diffusion of Caribbean labor services from the region to the metropole.

The main focus of the work centers on a subset of the Commonwealth Caribbean labor market—specifically, the nursing labor market. This market assumes priority because of its dominance in the British nursing labor market, and because we believe it has certain peculiarities which fall within the norms of the overall labor market. An additional factor for its study lies in the neglect that it has suffered. One is not referring to descriptive work of Michael Kendal or the halfhearted approach of Oscar Gish. Indeed, their work may be termed "seminal." However, the level of rigorous sophistication that is requisite of this market was crying out for attention.

Caribbean nurses literally dominated the foreign component of the British nursing labor market. In this paper we highlighted the important causal barometers of mobility. Objectively our primary purpose was the following: (1) to quantify the much discussed and alluded to push and pull factors of nursing labor services from the Caribbean to Britain; (2) to codify the policy options from an in-depth understanding of the parameters of the spatial diffusion of nursing services; and (3) to concretize the impact of out-diffusion of nursing services on the Caribbean nursing labor market, the sender country, and on the British nursing labor market, the receiver country.

BACKGROUND

In the first stage of the movement the people who lived in the rural Caribbean area migrated to the Caribbean "city" centers. The Caribbean entered an "underdevelopment syndrome."[1] It seems that this situation was a direct result of the links with the metropolitan economies. Development in the Caribbean was tailored to assist development in Britain, France, and other European countries. In essence, Caribbean labor markets were appendages of the metropolitan labor markets[2] or, as Sir Stanford Raffles said to the Duke of Somerset, on August 20, 1820, "The West Indies always look to the European market, and that alone."[3] In terms of frontier terminology, Caribbean economies were not "gold rush" economies for any length of time; they entered the "ghost town" economies stage very quickly.[4] They "fell" in a state of "dependent underdevelopment."[5] The dependent underdeveloped economies were harbingers of the displacement and disruption that caused the people of the Caribbean to seek employment in the cities, cities which were in actuality entrêpots for Europe. In general, the West Indian laborer operated in a market that was organized, regulated, and run by nonresident economic concerns.

During the late 1950s and early 1960s the Caribbean went through a neocolonial era of benign neglect. In accordance with the principles of economic development, overtures were made to modernize and attempts were made at creating viable economies out of the underdeveloping economies. Overtures came in the form of "local" industries, infant industries assistance, invitation to invest (from foreign capital), stimulation in the modern sectors of these dual economies, "shifts" from the agricultural sectors to the modern sectors a la A. W. Lewis, Fei and Ranis, B. Higgins, et al.

The process of economic development that was taking place in the Caribbean was "development" fostered by nonlocal capital. The bulk of the profits was exported to the metropolitan countries; minimal amounts were reinvested locally, and marginal consideration was given to the maldistribution of incomes in the society. There developed some economic improvements, such as bauxite and petroleum, for example, but the population continued to increase, the income gap continued to widen, underemployment and unemployment continued to increase. Meanwhile, the threshold of the demonstration syndrome[6] expanded, and the majority of the people got on the bandwagon of opting for goods and services with foreign labels. The governments were incapable of enforcing prices/income policies because they did not have the manpower and wherewithal to implement the policies. The Caribbean never attained the Rostovian "takeoff" stage because the only groups capable of catching up with the standards of living as obtained in the developed countries, were the *ten percenters* in the Caribbean economic echelon.

In the meantime, Britain, the main economic link with the Caribbean was going through a post–World War II labor shortage.[7] There was a shortage of skilled and semiskilled laborers; therefore, the government made provisions to downplay the 1920 Aliens Order so that the Ministry of labor could admit foreign laborers into the country to be employed in the industries which were in great need of labor. And several other attempts and schemes were implemented. The government and other public agencies were engaged in recruitment schemes designed to ease the labor shortages: textiles, building, domestic occupations, brickmaking, mining and quarrying, and agriculture.

Attempts were made to get labor from the European continent. The British labor market benefited from the Poles who resettled in Britain during the period 1946–51. The Poles were followed by the Germans and Austrians, who entered primarily to work in domestic occupations; Belgians and Italians also entered in substantial numbers. Between 1946–50, the British government went through many gyrations to solve the existing labor shortages. An estimated 457,000 European foreigners were in Britain at this time; some of them were students, but the vast numbers were assumed to be workers. Their high turn over was not conducive to the industrial nature of Britain. At this stage of the labor shortage, sights were focused on the Commonwealth as a guaranteed source of labor. Given the special "constitutional relationship" that existed between Britain and the Commonwealth, it was fairly easy for Britain to recruit Commonwealth citizens for its labor market. The West Indies featured prominently in supplying the needed labor.

In 1950 Barbados began an active policy of encouraging the diffusion of labor services to Britain. Barbados has a legitimate population problem, hence, when this *little Britain* sent a token of twenty hospital orderlies to work in Britain, the motive was the result of population pressures and the British labor market's needed for labor services from the Caribbean. In 1955, officials of the London Transport system went to Barbados to recruit men to work "on the buses." In 1966, recruitment was extended to Jamaica. J. Lyons and Company and British Rail entered the scene later. The success of these recruitment schemes led to what Monty Meth called "deliberate recruitment policies adopted by some management to meet their own *acute labor shortage*."[8]

West Indians entered Britain in large numbers until 1956 when there was a steady decline. The attitudes of British workers were changing. This was post-Suez, and Britain's labour market needs were declining. The 1958 Notting Hill, Shepherd's Bush, Kensall New Town, Paddington, and Maiden Vale disturbances, and the murder of a West Indian, Kelso Cochrane, on May 17, 1959, may have instilled some caution in the minds of West Indians traveling to Britain. For whatever reason, there was a noticeable decline in the number of West Indians entering Britain. The decline was only temporary, however, and the number picked up again in 1959, but it declined rapidly in 1962 with the introduction of the Commonwealth Immigration Act of 1962.[9]

The literature of migrants' entry into foreign countries consistently points to their attraction to those industries which are deficit in manpower, and which industries have some innate characteristics that the local population abhors. Some of the characteristics are unpleasant working conditions, arduous tasks, abominably low wages, extremely long working hours, and seasonality in labor demand.

Most of the West Indians in Britain are employed in jobs that are avoided by the local labor force.[10] West Indians, like other immigrants,[11] are found in jobs that are typified by their high insecurity, uncertainty and risk, low rates of pay, low status, and minimal chances of promotion. Some of the economic activities which have the inherent characteristics, as mentioned before, and in which large numbers of West Indians are employed are public transport and low level communication, catering industry, building and construction industry, industries concerned with the production of seasonal and cyclical goods and services, low echelons of the textile industry, and general unskilled labor. Fields such as banking, commerce, agriculture, mining and quarrying, insurance trading, and ship building have insignificant numbers of West Indians.

As the "recognition lag" of West Indians began to diminish, and as West Indians demonstrated that their attrition rate and job stability were important to them, there developed a noticeable deterioration in what appeared to be occupational downgrading of West Indian labor services. West Indians are now to be found in industries ranging from light engineering, food manufacturing, clothing, footwear, chemicals, vehicles, public transport, building and construction, laundries, and the health industry, principally, the nursing profession.

The latest data available to us seem to indicate that, in those occupations where there is great public contact and in which there are close knit groups, there is minimal representation from Commonwealth community citizens. Examples of the former are sales administration and management; examples of the latter are farming, fishing and forestry, mining and quarrying, and textiles.[12]

THE CARIBBEAN–BRITISH RELATIONSHIP: MARKET OVERTONES

The argument is often made that Britain is a "drainer" of labor services from the Commonwealth Caribbean (CC). CC citizens seem to constitute a natural source of labor services for the British health industry. Several factors stand out as vital in the superstructure of the British health market in relation to the entry of CC nursing input into the nursing labor market in Britain. Three factors will be mentioned: the nurse-trainees' mother tongue is English; the nurse-trainees' standard of education is very high, as a result of the "English" system in the CC; on a per nurse expenditure basis, the capital outlay of training a nurse in Britain is lower than in the Caribbean.[13]

Various estimates have been put forward in support of the dependence of the nursing labor market in Britain on overseas nurses. Our estimates indicate that about 30 percent of the presently constituted nursing labor force in Britain is from overseas: the vast majority of this overseas contingent is from the Commonwealth, and the largest component of this latter set is from the Caribbean. The evidence shows that over 90 percent of these nurses received their *basic nursing training* in Britain.

The nursing labor market (NLM) is very volatile.

The out-diffusion of British-born nurses establishes a gap in the NLM in Britain, and this gap is filled by the in-diffusion of overseas nurses. At this moment information is lacking and what is available is unreliable as to the extent of the outflow of nurses from Britain to overseas markets. It is evident, however, that the spatial diffusion of British-born nurses out of Britain is not small. In the early 1960s, according to Oscar Gish, almost 2,000 British-born nurses per year were entering the nursing labor market in the "Old Commonwealth" and the United States of America. This vacuum in the NLM in Britain was filled by input from the "New Commonwealth" countries; the CC contribution in this spatial inflow was very significant.

During the period 1960–72, the Commonwealth Caribbean contributed over 88,000 nurses to the NLM in Britain. This ranged from a first low of 5,289 (1960) to a high of 8,273 (1966) and a second low of 4,740 (1972).[14]

In the early 1960s inadequacy in the Caribbean nursing schools may be ascribed great weight in the outflow into the NLM in Britain. But there may have been more profound reasons which pushed the trainees out and pulled them into the British NLM. What are some of these factors?

The nursing labor market has features which are peculiar to its operations. CC nurses are trainees for the National Health Services (NHS) purposes, but they are laborers for labor market purposes. Unlike most other CC citizens the nurses do not enter the British labor market to seek employment the first time around. Initially, open-market factors seem to be of second order of importance. The fact that they left the Caribbean not for money only forces one to determine what are the underlying factors for the diffusion of their labor services into Britain. What are the parameters of decision making which caused the out-diffusion of nursing services into the nursing labor market in Britain? Can population pressure be a factor?

In Table 1 we look at the CC nurses (CCN) in the nursing labor market in Britain (NLM_m), the CC population, and the CCN per 10,000 CC population. The number of nurses diffused into the NLM gradually. The ratio showed movement from 13.4 per 10,000 population in 1960 up to a peak of 17.9

in 1966, and down to a low of 9.6 in 1972.

The rapid decline in the nursing ratio after 1966 may be a partial reflection of the passage of the British Government's White Paper of August 1965, which restricted voucher holders to 8,500 per year. Nurses enter Britain as voucher holders under category "B," that is, those applicants who possess specific skills or qualifications. These people need not have an offer of a job in Britain. The sharp decline in 1968 may be indicative of the restrictions imposed in March, 1968, relative to voucher holders. The small rally in 1969 and 1970 may be seen as a reflection of the fact that voucher holders in category B were curtailed to doctors, dentists, and trained nurses during this period. The decline in 1971 and 1972 speaks for itself.

DIFFUSION OF NURSING SERVICES INTO THE NLM_m AND THE CC POPULATION

What insights can be gained from the diffusion of nursing services into the NLM_m and this relationship to the CC population? The population increased steadily over the period of analysis from 3.9 million to 4.9 million, or about an average annual increase of about 2 percent. Did the relatively small increase have any significant underpinnings for the nurses' outflow? Was population pressure a factor in the movement of the nurses' outflow?

On an island by island level an argument can be advanced with regards to the nurses movement into the NLM_m and the population of the respective islands. In Table 2 data are presented of the islands depicting the population and the nurses' entry into the nursing labor market in Britain (NLM_m) per respective island population.

Using 1960 as a base, Table 2 shows that twelve out of seventeen islands sent a greater proportion of nurses into the NLM_m in 1970. Antigua, Bahamas, Barbados, British Virgin Islands, and Jamaica suffered decreases in the spatial inflow of nursing input. The decreases in these islands' contribution may be seen as a movement to alternative areas of training-work activities, as well as the growth and recognition of nursing schools in the Caribbean. It should be noted that the smaller islands picked up the burden of contribution. Is there any relationship

TABLE 1
CC NURSES DIFFUSION IN THE NURSING LABOR MARKET AND CC POPULATION
1960-1972

YEAR	CCN in NLM_m	CC POPULATION	CC/10,000 POPULATION
1960	5289	3,954,963	13.4
1961	5976	4,063,775	14.7
1962	6992	4,161,814	16.8
1963	6885	4,251,713	16.1
1964	7225	4,344,898	16.6
1965	7802	4,436,932	17.5
1966	8273	4,613,002	17.9
1967	8149	4,689,926	17.3
1968	7037	4,800,578	14.6
1969	7142	4,712,507	15.1
1970	7208	4,739,743	15.2
1971	6011	4,822,421	12.4
1972	4740	4,912,923	9.6

Sources: For sources on nurses data, see footnote 14

Population data were gathered from various Island sources as well as United Nations publications. The following are some of the main references: *Abstract of Barbados*, Barbados Statistical Service, Barbados, No. 6, 1969. (2) Barbados Statistical Service, *Digest of Statistics*, Barbados, Dec. 1972. (3) *Annual Statistica Digest*, Trinidad and Tobago, Port-of-Spain, Trinidad, 1970. (4) St. Kitts-Nevis-Anguilla Health Department, *Annual Report* 1960-1972. (5) *Population and Vital Statistics Report*, Department of Economic and Social Affairs, Statistical Office of the U.N., Series A, Vol. XXV, No. 2 Data as of April, 1973. (6) U.N. *Monthly Bulletin of Statistics*, Jan. 1971 - Sept. 1973, St/STAT/SER. Q, New York, 1971/1973. The Commonwealth of the Bahamas and Bermuda data were obtained from worksheets from the Bahamas, tabulations were done by us.

TABLE 2
CC POPULATION, 1960 AND 1970 AND CC NURSES PER 10,000 POPULATION

	A	B		
	Pop. 1960	Pop. 1970	CCN/A	CCN/B
Antigua	56,947	70,000	16.3	15.0
Bahamas	113,000	168,812	2.3	2.1
Barbados	242,274	241,378	40.1	34.0
Belize	90,343	119,863	.7	1.3
Bermuda	42,460	52,530	6.1	9.5
B. Virgin Island	7,378	10,484	5.4	2.0
Caymans	7,616	10,652	-	1.0
Dominica	59,916	70,302	3.3	8.5
Grenada	88,617	103,000	14.2	34.4
Guyana	558,769	740,090	6.7	9.3
Jamaica	1,609,814	1,890,700	16.2	13.0
Montserrat	12,157	12,300	16.5	17.1
St.Ketts-Nevis Anguilla	56,224	56,314	17.8	20.4
St. Lucia	86,194	110,064	4.4	6.6
St. Vincent	79,948	89,129	7.4	21.1
Turks & Caicos	5,716	9,609	-	24.0
Trinidad & Tobago	834,350	1,026,700	9.8	21.2

Sources: See the sources for footnote 14 and Table 1
Ratios were estimated by us. See also, *Statistical Abstract*
(Jamaica), Department of Statistics, Jamaica, April, 1973, for
the Jamaican data

between the change in the islands' population from 1960–70, and the change in the number of nurses per 10,000 population of the respective islands? This relationship will be explored later.

POPULATION DENSITY

Population density is often thought of as a push factor funneling labor services out of the CC into the British labor market. This density of population may be critical in the nurses leaving the Caribbean. It is a known fact that many of the islands are overpopulated in the socioeconomic sense. This means the islands are ''shouldering'' too many persons given their resource utilization capacity, and the inadequacy in the production and provision of goods and services to the masses of the people. The growth has been gradual moving from 37.5 per square mile in 1970 to 46.6 per square in 1972.[15]

In Table 3 we present a micro view of the density picture from the individual countries' point perspective. In 1960, the Bermuda Islands were the most densely populated, followed by Barbados, Grenada, St. Vincent, respectively, all above five hundred persons per square mile. The picture was similar in 1970. Bermuda headed the list with 2,388 up from 1980; Barbados fell by 5 down to 1454; Grenada went up by 112 to 774. St. Vincent went up to 594, an increase of 61, and Trinidad and Tobago registered a 98 increase, up to 519. In terms of nursing movement relative to populations, the countries with 100 or more were Jamaica, Barbados, Trinidad and Tobago, St. Vincent, Guyana, Grenada and St. Kitts-Nevis-Anguilla.

A cursory analysis of Table 3 will not reveal if there is any significant relationship between density of the respective islands and the CCN per 10,000 population of the respective islands. There seems to be no significant relationship between the two aggregates on a CC-wide basis. It could be argued that similar evidence exists on an island by island basis. In Table 4, data are presented from the island's perspective since aggregation of the data could have hidden some vital evidence.

From Table 4 it is observed that most of the countries which had densities of 100 or more in 1960 also had a nurse-to-population ratio of 10 or

more. The exceptions to this general observation on density and CCN/population were (1) Bermuda with 1,980 and 6.1; (2) Dominica with 196 and 3.3; (3) St. Lucia with 361 and 4.4; (4) St. Vincent with 533 and 7.4; and (5) Trinidad and Tobago with 421 and 9.8. The noticeable feature of this density and the number of CCN in the British labor market relative to the island's population is the fact that the latter figure closely approximates the nurse-to-population ratio in the respective islands.

The 1970 figures showed some remarkable shifts. The larger contributors showed a decline: there was a shift to the smaller units, but Trinidad and Tobago was the exception with a movement from 9.8 to 21.2, CCN/population.

LAND AND THE DIFFUSION OF NURSING SERVICES INTO THE NLM_m

Population density may not give adequate information about the movement of nursing services into the nursing labor market of Britain, NLM_m. Fundamental ideas may be gained from the agricultural sector wherein implicit pushes may be identified as causal in the outflow of nursing services from the CC to Britain. The outward movement from the agricultural sector is envisioned as a two sector movement: stage one involves a movement from the rural area to the CC city centers, and stage two involves a movement from the city centers to Britain. This two-stage movement is not a fool proof description because there is evidence to verify that many of the nurses who entered the British labor market were from the rural areas.

What of farmland and the inherent pushes of nursing labor services out of the CC into the NLM_m? Table 5 gives the data on the density of population per one thousand acres of farmland and the diffusion of nursing services into Britain from the respective CC country. Ten of the eleven units for which there were data available showed a decline in the farmland per capita: Barbados had a constant per capita farmland from 1960–70. The decline in farmland per capita could have stemmed from a reduction in the farmland under usage or if there was an increase in the population in the respective units, or if there was a combination of both effects leading to a de-

TABLE 3
AREA, DENSITY OF ISLANDS 1960-1970 AND CCN 1960-1970

	AREA*	DENSITY, 1960	DENSITY, 1970	NURSES, 1960	NURSES, 1970
Antigua	170.5	330	409	93	105
Bahamas	5,386	21	31	26	36
Barbados	166	1,459	1,454	982	820
Belize	8,866	10	14	6	16
Bermuda	22	1,980	2,388	26	50
B. Virgin Islands	67	110	156	–	2
Caymans	100	76	107	–	–
Dominica	305	196	230	20	60
Grenada	133	662	774	126	354
Guyana	83,000	7	9	375	687
Jamaica	4,411	365	429	2,604	2,450
St. Kitts-Nevis-Anguilla	152	370	370	100	115
St. Lucia	238	361	462	38	73
St. Vincent	150	533	594	126	354
Turks & Caicos	169	34	57	–	23
Trinidad & Tobago	1,980	421	519	814	2,208
Montserrat	32.5	368	372	20	21

Sources: For area, *Caribbean and West Indies Yearbook* (various years):
Density from our worksheets; Actual number of nurses were from the
Department of Health and Social Security Statistics and Research
Division. (See our Table 4).

*Square miles.

cline in the ratio.

Density of population per acre of cropland may also be brought into play to determine its influence, if any, in the diffusion process. Table 6 depicts the relationship of cropland per capita and nursing diffusion into the NLM_m.

Six units, for which there were data available, indicated declines in the per capita crop land; four

TABLE 4
POPULATION DENSITY AND DIFFUSION OF NURSING SERVICES INTO THE NLM$_m$

	DENSITY 1960	CCN/POP 1960	DENSITY 1970	CCN/POP 1970
Antigua	330	16.3	409	15.0
Bahamas	21	2.3	31	2.1
Barbados	1,459	40.1	1,454	34.0
Belize	10	.7	14	1.3
Bermuda	1,980	6.1	2,388	9.5
B.Virgin Islands	110	5.4	156	2.0
Caymans	76	-	107	1.0
Dominica	196	3.3	230	8.5
Grenada	602	3.3	774	8.5
Guyana	7	6.7	9	9.3
Jamaica	365	16.2	429	13.0
St.Kitts-Nevis-Anguilla	370	17.8	370	20.4
St.Lucia	361	4.4	462	6.6
St.Vincent	533	7.4	594	21.1
Turks & Caicos	34	-	57	24.0
Trinidad & Tobago	421	9.8	519	21.2
Montserrat	368	16.5	372	17.1

Sources:

See Table 3; density computed from our worksheets.

had no changes indicated, and one unit, Guyana, showed an approximate 16 percent increase, indicating among other things that a greater proportion of cropland was being reclaimed for usage versus the proportionate population growth rate.

THE FEMALE COMPONENT OF THE LABOR FORCE AND DIFFUSION OF NURSING SERVICES

Did the composition of the labor force in the CC

TABLE 5
CC POPULATION DENSITY PER ACRE OF FARMLAND AND
DIFFUSION OF NURSING SERVICES, 1960/1970

	DENSITY 1960	DENSITY 1970	CCN 1960	CCN 1970
Antigua	.9	.6	1.6	1.5
Bahamas	na	na	.2	.2
Barbados	.4	.4	4.1	3.4
Belize	na	na	.1	.1
Bermuda	na	na	.6	1.0
British Virgin Islands	na	na	-	.2
Caymans	na	na	-	.1
Dominica	1.2	1.0	.3	.9
Grenada	.8	.6	.3	.9
Guyana	5.3	4.7	.7	.9
Jamaica	1.1	1.0	1.6	1.3
Montserrat	1.4	1.0	1.7	1.7
St.Kitts-Nevis-Anguilla	.7	.5	1.8	2.0
St.Lucia	.9	.6	.4	.7
St.Vincent	.6	.4	.7	2.1
Turks & Caicos	na	na	-	2.4
Trinidad and Tobago	.6	.5	1.0	2.2

Sources: *Agricultural Statistics*, Series 2, Nos. 1-8, Federal Statistics Office,
Trinidad (1960): *Agricultural Census of Jamaica*, 1958 *Census of Agri-
culture*, 1968-69, Preliminary Report of the Agricultural Census Unit,
Dept. of Statistics, Oct. 1970. Vol.1, *Census of Agriculture, 1961*
(Barbados, Regional Council of Ministers, 1963), Land Areas: D. T.
Edwards. *Some Statistical Tables on West Indian Agriculture*, Insti-
tute of Social and Economic Research, Mona, Jamaica (1962). Carleen
O'Loughlin, *Economic and Political Change in the Leewards and Windward
Islands*, Yale Univ. Press, 1968, pp.66, Table 7. U.S. Department
of Agriculture, *Jamaica, Trinidad and Tobago, Leeward Islands, Wind-
ward Islands, Barbados, and British Guiana: Projected Level of Demand
Supply, and Imports of Agricultural Products to 1975*. ERS Foreign 94,
Washington (?), 1963. Carleen O'Loughlin, *A Survey of the Economic
Potential and Capital needs of the Leeward Island and Windward Islands,
and Barbados*, H.M.S.O. London, 1963 p. 144.
    *Nursing data were obtained from our worksheets: 100,000 population was
    used instead of 10,000 as in the earlier cases. Land area per 1000 acres.
    *It must be remembered that we are still considering the diffusion of
    nursing services per 100,000 population in these examples of land
    measurements. We are trying to discover what the analytical results would
    be if we moved from 10,000 to 100,000 population.

TABLE 6
POPULATION DENSITY PER ACRE OF CROP AND DIFFUSION OF NURSING SERVICES

	CROPLAND		NURSING DIFFUSION	
	1960	1970	1960	1970
Antigua	.3	.2	1.6	1.5
Bahamas	na	na	.2	.2
Barbados	.3	.2	4.1	3.4
Belize	na	na	.1	.1
Bermuda	na	na	.6	1.0
British Virgin Islands	na	na	-	.2
Caymans	na	na	-	.1
Dominica	.7	.6	.3	.9
Grenada	.6	.5	.3	.9
Guyana	.6	.7	.7	.9
Jamaica	.4	.4	1.6	1.3
Montserrat	.6	.5	1.7	1.7
St.Kitts-Nevis-Anguilla	.5	.5	1.7	1.7
St. Lucia	.5	.5	.4	.7
St. Vincent	.3	.3	.7	2.1
Turks & Caicos	na	na	-	2.4
Trinidad & Tobago	.4	.3	1.0	2.2

Sources: See sources following Table 5

have anything to do with the out-diffusion of nursing services from the CC to Britain? Specifically, did the female component of the labor force eventuate factors or characteristics precipitating an out-ward movement of nursing services from the CC? (Although the female component is stressed, it must be remembered that a significant number of CC nurses are males; however, the analysis will be

TABLE 7
FEMALE COMPONENT OF THE LABOR (WORKING) FORCE IN THE CC 1960 AND 1970

	1960	1970	% Change
Antigua	na	na	na
Bahamas	na	na	na
Barbados	34,900	32,900	-5.7
Belize	4,700	6,000	27.7
Bermuda	na	na	-
British Virgin Islands	400	1,000	150.0
Caymans	900	1,200	23.3
Dominica	9,700	7,300	-24.7
Grenada	10,000	9,800	-2.0
Guyana	36,700	30,100	-18.0
Jamaica	225,000	159,900	-29.0
Montserrat	1,800	1,300	-27.8
St.Kitts-Nevis-Anguilla	7,100	4,700	-33.8
St.Lucia	10,400	9,300	-5.8
St. Vincent	9,100	7,400	-18.7
Turks & Caicos	900	500	-44.0
Trinidad & Tobago	68,400	57,200	-16.4
Total	420,200	328,600	-21.8

Source: Adapted from G. W. Roberts, Working Force of the Commonwealth
         Caribbean at 1970, "A Provisional Assessment," Appendix, Table
         7 (Changes in Size of Male and Female Working Force for 14
         Commonwealth Caribbean Countries, 1960 and 1970); Paper
         presented to Inter-Disciplinary (Social Sciences) Seminar,
         University of the West Indies, Mona, Jamaica, February 1974,
         (Mimeo). The data for Antigua, Bahamas and Bermuda are not
         available due to the fact that these units held censuses
         independently of the other units, hence all of the data were
         not tabulated at the same time.

   *Anguilla's data are not included

developed from the perspective of the female sector of the labor force). In Table 7 data are presented on the female labor force (working force) and the changes therein, for base years 1960 and 1970.

As is observable from Table 7, the overall working force for women dropped by almost one-quarter since 1960. Of the fourteen units, three, Belize, British Virgin Islands, and the Caymans, registered increases, the other eleven units all showed declines. Does this large decline of 21.8 percent demonstrate a fall in the women's labor force and establish a case for the outflow of women's labor services to nonlocal labor market? It is a very difficult question given the fact that many nurses are recruited in Britain and not directly from the Caribbean.

GROWTH IN GDP AND THE DIFFUSION OF CCN SERVICES INTO THE NLM_m

Growth in GDP could serve as an agent of push/pull factor catering to the diffusion of nursing services out of the CC into Britain. As was discovered in this paper, this apparent logical outward thrust does not necessarily hinge on growth in GDP/GNP. To concretize the idea, GDP may be growing, and labor services may be flowing out or remaining within the local market of the GDP growth. Crucial to the discussion, too, is the fact that GDP differentials between the CC and Britain, for instance, may induce or may not induce outflows of labor services from the CC to Britain. Because the GDP aggregate has an uncertain diffusion direction, our aim is one of establishing what relationship exists between GDP per capita and the diffusion of nursing services into the NLM in Britain. Table 8 gives the data on GDP per capita for the CC in Eastern Caribbean dollars. These figures are compared with the nurses per 10,000 CC population. The GDP trend has been increasing over the period of analysis; this is not true of the CCN trend: it has been fluctuating. If we accept the thesis that GDP per capita is a measure of the standard of living, then we should notice some influence of per capita GDP on the nurses' movement into Britain. But the thesis may be weak in some respects.

THE CONDITIONS IN BRITAIN AND THE DIFFUSION OF NURSING LABOR SERVICES

Some *evident* pull factors may be examined to determine their force in pulling nursing labor services out of the Commonwealth Caribbean nursing labor market, NLM_{m-1} into the nursing labor market in Britain, NLM_m. As was developed elsewhere, two of the most pertinent indicators of the outflow of services from the CC (the inflow of services into Britain) are the labor force of Britain and the unemployment rate. The former should obviate the necessary conditions for the entry or nonentry of labor services into the British labor market. The latter ought to act as a barometer defining the magnitude of services that the labor market in Britain could accommodate. Together, these two labor market conditions may be interpreted as determinants of the necessary and sufficient conditions for any significant diffusion of labor services in the British labor market. In Table 9, data are given on the employed labor force in Britain, 1960–72, relative to the diffusion of nursing labor services into the NLM_m. A close analysis will reveal that the period 1964–68 demonstrated similar "characteristics" in the employed labor force in Britain and the entry of CCN into the NLM. We are not certain that this relationship is strong.

Finally, another measure of the conditions in Britain was examined in relation to the diffusion of nurses into the NLM_m. The average unemployment rate in Britain was considered in relation to the CCN entry into the nursing labor market in Britain. Table 10 presents data on the average unemployment in Britain and the CCN entry into the NLM_m. The information as to influence is not readily apparent. There is a slight inverse relationship. The significance of this is open although one would expect that conditions in Britain would affect the entry of nurses in the NLM_m. In periods of labor market "tightening", one should observe a falling off on CCN entering the NLM_m. In fact, unemployment rate is an accepted parameter in labor market demand-supply relationships.

TABLE 8
CC GDP PER CAPITA AND CCN PER 10,000 POPULATION, 1960-72

	GDP PER CAPITA*	CCN/10,000 POPULATION
1960	677.8	13.4
1961	710.9	14.7
1962	729.4	16.8
1963	758.0	16.1
1964	792.7	16.6
1965	824.0	17.5
1966	876.6	17.9
1967	914.1	17.3
1968	975.3	14.6
1969	1,092.4	15.1
1970	1,199.1	15.2
1971	1,274.3	12.4
1972	1,355.4	9.6

Sources: *Monthly Bulletin of Statistics*, 1960-72, United Nations,
New York. *National Accounts of LDC's* 1959-68, O.E.C.D.,
Paris, 1970. *National Income and Product Account*, 1972,
Dept. of Statistics, Jamaica, March 1973.
Statistical Abstract, 1972, Dept. of Statistics, Jamaica,
April 1973 ISER (Eastern Caribbean), *Abstract of Leeward
Islands, Windward Islands and Barbados, Barbados*, 1962.
Digest of Statistics (various years), St. Kitts-Nevis-
Anguilla, Basseterre, St. Kitts.

Owen Jefferson, *Post-War Economic Development in Jamaica*,
Institute of Social and Economic Research (ISER), (1971),
Mona, Jamaica. Huntley G. Manhertz, "The Mobilisation
and Allocation of Savings, National Savings Seminar, UWI,
Mona, Jamaica; (mimeo), no date.

*GDP per capita in Eastern Caribbean Currency (Dollar).
One EC$ J$. 21; or alternatively, EC$ 4.80 = J$2.00 =
1.00 = US$2.50. (These are only officially calculation
rates: the exchange rates have changed recently).

TABLE 9
EMPLOYED LABOR FORCE IN BRITAIN AND DIFFUSION OF NURSING SERVICES

	EMPLOYED LABOR FORCE		CCN ENTRY IN NLM_m
1960	24,845	millions	13.4
1961	25,081	"	14.7
1962	25,173	"	16.8
1963	25,207	"	16.1
1964	25,539	"	16.6
1965	25,764	"	17.5
1966	25,815	"	17.9
1967	25,449	"	17.3
1968	25,290	"	14.6
1969	25,245	"	15.1
1970	25,068	"	15.2
1971	24,633	"	12.4
1972	24,701	"	9.6

Sources: The Central Statistics Office, CSO, *Economic Trends*
Nos. 219-230, H.M.S.O., Jan-Dec, 1970-73.

Central Statistical Office, *Monthly Digest of Statistics*
H.M.S.O., London, Jan-Dec, 1969-73.

Data on CCN obtained as in Table 1.

ANALYSIS AND IMPLICATIONS

The conceptual framework of the problem considered in this paper mandated a methodological viewpoint which permitted us to use bivariate regression analysis and multivariate regression analysis.[16]

Under the bivariate analytical section ten equations were tested, specified according to theoretical and informed methods of analysis. Two dummy

TABLE 10
AVERAGE UNEMPLOYMENT IN BRITAIN AND CCN SERVICES IN-DIFFUSION

	UNEMPLOYMENT	CCN IN NLM$_m$
1960	1.6	13.4
1961	1.4	14.7
1962	1.9	16.8
1963	2.6	16.1
1964	1.7	16.6
1965	1.4	17.5
1966	1.5	17.9
1967	2.4	17.3
1968	2.4	14.6
1969	2.4	15.1
1970	2.5	15.2
1971	3.4	12.4
1972	3.9	9.6

Sources: *Economic Trends*, 1967-73, H.M.S.O. for Central Statistical
Office, London. (Reference is made to unemployment in
Britain, excluding school leavers: percentage rate.) Data
on CCN were obtained as from earlier tables in which they
were mentioned.

variables were incorporated in the equations with their anticipated purpose being that of capturing the impact of changes in the variables as well as capturing the effect of a policy decision—the British White Paper on Immigration curtailment.

The dependent variables were variations of the theme of the diffusion of nursing services into the British nursing labor market. On the bivariate side, we discovered that population pressures in the islands, and the employment/unemployment rate in Britain, were the critical factors of the diffusion of nursing labor service from the Caribbean to Britain.

On the multivariate side, the employed labor force in Britain, the change in the female component of the working force in the Caribbean, and GDP per capita in the Caribbean were all significant variables of diffusion determinants.

The findings have had cursory references in the literature. But, alarmingly, there was no rigorous analysis applied to testing the thoughts, even at the elementary level of sophistication, employed in this paper. The problem may have stemmed from the danger of collecting information from widely disparate sources, and then seeking to squeeze statistical purity out of or into the data (depending on one's methodological hue).

The contribution of the work revolves around the issue of nursing services as a vital component in the delivery of health care. Based on this partial development and subsequent detailed analysis, we were able to establish some theses about the diffusion of nursing services from the Caribbean to Britain.

We noted (1) that crushing socioeconomic conditions in the Caribbean push/pull West Indian men/women into the nursing profession in Britain. Population pressures and the changes in per capita gross domestic product were the main push factors; (2) the movement outward was also related to the structural rigidities in the absorptive capacity of the Caribbean nursing schools, and the Caribbean economies; (3) the diffusion of nursing services into Britain from the Caribbean exacerbates the demand for nursing services in the region, instead of mitigating the skill deficiency.

The development *cum* transformation implications of the immigration—or diffusion of services, as we prefer—for the Caribbean are many fold: (1) we argue that there is a need to equilibrate the needs of the Caribbean population for nursing services with the demand of the population for these services; (2) drastic changes are required in the nursing labor market conditions in the Caribbean so that there will evolve nursing services with the capacity of effectuating curative, preventive, and progressive patient care in the region; (3) nursing services in the Caribbean have to be radically transformed to keep abreast of the changing sphere of nursing and health care delivery. This means better health care delivery is needed in the region so as to establish a necessary condition of the retention of nursing and potential nursing services in the region; (4) the necessary and sufficient measures should be adopted to mitigate the impact of the

diffusion of nursing services from the region; these should be implemented via the improvement of work conditions, financial and nonfinancial remuneration, and the broadening and deepening of the scope of nursing services in the region.

What we outlined as set specific to the nursing labor market may be extended to the overall Caribbean labor market be it in Britain, Central America, or any other area of labor deficiency. Crucial to this diffusion of Caribbean nursing labor services to Britain, however, is the issue of investment.

Most of the Caribbean nurses who enter the nursing labor market in Britain begin basic training in that country. But the factor of concern for the Caribbean rests squarely on the initial educational investment of these members in the Caribbean. Given the fact that the Caribbean is a severely resource-scarce region, that capital formation is meagre and, *pari passu,* investment is low, there are some strong policy options which ought to be considered.

The Caribbean nurses' labor services are contributing to a British nursing labor market which would collapse were they not a part of it. It would seem that Caribbean authorities have a strong case for requiring that their countries be reimbursed for the initial (home) investment in the nurses. A few policy makers in Britain argue that the training of Caribbean nurses in Britain may be construed as aid to the Caribbean. This argument has several flaws. Firstly, the majority of the Caribbean nurses in Britain are recruited outside of a government-to-government interaction. Secondly, the rate of return of the nurses to the Caribbean is miniscule (the sender countries are not benefitting) and, thirdly, United Kingdom Council for Overseas Students' Affairs (UKCOSA) has documented evidence to substantiate that the foreign nurses' entry visas are "doctored", thereby permitting the nurses to stay on in Britain after the first level of nursing training.

By and large, the issue of the spatial diffusion of nursing services from the Caribbean to Britain assumes a dimension beyond simple treatment of push and pull factors of diffusion. A profound understanding, rigorous documentation of the causal determinants, and the development of possible policy options to mitigate the impact of the outward diffusion of the services were our tasks in this paper.

NOTES

1. By "underdevelopment syndrome" one means a country experiencing a group of socioeconomic conditions which, operating in concurrence, resemble the signs and symptoms of a disease.
2. This notion of the Caribbean economies as appendages of the metropolitan economics can best be seen in the discussion surrounding the thesis of plantation economies. The most up-to-date position of this plantation economy notion is found in the seminal work of G. L. F. Beckford, *Persistent Poverty: Underdevelopment in Plantation Economics in the Third World* (Oxford: Oxford University Press, 1972).
3. F. R. Augier and Shirley C. Gordon, (compilers), *Source of West Indian History* (Trinidad and Jamaica: Longman Caribbean Ltd., 1962), p.66.
4. See Sylvia Wynter, review article: "One Love—Rhetoric or Reality?—Aspects of Afro-Jamaicanism." *Caribbean Studies*, 12, (Oct. 1972) No. 3, 62–97. This is a review article of Audvile King, et al., *One Love* (London: The Bogle-L'Ouverture Publications, 1971).
5. This term was borrowed from the Commonwealth Caribbean Regional Secretariat, *From CARIFTA TO THE CARIBBEAN COMMUNITY* (Guyana: Georgetown, 1972), p.14. In actual fact this concept is the brain child of the New World Associates—"a loosely structured group of Caribbean intellectuals concerned with developing an indigenous view of the (Caribbean)." See Norman Girvan, "The Development of Dependency Economics in the Caribbean and Latin America: Review and Comparison," *SES*, 22, No.1 (March 1973), 1–33.
6. See S. B. Hendrickson, "The Demonstration Syndrome," *The Democrat*, (St. Kitts: Basseterre, 1971). Many development economists call this term the demonstration effect.
7. Sheila Patterson, *Dark Strangers: A Study of West Indians in London* (Middlesex, England: Penguin, 1965), p.1.
8. Monty Meth, *Here to Stay* (A Runnymede Trust Publication), (Middlesex, England: The Hillingdon Press, 1968), p.11.
9. Sources of data on estimated numbers of Commonwealth Caribbean citizens entering Britain, 1952–71: Hansard, pp.1038–39; Sheila Patterson, *Dark Strangers, A Study of West Indians in London*, p.350; Arthur Bottomley and George Sinclair, *Control of Commonwealth Immigration*, pp.46–47; *The Select Committee on Race Relations and Immigration*, H.C. 1968–69, 58-xxvii and H.C. 1969–70, 17-1 to xxviii, *Evidence*, p.9 and p.812; Dipak Nandy, *How to Calculate Immigration Statistics*, p.10; *Facts in Focus*, C.S.O. Table 13, "Population Movement," 1972, p.30.
10. Christ Mullard, *Black Britain* (London: George Allen and Unwin Ltd., 1973), pp.38–39. See also Paul Foot, *Immigration and Race Relations in British Politics*, (London, 1965).
11. Sheila Patterson (1965).
12. Sheila Patterson, *Immigration and Race Relations in Britain* (1969), pp.135–36; General Registrar's Office, Census 1961, Occupation Tables, H.M.S.O. (1966); Arthur Bottomley and George Sinclair, *Control of Commonwealth Immigration* (1970), p.41 and 43; and evidence to the Select Committee on Race Relations and Immigration, p.468–69.
13. Oscar Gish, *Doctor Migration and World Health*, Occasional Papers on Social Administration, No.43 (London: G. Bell and Sons, 1971), p.112.
14. Department of Health and Social Security, Statistic and Research Division (various years) *Overseas Born Student and Pupil Midwives in Training in the NHS Hospitals in England and Wales*, 1961–72. The British Council, *Overseas Students in Britain*, 1959/60–72. *Manpower Survey of Britain*, Digest of Health Statistics for England and Wales with Summary for Great Britain, 1971.
15. Data on density were obtained from our worksheets; data on area were obtained from *Caribbean and West Indies Yearbook* (various years).
16. The original version of this paper contained a section discussing more fully the methodology and presenting the statistical results of the analyses. This information can be found in "Note on the Spatial Diffusion of Nurses from the Commonwealth Caribbean to Britain: Quantitative Methods and Migration Studies," in Stephen R. Couch and Roy S. Bryce-Laporte, eds., *Quantitative Data and Immigration Research*. (Washington, D.C.: Smithsonian Institution, Research Institute on Immigration and Ethnic Studies, forthcoming 1979).

THE EFFECTS OF EMIGRATION ON THE SENDING COUNTRIES: SOME THOUGHTS AND PARALLELS BETWEEN THE AMERICAN AND RECENT EUROPEAN EXPERIENCES WITH "LABOR" EMIGRATION

Demetrios G. Papademetriou

Patrick Hillery, Vice President of the Commission of the European Communities (ECs) recently called the phenomenon of labor migration the "burning problem in Europe today."[1] Its reverberations are felt throughout Europe and strain the very essence of the labor importing advanced European systems. There are several dimensions to the migration of foreign workers: an obvious economic one, which is severely aggravated by the current international economic uncertainty; a sociocultural dimension, which is compounded by the sharply rising migrant-related infrastructure costs and the apocalyptic warnings of the cultural purists among the hosts; finally, these dimensions culminate in the crucial political dimension, which is becoming more salient with the increasing political consciousness and assertiveness among the migrants and the resulting indigenous backlash movement. Yet, until quite recently, both sending and receiving countries viewed labor migration as a panacea. In 1973, *The Economist* described the view of the latter in the following manner:

> Ten years ago they (the migrants) seemed to be the ideal answer to Germany's chronic labor shortages. Import a batch of young, healthy workers (medically checked before they are allowed in); keep them for a few years while they pay contributions into the state pension schemes they will never use; let them send wages home, because that helps to balance your persistent trade surpluses; then repatriate them to tell of the quick fortunes to be made, so encouraging the next batch to come. This way, their demands on the social infrastructure could be kept to an absolute minimum, while their economic usefulness was maximized.[2]

Although one could conclude from this statement that U.S. immigration is of a substantially different type from European labor migration (which in principle at least, is temporary, involves principally workers, and can be controlled to correspond to market fluctuations), it is an undeniable fact that the destination points of both types of this new immigration share a plethora of common features which, to varying degrees, reflect a certain systemic dependence on a continuous stream of new immigrants. Most of these features are attributed to the developmental levels attained by both European labor importers and the United States. These advanced industrial societies find themselves at a point on the development continuum where they experience a withdrawal of their work forces from the most onerous and worst compensated tasks, and, generally, from positions where the nonpecuniary disadvantages are most pronounced.

This socioeconomic restructuring of the employment habits of the indigenous labor forces, however, tends to precipitate selected but chronic labor shortages in the abandoned occupations. This development is endemic to what is frequently identified as the "postindustrial" condition which is characterized by, among a variety of other components, a *relative* abatement in both the intensity and the number of fundamental sociopolitical fissures arising from economic scarcity,[3] and intensifies the aspirations and expectations of the labor force. The postindustrial milieu, although only an ideal construct properly belonging to the future, is also characterized by the proliferation of technical and white collar occupations which must be filled by a better skilled and educated personnel. Consequently, the social consciousness and the wage demands of the indigenous labor are amplified to the point where they gradually abandon most low socioeconomic status occupations.

These structural developments encourage the articulation of a different set of systemic demands on the postindustrial societies. They include better working conditions, increased opportunities for social advancement, an equitable welfare infrastructure, and, in general, a better quality of life. As one would suspect, however, those occupations which have become incompatible with the new minimum social and economic expectations of the native workers are also indispensable to the economic well-being of advanced industrial societies. To perform these less agreeable, arduous, over-whelmingly menial, low in social esteem, and poorly compensated tasks, the postindustrial systems have had to rely increasingly on large numbers of foreign workers (in the European case recruited primarily from the developing countries which surround the Mediterranean Sea[4]).

Transitional societies, on the other hand, are im-mersed in the struggle for modernization—the cushioning and meeting (usually in part) of the demands of their rapidly mobilizing masses, and the attempts to alleviate the serious unemployment and underemployment pressures which reinforce the fissiparous forces attendant to efforts to catapult the society into a new set of membership patterns, or-ganizations, and commitments. The latter expand both the range of politically relevant human needs and the government services necessary to satisfy those needs.[5] Such societies, however, are ill-equipped to deal effectively with the onslaught of these new demands. Accordingly, and attributable precisely to the nature of the condition of "transi-tion,"[6] many governments view *regulated* emigra-tion of unemployed and underemployed workers (many of whom are in the process of mobilizing) as essentially beneficial. The uncontrolled loss, how-ever, of their already meager supplies of skilled[7] manpower—and usually of the most dynamic, progressive, and productive part of the population—precipitates a decline in investment and production and a consequent stunting of economic growth and development. At a minimum, the European experience has shown that the *un-regulated* emigration of labor underpopulates sev-eral areas and leads to demographic imbalances that in some labor exporting countries seem to point to an incipient and sporadic structural labor shortage of their own, as in agriculture (during peak sea-sons), the construction business, and other selected industries.[8]

It is obvious from these few introductory remarks that migration is a potent economic, social, politi-cal, and cultural issue. In the European case, it

involves approximately fifteen million people who have left their homes ostensibly in search of (better) employment at remuneration rates ranging from four times higher (for many highly skilled Yugoslav and Spanish workers) to seventy times higher than those offered at their home labor markets (for those migrants coming from the least developed regions of Turkey and the Maghreb countries). A large part of the responsibility for the dimensions of the problem lies with the frequent failure of labor ex-porters to critically evaluate the overall migration process and adjust their public policies to reflect a more systematic and comprehensive understanding of the phenomenon.

This presentation will focus principally on ex-plaining and assessing the effects of emigration from the perspective of the universe of the suppliers of the European labor needs, particularly those ef-fects which in my estimation are shared, to varying degrees, by most sending countries, regardless of the destination of their emigrating nationals. In fact, and beginning with the underlying assumption that the phenomenon of migration is effected and af-fected by—and subsequently affects—the overall development of a system, I will seek to re-appraise, in a somewhat unorthodox and critical manner, the effects of worker emigration on the development efforts of the countries of migrant origin.

In pursuing this objective, I will utilize the Par-sonian understanding of society as a "structured whole" composed of four analytically distinct, but strongly interdependent, subsystems—the ec-onomic, the cultural, the participational (social), and the political—along which change can be measured. Each of these distinct subsystems (or subcontinua), form one aspect of the multidimen-sional process of development which must comply with the key principle of "congruence," that is, the requirement that development, if it is to be harmo-nious (congruent), must take place rather synchro-nously along all subcontinua, since excessive re-liance on any one of them at the expense of the others will precipitate undue systemic stress and instability.

The economic dimension of emigration has been treated quite adequately by a variety of authors. I will turn my attention to the remaining three subsystems. Accordingly, the points of departure of the present work will be as follows: first, to the extent that a particular actor's culture is approaching the more modern or the more traditional end of the development subcontinuum, and a society's dominant values, belief systems, and relationship patterns alienate specific socioeconomic groups within it, a low level of cultural attachment is encouraged, thus making emigration a viable alternative. A commitment to rational authority, on the other hand, and a move toward the secularization of the perceptive, cognitive, and affective feelings of a people, as well as toward increasingly modern structures, institutions, and orientations, is likely to relieve some of the pressure for emigration—however indirectly—largely as the result of the effect of such orientations on facilitating development along the other subsystems, thus weakening many of the principally economic (but also social and/or political) reasons for emigration [9]

Secondly, the argument about the salience of *social* development for emigration is twofold. First, and in a manner similar to that articulated in regard with cultural development, unless the system attains at least moderate levels of role and structure differentiation (and an increasing degree of functional specificity), the newly mobilized (and already impatient) citizenry will be unable to secure a competent articulative and aggregative channel for its demands. Consequently, this unrelieved pressure, aggravated by the fast rates of poorly planned urban growth and unsystematic developments in the other societal realms, would tend to create an environment conducive to instability. The potential outlet to such frustration is not only aggressive and anomic behavior, but, and principally at a *subconscious* level, emigration. Second, by focusing on frequently articulated hopes (but only feeble efforts) by labor exporters to attract the most qualified among their own emigrants to return, I propose that, again, although economic matters are in the forefront of the migrants' priorities in deciding whether to return, social (and as I intend to argue subsequently, political) considerations are also quite important, although operating in a more indirect manner. Thus, unless measures are taken by labor exporters for the gradual accommodation of the legitimate demands of the newly mobilized[10] members of their societies, returning migrants, presumably already mobilized and with a new—and frequently militant—social and political conscience acquired while abroad, may be perceived by certain segments in the transition societies as a much larger sociopolitical liability than their economic worth.

Thirdly, political development is the last aspect of the multidimensional process of development. Although it cannot be properly advanced as *the* architect of change in all instances, it is an important regulator and guarantor,[11] a crucial sustaining force and a prerequisite for further growth, the tempering and sheltering of the societal infrastructure from extreme instability due to development-fueled strains, and the creating of the structures and institutions, as well as the atmosphere, most amenable to a climate of change. In effect, then, development along the political subcontinuum is a critical factor both in pacing the development of the other realms and providing the framework within which the atrophy (or hypertrophy) of the other subsystems can be averted and corrected. In the final analysis, it is the political plane which is better able to deal successfully with the cyclopean task of containing the cataclysmic effects of economic and social change and ordering further development.

In fact, a sending country's level of political development strongly influences an individual's decision to emigrate as it operates on the manifest (conscious) and latent (semi- and unconscious) levels of one's decision to emigrate, that is, respectively, the economic and the sociocultural-political realms. More specifically, an efficiently run governmental superstructure can be moderately effective in ameliorating participation (mobilization) induced stress,[12] it can encourage and assist in the creation of the technical/administrative infrastructure necessary for further development, particularly in the economic arena. The ensuing economic expansion will tend to create new job opportunities and will presumably absorb many of the un- and underemployed natives, while offering a favorable environment (in social and economic terms) for attracting skilled and semiskilled emigrants back.

The relationship of political development to

emigration, then, though indirect, can be explained as follows. It is highly probable that once a high level of socioeconomic development is attained (a level identifiable from the widening gap in the value of empirically measured indicators between that country, on the one hand, and a group of countries located further below it on the developmental continuum, on the other) the worker outflow valve will gradually be shut. Furthermore, when such a level is approached, a climate is created which provides both sociopsychological disincentives for external migration *and* socioeconomic incentives to return. It is this understanding, then, that dictates that attention be paid to the development problems of the less developed sending societies, and that an effort be made to assess the impact of emigration on each of the developmental planes.

THE COSTS OF THE EMIGRATION PROCESS

The costs of emigration for the sending countries manifest themselves on all four societal subsystems. As I will demonstrate below, the labor suppliers to the relatively controlled European labor markets profit much less from emigration than they expect and decidedly less than the receiving countries. Initially, and to reiterate a point discussed earlier, as a country attains a higher level of socioeconomic development and begins to exhibit an incipient capability to absorb some of its excess labor, uncontrolled emigration would tend to inhibit, and even arrest, substantial and badly needed further economic development and will have the effect of widening the competitive gap (in terms of development, wage differentials, services, and the like) between senders and receivers. Such inhibition of further economic development induces—in a circular manner—additional emigration since only through economic development can the developing actors hope to be able to occupy some of their labor released from agricultural activities.

The process through which such an adverse economic situation evolves is a lengthy one and starts with the first news of the existence of the emigration opportunity, a temptation reinforced by the tales and the conspicuous spending of the visiting emigrants. Feeding on the developing countries'

tendencies toward runaway *astyphilia* and, on the slow expansion of employment in the secondary and tertiary sectors, emigration accelerates the serious output decline in agricultural production.[13]

If emigration claimed only unskilled and unemployed labor, it could have had significant salutary effects for the sending countries—at least from the economic vantage point. The way the system has evolved, however, the advanced industrial societies frequently attract the better educated and qualified and the most dynamic, healthy, and productive part of the less developed countries' population. The deleterious effects of this process on the countries of origin are manifested at various levels. At the first level, as the badly needed and in critically short supply qualified workers (on whose training the sending countries have made an expensive investment) leave their countries, their jobs are taken by less qualified workers. This problem of the hemorrhage of qualified personnel is compounded by the fact that returning workers, by and large (and, in the European case, due to the selective eliminatory procedures of the importers), are the ones with the lower abilities from among those who left. This is a serious extrapolation but one which has been repeatedly documented.[14] In fact, all labor senders are disturbed with the depletion of their meager supplies of qualified personnel and are apprehensive that "the emigration of skilled workers whose education has been paid for by nonemigrants will lower the welfare of the latter group . . . in other words the emigration of recipients of subsidized education will harm nonemigrants."[15] As if to add insult to injury, the chimerical vision of large contingents of trained emigrants returning home after relatively short periods abroad eager to apply their skills and bring about the economic metamorphosis of their mother countries is consistently proving to be just that: chimerical. In reality, and as I have explained above, many of those who return have been trained in tasks which are irrelevant to the home country which usually lacks heavy and advanced industries, while many of the remaining ones, dismayed by the low salaries and social esteem accorded to industrial occupations, simply refuse to take such jobs and reemigrate—legally or illegally.

Neither are the vaunted remittances and transfers of savings the unquestioned panacea they are purported to be. Although they are an excellent source of badly needed foreign currency and play a crucial role in the sending countries' balance of payments equations, some of their economic consequences are rather distressing. Specifically, several studies of emigration to Europe show that remitted or transferred funds are usually expended injudiciously and conspicuously, in a manner that is uneconomical, unproductive, and often wasteful, usually toward the purchase of homes, clothes, and land. Finally, and significantly, remittances may also have an increasingly less favorable effect on the balance of payments, as well as an inflationary impact on the home economies, because they create demand and spending patterns for consumer goods produced abroad. In effect, the inevitable familiarization of the sending societies with foreign products tends to increase their economic and psychological value while simultaneously depressing that of the domestic goods. In a recent empirical study, Nikolinakos reports that the exposure of Greeks to German products (whether directly through the migrants themselves or their remittances) contributed to the remittances playing a decreasing role in counterbalancing the Greek trade deficit.[16]

It is probably obvious that the discussion has gradually shifted away from problems whose character is overwhelmingly economic and into areas fraught with serious *sociocultural* and *political* implications. One such area revolves around the emerging problem of the selective labor shortages experienced by some of the labor exporters (and the subsequent developing of an incipient labor importation flow into such countries), and particularly the sociocultural implications of such a flow. The factors contributing to such a development have already been alluded to. Suffice it to remind ourselves at this point that this unwelcome foreign contingent at the lowest end of the developing states' socioeconomic ladder, virtually ignored by appropriate legislation, carries with it a highly destabilizing potential and introduces these new ''receiving'' countries to some of the problems which face labor importers.

Most of the other sociocultural liabilities of emigration revolve around the individual, the family structure, and demographic considerations. Emigration is directly reponsible for a multitude of sociopsychological traumata, and for the subsequent creation of a class of social pariahs who live suspended between two cultures, leading essentially a very marginal existence at the very fringes of both societies. It also revolutionizes traditional family structures and contributes to the breakdown of authority and decision-making patterns and the alienation of children. Sociocultural changes emigration precipitates contribute to the transformation of society in its totality and in some instances even affect the senders' biological reproduction rates, particularly in areas where the incidence of emigration is heaviest. Frequent visits home or attempts at reintegrating into the mother society by such returnees result in introducing foreign ideas and perhaps unwanted sociocultural and political innovations on the indigenous culture.

Another serious and potentially destabilizing effect of returning emigrants is their contribution to the revolution of aspirations and the radicalizing influences of their imported industrial organization ideas. Indeed, the influx of syndicalist tendencies and freedom of organization, and of political expressionist ideas, are frequently anathema to the largely conservative regimes of the labor suppliers. Returning emigrants, then, present the power strata in their countries with a serious dilemma, in that their potential contributions to the economic development of their countries must be juxtaposed to the radicalization and syndicalist tendencies they surely will impart upon their fellow workers and citizens, thus, straining the sociopolitical infrastructure of the developing politics.

The final area of emigration-related liabilities concerns the demographic consequences of populations that already grow at declining rates and the subsequent sporadic actual declines in net active population, such as in Portugal and Greece, among European labor exporters. Consequently, regional demographic imbalances develop, favoring young children, women, and old people, which contribute to the further depletion of the countryside and the region's economic, social, and cultural deterioration.

THE BENEFITS OF THE EMIGRATION PROCESS

Under the rubric of "benefits" I will dwell briefly on a few rather ancillary advantages of migration and then I will proceed to appraise—in a critical and revisionist manner—two of the purportedly central salutary effects accruing principally to countries which export labor to Europe: the relief of their unemployment and the training of their workers. As has been repeatedly suggested, remittances and transferred savings are usually viewed as two of the more important gains of emigration. I want to reemphasize, however, that both are usually a mixed blessing. Another group of gains revolve around the significant savings accruing to the sending countries in terms of maintaining the unemployed, creating new jobs, and generally relieving some of the pressure in the home labor market and the social welfare infrastructure. A frequently articulated but dubious benefit of emigration is the relative decline in consumption and its attendant effect on easing the inflation pressure.[17] And a final ancillary (and little noticed) "advantage" of emigration is the substantial, though temporary, respite from some of the sociopolitical pressures for an immediate developmental transformation of the home societies into the ranks of the "developed" nations, particularly in sociopolitical terms.

One of the crucial "benefits" to the European labor exporters which remain to be assessed is the degree to which emigration performs one of the functions which are most frequently attributed to it, that is, the relief of unemployment. As European data conclusively demonstrate, however, the effect emigration has on unemployment (and with only the notable exception of Greece, which in 1974 appeared to have controlled the problem of official, registered unemployment) is at least exaggerated. Therefore, and as numerous economic studies have concluded, there is no significant correlation between emigration and unemployment.[18] On the contrary, emigrants are less likely to be unemployed and they can only be effectively replaced by another "elite" labor group, a commodity which countries of emigration have in an extremely short supply.

A last bitterly contested "benefit" of emigration concerns the degree to which, in the words of Böhning, migrant workers from developing countries "undergo an occupational and social apprenticeship in industrialized countries." Böhning states unequivocally that this argument "does *not* stand up to examination."[19] Although such an apprenticeship has been much vaunted, evidence that the expectation has never been fulfilled in the European scene goes back well over a decade.

The reasons for this failure revolve around the empirically confirmed observation that while a few migrants receive occupational training, the overwhelming majority of them are occupied in repetitive tasks whose most significant advantage is that they "train" foreign workers to adapt to the industrial life and rhythm and socialize them in the "achievement oriented behavioral norms of an industrial receiving country,"[20] both necessary prerequisites *but not sufficient factors* for economic development. Many skilled workers do not care to forego their newly found social and economic respectability and are reluctant to return to their home countries; while many of those who do return are unskilled workers, those who are skilled will be confronted with a situation where social and economic conditions at home have not changed substantially, industrial work still carries very low social esteem, wages are inadequate, and their families and children are often looked down upon and are socially ostracized. Such conditions prompt many of the returnees to reemigrate, while many among those who do stay deplete nearly all of their savings in search of socioeconomically acceptable employment. Additionally, it should also be recalled that many of those who return after only a short stay abroad have usually gained very little in terms of skills or industrial attitude, a thing that "effectively precludes the diffusion of innovative economic and cultural patterns from their side."[21] Thus, these returnees are of insignificant assistance to their home countries' efforts at economic development.

In conclusion, the close examination of European migration allows one to legitimately claim that the overall actual gains for the sending countries are only marginal, while the economic gains for the receiving countries are being outweighed by severe social and political strains related directly to the continuous presence of a foreign work force. Migration, then, as it is practiced today, is a less than adequate institution for all participants, both in economic and sociopolitical terms.

POLICY INITIATIVES

In this last part of the presentation, I shall seek to advance a set of proposed policy initiatives designed to reform the present system of European labor emigration and some recommendations on what supplying countries can do to ameliorate the situation.

First, I shall focus on the proposed avenues through which the sending countries can retain some of their *skilled workers* and control and regulate their emigration. At the outset, frequently articulated suggestions that emigration be prohibited should be dismissed as facile "solutions" of demagogue and chauvinists unworthy of serious consideration, as well as in violation of the Universal Declaration of Human Rights. Indeed, emigration has a variety of salutary effects on all development subcontinua which such a policy would deny. The energies of the exporters, then, should be directed toward identifying and improving the conditions which seem to fuel emigration.

Accordingly, and in the economic realm, an employment policy should be developed within the framework of a comprehensive economic and industrial policy. The latter should focus on vigorous programs of balanced regional and sectoral development, particularly of the most depressed areas and areas with a tradition of heavy emigration.

Labor emigration also has social, cultural and political dimensions. Therefore, positive action must be taken to revitalize cities, monitor their growth, and assist them to become trade, communications, and cultural centers in the expectation that such revitalization will also revive adjacent rural communities. In the scenario of such a successful policy, rural towns will attract rural migrants and, in tandem with successful policy of regional economic development, it can provide the means for the rejuvenation of the countryside and relieve some of the socioeconomic pressures for emigration to Western Europe.

Within this regional development policy, incentives must also be offered in an effort to attract internal migrants to return to such areas. Some ways in which they can be effectual are by absorbing relocation costs, encouraging geographic mobility, training, and retooling those who return and, finally, providing them with favorable loans for housing and, in general, augmenting the existing infrastructure so that it not only slows emigration (internal and external) but also attracts emigants back. All such proposals point to the need for a long term and reliable population policy and to the requirement that political initiatives toward this direction be developed. In view of the fact that emigration fails to offer senders most of the expected benefits, a rethinking of the migration system and formulation of new alternatives is imperative.

The second set of recommendations is integrally related to the first one, but focuses on the options open to countries of migrant origin in terms of selectively attracting their emigrants to return. Such a policy should revolve around incentives for the selective repatriation of their nationals and efforts aimed at facilitating the returnees' reintegration into the society's economic, cultural, social and political subsystems. Such policies must begin with active recruitment campaigns among one's nationals while they are still abroad, offering them favorable and not easily breached contracts, and information campaigns about the economic conditions and skills needed at home (even to the point of guaranteeing artificially high wages for certain badly needed specialized skills). Additionally, a plethora of fiscal incentives can be extended to the returnees, ranging from customs relief, preferential terms of currency exchange, free expert investment advice, facilitation of savings transfers, low interest loans, tax credits, preferential treatment for purchases made in badly needed hard currencies, and overall assistance in finding appropriate employment and adequate housing accommodations.[22]

In terms of the reintegration of the repatriates, the most serious problems arise in the sociocultural realm, particularly for the returnees' families, as well as in matters of political expression for the worker. The latter can be channeled through indigenous trade unions, however passive some of them may be. The former requires a concerted effort on the part of the sending governments both abroad and at home. The effort abroad should include the sponsoring of cultural activities and the education of migrant children in their parents' language, history, religion, and traditions. Upon return, an effort should be made to cushion the children from the trauma of maladjustment and allow them a more gradual transition into the home society through intensive special schooling and educational programs.

In conclusion, international migration is ripe for a radical reassessment which *must* involve both sending and receiving countries. The cooperative policies which would emanate from such a reassessment can be implemented within extant regional frameworks, such as the European Communities, the Organization of African Unity, or the Organization of the American States. The incentive for such cooperation is there: how to reform the system of migration so as to maximize the mutual benefits of the process. In view of the discussion in this presentation, migration has failed to address and resolve most of the problems it has been expected to resolve. Furthermore, the institution of illegal migration, which aggravates the problems examined above to an exponential degree, must be effectively addressed—a realization which may make some of the receiving countries more amenable to an international cooperative solution which would by sympathetic to the many problems of the sending societies.

NOTES

1. John M. Goshko, "Europe's New Immigrants," *The Washington Post*, July 28, 1974, p.C1.
2. "The Reserve Labour Army," *The Economist*, August 25, 1973. The passage is fascinating in that it illustrates the facile and shortsighted reasoning of the early exponents of migration. At the same time, the subtlety of the statement serves to underline the irony of the situation.
3. In making this statement I am fully cognizant of the question of whether such an abatement has indeed taken place. Suffice it to stipulate here that, although in need of strong qualifications, the abatement of economically motivated fissures has not been appreciably reversed.
4. The following are the major suppliers of foreign labor to Europe: Portugal, Spain, Italy, Yugoslavia, Greece, Turkey, Algeria, Morocco Tunisia.
5. This discussion has profited from Karl Deutch's exposition on the effects of social mobilization on the societal infrastructure. See his "Social Mobilization and Political Development," *American Political Science Review*, 55 (September, 1961), pp.493–514.
6. Transition is a development condition which exhibits a continuous process of ever shifting blends and mixtures of both tradition *and* modernity. Although all societies are thus transitional, the usage of the term *transition* will be reserved here for the universe of the less developed (or developing) actors. For a discussion of the frequently (but incorrectly) polar concepts of tradition and modernity, see Joseph R. Guiford, "Tradition and Modernity: Misplaced Polarities in the Study of Social Change," in *Political Development and Social Change*, ed. by Jason L. Finkle and Richard W. Gable (New York: John Wiley and Sons, Inc., 1971), pp.15–26.
7. This is a point of considerable intellectual erosion among most students of migration. Although statistics will point out that only a small percentage of the foreign workers are performing skilled duties, the fact remains that although the skill rates of migrants may appear insignificant when compared to those of the advanced industrial systems, for the developing countries they represent a substantial and disproportionate part of a very meager skill reservoir. Additionally, foreign workers are usually assigned—regardless of skills and at least for the first few years—to semiskilled repetitive occupations. A similar problem arises with education. Although the educational levels of migrants are low, they are consistently much higher than the average education attainment of those who remain behind.
8. Italy, Spain, Portugal, Yugoslavia, and Greece are particularly hard hit by this occurrence.
9. See especially Lucian Pye, "Introduction: Political Culture and Political Development," in *Political Culture and Political Development*, edited by Pye and Sidney Verba (Princeton: Princeton University Press, 1965), pp.7–8.
10. See Karl W. Deutsch's seminal work "Social Mobilization and Political Development," *American Political Science Review*, 55 (September, 1961), pp.493–514.
11. Helio Jaguaribe is the strongest advocate of the superordination of the political over the other subsystems. See his *Political Development: A General Theory and A Latin American Case Study* (New York: Harper and Row, 1973), pp.145–57.
12. See Samuel P. Huntington, and especially his idea of institutionalization in "Political Development and Political Decay," in *Political Modernization*, edited by Claude E. Welsh, Jr. (Belmont, California: Wadsworth Publishing Co., Inc., 1967), pp.208, 214–15; and *Political Order in Changing Societies* (New Haven: Yale University Press, 1968), pp.90–93 and *passim*.
13. See Ivo Baucic, "Some Economic Consequences of Yugoslav External Migrations." Paper presented at the *Colloque sur les Travailleurs Immigrés en Europe Occidentale*, Paris, June 5–7, 1974, pp.2–3. Although Baucic's model deals primarily with Yugoslavia it is remarkably applicable to most labor exporters. Also consult Evan Vlachos, "Worker Migration to Western Europe: The Ramifications of Population Outflow for the Demographic future of Greece," International Studies Association, Com-

parative Interdisciplinary Studies Section, Working Paper No.22, July, 1974, p.36.

14. For Yugoslavia, see Baucic, "Some Economic Consequences;" for Greece;, see B. Ch. Sjollena, "Return Migration and Development Aid," *Migration Today,* 5 (December, 1965) pp.14–23; and for Turkey, Duncan Miller and Ihsan Getin, *Migrant Workers, Wages, and Labor Markets* (Istanbul: Istanbul University, Institute of Economic Development, 1974), pp.51–62. The conclusions I have advanced are supported both by ILO estimates ("Migration of Workers as an Element in Employment Policy," December 22, 1973, p.97), and by Madeleine Trébous' superior effort, *Migration and Development: The Case of Algeria* (Paris: DECD, 1970).

15. See R. Albert Berry and Ronald Soligo, "Optimal Wage and Education Policies with International Migration," *Rice University Program of Development Studies,* Paper No. 25, 1972, p.29.

16. See his "Zur Frage der Auswanderungseffekte in dem Emigrationslandern," *Das Argument,* 13, 9–10 (December, 1971), pp.782–99.

17. It is generally estimated that the costs of creating new jobs for potential emigrants would be much higher than the average yearly amount of development aid expended by all advanced states.

18. See S. Paine, *Exporting Workers: The Turkish Case* (Cambridge: Cambridge University Press, 1974), p.123. See also the important collection of articles edited by Ronald E. Krane, *Manpower Mobility Across Cultural Boundaries: Social, Economic and Legal Aspects—The Case of Turkey and West Germany* (Leiden: E. J. Brill, 1975), particularly pp.197–200; also see Böhning, "Mediterranean Workers in Western Europe," p.37.

19. Böhning, "The Social and Occupational Apprenticeship of Mediterranean Migrant Workers in West Germany," in *The Demographic and Social Pattern of Emigration from the Southern European Countries,* ed. by Massimo Livi-Bacci (Firenze: Dipartimento Statistico Matematico, 1972), p.251.

20. See Böhning, "The Social and Occupational Apprenticeship," p. 251, and "Basic Aspects of Immigration and Return Migration in Western Europe," *International Labour Office,* World Employment Program, Migration for Employment Project, Working Paper, July, 1975, WEP 2–26/WP 1, p.29. For an excellent sutdy of the adaptation of foreign workers in the labor receiving countries see Robert Descloîtres, *The Foreign Worker: Adaptation to Industrial Work and Urban Life* (Paris: OECD, 1967).

21. See Krane, "Effects of Cyclical International Composition Migration upon Socio-economic Mobility," *International Migration Review,* 7 (Winter, 1973), pp.427–436; also Kudat, "International Migration to Europe."

22. "S.O.P.E.M.I.," 1974, p.32.

Part 3

Diplomatic/Political Implications of the New Immigration for the U.S. and Other Host Societies

IMMIGRANT FROM MEXICO:
THE SILENT INVASION ISSUE

Jorge A. Bustamante

One of the most widely accepted principles in sociology is that, if men define situations as real, they are real in their consequences.[1] A more vernacular version of this principle is that of "the self-fulfilling prophecy." These principles do not apply to all "prophesies," nor to all "definitions of the situation." An important factor puts at variance the social consequences of people's definitions of the situation. This factor is power.

Considering this factor, it could be postulated that the self-fulfilling social outcome of a "prophecy" varies directly with the magnitude of power of its proponent. A case in point is the definitions of the situation on the undocumented immigration to the United States produced by high government officials.

One such definition, authored by the Commissioner of the U.S. Immigration and Naturalization Service (INS), Leonard F. Chapman, Jr., has been as follows: "This [undocumented immigration] is completely out of control. It's a national dilemma that threatens to worsen rapidly. We're facing a vast army that's carrying out a silent invasion of the United States."[2]

This paper discusses some of the social consequences of definitions of the situation which rise to the social arena endowed with the power of a public office. It is not within the scope of this paper to discuss the sincerity of high government officials in their public statements. It is the purpose of this paper to discuss the extent to which these statements shape social realities that affect the content of social relations.

During the fiscal year that ended in June 1974 the INS located 780,991 undocumented immigrants. Ninety-one percent of these arrests were Mexican citizens. It should be pointed out that this figure was based on arrests not on different individuals, since one could have been arrested several times in one year.[3] Number of arrests of undocumented immigrants by the INS have been increasing at an ap-

proximate rate of 20 to 25 percent per year for the last ten years.[4] It has been recognized by the INS, however, that figures on apprehensions of undocumented immigrants are more a function of manpower and funds available to INS than changes in the number of actual undocumented immigrants in the United States.[5] Nevertheless, few people would doubt that the undocumented immigration involves a large number of people.

The question on the size of undocumented Mexican immigrants becomes relevant for the general public to the extent that an association, real or ideological, is established between their living or working conditions and the presence of undocumented immigrants, outsiders by definition.

The authority attached to the position of the Commissioner of INS becomes the foundation for the credibility of definitions of the situation for the general public. One definition is the magnitude of the situation and the other is the nature of its impact upon the general public. As for the first, Commissioner Chapman further states in February 1975 that there were at least 4 to 5 million, and maybe as many as 10 to 12 million, undocumented immigrants in the United States at that time.[6] As for the nature of its impact upon the American people, the situation is repeatedly defined as being a national crisis and a threat: a silent invasion.

In 1975, General Chapman said to a crowd in Miami: "This is not only an alarming social and economic problem, but one that our service is incapable of dealing with at this time. . . . The population explosion in Latin America is bound to be harmful to the employment picture in Florida."[7]

In this statement an association clearly appears between immigration and a threat to local working conditions. This association precedes General Chapman by almost one hundred years and was made by the nativist groups that harassed the German immigrants;[8] recall the agitation of the Know-Nothing Party and the outbreaks of mob violence against the Irish and the Germans.[9] The association between immigration and a threat to working conditions was also reported on and made by the team of scholars that produced the famous Dillingham Immigration Commission Report in 1911.[10] In some regions of the United States some unions were born making that association.

> The Caucasian and Asiatic races are unassimilable. Contact between these races must result, under the conditions of industrial life obtaining in North America, in injury to the former, proportioned to the extent to which such contact prevails. The preservation of the Caucasian race upon American soil and particularly upon the west shore thereof necessitates the adoption of all possible measures to prevent or minimize the immigration of Asiatics to America.[11]

Historical evidence has been presented[12] on the coincidence between epochs of state of alarm on the part of the general public regarding (1) impact of immigration upon working and living standards, (2) downswings of the economy with high percentages of unemployment, and (3) emergence of restrictive measures against immigration.

In times of high unemployment in the United States such as the current one, a concern for empirical foundations on the part of "official" definers of the immigration situation appears inversely related to the degree of threat imputed to the situation. In spite of a general recognition that statistics on apprehensions produced by INS represent events (the apprehension), and not different individuals, there is a consistant reference to figures on apprehensions as if they were on people:

> Last year the Immigration Service apprehended nearly 80,000 illegal aliens—equal to more than half the population of the City of Houston. Though this was 10 times the number we apprehended just a decade earlier, it was probably no more than one out of four who enter the country illegally; or enter legally as a student or visitor and then simply found a job and stayed here illegally. That means there were probably 3 million illegal additions to our population and work force last year alone. This situation has been growing out of control for several years, and the number of illegal aliens currently here may be as great as 10 or 12 million.[13]

Beyond the ideological implications of such a

case,[14] the point here is that there are sociological implications of a persistence on the part of high government officials in defining the situation as "real." Credibility at the social level has never been conditioned solely by empirical evidence, thus the area of social values becomes of particular importance when situations defined as real become real in their consequences. When a recent report suggests that the percentage of Mexicans in the total of undocumented immigrants might be no more than approximately 60 percent,[15] one could think that the difference between the 91 percent of the total of apprehensions reported for fiscal year 1974, and the real proportion of Mexicans in the total picture of undocumented immigrants, is due to discriminatory social values and certainly to discriminatory practices. If this were the case, statements that involved Mexican immigration which were not supported by empirical evidence would not help to prevent such discrimination from happening, but in fact would do the opposite.

THE DEBATE ON THE LESKO REPORT

The case of the Lesko study is of particular importance in the sociological context of the self-fulfilling prophecy syndrome. In an effort to find objective bases to establish the size of the undocumented immigration to the United States, as well as its impact upon the economy and society of this country, INS announced the availability of one million dollars for contract research on these questions. On October 15, 1975, Lesko Associates of Washington, D.C.,[16] submitted a report entitled, *Final Report: Basic Data and Guidance Required to Implement a Major Illegal Alien Study During Fiscal Year 1976.*

Findings of this report contained two separate estimates of the size of the undocumented immigrant population in the United States. The first estimate, which is presented as "analytically defensible," refers to "the size of the Mexican national segment of the total illegal population," and it is 5,200,000. The second estimate refers to the total of illegal aliens in the U.S. during mid-1975, and it was set at 8,180,000.

The first estimate derived from a formula on a

function of the estimated change in the number of undocumented residents between 1960 and 1970 and a portion of the number of apprehensions during the decade. In other words, the number of undocumented immigrants from Mexico is equal to the number who were in the United States at the beginning of the year, minus those who were caught at some point other than entry, times a constant number.

The second estimate, described as an enlightened, professional estimate, was based on a logical process of consensus from professionals in the business of dealing with the illegal alien problem and, more importantly, who are not officially connected with INS. The Delphi method was used with seven individuals as Delphi panel members. Panelists were asked in three rounds to make estimates as to the number of undocumented workers in the United States.

The close coincidence between the estimates of Lesko Associates, and the figures so widely used by General Chapman in reference to the size of the undocumented immigration, have raised serious questions from at least three sources.

One of these sources was the Director of the U.S. Bureau of the Census, Mr. Vincent P. Barabba. In response to a personal inquiry from Congressman Herman Badillo, Mr. Barabba responded by letter dated December 23, 1975. Sections of this letter seem to be particularly relevant to the discussion presented in this paper:

> In our opinion the estimates of the current illegal alien population shown in the study are based on weak and untenable assumptions, and add very little to our knowledge of the size of the illegal alien population.

> The formula for estimating Mexican illegal immigration for 1970–1975 in the Lesko report is based on the unsupported assumption that illegal immigration is consistently related to the number of aliens apprehended at points other than at entry and that this ratio has remained at the level estimated for the 1960–1970 decade. The estimating formula, complex as it may appear, can be reduced to a function of the estimated change in the number of illegal residents between 1960 and 1970 and a portion of the number of apprehensions during the decade. In effect, this relationship amounts to saying that Mexican illegal immigration is equal to some multiple of the number of Mexican aliens apprehended at other than entry

points. For 1960–1970, this factor was estimated to be 2.1. The same factor was arbitrarily assumed to apply to the 1970–1975 period. Many variables, including increased efficiency of the Immigration Service, can affect the number of apprehensions. These variables may have no effect on illegal immigration or may cause an increase or decrease in illegal immigration.[17]

Some points could be derived from the above quotation: (1) lack of scientific validity of the Lesko report's estimates; (2) lack of reliability of the Delphi method as a basis for quantitative measurement; (3) coincidence in the range of estimates used by Federal and local officials prior to the Lesko report findings and the range of estimates produced by this report; (4) unjustified complexity of a formula based on untenable assumptions for the production of an estimate presented by the authors of the Lesko report.

A study requested by Congressman Badillo and undertaken by researchers with the Congressional Research Service of the Library of Congress was filed as a report entitled, ''Critique of the Estimates of the Number of Illegal Aliens in the United States made by Lesko Associates.'' The conclusions of this report are consistent with the two others cited above.

In spite of the conclusions of these and other studies, Lesko Associates' estimates are still being used by INS officials as basis for a further definition of the situation in regard to both the Mexican and the total undocumented immigration population.[18] Indeed, the Lesko report became a source of validation of estimates previously used by the Immigration and Naturalization Service. A study which was made in the name of science became a source of social legitimacy for a *fait acompli*, namely, a previously made definition of the size of illegal immigration to the United States. The Immigration and Naturalization Service's continued use of the Lesko study findings after being notified of other studies questioning its scientific validity could be conceived as a case of what Francis Bacon called ''seeking legitimacy by appeal to authority.'' This is certainly a case for the sociology of knowledge in as much as it involves a process of a social construction of reality from a basis of power rather than facts.

In this process several elements and actions appear combined. First, the magnitude of power corresponding to a federal official in relation to either access or visibility for mass media communications. Second, the degree of legitimate authority attached to actions within the jurisdiction of a given governmental office. Third, the action of defining a situation as real for the general public. Fourth, asking a selected group of recipients of the previously made definition of the situation to describe that situation in the absence of other sources of information. Fifth, attaching the notion of science to the answers of a selected group produced in the absence of other data than what included the authority's definition of the situation. Sixth, achieving social legitimation for actions designed for goals that were born in advance and in correspondance to those for third.

The goals referred to in the latter point could be inferred from a remark reportedly made by President Ford to representatives of a Texas mass media network on April 22, 1976 (according to a note of the United Press International published in Mexico by the newspaper *El Dia*). The translation from Spanish of the words quoted from President Ford by this source is as follows: "The main problem is how to get rid of those 6 to 8 million of aliens who are interfering with our economic prosperity."

There is no doubt that the figure of 6 to 8 million has stuck in the minds of a great number of people in the United States, including the President. What is important about an apparent concensus on a believed size of the undocumented immigration is not only that it has remained in spite of evidence of its lack of foundation; what is important is the social effect of a self-fulfilling prophecy.

The role of the Lesko report in fulfilling the prophecy should not be underestimated. It provided a touch of legitimacy by appeal to a socially recognizable notion of science. The use of the Delphi technique by Lesko Associates seems, from the cited criticisms, like a *rite de passage* of magic connotations, one in which an original definition of the situation appears as being approved by the oracles with a sacred stamp of science. If it had been reported as it was, that statistics on apprehensions were not on people but on events[19] and, therefore, there was no statistical base to speak about the size of the undocumented immigrants population, how was it that INS accepted the results derived from the Delphi technique? What in fact this technique involved, in the case of its use by Lesko Associates, was (1) the public was given a judgment on the nature and size of a particular problem (undocumented immigration) by a legitimate authority; (2) there were no other data sources available to check that judgment; (3) a selected group of that public who had heard that judgment was asked their educated opinion on the size of the problem; (4) that selected group reproduced, in the absence of other information, what they had heard from the news media as an accepted estimate, that is, the original definition of the situation.

Another important factor of the Lesko report in fulfilling a prophecy was their use of "a complex formula" to arrive at their estimates on the Mexican undocumented immigration. According to the devastating criticisms, particularly that from a detailed analysis of the formula made by Daniel Melnick of the Congressional Research Service, that "complex formula" seems also more like an exorcism than a scientific procedure.

From those criticisms cited above it could be argued that the persistent acceptance of the Lesko findings, however preliminary, is not based on a social framework of knowledge based on science; rather, it is based on another framework of knowledge, perhaps magic.

Coming back to the social effect of a self-fulfilling prophecy, some reference will be made now to the social effects on attitudes and behavior of a generally accepted definition of the undocumented immigration situation.

The National Socialist White People's Party issued and distributed in the streets of San Diego (during the third week of April 1976) a leaflet which read:

STOP ILLEGAL ALIENS! Every month thousands of illegal aliens pour into San Diego County. TAKING YOUR JOBS! SPENDING YOUR TAX DOLLARS! USING YOUR PUBLIC SERVICES! SENDING THOUSANDS OF DOLLARS BACK INTO MEXICO! IF YOU KNOW WHERE THEY WORK, IT IS YOUR DUTY TO REPORT IT TO THE IMMIGRATION DEPARTMENT OR BORDER PATROL. IF YOU WANT TO WORK FOR WHITE

AMERICA JOIN US! National Socialist White People's Party (The address for the National Headquarters in Washington and for the San Diego Unit are included in the leaflet.]

The point is not how representative this view is among the general public. It is unquestionable that both the U.S. government and the American public at large have demonstrated historically their rejection of nazi ideological premises. The point is the association made between some of the definitions provided and frequently cited by INS officials, such as taking your jobs, spending your tax dollars, and so forth, and an extremist ideology. Certainly, INS could not be blamed for this association. But it could be blamed for insisting on those definitions in spite of reports that counter them.

A recent study, made under the direction of David North and released by the Department of Labor, reported that, contrary to a general belief, Mexican illegal aliens receive wages that average $2.33 an hour.[20] It should be pointed out that approximately 54 percent of Mexican aliens apprehended are expelled before they are able to find a job, according to our own research and according to INS statistics on apprehensions. North's study also finds that the majority of the undocumented immigrants pay taxes and social security; however, they do not benefit from them to the extent, or near to it, of their contribution.

As for the effects of official definitions of the situation on behavior, it should be pointed out that the Mexican Consulate of San Diego has reported the increasing practice of assaults by groups of juveniles against Mexican undocumented immigrants as they enter surreptitiously into the United States. According to the Mexican Consulate authorities, a characteristic of these assaults is that the attack is accompanied with racist remarks and insults to Mexico and the Mexicans.

The phenomenon of the undocumented immigration from Mexico derives basically from two interrelated factors: a demand for cheap labor in the United States, and trends of unemployment, underdevelopment, poverty, and population in Mexico. In the absence of the factors produced by any one of the two countries, the phenomenon would not exist. This means that no solution will be reached by

unilateral measures taken by only one of the countries. This also means that whatever measure is taken by one country without taking into account the intervening factors from the other side of the border will not only maintain the unsolved problem but may worsen it. The international interrelatedness of the problem also means that any realistic solution to the problem could come only from a binational approach to it. Finally, this means, that the maintenance of the effects of unfounded definitions of the situation will not help prepare a public atmosphere in which international negotiations could achieve more than mutual accusations.

NOTES

1. This principle was first developed by W. J. Thomas in *The Child in America: Behavior, Problems and Programs* (New York: Alfred A. Knopf, 1928), p.81.
2. L. H. Whittemore, "Can We Stop the Invasion of Illegal Aliens?" *South Bend Tribune*, 29 February 1976. The author quotes Commissioner Chapman.
3. Julian Samora, *Los Mojados: The Wetback Story* (South Bend: University of Notre Dame Press, 1971), p.87.
4. U.S. House of Representatives, Ninety-fourth Congress, First Session, Report No.94–506, September 24, 1975, p.4.
5. Op. cit., p.5.
6. U.S. House of Representatives, Report No.94–506, p.5.
7. *New York Times*, Sunday, 21 December 1975, p.27.
8. John Higham, *Strangers in the Land: Patterners of American Nativism, 1860–1925* (New Brunswick, New Jersey: Rutgers Hall, 1970).
9. Isaac Hourwich, *Immigration and Labor* (New York: G. P. Putnam, Sons, 1912), p.73.
10. U.S. Senate Immigration Commission, *Reports of the Immigration Commission* (Washington, D.C.: U.S. Government Printing Office, 1911).
11. Ibid., Vol.23, p.170.
12. Jorge A. Bustamante, "Espaldas Mojadas: Materia Prima para la Expansión del Capital Norteamericano," *Cuadernos del CES* (México: El Colegio de México, 1975).
13. Vernon Brigs, "Illegal Migration Turning into a Human Onslaught," *Houston Chronicle*, Sunday, 16 February 1976, section 3, p.25. The author is quoting General Leonard F. Chapman, Jr.
14. See Jorge A. Bustamante, "Structural and Ideological Conditions of the Mexican Immigration to the United States," *American Behavioral Scientist*, 19, No.3 (January–February 1976), pp. 364–376.
15. David North and Marion F. Houston, "Illegal Aliens: Their Characteristics and Role in the U.S. Labor Market," unpublished "executive summary," (Washington, D.C.: Department of Labor, 1976).
16. Lesko Associates, a consulting firm signed Contract No.CO–16–75 with the Office of Planning and Evaluation of INS.
17. Mimeographed copy of a letter from Mr. Vincent P. Barabba to Congressman Badillo of December 23, 1975. It

is mentioned in the letter that a copy was sent to Mr. Leonard F. Chapman, Jr., Commissioner, Immigration and Naturalization Service.

18. See "U.S. Job Market Pinched by Alien Trespassers," in *U.S. News & World Report,* January 26, 1976, p.84.

19. Julian Samora, *Los Mojados: The Wetback Story,* Appendix Two.

20. North and Houston, op. cit.

THE IDEOLOGY OF COLONIALISM: EMIGRATION AND NEO-MALTHUSIANISM IN CONTEMPORARY PUERTO RICAN SOCIETY

Manuel Maldonado-Denis

Let us proceed from an incontestable demographic fact which Dr. José Luis Vázquez Calzada, one of our most distinguished demographers, describes for us as "one of the largest population exoduses registered by contemporary history." The magnitude of this exodus can be seen in the following statistics: between 1898 and 1944, approximately 90,000 people emigrated from Puerto Rico to the United States. During the 1940s, 150,000 Puerto Ricans emigrated; in the 1950s, 400,000. This leads Vázquez Calzada to claim that by adding the number of children who would have been born to the total number of emigrants (had they remained on the island) we arrive at the conclusion that, between 1940 and 1960, the Island lost approximately one million people as a result of mass emigration.[1] At the same time, Vázquez Calzada indicates that, during the 1950s, 70 percent of the emigrants were between the ages of 15 and 39.

We are clearly dealing with a massive emigration, in spite of the fact that some 50,000 Puerto Ricans returned to Puerto Rico during the 1950s, and 253,212 during the 1960s. During this same period 586,636 Puerto Ricans emigrated to the United States, leaving a net emigration balance of 253,212 in the 1960s.[2] These figures mean that in the period from 1945 to today, more than a half million Puerto Ricans have emigrated to and settled in the metropolis. This helps explain why there are, conservatively speaking, a grand total of one and a half million Puerto Ricans on United States soil, a figure that could be expanded to two million if we consider the fact that third generation emigrant *boricuas* should be counted as well. If one-third of the Puerto Rican population is found outside of the national territory, this has profound consequences not only for the destiny of Puerto Rico as a Spanish-speaking country but also for the development of the struggle for independence and socialism.

The cultural as well as the political consequences resulting from these demographic changes demand our most careful attention. First of all, it is necessary to study how the Puerto Rican ruling class has perceived the emigrant exodus as well as the solutions they have tried to implement. In the same vein, we are interested in knowing the rationalizations of the ruling class concerning an alleged "necessity" for the exodus. In other words, once we have examined the historical-structural transformations that have produced and reproduced the emigration problem, we may then examine the arguments used by the defenders of the colonial-capitalist mode of production when these defenders try to offer *their* conception of the causes and effects of emigration.

We must begin with what might be called the ideology (using the term in its Marxist sense) of those who judge that Puerto Rican emigration has been something "inevitable": that Puerto Ricans have emigrated in great numbers to the United States because of prospects of better and fuller horizons in the heart of a new "promised land." According to this thesis, the emigration has been purely voluntary since Puerto Ricans, rather than having been forced to emigrate, have done so in the exercise of their own free will. Given this reality, one has to accept as a *fait accompli* that there are no alternatives given the smallness of the Island, its population density, and its high rate of unemployment and underemployment. In other words, for the ideologues of mass emigration this is essentially a remedy—disagreeable but necessary—for solving other social problems of great importance that afflict us. Perhaps the best example of what we mean is to be found in an editorial in the newspaper *El Nuevo Día* (February 27, 1974), where many of the points of view just expressed are brought together and the "inevitability" of Puerto Rican emigration is accepted. Although this newspaper represents the position of the Partido Nuevo Progresista, its criteria transcend party lines and form part of a world view prevalent among the class that clings to colonial power in Puerto Rico:

> In short and long terms, the most serious problem of Puerto Rico is its somber population density. Judging from the declarations of Secretary of Natural Resources, Cruz A. Matos, in a symposium held at the University of Puerto Rico, the population density of our island is presently 875 people per square mile, resulting in a total population of 2,905,625 in comparison with the 2,712,033 inhabitants which was the official figure of the Federal census of April, 1970. Taking these figures as a base, we can calculate that in 1980 our island will have 3,200,000 inhabitants.
>
> One will therefore see that since Puerto Rican life already demands more living space, one will have to look for a livelihood in the lands of promise of the American world. The problem also raises the inescapable obligation of preparing the Puerto Rican with the necessary working and professional skills and with the command of other languages, so that he might make a living and progress economically and competitively in the new lands.
>
> The lands which attract are, of course, those of the United States of America, where we can advantageously develop in the economic, social and political orders, because we're already citizens, and the advantage will be greater if in our schools we include not only the command of English, but also the acquisition of disciplines with high economic yield.
>
> And other lands of promise might also be immense Brazil or any other country of South or Central America.
>
> Concurrently, and as a fixed policy of all our governments, we are obliged to increase the island's production on all levels, as an imperative patriotic duty.
>
> As we see it, it will be an inevitable exodus, and many Puerto Ricans will have to get used to carrying their small homeland, as Gautier Benitez would say "like the memory of a profound love," in their nostalgia and affection and to giving practical application to the Latin aphorism *ubi bene, ibi patria*—wherever one is well, there too is the homeland.

The principal ideological mouthpiece of the other colonial party, the Partido Popular Democrático, tells us the same thing with even greater impudence. Reference is here made to that ineffable homonym of Chile's *El Mercurio,* San Juan's *El Mundo,* which on June 22, 1975, editorialized:

> We Puerto Ricans ought to be profoundly concerned with the arisen change in the migratory tendency. Contrary to what has been going on for decades, more of our countrymen are returning to the Island than leaving it.
>
> In the face of this turn of events which characterizes today's migratory movement, the importance of the massive exodus of Puerto Ricans to the United States, particularly in the 1950's and 1960's, becomes even more significant for us than before. Those who return find many jobs and aggravate the unemployment problem in the country. Now that these brothers are returning perhaps we'll be able to see, in all its crude reality, the enormous, snowballing problem of overpopulation that we are faced with in this small piece of land we call Puerto Rico.
>
> There are almost two million Puerto Ricans in the United States, of whom many will return to the Island sooner or later. It is easy to imagine what would occur if all those Puerto Ricans who live in the United States decided to return to Puerto Rico. *And it is easy to calculate what would have happened with our progress if they had never abandoned the Island to go to the United States in search of work.*
>
> We are already more than three million here. And another two million over there. From the human and ecological points of view, Puerto Rico is rapidly becoming a place where one won't be able to live.

This thesis is representative of a whole conception of the economic development of Puerto Rico within the context of its relation to the United States and has been endorsed on multiple occasions by the Administrator of Fomento Económico (Economic Development), Mr. Teodoro Moscoso. Nevertheless, Mr. Moscoso has been more explicit than the editors of *El Nuevo Día* and *El Mundo,* and in several published declarations (*El Mundo,* April 4, 1974) seeks to tie the emigration problem to the variables of unemployment and a high birth rate. Therefore, in the quoted dispatch, Mr. Moscoso admits that the rate of unemployment is officially 12 percent, although the real rate could be as high as 30 percent. But the problem of unemployment, he adds, will not be solved if something is not done to control birth rates in Puerto Rico. Here, then, is the complement of Puerto Rican emigration: population control. Both phenomena march hand in hand as part of the strategy designed by Fomento Económico for the development of Puerto Rico.

What has been quoted thus far could be taken as a simple position of a newspaper or of a public functionary. But when we receive a report from a subcommittee of the governor of Puerto Rico about "work, educational and training opportunities," signed by Dr. Luis Silva Recio, Secretary of Labor; Mr. Teodoro Moscoso, Administrator of Fomento Económico; Dr. Ramón A. Cruz, Secretary of Public Education; Dr. Amador Cobas, President of the University of Puerto Rico; and technicians of the Planning Board and Department of the Budget, we face a very different kind of reality. We are dealing with nothing less than a statement about the standards that should guide the government of the "Free Associated State" in matters such as employment and education. The report, submitted to the governor in November 1973, could not be more explicit in its conclusions and recommendations:

We can conclude from the lessons of history of the last decades that: (1) the unemployment problem has been, continues to be and will be for many years one of the fundamental economic problems of Puerto Rico; (2) the government has tried to solve the unemployment problem through the creation of the most jobs possible and, indirectly, through the reduction of the working force, making a limited and a bit concealed effort to reduce the birth rate; (3) the emigration of the unemployed who voluntarily have decided to leave, has constituted the *escape valve* that has prevented unemployment from acquiring catastrophic proportions. The projections of the Planning Board, based on the natural growth of population, emigration and rates of participation, state that the annual growth of the work force will average 28,000 people annually from 1975 to 1985. Therefore, if we want to reach our goal of 5 percent unemployment here in 1985, we will have to substantially change the present tendencies with respect to supply and demand of jobs. In order to achieve this, the government will have to draw up a plan of action that will produce a reduction in job demand by means of a series of measures related to: (1) a migration program that results in a lesser influx of people returning to Puerto Rico and possibly a greater flow out of Puerto Rico; (2) an active program of keeping the greatest possible number of young people in the school system. The birth control program, which is also urgent and necessary, would come to have an effect on the work force after 1985.[3]

We should note the term "escape valve" in the present context. It obviously has to do with a simile whose reference point seems to be a pressure cooker about to explode. The pressure cooker in question is Puerto Rico, which threatens to blow up because of an excess of accumulated steam (the population). The escape valve (emigration) will go on being the antidetonator. But emigration alone is not enough. It is also necessary to reduce population growth as much as possible.

In the quoted report, we are given the following statistics: of the 485,948 women of child-rearing age in Puerto Rico, excepting the municipality of San Juan, 160,365 are sterilized. This leaves a "potential clinetele" of 325,585 women, of whom approximately 75,000 are already taking advantage of the medical and contraceptive services of the Department of Health and the Puerto Rican Association of Family Welfare. In the same report, we discover that "almost 33 percent of the female population of child-rearing age are sterilized." But this, apparently, is not enough since we have seen that it is still necessary to sterilize the "potential clientele" mentioned before.

In order to implement this plan, the government of the "Commonwealth of Puerto Rico" has created a subsecretaryship in charge of "Family Planning" presently headed by Dr. Antonio Silva Iglesias.

Dr. Silva Iglesias has taken up his charge as supreme "family planner" of Puerto Rico with the fervor of a crusader. According to his plans there ought to be established a minimum of 25 voluntary sterilization centers throughout the island, in each of which "in principle would be performed a total of 10 sterilizations per week." Dr. Silva Iglesia's goal is the sterilization of some 5,000 Puerto Rican women a month, with the eventual objective of arriving at zero population growth. In his own words, the Family Planning program "has as its chief objective the reduction of the rate of population growth so as to bring about a better socioeconomic balance. Toward those ends and voluntarily, the program will provide medical and educational services offered to reduce the birth rate so as to result in zero population growth."[4] With respect to the criteria for carrying out the sterilizations, there is only the consent of the patient. But Dr. Silva has a more ambitious goal. According to him, up to now sterilization has been a costly surgical operation, which explains why 70 percent of sterilized women are in high income brackets. Therefore, the Family Planning program is interested in the poor women of Puerto Rico or, in Dr. Silva's words, "It seems to me that a person of limited resources and of a large family ought to be sterilized."[5] There is no need to go on. We are dealing with a neo-Malthusian plan directed towards the massive sterilization of proletarian and peasant Puerto Rican women.

But nothing reveals better the mentality of the director of Family Planning than his perception of the need for these sterilization programs for the Cuban exiles in Puerto Rico whose total number is estimated at some 50,000. With his typical candor, Dr. Silva Iglesias affirmed: "The Cuban Immigration has not been dangerous in economic terms because those who have arrived from Cuba for the most past are well educated. *The return of the Puerto Ricans living in the United States would indeed be dangerous.* And presently, more Puerto Ricans are settling in the Island than in the United States."[6]

We have come full circle. We are again faced with Puerto Rican emigration with a twist: it is now seen as a "danger" because our countrymen are deciding to return to their homeland. Clearly, once again here is the inextricable relation between emigration, unemployment, overpopulation, and birth control, all seen, not as an isolated social phenomenon, but rather as integral parts of that "organic totality" which is Puerto Rican society in the twentieth century.

As you can see, the "escape valve" is not sufficient as an antidote for the "population explosion." It is also necessary that the emigrants do not return to Puerto Rico. In other words, and in order to continue with the use of "explosive" images, it is a matter of hurling out of the national territory thousands and thousands of Puerto Ricans—the immense majority of whom are unemployed—with the vigilant and, as we have seen, expressed hope that they will never again return to settle on Puerto Rican soil. Further, it is not just that proletarian and peasant Puerto Ricans should go to the metropolis, but also that the Puerto Rican people should stop growing demographically until said growth is reduced to zero. As the reader will see, this represents an inverted causality, which claims that the existing

unemployment in Puerto Rico does not rest on the structural changes which have taken place in the Puerto Rican economy during the last thirty-odd years, but rather is the primary effect of excessive population growth. And for great ills are prescribed great cures. We will wipe our massive unemployment through massive emigration and massive sterilization. These are cures which obviously mean that Malthus' ghost has been revived by the ideologues of imperialism in order to try to ward off the prevailing presence of Marx.

In truth, the Puerto Rican ideologues of massive emigration and neo-Malthusianism repeat plainly and simply the known arguments related to the "world population explosion" and its catastrophic consequences. Catastrophic, to be sure, for the capitalist countries like the United States which represents only 5 percent of the world population while enjoying more than 50 percent of the earth's wealth. But there is more. We are referring to an entire ideology dealing with the causes of economic antidevelopment and development which is none other than W. W. Rostow's well-known thesis of the stages of economic growth. When one outlines this thesis with all its corollaries, the ideologues of colonial capitalism speak of Puerto Rico as if it were an industrially developed country and they therefore refuse to see us as part of the exploited and underdeveloped peoples of the Third World. But, at the same time, they find themselves forced to admit that this economic growth is not self-sustaining and that their plans for economic development depend on the massive influx of foreign capital attracted by the lure of tax exemptions, low salaries, and an abundant labor supply. When this influx is paralyzed, the false development will become paralyzed as well.

We consider it essential to point out that such arguments are not only fatalistic but also false. We see this at both the global and national levels. First let us look at the problem from the point of view of our national reality.

According to the prophets of fatalism, our society is eternally condemned to underdevelopment and poverty. Our only salvation is thus found in population control, emigration, and the importation of capital because we are a small country, overpopulated, and lacking in natural resources. Given this inflexible reality, all we can do is resign ourselves to our fate and increase more and more our dependence on North American capitalism. It is of little importance that desposits of copper and other minerals have been discovered with a value approximated in billions of dollars; that there is evidence of the existence of petroleum in our subsoil; or that we have an exceptional future in the technological exploitation of agriculture, especially sugar cane. None of this is important to those who still repeat that we lack natural resources and that we are small and overpopulated.

It is clear that Puerto Rico has a high population density. But population density is not automatically the primary determinant of poverty and unemployment. Compare the population densities of Haiti and Holland. We will immediately see that Haiti is an underdeveloped country with a low population demnsity, while Holland is a highly industrialized capitalist country with a high population density. The difference between the two is not to be found simply in population density but in the economic bases of development of both countries. The ideologues of neo-Malthusianism are thus forced to look for new arguments when confronted with these realities. What they overlook—very conveniently of course—is the essential difference between the development of the rich capitalist countries and the antidevelopment from which the poor countries of the Third World systematically suffer.[7]

Seen in this way, the problem presented acquires other secret dimensions for neo-Malthusianism. The root of Puerto Rico's unemployment and underdevelopment ought to be found in the relationship between the colonial society, the capitalist metropolis, and the capitalist division of world labor. The definitive bankruptcy of *Fomento* is nothing more than the culmination of the bankruptcy of a strategy for development whose fragile foundations gave way as soon as the first serious crisis of world capitalism occurred after the Great Depression.

We would be shortsighted, nevertheless, if we lost sight of the global character of neo-Malthusianism as the ideology and strategy of imperalism in its growing confrontation with the raw material producing countries of the Third World which today claim control of their natural resources.[8] The same thing can be said for the strategy of North American monopoly capital which seeks to limit population growth of those they call "national minorities," that is, Blacks, Puerto Ricans, Chicanos, and others *within its national boundaries*. All this forms part of the world view which the ideologues of imperialism have with respect to worldwide counterrevolution. Puerto Rico is one chip more on the table, but an important chip.

Actually, the neo-Malthusian thesis in its various versions is a prescription for attempting to detain the international revolutionary process. Just as Malthus himself would have done in his day, this ideology is directed against population growth and what this growth represents as revolutionary potential.

The ideologues of emigration and neo-Malthusianism in Puerto Rico identify with the bourgeoisie of the capitalist countries and express in the same way the class antagonisms that underlie said ideology. The Puerto Rican intermediary bourgeoisie wants to continue profiting from its privileged relationship—notwithstanding a subordinate one—with the metropolis by promoting the exportation of a cheap labor force while it goes on to cut the fallopian tubes of an ever increasing number of Puerto Rican women. With these measures they hope to ward off the crisis which becomes deeper every day.

Nothing said so far here should be interpreted as meaning that we oppose family planning under no uncertain terms. What we do oppose is that such planning utilize the most irreversible and drastic method of all, that of massive sterilization, as a kind of panacea for all social problems. Seen properly, true family planning ought to be conceived as part of worldwide social planning. From this point of view, this kind of planning is not only not in conflict with socialism, but, in fact, it can only be implemented within the bounds of a socialist society. It is precisely in a society such as ours, where true social planning does not exist, that family planning acquires the Orwellian characteristic of being the direct opposite of what its name suggests. That is why the apocalyptic prophets of the population catastrophe.[9] In fact, the most recent scientific analyses completely invalidate the interpretation mentioned above. Demographic growth must be seen in its fullest context in a *human society*.

This is the focus which ought to prevail among the apostles of the improperly titled "Family Planning'' in Puerto Rico. But that would be too much to ask of those who are bound to the imperialist world view of demographic growth.

The ideologues of neo-Malthusianism and massive emigration have attempted to offer rationalizations for the social practices which they commit against Puerto Rican integrity. The system itself, whose flagrant injustices they attempt to cover up, is passing through the most profound crisis of its history. In this context, colonialist ideology becomes shrill and hysterical. Having lost the bases of its spurious legitimacy, these ideologues are not left with any other recourse but to appeal to naked power and brute force. They are not yet capable of sweetening the pill. Reality does not permit this. Now they are limited to justifying the unjustifiable as a last resort born of desperation. These are the bitter fruits of the ideologues of a system in economic, moral, and spiritual bankruptcy like the one in which it has fallen to the lot of us Puerto Ricans to live in this historic moment.

NOTES

1. José Luis Vázquez Calzada, ''La Emigración Puertorriqueña: Solución o Problema,'' *Revista de Ciencias Sociales,* 8, No.4 (December 1963).
2. José Hernández Alvarez, *Return Migration to Puerto Rico* (University of California, 1967). Also, Vázquez Calzada, ''Aspectos Demográficos de la Emigración,'' (manuscript). For the study of the return to Puerto Rico, see also the recent study by Celia Fernández de Cintrón and Pedro Vales Hernández, *Return Migration to Puerto Rico* (Centro de Investigaciones Sociales, University of Puerto Rico, 1974).
3. Informe del Subcomité del grupo de trabajo del Gobernador Area I, *Oportunidades de Empleo, Educación y Adiestramiento* (November 1973), p.65 (manuscript).
4. *El Mundo,* 20 April 1974.
5. *Avance,* 10 June 1974, p.15.
6. Ibid., p.16.
7. I use the term ''antidevelopment'' in this context following the felicitous conception of Héctor Malavé Matta when he describes it as that ''incessant superficial metamorphosis of prolonged colonization.'' Héctor Malavé Matta, *Formación histórica del antidesarrollo en Venezuela* (Havana: Casa de las Américas, 1974).
8. This preoccupation, just like the new imperialist strategy to confront the demands of the Third World, can be seen in Secretary of State Kissinger's speech before the U.N. on September 2, 1975 (*New York Times,* 2 September 1975). See also Jose Consuegra Higgins, *El control de la natalidad como arma del imperialismo* (Buenos Aires: Galerna, 1969).
9. We should now add to the list of apocalyptic prophets Professor Juan Sánchez Viera, fiery ideologue of the population catastrophe. But no one overlooks, of course, the epitome of the Family Planners, Dr. Silva Iglesias. In some of his recent declarations, the delirious context of which cannot escape the careful reader, he says: ''If Puerto Rico's population growth is not controlled to a substitute population rate, population density will reach a crisis of such magnitude as is only contemplated in the novels of science fiction. It is well known by behavioral psychologists that *when experimental animal populations* are confined in limited areas, a marked antisocial behavior develops among them, such as cannibalism, low tension resistance, homosexuality, and other problems. This experience could well be what we are beginning to see in our society,'' *El Mundo,* 22 July 1975. Note the analogy between the animal and social world and that the speaker is the Associate Secretary of Health for Family Planning.

GREEK-AMERICANS AND THE TURKISH AID ISSUE
1974–75

Sallie M. Hicks and Theodore A. Couloumbis

In July 1974, a coup d'etat planned and supported by the Greek military junta under Dimitrios Ioannides led to the temporary downfall of Archbishop Makarios, the President of Cyprus. Turkey, arguing that the Turkish-Cypriot community (18 percent of the population) was in danger, and looking for an opportunity to expand its own presence on the island, decided to intervene militarily. The net result of two massive Turkish strikes in July and August 1974 was a refugee population of approximately 210,000: 180,000 Greek Cypriots and over 30,000 Turkish Cypriots. The Turkish army—40,000 strong—occupied 40 percent of Northern Cyprus.

The Greek-American community in the United States was swift in responding to the plight of the Greek Cypriots. Concern was expressed over two issues: help for the refugees, and U.S. military aid to Turkey. Attention was focused primarily upon Turkey's second strike which was labelled as aggressive and morally reprehensible. Greek Americans pointed out that Turkey had used U.S. military arms and supplies, although U.S. laws prohibit the use of U.S.–supplied arms and equipment by NATO member nations for purposes other than self-defense, internal security, or collective arrangements consistent with the United Nations Charter.

What ensued over the next year was a heated and continuing debate between some members of Congress and the Executive. Congress, contending that American arms had been used illegally, favored a military arms embargo against Turkey until progress toward a peaceful settlement of the Cyprus issue could be demonstrated. Congressional action promoting such an embargo was initiated in September 1974, and an arms embargo took effect on February 5, 1975. The Executive, fearful that Turkey might take offense and withdraw from NATO, countered that a continuation of the arms flow to Turkey was necessary in order to provide the U.S. with "leverage" during peace negotiations. Fur-

ther, the administration counseled against congressional involvement in tactical (day-to-day) applications of U.S. foreign policy and warned against congressional restrictions motivated by Greek-American ethnic pressures.

AMERICAN PRESS REACTION

The American media, particularly the press, followed the congressional-executive debate over the Turkish arms embargo with interest. Views expressed in the columns and editorials of the major northeast newspapers (*Baltimore Sun*, *Christian Science Monitor*, *New York Times*, *Washington Post*, and *Washington Star News*) seemed to echo the administration line: downplaying questions of morality and legality in favor of political "realism" and national interest. Turkey, the argument ran, was militarily more strategic and vital to NATO than was Greece. Congress was pictured as the willing victim of a small but potent Greek-American "lobby." Greek Americans were portrayed as "emotional," "abusive," and "relentless," and they were accused of damaging not only U.S. national interest but also Greek national interest. One columnist labeled the "ethnic foreign policy-making" which culminated in the decision to ban arms to Turkey as a "rising menace" tantamount to communism in its potential destabilization of U.S. foreign policy.

It is quite possible that the press, by bringing Greek-American ethnics into the limelight, lent the so-called Greek lobby a certain legitimacy and *perceived* potency in the eyes of the public that was and is most likely beyond their *actual* strength. It is more likely that timing, the merits of the issue, Greek-American support, and a large number of other variables worked in combination to sway the Congress.

Two aspects of Greek-American influence were examined in order to shed light upon this controversial question of Greek-American impact on United States foreign policy. They were Greek-American potential for influencing policy decisions and Greek-American effectiveness in influencing policy decisions. How pervasive were Greek-American ethnic networks, and what types of channels were used to voice political concern for the Cyprus issue? What correlations, if any, were there between the numbers and percentages of Greek-American constituents and congressional voting patterns?

GREEK-AMERICAN ETHNIC NETWORKS

It is possible to trace ethnic reactions to the Cyprus situation at three different levels of organizational sophistication ranging from the informal (religion and kinship) to the formal (special purpose groups that consciously use "ethnicity" and ethnic symbols to draw support).

Religion

The Greek Orthodox Church in the United States is perhaps the most important informal ethnic channel. Religion and ethnicity are virtually synonymous among Greeks, and the organizational structure of the Greek Orthodox Church in the United States is such that "grass roots" support can be harnessed quickly and effectively. When questions first arose concerning the morality and legality of continuing U.S. military aid to Turkey, it was the priests, in their dual role as preservers of the religious tradition and guardians of Hellenism, who began using their sermons to rouse the Greek-American communities to action. Money for Greek-Cypriot refugee relief was collected during services, and petitions urging U.S. congressmen and senators to impose a military embargo on Turkey were circulated among the congregations.

The administration was not unaware of the role and position of the Archbishop of North and South America and his staff. In October 1974, Secretary of State Henry Kissinger attempted to convince the Archbishop that the Greek government was not adverse to the continuation of the U.S. arms flow to Turkey. Had Kissinger's effort to "reinterpret" the issue and channel it through the Archbishop succeeded, it is safe to assume that a critical rift within

the Greek-American community would have developed over the interpretation of the Turkish aid issue.

National Ethnic Organizations

National ethnic organizations can be thought of as semiformal networks. The American Hellenic Educational Progressive Association (AHEPA) is today the largest and oldest of the nationwide Greek-American organizations with approximately 22,000 members. Between the Church and AHEPA, most elements of the Greek-American community are represented. Like the Greek Orthodox Church, AHEPA is organized in such a way as to facilitate the activation of large-scale "grass roots" campaigns. Local chapters of AHEPA exist in almost all states of the Union. It would not be presumptuous to say that although other Greek-American organizations exist, AHEPA is *perceived by non-Greek Americans* as representative of and spokesman for Greek Americans and their interests.

During the congressional-executive debate concerning Cyprus, the Washington location of the Supreme Lodge put the AHEPA national officers in the ideal position of "watchdogs" of the U.S. Congress in the sense that they could easily survey the unfolding drama, note nuances, and report back to the group. Again, the administration was not blind to the importance of AHEPA officers within the Greek community. On several occasions Kissinger invited various AHEPA members to his small discussions with congressional representatives in an attempt to explain and "sell" the administration point of view.

The press and radio

In addition to national organizations such as AHEPA, the Greek-American press and radio were indispensable in dispersing information among Greek Americans throughout the United States. From our data we estimated that approximately 159 Greek-American radio programs existed on various stations at one time or another between the years 1965 and 1975. Most programs were broadcast for one-half hour to two hours weekly. And, as of 1975, there wre approximately 30 Greek-American newspapers with circulations ranging from 1,000 to over 27,000.

The Greek lobby

The situation on Cyprus and the sense of urgency attached in reacting to it allowed Greek Americans temporarily to bury some of their ideological and personal differences and to form organizations either for the purpose of supplying relief help for the large Cypriot refugee population or for lobbying the U.S. Congress. The two most well-known lobby groups are the United Hellenic American Congress (UHAC) and the American Hellenic Institute (AHI). The UHAC is the brainchild of Archbishop Iakovos. Its membership is made up of strong lay and clerical church supporters. Its headquarters is in Chicago and it has, up until now, specialized in letter writing and telegram/telephone campaigns. In contrast, a long line of former and current AHEPA officers are listed among the names on AHI's board of directors. AHI has its headquarters in Washington, D.C., and it utilizes AHEPA channels just as UHAC utilizes religious channels to launch letter writing campaigns that are meant to generate spontaneous, grass roots concern for the Cyprus issue. In actuality, these campaigns are often perceived by legislative assistants as orchestrated drives primarily because the content of the letters is so uniform. While the United Hellenic American Congress and the American Hellenic Institute are united in their condemnation of Turkish use of military force in Cyprus, they are more often competitive than cooperative.

In addition to AHI and UHAC, other Greek-American organizations, such as the Free Cyprus Coalition and the United Hellenic Association, have arisen in response to the Cyprus issue. The staying capacity of many of these organizations is questionable given the ad hoc nature of their organizational structures and the highly inadequate sources of funding for their activities.

GREEK AMERICANS AND CONGRESSIONAL VOTING PATTERNS

Turning to the question of Greek-American effectiveness in influencing foreign policy deci-sions, we examined the degree of correlation, if any, between the number and percentage of Greek Americans in each state and congressional district and the way in which their respective congressional representatives voted on a set of issues pertaining to the Turkish arms embargo. If the administration and the press were correct in asserting that Congress was sacrificing foreign policy in favor of personal and political "survival" interests then, logically, members of Congress from states or districts with a large Greek-American constituency would have voted for an embargo. We limited our selection of issues to a one-year time period, from July 1974 through July 1975.

The Senate

We used the 1970 U.S. census tracts in order to determine both the number and the percent of Greek Americans in each state. The absolute figure was included on the supposition that sheer numbers may have been more impressive to the senators than the actual proportion of Greek Americans in the population. In order to test our hypothesis, we selected a set of nine motions pertaining to the Turkish aid question for which there were roll call votes. These nine issues were taken from the voting records published by one of the Greek lobby groups. Senators were recorded as voting (1) in favor of a Turkish arms embargo, (2) against such a move, or (3) they were absent and were counted, for our purposes, among the missing values. In general, a vote in favor of the embargo corresponded to a vote against the administration's announced position.

A simple Pearson correlation test was used to assess the strength of relationships. If the 0.3 correlation commonly accepted by social scientists is posited as the cutoff point for indicating relationships of significant strength, then on *none* of the motions did the number or percent of Greek Americans covary with the way the Senators voted on the Turkish aid issue.

In breaking our sample down into two smaller subsamples according to party affiliation, we found that Democrats as a general rule voted for the embargo on all nine motions. The Republicans were more evenly split on the question, and a relationship did exist between the number of Greek Americans in the individual states and the way in which Republican senators from those states voted on *some* of the issues. If there was any truth at all to the administration and press picture of a Senate yielding to domestic pressure politics, it was members from the president's own Republican party who were the "culprits." On most, though not all, motions a greater relationship existed between the absolute numbers of Greek Americans rather than the proportion of the total population which they represented in a given state.

The House

We attempted to assess whether the charges of pressure politics made in the press and by the administration were any more valid in the House than in the Senate. It was in the House that the administration suffered its most glaring defeats on this issue. Certainly, at the congressional district level, allegations of ethnic politics seem, at first glance, more plausible. Given the constraints of data availability, only four states were chosen as a sample: Illinois, New York, New Jersey, and Massachusetts. Thus, it must be borne in mind that our sample, predominantly representative of the northeast United States, is regionally biased, although it is probably biased in favor of the administration and press line because these were the states with the largest number of Greek Americans. We also added a new indicator, the total number of *ethnic* Americans in each of the districts. Our assumption was that congressmen may not distinguish between ethnic groups, particularly on issues where there appears to be no other sizeable ethnic group opposition. From July 1974 through July 1975, our Greek lobby source listed eight congressional motions which related directly to the question of military aid and sales to Turkey.

According to the Pearson correlation test, the relationships between the size of the Greek-American constituency and the voting behavior of House members were stronger than those found in the Senate. However, on only three of the eight issues was there a correlation greater than 0.3. In looking at the totality, it appears that, even in the House, Greek Americans had little or no effect on a representative's vote. What is interesting, however,

is that on all eight issues there was a correlation (greater than 0.3) between the number of *ethnic* Americans in a district and congressional voting patterns. The possibility, therefore, exists that perceptions concerning the size of ethnic constituencies, regardless of their individual composition, will affect congressmen's voting patterns, at least on issues salient to one or more ethnic groups and on issues that do not represent a threat to any other existing or sizeable American ethnic group.

In separating the sample into two subsamples reflecting party affiliation, it became apparent, as in the Senate, that Democrats *en masse* had voted in favor of an arms embargo. Unlike the Senate, Republican members of the House shifted voting patterns more often, and they tended on the whole to be more in favor of embargo measures. On five of the eight motions a significant correlation existed between the size of the Greek-American constituency and the way in which the Republican House member voted. Only Republicans with a high proportion of Greek-American constituents continued to vote in favor of an embargo by the time of the July 1975 motion.

CONCLUSIONS

The results of our preliminary investigation would seem to indicate that Greek-American attempts to influence members of the Senate or the House on the issue of aid to Turkey were not very effective. Any relationships that do exist between Greek Americans as a voting bloc and congressional voting patterns are small, more prevalent in the House of Representatives, and more apt to occur among Republican members of the House or Senate than among Democrats. If the administration was at all correct in criticizing the Congress for practicing ethnic politics, it was the Republican party members that fit the profile.

Of course, we have attempted to measure only the correlations between the number of Greek-American constituents and congressional voting patterns. We have not attempted to measure other types of possible lobby influence such as possible pressures exerted by wealthy and influential Greek Americans.

Although we attempted to minimize the effect of

other issues upon our voting study by selecting an issue area that was fairly clear-cut, in reality no issue should ever be looked at in a vacuum. Most of the motions we examined, for example, were amendments attached to larger bills such as the Continuing Appropriations Bill. Moreover, a very plausible case could be made that voting patterns on the Turkish arms embargo issue followed rather closely those found on other similar foreign aid issues. The administration suffered similar setbacks, for instance, on its requests for aid to the dying Thieu regime of South Vietnam, for aid to the repressive Chilean military junta, and for support of clandestine operations in Angola. Can a North Vietnamese or a Chilean-American lobby be credited with these antiadministration successes?

Moreover, there is an important distinction to be made between voting "pro-Greek," "antiadministration," "anti-Turkish aid," or even "anti-Turkish." Each of these phrases implies different underlying motivations. There were a number of conservative Republicans, for example, whose vote to discontinue aid to Turkey might better be ex-plained in terms of their growing disillusionment with Kissinger's policy of detente. Moreover, there were a number of representatives of the Black Caucus whose vote to discontinue aid to Turkey might better be explained in terms of their concern with the trafficking of narcotics in American cities. Their vote, in other words, was an expression of disapproval over Turkey's decision to renew the production of opium.

Finally, critics who have claimed that there were and are no Greek-American lobby groups or constituent pressures are incorrect. Informal and formal ethnic organization lends itself to mobilization on particular foreign policy issues. On the other hand, critics who have claimed that a "Greek lobby" was the determining factor in the congressional decision to cut off military aid to Turkey are also incorrect. Statistical evidence does not confirm the allegation made in the press and by the administration that members of Congress, in voting for an embargo, were yielding to ethnic pressures. The truth probably lies somewhere on the middle ground.

ENVIRONMENTAL CONSERVATION AND IMMIGRATION: A NEW RACIST IDEOLOGY?

Anthony H. Richmond

Immigration policies, like other government decisions, are thrashed out in a political arena and are an accommodation to conflicting interest groups and their respective ideologies. Actual legislation and regulations governing the admission of immigrants have tended to swing between the two extremes of a complete "open door" policy, and one of an almost total exclusion of all but a small number of people with preferred qualifications and national backgrounds. The interest groups most often supporting a larger and more diversified immigration flow have included, firstly, transportation companies and all those associated with the travel industry, which depends for its livelihood on the promotion of large population movements. Secondly, the proponents of immigration generally include large land owners and developers for whom a larger population is a prerequisite for economic growth. The classical example of a combination of these two interests was that of the Canadian Pacific Railway (CPR) which, as part of its contract with the federal government in Ottawa for the development of a railway to the west coast, received large land grants in the prairie provinces of Canada. The CPR became one of the largest promoters of immigration at the turn of this century. Thirdly, capital investors and employers generally tend to favor immigration. Employers and managers in expanding new industries frequently require large numbers of skilled workers which cannot always be supplied domestically; at the same time, employers in declining and marginal industries are interested in immigrant workers when they can be persuaded to work for wages or under conditions that are less attractive to the existing populations of the receiving society. Generally in favor of further immigration are the representatives of immigrant groups themselves and ethnic minorities who, through chain migration and "family reunion," hope to increase their numbers and strengthen their influence in the new country. These interest groups generally espouse a liberal ideology which emphasizes freedom of movement as a human right, equality of opportunity and access to resources, cosmopolitan values, cultural pluralism, and the desirability of nondiscrimination in immigration policies.

Those interest groups more often opposed to immigration include both organized and unorganized labor, which frequently see immigration as a potential source of competition for scarce resources, and as undermining labor unions and wage levels. Immigration is seen as particularly threatening at times of economic recession and high unemployment. Secondly, opposition to immigration is very frequently expressed by the socially mobile and less secure sectors of the middle classes, particularly those who have espoused particular moral, religious and nationalistic values which they feel would be threatened by a large influx of "aliens." Thirdly, the ranks of those opposed to immigration may sometimes be joined by an older generation of immigrants or their children who perceive further waves of immigration as threatening the precarious *modus vivendi* they have established with the receiving society. The opponents of immigration may be joined by those for whom hostility toward immigrants and ethnic minorities is an expression of a basic authoritarian personality.

The immigration policies of major English-speaking countries such as Great Britain, the United States, Canada and Australia have always been influenced by racism and bigotry, although the economic interests favouring immigration have sometimes been strong enough to overcome these attitudes. At other times, immigration policies have exhibited a compromise whereby a controlled and selective immigration policy was pursued favoring the dominant race or nationalities already established in the new country. In English-speaking countries, the prejudice and discrimination against non-Anglo-Saxon immigrants has been often explicit and outspoken. At other times, its expression has been covert. Today, it is no longer respectable for intellectuals, scientists and politicians to express racist views openly or to advocate explicit discrimination. Theories that attribute genetic inferiority to certain races, nationalities, or classes are no longer popular and command only eccentric support. Furthermore, racial discrimination is not politically expedient when trade and diplomatic relations with the Third World must be promoted. However, even when belief in the racial superiority of the British and some other Western European nationalities was fashionable (and even defended by eminent biologists and social scientists), it was quite common to provide other arguments for restricting immigration and particularly for excluding certain races and nationalities.

From an academic point of view, there is some dispute whether these alternative defenses of exclusionary immigration should, strictly speaking, be described as "racist." Two leading authorities on race relations and immigration in Britain take opposing views on this question. Looking at it from the point of view of the history of social thought and the influence of Social Darwinism on race relations, Michael Banton had argued that only when genetic inferiority and superiority are ascribed to certain populations as a justification for differential treatment should the theory or argument be defined as an example of "racism."[1] The alternative view is expressed by John Rex who has stated that, while a race relations situation would always be marked by some appeal to a deterministic theory, that theory might not always be a biological or genetic one but might be based upon religious, cultural, historical, ideological, or sociological grounds.[2]

Subsequently, Rex elaborated this point. He argued that to confine the term racism to the use of genetic theories would be to "trivialize the sociology of race relations almost beyond belief." He suggested that racist ideas must be examined in the context of the sociology of knowledge and the relation between ideas and social structures. He also pointed out that there has been a resurgence in popularity of explicitly racist theories and other Social Darwinistic perspectives among some biologists and psychologists.[3] If Social Darwinism is defined, broadly, as the advocacy of social

policies on the basis of false biological analogies, then the use of arguments based upon ecology, conservation, and environmental protection to support exclusionary immigration policies must be regarded as another manifestation of racism in disguise. In effect, the proponents of restrictive immigration policies appear to be saying that if we can no longer ensure that the majority of immigrants will be Caucasian, then let us find some convincing argument for having none at all, or very few! As such, it is the latest in a long line of euphemistic arguments and policies that have been used at various times, in different countries, to justify immigration restriction and, particularly, the exclusion of nonwhite immigrants from Britain, Canada, Australia, and the United States.

In order to avoid the semantic dispute between Banton and Rex, I shall call these indirect arguments "quasiracist." A key element in all of the arguments used and devices adopted to justify exclusion and discrimination is the self-interest of the existing inhabitants and settler communities in the receiving societies. Intrinsically, the various arguments and the laws and regulations had a rational basis. However, it was the deliberate manipulation and exaggeration of these considerations which enabled them to be utilized in a highly restrictive and discriminatory way. Thus, rational considerations became ideologically distorted.

EXAMPLES OF IDEOLOGICAL DISTORTION

The history of immigration and its control in various countries is repleet with examples of the ideological distortion of otherwise rational arguments and policies. The misuse of legitimate concerns regarding conservation, environmental protection, and population growth is only the latest in a long list of similar cases. For example, the prevention and control of the spread of infectious and contageous diseases is a proper concern of any government. The immigration regulations of almost all countries include provisions for the medical inspection of potential immigrants and other public health provisions relating to transportation. However, one of the most frequent stereotypes promoted by those opposed to immigration, or to the entry of particular races or nationalities, is that which suggests the unwanted group may be responsible for spreading loathesome diseases. Charles Price, in his study of restrictive immigration to North America and Australasia, mentions this as one of the elements in an inquiry into immigration into Australia in 1854; it was among the allegations made by those opposed to immigration from Eastern Europe to Britain and the United States at the turn of the century.[4]

In Canada in 1911, a draft order in council would have prohibited "any immigrant belonging to the Negro race, which race is deemed unsuitable to the climate and requirements of Canada" from landing in Canada. However, this order was vetoed. Instead, medical inspections at the U.S.–Canada border were used to prevent black would-be migrants from entering the country.[5] At about the same time (in 1908) Canada introduced its notorious "continuous journey regulations." Ostensibly, these were a public health measure designed to prevent the spread of disease from ships stopping at intermediate ports. However, their real purpose was to exclude East Indians from Canada. Unlike the Chinese and Japanese, the East Indians were British subjects and could not legally be excluded. However, the government was aware that there was no shipping line plying directly between India and Canada. The most infamous incident arising from this occurred in 1914 when 375 passengers were anchored off Vancouver, but were refused entry into Canada because of the noncontinuous journey regulation. The ship remained in the harbor for two months and there were violent antiOriental demmonstrations.

Concern for the external security of the particular country and fear of war and invasion have been the basis for exclusionary immigration policies and for discimination against racial and national minorities. Australia's white immigration policy was prompted very largely by defense considerations and fear of being surrounded by Asian countries. Even after the Second World War, defense considerations were still being used as grounds for promoting British and European immigration to the exclusion of Asians. In Canada and the United States, the discriminatory treatment of Japanese residents, and their American- and Canadian-born children who were citi-

zens, are further examples of the sometimes hysterical anxieties to which these considerations can give rise. After the Second World War, Canada repatriated a large number of Japanese, although it has since been recognized that the fear of invasion and the security threats were grossly exaggerated.

Internal security and the question of subversion has frequently been used as a gound for excluding particular nationalities. At the turn of the century these fears were frequently expressed in Britain and the United States with regard to eastern European immigration. At that time the boogey men were the so-called "anarchists." More recently, the passage of the McCarran Act in the United States in 1952 (despite President Truman's veto) was an example of the use of the fear of communism, and concern with questions of internal security, as a way of excluding potential immigrants from Asia and parts of Eastern Europe. Subsequently, the President's Commission on Immigration and Naturalization criticized the Act of 1952 because it promoted a claim of Nordic supremacy, discriminated in favor of the nations of western and northern Europe and against those of southern and eastern Europe, the Near East, and Asia. In responding to the Commission's report, Senator McCarran claimed that his act "does not contain one iota of racial or religious discrimination. It is, however, very tough, very tough, on communists, as it is on criminals and other subversives."[6]

Closely related to questions of internal security were the frequent allegations that immigrants are more likely to exhibit criminal tendencies. Such views had been expressed frequently by opponents of immigration in Britain, Canada, and elsewhere. The chief of police in Toronto is on record as having frequently blamed immigrants for a rise in the crime rate. These assertions are made notwithstanding the fact that all systematic studies support the conclusion that the crime rates of the foreign born are generally lower than those of the native born populations of the countries concerned.

One of the most frequent concerns expressed by those opposed to immigration has been that immigrants will provide a pool of cheap labor, be used as strike breakers, and generally threaten the improvements in wages and working conditions achieved by labor unions. Such fears are often associated with stereotypes of racial minorities whose material standards and dietary habits supposedly enabled them to live "off the smell of a rag." Such views provided a rationale for such discriminatory legislation as the requirement that potential immigrants must be in possession of certain sums of money and, in the case of Canada, the imposition of taxes on Chinese immigrants. In 1885, the amount was $50.00 on entry and was gradually increased to $500 in 1903.

The alleged inability of certain races and nationalities to assimilate into the receiving society has been a common basis of exclusion and discrimination. The Canadian Immigration Act of 1952, which was the legislative authority for immigration regulation until 1977, contained clauses which permit regulations to be made that would exclude immigrants on the basis of "peculiar customs, habits, modes of life or methods of holding property in his country of birth or citizenship;" and "his probable inability to become readily assimilated."[7] (These clauses were omitted from the new Act of 1977 now in force.) Studies carried out on behalf of the United States Immigration Commission of 1907 distinguished between the "new" and old immigrant flows, and alleged that the former exhibited lower rates of naturalization and other indications of slower assimilation. Subsequent research showed these claims to be unfounded and largely a consequence of not taking into account the different periods of immigration of the immigrant groups concerned. Nevertheless, census monographs in Canada, for the years 1921 and 1931, perpetuated the same myths with regard to the eastern and southern European groups compared with the British and others from northern and western Europe.

In Australia, Charles Price has shown that a desire for social homogeneity was a major factor in promoting the white Australia policy.[8] Among the discriminatory measures adopted in various countries to exclude particular nationalities were the notorious "literacy tests," such as those incorporated into the Commonwealth Immigration Restriction Act of 1901 in Australia. This prohibited "the entry into Australia of any person who, when asked to do so fails to write out at dictation, and sign in the presence of an officer, a passage of 50 words in length in a European language."[9] Similar legislation was introduced in British Columbia in 1900 and repeated annually until 1908, despite some question at the federal level as to the legality of such regulations. In Canada, the alleged unsuitability of the climate for settlement by blacks and Asians had been used as a reason for exclusion as recently as 1955.

Related to the question of social homogeneity is the concern that a racially and ethnically diversified immigration will give rise to religious and ethnic strife. This is often expressed as an exaggerated concern for the welfare of the immigrants and ethnic minorities themselves. Such notorious opponents of black and Asian immigration to Britain as Enoch Powell have argued a case for repatriation on the ground that this would benefit the immigrants themselves as well as white Britishers.[10]

All the examples I have given of "quasiracist" attitudes and policies have one element in common: they all have a superficial plausibility and an element of apparent rationality. Few people would wish to question the desirability of preventing the spread of disease, resisting threats of invasion, taking precautions against the subversion of democratic institutions, preventing crime, racial and ethnic conflict, or undermining the living standards of workers. However, all of these good causes can be used to misrepresent and distort the real situation. And, as the more or less conscious deceptions and disguises of human interest groups, these plausible arguments must be recognized as ideologically racist.[11]

ENVIRONMENTAL CONSERVATION AND IMMIGRATION

Since the mid–1960s, most English-speaking countries have relaxed to some degree the discrimination that previously existed against black and Asian immigration. Great Britain is an exception in that, as far as immigration from Commonwealth countries was concerned, an open door policy was pursued so long as the numbers arriving were comparatively small. When the numbers began to increase, in the late 1950s, the government felt obliged to introduce the first of a series of Commonwealth immigration acts which restricted the admissibility of those from present or former Commonwealth countries, even those carrying British passports. In practice, however, the number actually entering the United Kingdom has continued to be quite substantial to the present day.[12] In the United States, the major departure from previous regulations came in 1965 when priority was given to reuniting immigrant families and permitting the entry of professional persons and other workers in short supply in the United States. A revised quota system was put into effect in 1968 which tended to reverse the previous priorities placing severe limitations on Western Hemisphere immigration. In Canada, all formal discrimination by race or national origin was removed from immigration regulations in 1962. Since then the proportion of black and Asian immigrants has risen to almost one-third of the total in recent years. Australia moved more slowly in removing restrictions on Asian immigration, but the numbers admitted for permanent residence did increase during the 1960s and all formal restrictions were removed in 1974.[13] Concurrently with this liberalization of actual immigration policies, there has been a backlash of opposition from certain groups. The emphasis upon highly qualified immigrants, particularly in Canada and Australia, had led to an increase in opposition to immigration from some professional groups such as medical doctors and university teachers. A new manifestation of Social Darwinism has appeared in recent years and is being used to rationalize exclusionary immigration policies. The underlying premise of the new argument for reducing immigration is as superficially plausible as those offered in earlier years. It is derived from recent developments in our understanding of the delicate balance of ecological forces that sustain our population on earth. Few would deny the reality of a population and resource crisis at the global level. Present rates of population growth, particularly in developing countries, will put serious pressures on food and energy resources. It is generally agreed that mass emigration will not solve the population problem. The solution lies in more effective fertility control, greater productivity, and a more egalatarian distribution of resources. However, arguments based upon the need to reduce urban congestion, prevent further environmental pollution, and reduce energy and resource consumption are now being used to support exclusionary immigration policies.

Indeed, the most outspoken opposition to immigration in Canada and Australia has come from influential lobbyists and spokesmen who argue that, contrary to the traditional view, these countries have reached, or will shortly achieve, an optimal level of population relative to the available productive land, energy resources, and other ecological considerations. Linked with these views are expressions of concern at the level of urbanization and metropolitanization of the populations of these countries. These arguments are being put forward by some of the most eminent scientists, including biologists, medical doctors, and demographers.

In Australia, the argument against immigration on environmental grounds was first put forward by Professor Fenner, Director of the School of Medical Research at the Australian National University in 1971. He claimed that, "Australia is far more vulnerable than the other large centres of Western culture, North America and Europe, to the damaging effects of a large number of people."[12] He went on point out that Australia suffers from an arrid climate and that, relative to its size, its ecosystems are much more fragile. This led him to conclude that a substantial lowering of the rate of population growth in Australia was desirable, including, among other things, a reduction in immigration.[14]

Very similar views were echoed in Canada, where the large Arctic and sub-Arctic territories are also recognized as ecologically fragile and incapable of supporting large populations. At seminars sponsored by the Conservation Council of Ontario, in 1972 and 1973, biologists argued, "Canada is already over-populated in terms of its sustainable carrying capacity, and this means that a lot of debate about the action alternatives can be avoided if this point is understood."[15] Arguments against immigration were also advanced in Canada on behalf of environmentalists at hearings of a Special Joint Committee of Parliament, in 1975. For example, a spokesman for British Columbia's Wildlife Federation argued that the Greater Vancouver and lower mainland areas of British Columbia should be protected from further immigration "until we can reconcile the numbers of people that can be accommodated without destroying our liveable regions." The same view was put forward by the President of the Conservation Council of New Brunswick who suggested that "immigration into Canada must be reduced drastically and, eventually, almost to zero."[16]

In its report, the Science Council of Canada examines Canada's available agricultural land, food supplies, energy and capital needs, labor force, and population options. While recognizing that, due to the very low birthrates at the present time, Canada may well be faced with a severe labor shortage from the mid–1980s onwards, the committee came down firmly against increased immigration as a solution to this problem. The principal recommendation of the report is that Canadian population growth should be slow. "The country should adopt a long-term population policy to achieve this slow growth. An initial target of 28–30 million for the year 2000 seems reasonable, assuming that the fertility rates remain between 1.8 and 2.1. An annual net immigration (immigration minus emigration) of about 50,000 per annum would achieve this goal." They go on to say that in view of the uncertainty about fertility levels, immigration programs should be reviewed at last every five years.[17]

It is interesting to note the suggestions made in the course of the report by members of the science council as a means of compensating for the possible labor shortages that would follow from slow population growth and a restriction on immigration. They include the following:

(1) Canadians should work harder;
(2) Canadians should give up any idea that the future of society will be leisure oriented;
(3) Increased labor force participation rates by women and youth should be encouraged;
(4) Older members of the labor force should postpone their expected retiring age and remain in work;
(5) Canadians should be prepared to do more of the "traditionally unpopular jobs," usually left to immigrants!

It should be emphasized that, both in Canada and Australia, at the official level alternative arguments favoring the maintenance of moderate levels of immigration have so far prevailed, notwithstanding the influential stature of those opposing immigration on environmentalist grounds. Professor W. D. Borrie, in his report to the Australian government based upon the National Population Inquiry, pointed out,

> the minority who have advocated zero growth have been very articulate, strongly dominated be elite educational groups, with their argument often backed by deep understanding of the Australian environment and ecology. The associated aspects of conservation, the onset as quickly as possible of the stationary state, and controlled consumption to minimize the wastage of non-renewable resources, are set not only as a goal for Australia, but for humanity at large.[18]

Those opposing immigration have generally associated themselves with the zero population growth movement. In Canada, the ZPG propaganda has included the publication of graphs showing the possible consequences of a net immigration in the order of 500,000 per annum. Nowhere is it noted that net immigration to Canada has rarely exceeded 100,000 and, in recent years, has been closer to 75,000 per annum. The same organization published a picture in a number of Canadian newspapers representing Canada as a young woman with an unwanted pregnancy. The context made it clear that opposition was not only to high birthrates, but also to immigration.

The zero population growth movement in the United States has also been vocal in its opposition to immigration. The danger of the ZPG movement diverting attention from the real causes of environmental damage and excessive energy consumption has been noted by Philip Hauser, who pointed out that "it is ironic that at this point in history, demographers should have to take issue with 'angry ecologists' overstating their case and using 'the population explosion' as a major enemy in their effort to stem environmental pollution. There are two dangers inherent in this situation. One, the danger that the problems of environmental pollution and the population explosion may be used as a smoke screen to obscure other problems that should have priority, including the problems of slums, racism and the 'urban crisis' in general. Second, the overstatements of the case . . . may do great harm if boomerang effects follow."[19]

Nothing I have said in this paper should be construed to mean that, at a global and a national level, we should not be taking positive steps to achieve fertility control, to reduce excessive consumption and wastage of energy and other resources, and to prevent environmental pollution. However, to argue that the existing levels of immigration to countries such as Britain, Canada, Australia, or the United States should be stopped or substantially reduced, for purely ecological reasons, must be recognized as an ideological proposition serving the interests of the more affluent segments of the world's population. Such an argument could only be sustained if it were considered that the environments presently enjoyed (and often spoiled) by affluent nations must be perpetually protected from habitation by the less advantaged. Not only would such policies be contrary to fundamental human rights, but they would place serious obstacles in the way of those people from developing countries who seek to improve their own material conditions and career opportunities through geographic and social mobility. Completely unrestricted immigration would undoubtedly disrupt the economic and social systems of advanced societies, but moderate levels of immigration are well within the absorbtive capacity of these countries. Indeed, in the long run, the declining rates of growth of population in post-industrial societies (and the imminent absolute decline of population in some western European countries) will mean positive net immigration will be to their own economic advantage. Only through immigration (on a scale large enough to compensate for outward movements of population and the effects of an aging population) will it be possible to sustain the levels of economic productivity necessary to provide adequate health and welfare services, including those directed toward the elimination of environmental pollution. I suggest that the opposite view, now expressed by those who uphold the virtues of a "steady state," who urge limits to growth, and who use environmental conservation as

an argument against immigration, is new ideology designed to protect the privileges of the affluent. It can appropriately be described as racist, or at least "quasiracist," because its implementation would mean a substantial reduction in black and Asian immigration to countries such as Canada and Australia, just as the formal legal barriers to their admissibility have been removed.

NOTES

1. Michael Banton has elaborated this point of view in the following publications: as editor of *Darwinism and the Study of Society* (London: Tavistock, 1961); and author of *Race Relations* (London: Tavistock, 1967); and "What Do We Mean by Racism?" *New Society* 341 (10 April 1969):551–54.
2. John Rex, *Race Relations in Sociological Theory* (London: Weidenfeld & Nicolson, 1970), p.159.
3. Idem, *Race, Colonialism and the City* (London: Routledge & Kegan Paul, 1973), p.221.
4. Charles Price, *The Great White Walls Are Built: Restrictive Immigration to North America and Australasia, 1836-1888* (Canberra: Australian National University Press, 1974).
5. Harold Troper, *Only Farmers Need Apply: Official Canadian Government Encouragement of Immigration from the United States, 1896-1911* (Toronto: Griffin House, 1972), pp.121–46.
6. B. M. Ziegler, ed., *Immigration: An American Dilemma* (Boston: D. C. Heath, 1953), p.113.
7. Immigration Act RSC 1952, C. 325 (Ottawa, Canada: Queen's Printer, 1952).
8. Price, op. cit.
9. *Commonwealth Immigration Restriction Act of 1901,* Act number 17 (Melbourne, Australia, 1901).
10. Paul Foot, *The Rise of Enoch Powell* (Haimondsworth: Penguin Books, 1969), p.125.
11. Karl Mannheim, *Ideology and Utopia* (London: Kegan Paul, 1936), pp.238–39.
12. Anthony H. Richmond, "Black and Asian Immigrants in Britain and Canada: A Comparison," *New Community* (Winter/Spring 1975–76):501–16.
13. Idem. and G. Lakshmana Rao, "Recent Developments in Immigration to Canada and Australia: A Comparative Analysis," *The International Journal of Comparative Sociology* 17 (1977):183–205.
14. F. J. Fenner, "The Environment," in Australian Institute of Political Science, eds., *How Many Australians? Immigration and Growth* (Sydney: Angus & Robertson, 1971), p.46.
15. Ontario Conservation Council, *A Population Policy for Canada? The Proceedings of Two Seminars on the Need for a Canadian Population Policy, the Impact of People on the Environment* (Toronto: Ontario Conservation Council, 1972–73), p.29.
16. Canada, Senate/House of Commons, *Proceedings of the Special Joint Committee of the Senate and of the House of Commons on Immigration Policy*, 30th Parliament, 1st sess., 1974–75–76, vol. 25, pp.17–19; vol. 31, pp.50–52.
17. Science Council of Canada, *Population, Technology and*

Resources, report no.5 (Ottawa: Supply and Services Canada, 1976), pp.20-23.

18. W. D. Borrie, *Population and Australia: A Demographic Analysis and Projection,* First Report of the National Population Inquiry, vols. I and II (Canberra: Australian Government Publishing Service, 1975), p.711.

19. Philip Hauser, "Zero Population Growth," *Population Index,* vol. 36, no.4 (October-December 1970), pp.455.

Part 4

Domestic Implication of the New Immigration for the U.S. and Other Host Societies I: Occupations and Services

KOREAN IMMIGRANT: SMALL BUSINESS IN LOS ANGELES[1]

Edna Bonacich, Ivan Light, and Charles Choy Wong

Anyone familiar with the city of Los Angeles who has not driven through the downtown area in the last two or three years would be astonished at the transformation of the Olympic Boulevard area between Crenshaw and Hoover. The change has been dramatic enough to attract the attention of a national news magazine:

> It's called Koreatown, a 2–mile stretch along Los Angeles's busy Olympic Boulevard, where 45,000 Korean immigrants have settled into new lives during the last five years. What used to be Mexican-American, Japanese and Jewish stores and businesses are now mostly Korean, with giant Oriental letters spread across their low-slung storefronts.[2]

Small business is flowering among the Koreans in Los Angeles.

This paper is a tentative statement of some of our early findings and ideas regarding Korean small business. We plan to pursue the study further, testing some of the hypotheses developed here.

BACKGROUND

The Korean community in the United States in general, and Los Angeles in particular, is by and large a new one, a product of the change in U.S. immigration laws in 1965. However, a small community had been established prior to this. The first Koreans who came to the U.S., starting in 1883, were diplomats, political refugees, students, and merchants.[3] Emigrants began coming in 1899,[4] arriving in any numbers only after 1903.[5] Between 1903 and 1905, over 7,000 Korean emigrants went to Hawaii,[6] and another 1,000 to the American mainland.[7] Many of the Hawaiian settlers moved on to the mainland.[8]

The immigration was rapidly curtailed by the establishment of Korea as a Japanese protectorate in 1905, leading to annexation in 1910. On the emigration side, Japan restricted passports for Koreans wishing to migrate to the U.S.,[9] while on the immigration end, Koreans were treated as Japanese (much against their will), being subjected to all the anti-Japanese agitation. Thus, the Asiatic Exclusion League, founded in 1905, was first known as the Japanese and Korean Exclusion League.[10] The presidential order of 1907 cutting off indirect immigration from Hawaii to the mainland, the Gentlemen's Agreement of 1907–1908, and the Exclusion Act of 1924, all aimed primarily at the Japanese, adversely affected Korean rights to immigration. As a result, the number of Koreans in this country was always exceedingly small.

The Immigration and Naturalization Act of 1965 altered this picture. It abolished discriminatory quotas based on national origins and set an overall annual limit of 170,000 from the Eastern Hemisphere (territories outside the Americas). Each country is now restricted to a maximum of 20,000 per annum. Both limits exempt immediate relatives of American citizens, including minor children, spouses, and parents.[11] Within the limits, preference is given to other relatives and workers with skills deemed necessary to the American economy.

An unanticipated consequence of the new law has been a sharp rise in immigration from Asia.[12] The Korean proportion of this immigration has gradually been rising to the point where Koreans make up over one-fifth of Asian immigrants. As of 1975, they are the third largest group entering the U.S., falling behind only Mexicans and Pilipinos.[13] In addition, another 176,013 nonimmigrants arrived from Korea between 1965 and 1975,[14] some of whom, among them students, have remained to swell the ranks of the immigrants.[15]

The 1970 census found 70,598 Koreans in the United Stated, 9,395 of whom lived in Los Angeles/Long Beach SMSA.[16] This is widely believed to have been an undercount, the national

TABLE 1
Korean, Asian, and Total Immigration to U.S. for
Fiscal Years 1965-75

YEAR	TOTAL	ASIAN	KOREAN	ASIAN % OF TOTAL	KOREAN % OF ASIAN	KOREAN % OF TOTAL
1965	296,697	20,683	2,165	7.0	10.5	0.7
1966	323,040	41.432	2,492	12.8	6.0	0.8
1967	361.972	61.446	3,956	17.0	6.4	1.1
1968	454,448	58,989	3,811	13.0	6.5	0.8
1969	358,579	75,679	6,045	21.1	8.0	1.7
1970	373,326	94,883	9,314	25.4	9.8	2.5
1971	370,478	103,461	14,297	27.9	13.8	3.9
1972	384,685	121,058	18,876	31.5	15.6	4.9
1973	400,063	124,160	22,930	31.0	18.5	5.7
1974	394,861	130,662	28,028	33.1	21.5	7.1
1975	386,194	132,469	28,362	34.3	21.4	7.3
	4,104,343	964,922	140,276	23.5	14.5	3.4

Source: U.S. Department of Justice. Immigration and Naturalization Service, Annual Report 1974 and 1975. Table 14.

figure at that time probably exceeding 100,000.[17] Recent immigration has raised the national estimate to 270,000 in 1976.[18]

In 1975, about one-quarter of entering Koreans reported Los Angeles as the place where they were residing.[19] It is generally acknowledged that Los Angeles is the major center of Korean American settlement.[20] A recent estimate[21] places the Los Angeles community at approximately 70,000 and growing.

THE PROBLEM

Immigrants who came to the United States from Asia before 1924, when immigration was effectively cut off, showed an unusual propensity to enter small business. Light[22] found that, in California in 1929, Chinese and Japanese owned thirty-one percent more retail stores than one would expect from their numbers. In a study of the Japanese in Seattle before World War II, Miyamoto[23] points to "the overwhelming dominance in their lives of the 'small shop.' " And many other studies support this point. Their "success" in small business derived from an ability to undercut competitors. They tended to be thrifty, working long hours and reinvesting a high proportion of profits. And they were able to utilize communal solidarity to distribute resources (including capital, labor, and information) more cheaply than competitors, and to control internal competition to some extent. Signs of small business concentration are evident even at this stage. Givens[24] enumerated seventy-three small businesses, thirty-three of which were fruit and vegetable stands.

The new immigration from Asia, of which Koreans are one example, is very different from the old in two important ways. First, the immigrants themselves are no longer a largely uneducated peasantry. This is partly a function of developments in the countries of emigration, where universal education has become commonplace, and partly a product of U.S. immigration policy which selects for skill and education. The Korean minority is a highly educated one.

The second change has occurred, not among the immigrants, but in the context into which they are moving. The U.S. economy has been transformed since 1924 from one in which there was considerable small business and self-employment, to a highly centralized economy with a small number of owners of large amounts of capital. A recent government study states: "In the middle of the nineteenth century, less than half of all employed people were wage and salary workers. By 1950 it was 80 percent, and by 1970, 90 percent."[25] This "proletarianization" continues even today, though it clearly must slow down as it reaches the limit.

Centralization has been accompanied by increasing efficiency. Technology has been introduced in many phases of production and distribution, increasing speed and reducing error. Scientific management has led to greater control over the work process.[26] Vertical integration, linking the production and distribution process under one corporate umbrella, increases reliability of supply and eliminates the middleman. As a result, costs have been cut, seeming to eliminate the possibility of undercutting by small business. No matter how thrifty, and how cheap the labor, it would appear that the mom-and-pop grocery store (for example) could not undersell the highly efficient supermarket. These shifts in the economy have a direct impact on traditional areas of Asian concentration, displacing such traditional industries as truck farming, hand laundry, restaurants, wholesaling, and retailing by mechanized agribusiness and chain stores.

Despite these forces, Korean immigrants show a marked movement into small business. Our problem is to understand how this happens against seemingly insuperable odds. More important, perhaps, is to consider why it happens in an economy which is clearly moving in the opposite direction.

METHOD OF STUDY

The approach used in this study can be described as "fieldwork." We have used a variety of information sources, taking advantage of what was available rather than creating a new data base by systematically surveying the community. It is our assumption that much taken-for-granted information is available in a community such as the Koreans in Los Angeles, and the problem is one of finding out where to obtain it. The data can be divided into two types: written materials and interviews. In interviewing, we have sought people who were likely to have information ranging beyond their own experience; interviewees have been treated as informants, not respondents.

The study is incomplete and will continue. The strategy followed so far admittedly emphasizes the leadership's perspective and down plays the experience and viewpoint of the humblest members of the community. Still, some of the studies we cite have tried to reach a broad spectrum. And, we plan to conduct a telephone survey of some individual businesses in order to counter this weakness.

THE NATURE OF KOREAN BUSINESS

Extent

The 1975 Directory of the Korean Association of Southern California, and its 1976 Supplement, list around 2,000 "firms" in their yellow pages. Some of these (54 alumni associations, 100 churches, and 126 nonprofit organizations) are not, strictly speaking, businesses, though in some cases, as in the minister of an independent church, the person in charge may be close to self-employment. On the other hand, the directories are widely acknowledged to be an undercount, with a higher probability of listing businesses with a Korean clientele. Even towards the end of 1975, it was estimated that there were around 4,000 Korean enterprises in Los Angeles County.[27]

While there are clearly "many" Korean businesses in Los Angeles, are Koreans more likely than others to enter small business? Assuming the population is 70,000, and household size (based on the 1970 census) is 4.4, the number of households in the community would be about 16,000. Taking the estimate of 4,000 businesses as accurate, about twenty-five percent of Korean families are currently in business for themselves.

BUSINESS LINES

Korean business tends to be concentrated in certain lines. They are likely to be in wholesaling and retailing, in service "shops" such as barber shops or restaurants, and in the independent professions. They tend to concentrate in "middleman" occupations, mobilizing resources to provide a service to a client which the client might have provided directly for him or herself. There is some light manufacturing, especially garment industry subcontracting, in which the enterprise takes on one small part of the production process, such as sewing up, and which, from the entrepreneur's point of view, resembles labor contracting. On the whole, however, Korean business tends to avoid manufacturing or heavy industry (See Table 2).

It should be noted that, despite self-employment, Korean businesses are not all independent. A number, notably gas stations (auto service stations) and some of the restaurants (for example, hamburger stands) are franchised from larger corporations. Similarly, insurance agencies may be branches of larger operations.

Korean business lines appear to be typical of "middleman minorities."[28] They tend to avoid concerns which tie up capital, preferring easily liquidable lines of business. There is some tendency to speculation. When a particular line shows high profits, a number of Korean entrepreneurs will rush into it in the hopes of reaping the gains. The wig business, for example, experienced this kind of boom between 1970 and 1972, and has since been declining, perhaps because of oversaturation.

Size of businesses

In 1972, a study of businesses was conducted by the census bureau. It found 1,201 Korean businesses in the United States and 298 in Los Angeles, obviously an undercount.[29] The mean gross income for Korean businesses was $54,820 per annum. Only twenty-one percent had any paid employees, and of these the average number of employees was six.

In a study of 278 Korean businesses in the Olympic area of Los Angeles, David Kim[30] found that about seventy percent were what he describes as "small scale"; this finding was supported by the Subcommittee on Equal Opportunities[31] which describes the Olympic area businesses as follows: "The vast predominance of these small businesses are low capital investment and leasehold establishments." There are, however, exceptions to this picture, especially among trading companies, import-export establishments, and wholesale firms.[32] Even so, the operation itself can still be small.

Clientele

Koreans make up a significant portion of the clientele of Korean businesses. Kim[33] estimates that slightly over half of the customers of Korean businesses in the Olympic area are Korean. This is not surprising given that the Olympic area is the

TABLE 2
Korean Firms in Los Angeles, 1975-76

MALES

	TOTAL				NON AGRICULTURAL			
	1960	1965	1970	1973	1960	1965	1970	1973
Wage and Salary	81%	85%	88%	89%	87%	89%	91%	92%
Self Employed	17	15	12	11	13	11	9	8
Unpaid Family	1	1	0	0	0	0	0	0
	44,485	47,034	48,959	51,963	39,807	43,304	46,098	49,130

FEMALES

Wage and Salary	88%	90%	93%	93%	91%	92%	94%	94%
Self Employed	7	6	5	5	6	6	4	4
Unpaid Family	5	4	3	2	2	2	2	1
	22,196	25,146	29,668	32,447	21,151	24,290	29,066	31,828

Source: U.S. Bureau of Census. Statistical Abstract of the United States: 1974 (95th edition). Washington, D.C., 1974: Table 567.

center of Korean residence. One would expect that businesses located elsewhere in the city would rely much less on a Korean clientele.

There is some variation in clientele by line of business. Restaurants and grocery stores cater more to Koreans; gas stations, liquor stores, and wig shops, to non-Koreans. Entrepreneurs may change the ethnicity of their clients during the course of their careers, as they move, for example, from gas stations to grocery stores, or from grocery stores to liquor stores. These shifts occur fairly frequently, suggesting that an ethnic clientele is not an essential feature of Korean businees.

It is possible that Korean businesses which do not cater to other Koreans tend to have a dispro-portionately large disprivileged minority clientele. At least, we have been told that wig stores and liquor stores tend to be concentrated in the black ghettos and Spanish-speaking barrios of the city.[34] Having a black and chicano (and perhaps poor white) clientele suggests that Koreans may be acting as a commercial and service class to the poorer strata of society, and bearing the brunt of their hostility.

In sum, Korean entrepreneurs concentrate heav-ily in trade and service, rather than in production of

TABLE 3
Class of Worker or Employed Persons by Sex,
1960-75, for Total and Nonagricultural Workers (in
thousands, 14+ years for 1960 and 1965, 16+
years for 1970 and 1973)

Accounting and Income Tax	17	Computer Processing Institute	4
Advertising Company	6	Construction and Architect	21
Alumni, High School	23	Certified Public Accountant	14
Alumni, University	31	Delivery Service	9
Answering Service	2	Dental and Laboratory	26
Art and Interior Design	7	Department Store	2
Auto Body Shop and Repair	20	Driving School	10
Auto Dealer	21	Electric Appliances Sale and Repair	14
Auto Service Station	160	Embroidery Company	1
Auto Supply and Rent	3	Employment Agency	1
Auto Wrecking	2	Flower Shop	16
Ba Dook	1	Funeral Parlor	1
Bakery	4	Furniture	5
Bank and Loan Company	13*	Gallery	8
Barber Shop	4	Gift Shop	14
Beauty Salon	11	Grocery, American Food	138
Bicycle	2	Grocery, Fish and Meat	10
Book Store	3	Grocery, Oriental Food	46
Broadcasting	7	Grocery, Wholesale	15
Cabinet Shop	3	Gymnasium	34
Carpet and Curtain	3	Hardware	1
Church	100	Health Center	1
Clothing, Children	2	Hospital	5*
Clothing, Manufacture	28	Insurance Agency	49
Clothing, Men and/or Women	32	Investigation	1
Clothing, Tailor	6	Iron Works	1
Coffee Shop	9	Jewelry	8

Table 3, continued

Laundry and Cleaner	8	Real Estate	26
Law Office and Immigration Consultant	20	Restaurant	115
Liquor Store	63	Restaurant Fixture	1
Maintenance	52	Schools	26
Maintenance Supply	1	Sewing Machine and Vacuum	2
Marriage Office	1	Shoe Store and Repair	34
Medical Doctor	36	Sign Company	3
Music Instruction	16	Sporting Goods	10
Newspaper	9	Stationery and Office Supply	8
Night Club	17	Temple	4
Non-Profit Organization	126	Theatre	2
Notary Public	3	Trading Company	158
Optical and Optometrist	3	Travel Agency	31
Oriental Health, Acupuncture	2	Trophy	3
Oriental Health, Massage	5	Tropical Fish	1
Oriental Health, Herb and Herb Pharmacy	23	TV and Radio Sales and Repair	26
Painting	9	Wig and Beauty Supply	152
Pharmacy	3	Miscellaneous	4*
Photo Studio	8		
Photo Typesetting	1	Total	1,995
Printing	7		

Source: *Korean Directory of Southern California*, 1975. Los Angeles: Korean Association of Southern California and Keys Printing Company, 1975; and *Supplement to Korean Directory of Southern California*, 1976. Los Angeles: Korean Association of Southern California and Keys Printing Company, 1976.

* Rough estimate, unclear from names which ones are Korean.

commodities. Their businesses are small in size and rely little on the use of wage labor. And their clientele is not confined to the ethnic community. These characteristics suggest that the Koreans are becoming a ''middleman minority'' or ''marginal trading people.'' Such groups are commonly found in economies where most people are producing for their own subsistence, and where an alien group comes in and monopolizes what little trade there is. That a similar group concentration should arise in an advanced capitalist society, where commerce is the mode of the day, is puzzling indeed.

HOW KOREAN BUSINESS
IS ESTABLISHED

The question of how Korean immigrants get into small business is problematic because most come without prior experience. Entrepreneurship is not something they fall into "naturally" or out of habit, but must be acquired on arrival. In this sense, despite higher levels of education, the new Korean immigrants are not unlike the pre-1974 Asian immigrants who tended to be laborers lacking in business skills, but who nevertheless were able to move into the petite bourgeoisie. The old immigrants relied on two major mechanisms for advancement into business: thrift and the efficient utilization of community resources. The Koreans use both of these means and some new ones, too. We shall consider four factors which aid in the movement to entrepreneurship: (1) thrift, (2) the use of communal resources, (3) the use of public resources, and (4) the role of the Korean government.

Thrift

Koreans are thrifty in two important ways. They amass capital by saving their earnings, and they and their families work long hours for little immediate remuneration.

Regarding capital, despite government restrictions on the amount one can take out (the upper limit is $1,400), some Koreans do come with capital in hand, sometimes with $50,000 to $60,000 cash. Apart from smuggling it out illegally, an important segment of the Los Angeles community came indirectly from Koreans working in Germany and Vietnam, as coal miners, nurses, and engineers,[35] and may have collected some capital there. The most common pattern, however, is to come with little and work hard for two or three years until one has saved about $20,000 to invest in a business. The wife typically works in a garment factory (about ninety percent of wage-earning Korean women are said to work at sewing),[36] and the husband may carry two jobs, perhaps working as a janitor or gas station attendant. Wages in these jobs are low, making it difficult to save up. The aspiring entrepreneur must sacrifice living standards for a while.[37]

Korean thrift is shown not only in lack of spending, but also in hard work. As we have seen, a Korean family is likely to put in more time at work than the average American family before they acquire a business of their own. The pattern continues after self-employment has been attained.[38]

Communal Resources

The Koreans form a highly organized community. There are numerous associations and organizations which form hierarchies and overlap. According to one source, there are between 500 and 600 associations, and nine out of ten Koreans in Los Angeles belong to at least one, and most to more than one.[39] *The Korea Times*[40] reports that there are over seventy community organizations; the Korean Consul provided us with a list of fifty six organizations. Especially important, from the point of view of business development, are occupational and trade associations (See Table 4).

Community organization is important for business development. It aids in the efficient distribution of resources through the community. Even organizations which do not have an overt economic purpose, such as alumni associations or churches, still serve this function by bringing people together and providing chains of communication; indeed they may be more important in supplying communal support for small business than organizations formally geared to that end. A number of resources are communally generated and distributed, including capital, labor and jobs, clients, and information. In addition, community organization can help to control internal competition.

Among early Chinese and Japanese immigrants, the pooling of capital, especially through rotating credit associations, was an important advantage in gaining a foothold in business.[41] Rotating credit is found among the Koreans and is called *gae*.[42] A group of friends or members of an organization pool money together and give it to one member. They do this on a regular basis, shifting the recipient until everyone has had a turn. While a *gae* may be used to purchase consumer items, such as cars, they are also used to raise business capital. A large *gae* will include about twenty participants and raise $10,000 for each.

TABLE 4
Occupational Organizations among Koreans in
Los Angeles

	Membership
American Korean Businessmen's Association	
Korea Hair Product Association of America	20
Korea Musician Union Association	
Korean-American CPA Society	12
Korean Artists Association of Southern California	50
Korean Chamber of Commerce and Industry of	
Southern California	200
Korean Dental Association of California	80
Korean Entertainers Association	80
Korean Food Association of Southern California	15
Korean Medical Association of California	200
Korean Ministers Association of Southern California	200
Korean Musicians Association of California	50
Korean Nurses Association of Southern California	400
Korean Oriental Herb Doctors Association of USA	17
Korean Petroleum Dealers Association of California	85
Korean Pharmacist Association of California	300
Korean Photographic Association of California	
Korean Scientists and Engineers Association	46
Korean Society of Engineering Science and	
Professional Management of Southern California	70
Korean Traders Club of Los Angeles	45
Korean Travel Agency Association of California	7
Na U Club (Businessman's Club)	37

Apart from rotating credit, partnerships and private loans from family and friends are other means of acquiring capital which rely on "communal resources." However, the sole proprietorship based on the saving up of one's own capital is probably the most common form.[43]

The early Asian immigrants developed a system of labor paternalism which is still evident among Koreans. Preference is given to members of the ethnic group in hiring, but work conditions are poor, the hours long, pay low and irregular, and membership in unions not contemplated. Indeed, in the garment industry, violations of labor standards have received some state agency attention. Despite these conditions, the employees have something to gain. They receive employment in a job market where unemployment is high and where poor English may be a severe handicap. In addition, they may receive on-the-job training and aid towards setting up a business of their own. In exchange, the employer obtains a reliable, loyal, and cheap worker. This employer "bargain" is cemented through ethnic allegiance.

Another feature of old Asian enterprises was a special relationship with ethnic community clientele. Fellow Asians would patronize Asian stores when they could, and would in turn get a special price or better credit arrangement. Among Koreans, this does not occur overtly; if a Korean and non-Korean walked into a Korean store they would pay the same price for the same item. However, Korean clients do receive preferential treatment through such indirect channels as advertisement in the vernacular press, and referrals through Korean associations.

Information and training are important resources which the community can effectively mobilize. The ethnic press plays an important role in the process. In Los Angeles, there are four Korean daily newspapers, two weeklies, and two Korean television stations each broadcasting a two-hour weekly program. Through these channels Koreans are given up-to-date information on business trends. For example, they can read articles on how to manage a business and how to avoid being cheated. And, they can advertise.

Community organizations are also important sources of information. The Korean Chamber of Commerce runs lecture series and classes, some of which provide instruction in business. The Asian Community Service Center operates a Korean hotline. Among other things, it offered aid in seventy-one cases of business and job counseling in 1974.[44]

Private Korean concerns also aid in the efficient distribution of information. There are businesses which specialize in providing information as a service. For example, one real estate agency locates small businesses being sold around the city, providing this information to prospective Korean buyers.

Another resource which is efficiently passed around the community is businesses themselves. Once a shop is in the hands of Korean, chances are the next owner will be a Korean.[45]

Apart from distributing resources efficiently and cheaply, the Korean community could perform the function of controlling internal competition, as did trade guilds in earlier Asian communities.[46] Korean businessmen and leaders of the community are aware of the advantages of agreements over spacing and price policy. While some attempts have been made to institute them in the grocery business, for example, the pressure of competition, and the continued influx of new immigrants anxious to get established in similar lines makes such agreements almost impossible to sustain. In addition, some of the most recent immigrants are coming with more capital, making it less essential for them to join in agreements with their poorer compatriots. In the long run, however, we expect that internal competition will come under organizational control.

The ability of the Korean community to mobilize its own resources is impressive. However, there is another, less rosy side to the picture. Not only does the community "help its own"; it "exploits" them. There is a flowering of adjustment services, such as business or immigration consultants, whose living depends on the problems and aspirations of newly arrived countrymen. There is a tendency to charge fees for all services. The labor contractor takes advantage of the difficult circumstances of new immigrants to turn a good profit. Indeed, the use of unpaid family labor, or nonunion low-wage workers, is a form of exploitation. In general, older immigrants climb up the economic ladder on the backs of newer immigrants, a prevalent practice among pre-1924 European immigrants in the east. It is a system that works to everyone's advantage so long as immigration continues. Should the influx from Korea suddenly be curtailed, however, the latest arrivals could be trapped at the bottom of the economic ladder.

Noncommunal resources

Unlike earlier Asian immigrants, who developed a reputation for low dependence on the public, the Koreans are determined to make use of all resources. They want to get full value for their tax dollar, and are not reluctant to use political means to get it. In other words, there has been a shift from the "quiet Asian" image. For example, aspiring Korean businessmen do not only rely on their own or friends' savings to finance their enterprises. Many turn to American banks or to the Small Business Administration.

The community helps tap noncommunal resources. Community organizations and the press will direct people to public agencies, such as the Office of Minority Business Enterprise (OMBE), the Asian American National Business Alliance (AANBA), and the Interracial Council for Business Opportunity (ICBO), which can give them business assistance.

The Korean community tries to exert political pressure to further its interests. There is an attempt to get the community to support particular political candidates and to deliver the votes on election day. In 1972, the Korean American Political Association supported Jerry Brown for governor, Marvyn Dymally for lieutenant governor, and March Fong Eu for secretary of state.

The community tries to gain access to government officials to make sure its needs are met. It pressured the Los Angeles Police Department into doubling the police protection in the Olympic area. It induced the mayor to appoint a Korean aid to act as a liaison with the community.[47] Some of the data which this paper uses come from "advocacy research," in which a member tries to gain public

assistance for the community.[48] In addition, the ethnic press urges that Koreans be good citizens, while encouraging them to exercise the rights of citizenship.

Korean government

Another resource Korean immigrants can use, which was not available to earlier Asian immigrants, is aid from their home government. The South Korean government encourages emigration, with the idea of sending its less wealthy elements overseas and helping them to get rich there. They will either come home or send back some of their wealth, enriching Korea either way. As we have seen, Korea sets a very low limit on the amount of money an individual can take out. There is also a limit on who can emigrate, restrictions being erected against those with assets of $25,000 or more.

The government of Korea helps local businesses in at least two ways. First, it aids in training and disseminating information; some of the classes in entrepreneurship run by the Korean Association are taught by visiting dignitaries. Second, and more important, it helps to provide capital. There are now two Korean banks in Los Angeles: the Korea Exchange Bank (specializing in international trade) and the Korea Exchange Bank of California (which is more concerned with local-oriented business). In addition, the government provided matching funds to help the local community purchase a Community Center building, which houses some of the top organizations of the community.

South Korea benefits from the development of local business because it helps to establish export outlets. The Korea Exchange Bank, which deals mainly with local importers of Korean products, has an annual loan volume of $100 million. Two lines of exports are of special importance: hair products and clothing. It is a fact, Korea produces most of the world's wigs. Its dominant position depends on the use of cheap, female labor which is paid about 50,000 won ($100) per month. There is "vertical integration" in this line in that Korean importers use local Korean small businesses as their chief retail outlet.

The scale of clothing importation is much larger and of far greater potential importance. According to a number of sources, the Los Angeles garment industry is now controlled by Jews, but the Koreans are starting to make a crack in the edifice. Although there is some local manufacture, the Jews depend on importing from "cheap labor" countries such as Brazil and Taiwan. As yet, they do not import from Korea, leaving that trade to Korean importers. About twenty percent of the clothing imported to the U.S. now comes from Korea. Unlike the wig business, the major outlets are not Korean small shops, but large volume Jewish-owned retailers with multimillion dollar annual sales.

The local Korean press plays a role in Korea's efforts to establish export outlets. Three of the local papers are versions of Seoul newspapers, with a section changed to provide local news and advertising. In turn, the Seoul papers are sponsored by major corporations and conglomerates in Korea.

Another benefit to Korea in aiding local business is the sending back of remittances to families in the homeland. The Korea Exchange Bank handles most (though not all) of these, and reports that it sends back about $5 million per annum.

It should be noted that the Korean government's activities in the local community are not all viewed in a positive light. There is considerable negative sentiment towards the Park regime, which is not surprising given that a number of local Koreans emigrated for political reasons. There is concern that the Korean CIA has operatives in Los Angeles, based in the Consul-General's office, to make sure the emigrant community is not too critical of Park Chung-hee.[49] Strong business ties with Korea lead many community members to subdue their criticisms of the government in the interests of perpetrating good economic relations.

"Success" of businesses

We have been describing four mechanisms by which Koreans "succeed" in business. But how successful are they really? There is some disagreement over the answer to this question.

While Korean businesses may have a better chance of survival than other minority-owned businesses, bankruptcy and failure is not unknown among them. The Small Business Association, for example, reports that it faced a problem of a series of failures in Korean-owned liquor stores. However, this record did not extend to other business lines.

If we mean by "success" making millions of dollars, or even hundreds of thousands, Korean enterprise could not be deemed successful except in rare instances. Typically, the firm must struggle and its owners work excessively hard in order to keep it going. If, on the other hand, we mean by "success" survival and modest growth to the point where many people can make a decent living by American standards, we must conclude that Korean immigrant enterprise is largely successful. Indeed, their great overrepresentation in small business would seem to put it beyond dispute.

"Success" in business is not instantaneous. It typically takes two to three years of very hard work and abstinence to get established. But, after this initial breaking-in period, many Korean families are well on the road to becoming established.

This should not be taken to mean there is no poverty in the Korean community. Poverty does exist, especially among the most recent immigrants, and many people are underemployed and earning below their capacity. In particular, many Koreans enter the U.S. with professional training and are given preference by the immigration authorities because of these skills, only to find on arrival that they cannot pass state licensing examinations, in part (and perhaps entirely), because of language difficulties. In one notorious case, pharmacy, they are not even permitted to take the examination.[50] "Success" in small business must be seen in the context of failure to become established in one's chosen profession.

Another sign of "success" is that Koreans are able to climb up a kind of business ladder. They typically start with a business which requires little capital, such as a gas station or wig shop. As their stake increases, they move on to a grocery store. Requiring still more capital, perhaps $100,000, are liquor stores and restaurants. At the top of the ladder is real estate. We heard that Koreans are investing in land in the Antelope Valley, near the projected new

Los Angeles international airport. They also purchase rental real estate, again suggesting a "middleman" role. This kind of business succession helps to explain the preference for liquidity of assets, apart from sojourning.[51] Koreans want to "get rich quick," and the way to do it is not to sink too much capital into any particular business.

As we said earlier in this paper, it is difficult for small business to compete successfully with efficient, capital-intensive, large corporations. How then are the Koreans able to succeed? The four factors discussed above help to lower the costs of Korean enterprise relative to other small business. Whether or not they lower them sufficiently to compete effectively with big business is another question. In some cases, for example, grocery stores, Koreans are unable to undersell the supermarkets, and depend for survival on carrying special products such as Korean foods, on staying open long hours, and on location. Similarly, Korean restaurants depend less on cheapness than on the exotic quality of their meals, and catering to the ethnic clientele. In other cases, for example, wig shops, their success depends on advantageous access to the sources of supply. In still others, Koreans have capitulated to corporate control, and purchase franchises from big business rather than trying to fight against it.

However, there are still cases, we believe, where the "cheapness" of the Korean firm enables it to be competitive. For example, janitorial services and sewing factories, which subcontract from big business, must be cheaper than the corporations could provide for themselves by hiring directly. The cheapness here lies in being able to mobilize immigrant "cheap labor," to utilize paternalistic ties with the workers in order to subvert discontent and avoid unionization, and to bear the costs of management. The profit margins of such enterprises are often slim, and the owner may work alongside his employees, making it difficult for the workers to develop a working-class consciousness against him. If they did, of course, the costs of the enterprise would rise and it would cease to exist.[52]

THE KOREANS ENGAGE IN SMALL BUSINESS

The reasons why Koreans enter small business in an economy which is moving in the opposite direction can be discussed under two headings: the immediate reasons as experienced and articulated by the Koreans themselves, and the larger forces in the social system which the participants may not be aware of. The following discussion presents possibilities, not conclusions.

Immediate reasons

One of the most frequent reasons given for entering small business is the lack of adequate alternatives. According to Kim Ha Tai, "When it comes to getting employment in American firms, factories, public and private institutions, there is a great deal of difficulty in securing jobs due to discrimination and language barriers."[53] This and licensure problems (which may indeed be seen as discriminatory) severely restrict Korean job opportunities in the general economy.

A second commonly articulated reason concerns the immigration itself. The Immigration and Naturalization Service will adjust the status of persons who are self-employed on the assumption that they contribute to the American economy.[54] Once established, the business can be used for sponsoring other relatives, since assurance can be provided that they will be employed and not become a public burden. Small business helps the process of chain migration, while the immigration aids the business with a continuing stream of "cheap labor."

Both of the above reasons imply that Koreans enter small business against their will, or at best are so constrained that they have little choice. We question this, believing that many Koreans would enter small business even if they had better job opportunities in the surrounding society and were not faced with immigration problems. This brings us to a third frequently mentioned reason: to provide education for their children. This suggests Koreans view entrepreneurship as a way to make money. Education for one's children is one of the goals which can be achieved with wealth.

It seems the Koreans see this country as a land of economic opportunity. They have bought the "American dream" while, paradoxically, most Americans have given up on it (at least judging from the low and decreasing level of self-employment). It is puzzling that immigrants are better able than the natives to see, and take advantage of, opportunities for self-employment. Perhaps the answer lies in the larger social system.

Larger reasons

Unarticulated reasons for concentrating in small business can be divided into two types: those which come from the Koreans themselves (internal factors), and those which come from the American social system. One internal factor concerns the level of economic development in South Korea. Koreans come from an economy where small business is still very much alive. That they aspire to enter it is, therefore, not at all surprising. The fact that Korea is a poorer country than the U.S. also encourages Koreans to be thrifty. They may be willing to live for a while on a level that an American would consider very low, but does not compare unfavorably with the Korean level of living.

We believe there is truth to this explanation, yet a puzzle remains. Given that the Korean approach of thrift and self-denial works and proves there are still opportunities for small business within American advanced capitalism, why do not Americans pursue the same path? The answer, we hypothesize, lies in a subtle issue of consciousness. Monopoly capitalism has made the American people into an army of wage and salary workers who have essentially given up the American dream. The reasons for this are not just resignation; they are unwilling to pay the costs of small business. How many Americans would be willing to keep a shop open seven days a week, fifteen hours a day? The fact is, the American working class has fought long and hard for a comfortable and secure life. They value leisure time and the right not to have to work too hard for long hours. They value job security and the comfort of not having to worry about the job folding. Needless to say, not all American workers have attained these goals, but we would contend that even the unemployed in the ghetto share them,[55] preferring an eight-hour-a-day job with reasonable pay and fringe benefits, to the risky and hard-working life of the small entrepreneur. For Koreans, in contrast, hard

work, long hours, thrift, taking economic risks (admittedly minimized by communal support) are not yet alien, since Korea has not yet experienced a labor movement on a scale remotely approaching the United States. In a word, there is a "split labor market"[56] between locals and Korean immigrants which, in this case, takes a petit bourgeois form.

But, apart from internal factors, are there any forces within American monopoly capitalism which encourage Korean immigrants to enter small business? We shall consider three possibilities: that the "system" pushes them into playing a middleman minority role, that gaps are left by monopoly capital which Koreans can fill, and that the immigrants themselves create small business niches which monopoly capital finds useful.

The first possibility is that the "system" helps to create Korean small business. It uses Korean immigrants to play a "middleman minority" role[57] to the masses, especially disprivileged minorities. Koreans are interposed between the corporations and the people, helping to distribute corporate products, and bearing the brunt of hostility, crime, and low profits accruing to retailers and service shops in poor areas.

To sustain this view, we would have to show that the corporations (or the government representing their interests) somehow act to encourage Korean small business. There are a number of points that support such an interpretation. The policies of the Immigration and Naturalization Service, as we have seen, help to push Koreans into small business, and the Small Business Association helps to provide some of the wherewithal. The largest number of SBA loans to Koreans were given to liquor store operators—33 out of 101, totaling $2,850,550 from 1971–74,[58] and Korean liquor stores are quite likely to operate in the ghetto and barrio. Franchising is another mechanism whereby one can see a direct link between corporations and using the Korean small entrepreneur as an outlet which bears many social and economic costs.

Against this interpretation is the fact that Koreans help to distribute not only American, but also Korean corporate products. In the wig, garment, and some food products industries, they are at odds with local big business. Also, American financial institutions do not unambiguously support middleman-type firms. Despite the large number of SBA loans to liquor stores, Korean garment manufacturers received much larger loans, averaging $450,000 compared to $86,000 for a liquor store.[59] And in an interview with an SBA representative, we were told that they prefer to finance nonretail businesses, thereby encouraging more circulation of funds within a community. Retailing is seen as draining money out of the community and sending it straight to the supplier. The Small Business Association expresses a preference for manufacturing, which creates jobs within the community. Similarly, private banks seem to favor manufacturing. These facts suggest that the middleman role is less than encouraged by big business or the government.

The second approach is to see monopoly capitalism as less active in the development of Korean business. The large corporations leave gaps in the economy which prove inefficient for them to fill. The corner grocery store between two shopping centers, satisfying the demand for the occasional few items needed between weekly shoppings or at odd hours, is a case in point. Many services, like hair cutting or shoe repair, are left to the small entrepreneur, perhaps because there is little economic advantage in large-scale operations. Similarly, the ghetto and barrio, with their high crime rates and credit problems, may be deserted by the corporations for more profitable locations. In other words, the edifice of monopoly capitalism may be somewhat porous, leaving niches which the enterprising small businessperson can take advantage of.

This view fits with "dual labor market theory,"[60] which sees the economy as divided into core and peripheral industries. The former, such as steel and automobile manufacturing, are highly centralized in the hands of a few giant corporations. They have well-developed technologies, are capital-intensive, and their labor force is unionized and relatively well-paid. The peripheral industries deal with more perishable items (for example, food, clothing) in which control of the market is much more problematic. They tend to be the opposite of the core industries in terms of the factors mentioned, that is, they have low technological content, are labor in-

tensive, and tend to have nonunionized, low-paid workers. The "service economy" tends to fall among the peripheral industries.

Whether or not these "gaps" in corporate domination will remain is another question. Some would argue that they are technologically determined so that it will never be efficient for big capital to take them over. We are inclined to believe, rather, that they are signs of "uneven development," and will inevitably fall prey to centralizing pressures. The service industries tend to be newer and are therefore less "advanced" in their organization, but sooner or later a few large corporations will dominate these too. (This is not to say that new undeveloped pockets will not emerge in the future. Indeed, uneven developments may be a chronic condition in advanced capitalism. But the points of underdevelopment shift over time.)

Meanwhile, Koreans help to fill the gaps with small businesses which are able to run fairly efficiently. Since they tend to keep prices down, Koreans make it harder for the big corporations to enter their fields. In other words, Korean enterprise can be seen as a retarding influence on the total "monopolization" of the economy. If we accept this interpretation, it makes sense that INS and SBA support Korean entrepreneurship, since the U.S. government reflects the interests not only of the corporations, but also of those who would like to contain their power. The very existence of the SBA suggests this. Because Koreans have the desire and know-how to pursue self-employment, they help us all to slow down the inevitable advance of monopoly capitalism.

This brings us to the third interpretation, namely, that Koreans actively create small business niches within monopoly capitalism. This seems to be the case in a few lines, namely, garment industry subcontracting and maintenance companies. In the garment industry, for example, sewing could be done in large factories under assembly-line conditions. That it is subcontracted to small sweatshops, of which Korean-operated shops are only one example, suggests that they are able to produce the goods for less.

Unlike retailing and service shops, the garment factory and maintenance business have the characteristic of using large labor pools. The firm owners are almost in the business of labor contracting to the large corporations, except that they retain some control over the labor process. The role of the Korean entrepreneur, then, is to help the corporations exploit cheap immigrant labor, which, through paternalism and community ties, is kept docile and nonunionized. Korean shops perform a service for the corporations which the latter could not achieve on their own. One might note that SBA is aware of substandard labor conditions in Korean garment factories and other businesses, yet chooses not to turn them in to the authorities. While the rationale is to allow a struggling new business a little legal leeway, the consequence is to permit the continued exploitation of immigrant "cheap labor."

In these cases, the relationship of Korean enterprise to monopolization is more ambiguous. By providing big corporations with cheap labor to fill at least part of their work requirements, Korean entrepreneurs are aiding the corporations in cutting costs, thereby enabling them to compete more effectively. On the other hand, the Korean organizers of these labor pools are themselves a form of decentralization, though we should note that they "control" a very small segment of the production process, and have virtually no say in the larger scheme.

This kind of creation of niches in the corporate structure seems to depend heavily on immigration. It is the newest immigrant who is likely to work in the sweatshops until he or she has amassed enough savings to set up a business. As such, this process is probably short-lived. Once immigration slows down, it is unlikely to persist for very long.

Of the three interpretations, we believe that the second and third both have some cogency. The monopolization of the economy is incomplete, allowing enterprising Koreans to take advantage of the less developed areas, especially services and small trade. So far, we find little support for the idea that the big corporations encourage the Koreans to play the middleman role in minority areas. The role of big business seems more passive; they find the poorer areas to be less profitable, and leave them to immigrants who are willing (or forced through lack of alternatives) to accept the reduced profit margins and higher crime rate. On the other hand, particularly in the garment and maintenance industries, Korean immigrants do appear to be able to create niches in the economy which they can run more cheaply, because of the nature of the labor supply, than can the corporations. This type of small business may be more important to monopoly capitalism, and be a significant reason for its receiving institutional support. Also, the United States government may be implicated, rather indirectly, in this whole process by helping to prop up the Park regime which in turn helps to keep Korean labor cheap.

Two questions relating to the future remain. First, what will happen to Korean entrepreneurship if, as we predict, monopoly capitalism continues to extend its influence into all branches of the economy? One possibility is that this process will never be complete, as new industries will always be emerging. Another is that Koreans will adapt in the form of running semiindependent shops. Franchising is a system in which monopoly capital can utilize the initiative, energy, and resources of the small entrepreneur, and we may come to see more Koreans following this path.

The second question concerns the issue of race relations. Middleman minorities have notoriously been ill-received by the communities in which they reside. They face antagonism from their clientele, business competitors, and organized labor.[61] Already some signs of irritation are emerging. Los Angeles labor unions have held demonstrations against garment importers who bring in clothing from "cheap labor" countries. And, as we said earlier, the Division of Labor Standards Enforcement has investigated local sweatshops. Neither of these instances have singled out the Koreans; indeed, in the larger scheme of things in the garment industry, the Koreans are still not all that visible. Apart from the garment industry, we have heard small rumblings about competition between Koreans and other retailers. And crime against Korean shopkeepers suggests the possibility of antagonism from the clientele. There have been some cases of murdered store owners. On the other hand, it has not been suggested that Korean entrepreneurs are singled out as special targets of crime, and we have been told that they are careful to protect themselves from being seen as "alien shopkeepers" by hiring a member of the group where they are located to serve behind the counter.

While the signs of friction are minimal so far, the potential for intergroup conflict seems large, especially if Korean business continues to grow at the current rate, and spreads all over the city. At the moment, Koreans do not particularly stand out amidst the cultural heterogeneity of an immigrant center like Los Angeles. But the day may come when a new anti-Asian agitation surfaces in Southern California.

NOTES

1. The research was supported by the National Science Foundation under grant Soc. 76-12348.

2. *Newsweek*, 26 May 1975, p.10.

3. Warren Y. Kim, *Koreans in America*. Los Angeles: Po Chin Chai, 1971, pp.3-4 and Hyung-chan Kim and Wayne Patterson, (eds.) *The Koreans in America, 1882-1974* (Dobbs Ferry, New York: Oceana, 1974), p.v-2.

4. Hyung-chan Kim, "Some Aspects of Social Demography of Korean Americans," *International Migration Review*, vol. 8 (Spring 1974), p.24.

5. Lee Houchins and Chang-su Houchins, "The Korean Experience in America, 1903-1924," *Pacific Historical Review*, vol. 43 (November, 1974) pp.553-54; Warren Y. Kim, *Koreans in America* (Los Angeles: Po Chin Chai, 1971), p.4; and Linda Shin, "Koreans in America, 1903-1945," in Amy Tachiki, Eddie Wong, and Franklin Odo, (eds.) *Roots: An Asian American Reader* (Los Angeles: University of California at Los Angeles, Asian American Studies Center, 1971), p.200.

6. Kim and Patterson, op. cit, p.v.

7. Kyung Lee, *Ethnic Enterprise in America* (Berkeley: University of California Press, 1972), p.18.

8. Shin, op. cit, p.201.

9. Warren Y. Kim, op. cit.

10. Roger Daniels, *The Politics of Prejudice: The Anti-Japanese Movement in California and the Struggle for Japanese Exclusion* (Gloucester, Mass.: Peter Smith, 1966), pp.27 and 126.

11. Elliott Abrams and Franklin S. Abrams, "Immigration Policy - Who Gets In and Why?" *Public Interest*, vol. 38 (Winter 1975), p.4.

12. Monica Boyd, "The Changing Nature of Central and Southeast Asian Immigration to the United States: 1961-1972," *International Migration Review*, vol. 8 (Winter 1974), pp.507-19.

13. U.S. Department of Justice, Immigration and Naturalization Service, *Annual Report: Immigration and Naturalization Service* (Washington, D.C., 1975), Table 14.

14. U.S. Department of Justice, ibid., 1974 and 1975, Table 15.

15. James Alsop Thames, "Korean Students in Southern California: Factors Influencing Their Plans Towards Returning Home." Ph.D dissertation in Education, University of Southern California, 1971.

16. U.S. Department of Commerce, Bureau of Census. *Census of Population: 1970, Subject Reports, Japanese, Chinese and Filipinos in the United States* (Washington, D.C.: 1973), Tables 48 and 49.

17. Eui-Young Yu, "A Comment on the Number of Koreans in the 1970 U.S. Census of Population," Korean Student Association of Southern California, no.5, 1974, p.35 and California Advisory Committee to U.S. Commission on Civil Rights, *Asian American and Pacific Peoples: A Case of Mistaken Identity* (Washington, D.C., 1975), pp.16-18.

18. Idem, "Koreans in America: An Emerging Ethnic Minority," paper presented at the Annual Meeting of the American Sociological Association, New York, August 30 to September 3, 1976.

19. U.S. Department of Justice, op. cit. 1975, Table 12A.

20. David Y. Lee, "Organizational Activities of the Korean Community" (master's thesis, University of California at Los Angeles, 1974), p.8.

21. Yu, "Koreans in America," op. cit.

22. Ivan Light, *Ethnic Enterprise in America* (Berkeley: University of California Press, 1972), p.16.

23. Shotaro Frank Miyamoto, "Social Solidarity among the Japanese in Seattle," *University of Washington Publications in the Social Sciences* II (Seattle, Washington: University of Washington, December 1939), p.70.

24. Helen Lewis Givens, "The Korean Community in Los Angeles County" (master's thesis, University of Southern California, 1939), p.48.

25. Special Task Force to the Secretary of Health, Education and Welfare, *Work in America*. Cambridge, Massachusetts: MIT Press, 1973, p.21.

26. Harry Braverman, *Labor and Monopoly Capital: The Degradation of Work in the Twentieth Century* (New York: Monthly Review Press, 1974.)

27. Dong-a Ilbo, October 28, 1975.

28. Edna Bonacich, "A Theory of Middleman Minorities," *American Sociological Review*, vol. 38 (October 1973), pp.583-94.

29. U.S. Department of Commerce, Bureau of Census. *Minority-Owned Businesses - Asian Americans, American Indians, and Others* (Washington, D.C., 1972), Tables 2 and 4.

30. David Kim, "Business Development in Koreatown, USA," student paper in Architecture and Planning, University of California at Los Angeles, 1975, pp.22-23.

31. U.S., Congress, House Committee on Education and Labor, Subcommittee on Equal Opportunities. *Koreans in Los Angeles: Employment and Education, Hearings on H.R. 9895*, 93rd Cong., 2nd sess., 1974, p.183.

32. David Kim, op. cit., p.36.

33. Ibid., pp.30-31.

34. House Subcommittee Hearings, op. cit., pp.183-84.

35. L. Clay Terry and Valiant R. Stull, "An Independent Study of the Los Angeles Korean Community and Its People," student paper, California State University at Los Angeles, 1975, pp.31-32.

36. House Subcommittee Hearings, op. cit., p.18.

37. *The New Korea*, 29 May 1975.

38. *The New Korea*, 6 March 1975.

39. Terry and Stull, op. cit., pp.34-35.

40. *The New Korea*, 5 June 1975.

41. Light, op. cit.

42. Terry and Stull, op. cit., pp.37-39.

43. David Kim, op. cit., pp.41-42.

44. *The New Korea*, 26 December 1974.
45. Terry and Stull, op. cit., p.34.
46. Light, op. cit., pp.68-69.
47. *The New Korea*, 22 May 1975.
48. For example, House Subcommittee Hearings, op. cit.; California Advisory Committee, op. cit.; and California Advisory Committee to U.S. Commission on Civil Rights, *A Dream Unfulfilled: Korean and Filipino Health Professionals in California* (Washington, D.C., May 1975).
49. Terry and Stull, op. cit., pp.46-47.
50. California Advisory Committee, *A Dream Unfulfilled,* op. cit.
51. Bonacich, op. cit.
52. Dean Lan, "The Chinatown Sweatshops: Oppression and an Alternative," *Amerasia Journal*, vol. 1 (November 1971), pp.40-57.
53. Kim Ha Tai, *The New Korea*, 13 March 1975.
54. Terry and Stull, op. cit., pp.33-34.
55. Edna Bonacich, "Advanced Capitalism and Black/White Race Relations in the United States: A Split Labor Market Interpretation," *American Sociological Review*, vol. 41 (February, 1976), pp.34-51.
56. Idem, "A Theory of Ethnic Antagonism: The Split Labor Market," *American Sociological Review*, vol. 37 (October 1972), pp.547-59.
57. Hubert M. Blalack, Jr., *Towards a Theory of Minority Group Relations* (New York: John Wiley, 1967), pp.79-84.
58. David Kim, op. cit., p.42.
59. Kim, ibid., pp.42-43.
60. For example, David M. Gordon, *Theories of Poverty and Underemployment* (Lexington, Massachusetts: D. C. Heath, 1972).
61. Bonacich, "Middleman, Minorities," op. cit.

IMMIGRANTS AND THE MEDICAL CARE SYSTEM: THE EXAMPLE OF THE PORTUGUESE

Lois Monteiro

One of the concerns about National Health Insurance voiced by health care policy makers is that the equity of access to medical care which should be the right of all Americans be assured with a national health program. The accessibility of care, and the barriers which individuals meet in obtaining needed care, have been studied by economists and sociologists. These scholars have emphasized economic and geographical barriers to access, but the literature also includes examinations of other barriers, such as patterns of physician distribution and cultural differences in illness perception. This paper will examine the factors related to access to and use of medical care among one subpopulation, immigrants of Portuguese origin.

BACKGROUND

The extent to which immigrants use medical care is of importance for a number of reasons. As Wessen has pointed out, migrants probably represent a rather unique epidemiological subgroup, whose health status can be expected for a variety of reasons to differ from that of nonmigrants and of the host population. Environmental change, altered social and psychological circumstances, shifts in exposure to transmissible diseases, and dietary changes, are some of the specific variations in social, physical, and biological environments which, for the migrant, may be reflected in physical and psychosomatic illness and in need for medical care. Wessen argues that "if epidemiologists should wish to study the health effects of change, migrants seem a tremendously attractive population to study."[1] Yet there has been, in the United States at least, little emphasis on the immigrant in the recent literature on medical care and health services.[2] Part of this problem stems from the fact that the major source of health data on the United States population, The National Health Survey, conducted regularly by the National Center for Health Statistics, does not contain information on ethnicity or country of birth of those persons from whom the health data is obtained. The variables available from this source that have been the major interest of health care utilization studies are age, sex, residence location, income, and race. Health studies of ethnic groups have for the most part been conducted on data collected in local surveys, and have focused heavily on the Mexican American group,[3] while immigrants and the foreign-born population in general have been of greater interest to researchers in the population and fertility field, who have considered immigrant use of particular health services related to family planning resources.

A comprehensive study of immigrants' use of medical care services has been conducted by Shuval in Israel, a country where the level of immigration has been extremely high, and where the use of medical services through a national medical services system has also been very high. Shuval and her associates felt that extensive immigrant use of Israeli medical services was due not only to medical (illness) reasons, but also related to particular (nonmedical) psychological needs of the immigrant group, and that for the resolution of these needs the immigrant may try to get help from the medical care system. As examples of these nonmedical needs she cited the need for social contact and for interpersonal communication (she defines these as the need for catharsis and for a sympathetic ear), the need for a means of coping with failure, and the need for integration into the society. Her research situation demonstrated various associations between immigrants and clinic utilization as follows:

> High frequency of utilization is concentrated among those segments of the population which have not yet entered fully into the mainstream of Israeli life. The sick role apparently serves as a mechanism to aid immigrants in the process of adjustment to a new

social system. What is more, there is evidence that utilization rates fall off with time, presumably as immigrants assume the new social roles required of them and as they adapt to the social system. While it is possible that newly arrived immigrants are sicker and their level of health might improve with time, this research strongly suggests that certain social and psychological needs may also be motivating entry into the sick role as well as clinic attendance.

This pattern suggests that the medical institution fulfills an early socializing role for new immigrants, satisfying certain of their needs so that with time they no longer require the institution as much.[4]

However, in the Israeli system ("Kupat Holim"), there is almost free access to care, and financial barriers do not present the deterrents to use of services there that they do in this country.

SAMPLE SELECTION

This study will examine data collected from Portuguese ethnics in the state of Rhode Island, an area that researchers at Brown University have used for a series of local health surveys over the past ten years.[5] The central data source for the study was a survey of sixty-four families who resided in two "high immigrant" areas. The study areas were selected on the basis of 1970 census information which compared the location of residence of the individual in 1970 with his residence in 1965. Each of the selected census tracts had, in 1970, approximately 500 persons who had been living abroad in 1965. In addition, these areas were known to the researcher as places of high concentrations of Portuguese ethnics. Once the census tracts were selected the local school departments were contacted to determine if there were known residential subconcentrations of more recent immigrants within the larger census tract and, on the basis of these suggestions, residential areas to be surveyed were delimited. A ten percent sample of household addresses within the designated areas was selected from city directory lists of residential units in the area. Since the survey was to be limited to Portuguese ethnics, a screening question was used to determine eligibility for interview.

Due to limited time available for the survey and the difficulty in finding only the new immigrant, the survey was opened to all Portuguese ethnics. Persons living at selected addresses who said they were not of Portuguese origin were not interviewed. The interview questionnaire was printed in Portuguese and the interviews were conducted in that language, except in those households where a native born person was interviewed. By fortuitous circumstance, the social services department in one of the areas selected for the interviews had two C.E.T.A. temporary employees who were available to do the interviews. These were local young women with bilingual facility. The interviews in the other areas were conducted by two different Portuguese-speaking persons, one of whom also was of Portuguese ancestry. Of the 64 households that were eligible and interviewed, the year of immigration for the household was as follows:

Recent immigrants (1965 or after): 31 households, 48 percent;

Earlier immigrants (before 1965): 16 households, 25 percent;

Native-born households: 17 households, 27 percent.

The place of birth of the household heads was as follows:

Continental Portugal: 9 households, 14 percent;
Sao Miguel, Azores: 31 households, 48 percent;
Other Azores islands: 7 households, 11 percent;
United States: 17 households, 27 percent.

PORTUGUESE IMMIGRATION TO THE UNITED STATES

While the interest of this study is in new and current immigration, the record of Portuguese immigration to the United States actually dates from the seventeenth century when some Sephardic Jews no longer welcome in Portugal settled in New York and Newport. During the 1800s, many persons from the Azores served aboard American whalers and then settled in the United States, particularly in California and New England. In the early 1900s, pressed by the economic and political situation in their homeland, thousands of continental and Azorian Portuguese emigrated to become millworkers in the textile centers of the east coast, with New England, and especially the Fall River, Massachusetts, and Providence, Rhode Island areas as major foci for settlement. The Portuguese immigrants to California turned to farming. In the 1960s, when immigration restrictions were again relaxed, Portuguese immigrants, especially Azorean Portuguese, once more began to enter the country.

Although as a national ethnic group the Portuguese immigrants have not been highly visible, they have been, in recent years, one of the ten major sources of United States immigration. The Portuguese in 1969 ranked fifth as a sending country, with 17,567 United States immigrants, and from 1970–73, fluctuated between sixth and seventh in rank, with the number of immigrants ranging between 10,000 and 13,000. In the decade between 1964 and 1973, there were 91,397 immigrants to this country from Portugal. Furthermore, since 1962 when alien registration began, Portugal has been one of the ten countries which contributed nearly two-thirds of the registered permanent aliens in the United States.[6]

As has been noted, these immigrants have tended not to disperse geographically but to gravitate to the established Portuguese centers. As one writer put it, "Oakland is the Portuguese capital of California."[7] Gibson, in his work on the U.S. alien population, reported on the preference of new immigrants for California, "In 1969, a predominant number of immigrants from Mexico, Canada, and the Far East chose to live in California. . . . Some 20 percent of all new Portuguese immigrants chose to reside in California."[8] According to the annual reports of the Visa Office, an even greater proportion of Portuguese immigrants, about one-third, chose Massachusetts as their destination site in 1972. In Rhode Island, which received about 10 percent of the total Portuguese origin that same year, out of 2,476 immigrants entering the state, 1,143 were from Portugal. At the time of the 1960 census, 6,665 Rhode Island persons cited Portugal as their place of birth (7.7 percent of the state's foreign-born population). By 1970, in Rhode Island this figure had more than doubled to 14,582 persons who were born in Portugal or the Azores.

Immigration Service reports give some informa-

tion on the recently immigrating Portuguese population. The total immigration to the United States from Portugal during the three years of 1968, 1969, and 1970 was 41,935 persons. Of these, 13.8 percent, or 5,816 persons, intended to settle in Rhode Island; thus, a large proportion of the difference between the 1960 and 1970 census figures is accounted for by immigrants in those last three years. Alien registration reports, another estimation of immigrants, showed that in 1970 there were 11,421 Portuguese aliens who were registered as living in Rhode Island.

Some statistics on the national Portuguese ethnic population are available from the 1970 census. Table 1 shows the distribution of persons of Portuguese stock in the United States as reported in 1970. The concentrations of these persons in California, Massachusetts, and Rhode Island is evident. A similar distribution pattern can also be seen in Table 2, which displays the 1970 census figures on persons who reported that Portuguese was the language spoken in their home (mother tongue). Table 3, based on Immigration Service figures, shows the size and distribution of the Portuguese immigrant flow between 1970 and 1974. This table indicates a shift of preference of new immigrants away from California to the metropolitan areas of New York and New Jersey.[9]

IMPACT OF NEW IMMIGRATION ON LOCAL MEDICAL CARE DELIVERY SYSTEM

In the introductory section of this paper, it was suggested that immigrants can be expected to evidence greater need for medical care than the host population, and that immigrants, in the Israeli situations at least, have a high rate of use of medical care. However, a contradictory research finding has appeared in a study of Chinese immigrants in the Boston area which suggests that in the United States, medical care services may be underutilized. For that immigrant group, the authors felt that the reason for underutilization was related to the Chinese skepticism regarding Western medicine.[10]

The most immediately visible impact of the new wave of immigration on the health system in Rhode Island is found at the largest general hospital, a five-hundred bed facility which serves the state's medical community. There, at Rhode Island Hospital, as one waits for the main elevator one sees a large notice in Portuguese, explaining visiting hours and visitor regulations. In addition, at the side of this notice are pamphlets, also in Portuguese, which invite the visitor to *Seja Bemvindo* (feel welcome), and then go on to give the rules for visitors. In addition to this outward manifestation of the impact of the Portuguese-speaking community, the hospital maintains a staff of Portuguese interpreters to act as intermediaries for both hospitalized and outpatient Portuguese clients. An estimate of the proportion of Portuguese patients using the outpatient facilities is available from a survey of pediatric clinic users in which eighteen percent of the clinic's patients were of Portuguese or Spanish-speaking origin.

Neighborhood health centers, in which medical care is provided to small geographic areas, were developed by the Office of Economic Opportunity during the 1960s in a national effort to serve poverty populations which were in need of medical care (for example, ghetto areas in particular). A series of such centers has been established in Providence, Rhode Island, and one of these is located in the Portuguese ethnic section of Providence. That center serves an almost entirely Portuguese ethnic population of about eight thousand persons, of whom about one thousand are recent immigrants. The center provides ambulatory care for residents of the area, and has a largely Portuguese-speaking auxiliary staff, with English-speaking physicians and nurses.

The impact of the immigrant group on other medical care facilities has been less visible, although through the survey data which will be presented, we can get an indication of the impact on the private medical-care practitioners. First, however, let us consider one medical service which has had some stronger response to the immigrants, the psychiatric specialty group. With psychiatric care depending heavily on verbal interaction, the problems that foreign-language-speaking persons present for psychiatry could be expected. Since Portuguese is not a commonly known language, the possibilities for a patois type interaction are limited.

But, in addition to verbal facility, psychiatric services require that the client and provider share a perception of the situation and of the need for services. Such a shared perception is important to some extent with all medical care but is greater in psychiatry. The recognition of the existence of illness requires that a change in bodily function be perceived as an indication of illness. To take on the sick role, and behave in expected ways in relation to medical care, a person must view his behavioral or physical phenomena as a symptom of illness. For example, medical anthropologists have shown that in some cultures certain physical changes might not be considered as an illness and, consequently, would go untreated. Some ethnic groups have been shown to be less likely to report symptoms of a certain type or to be less sensitive to pain.[11] Since symptoms of psychiatric or behavioral illness may often be subtle and easily defined as a nonsickness, a shared perception (by client and therapist) of certain behavior as illness may be difficult to achieve when the therapist is confronted with a patient from an unknown culture, and when verbal communication is hampered as well.

The psychiatric group at the Brown University Medical School and its teaching hospitals has seen the problem of the new immigrants to the area and recognized the importance of learning about the Portuguese culture. The psychiatric services have held teaching rounds on the subject, using consultants from the university's Portuguese and Brazilian Studies Center. The psychiatric group has been particularly interested in religious and superstitious beliefs which would especially hamper therapy.

THE IMMIGRANT HEALTH SURVEY

In the past decade, health surveys, as we have noted previously, have been done on local and national populations to gather baseline data on the needs for services, data that can then be used for decisions by health planners. For example, PL 93–641, the National Health Planning and Resources Development Act of 1974, requires that planning for and coordination of local health care spending be under the supervision of local "health systems agencies." The law requires the health systems agencies to gather and analyze data on health in their area so that rational decisions can be made about health-care spending. Those states and metropolitan areas with large immigrant populations would seem compelled by the legislation to learn more about the health needs of these ethnic groups, and investigations of immigrant health care may become more important in the next few years as the agencies begin their planning. Incidentally, since the board of the local health systems agencies must, by law, be comprised half of consumers, and half of providers, and be representative of the area served, the immigrant group should have further impact on health planning through this mechanism.[12]

The findings from the survey of sixty-four immigrant Portuguese families provide some interesting data on the health of the respondents and their use of medical care services. Table 4 gives a general overview of the differences between the new immigrants and the rest of the Portuguese group on the health measures. In each of the 64 families, one member (usually the wife of the household head) reported on the whole family. This technique is commonly used in health surveys, but may introduce some bias. However, it is generally felt that the mother can best answer about the health of the children, and the bias introduced is minimal, relating mostly to her reports about adult household members. Data was thus collected on 253 family members, of whom 131 were in post-1965 immigrant households, 72 in earlier immigrant households, and 49 in households with a native-born head of Portuguese ancestry.

The findings on health status suggest that the new immigrants are in better health than are the other sample members. The new group had a smaller percentage who said they had an illness (answered "yes" to the question, "Do you have any sickness or physical incapacity?"), and they also had a smaller percentage who said they had a longstanding illness of more than three months duration. With regard to the first question about any illness, 19 percent of the new immigrants had an illness, compared to 33 percent of the rest of the sample. Similarly, 5 percent of the new immigrants, compared to 10 percent of the remaining sample, had a chronic illness. Twenty-eight percent of the recent immigrant group, compared to 42 percent of the other group, said that during the previous year they had experienced at least one day in which illness forced them to stay in bed. Data which is available on the total Rhode Island population for the last two measures, chronic conditions and disability days, show a smaller proportion of chronic conditions among new immigrants than among the general Rhode Island population (5 percent compared to 29 percent), but about the same proportion of both groups had experienced a "sick day" (28 percent compared to 25 percent).

Immigrants are to some extent screened for exclusion of persons with serious illness, and the lower chronic conditions rate may reflect this selective process. Their present illness rate as indicated by the sick days measure suggests that, in this respect, the immigrants are not much different from the host population.

The low figures on illness experience might well be also a reflection of some unwillingness on the part of newer immigrant respondents to admit to illness. A number of social-psychological factors could influence these reports, including suspicion or uncertainty about why the interviewer, a stranger, would want the information, and fear of how a negative report would be used. Assurances of anonymity might carry little weight with persons unfamiliar with the United States tradition of public opinion polls. Corroborating evidence to support the idea that illness was underreported is fortunately available from another survey,[13] done in the same area, at the same time, with the same interviewers, but with a different set of questions that were primarily about education and language and that also included a few illness-related items. Those persons were given a list of conditions and asked if *anyone* in the household (identification of the victim was not asked) suffered from the condition. From that list the following conditions were admitted:

Diabetes, 5 percent of the households
Heart trouble, 19 percent
High blood pressure, 19 percent
Asthma, 7 percent
Kidney trouble, 25 percent
Stomach problems, 28 percent.

For all except the last of these conditions, there was no difference between new and old immigrant households in the proportion reporting the condition. For "stomach problems," there was a significant difference between the groups with the condition being reported in 46 percent of the recent immigrant households compared to 18 percent of the remaining sample. With the data we have, we can only speculate on why this particular condition should have been so frequently reported. Perhaps stomach upsets are a reflection of the stress and tension of the immigrant status or of the food changes related to immigration. It is also possible that "stomach trouble" may be a catch phrase used by Azorians to stand for a variety of indefinite symptoms; for example, rather than saying "I just feel rotten," the phrase would be "I've got a belly ache." This is common in Brazil where *figado* (liver) covers indispositions from headache to intestinal cramps. However, since the reports of stomach trouble are much lower among the earlier immigrant cohorts, the best explanation of the finding would seem to be the physical (tension and eating habits) rather than the folk illness source.

SOURCES OF IMMIGRANT MEDICAL CARE

In addition to displaying the findings of immigrant health status, Table 4 shows the extent to which the immigrants were associated with particular sources of medical and dental care. The first measure listed, "percent with a regular doctor," was based on the question, "Is there a particular doctor whom you would visit or telephone if you had a problem related to your health?" Eighty percent of the new immigrants and 89 percent of the remaining Portuguese sample, as well as 89 percent of the Rhode Island population, said they had such a doctor. In nationwide surveys, about 67 percent of the population reported they regularly used a particular physician, and another 18 percent used a clinic regularly. Thus, although a smaller proportion of the new immigrants had a regular physician, the percentage was still above the national figure for such medical care use, and close to the proportion for the rest of the Rhode Island population. With regard to the next measure listed, the proportion of

new immigrants who were also affiliated with another, second physician beyond the regular care source was small (18 percent) compared to the Portuguese ethnic group (26 percent), and both were low compared to the Rhode Island population (53 percent). This measure shows the extent to which the immigrants depended on a single provider, such as a general practitioner, for all their care rather than using different specialists for different conditions. The latter pattern of specialist use probably requires that the patient have a rather sophisticated knowledge of the provider system; for example, another study of provider relationships has shown that such a pattern was favored by more educated, higher income respondents.[14] There was little difference between the two Portuguese groups on the percent who visited the doctor (48 percent), but both were somewhat lower than the figure for the total population (55 percent).

Sharp differences between the new immigrants and both the longer established Portuguese and the total population appeared with the last two measures in Table 4, dental services. Fifty percent of the new immigrants, compared to 80 percent of the other Portuguese ethnics, said they had a dentist. An even smaller proportion of the new immigrants had visited a dentist during the previous year, 22 percent of these persons, compared to 35 percent of the other Portuguese and 47 percent of the state's population. These differences are statistically significant and show that dental care is being neglected or delayed by the immigrant group.

The data allow for more complex analyses of the relationship of the Portuguese immigrant and Portuguese ethnic groups to the medical care system when, for example, other variables are introduced as controls. We were able to control for age, a variable which is related to the need for, and relative use of, services; to control for the type of medical care source used; and to consider the mean number of physician visits for each category of age and immigration status. These relationships are displayed in Tables 5 and 6.

First, let us further consider (Table 5) the medical care provider source with which the person is affiliated. That is, does the person usually receive care from a private physician or from a place such as a hospital or work clinic, or does the person have no regular source of medical care? Table 5 shows these findings.

We have noted that, when taken as a whole, the immigrant and Portuguese ethnic groups did not differ markedly from the statewide population on the use of a private physician as a regular source of care. However, when the figures are broken down by age and immigration status, the groups do clearly differ especially in regard to the proportion who had *no* regular source of care. Almost all of the native-born Portuguese ethnics (98 percent) had an affiliation with some kind of care source (88 percent with a private doctor, 10 percent with a place), and only 2 percent of this subgroup had no source of care. For the pre-1965 immigrant group, only 4 percent were without a source of care, since 91 percent used a private physician and 4 percent used a place of care. But the percentage of new (post-1965) immigrants with no usual care source was much higher, 12 percent, with 80 percent using a private doctor and the remaining 8 percent a place of care. For the Rhode Island area, where the proportion of the total population without a care source is around 5 percent, this group of new immigrants can be considered to represent a medically underserved population.

The age breakdown that is also shown in Table 5 indicates that the bulk of these underserved persons are in the child and young family ages (under 49 years). The disparities are largest in the under 18 year old group, where all (100 percent) of the children in the pre-1965 immigrant households, and all in the native-born Portuguese households, were reported to have a medical care affiliation, yet 10 percent of the new immigrant children had no usual source of care. The differences in the 18 to 49 year old group are also striking, for 17 percent of the post-1965 immigrants in this age category had no usual care source. Since illness is generally less prevalent among persons in the earlier years of adulthood, one might expect this group to have a relatively high proportion of persons who do not "need" regular medical care. Yet the figure of 17 percent is much higher than would be expected.[15] These findings, particularly with regard to the 0–18 year olds, are important from the viewpoint of pre-

ventive medicine and public health, for they suggest that the immigrant group is not receiving maintenance health care. Most of the medical visits of children are well-baby checkups, to receive immunization and to detect abnormalities at an early age. Children with no medical care source may no doubt see some medical provider for acute situations (for example, an emergency room visit for croup) but will not have the benefit of regular preventive and health maintenance care. This group should be of serious concern to the state's health planners, and might be a target group for a public immunization program or for federal programs of child health and welfare.

The proportion of younger adults without a regular care source has some interesting implications. From a policy viewpoint, such unserved persons might well be reached by improved industrial health programs. More importantly, Shuval's study of immigrants in a system where there is free medical care showed that persons in similar circumstances will use, and use heavily, medical care when they have access to it.[16] In the present U.S. system, access to medical care is most readily available to the old and the poor. But the 18–49 year old immigrants are for the most part working, blue-collar, marginally paid employees, ineligible for medicaid and, it is likely, some economic barrier to medical care does exist for the group. In Davis' survey, for 16 percent of the households, the respondents said "yes" to the question, "During the past year has any member of your household ever needed the services of a doctor but did not go to see the doctor because of lack of money?"[17] The introduction of a national health insurance program covering this pool of potential users would probably result in a much greater use of services for nonacute and, if Shuval's findings are generalizable, for "nonmedical" psychological reasons. In this perspective, it is worthwhile to recall the high reports of "stomach trouble" among the post-1965 Portuguese immigrants, and to again suggest that psychosomatic elements may be related to these reports.

One other piece of information suggests that Rhode Island's Portuguese ethnic population is less likely than other state residents to be receiving preventive health services. As part of a study on early cancer detection, a statewide survey asked women whether they had had a Pap test for uterine cancer within the previous five years, and whether they practiced self-examination for early breast cancer detection.

Portuguese women, compared to women of Italian, Irish, or French-Canadian background, were less likely to practice breast examination. Even among women in the younger (25–44) age group, 56 percent of the Portuguese, compared to 70 percent or more of the women in other groups, practiced this prevention measure. With regard to the uterine cancer test, 48 percent of Portuguese ethnic women under age 65 had *not* had such a test within the previous five years. Among the other ethnic groups the figure was about 26 percent. One could speculate that Portuguese women may for cultural reasons be hesitant to submit themselves to such an intimate physical procedure. Nevertheless, the pattern of affiliation with physicians also could be a factor in this failure to receive preventive services.

The mean number of visits to a physician or other care source during the year serves as another measure of the relative access to care of the immigrant subgroups. Of the three, the native-born group, with 2.8 visits, had the highest visit rate, and the rate for the pre-1965 group was only slightly lower, 2.4 visits. The post-1965 group, however, had a much lower rate of visits, with a mean of 1.9. Interestingly, the greatest disparity among the subgroups was found among the youngest household members (under 18 years old). The pattern again corroborates the relatively lower access to medical care of the newer immigrants, and especially for the children in these immigrant households.

IMMIGRANT USE OF FOREIGN-TRAINED PHYSICIANS

Table 6 presents some interesting data on the characteristics of those private physician sources which are used by the immigrant group.

The interviewer asked not only whether the individual had a regular source of care, but also asked the respondent to name the physician or place used for care. Through a file of licensed Rhode Island physicians which is compiled by the Rhode Island Department of Health, and lists the place of education and other characteristics of each physician in the state, it was possible to determine whether a physician named as the source of care was a foreign medical graduate trained in Portugal. This was done to determine whether the medical care of the immigrant group was received primarily from foreign medical graduates (FMG), whose presence in and admission to the United States have been an issue to policy makers in medicine and immigration in recent years. Heavy use of Portuguese FMG's by the Portuguese immigrants might be an argument for a policy which would balance the entry of immigrant and physician FMG streams so that the immigrant group could be served by compatible physicians. A contradictory argument could also be presented, namely, if, as some have claimed, FMG's are more poorly trained than United States physicians, then the immigrant group as heavy FMG users might be receiving "second-rate" medical care. A decrease in the admission of FMG's would change this by forcing the immigrant group to use a different source of supply for medical care, the United States trained physician.

As Table 6 shows, native-born Portuguese ethnics (under age 50) were the least likely to be affiliated with Portuguese trained physicians. This is especially clear in the case of children in native-born Portuguese households.[18] On the other hand, the early (pre-1965) immigrants had the largest proportion of affiliations with Portuguese trained physicians. For example, 80 percent or more of the affiliations of this group at each age level were with Portuguese FMG's, and the group as a whole was the heaviest user of Portuguese trained doctors. Contrary to what might have been expected, a smaller proportion of recent (post-1965) immigrants were using Portuguese FMG's than were earlier immigrants. Just over 50 percent of the affiliations of recent immigrants were with Portuguese doctors, compared to about 80 percent of the affiliations of the pre-1965 immigrants. This suggests that newer immigrants have less access to the Portuguese doctors. Since the groups are from the same locale, geographical inaccessibility can probably be ruled out. Financial access as discussed above could be a reason; however, the supply and demand factor of physician distribution and scarcity is also a likely reason. If the Portuguese physicians have heavy case loads built up from earlier pre-1965 immigrants, they may be unable to take on further patients from the stream of recent immigrants, forcing the group to select non-Portuguese physicians through necessity rather than by choice. Whatever the reason, the pattern of medical care affiliation of post-1965 immigrants resembles that of the native-born ethnics rather than the pre-1965 immigrants.

SUMMARY

We have been concerned in this report with the interface between the immigrant population and the medical care system. Although immigrants represent only a small proportion of the consumers of medical care in the United States, the group, because of its unique nature, may have a disproportionate impact on the system. We reviewed some of the problems of the immigrant group as a potentially high-need population with regard to medical care, and as a group which in some systems is a high user of medical services. The empirical data used in the analysis were collected from a survey of one immigrant population in one state. We realize that, because health and illness behavior are culturally related, and because access to medical care facilities varies in different geographical settings, further research on immigrants of diverse background in multiple settings would be required for generalization of our findings to the whole post-1965 immigrant group. Nevertheless, some issues presented by the immigrants for health care delivery systems should be cross-cutting, as for example, the issue of the patient's inability to speak English, and his unfamiliarity with the appropriate "sick role" (the behavior expected of the sick person by his society). The issue of minority consumer input into the policy-making bureaucratic mechanism is also cross-cutting, as are the problems of the economic burden on health care to the lower income, but above poverty level, family which is ineligible for federally funded medical care.

The empirical findings presented here showed the immigrants to have a relatively low level of need for services, at least according to their perceptions of whether they have any illnesses, have a chronic illness, or were sick enough to stay in bed at any time during the previous year. Although it is possible that physical examinations might show a discrepancy between perceived need and actual need for care, a person's action to use the medical care system is related to a perceived need; thus, perceived need may have a greater impact on use of care than will actual need.

The findings on the use of medical services by the survey population are of more importance. Although a majority of the immigrants were found to have some affiliation with a source of medical care, the group made fewer medical care visits (even with age controlled), and a disturbing proportion of the post-1965 immigrant group had no regular source of medical care. This was the case for 10 percent of the children in the post-1965 immigrant families, and for 17 percent of those in the 18–49 age group. The ramifications of this are important, for it means that these persons are "outside" the health care system, receive episodic and fragmented services for acute conditions, and probably are not receiving the benefits of preventive or health maintenance services that a regular care source can provide. The data suggest that economic factors and the availability of Portuguese physicians may be related to this pattern of affiliation with sources of care.

NOTES

1. Albert F. Wessen, "The Role of Migrant Studies in Epidemiological Research," *Israel Journal of Medical Sciences* 7 (December 1971), pp.1584–97.
2. In the earlier period of the wave of immigration that took place at the turn of the century, immigrant health, particularly with regard to communicable disease, was of some social concern. For example, the famous Nurses' Settlement house at Henry Street in New York was established to deal with the health problems of East European immigrants on New York's lower east side.
3. Margaret Clark, *Health in the Mexican American Culture* (Berkeley: University of California Press, 1959); E. Berkanovic and Leo Reeder, "Ethnic, Economic and Social-Psychological Factors in the Source of Medical Care," *Social Problems* 20 (Fall 1973), pp.246–59; Bonnie Bullough, "Poverty, Ethnic Identity, and Preventive Health Care," *Journal of Health and Social Behavior* 13 (December 1972), pp.347–59; and Robert Roberts, "Spanish Language Health Survey Interviews," paper presented at

the American Sociological Association, Session 81, New York, August 1976.

4. Judith Shuval et. al., *Social Functions of Medical Practice* (San Francisco: Jossey-Bass, Inc., 1970), p.190.

5. Harold Organic and Sidney Goldstein, "The Brown University Population Research Laboratory: Its Purposes and Initial Progress," in *The Community as an Epidemiologic Laboratory: A Casebook of Community Studies*, Irving I. Kessler and Marton L. Levin, eds. (Baltimore: The Johns Hopkins Press, 1970); and Lois A. Monteiro, *Monitoring Health Status and Medical Care* (Cambridge: Ballinger Publishing Company, 1976).

6. Charles Keely, "Immigration: Considerations on Trends, Prospects and Policy," in Charles Westoff and Robert Park, eds., *Demographic and Social Aspects of Population Growth*, Commission on Population Growth and the American Future, Research Reports 1 (Washington, D.C.: Government Printing Office, 1972), p.190.

7. Joanne B. Purcell, "Traditional Ballads among the Portuguese in California: Part I," *Western Folklore* 28 (1969), p.1.

8. Marvin Gibson, "Alien Population in the United States: Changing Residence Patterns," *Immigration and Naturalization Reporter* 19 (October 1970), pp.23–24.

9. U.S. Department of State, Visa Office, *Annual Report* (Washington, D.C.: U.S. Government Printing Office, 1972); U.S. Bureau of the Census, Census of Population: 1960, *Detailed Characteristics*, Final Report, PC(1)–D41, Rhode Island (Washington, D.C.: U.S. Government Printing Office); Idem 1970; U.S. Department of Justice, Immigration, and Naturalization Service, *Annual Reports* (Washington, D.C.: Government Printing Office).

10. F. P. Li, et. al., "Health Care for the Chinese Community in Boston," *American Journal of Public Health* 62 (April 1972), pp.536–39.

11. Mark Zoborowski has demonstrated this phenomenon among Jewish and Anglo-Saxon groups in his paper, "Cultural Components in Response to Pain," *Journal of Social Issues* 8 (1952), pp.16–30.

12. In Rhode Island, where the choice of board members is now being made, the nominations include representatives of the Portuguese community as an "ethnic minority."

13. Norman Davis, "Social Service Delivery in the Portuguese-American Community in Rhode Island" (Master's thesis, Lyndon B. Johnson School of Public Affairs, University of Texas at Austin, 1976).

14. Jennie Kronenfeld, "How People Use Medical Care—A Study of Provider Client Affiliations" (Doctoral dissertation, Brown University, 1976).

15. In the statewide survey, 8 percent of 18–30 year olds had no regular care source.

16. Shuval, op. cit., p.190.

17. Davis, op. cit., p.27.

18. None of the Portuguese trained physicians is a pediatrician.

SOCIAL SERVICES TO NEW IMMIGRANTS: A PASSPORT TO SUCCESSFUL ADJUSTMENT

Murali Nair

In this paper, I am drawing upon my own personal past experience in working with new immigrants as a social worker, as well as upon my present research in the area of social services to new immigrants.

The purpose of this paper is to take our problem, namely, the improvement of social services to new immigrants, and put it in its context by analyzing the existing situation, and then discuss the services available in other countries, since the experience of those countries will contrast with our own and may inspire us to make innovations.

INTRODUCTION

This country was built by immigrants, and even the native Americans, the American Indians, came to this continent from some other place. In certain respects conditions today are more favorable to immigrants than they have been. Earlier, the Darwinian struggle to survive was mitigated only if one had relatives or friends already here. There is an historical relationship that has existed between social work and the "new immigrant." The new immigrants were social work's earliest clientele, especially in the Settlement House Movement. Today, only few social agencies, unfortunately, understand the problems of new immigrants. Social workers are unlikely to know anything about the culture of the new immigrants or to speak their languages.

At present, the United States is one of the major immigrant-receiving countries in the world. We attract about 370,000 new immigrants every year. They come from all the continents, with different cultural and language backgrounds. Even though the character of modern immigration has changed, with many more of the newcomers in the professional and intellectual classes than formerly, the problems of adjustment faced by them are just as important, complex, and acute as the problems confronted by the earlier immigrants. In fact, in some respects their difficulties are greater, for they are coming to a tremendously complicated urban environment in which they must cope with relocation, automation, psychological stresses, and a host of other factors undreamed of on the frontier. Aside from the government's help in the resettlement of refugees, largely in the form of transportation and relief subsidies, the United States has never officially aided in the adjustment or assimilation of immigrants. It is the only major country where this is the case.[1] A very few voluntary agencies are responsible for assisting the new immigrants in settling. The *need* for services to assist the newcomers is *unlimited,* but the *resources* are very *limited.* We ought to reexamine the question of the extent of our collective duty to assist newcomers in their initial adjustment.

ADJUSTMENT PROBLEMS RELATED TO IMMIGRATION

Let us first of all examine why people immigrate: sometimes there is a chain migration process, in which the migrant follows relatives or friends. Often there are few jobs at home, and one hears that there are plenty of jobs abroad. In addition, there may be other frustrations or dissatisfactions and the hope of resolving them through migration. There are many other possible factors, including chance, accident, or a sudden whim or impulse. There are usually several forces at work; rarely can an individual's motivation be reduced to a single factor.

In immigration, some disturbances of social identity and self-image are to be expected, and in this sense immigration has a desocializing effect.[2] So, if we perceive immigration as a process of desocialization, then adaptation may be seen as a process of resocialization. As the immigrant adapts, desocialization tendencies are slowly eliminated while resocialization forces expand. He makes an effort to reestablish role-set, to rebuild the connections between self-image and role-image, and to achieve a real social status. Adaptation is not a well-ordered sequence, with regular phases of adjustment, but a fluid exchange between immigrant and society. Inputs are determined by the social situation, and also by the changing ability of the immigrant to accept change. Some researchers suggest that, in order to combat isolation and loneliness, which engender psychological disturbances, the receiving countries should provide a warm reception and immediate access to social networks.[3]

Oscar Handlin describes the experiences of immigrants who came to the United States as follows: "They lived in crisis because they were uprooted. In transportation, while the old roots were sundered, before the new were established, the immigrants lived in an extreme situation. The shock and the effects of the shock persisted for many years; and their influence reached down to generations which themselves never paid the cost of crossing."[4]

Upon arrival in a new country, the immigrant faces a task of integration into a new culture which is associated with psychological stresses and strains, and these have become magnified with the complexity of modern social organization. The modern immigrant must accept the established social framework, and he no longer has the freedom of the original settler to simply bring his own ways with him.[5]

Some immigrants who have been here for a long time won't bother to help the newcomers and instead show resentment and say, "We made it the hard way—why should they get extra help?" From time to time, the native-born people express opposition to the large influx of new immigrants in their country, and sometimes question how well these new people are adjusting to the life in the host society.

One of the pressing problems the immigrant must deal with is adjusting the illusion he held about his new country to what the realities are.[6] He must cope with the immediate practical problems of housing, education, employment, and the task of learning the language. Along with these practical problems, the immigrant must be psychologically comfortable with the American culture, and able to adjust to it without culture shock or conflict with the culture of his homeland. Another problem is that immigrants often suffer in silence, not wishing to bring the

attention of the government upon themselves, for they fear it might lead to their deportation. All in all, there happens to be a need to reexamine the whole situation and develop new social policies which will help immigrants feel welcome and become true participants in the life of our country.

SOME OF THE PRESSING SOCIAL SERVICE NEEDS OF NEW IMMIGRANTS

Due to unfamiliarity with his new social environment, the immigrant, at a crucial turning point in his life, often finds that his ability to perform his major roles as bread winner and parent are seriously challenged. One researcher[7] has observed a remarkable similiarity between the needs of the new immigrant and the needs of the new-born human being—the need for belonging, the need to be loved, understood, and supported, but not to be dominated, pampered, or spoiled—the needs that enable the child to develop into a sound, mature person, satisfactorily integrated with his family, community, and society.

The immigrant has basically the same needs as other people, but because he finds himself in a new country with new customs, his needs may be intensified and the satisfaction of his needs may be more difficult. His family ties have been broken by leaving the old country; he may have to change his occupation and, as a result, suffer from insecurity and an inability to establish a new identity and status for himself and his family.

Many of the needs of the new immigrants are needs common to all immigrants, rather independent of the individual personality. Among them is the drastic need to change culture, to enter successfully into a cultural community substantially different from the one in which the individual has lived before. At this point, a substantial measure of carefully planned help seems required for the effective settlement of newcomers.

One of the Canadian studies[8] proved that services which have been designed and staffed for native people are inadequate to meet the needs of new immigrants, and their personnel have lacked knowledge of the culture of newcomers. The two hundred families studied had problems in employment, finances, health, housing, education, and family life, and yet failed to use the community services which could have given help in these areas. They turned to relatives, friends, the doctor, or the priests in time of need.

If the adjustment needs of the new immigrant is not met—needs such as making a living, finding a suitable vocation, and building up personal and family stability—he may withdraw into a protective shell of aggression, bitterness, new hostility, and silent and negative suffering. This will cut deeply into the effectiveness of the new immigrant and his family in the adjustment process. Entering a new cultural community requires quick and ready learning of innumerable matters completely familiar to the person who has grown up in that setting. While this assimilation of knowledge is not identical to the learning of the new language, the two are frequently confused. The person who can follow the directions of a subway map or a street directory, who has learned to read strange timetables with accuracy, may still fail completely to grasp significant differences between his traditional set of values and his traditional behavior, and the accepted behavior of the community into which he has entered. The new immigrant needs technical guidance, namely, information and referral services to certain community facilities. At present, in most cases, he may learn about these resources late and by accident, or from other newcomers who have gone through similar experiences. When we talk about social services, it does not mean that every immigrant needs to have all services provided, but if they do need them they should not be regarded as unnecessary luxuries.

THE PRESENT SOCIAL SERVICE AND NEW IMMIGRANTS

In the United States, only certain voluntary agencies are responsible for assisting the new immigrants. They provide information and referral services, English language instruction, education for citizenship, and interpreter and translation services. Some agencies are also involved in long-term case work and group work services.

At present, three types of social agencies try to provide assistance to newcomers: (1) nonsectarian agencies, like the International Institutes in major cities; (2) sectarian agencies, like the Catholic Migration and Refugee Services, the Hebrew Immigrant Aid Society, and the Lutheran Immigration and Refugee Service; and (3) ethnic agencies serving one specific immigrant group, such as the Italian Welfare League, National Chinese Welfare Council.

As far as the new immigrants' settlement is concerned, it seems that government is not interested in setting up programs. It takes a position of, "Let the immigrants assimilate in the local community and, later on, if they develop complicated problems, there are established traditional social agencies such as family service agencies, child welfare agencies, and mental health clinics which can handle their needs."

SOCIAL SERVICE PROGRAMS IN AUSTRALIA, CANADA AND ISRAEL

Now, let us examine briefly how the other major immigrant-receiving countries cope with this issue of social services to newcomers, and see whether we can learn something new from their experience. I will discuss mainly the role played by the governmental agencies in Australia, Canada, and Israel in providing social services to new immigrants at the initial stages of their stay in these countries.

Australia

In Australia, governmental organizations undertake the pre- and postorientation and counseling of immigrants. And, in the after arrival period, there is an outstanding cooperative relationship between the government and the voluntary sector carried out by the Good Neighbour Councils, composed both of government staff and public volunteers, and active in counseling orientation and promotion of the migrant's integration into the community in a number of ways. There is an establishment of Migrant Social Workers, under the Migrant Community Services Branch of the central government, which provides a professional social worker service for immigrants whose problems are more complex. Then there are Migrant Welfare Officers, some multilingual and some bilingual, with special training in the ethnic-cultural backgrounds of different immigrant groups. The work of these welfare officers is to provide counseling and referral services on the problems and difficulties faced by newcomers. These officers maintain close liaison with Australian and State Government Departments, Voluntary organizations including religious bodies and Good Neighbour Councils, hospitals and medical centers, and major employers. Certain Migrant Officers are attached to schools to help with problems in the school-home context; they counsel teachers, parents, and children, assist with interviews and enrollment formalities, translate documents, and visit homes.

The Telephone Interpreter Service operates in all major immigrant receiving centers in Australia. The service consists of a core of departmental interpreters, assisted by private community interpreters, who operate the center on twenty-four hours per day, seven days per week. They provide interpreting assistance in over one hundred languages and dialects. Moreover, the department provides grants to community agencies that work with new immigrants. This scheme was designed to extend financial assistance to selected voluntary agencies to enable them to employ qualified social workers to help migrants with major settlement problems. It was also developed in recognition of the increasing involvement of voluntary agencies in providing assistance to migrants in need.

Canada

The Canadian government (in the White Paper of 1966 and the Green Paper of 1974) acknowledged an underlying principle: "If immigration is in the national interest, then it is the responsibility of Canadian society to provide services to help immigrants over some of the psychological, social and economic barriers to integration. Services to immigrants not only reflect concern for the welfare of those who join the Canadian community, but are also an essential aspect of policy to ensure that the immigration process efficiently serves the nation's social and economic interest."[9] The services currently available to immigrants can be classified into two areas: (1) services provided to prospective immigrants abroad; and (2) postimmigration services (services designed to help immigrants to acquire financial security and to maximize their employment opportunities; and services designed to help the immigrant over such initial obstacles to adjustment as language differences and lack of familiarity with Canadian ways.)

Services Provided to Prospective Immigrants Abroad. Selection officers abroad offer prospective immigrants counseling and information regarding life in Canada, as well as employment opportunities. Some provinces maintain offices abroad to encourage immigration to their provinces (subject to federal acceptance) and to disseminate information. Selection officers also receive information provided by Canadian Manpower Centres about adjustment problems currently being experienced by recent immigrants.

Postimmigration Services. A number of services are available to immigrants upon their arrival at a Canadian port of entry. These include a "Welcome Kit" prepared by the Department of Manpower and Immigration, containing information about social services, initial employment and training, and assistance with transportation to final destinations. Counseling and interpreter services are provided in major arrival centers by federal and provincial officials and representatives of voluntary agencies.

If an immigrant's community of destination does not have a federal government agency (Manpower and Immigration Centre), the department officials make special arrangements with local, provincial, or voluntary agencies to ensure that the new immigrant obtains any necessary help. Immigrants who become ill after admission at a port of entry, and prior either to their arrival at their final destination or their getting gainful employment, are provided, if necessary, with hospital, medical, and dental care at the federal government's expense. Besides the counseling and information services made available to immigrants by the federal government, provincial and some municipal governments, and voluntary social agencies also provide a variety of services to new immigrants.

The Ontario government has initiated a project in Toronto, called "Welcome House," designed to bring together in one place a number of services provided by federal and provincial government and voluntary agencies. Thie center provides counseling, information and referral services, interpreter services, English classes, day care services, group orientation services, and other assistances to new immigrants in Toronto.

Now the federal government is working closely with other levels of government, as well as with voluntary agencies, through their Settlement centers, to improve the planning and delivery of immigrant services. Their aim is to maximize the effectiveness of existing services, as well as to expand and improve the quality of services available to new immigrants in Canada, mainly in the area of financial assistance, job counseling, information and referral services, social counseling, centers for community contact, and other general forums relevant to immigrants' concerns.

Israel

Israel is the only country in the world that accepts immigrants (Jewish) on a nonselective basis. In order to minimize the difficulties of new immigrants' initial adjustment, specially trained social workers provide counseling services at the airport and refer the newcomers to the social agencies nearest to their place of destination. Immigrant families in need of special assistance not detected this way are usually identified in the early stages of their residence in Israel by "absorption workers" and are transferred to social service care.

At the port of entry, every immigrant family receives a monetary grant in accordance with family size in order to assist the family during the first few days in the country. Sole supporters of households without income or in need receive monthly subsistence allowances. Moreover, every immigrant family, upon moving into an apartment, receives basic furniture and other furnishings. Every family is entitled to assistance in finding and acquiring housing.

A wide number of possibilities are available to the new immigrants interested in learning Hebrew: intensive residential and nonresidential Hebrew language centers, as well as evening classes in the various locations of immigrant population. Professional employment counseling services are provided to all immigrants as soon as they enter the country. In the social absorption of the family, emphasis is placed on integrating all members of the immigrant families with the various institutions of the community: nursery, day care center, kindergarten, school, health centers, employment center, club, synagogue, and the like. The integration of immigrant families on the neighborhood level is assisted by community workers who attempt to induce immigrants towards active participation in house and neighborhood committees. They also organize social and cultural activities, including meetings with Israeli citizens of long residence. In most neighborhoods, women volunteers accompany the new immigrant in his or her first contact with the health agency, employment office, school, kindergarten, Hebrew language center, and the like. They also call the immigrant's attention to cultural activities (which they often help organize) that are available in his or her area.

About one-third of all families coming to Israel receive particular care. Follow-up studies have shown that at the end of two years 96 percent are able to continue functioning without further social work intervention.[10]

POSSIBLE SOCIAL SERVICES THE UNITED STATES GOVERNMENT COULD PROVIDE

In all the countries we have looked into, immigration is the responsibility of the central government. We all know that the United States admits immigrants relatively freely, but once they are in, the government doesn't want to play any role in providing services for them. The only exception is when refugees come to this country. The government has spent a substantial amount of money for Cuban and Vietnamese refugees. It transports the refugees to the United States, examines them medically, and screens them as to their occupational skills and experience and provides initial counseling. Moreover, the government has provided financial assistance to voluntary agencies all over the country to run different social programs for this group of newcomers. And the government steps in again to pay any welfare or public relief costs if the refugees should become unemployed or need other emergency assistance.

Here our concern is new immigrants who are

coming to the United States not as refugees. Our discussion is on the question of whether the government ought to play any major role in providing services for newcomers. Let us examine the two main phases of immigrant adjustment and some of the basic needs the governmental agencies could provide.

Phase one: Preimmigration services (in the old country)

Most of the immigrants' applications to immigrate are processed in their home countries, and the immigration officers interview them there. It is at that point that the government should initiate the first stage of social services by providing general information about the new country, the different services available to them once they are in the new country, and how to go about getting them. This information could be provided in several ways, either through individual counseling or through group orientation. It would also be a good idea to provide English classes to prospective immigrants in their own countries, either our own classes or classes set up by voluntary agencies in that country. Perhaps attendance should be required before we let the person immigrate to this country. At present, the United States Information Service Centers provide group orientation about different aspects of American life to students in different countries who are planning to come here for higher studies. It would be a good idea if we could provide at least that much service to new immigrants even before they leave their home countries. This would alleviate some of their anxiety and lessen the culture shock the immigrants may face in this country.

Phase two: Postimmigration services at the time of arrival

Here our concern is what happens when the new immigrants arrive. At present, the immigration officer at the port of entry does the final processing of the immigrant visa. There is no social service program at this point; the government expects the new immigrant to find his own way around. But he needs at least general information about housing, education, health care facilities, and social clubs.

If the immigration officer at the port of entry provided basic information about different community resources available to new immigrants, that itself would solve a lot of problems for the immigrants. Our government should think about the importance of providing at least the access services to new immigrants; other pressing needs could be met by voluntary agencies specializing in the area of social service to new immigrants. However, the services provided by the voluntary agencies are also not adequate for the newcomers; improving them will be possible only if our government gives these agencies more than the very small subsidies they now receive.

CONCLUSION

I would like to emphasize the importance of regularly introducing the newcomer to the common resources of the American community, which he will need to use in order to learn, to understand, and to help himself. These resources provide information and techniques for dealing with the wide range of real problems which any newcomer must tackle at once: finding a place to live, learning where to look for jobs and how to apply for them, buying food and household goods and using the typical equipment of the American home, and using the American means of public transportation and communication.

The very fact that these resources exist may be news to some immigrants (especially immigrants from rural, developing nations). Others may know of such resources in a vague way, from experience in the home countries, but anticipate a different scope; in short, entirely different institutional behavior.

The social workers have to determine whether or not the immigrant needs these informative services and, if he does, should be prepared to provide services in the fields of health, education, employment, income maintenance, housing, and other personal social services. Though we accept immigrants in this country, we are not convinced that we really need them or want them. We tend to show our ambivalence in unreasonable and impossible demands for conformity and "quick assimilation," or, it may be, we praise their contributions to our life, especially "their wonderful folk dances," or we remain vastly indifferent to them, tossing them all into "the melting pot," from which, of course, we exempt ourselves. We should want them even if in not unlimited numbers, because they can add to our cultural vitality. But this they can do only if they adjust to our way of life. And to do this successfully, the aforementioned services should be made available to them.

NOTES

1. William S. Bernard, "Services for Foreign Born," in *Encyclopedia of Social Work* (Washington, D.C.: National Association of Social Workers), p.197.

2. S. N. Eisenstadt, *The Absorption of Immigrants* (Glencoe, Illinois: The Free Press, 1955).

3. B. W. Bar-Yosef, "Desocialization and Resocialization: The Adjustment Process of Immigrants," *International Migration Review,* Vol. 2, No.1 (1968), pp.27–45.

4. Oscar Handlin, *The Uprooted* (London: Watts, 1953), p.51.

5. Wilfred D. Borrie, *The Cultural Integration of Immigrants: A Survey Based on the Papers and Proceedings of the UNESCO Conference Held in Havana* (UNESCO: 1959).

6. Nicholas Zay, "Adaptation of the Immigrants," *Canadian Welfare* (February, 1963), p.42.

7. A. A. Weinberg, *Migration and Belonging: A Study of Mental Health and Personal Adjustment in Israel* (The Hague: Martins Nijhoff, 1961).

8. Spencer and Grygier, *The Integration of Immigrants in Toronto* (Toronto: Social Planning Council of Toronto, 1966).

9. Canada, *White Paper* (Ottawa: Queen's Printer, 1966), p. 18.

10. Israel, *Assistance Program for Immigrant Families in Israel* (Jerusalem: Ministry of Immigrant Absorption, November, 1975).

THE NEW IMMIGRATION IN CANADA:
IMPACT AND MANAGEMENT

John Hucker

At the outset I should like to issue two disclaimers. First, while I have been associated with a Canadian government task force which has been preparing a new immigration act, I am in no sense a spokesman for the government of Canada. The remarks that follow are made in a wholly personal capacity. Secondly, I am not a sociologist and what follows does not purport to be a scholarly paper based upon empirically verified data. Rather, it is an attempt to sketch some significant past and present features of the Canadian legal system in its approach to regulating migration to Canada.[1]

Historically, there are parallels between the Canadian and United States immigration experience. An initially open door policy gave way in both countries to early legislative efforts to reduce immigration, particularly when this was of a nonwhite variety. Thus, both countries attempted to reduce or eliminate Asian immigration in the late nineteenth century and, in fact, a Chinese Immigration Act remained on the statute books in Ottawa until as late as 1947. Worthy of note is an Order-in-Council of 1908 which, ingeniously, prohibited from admission persons who travelled to Canada otherwise than by continuous journey from their country of origin. Coincidentally, there existed no direct sea link between Canada and India, so that intending immigrants from that country had to board ship either in Hong Kong or Japan, thereby rendering themselves inadmissible. As well as being indicative of attitudes then prevailing, the technique used to bar East Indians illustrates a prominent feature of the Canadian immigration regime: its reliance upon regulations and subsidiary lawmaking as vessels for the implementation of policies. In fact, Parliament has passed only three major immigration acts this century, the most recent having been enacted in 1952.

An important feature of the Canadian Constitution is the shared jurisdiction over immigration conferred upon the federal and provincial governments. Although Ottawa's power is paramount, the provinces have from time to time played significant roles in immigration to Canada. At the turn of the century, British Columbia enacted a number of laws aimed at curtailing the influx of immigrants to that province. Many of these were blatantly racist in character and some were disallowed by Ottawa, not, I should add, out of any sensitivity to the rights of the groups affected (notably Chinese), but rather because the province's initiatives were viewed as incursions into a field occupied by the federal government. On a more positive note, the post–World War II period saw activity by several provinces in the recruitment of immigrants, particularly those possessing skills which were domestically in short supply.

At the present time Quebec is the province manifesting the greatest interest in immigration. Since 1968, it has had its own Immigration Act, as well as a minister and government department responsible for immigration matters. The major concern of Quebec has been to recruit francophone immigrants to sufficient numbers to counteract its declining birthrate and the negative implications this has for the survival of linguistic and cultural sovereignty in that province.

The relationship between the federal and provincial governments has had its uneasy moments, but recent years have seen cooperation between Ottawa and those provinces whose labor and other needs have generated on ongoing interest in the immigration process. Nontheless, while receptive to provincial initiatives, Ottawa has consistently asserted its prerogative to have the final voice in actual selection and admission to Canada. The federal government also operates various schemes intended to assist immigrants in making the necessary adjustments to Canadian life. Again, however, the provinces (as well as voluntary agencies) play an important role. They are responsible under the constitutional division of powers for such matters as education, health care, and welfare (although federal funds constitute an essential component of many provincial programs). Civil rights also fall within provincial jurisdiction, and all provinces now have human rights commissions, empowered to enforce laws requiring equality of treatment. In Quebec, the immigrant's freedom to choose an education for his children has recently confronted a government policy designed to buttress the French language, whereby nonfrancophone immigrants have been required—not always willingly—to send their children to francophone schools.

Except for the unique case of Quebec and periodic special movements of foreign workers, active recruitment programs are largely a feature of the past. Canada's relatively advanced position in the world's economic league has for some time prompted applications far in excess of the number of immigrants actually admitted. The overtly discriminatory features of Canadian immigration law were reduced in 1962 by changes to the regulations, and eliminated as a result of the establishment of new, universally applied selection criteria in 1967. The 1967 regulations created three basic classes of immigrants.

Sponsored dependents are the close relatives of citizens or permanent residents of Canada. They essentially encompass the nuclear family, that is, spouses, fiances, minor children, and elderly parents. Once the family relationship has been established and basic health requirements met, the persons concerned are admissible without the need to satisfy any additional selection norms.

The *nominated* category consists of more distant relatives of Canadians or permanent residents. Included are nondependent children and brothers and sisters, and other members of the extended family. Applicants are assessed on a points system under which they need to score fifty out of a possible maximum of one hundred. Under the 1967 scheme, the family relationship itself, depending on its closeness and whether or not the nominating relative was a citizen, accounted for as many as thirty of the necessary fifty points. Other factors taken into account were age, education and training, and oc-

cupational skills and demand. As well, up to fifteen points could be awarded as a result of a personal assessment by an immigration officer of the individual's suitability as a candidate for immigration to Canada.

The final category is the *independent* immigrant. He is required to amass his necessary fifty points on the basis of the factors mentioned above for the nominated group but without the additional boost from the points awarded for family relationship. These are replaced by points assessed for arranged employment, knowledge of English and French, and area labor demand.

On the basis of this brief description, what can be said to be the objectives of the Canadian immigration program? An earlier participant at the present conference adverted to family reunification as the prevailing goal of United States immigration and suggested that Washington has resisted efforts to utilize immigrants as a pool to service American industry. He went on to contrast this with economically oriented immigration systems, among which he counted that of Canada, and which he described as being "total disasters." I think this last remark would come as a considerable surprise to the Canadian government, which has for some time favoured an approach combining elements of family reunification and labor needs. The sponsored category is the most obvious manifestation of the former objective, while the independent category is structured as an economic group. The nominated class falls somewhere in between. Initially, nominated applicants were viewed primarily as a family group. However, more recently the category has shifted or been channelled into the economic wing of Canada's immigration program. Probably economic considerations were always the most important motivating factor for members of the extended, as opposed to the nuclear family. This economic reality was acknowledged by changes in 1974 to the points system governing independent and nominated applicants.[2] Since that time both groups have been required to show evidence of occupational demand for their services, either by arranging definite employment or by being a member of a designated occupation.

What has been the effect of the 1967 selection

system upon the immigration movement to Canada? The obvious change, and again the parallels with the United States are clear, has been the decline in the total percentage of immigrants from traditional source countries. Thus, the 1966 figures showed that 76 percent of immigrants to Canada were from Europe; by 1973 this had declined to 39 percent. During the same period there was an additional shift from northern to southern European source countries, notably Portugal and Greece. As immigration from Europe declined, the percentage of immigrants from Asia climbed from 6 percent in 1966 to 23 percent in 1973.[3]

These developments were inevitable once the decision had been taken to move to a universally applied selection system. However, the change in the makeup of the immigrant movement has occurred without any amendment to the present Immigration Act which has been in force since 1952. The act itself contains a number of anomalous and outmoded provisions, including prohibitions against the admission of epileptics, homosexuals, and various other groups whose threat to the Canadian body politic is at best obscure. In 1973, the then Minister of Manpower and Immigration, Robert Andras, announced that he was initiating a broad-ranging review of all facets of Canadian immigration law and policy with a view, ultimately, to introducing new immigration legislation. The first stage in this process was the publication in early 1975 of a government Green Paper on Immigration.[4] This reviewed the history of Canadian immigration and canvassed various future policy options. It did not recommend any particular approach, nor did it commit the government to a specific course of action beyond that of maintaining a nondiscriminatory admissions policy. Intended to serve as a catalyst for an informed public discussion of the issues at stake, the Green Paper itself met with a mixed reception, being criticized for the inadequacy of some of its scientific data and condemned in some quarters for the veiled prejudices which were seen to lurk between the lines of its bureaucratic language.

Publication of the Green Paper was soon followed by the establishment of a Special Joint Committee of the House and Senate. The committee was charged with responsibility for examining the pro-

posals contained in the Green Paper and submitting a report to Parliament. It travelled to various Canadian cities in order to take the pulse of the Canadian public, or at least of that segment of which was sufficiently interested to make itself heard. Perhaps unsurprisingly, its hearings were utilized as a forum by various fringe groups, some arguing for a total suspension of immigration and others advocating entry into Canada for all who wished to come. The committee heard the Immigration Department denounced as blatantly racist and at the same time harangued for following an open door admissions approach. One thing the hearings showed is that immigration is a politically volatile issue which in Canada is likely to generate few political kudos for any government which takes action (whatever the action might be) on the immigration front. In view of the furor created by the Special Joint Committee hearings, the present government, whose popularity is hardly at a peak, would probably prefer to see the issue of immigration disappear. However, it has publicly announced its commitment to introduce a new immigration act in the near future, and has suggested that this may be expected to follow closely the path charted by the report of the committee, which was tabled in Parliament in the fall of 1975.[5] What then can we expect in the future as Ottawa attempts to develop a system for regulating immigration to Canada during the final quarter of the twentieth century?

The first major issue which was addressed by the Special Joint Committee is the appropriate level of immigration. During the postwar years, immigration to Canada has generally fluctuated between 100,000 to 200,000 per year. The significance of this figure can be realized when it is compared to an annual immigration to the United States of some 400,000 people. The Canadian approach would mean an annual intake of between one and a half and two million immigrants a year if transposed to the U.S. context.

In recent years there has been pressure to reduce the number of immigrants entering Canada. The rationales offered for a reduction or cutoff of immigration have included the economic and environmental, as well as the supposed dangers of overstraining domestic tolerance of immigrant groups with "novel and distinctive features," to quote the Green Paper. However, the report of the Special Joint Committee did not suggest any drastic reductions but rather a stabilization of the immigrant movement at a level of around 100,000 per year as long as present fertility rates prevail. The committee expressly rejected the view that Canada could prosper with a closed door policy.

The committee called for significant modifications to the present system of immigration management. Today, no annual figure (target, ceiling, or quota) is announced or fixed by Canadian law. Of course, management does occur in various ways, including the staffing and location of overseas offices, the establishing of processing priorities, and periodic adjustments to the points system. The committee asserted that a principal objective of a new immigration policy should be "the regulation of immigration flow to achieve desired population growth," and suggested that this could be accomplished by setting an annual target and developing processes for determining and keeping close to that target. It also emphasized that any target should be announced only after consultation with the provincial governments.

It seems likely, therefore, that any future legislative initiatives will be in the direction of a more overtly managerial and structured approach to the immigration movement.

A concomitant of the concern with levels has been the maldistribution of immigrants within Canada. At present, while additional points may be awarded for a person who indicates that he intends to settle in an area of high labor demand, once he has been granted admission there is no guarantee he will remain there or indeed that he will ever reach his stated destination. In recent years, the three major cities of Vancouver, Toronto, and Montreal have acted as magnets for immigrants, as also for signficiant elements of the domestic labor force. Estimates have suggested that as many as fifty percent of the total immigration movement may end up in Toronto within one year of arrival in Canada.

The committee favored retention of a points system for selecting immigrants but had serious reservations about the concept of "area demand," under which points are allocated on the basis of employment levels in different regions of the country but ignoring more localized manpower needs as well as the desirability of encouraging people to settle away from large urban areas. It observed:

> Instead of giving points to immigrants for going to major cities like Toronto. . . . the Committee proposes that area demand be substantially modified and used experimentally to encourage prospective immigrants to settle in communities where population growth is desired and is compatible with regional development plans. It would be important to work closely with provincial authorities to ensure that they agreed that immigrants were desired and jobs were available in the designated communities, and that the services immigrants require would be provided.[6]

The committee went on to recommend that a person who was prepared to settle in a designated locality should be given line-jumping privileges if he signed a written contract to remain in his agreed location for a minimum of two years. In the absence of special circumstances—for example, an inability to find work or supervening health or family problems—the person would not be released from his agreement and, in fact, would face removal from Canada for failure to comply with the terms of his initial admission.

Not surprisingly, this particular proposal proved to be the single most controversial feature of the committee's report. It was seen as reviving the spectre of indentured labor and, at the more practical level, posing intractable problems of enforcement. How does one monitor the movements of a large group of people for a period of two years without introducing the accoutrements of a police state?

Of perhaps greater concern is the likely impact upon societal attitudes of any decision to implement a scheme similar to that envisaged by the committee. There is some evidence that Canadians are becoming less favorably disposed towards immigration. In part this may be seen as a consequence of recent economic stagnation with its resultant reduction in employment opportunities. Public perceptions of immigrants as a group apart, often ethnically distinct and filling positions at the lower end of the socioeconomic continuum, may well be reinforced by any official action which further singles them out as the pawns in a demographic game plan.

The present time is a watershed in Canadian immigration policy. Legislation is imminent and the preliminary stages of its gestation have precipitated isolated but disturbing manifestations of racist and antiimmigrant sentiment, which is not likely to be influenced by data showing that immigrant demands upon social services are generally less than average and that the crimogenic tendencies of immigrants are lower than that of equivalent control groups within the broader Canadian community. It is a trite observation that laws do not change public attitudes; nonetheless it is hoped that the govern- ment in its legislative program will reaffirm the continued place of immigration in Canada's future.

NOTES

1. John Hucker, "A Synopsis of Canadian Immigration Law," *Syracuse Journal of International Law,* 3 (1975), p.47.
2. Tienhaara, *Canadian Views on Immigration and Population* (Ottawa: Department of Manpower and Immigration, 1974).
3. Department of Manpower and Immigration, Annual Statistics (Information Canada, Ottawa).
4. *Green Paper 1975–A Report of the Canadian Immigration and Population Study,* four vols. (Ottawa: Dept. of Manpower and Immigration).
5. Report of Special Joint Committee on Immigration Policy (Government of Canada, November 6, 1975).
6. Ibid.

Part 5

Domestic Implications of the New Immigration for the U.S. and Other Host Societies II: Minorities

THE ECONOMIC IMPACT OF THE NEW IMMIGRATION ON "NATIVE" MINORITIES

Christina Brinkley-Carter

INTRODUCTION

It is recognized that the United States has been and is a country of immigrants. It has been one of several geographic outlets for eighteenth and nineteenth century European population growth and sociopolitical turmoil. During the twentieth century the United States has restricted immigration by the application of various quantitative and qualitative formulae. The quantitative restrictions stemmed principally from a concern to preserve a high degree of homogeneity in the national origins and ethnicity of immigrants rather than any belief in cultural diversity. The qualitative features add "new" citizens most rapidly (and those with work visas) to the professional, technical, and skilled sectors of the labor force. Among native-born citizens at least two observations can be made: (1) a fairly high proportion of our citizens—roughly one-fifth to one-third—cannot be accommodated by our socioeconomic structure, that is the structure and its institutionalized services seem incapable of meeting their needs in education, health, or labor force participation; and (2) the low economic and social position of "native" minorities, that is, those minorities whose roots extend beyond four generations appears to be an ever present constant. Their absorption into the upper quarter of the labor force structure has been miniscule. Thus, it is an appropriate question to ask: To what extent is the U.S. labor force structure absorbing both immigrants and native citizens? Further, how does the absorption of one group affect that of the other? And, what are the policy implications in relation to immigration and manpower planning? To examine one part of the economic impact of immigration, this presentation contrasts the absorption of recent immigrants and "native" minorities into the labor force structure.

Research on the economic impact of immigration has focused largely on the "brain drain" in relation to country of origin, or welfare costs to the receiving country. This paper rests in part on the assumption that considerations of welfare costs to the receiving country have been one-sided: such considerations have been concerned principally with savings in educational expenditures for experienced, skilled manpower. Another much ignored component of welfare costs is the human capital investment and subsequent, perhaps lifetime welfare costs for native-born citizens who attend U.S. schools but are not educated, who have jobs but are unskilled, who receive "free" health care, and who have families but cannot support them.

DATA AND METHODOLOGY

This presentation focuses on the distribution and entry level of native minorities and immigrant workers in professional, technical, and kindred occupations. This is one of the fastest growing sectors of the labor force, and is therefore open to absorbing larger numbers of entrants than any other sector. "Employment growth in this major group will continue to be faster than all others, from 11.5 million in 1972 to about 17 million by 1985. This is about one and one-half times the annual rate of employment increase projected for all occupations combined."[2] This factor, combined with immigration laws that stress occupational quality, thereby favors those entry level participants who are highly skilled immigrants. Simultaneously it is also the major sector upon which developing populations must look to analyze, plan, etc., for economic mobility.

The basic data were reported in the 1970 U.S. Census Bureau's PC (1)–D Series of *Detailed Characteristics: U.S. Summary,* and selected volumes of the PC(2) Series, *Subject Reports.* The occupational data utilized are reports of employed persons in the experienced civilian labor force, sixteen years of age and over. Data are presented for thirty-six *major* occupations that compose the intermediate classification of "professional, technical and kindred workers." This level of specificity provides both a more accurate description of labor force participation, and highlights the tremendous variance in more broadly defined occupational groupings.

Such data reflect primarily the present as a consequence of the past. Alone, they are not suitable for planning the economic development of populations. Knowledge of the labor force composition *in conjunction with manpower need estimates* provide a foundation for program planning, monitoring, and evaluation as well as for the assignment of training priorities. Thus, in addition to a descriptive summary of the experienced professional labor force, estimates of *manpower need* were derived also.

Manpower need estimates were determined in the following manner. First, for each occupational category, percent minority of the total employed was determined. Second, in relation to the total population, the proportion represented by a given minority was determined. "Equity" is defined as the number of a minority that is equivalent to that minority's proportion of the total population. It is assumed that integration economically of native minorities, *throughout* the labor force structure, is a societal goal as so often stated. Thus, third, the "number assuming equity" is the product of the total employed per category and a minority's proportion of the total population. Fourth, the number assuming equity is compared then with the observed number employed. The resulting datum represents an estimate of manpower need, indicating the approximate increase of minority persons necessary to achieve equity as of 1970.

Specific data for native and Asian-American were not available in published census reports;[3] therefore, these data were derived indirectly. The basic assumption underlying the derivation was that the known distribution of minority persons among the categories of a major occupation group would not differ significantly by ethnic identification. Since the census does provide general data on the total employed by ethnic identification and *major* occupation groups,[4] then the product of the reported total and an averaged value of "known minority

proportions"[5] per occupational category, would indicate approximately the number of persons employed for another ethnic group. *The employment data derived in this manner tend to be biased in a positive direction; that is, they represent generally maximum numbers of employed persons, thereby resulting in underestimates of manpower need.*

The "need data" pertain to need as of 1970 and tend to be underestimates resulting from the following constraints: (1) the period of data collection; (2) the census' underenumeration of minorities; (3) population growth; (4) continued change in the labor force structure; and (5) changing job qualifications.

(1) The data were collected in 1970, not 1976, and represent therefore manpower need estimates as of 1970. During the past six years, there has been an increase in minority representation in a few selected areas, but correspondingly for every minority entrant, there are 10–1,000 or more nonminority entrants, thus preserving the overall existing minority-nonminority ratios. This fact is generally overlooked, particularly in much of social science and media reports. In addition there are indications of retrogression: for example, the continued significant proportion of low income "native minorities," at a subsistence or less income level; an increasing proportion of "working poor"; increasing costs of undergraduate and graduate education hitting both middle and low income persons; and an overall decrease in the already infinitesimal number of minority graduate students. For the vast majority of professional and technical occupations, graduate training is a prerequisite. Considering these trends, it is improbable that the need picture is less dismal than described.

(2) Minority populations continue to be significantly underenumerated by the census. This pertains particularly to native Americans, Afro-Americans and Americans of Spanish heritage. Postenumeration surveys and census survival ratios provide a basis for estimating the extent of underenumeration and correcting part of the error, but the 1970 census data have not been corrected. These data are utilized generally without any correction, and often without any reference to the fact of underenumeration.

(3) Minority population growth is somewhat greater than total population growth. Such trends indicate that minorities constitute a slightly greater proportion of the total population than indicated by the census; a corresponding planned rate of entry per occupation should reflect this fact.

(4) As a proportion of the total labor force, professional and technical groups are increasing and are expected to continue to increase through 1985,[6] as indicated earlier. This anticipated rate of growth has not been included in our calculations of manpower "need," but should be for program planning.

(5) Job qualifications have been increasing, generally requiring more education and relevant work experiences, principally the former. Educational requirements are often far greater than necessary for the tasks and responsibilities commensurate with a given occupation. Nevertheless, more and more jobs are requiring more and more education, and education is less accessible to the poor and minorities.

NATIVE MINORITIES AMONG PROFESSIONAL OCCUPATIONS

Tables 1–3 give the distributions of native minorities in professional occupations and the corresponding estimates of manpower need assuming equity. Table 1 shows the number and percent of professional workers by occupation and ethnicity. Generally, the representation of minorities is one-half or less of their respective proportion of the total population. Afro-Americans compose 5.4 percent of professional and technical workers; Spanish heritage, 2.3 percent; native American, 0.16 percent; and Asian-Americans, 0.43 percent. Of the total U.S. population, these groups equal respectively 11.1, 4.6, 0.37, and 0.67 percent.

In Table 2, for each minority group, the number employed can be compared with the number who "ought to be" in a given category, and the additional manpower needed to achieve an equitable position. A figure in parentheses indicates that the present number of labor force participants exceeds the number necessary for equity. Note that this list of occupations consists of nineteen broadly

defined professional areas, eight of which have been divided further. (A detailed classification includes more than 100 professional and technical categories.) Of the nineteen, an estimate of manpower need appears in (a) 18 categories for Afro-Americans; (b) 19 categories for Americans of Spanish heritage; (c) 13 for native Americans; and (d) 9 for Asian-Americans.

Keep in mind that these data represent *minimum* estimates of immediate program goals. More precise estimates could be derived by incorporating adjustments for the factors mentioned earlier regarding "data constraints."

To summarize the contents of Table 2, I have indicated in Table 3 the percentage increase in the present number of persons employed that is necessary to meet a position of equity. A percentage equal to or greater than 100.0 indicates that the present number employed should be doubled, 200.0 indicates a tripling, and so forth. Table 3 shows that overall the number of employed persons should be doubled in the majority of occupations. The general finding for each minority group is as follows:

(1) in 24 of 36 categories for Afro-Americans, the number of employed persons should be *at least* doubled; an increase greater than 200.0 percent is indicated in 16 categories;

(2) for persons of Spanish heritage, the number employed should be doubled in 21 categories, and at least tripled in 7 of these categories;

(3) for native Americans the employed should be increased by 100.0 percent or more in 16 categories, and at least tripled in 9 of these categories.

(4) in 11 occupational areas, the number of Asian-Americans should be at least doubled. As contrasted with other minorities, a somewhat higher proportion of Asian-Americans are employed in professional, technical, and managerial occupations, but this proportion does not equal the proportion of Asian-Americans in the total population. In addition, the Asian-American constituency may be affected directly and significantly by recent immigration rather than any change in the position of "native" Asian Americans.[7]

TABLE 1

PROFESSIONAL AND TECHNICAL WORKERS IN THE EXPERIENCED CIVILIAN LABOR FORCE BY ETHNICITY: UNITED STATES, 1970[a,b]

OCCUPATION	TOTAL	AFRO-AMERICANS		SPANISH HERITAGE[d] AMERICANS		NATIVE-AMERICANS		ASIAN-AMERICANS	
		NUMBER	PERCENT[c] (cf. 11.1)	NUMBER	PERCENT[c] (cf. 4.6)	NUMBER	PERCENT (cf. 0.37)	NUMBER	PERCENT (cf. 0.67)
Accountants	712,413	16,886	2.4	15,404	2.2	371	0.05	1,044	0.15
Architects	54,834	1,191	2.2	1,553	2.8	409	0.75	1,153	2.10
Computer Specialists	258,215	8,608	3.3	5,478	2.1	446	0.17	1,257	0.49
Engineers	1,210,211	13,374	1.1	25,551	2.1	1,407	0.12	3,958	0.33
Aeronautical & Astronautical	67,657	748	1.1	1,833	2.7	313	0.46	881	1.30
Civil	172,742	2,417	1.4	4,811	2.8	343	0.20	966	0.56
Electrical & Electronic	281,131	3,722	1.3	6,360	2.3	293	0.10	825	0.29
Mechanical	179,600	1,786	1.0	3,321	1.8	233	0.13	655	0.36
Other Engineers	509,081	4,701	0.9	9,226	1.8	224	0.04	630	0.12
Lawyers & Judges	260,066	3,236	1.2	3,783	1.5	222	0.09	623	0.24
Librarians	101,233	6,839	6.8	1,478	1.5	673	0.66	1,896	1.87
Mathematical Specialists	12,427	750	6.0	181	1.5	614	4.94	1,730	13.92
Life & Physical Scientists	205,407	6,392	3.1	4,711	2.3	466	0.23	1,245	0.61
Chemists	96,754	3,332	3.4	2,175	2.2	--	--	--	--
Physicians, Dentists & Related Practitioners	494,464	9,614	1.9	13,048	2.6	1,281	0.26	3,608	0.73
Dentists	87,851	1,983	2.3	1,164	1.3	293	0.33	825	0.94
Pharmacists	97,185	1,917	2.0	1,717	1.8	306	0.31	863	0.89
Physicians, Medical & Osteopathic	255,606	5,084	2.0	9,362	3.7	463	0.18	1,303	0.51
Other Related Practitioners	53,822	630	1.2	805	1.5	219	0.41	616	1.14
Registered Nurses, Dietitians, & Therapists	904,946	71,162	7.9	18,587	2.1	3,372	0.37	9,493	1.05
Dietitians	37,668	7,735	20.5	986	2.6	1,896	5.03	5,339	14.17
Registered Nurses	818,798	60,240	7.4	16,607	2.0	769	0.09	2,165	0.26
Therapists	48,480	3,187	6.6	994	2.1	706	1.46	1,989	4.10
Health Technologists & Technicians	263,696	24,566	9.3	9,778	3.7	1,068	0.41	3,005	1.14
Religious Workers	228,391	12,951	5.7	3,282	1.4	582	0.25	1,639	0.72
Social Scientists	110,010	3,102	2.8	2,328	2.1	405	0.37	1,139	1.04

TABLE 1 continued

Social & Recreation Workers	273,608	42,368	15.5	11,269	4.1	1,606	0.59	4,521	1.65
Teachers	3,265,488	244,185	7.5	65,349	2.0	2,573	0.08	7,244	0.22
College & University	490,691	17,102	3.5	11,129	2.3	471	0.10	1,328	0.27
Elem. & Prekindergarten	1,558,736	150,092	9.6	29,270	1.9	943	0.06	2,655	0.17
Secondary	1,011,164	61,875	6.1	19,948	2.0	663	0.07	1,866	0.18
Other	131,636	5,429	4.1	2,537	1.9	496	0.38	1,395	1.06
Engineering & Science Technicians	826,904	27,949	3.4	26,972	3.3	1,098	0.13	1,532	0.19
Draftsmen & Surveyors	330,559	8,303	2.5	12,118	3.7	506	0.15	--	--
Electrical & Electronic Engineering Technologists	149,750	5,069	3.4	5,754	3.8	592	0.40	--	--
Technicians, except Health, Engineering & Science	159,885	4,212	2.6	4,630	2.9	234	0.15	1,278	0.80
Airplane Pilots	51,295	172	0.3	1,286	2.5	--	--	--	--
Writers, Artists & Entertainers	791,227	27,068	3.4	24,322	3.1	1,319	0.17	1,497	0.20
Actors & Dancers	11,396	777	6.8	625	5.5	--	--	--	--
Authors, Editors & Reporters	69,169	1,678	2.4	948	1.4	--	--	--	--
Other Professional, Technical & Kindred Workers	1,427,807	103,863	7.3	33,686	2.4	792	0.08	2,221	0.16
TOTAL	11,561,032	628,316	5.4	271,390	2.3	18,938	0.16	50,083	0.43

a   Source: U.S. Bureau of the Census, Census of Population: 1970. (1) DETAILED CHARACTERISTICS: Final Report PC (1)-D1, *United States Summary*. Washington, D.C., Government Printing Office, 1973, Table 224. (2) SUBJECT REPORTS: Final Report PC(2)-IF, American Indians and Final Report PC(2)-IG, Japanese, Chinese and Filipinos in the United States. Washington, D.C.: GPO, 1973, Table 7.

b   Data for Native-Americans and selected Asian-Americans extrapolated. See text for explanation.

c   Assuming equity this percentage should equal 11.1 for Afro-Americans; 4.6 for those of Spanish Heritage; 0.37 for Native-Americans, and 0.67 for selected Asian-Americans.

d   The category of "Spanish Heritage Americans" is a composite of the following: (1) In 42 states and the District of Columbia, this population is identified as "Persons of Spanish language"; (2) in five Southwestern States (Arizona, Colorado, New Mexico, California and Texas), these are "persons of Spanish language or Spanish surname"; and (3) in three Middle Atlantic States (New York, New Jersey and Pennsylvania), the population of Spanish heritage consists of persons of Puerto Rican birth or parentage.

TABLE 2
ESTIMATED MANPOWER NEED BY ETHNICITY FOR PROFESSIONAL AND TECHNICAL OCCUPATIONS: UNITED STATES, 1970[a]

OCCUPATION	A. ESTIMATES FOR AFRO-AMERICANS			B. ESTIMATES FOR SPANISH HERITAGE AMERICANS[b]		
	NUMBER IN EXPER. CLF	NUMBER ASSUMING EQUITY	ESTIMATED MANPOWER NEEDS	NUMBER IN EXPER. CLF	NUMBER ASSUMING EQUITY	ESTIMATED MANPOWER NEEDS
Accountants	16,886	79,078	62,192	15,404	32,771	17,367
Architects	1,191	6,087	4,896	1,553	2,522	969
Computer Specialists	8,608	28,662	20,054	5,478	11,878	6,400
Engineers	13,374	134,333	120,959	25,551	55,670	30,119
Aeronautical & Astronautical	748	7,510	6,762	1,833	3,112	1,279
Civil	2,417	19,174	16,757	4,811	7,946	3,135
Electrical and Electronic	3,722	31,206	27,484	6,360	12,932	6,572
Mechanical	1,786	19,936	18,150	3,321	8,262	4,941
Other Engineers	4,701	56,508	51,807	9,226	23,418	14,192
Lawyers & Judges	3,236	28,860	25,631	3,783	11,963	8,180
Librarians	6,839	11,237	4,398	1,478	4,657	3,179
Mathematical Specialists	750	1,379	629	181	572	391
Life & Physical Scientists	6,392	22,800	16,408	4,711	9,449	4,738
Chemists	3,332	10,739	7,407	2,175	4,451	2,276
Physicians, Dentists & Related Practitioners	9,614	54,836	45,272	13,048	22,745	9,697
Dentists	1,983	9,751	7,768	1,164	4,041	2,877
Pharmacists	1,917	10,788	8,871	1,717	4,471	2,754
Physicians, Medical & Osteopathic	5,084	28,372	23,288	9,362	11,758	2,396
Other Related Practitioners	630	5,974	5,344	805	2,476	1,671
Registered Nurses, Dietitians, & Therapists	71,162	100,449	29,287	18,587	41,628	23,041
Dieticians	7,735	4,181	≐3,554	986	1,733	747
Registered Nurses	60,240	90,887	30,647	16,607	37,665	21,058
Therapists	3,187	5,381	2,194	994	2,230	1,236
Health Technologists & Technicians	24,566	29,270	4,704	9,778	12,130	2,352
Religious Workers	12,951	25,351	12,400	3,282	10,506	7,224
Social Scientists	3,102	12,211	9,109	2,328	5,060	2,732
Social & Recreation Workers	1,606	1,012	(594)	4,521	1,833	(2,688)
Teachers	2,573	12,082	9,509	7,244	21,879	14,635
College & University	471	1,816	1,345	1,328	3,288	1,960
Elem. & Prekindergarten	943	5,767	4,824	2,655	10,444	7,789
Secondary	663	3,741	3,078	1,866	6,775	4,909
Other	496	487	(9)	1,395	882	(513)
Engineering & Science Technicians	1,098	3,060	1,962	1,532	5,540	4,008
Draftsmen & Surveyors	506	1,223	717	--	--	--
Electrical & Electronic Engineering Technologists	592	554	(38)	--	--	--
Technicians, except Health, Engineering & Science	234	591	357	1,278	1,070	(208)
Airplane Pilots	--	--	--	--	--	--
Writers, Artists & Entertainers	1,319	2,928	1,609	1,497	5,301	3,804
Actors & Dancers	--	--	--	--	--	--
Authors, Editors & Reporters	--	--	--	--	--	--
Other Professional, Technical & Kindred Workers	792	5,283	4,491	2,221	9,566	7,345
TOTAL	18,938	42,776	23,838	50,083	77,459	27,376

As expected, in order to achieve a more equitable labor force structure, there must be a significant increase in native minority representation. We have indicated in part where that need occurs and to what degree because both indicators are important in determining manpower and community development policies. Another key consideration in the design of such policies is immigration. Immigration has become a related, major issue because of its direct contribution to growth sectors of the U.S. labor force, and its possible function as an alternative to a native-born labor force supply.

THE NEW IMMIGRATION AND PROFESSIONAL OCCUPATIONS

Inasmuch as the annual number of immigrants equals far less than one percent of the U.S. popula-

TABLE 2 continued

OCCUPATION	C. ESTIMATES FOR NATIVE-AMERICANS			D. ESTIMATES FOR ASIAN-AMERICANS		
	NUMBER IN EXPER.CLF	NUMBER ASSUMING EQUITY	ESTIMATED MANPOWER NEEDS	NUMBER IN EXPER. CLF	NUMBER ASSUMING EQUITY	ESTIMATED MANPOWER NEEDS
Accountants	371	2,636	2,265	1,044	4,773	3,729
Architects	409	203	(206)	1,153	367	(786)
Computer Specialists	446	955	509	1,257	1,730	473
Engineers	1,407	4,478	3,071	3,958	8,108	4,150
Aeronautical & Astronautical	313	250	(63)	881	453	(428)
Civil	343	639	296	966	1,157	191
Electrical & Electronic	293	1,040	747	825	1,884	1,059
Mechanical	233	665	432	655	1,203	548
Other Engineers	224	1,884	1,660	630	3,411	2,781
Lawyers & Judges	222	962	740	623	1,742	1,119
Librarians	673	375	(298)	1,896	678	(1,218)
Mathematical Specialists	614	46	(568)	1,730	83	(1,647)
Life & Physical Scientists	466	760	294	1,245	1,376	131
Chemists	--	--	--	--	--	--
Physicians, Dentists &						
Related Practitioners	1,281	1,830	549	3,608	3,313	(295)
Dentists	293	325	32	825	589	(236)
Pharmacists	306	360	54	863	651	(212)
Physicians, Medical &						
Osteopathic	463	946	483	1,303	1,713	410
Other Related Practitioners	219	199	(20)	616	361	(255)
Registered Nurses, Dietitians,						
& Therapists	3,372	3,348	(24)	9,493	6,063	(3,430)
Dietitians	1,896	139	(1,757)	5,339	252	(5,086)
Registered Nurses	769	3,030	2,261	2,165	5,486	3,321
Therapists	706	179	(527)	1,989	325	(1,664)
Health Technologists &						
Technicians	1,068	976	92	3,005	1,767	(1,238)
Religious Workers	582	845	263	1,639	1,530	(109)
Social Scientists	405	407	2	1,139	737	(402)
Social & Recreation Workers	42,368	30,370	±11,998	11,269	12,586	1,317
Teachers	244,185	362,469	118,284	65,349	150,212	84,863
College & University	17,102	54,467	37,365	11,129	22,572	11,443
Elem. & Prekindergarten	150,092	173,020	22,928	29,270	71,702	42,432
Secondary	61,875	112,239	50,364	19,948	46,514	26,566
Other	5,429	14,612	9,183	2,537	6,055	3,518
Engineering & Science						
Technicians	27,949	91,786	63,837	26,972	38,038	11,066
Draftsmen & Surveyors	8,303	36,692	28,389	12,118	15,206	3,088
Electrical & Electronic						
Engineering Technologists	5,069	16,622	11,553	5,754	6,888	1,134
Technicians, except Health,						
Engineering & Science	4,212	17,725	13,513	4,630	7,346	2,716
Airplane Pilots	172	5,694	5,522	1,286	2,360	1,074
Writers, Artists & Entertainers	27,068	87,826	60,758	24,322	36,396	12,074
Actors & Dancers	777	1,309	532	625	524	(101)
Authors, Editors & Reporters	1,678	7,678	6,000	948	3,182	2,234
Other Professional, Technical						
& Kindred Workers	103,863	158,487	54,624	33,686	65,679	31,993
TOTAL	628,316	1,283,274	654,958	271,390	531,807	260,417

a Source: U.S. Bureau of the Census, Census of Population: 1970. (1) DETAILED CHARACTERISTICS: Final Report PC(1)-D1, United States Summary (Washington, D.C., 1973), Table 224. (2) SUBJECT REPORTS: Final Report PC(2)-1F, American Indians and Final Report PC(2)-1G, Japanese, Chinese, and Filipinos in the United States (Washington, D.C., 1973), Table 7. Note: Data for Native-Americans and selected Asian-Americans extrapolated. See text for explantaion.

b The category of "Spanish Heritage Americans" is a composite of the following: (1) In 42 states and the District of Columbia, this population is identfied as "Persons of Spanish language"; (2) in five Southwestern States (Arizona, Colorado, New Mexico, California and Texas), these are "persons of Spanish language or Spanish surname"; and (3) in three Middle Atlantic States (New York, New Jersey and Pennsylvania), the population of Spanish heritage consists of persons of Puerto Rican birth or parentage.

tion, the economic effect on U.S. citizens generally and native minorities in particular has rarely been considered. Between 1961 and 1970, the annual number of newly naturalized citizens entering professional and technical occupations increased from 21,455 to 46,151. (The former figure equalled 7.9 percent of 1961 immigrants, and the latter equalled 12.4 percent of 1970.) From 1967–70, the number of professional and technical workers admitted were as follows: 46,151, 40,427, 48,753, and 41,753

TABLE 3
SUMMARY OF MANPOWER POSITION: PERCENTAGE INCREASE IN CLF PARTICIPATION NECESSARY TO MEET MANPOWER GOALS, 1970.

OCCUPATION	AFRO-AMERICAN	SPANISH HERITAGE	NATIVE-AMERICAN	ASIAN-AMERICAN
Accountants	368.3	112.7	610.5	357.2
Architects	411.1	62.4	-50.4	-68.2
Computer Specialists	233.0	116.8	114.1	37.6
Engineers	904.4	117.9	218.3	104.9
Aeronatical & Astronautical	904.0	69.8	-20.1	-48.6
Civil	693.3	65.2	86.3	19.8
Electrical & Electronic	738.4	103.3	254.9	128.4
Mechanical	1016.2	148.8	185.4	83.7
Other Engineers	1102.0	153.8	741.1	441.4
Lawyers & Judges	792.1	216.2	333.3	179.6
Librarians	64.4	215.1	-44.3	-64.2
Mathematical Specialists	83.9	216.0	-92.6	-95.2
Life & Physical Scientists	256.7	100.6	63.1	10.5
Chemists	222.3	104.6	--	--
Physicians, Dentists & Related Practitioners	470.9	74.3	42.9	-8.2
Dentists	391.7	247.2	10.9	-28.6
Pharmacists	462.8	160.4	17.6	-24.6
Physicians, Medical & Osteopathic	458.1	25.6	104.3	31.5
Other Related Practitioners	848.3	207.6	-9.1	-41.4
Registered Nurses, Dietitians & Therapists	41.2	124.0	09.7	-36.1
Dietitians	-45.9	75.8	-92.7	-95.3
Registered Nurses	50.9	126.8	294.0	153.4
Therapists	68.8	124.3	-74.6	-83.7
Health Technologists & Technicians	19.1	24.5	8.6	-41.2
Religious Workers	95.7	220.1	45.2	-6.7
Social Scientists	293.6	117.4	0.5	-35.3
Social & Recreation Workers	-28.3	11.7	-37.0	-59.5
Teachers	48.4	129.9	369.6	202.0
College & University	218.5	102.8	285.6	147.6
Elem. & Prekindergarten	15.3	145.0	511.6	293.4
Secondary	81.4	133.2	464.3	263.1
Other	169.1	138.7	1.8	-36.8
Engineering & Science Technicians	228.4	41.0	178.7	261.6
Draftsmen & Surveyors	341.9	25.5	141.7	--
Electric & Electronic Engineering Technicians	227.9	19.7	-6.4	--
Technicians, except Health, & Engineering Science	320.8	58.7	152.6	-16.3
Airplane Pilots	3210.5	83.5	--	--
Writers, Artists, & Entertainers	224.5	49.6	122.0	254.1
Actors & Dancers	68.5	-16.2	--	--
Authors, Editors & Reporters	357.6	235.7	--	--
Other Professional, Technical, & Kindred Workers	52.6	95.0	567.0	330.7

respectively.[8] (The Bureau of Labor Statistics expects this trend to continue.) The numbers cited equal or exceed the total of U.S. minorities entering the professions annually.

The occupational position of ''new'' immigrants as contrasted with Afro-Americans is shown in Table 4. These data refer only to ''naturalized'' immigrants.

TABLE 4
NUMBER OF AFRO-AMERICANS IN THE CLF;[a] AVERAGE ANNUAL NUMBER OF PROFESSIONAL AFRO-AMERICANS AND IMMIGRANTS ENTERING THE U.S. LABOR FORCE, 1967-1970; AND THE ESTIMATED AVERAGE ANNUAL OPENINGS TO 1980 BY OCCUPATION

Occupation	Afro-Americans 1970 (1)	Average Annual Number of Professional Entrants, 1967-1970		Average Annual Openings to 1980 (4)
		Immigrants[b] (2)	Afro-Americans (3)	
Natural Scientists	6,392	2,384	622	24,100
Social Scientists	3,102	514	255	5,500
Physicians, Surgeons and Dentists	7,067	3,440	45	29,200
Nurses (incl.student)	71,162	5,572	4,129	69,000
Other Medical and Related Fields	27,113	2,250	2,168	50,000+
Engineers	8,673	8,586	662	46,480
Other Technology and Related Fields	32,650	7,155	3,755	44,520
Editors and Reporters	1,678	260	65	
Lawyers and Judges	3,236	316	132	14,000
Professors and Instructors	17,102	1,716	1,461	10,800
Social and Welfare Workers	42,368	295[c]	3,512	19,700
Teachers: Elementary, Secondary,n.e.c.	217,396	5,974	10,842	90,000
Other PT and K, n.e.c.	103,863	4,240	8,947	100,000+
Total	541,802	42,702	36,595	-

[a]CLF=Civilian Labor Force.

[b]From Judith Fortney, "Immigration into the U.S. with Special Reference to Professional and Technical Workers," p. 216 in U.S. Commission on Population Growth and the American Future. Vol. I of Commission research reports. Washington, D.C.: GOP, 1972.

[c]Excludes group workers.

The issues being raised have an even stronger quantitative foundation if data were more readily available for persons with various types of visas, particularly permanent work visas, and for illegal immigration. The latter may contribute significantly to the reduction of unskilled and semiskilled positions available for U.S. citizens. Rough estimates picture illegal immigration to be twice the size of legal immigration.

For comparative purposes, column 1 of Table 4 shows the total number of Afro-Americans in the civilian labor force by occupation as of 1970. For 1967 through 1970, columns 2 and 3 show the average annual number of immigrants and Afro-Americans entering a given occupation. In ten of thirteen categories, the number of immigrants exceeds the number of Afro-Americans. Given that Afro-Americans constitute the largest proportion of native minorities, then the data imply further that the number of immigrants and their rate of entry into professional occupations generally exceeds the corresponding numbers and rates for native minority entrants. Column 4,[9] average annual openings to 1980 by occupation, indicate that a sufficient number of openings may exist to accommodate both groups. But *both* groups are not being accommodated.

The economic development of native minorities cannot be accomplished without access to the higher skill and income levels of the labor force. Immigration is one of several supply and demand factors that affect such access. It is a supply factor resulting from the interaction of qualitative features of our immigration laws and procedures, and the correspondingly high occupational level in which immigrants tend to enter the labor force.

Given the patterns of institutionalized racism in our social and economic structure, a supply of immigrant labor represents an alternative to hiring native minorities. There are at least three bases for this assertion: (1) the historical pattern of immigrant and native minority participation in the labor force; (2) the stratification of and among native minorities; and (3) the psychological perspective of nonminority citizens that tends to automatically assign superiority in skill and being to the majority of immigrants, for example, the anglophiles.

In addition, both aggregated and individual mobility depend partially upon societal conditions for mobility, such as population and economic growth rates. Recent U.S. trends indicate less growth in both areas and, at least implicitly, the reduction of fertility to zero population growth is strongly supported. The economic position of developing populations becomes more rigid as population growth decreases. Although immigration adds annually less than one-hundredth of a percent to our total population, the corresponding number appears to have a significant effect on the distribution of U.S. citizens in the labor force. Given this situation, is it not contradictory to stress the reduction of fertility among U.S. citizens while allowing legal and illegal immigration in increasing numbers?

CONCLUDING REMARKS

It appears that the continuation of legal and illegal immigration removes a significant number of jobs from accessibility to all citizens and native minorities in particular. Our conclusion is appropriately a cautious one, because our analysis is preliminary and further examination is needed of both this question and related issues. The analysis should be expanded to include the entire civilian labor force as well as other factors.

We recognize that the economic and social position of native born citizens is dependent in part on other economic factors—both international and domestic. Such factors include

(1) the movement of many unskilled and semi-skilled work tasks to geographic areas outside the continental U.S., where wages are far cheaper;

(2) that U.S. entrepreneurs can pay less salary and fewer benefits to immigrants and simultaneously circumvent U.S. labor union requirements (fear of losing their jobs and/or deportation causes immigrants to say little);

(3) the ability of professional and technical groups to implement entry-level requirements that are perhaps met more easily by immigrants than native minorities;

(4) the underutilization or underemployment of present labor force participants; and

(5) welfare costs associated with the waste of human resources.

To answer our original question: although it appears that the upper quarter of the labor force is capable of absorbing both immigrants and native born citizens, immigrants and native born white citizens appear to be in more favored positions than native minority citizens. Further research is needed to make a less cautious statement, but if these data and U.S. history provide some evidence [in support of this conclusion], then undoubtedly the absorption of immigrants does affect the economic position of native born citizens. The policy implication is a difficult one but one that we must consider; that is, the restriction of immigration until the labor force needs, and opportunities for economic mobility, of U.S. citizens exist in practice as well as in theory.

NOTES

1. A term applied to non-European minorities, because they have been citizens for many generations. See Jose Hernandez, *People, Power, and Policy: A New View on Population* (Palo Alto, California, 1974), p. 97.

2. Neal H. Rosenthal, ''Projected Changes in Occupations'' in *The U.S. Economy in 1985: A Summary of BLS Projections,* Bulletin #1809, U.S. Department of Labor, Bureau of Labor Statistics (1974), p. 18.

3. Such data are available from the 1970 Census Public Use Sample data files.

4. There are twelve major occupation groups as follows: professional, technical, and kindred workers; managers and administrators except farm; sales workers; clerical and kindred workers; craftsmen and kindred workers; operatives except transport; transport equipment operatives; laboreres except farm; farmers and farm managers; farm laborers and farm foremen; service workers except private household; and private household workers.

5. That is, what proportion of Afro-American professionals are in a particular occupation? The same question was applied to Spanish heritage persons. The proportions found were averaged.

6. Rosenthal, op. cit., p. 18.

7. See Table 9 in Judith A. Fortney, ''Immigration into the United States with Special Reference to Professional and Technical Workers,'' in *Demographic and Social Aspects of Population Growth,* Charles F. Westoff and Robert Parke, Jr., Editors, vol. 1 of commission research reports, U.S. Commission on Population Growth and the American Future) (Washington, D.C.: Government Printing Office, 1972), pp. 205–32.

8. Judith Fortney, p. 216.

9. Joan Slowitsky, ''Occupational Outlook Handbook in Brief 1974–75 Edition,'' Reprinted from *Occupational Outlook Quarterly* 18, No. 2 (Summer 1974), U.S. Department of Labor, Bureau of Labor Statistics.

DOMESTIC POLICY IMPLICATIONS AS THEY RELATE TO BLACK ETHNIC GROUPS IN AMERICA

B. William Austin

THE PROBLEM

One of the most perplexing issues facing policy makers and program administrators today is, "Why is it that so many policies, programs, and social services directed toward blacks have failed to significantly improve their social and economic status?"

Public school administrators are in a quandry as to why many of their instructional innovations fail to significantly raise the achievement level of most of their black students. Directors of social service agencies are puzzled as to why their services and outreach programs do not reach many needy black families, and fail to significantly enhance the quality of life of those that are reached. And managers of job-training and other work-related programs continue to be frustrated in their efforts to obtain meaningful employment opportunities for underemployed and unemployed blacks.

The reasons for the failure of many of these policies and programs are numerous: the lack of participation of blacks in the planning and design of the programs, the inadequacy of financial and manpower resources for implementing them, the lack of genuine commitment toward achieving the stated program goals, and so on. But one factor that is common to most ineffective social policies and programs is that they are based on misconceptions about the attitudes, values, and life styles of black people. Perhaps, the most serious misconception is that blacks are presumed to be a racially homogeneous group devoid of any culture that is distinct from the "average" white American. It is for this reason that a not insignificant minority of white social scientists still contend that blacks should not be characterized as an ethnic group because they have no culture that is distinct from "typical" white Americans.

According to this conventional wisdom, the only culture that the majority of black Americans has is a "culture of poverty" which is fundamentally the same for all poor people, whether they be Puerto Rican, Chicano or non-Spanish-speaking whites. Since this universal "poverty culture" is characterized by low achievement orientation, alienation from work, family instability, and high rates of illegitimacy and crime, according to the conventional view, the programs and services directed toward the poor, regardless of their ethnicity, should be primarily designed to do the following: inculcate an achievement motivation, create a work ethnic, implant norms about the sanctity of the nuclear family structure, and instill proper moral values. The poor, by definition, cannot already possess these positive orientations—otherwise, they would not be poor! This is why the deficit model is still the basis for most policies, programs, and services directed toward black people today.

At the same time, however, it must be noted that even the conventional view of blacks as a "nonethnic" group acknowledges, on occasion, the existence of a minority "culture" within the black community—the life styles of the so-called "middle class." But since, according to this view, the life styles of middle-class blacks largely mirror those of middle-class white America, even these patterns, if they can be called cultural, are not seen as distinct from the "typical" culture of white America. Consequently, most contemporary policies, programs, and services designed for middle-class blacks are based on the unwarranted assumption that they are largely replicas of middle-income white America.

This is not to say that there are not many behavioral patterns, attitudes, and values that black Americans have in common with white Americans—because they do. But policy makers and program administrators must also be aware of differences in life styles and cultural patterns so that their policies, programs, and services can be sensitive to similarities *and* differences between ethnic groups as well as *within* them. For, attitudes, values, life styles, and other cultural patterns among black Americans differ not only from those of similar income white Americans, but from similar income blacks as well—because of the existence of ethnic subgroups within the black community.

BLACK ETHNICITY

Ethnic groups for the most part are derivations of conquest or mutual acceptance and amalgamation of groups of people. Ethnic groups may be formed by such forces as mentioned previously, but this does not explain ethnicity, the feeling of belonging.

The feeling of ethnicity can be seen among American blacks. The American black population is composed of racial and ethnic mixtures made up predominately of Africans, American Indian, English, Scotch, Irish, and French, and so the American black is a somewhat new ethnic entity.

The mulatto class which arose out of the slave experience marked the beginning of the changing of the African slave into the political category today called *black Americans*. The African slave and freed man fused with the European and the American Indian to form a distinct group of people. It was not, however, the intermingling of these groups alone which made the "colored" community in America. It was, however, the legal code of the country which dictated political policy in this area. It is hard to say what would have happened had there been no legal code defining who was to be considered "colored" or "Negro." But as it was, anyone with recognizable African blood, or acknowledged such, was politically "colored" or "Negro." Unlike the West Indies and South America, the American social and legal system did not allow for, or more specifically, had no need for a buffer group of mulattoes between themselves and blacks. As such, political or social sanctions did not uphold the mulatto class as different from the African in the eyes of the law or the society.

It is apparent, however, that the blacks, the mulattoes, the creoles, and the Indian-African groups all formed groups of their own within the broader view of their political status. These were based on kindred and types of cultures which they created for themselves.

By the 1950s, the dominant legal status of all people of African descent in America forged them even closer together even though they were of different colors, backgrounds and cultures, which were only minor variations on the same theme. The Negro or colored population was still rather unorganized. Intellectuals, political spokesmen, religious leaders, and scholars had worked tirelessly to solve the identity crises of the Negro people. But the task was a monumental one. The identity crisis stemmed from the ambiguity of being nonwhite in a white society. Even though there were definite broad cultural ties among all of these Americans, there were, in fact, large areas which separated them. When Martin Luther King, Jr., pulled together what was to become the most formative proof of a national identity among Negroes in America, the Civil Rights Movement, he all but solved the broad political identity crisis.

As a black minister, King understood the religious strain that runs so deeply through this population. Much of their frustration, which stemmed from their being discriminated against and thus segregated from the mainstream of American society, was due to their nonwhite status. The most viable and independent institution among nonwhite America is the church, an institution formed out of protest against segregation and one of the most powerful crusaders for justice in American life. This religious fervor was shared by almost all black Americans, the rich and the poor, the fair and the dark, the rural and the urban, the educated and the illiterate. Thus, King used the legitimate spiritual forces of the church in its historic role of protest to undergird his movement for destroying segregation, welding together, for a time, the broadest coalition of groups in the nonwhite spectrum. From that point on, others have been able to build upon that foundation.

Even though this political concept, "black Americans," includes all people who are of African descent in America, this is only one level of a multilevel identity which is true not only for blacks, but for most Americans. The reasons for black multilevel identity are, indeed, quite different in origin, scope, and longevity from that of whites, but they do exist. The political concept, "black Americans," may, indeed, provide the necessary political umbrella for conceptualizing black national identity. But this should not obscure in any way the fact that, in the realm of the social, black American ethnic groups with distinct languages and/or dialects, customs and manners, religious and family structures do exist.

One may sum this up in the following remarks pointing toward a theory of ethnicity.[1] In the history of peoples, for a variety of causes—physical differences, legal inequalities, arising from slavery or conquest—"we" and "they" groups rooted in consanguineous relationships arise and acquire what have been called "social definitions" by sociologists. This last point is seen in the case of the man who can "pass." The "passer" is a man who, if he conceals his ancestry from the "they" group, will be accepted by them as one of their own on the basis of his physical characteristics. He looks like them and they do not go further with it. Yet why does he refuse to pass on a permanent basis? The answer to this question points to an understanding of what ethnicity is and the power it has in the life of men.

Two points arise. The first is the force of loyalty to one's kinsmen and friends. This is what I call the *sentiment* of ethnicity. The term ethnicity has its roots in the Greek word for *nation*, meaning a people with common descent. This is why ethnic relationships are generalized kinship relationships. The loyalty to one's ethnic group, the solidarity this creates, and the guilt created by disloyalty are all an outgrowth of family solidarity. Sentiment, then, is that feeling of attachment which holds one's loyalty to the group through desire to belong rather than by force of law or mere social precedent.

The second point is that this attachment to kin, and the preference for one's own is fortified by differences in ways of life between ethnically distinct groups. Differences of religion and language are the most important ones. But people of different religion—to the extent that they marry with other coreligionists—perpetuate the cultural group as an ethnic group. The cultural differences intensify the bond and the self-consciousness of belonging to "us" rather than to "them." However, even where the cultural differences become fewer, the family loyalties remain. This is the heart of the matter. People find themselves locked into a situation where no one really can change the ethnic differentiation. The group may or may not be headed toward extinction as a social group, but it exists in the here and now. If a white man or many white men simultaneously resolve to be color-blind from now on, it does not really alter the relationship of the black man with his own relatives and friends which has been formed in a prior context.

Many people have concerned themselves with the question of whether or not blacks have a separate culture. Many say that they can understand why Italians or Jews remain as entities. Why blacks? Where is their culture? Many blacks ask the same question and have, indeed, insisted that there is a separate black culture. Howard Brotz has argued in his *Black Jews of Harlem* that the difference in social behaviors between whites and blacks in the United States might best be described as a *style* rather than a culture.[2] His argument is based on the fact that the term *culture* implies something fundamental about a way of life, such as the belief and practices shaped by different religions. Regardless of whether one accepts this view or not, the fundamental point I wish to emphasize is that the attachment to one's kin would remain if the differences in behavior were fewer than they are now. This is what Myrdal did not adequately understand, and what Glazer and Moynihan[3] have understood. Thus, the heart of this definition of an ethnic group is the subjective feeling of identification of its members.

BLACK ETHNIC GROUPS

The previous theoretical discussion concerning black Americans' identity and ethnicity provides the jumping off point for understanding the existence of black ethnic groups. Now, one can logically ask the question, do all these individuals called black Americans who do not look alike, speak the same language or dialect and, in many cases, do not share the same culture, form one homogenous ethnic group?

The American nation is composed of many ethnic groups formed as a result of mass immigration. Only one major American ethnic group other than the American Indian cannot be classified as immigrants; this group is composed of Africans who were brought involuntarily to America. Even so, there are among this group, broadly called "black Americans," persons of varied ethnic and cultural origins who did immigrate *freely* to the American shores. Little, if anything, is known about these many black ethnic groups. In the past, research literature and statistical data tend towards a blanket approach, describing, depicting, or analyzing them in terms of color rather than cultural differences. The one exception seems to be some data on British West Indian immigrants around the 1930s.

From as early as 1820, some blacks have sought entry into the United States. With regard to systematic empirical studies of foreign-born blacks or the descendants of foreign-born blacks, however, Ira de A. Reid's 1934 classic, *The Negro Immigrant*, has stood virtually alone for more than 40 years.[4] It is true that there has been a sharp rise in studies on Caribbean blacks in recent years, but most of them focus on blacks in the United States—with the exception of recent articles by Roy Bryce-Laporte.[5]

According to official census figures, approximately 1,216,938 West Indians and 82,317 Africans have come to America since 1820. I should like to note that the majority of the African immigration does not represent West Africa, but rather the northern and southern parts of the continent. If you were to compare these figures of black immigration with those of Europeans, the facts are devastating. The figures for Europeans range from 45 to 48 million during the same period. The real impact of the one and a half million immigrants in the black community, as well as society in general, is a vastly unexplored area. This is clearly accentuated by a recent report in the October, 1973, *Encore* magazine concerning illegal Jamaican immigration.[7] From their investigative research, they were able to determine that two out of every three Jamaicans living in the United States were doing so illegally.

If this assertion can be taken seriously, the number of black immigrants would double the previously cited figure if we can assume that other groups are doing the same, and there is reason to believe that this is so. As such, the number of foreign-born blacks within the United States could well be over two and a half to three million such individuals.

Examining the latest immigration figures, those groups of which Reid spoke continue to make up the bulk of black immigration. These groups are Africans, Barbadians, Dominicans, Haitians, Jamaicans, Trinidadians, Panamanians, and Guyanese.

Selecting three of these groups, one is impressed by the heavy concentration of these three groups in large metropolitan areas. Immigrants from Haiti, Jamaica, and Trinidad and Tobago tend to come to New York. In percentages, this is 78 percent of all Haitians, 63 percent of all Jamaicans, and 59 percent of all Trinidadians. The remainder of the immigrants are divided between several states and specific cities: Miami, Boston, Cambridge, Newark, Baltimore, and Philadelphia. Thus, among the immigrants, the knowledge of family and a large colony of fellow countrymen in residence serves to pull certain groups to specific areas.

According to Charles Valentine's research[8], in northern cities there are at least fourteen different Afro-American subgroups within the American black population. This kind of variety has many implications for the black community as well as the larger society.

IMPLICATIONS

Black foreign ethnics in the United States are highly urban, almost 100 percent. Along with being urban, they are concentrated in large numbers in the most urban of American cities, New York. This is important for several reasons: New York City is the acknowledged leader in the entertainment and financial fields, as well as the arts and letters.

Southern-born blacks warrant our special attention as a result of their tremendous out-migration from the southern states to other parts of the country. They are, without doubt, a cultural group with language (dialect), customs and manners, religion and family structure peculiar to their group. As of now, little systematic study has been made of the group relating to their status and progress since leaving the South. While volumes seem to exist concerning southern-born blacks, one is shocked at the lack of empirical data on the southern black as an ethnic subgroup in the United States.

The scientific literature is replete with studies describing various life styles among blacks inside and outside the South, in urban and rural areas, and in large- and small-sized communities. The works on rural blacks by Charles S. Johnson,[9] on blacks in metropolitan areas by Clayton and Drake,[10] and on blacks in rural and urban areas and in large and small communities by E. Franklin Frazier[11] continue to stand out as hallmark studies on the black community. But almost all of these classic studies attempted to account for the variations among blacks in attitudes, aspirations, values, and life styles on the basis of class or socioeconomic differences and not in terms of subcultural or ethnic differences among blacks. Because of the class bias of most past and present social research, black subcultures have tended to be examined in isolation from one another, thus precluding comparative analysis of ethnic subgroups within the black community.

It is surprising to note that, of the numerous studies that have been conducted on northern and southern blacks, for example, relatively few have compared the two as ethnic subgroups in their own right. There are several notable exceptions, of course. Frazier's work, *Negro Youth at the Crossways*[12] attempts to contrast the attitudes, values, and goals of black youth in a deep south community with those of black youth in a border community. Moreover, Charles Johnson's study,[13] *The Negro College Graduate*, contrasts the marital patterns of not only southern-born and northern-born mothers of black college graduates, but contrasts the marital patterns of foreign-born and native-born mothers of college graduates as well.

Interestingly, some of the most sensitive descriptions of different ethnic subcultural patterns among blacks in recent years have been provided not by social scientists, but by black novelists, poets, and playwrights.

DOMESTIC POLICY IMPLICATIONS

In recent years, the southern migrants who were of a somewhat different background than the scholars and intellectuals who preceded them have been singled out as the reason for the troubles of the urban North. Sociologists, among others, have described the lack of family stability of these people in relationship to other groups. Most, if not all, are based on thoughts and assumptions rather than fact. Presently, studies are being issued which contradict these prevailing generalizations about southern blacks. The National Urban League Research Department has uncovered surprising facts as a result of an analysis of Census Bureau data on the characteristics of *Negro Immigrants to Selected Metropolitan Areas*.

When analyzing the Detroit Standard Metropolitan Statistical Area (SMSA) data, there is clear evidence to contradict the southern black riffraff stereotype. Detroit is an especially good example because more than half (51 percent) of the blacks residing there in 1970 were born in the South.

A comparison of the data provided for black males of the primary earning years (aged 25–64) shows that those from the South have a slightly higher employment rate, higher average earnings, and substantially less schooling. Also, the southern-born appear to be more family oriented than their northern counterparts, and are more likely to be married and living with their spouse.

Taking these shortcomings into account, the southern-born appear to have higher earnings at every level of schooling except for the college groups. The model earnings of each age- and school-level group are within the census interval of 6.0 to 9.9 thousand dollars, and increased earnings are apparent within age groups as the level of schooling rises.

Differences between the southern- and northern-born are reduced when school levels are combined within age groups, in part, because relatively more of the northern-born have had some college, and relatively more of the northern-born college groups are in the earnings interval of 15.0 and above. Similarly, the average earnings of the older southern subgroup with only some high school is less, in part, because most (53 percent) of the older southern-born have not had more than eight years of schooling.[14]

These data state specifically that there are horrible and misleading ideas floating about concerning the impact of southern blacks on the urban North. More importantly, such misconceptions have been the basis for many important social policies formulated for this group which have failed. For example, in 1971, Dr. Daniel H. Kruger of the Michigan State University School of Labor and Industrial Relations testified at hearings before Senator Walter

Mondale's Select Committee for Equal Educational Opportunity, that, "We [Michigan] inherit the educational deficiencies of the school systems of other parts of the country."[15] Dr. Kruger was explaining the reasons for the problems affecting the Detroit and the Michigan educational school system. The state was placing the blame on southern blacks and Mexican Americans, when, in fact, the census data were revealing just the opposite, at least for black Americans.

Such policies have failed because they are not based on a systematic analysis of the variety of socioeconomic and cultural patterns within the black community. For example, in many ways Detroit is quite different from New York City, Atlanta, and Los Angeles. Each should be viewed for its own peculiarities rather than as a monolithic, homogeneous "black community." This kind of approach takes into account the varying ethnic groups, the power of ethnicity, and the special problem in understanding, in a more meaningful way, the "black communities."

If one is to develop effective social policies, programs, and services for various groups, then it is imperative that one has sufficient knowledge of significant variations within minority groups as well as between them. For example, many teachers in ghetto schools are ineffective because they fail to realize that black children come from a variety of social, cultural, and ethnic backgrounds.

SUMMARY

If cultural variations among native-born American blacks are not taken into account, it is not surprising that national policies and programs are also insensitive to cultural variations between native born and foreign-born blacks. Most Americans are unaware of the fact that over one million blacks in the United States today are either foreign-born or are the descendants of immigrants from the Caribbean, Central America, or Africa. In fact, Caribbean, or "West Indian" blacks as they are more popularly called, have made and are still making significant contributions to the advancement and heritage of blacks in America. Most of their contributions, however, have largely gone unrecog-

nized because of the monolithic view of the black community as ethnically homogeneous.

Thousands upon thousands of blacks are coming to America each year, with the bulk of this immigration consisting of Barbadians, Jamaicans, Trinidadians, Haitians, Panamanians, Guyanese, Dominicans, and Africans. Because most school systems are unaware of the variety of black ethnic subgroups, many black children from foreign backgrounds are being erroneously classified as "retarded," "hyperactive," and "antisocial" because of their cultural speech or behavioral patterns.

Most national policies and programs for blacks today fail to take account of important variations in life styles and other cultural patterns between northern and southern blacks, as well as domestic and foreign-born blacks.

NOTES

1. B. William Austin, "Why Ethnicity is Important to Blacks," *Urban League Review,* Vol. 1, No. 2, Fall 1975, pp.13–17.
2. H. Brotz, *The Black Jews of Harlem* (London: Free Press of Glencoe, 1964).
3. N. Glazer and D. Moynihan, *Beyond the Melting Pot* (Cambridge, Mass.: The M.I.T. Press, 1963).
4. Ira de A. Reid, *The Negro Immigrant: His Background, Characteristics and Social Adjustment, 1899–1937* (New York: Arno Press and the New York Times, 1969).
5. Roy Simon Bryce-Laporte, "Black Immigrants," *Journal of Black Studies* (September 1972).
6. *1973 Annual Report: Immigration and Naturalization Service,* United States Department of Justice, Immigration and Naturalization Service, Washington, D.C. 1974.
7. Les Payne and Knut Royce, "Don't Send Me All of Your Poor," *Encore* Vol. 2, No. 10, October 1973, p.55.
8. Charles A. Valentine, "Deficit, Difference, and Bicultural Models of Afro-American Behavior." *Harvard Educational Review,* Vol. 42, No. 2, May 1971, p.140.

   A. Afro-English speakers:
      1. Northern-urban U.S. Blacks
      2. Southern-rural U.S. Blacks
      3. Anglo-African West Indians
      4. Guyanese
      5. Surinam Takitaki-speakers
      *6. West Africans

   B. Afro-French speakers:
      7. Haitian Creole-speakers
      *8. Other French West Indians
      *9. French Guianans
      *10. Louisiana Creoles

   C. Afro-Spanish speakers:
      11. Black Cubans
      12. A-B-C Islanders Papiamento-speakers

*13. Panamanians
*14. Black South Americans

 * Groups not yet observed.

9. Charles S. Johnson, *The Negro College Graduate* (New York: Negro University Press, 1969).

10. Horace Clayton and St. Clair Drake, *Black Metropolis: A Study of Negro Life in a Northern City* (New York: Harper and Row, 1962).

11. E. Franklin Frazier, *Black Bourgeoisie* (Glencoe, Illinois: Free Press, 1957).

12. E. Franklin Frazier, *Negro Youth at the Crossways* (Washington, D.C.: American Council on Education, 1940).

13. Johnson, op. cit.

14. "Black Migration and Its Influence on Political Thinking of High School Students," National Urban League Research Department, 1974. Also see U.S. Bureau of the Census, Census of Population: 1970. Supplementary Reports, PC (S1)-47, *Negro Immigrants to Selected Metropolitan Areas* (Washington, D.C.: U.S. Government Printing Office, 1973).

15. *Hearings Before the Select Committee on Equal Educational Opportunity of the United States Senate*, 91st Congress, 2nd Session, 1978, p.407.

IMMIGRANTS AND EMPLOYERS:
A SOCIOLEGAL PERSPECTIVE

Bradley W. Parlin

OVERVIEW: THE SOCIOLEGAL SETTING

While sociologists, most often demographers, have investigated a wide range of immigrant and immigration-related issues, there is, overall, a paucity of research on the employment experiences faced by immigrants who seek employment in the U.S. labor market. A review of the research literature on the employment adjustment of immigrants often reveals soft generalizations based on sometimes insensitive data-gathering techniques. The character of the adjustment process—the interactive relationships of American employers and immigrant candidates for employment—are obscured by generalizations.[1]

The starting point of this investigation into the labor market experiences of immigrants must include a consideration of the sociolegal environment which may facilitate or hinder immigrants' employment adjustment.

THE SOCIAL MILIEU

The sentiments of contemporary Americans toward immigrants have obvious implications for the immigrants' fortune on the labor market. However, a confident assessment is difficult due to the divergent evidence in this regard.[2]

The legal status of an immigrant in the U.S. labor market is intimately linked to his being a noncitizen until naturalized and the vicissitudes of legal definition. While employment discrimination against noncitizens clearly violates the spirit of the law, it does not violate the legal interpretation of the 1964 Civil Rights Act. Thus, while "Title VII protects all individuals from unlawful discrimination *whether or not a citizen of the United States*," an employer may refuse to hire noncitizens and not be guilty of national origin discrimination.[3]

Four recent Supreme Court decisions directly influence the labor market viability of noncitizen (alien and immigrant) candidates for employment. Two of the decisions involve public sector (state and federal agencies) employment practices, while the remaining two apply to the private sector.[4] The June 1973 decision provides that state agencies may not discriminate against noncitizens.[5] The June 1976 decision abolishes the citizenship requirement for taking the Federal Service Entrance Examination making citizenship discrimination illegal for the federal government.[6]

In the private sector, the November 1973 decision allows private employers to legally discriminate against noncitizens through citizenship exclusion policies.[7] Finally, the February 1976 decision, which allows states to levy sanctions against private employers who hire illegal aliens, increases the probability that employers will utilize the citizenship exclusion policies made legal by the Espinoza Decision.[8] Writing the dissenting opinion in the Espinoza Decision, Douglas argues "that discrimination on the basis of alienage always has the effect of discrimination on the basis of national origin."[9] He concludes that

> the first generation has the greater adjustment to make to their new country. Their unfamiliarity with America makes them the most vulnerable to exploitation and discriminatory treatment. They, of course, have the same obligations as American citizens to pay taxes, and they are subject to the draft on the same basis, but they have never received equal treatment in the job market.[10]

In sum, the implications of the sociolegal milieux of the immigrant entrant into the labor market are suggestive. If there are any substantial antiforeign sentiments among employer representatives, the legality of citizenship exclusion policies permits and encourages employment discrimination against immigrants. Do employers avail themselves of the legal opportunity to discriminate, thus placing ascriptive barriers before the immigrant in his quest for economic independence? This is the empirical question the remainder of this paper addresses.

IMMIGRANTS AND EMPLOYMENT

It is beyond the scope of this paper to explore the labor force experience of all classes of immigrants. In this paper, our central concern is with employment prospects for "immigrant professionals" who are new graduates from U.S. colleges and universities, and who become legal immigrants through the conversion of student to permanent resident visas.

Foreign student nonreturn

The Immigration Act of 1965, by abolishing the national origin quotas and giving preference to those with skills in short supply in the United States, contributed substantially to the increasing number of foreign students who immigrate.[11] The mechanism of foreign student immigration is the conversion of his or her visa. Students enter the United States on either an F (student) or J (exchange visitor) visa. Holders of either visa may remain in the United States for training for a period of eighteen months after the conclusion of their university programs. The important difference between these visa statuses is that the F visa holder can easily extend his stay indefinitely by converting to an immigrant visa, while the J visa holder is almost never able to gain an exit waiver.[12] The effect of visa status for immigrants is evident in Niland's observation that for engineers, the F visa accounted for ninety-nine percent of all engineering immigration to America from five Asian countries.[13]

Thus, a significant component of immigrant professionals is drawn from what is called the foreign student nonreturn (FSNR) component. Although there are no official statistics on the FSNR component of total immigrants, Thomas states that "the numbers are very high. A cultural attache at a Middle Eastern embassy recently said that, of Iran's 6,000 students in America, only about 50 percent are returning. The same seems to be true of students from countries such as India, Korea, Egypt, Pakistan, Greece, Columbia, and Jordan."[14] Similarly, Niland estimates that the FSNR

component accounted for approximately twenty-seven percent of the total immigration to the United States in 1968.[15] In addition, Ritterband notes that "almost half of the science, technology, and medical immigrants from the developing nations come to the United States as students or trainees."[16]

In short, the new graduate foreign student comprises a significant proportion of immigrants from the professional and technical occupations. Yet, little is known about his employment prospects and experiences in the United States. Thus, the remainder of this paper will focus upon a brief report of some of my research findings in order to arrive at a preliminary assessment of the employability of immigrant professionals who enter the U.S. labor market.

Employability

The concept of employability has been primarily the domain of labor economists and only recently has been introduced to the sociological literature by Hodges.[17] *Employability* refers to the relative desirability of a category or class of candidates for employment to potential employers; and the absence of a literature addressing the experiences of immigrants in the labor market precludes any kind of sensitive appraisal of the employability of this group.[18]

Conceptually, employability is a premise of the "queue" theory of the labor force, "in which workers are arrayed according to their employability, i.e., desirability to employers. Those at the head of the queue are the most desirable employees: first hired and last fired."[19]

The studies

The results of a case study comparing citizen and immigrant professionals in terms of their employability reveal patterns of employment discrimination against noncitizens. The comparison of the 621 citizens with the 141 immigrant professionals on four indices of employability controlling for ability (grade point average) suggests the immigrant is marginal in the labor market.

While this employer was willing to interview new graduate immigrants, but not alien candidates, for professional employment, there was clearly employment discrimination against immigrant candidates in the recruitment process. Citizens were found to be considerably more employable than immigrants. In addition, non-Western noncitizens were considerably less employable than Western noncitizens. Significantly, the desirability of immigrant applicants in the case of this employer appears to be based on factors other than those related to merit or competence such as college or university grade point averages. If we then concur with Hodges that "discrimination in employment practices occurs when a person is displaced from the position he holds in the queue by virtue of his employability and replaced by some less qualified prospective employee,"[20] it can be concluded that there is discrimination against immigrants in the scientific labor market. Were the discriminatory hiring practices found in the study unique to the industrial organizations studied or is employment discrimination against noncitizens commonplace?

In order to extend this investigation into the employability of immigrant professionals, it will be useful to consider the tripartite relationship among noncitizens (aliens and immigrants), American employers, and the placement organizations of U.S. universities.

Many immigrant professionals, particularly the new graduates who comprise the foreign student nonreturn (FSNR) element, and who are the focus of this study, enter the labor market through university placement centers. The placement centers encourage both employers and students to utilize their services to facilitate the recruitment process. Students benefit from exposure to many and varied potential employers. Employers benefit by the efficiency of exposure to a large pool of well-trained potential employees; and the university, through its placement center, most efficiently markets its products. The university placement center, then, is a publicly supported employment agency for the institution's graduates.

Employment agencies have always been important gatekeepers in maintaining discriminatory hiring practices through exclusion policies that select certain categories of candidates for employment with prospective employers. David Dressler, for example, notes that, "in the late 1930's, according to surveys, employment agencies estimated that as many as 95 percent of their job orders specified 'no Jews.' "[21] Although exclusion policies on the criteria of race, sex, religion, and national origin are formally banned under Title VII of the 1964 Civil Rights Act, many employers and placement centers maintain exclusionary policies with respect to citizenship. Employers often require citizenship as a condition of employment, and placement centers frequently allow recruiting employers who so desire to exclude noncitizens from campus employment interviews.

In the case of the university placement center, the mechanism for noncitizen exclusion is the employer data sheet (EDS). The EDS is a form sent by the placement organization to employers who plan to recruit new graduates. The companies are asked to specify on the data sheets the degree areas for which they plan to recruit, the types of jobs available, the locations of the jobs, and so on. Questions regarding whether or not citizenship is a requirement for employment with the recruiting organization are found on placement organization forms in colleges and universities across the United States. The EDS, then, becomes a potentially useful source of information regarding the employability of immigrant professionals, since any tendency to exclude noncitizens from the recruitment process a priori places a barrier against both aliens and immigrants in their search for employment.

Two approaches, both utilizing placement center EDS forms, characterize this phase of research. First, I will summarize the responses of a sample of 168 employers to university placement center EDS's at three universities that provided prospective employers with the option of placing blanket exclusions against noncitizens as potential candidates for employment with their companies, in order to determine the desirability of noncitizens as candidates for employment. Briefly, then, the proportion of a sample of employers who avail themselves of the opportunity to discriminate against noncitizens, and therefore immigrant professionals, becomes an index of employability that will provide important insights into the labor market desirability of this minority. The second approach derives from an analysis of the propensity of fifty-eight university placement organizations to allow recruiting employers the opportunity to exclude noncitizens from access to the recruitment process. This index will further illuminate the relative desirability or marginality of the noncitizen and immigrant professional in the marketplace, since it reflects either discriminatory policies of placement center administration, or placement center responses to discriminatory personnel policies of recruiting companies or both. This phase of the investigation will permit preliminary reflections concerning the relationship between the ascriptive aspects of citizenship status and the employment prospects available to immigrant professionals in the scientific labor market.

The data to be reported were gathered from three universities and cover one recruiting year (fall to spring, 1974). The information derives from EDS's of three placement centers at moderate-sized universities; two were state universities and one was a private technical college. All three placement centers provided recruiting employers with the option to exclude noncitizens from interviews with company representatives through the citizenship exclusion question on the EDS. There were a total of 100 organizational employers who recruited at University A, 35 at University B, and 33 at University C.

The organizational recruiters at these three schools represent a wide variety of organizational categories, including manufacturing, aerospace, insurance, public agencies at federal, state and local levels, public accounting firms, electronics industries, retail merchandising firms, and many of the *Fortune 500* blue chip corporations. All were equal opportunity employers.

The overall responses of the 168 employers recruiting at the three universities reveal the marginal employability of immigrant professionals. Over two thirds (67 percent) of recruiting employers discriminate in some way against noncitizens. Almost half (43 percent) of the recruiting organizations require citizenship as a condition for employment interviews, while 24 percent indicated their willingness to interview noncitizens according to certain stipulations.[22] Only 7 percent were unqualifiedly willing to interview noncitizens, and 26 percent did not respond to the exclusionary question. In short, discriminatory hiring practices with respect to noncitizens appear to be commonplace. Interestingly, two of the recruiting organizations that

would not consider noncitizens as applicants include a major university graduate school that was actively recruiting minority applicants for its graduate program, and a large religious missionary organization engaged in recruiting male and female spiritual leaders and church officials.

In terms of employability, we can conclude that the immigrant professional is at a clear disadvantage in the labor market. The ascriptive effect of citizenship status is apparent. A significant proportion of organizational employers routinely exclude noncitizens from the recruitment process. And, most important, the universities that hosted the sample companies provided the company representatives with the opportunity to discriminate. The subject of the following section will be the university-employer complicity.

To broaden the base of investigation, the researcher contacted 164 colleges and universities in the midwestern part of the United States and sought their EDS's to ascertain whether or not discriminatory questions were included. The decision to confine this investigation to midwestern colleges and universities was basically logistic. We could think of no important reason why midwestern universities would be unique on this issue. Schools were selected from *Lovejoy's College Guide*.[23] All schools with university or college status, with student populations of 3,000 or more, throughout ten states were contacted. Of the 164 schools contacted, 106 had university status and the remaining 58 were colleges.

During February 1974, letters requesting EDS's were sent to the institutions. One hundred and thirty of the schools responded to the inquiry, 58 of which sent EDS's and became the subsample for further analysis. The remaining 72 either did not utilize EDS's or declined to provide them. Although the low return rate of EDS forms among the respondent school organizations inhibits gross generalizations, the findings indicate that the option to exclude noncitizens from interviews is not restricted to the three universities on which the previous research was focused.

Eighteen of the schools in the sample were privately supported, while 40 out of 58, or 68 percent, of the schools were public institutions. The data indicate that a substantial number of the universities and colleges provide recruiting employers with the option of excluding noncitizen students from employment interviews with their organizations. Among the forty public institutions, fifteen (37 percent) include discriminatory questions. Among the eighteen large private schools in the subsample, fifteen (85 percent) facilitated discrimination against noncitizens by bringing the option to the employers' attention with the question of whether or not they would interview noncitizens. In short, over half (51 percent) of the subsample schools allowed employers, who utilized their placement facilities to recruit new graduates, to refuse employment interviews to noncitizens.[24]

This research has presented strong evidence that immigrant professionals may often experience employment discrimination in the competition for jobs in the U.S. labor market. The case study findings suggest that compared with citizens, immigrants are less likely to be granted interviews and offers of employment from an employer. Immigrants are routinely screened out of the recruitment process by employers who, through citizenship exclusion policies, place discriminatory barriers before alien and immigrant candidates for employment. In addition, many universities encourage employment discrimination against immigrant professionals by allowing employers to exclude them from access to employment interviews on campus recruit visits.

The foregoing synthesis of exploratory studies concerning the employability of immigrant professionals has generated more questions than answers (as is always the case with research) and, given the preliminary character of my conclusions, I am hopeful that my findings might provide a benchmark from which future investigations into immigrant labor market experiences might begin.

POLICY IMPLICATION

The United States has long benefited from immigrant labor and, as Fortney suggests, "The contributions that immigrants have made to American science and other professions [are] . . . intimately related to American legislative idiosyncracies."[25] The most recent manifestation of Fortney's generalization finds its focus in legislative changes occurring in the mid–1960s. The Immigration and Nationality Act of 1965 introduced skill discrimination in the immigrant selection process: "Under the new Act, preference was given to persons with skills which the Secretary of Labor deemed 'especially advantageous' to the United States."[26] Occurring at a point of acute shortages of engineers and scientists in the U.S. labor market, the effect of the American skill discrimination policy was to contribute greatly to the sharp influx of immigrant professional and technical workers in the 1960s and to the United State's stellar role in the so-called brain drain controversy.

This debate, in turn, spawned polar reflections on the propriety of U.S. immigration policies that remain unresolved today. While the intensity of this debate has been on the wane with the decline of the U.S. aerospace efforts, and the widespread unemployment of engineers and scientists (both citizen and noncitizen), it is my position that the Espinoza decision requires a reconsideration of the importance of the dispute. This is especially so since these arguments continue to legitimize or compromise present immigration policy.

The critics of U.S. post–1965 immigration policy tend to focus on its exploitive dimension and view the United States as

> an often ungrateful recipient of a costly gift of human capital. Scientists, engineers and physicians of foreign origin are, in effect, providing foreign aid to the United States in a reversal of the more heralded flow of economic and technical assistance. Although no neat credit/debit balance can be struck, the professional manpower to which this country falls heir represents a capital investment in education and training equivalent to millions of dollars.[27]

From this perspective the United States, because of the pull of its immigration policies, is primarily serving its own interests with little regard for the costs to developing nations or individual immigrants. The costs to developing nations, while difficult to measure, are undeniable and substantial.[28] These include the monetarily expensive gift of human capital and the loss of the social potential of exceptional people by the society. There are strong arguments that propose that in the long run, because of remittance and other monetary returns, the gift will be repaid to the benefit of the donor country.[29] It is difficult to reconcile, however, the social loss of the immigrant professional as a catalyst for change. The committee on the International Migration of Talent stresses the crucial role of professionals in nation building:

> Persons with highly developed talent have several indispensable roles to play in the development process: (1) they constitute the intellectual bridge to the developed world, that is, they assess and adapt relevant ideas and technologies originating elsewhere; (2) they develop, maintain and manage the productive processes, the resources, and the complex structures of modern society; as the intellectual elite, they bring about the structural and institutional changes necessary if a nation is to become a modern state; and (3) their irreplaceable efforts, and the standards they set, heavily influence the educational and other institutions which shape future generations of educated persons.[30]

Thus, from one point of view, United States immigration policy contributes to perpetration of economic inequality between the developed and developing nations and should be modified to correct what is suggested to be a self-serving injustice. As the committee suggests, "the more advanced nations should reduce, or halt entirely, the migration of highly trained people by changing their immigrant laws or shifting their interpretation of these laws."[31] Similarly, if somewhat more acerbic, James Perkins argues for closing "selfish loopholes—the special waivers that allow students to stay here in our national interest . . . if they can teach a foreign language or be useful to the Defense Department."[32] He strongly rejects the "general exploitation of foreign students by the diploma mills; the all-too-easy solution to our need for teaching assistants, laboratory aides, and medical workers, offered in the name of scholarships or fellowships."[33]

While the critics of U.S. immigration policy focus on the national and individual exploitation of immigrant professionals, proponents pay homage to the individual freedom and welfare of immigrants. Defenders of U.S. immigration policy draw "inspiration from the tradition that learned men for centuries have crossed borders in the pursuit and practice of truth. Their ideal is that this should remain a self-evident virtue and a cherished tradition."[34] Thus, U.S. immigration policy, by encouraging the free flow of skilled manpower, contributes to "a beneficial process, since it results from the free choices of the individuals concerned" and thereby "may be said to increase potential world welfare."[35] Some observers are less certain of the beneficial consequences of U.S. policy. Thomas Mills, for example, emphasizes that "there still remains the nagging doubt of whether mankind is better served by the over-concentration of such manpower in a single country."[36] In addition, Brinley Thomas points out that the assumption underlying the proponents of U.S. immigration policy is "what is good for the United States is good for the world." He goes on to suggest that this "is no more self-evident than the other old chestnut: What is good for General Motors is good for the United States."[37]

It is my supposition that the research findings reported, and the implications of the Espinoza decision, combine to compromise seriously the viability of the arguments that support current U.S. immigration policy. The crux of this matter lies in the inconsistency between the philosophical basis of U.S. immigration policy and the legal status of the immigrant in the labor market. Recall that the essence of the defense of present policies is in the idea that men should be free to pursue knowledge wherever that pursuit might lead them. Therefore, from this point of view, infringements on freedom such as discrimination and bigotry are logically abhorrent, being in opposition to the ideals of freedom and the universalism of science. Walter Adams and Joel Dirlam, for example, propose that "Nations aspiring to wealth, growth, and power cannot afford to tolerate discrimination against individuals on grounds of national origin, caste, tribe, political affiliation, family connection, etc."[38]

Citizenship discrimination in the employment sphere was effectively legalized and sanctioned by the Espinoza decision, thereby leaving legal immigrants to the United States without protection from discriminatory hiring practices of organizational employers. We have seen that employers and university placement centers do in fact discriminate against noncitizens (aliens and immigrants) in the recruitment process. Clearly, employment discrimination against immigrants, professional or otherwise, is inconsistent with the philosophical basis of U.S. immigration policy. It is difficult to reconcile attracting immigrants to skill areas in short supply in the U.S. labor market with not providing them with protection from discriminatory hiring practices upon their arrival. This is also inconsistent with the philosophical underpinnings of U.S. immigration policy, the spirit of the 1964 Civil Rights Act, and the value of social equity. American policymakers could well find guidance from Mills, who feels that, "The social and economic welfare of the individual . . . should be the most important aspect of migration of scientists and engineers as with others."[39]

The resolution of the dilemma posed by the interface between United States immigration policy and the legal status of the immigrant in the U.S. labor market is a complex matter. If one finds, as I do, that the free flow of men and ideas in pursuit of art and science is a worthwhile goal, then the United States should provide protection for immigrants in the labor market by extending Title VII of the 1964 Civil Rights Act to include alienage as a covered classification. In addition, as others have proposed, the United States could substantially invest in training programs to overcome the shortages of high-level manpower,[40] and consider immigration policies and procedures that will not contribute to the perpetuation of the inequalities between less developed nations and developed nations.[41] Developing nations feeling the pinch of the loss of highly trained manpower can constrict the outflow of immigrant professionals through the manipulation of their national policies and procedures.[42]

Since immigrant professionals are encouraged to become citizens and new entrants into the labor market, it seems equitable to offer them protection on a basis similar to that afforded citizens. Policy analysts might usefully ponder the effect of citizenship discrimination on foreign relations and policies. Many noncitizens, aliens and immigrants alike, out of personal choice—possibly influenced by the frustration of facing discriminatory practices in establishing economic independence—return to their homelands to become members of the political elite. One cannot help but wonder how their experiences while in this country might affect their future roles as policymakers in relationships with the United States.

NOTES

1. See David North, *Immigrants and the American Labor Market* Manpower Administration Research Monograph No.31 (Washington, D.C.: U.S. Department of Labor, 1974), p.5; and Frank Mott, "The Immigrant Workers," *Annals of the American Academy of Political and Social Sciences* 367 (September, 1966).
2. John Higham, *American Issues Forum* 4 (San Diego, California: University of California Press, 1975).
3. U.S. Supreme Court No.72–671, November 19, 1973. *Cecilia Espinoza, et al. Farah Manufacturing Company, Inc.* (Commerce Clearing House, 1973), p.6023.
4. Ibid., pp. 6020–25; *Wall Street Journal,* 2 June 1976, p. 1; and Austin Fragomen, Jr., "U.S. Supreme Court's Decision on Non-Citizenship," *International Migration Review,* 8, No.1 (1976), p.78.
5. Fragomen, op. cit.
6. *Wall Street Journal,* 26 February 1976.
7. U.S. Supreme Court, op. cit.
8. *Wall Street Journal,* 2 June 1976.
9. U.S. Supreme Court, op. cit., p.6025.
10. Ibid.
11. For explorations into the consequences of the Kennedy-Johnson legislation, see "The New Immigration," *Annals of the American Academy of Political and Social Sciences,* 367 (September, 1966), pp.1–4; and *International Migration Review,* 4, No.3 (Summer 1970); 5, No.3 (Fall 1971); 5, No.4 (Winter 1971); and 6, No.1 (Spring 1972).
12. See John Niland, *The Brain Drain of Highly Trained Engineering Manpower from Asia to the United States* (Lexington, Massachusetts: D.C. Heath, 1971), p.67, and Paul Ritterband, "Law, Policy, and Behavior: Educational Exchange Policy and Student Migration," *The American Journal of Sociology,* 76 (July 1970), pp.72–74, for detailed treatment of visa allocation procedures and consequences.
13. Niland, op. cit., p.7
14. Brinley Thomas, "From the Other Side: A European View," *Annals of the American Academy of Political and Social Sciences,* 367 (September 1966), p.71.
15. Niland, op. cit., p.6.
16. Ritterband, op. cit., p.72.
17. Robert Hodges, "Toward a Theory of Racial Differences in Employment," *Social Forces,* 52, No.1 (September 1972). For conceptual explications of employability in sociology and economics, see Hodges, ibid., pp.16–31; and Lester Thurow, *Poverty and Discrimination* (Washington, D.C.: The Brookings Institute, 1969).
18. Hodges, op. cit., p.16.
19. Hodges, ibid., p.16.
20. Hodges, op. cit., p.17.
21. David Dressler, *Sociology: The Study of Human Interaction* (New York: Knopf, 1969), p.542.
22. The stipulations include the possession of a permanent resident visa or a commitment to return to the homeland to work as a national in international divisions of United States firms.
23. Clarence Lovejoy, *College Guide: A Complete Reference to*

American Colleges and Universities (New York: Simon and Schuster, 1953).

24. There can be no doubt that the noncitizen students' attitudes toward U.S. social structure are influenced by labor market experiences that involve elements of discrimination. Because many of the PTK, FSNR components of immigrants to the United States remigrate to assume important positions in the social infrastructures of their home countries, questions surrounding their attitudes and adjustment experiences take on added importance. Preliminary results of a study recently completed by this researcher suggest that noncitizen students do indeed see themselves as a handicapped minority in the labor market. However, broadbased systematic longitudinal research is requisite to provide definitive answers to questions on the impact of discrimination on immigrant adjustment.

25. Judith Fortney, "Immigrant Professionals: A Brief Historical Survey," *International Migration Review* 1, No.1 (1972), p.50. Also see Gerald Rosenblum, *Immigrant Workers* (New York: Basic Books, 1973); and Abba Swartz, *The Open Society* (New York: Morrow, 1968)—both of whom examine the historical relationship between immigration legislation and the occupational composition of immigrants.

26. Fortney, op. cit., p.55.

27. Thomas Mills, "Scientific Personnel and the Professions," *Annals of the American Academy of Political and Social Sciences* 367 (September, 1966), p.41.

28. This point is widely elaborated by both critics and proponents of U.S. immigration policy. See, for example, Thomas, "From the Other Side," loc. cit.; Robert Meyers, " 'Brain Drains' and 'Brain Gains,' " *International Development Review* 9, No.4 (December 1967); William Glaser and G. Christopher Hobers, "The Migration and Return of Professionals," *International Migration Review* 8, No.2 (1974); Acueil Ahmad, "Gain-Drain Ratio in the Global Exchange of Scientific and Technical Manpower," *Journal of Asian and African Studies* 5, No.3 (July 1970); and High Folk, "The Brain Drain and Economic Development" (paper presented at the Midwestern Economics Association Meeting, Detroit, Michigan, April 1970).

29. See, for example, Harry Johnson, "An 'Internationalist' Model," in *The Brain Drain,* ed. Walter Adams (New York: Macmillan, 1968). Johnson argues that "normally such migration—like any profit-motivated international movement of factors of production—may be expected to raise total world output and, therefore, ... be economically beneficial to the world as a whole," p.83. Indeed, "it should be noted that the country of emigration generally obtains some gains from the emigration of educated people,

which may provide indirect compensation for any losses incurred" (p.83).

30. The Committee on the International Migration of Talent, *Modernization and the Migration of Talent,* a report from Education and World Affairs (1970), p.42.

31. Ibid., p.75. For a more thorough treatment of the unique role of the United States as an attracter of highly trained talent, see Justus Van Der Kroef, "The U.S. and the World's Brain Drain," *International Journal of Comparative Sociology* 2, No.3 (1970), pp.220–39.

32. James Perkins, "Foreign Aid and the Brain Drain," *Foreign Affairs* (July 1966), p.618.

33. Ibid., p.619. The Committee on the International Migration of Talent (op. cit.) observes that "large parts of the hospital systems of both the United Kingdom and the United States would collapse if migration of physicians from less developed countries were suddenly to cease" (p.49). Thomas, "From the Other Side," op. cit., adds the caution that "we must beware of the simple view that the principles of the free society impel us to regard all free international movements of human capital as inherently desirable." (p.72).

34. John Niland, *The Asian Engineering Brain Drain* (Lexington, Massachusetts: D.C. Heath and Co., 1970), p.8.

35. Walter Adams, ed., *The Brain Drain* (New York: Macmillan, 1968), p.75.

36. Mills, op. cit., p.42.

37. Thomas, "From the Other Side," op. cit., p.69.

38. Walter Adams and Joel Dirlam, "An Agenda for Action," in Adams, op. cit., p.259.

39. Mills, op. cit., pp.34–35.

40. See the Committee on the International Migration of Talent, op. cit., p.71.

41. This approach is based on the observation that "there is a clear, common tendency among the richer countries to give various kinds of preference to highly trained people. This general evolution of immigration laws and regulations is a clear response to the sharply rising demand in all developed societies for persons with high levels of education, and to the fact that the advanced countries have not trained enough of their citizens to fill all of the jobs generated by their economic and social systems." Committee on the International Migration of Talent, op. cit., p.75. See also Khoshkish, op. cit.

42. See, for example, W. R. Bohning's discussion of "Immigration Policies of Western European Countries," *International Migration Review* 7, No.2 (1973) pp.155–63; Paul Ritterband, "Law, Policy, and Behavior: Educational Exchange Policy and Student Migration," *American Journal of Sociology* 76 (July 1970).

THE MEXICAN ILLEGAL ALIEN AND
THE U.S. BORDER COMMUNITY

Julius Rivera

The United States shares with Mexico a 2,597 kilometer border line extending from San Ysidro-Tijuana on the Pacific to Brownsville-Matamoros on the Gulf of Mexico. The geographic boundary that brings together the two countries makes them participants in similar opportunities, and similar problems. However, occupying different levels in socioeconomic development makes them take different perspectives with regard to the same opportunities and problems. One instance of these is the population pressure. As a fully industrialized nation, the United States has seen a concomitant decline in population growth, and the border region, poor in industrial raw materials and with low population densities, has not required special attention for general socioeconomic growth. Mexico, on the contrary, finds itself at a transition level, attempting to industrialize both in manufacturing and in agriculture without having resolved the problem of urbanization and urbanism. Urbanism in particular implies a new style of living, and the bulk of Mexican population seems to hold steadfastly to rural values. One of these values is the still clear emphasis on large families.

Without doubt, both the average family size and the annual population growth rate for the country have declined while, at the same time, a relatively steady economic growth has been maintained. Nevertheless, since this economic growth has not been balanced between urban and rural life, and since other factors, such as education, have not given full support to economic growth, the population pressure has not relented to respond to this growth. Thus we have a continuing migration from the rural areas to the cities in and out of the country. This latter form of migration (out of the country) is compounded by an underdeveloped urban infrastructure that makes living in Mexican cities not much better than living in the rural areas.

Lest this analysis of the Mexican conditions appears exceedingly harsh, it should be tempered with the thought that the geographic configuration and the natural resources of the country are not the most conducive to rapid socioeconomic development. Moreover, Mexico inherited from the colonial experience a class and land tenure systems that the Revolution itself was not able to alter sufficiently to fit the new society. Regardless of the variables involved in Mexico's demographic explosion, one of the largest in the hemisphere and in the world, there is a related fact that engages our attention today. It is that the United States is immediately affected by Mexico's population growth, especially along the border.

In this paper we will be concerned, first, with the population pressure that Mexico exerts on the border and the response from the United States, with emphasis on some critical age brackets. Second, we will analyze the cultural aspects of the migration problems in terms of mutual expectations (community U.S. versus migrant worker and vice versa), and in terms of "the definition of the situation." Third, the structural problem will consist of a comparative analysis of Mexican and United States communities, focusing on the ecological, the general social, and the specific organizational aspects of such communities, and on how the illegal alien "fits" and does not "fit" into these structures. In closing, some policy recommendations will be made for possible application at the international, cross-national, regional, and local community levels.

POPULATION PRESSURE

It is interesting that, in two-thirds of the municipios and in three-fourths of the counties along the border, the sex distribution for age bracket 0–14 is smaller for females than for males. In other words, in large proportions of municipios and counties there are more boys than girls of this age, especially on the U.S. side. In the next age bracket

(15–29), the proportions turn in the opposite directions especially on the Mexican side where only eleven municipios out of thirty-seven show a percentage smaller for females than for males. In other words, there are more females than males for this age in most municipios and counties especially on the Mexican side. There does not seem to be an explanation at the present for the consistently lower percentage of females in the 0–14 age bracket. On the other hand, it is well known that young women, particularly in their twenties, do tend to move to urban and urbanizing areas. This is clearly true in the border municipios where not only a great variety of service activities are performed by young females but because of the *maquiladoras* (firms manufacturing products on contract for U.S. companies) where young women find excellent work opportunities. In the U.S. counties it is retail stores that primarily attract young women. With few exceptions explainable by census errors, the percentages consistently indicate these trends. Twenty six out of thirty-seven municipios characteristically exhibit this phenomenon compared with fourteen out of twenty-five counties.

Now, in terms of job seekers and job holders, on the U.S. side these proportions are very important because they imply pressures on the labor market both legal and illegal. Daily commuters, mostly young women, tend to find employment in small retail stores, restaurants, and the like. Maids (about 9,000 of them in El Paso) tend to cross the border with shopping permits or they simply cross the river at various points from time to time, escaping apprehension.

Young men do not cross the border to find employment locally unless they have family and organizational connections. They cross to migrate north, to Los Angeles, Denver, Houston, or Chicago and to large industrial cities of this type.

It is well-known that migrants, regardless of their legal status, are characteristically young. Of the critical age brackets, the one most likely to be affected by migration is the group of 15–29 year olds.

About 72,000 people migrated legally from Mexico last year. Forty thousand did it within the numerical limitation system for the Western Hemisphere, and thirty-two thousand under the provisions of the law that allows members of the immediate family to reunite in the United States. It is probable that a similar number will come under the same conditions in 1976.

Nobody actually knows how many illegals enter the U.S. every year. What we do know is that over 788,000 were apprehended in 1974 and over 766,000 in 1975. Naturally, most of these came from Mexico (680,000 in 1975).

The response to this latter type of migration in the U.S. is well-known. It has ranged from suggestions of massive deportations reminiscent of the ones in the 1930s and 1950s to a sort of controlled amnesty, for which there also have been some precedents.[1]

THE COMMUNITY CULTURE AND THE NEW IMMIGRANT

Every social scientist is familiar with the dictum of W.I. Thomas that "when people make the situations real they are real in the consequences." The reality of the situation, however, often depends on the perspective one takes. Regarding the situation of the illegal alien the U.S. communities are divided into many forms. And so it is for the Chicano community in particular.

In the north, the reality of the illegal alien does not acquire the complexities of which we are fully aware along the border. To begin with we live in a truly bilingual community. This is so not only because the Mexican side speaks mainly Spanish. It is likewise true because a large amount of the population on the U.S. side speaks Spanish also. In proportion to the total population of each county the Spanish-speaking/Spanish-surname ratio ranges from 12.8 in San Diego to 97.8 in Starr County, Texas.[2]

Thus, there is an ethnic continuity across the border from Mexico into the U.S. of which language is not the only expression. There is music, art, theater, rituals, family ties, organizations, anything that is cultural. In this perspective for the new immigrant, crossing the line does not mean transferring entirely to a new cultural setting, and the receiving community is in turn hardly altered by his presence. He often even goes unnoticed. His legality or illegality is actually irrelevant. If the issue of the presence of the alien were not raised, usually by outsiders to this cultural community, his shadow would dissolve quietly as it were in the larger society. When it is raised, the Chicano community itself takes contradictory positions, joining forces, one may add, with the various segments of opinion in the general U.S. public.

If Chicanos work for local or federal law enforcement agencies—the local police force, the border patrol, immigration or customs—and many Chicanos do, they would tend as I have witnessed to support the position of Mr. Chapman, the previous director of the U.S. Immigration and Naturalization Service. In his view there is an urgent need for more fences along the border and more law enforcement agents. To accomplish these goals an additional budget of about 50 million dollars is required. Some interest groups follow this perspective. One of them is not a group in the strict sense of the term but a segment of the population concerned with the increasing wave of burglaries and rapes. The natural scapegoat is the illegal alien even when the two types of crimes mentioned are not related. In a recent letter to the editor,[3] an Anglo citizen criticized the presidential candidates for not having any plans to stop the illegal Mexican invasion of our country.

A second group is, of course, organized labor. Chicanos and non-Chicanos in this group fear the competition of the commuter and of the illegal alien. At one time Cesar Chavez had shared these concerns. It appears now that he is leaning toward what I have called the internationalistic branch of the Chicano movement.[4]

The Chicano internationalist, together with radical labor sectors and intellectuals in the U.S. and Mexico, has based his position on some interesting premises. The first one is that the U.S.–Mexican border line is not only artificial but illegal or, more precisely, illegitimate. It is the product of an unjust war, condemned at the time by some distinguished North Americans, that the treaty of Guadelupe Hidalgo could not make right.

The second premise is the unity of Aztlan, a historico-mythological land travelled freely by the Aztecs and some other Indian ancestors, that the modern nation state has split physically but cannot break ethnically and morally. It is then, in the third place, the unity of La Raza, the Mestizo, the product of the Spanish father and the Indian mother,

whose blood and cultural heritage has established networks of kinship, language, symbols, ways of life, and values that transcend national boundaries making them irrelevant.

Finally, in the mind of the more radical, it is a basic human right to work wherever work is available, and this right cannot be determined by the employer or by the government that represents the employer. It is not fair that, when the employer needs cheap labor, laws can be produced or ignored and treaties drawn to import this labor. Once he is needed no more, the working man is released and returned home by so-called "voluntary" deportations and repatriations. Thus the needs of the employer are attended but not the needs of the worker.

These ideas may suffice to summarize the position of the internationalist. It is diametrically opposed to the previous one that may be called the official or the nationalistic position.

There is a third position in addition. It may be called the nonposition. It is an attitude found in the Chicano as well as in the Anglo communities that consists in acknowledging the problem but considering it the concern of government bureaucracies. This attitude, however, is not deep in the Chicano community at least along the border. When pressed, this Chicano tends to side with the internationalist, although not for the same reasons. He finds embarrassing to deny to others the access that he or his ancestors had years ago when a new life began in the U.S. with illegal migration. According to the local office of the U.S. Catholic Immigration Service, most of the new legal immigrants had at least two previous experiences in the U.S. as illegal workers.

COMMUNITIES ON THE MIGRANT STREAM

The geoecological conditions of the border on both sides are not very conducive to the sustenance of subhuman and human life. With the exception of some fertile areas in western Chihuahua and in the state of Tamaulipas, practically all of the other land in Baja California, Sonora, some in Chihuahua, Coahuila, and Nuevo Leon, and again large portions in Tamaulipas is desertic.

The U.S. side is not much different. Naturally

fertile soils are found along the Rio Grande; the others have been reclaimed by irrigation. These are located in the Imperial Valley in California, some in Arizona and New Mexico, and some in the lower Rio Grande, especially from McAllen to Brownsville. Most of the land, as in Mexico, is desertic and semidesertic with the same type of vegetation and animal life.

The transportation system in northern Mexico is good when moving north and south but very deficient when going east and west. There is no road running all the way from Matamoros to Tijuana. There are stretches, some of them good, between Matamoros and Reynosa, between Reynosa and Ciudad Acuna, between Ojinaga and Juarez, between Agua Prieta and Nogales, and between Magdalena and Tijuana. No train in northern Mexico runs east and west except in a stretch between Sonora and Baja California.

Needless to say, in the U.S. southwest transportation is by contrast excellent in practically every direction.

In another work, I have divided the border area in ten cross-national regions that appear as obvious invitations to move from south to north or from north to south. In fact, for at least eight hundred years some of them have been traveled by peoples of the southwest. There is some evidence that the Aztecs initiated in one of these regions (what is today New Mexico) their pilgrimage toward central Mexico, and that later they built some outposts here for the empire. The Spaniards developed at least two clear routes in the west and through the central region, one toward San Francisco and the other toward Santa Fe. The construction of the railroads by the Porfirio Diaz regime ended in seven ports on the U.S. border linking the two nations for the movement of people and commodities. During the Mexican Revolution, thousands of refugees headed north through all these regions but especially through El Paso-Juarez and Nogales. And throughout all this century laborers from Mexico have come, contracts or no contracts, treaties or no treaties, according to the law or outside the law, mainly because they are needed or, if not, because their services are utilized for pay in any case. The ecological conditions of the area have always facilitated their movement.

The economy of the southwest has always been closely interrelated with the economy of northern Mexico. Whether it was cattle, agriculture, railroads and highway construction, mining or manufacturing, the Mexican laborer was there, and as often the North American capital and engineering skills were there. As a result of this interdependence of the regional communities, local communities have grown as twins along the border. And the people have come for the most part from central Mexico, from Jalisco, Durango, Zacatecas, Nuevo Leon, and Sinaloa. According to the 1970 Mexican Census, 50 percent of the 1.7 million migrants to the border communities had come from the states just mentioned. From the named states had come 53 percent of those who had lived in these cities for more than eleven years,[5] that is, since before 1960.

There is certain order in this migratory movement northbound. Often a migrant leaves his home community as a single person in search of work; in another town he gets married and perhaps has his first child; in another, still, he has a second child; later a third child might be born either in a border city or in the U.S., probably during an illegal second entry when the man could bring along his whole family. His legal entry may imply his final settling in the place where he could find permanent work during his illegal pilgrimage.

It is very probable that once on the border the future illegal alien will occupy a marginal position in the community, and that once in the U.S. he will become part of a subterranean culture with few linkages in the regular community. He is in a very different position from the one occupied by the new immigrant. When the subterranean culture becomes a burden in the ranks of unemployment it is not on the new immigrant's account because when he enters the country he has a guaranteed job. Only a frequent delay (from 3–6 weeks) in obtaining a social security card may keep him out of work temporarily. The new immigrant may not exert any pressure on the health services of the community because he had to have a full physical check up before his immigration. He might be, if he has a family, a burden on the educational facilities of the community, but later on when he acquires property he would be making his fair contribution in this area.

By contrast the illegal alien along the border is no burden at all in any of those eventualities. He does not stay very long if he does not find a job; unless, of course, he decides to migrate into the interior of the country, he will return to Mexico. If he gets sick he will immediately cross the border back home for inexpensive or free medical care. Since he is not married, or has not brought his family with him, his children will not utilize the community educational services.

That the illegal alien moves in a community of his own may be exemplified by three levels in the occupational structure of the border communities in which they tend to fit best in relatively large numbers.

The first is the low skill jobs in small industrial enterprises and services, such as machine shops, automotive service stations, housing, and restaurants. The second is the seasonal farm laborers on which most of small agriculture depends. In the fall of 1974, when INS decided to put a halt to the constant inflow of undocumented workers into the farms along the Rio Grande, multiple small acreages of chili pepper, cotton, onion, and the like went unharvested. The Texas Employment Commission could not supply the needed labor and appeals by the media were of no avail. The third is the domestic labor force. Although considered a luxury that even middle income people can afford, domestic service acquires the character of a need in the lower income brackets. At this level married mothers often hire girls from Mexico so they can hold jobs to supplement their husbands' income. Single mothers frequently seek this help as well.

These sorts of activities are parts and parcels of the border communities although marginally all the same. Each one of them has become institutionalized and has a culture of its own.

It appears that the border cities have a unique position along the stream of northbound Mexican migrations. Here the illegal aliens are rather illegal commuters or truly undocumented workers.

It seems that there is a second tier of cities where there may occur a second screening of migrants. It is the tier extending from Corpus Christi and Houston on the Gulf of Mexico to San Diego and Los Angeles on the Pacific. This tier includes such cities as San Antonio, Austin, Dallas, and Lubbock in Texas, Las Cruces and Albuquerque in New Mexico, Tucson and Phoenix in Arizona. Large Spanish-speaking enclaves exist in these cities and presumably good employment opportunities in marginal occupations. Besides, it may be here where they pick up a little English and more specific information to continue their search for work further north.

Then comes tier three where the Mexicans find stiff competition with other nationals seldom found in the southwest with the exception of Houston and Los Angeles. And it is here, people in the southwest presume, where, as a result of this fierce competition, the illegal alien becomes visible and most of the noise is made around and in the halls of Congress. For at least some articulate people in the southwest, the illegal alien is a problem for bureaucrats and politicians that have not lived in, do not represent, and do not speak for the southwest.

CONCLUSIONS AND RECOMMENDATIONS

If the U.S. government and its agencies are genuinely interested in slowing down immigration in general and in containing the illegal alien inflow in particular, in a drastic reversal of its socioeconomic traditions, placing the blame on the migrants, as it appears to be doing now, is not the wisest approach. Most of the migrants are and have been ''economic refugees,'' to use the expression of Mr. Luis Velarde of the Catholic Immigration Service in El Paso. Therefore, through international agencies, the U.S. has to enter into reorganizing programs of national and regional development to level somewhat the disparity in international economic growth. Studies made by Cornelius and Diez-Canedo have clearly indicated that, given fair opportunity structures in their homelands, most people do not tend to migrate. I have also found this in my interviews with migrants and nonmigrants along the border.

Hunger cannot be stopped by erecting more or higher and stronger fences along the border, and with increasing the number of patrol cars and policemen. A distinguished businessman and civic leader from Ciudad Juarez has warned against the building of a Berlin Wall along a border that has meant for generation of Mexicans and North Americans a community, a neighborhood not a battle ground.

The social, cultural, and economic interdependence of the border communities and of the border regions must be recognized and respected in any attempts to strictly regulate the immigration flows. Which means that the present dual immigration policy must continue. Local authorities, businessmen, and civic leaders from both sides of the border have for years been engaged in finding local solutions to local problems. Any federal program must take into consideration these efforts, must consult with the local constituencies, and must sutdy the local interdependencies utilizing local talent. The border region is getting tired of being treated as a colony by colonial powers, of being administered as a colony by colonial administrators, of being studied as a colony by colonial intellectuals, and of being advised as a colony by colonial advisers.

In this view, at least some activities of immigration administration must be decentralized, placed in the hands of city, county, and state authorities, and given revenue sharing to function.

In the meantime, some labor policies must be set loose for local employment agencies to administer. For example, there is no reason why a small farmer cannot save his harvest by employing laborers from Mexico on a temporary contractual basis just as the present day commuters cross the border every day to work. There is no reason why small construction jobs cannot be allowed to be done in similar fashion and there is no reason to tie the clamps on domestic workers. Each farmer, each construction workman, each housewife would arrange the appropriate permit to hire help in a fully capitalistic competitive labor market.

Another alternative would be to raise the minimum wage high enough to make low paid jobs attractive to citizens. However, the consequences could be disastrous because then small business would continue to disappear from the scene at an even higher rate, and without more tight controls the illegal inflow would rise. More tight controls are perhaps not welcome in our system of government.

Characteristically, the Western Hemisphere has traditionally allowed and even welcomed the relatively free flow of people between nations. It would be a sad day when this flow would be fenced out, making each nation either an economic castle to be conquered or an economic prison from which to escape. Thus, we return to the first alternative. There are enough resources in the countries affected by out-and-in-migration. There is plenty of talent in the United Nations, in the Organization of American States, in the World Bank, in the Interamerican Development Bank, and in other international agencies to put together programs of social and economic progress for the migrant-sending nations. These programs must consider local conditions and local cultures.

There must be other alternatives and other strategies, because the fact remains that we live in a free world and in a free society, and that whatever we do must be based on this fundamental consideration.

NOTES

1. See Immigration and Nationality Act of 1924 and its amendments of 1958 and 1965.
2. Source Table 5 in Julius Rivera, Oscar Martinez, and Robert Schmidt, *Profiles of the Border Cities* (El Paso: University of Texas at El Paso, forthcoming).
3. El Paso *Times*, 27 October 1976.
4. Dworkin and Dworkin, *The Minority Report*, (New York: Praeger, 1976).
5. Secretaria de Industria y Comercio, *La Frontera Norte* (San Mateo Tecoloapan, Estado de Mexico: Impresos y Editora Mexicana, Abril de 1975), p.47.

NEW IMMIGRATION: IMPLICATIONS FOR THE
UNITED STATES AND THE INTERNATIONAL COMMUNITY

E. Aracelis Francis

This paper was prepared for presentation at a panel charged with the responsibility of addressing the domestic implications of the new immigration for the United States and other host societies. And, the author seeks to examine the issue of foreign labor in the United States Virgin Islands, which is closely related to the peculiar situation of the unincorporated territories of the United States.

Perkins[1] states that the attempts of the United States to deny, to reduce, and to liquidate dependency are more instructive than our experience in facing up to its reality or in defining its significance and its role in the U.S. system of government. While the Constitution does not specifically set forth detailed policies regarding governance of areas which have not become states, it recognizes such areas, which indeed existed at the time of its adoption, by the provisions of Article IV, Section 3 which stipulates that "new states may be admitted by the Congress into this Union" and that "The Congress shall have power to dispose of and make all needful rules and regulations respecting the territory or other property belonging to the United States."[2] An unresolved question for the United States is what policies or objectives should be utilized in addressing the special problems of those territories where size, language, customs, culture, and distance from the mainland make the extension of statehood a remote possibility.

Perkins[3] states that the success of the domestic political experiment has made it possible for Americans to overlook the dilemma of power when it cannot be limited, shared, or abdicated, and when its exercise is complicated by pronounced economic and cultural differences. Consequently the scattering of lesser territories which have come under control of the United States, such as the Virgin Islands, Guam, U.S. Samoa, and the Trust Territories, have not been important issues of national concern. Earlier attempts by Presidents Roosevelt and Taft to designate a single department "to supervise or assume headship over all our island possessions" met resistance in Congress because the establishment of a U.S. "colonial office" would represent an acknowledgment that the United States was to remain an imperial republic. In the absence of adequate foresight and controls, decisions regarding the permanent relationship between the United States and the major dependencies have been reached by trial and error.

This attitude has had severe consequences for the Virgin Islands, as the issue of the political relationship between the Virgin Islands and the United States has not been adequately addressed nationally or locally, and the significance of this problem for the future of the Islands and its people remains unacknowledged. It has been observed[4] that the action of renouncing its "empire" committed the United States to moving towards the profoundly imperialistic objective of refashioning the societies of its dependencies with an eye toward their eventual qualification for self-government modeled after the U.S. system. Yet because there frequently was little thought given to the consequences of actions imposed upon the territories by the federal government, even the exercise of good intentions could not prevent the forces of American controls from being deeply shaken and firmly shaping the dependent societies into sometimes grotesque and unexpected forms.

In the Virgin Islands this has resulted in a colonial mentality that (1) remains unacknowledged; (2) has resisted identification with the movements toward independence in the rest of the Caribbean; (3) has denounced the assertions of black power as inappropriate in a society where political power purportedly resides with the native population; and (4) has made discussions of alternative approaches to United States rule and the question of nationality impossible.

Since 1964, the Subcommittee III of the United Nations Special Committee of twenty-four has examined the status of the United States Virgin Islands and has affirmed that the Declaration on the Granting of Independence to Colonial Countries and Peoples applies fully to the territory. However, the United States has not agreed to permit the Special Committee to send a visiting mission to the Virgin Islands in order to ascertain the views of the people and the extent to which they are aware of the options open to them with regard to their future political status.[5] In 1973, the United Nations Committee on Colonialism, without vote, adopted a report stating that an "urgent need remains for the administering power to take measures in order to encourage the people to enter into full and free discussion of all alternatives available to them." The report indicated that in the United States Virgin Islands there has been "a lack of significant constitutional progress" toward self-determination and independence, and requested the United States to set up a program of political education in the Virgin Islands to explore alternatives to continued United States control.[6] This report generated very little local discussion. One Virgin Islands newspaper, however, expressed the opinion that the United Nations was motivated by a desire to embarrass the United States, that it had enough problems of its own, and that it did not need to meddle in the internal affairs of the Virgin Islands.[7]

Lewis states that in many ways the central reason for the malaise in the Virgin Islands is its continuing status as an "unincorporated territory" of the United States. That status is one in which citizenship in the Islands does not carry with it the full plentitude of rights which inheres in citizenship in any of the fifty states.[8] The constitutional provisions which give guarantees and safeguards for all American citizens may actually be straitjackets for the native Virgin Islanders. Macridis believes that the time may have come for a careful and discriminating "contracting out." In his opinion, as long as the Constitution and congressional legislation are supreme, genuine self-government adapted to local needs cannot be instituted, especially since the federal judiciary, sworn to uphold the Constitution, is the final judge.[9] The dilemmas of territorial status

and American citizenship highlight the critical issues that are basic to an understanding of the problems created by the foreign labor program in the Virgin Islands.

By the early 1950s, the attempts to stimulate native industries through protective legislation had failed. The Virgin Islands Corporation, a New Deal venture whose objective was to improve the economic conditions of the Islands, also had limited success. Moorhead[10] describes the period from 1936 to 1954 as a time of grace for native leaders, an opportunity to understand that the needs of the society required a social revolution of a national character to sever the chains of colonialism. It was incumbent upon the native leaders to analyze the need for a government bureaucracy and the lack of native capital as due to colonialism, and thus educate the masses to the need for independence and sovereignty. Instead, the leaders disseminated a fear of independence, supposedly based on the society's lack of natural resources.[11]

Given such a limited understanding of the condition of the Islands, it was not at all surprising that the thrust of the local legislators was towards improving the political relationship between the United States and the Virgin Islands. By 1954, a Revised Organic Act was passed by the U.S. Congress. Only two of the four demands of the Organic Act Committee of the local legislature were passed. The four demands were (1) an elective governor; (2) a single legislature; (3) a single treasury; and (4) a resident commissioner in Washington, D.C. Gordon Lewis views them as primarily concerned with strengthening the bargaining power of the Islands in the grossly unequal relationship between the popularly elected local legislature and the presidentially appointed chief executive.[12] The Revised Organic Act provided for a single legislature and a single treasury. The Islands were to wait until the early 1970s to have their other demands met. Additionally, the 1954 Act formally defined the Virgin Islands as an "unincorporated territory", prohibited language requirements for voters, granted the Islands the use of federal funds derived from Internal Revenue on articles produced in the Virgin Islands, but required that projects approved by the local legislature also be approved by the

Secretary of Interior, and gave the Secretary of the Interior the power to appoint a government comptroller to audit and settle all accounts pertaining to the revenues and receipts of the government of the Virgin Islands.

Bough writes that Senator Butler, in his report to the Senate on the 1954 Revised Organic Act, stated that the Act was intended to grant a larger measure of self-government to the Virgin Islands, but a close study of the 1954 Act casts doubt on this statement.[13] Lewis described the 1954 Organic Act as a counterrevolution, since it left unchanged the governor's power of suspensive veto and the president's power of final veto, and actually reduced the previously accredited prerogatives of the elected legislature and increased those of the executive branch. For example, the governor was given far reaching discretionary powers to reorganize the administrative machinery, and fresh powers to appoint administrative assistants for St. Croix and St. John without legislative ratification, but existing legislative powers, such as the right of the legislators to set their own salaries, were limited.[14] Thus the stage was set for the economic development of the Islands as the political powers of the elected representatives of the people were curtailed, and power was vested in the appointed governor and the absentee United States president and the Congress. There still remained one missing ingredient for the development of the Islands by foreign capital—an unlimited supply of unskilled or cheap labor. Groups such as the Chamber of Commerce and the Hotel Association felt that a free ingress and egress of foreign labor was needed to supplement an insufficient supply of local labor. They also argued that certain jobs were so undesirable (sugar cane harvesting) and/or seasonal (the winter tourist industry) that the local labor force was unwilling to do them. They agitated for the extension of Section 101 (a) (15) (H) and 214 (c) of the 1952 Immigration and Nationality Act, which addressed the admission of temporary alien workers into the United States to perform services or receive training on a temporary basis. The Immigration and Naturalization Service, however, took the position that many of the jobs in the Virgin Islands were not temporary and, therefore, this section of the act did not apply. The business community responded by

presenting written petitions to the subcommittee of the House Committee on Interior and Insular Affairs, which held hearings in St. Thomas in February 1954 on immigration and labor problems. The Immigration and Naturalization Service replied to an inquiry from the chairman of the committee that the Service "has no authority under the present immigration laws to authorize the importation of the labor desired by the petitioners."[15] This, however, was only a minor setback for the business groups.

In December, 1954, a special subcommittee of the House Committee on the Judiciary held hearings in the Virgin Islands on the need for alien labor. The subcommittee heard the views of three principal groups: the Legislative Assembly of the Virgin Islands, the Chambers of Commerce and the Hotel Association of the Virgin Islands, and Organized Labor. Although the Legislative Assembly "apparently" favored the importation of labor, it was not by the two-thirds majority necessary to pass a resolution to that effect. The opposition expressed the fear that there might be an oversupply of local labor in the future, and that the presence of alien workers would complicate such a situation. The Chambers of Commerce and the Hotel Association of the Virgin Islands were the proponents of the most liberal recommendations for the admission of alien workers, and recommended "free ingress and egress" of workers when a certification of the lack of labor was made by an individual or firm. Organized labor was the most hostile to the idea of the admission of nonimmigrant labor. They argued that the "free ingress and egress" proposal of the Chambers of Commerce was definitely unacceptable and held that the certification system then required under the petitioning procedure was satisfactory. They denied the existence of labor shortages in certain areas and emphasized that, before any foreign labor was imported, every resident Virgin Islander should be employed, and that this should be followed by the tapping of other U.S. sources for the required labor. They recommended the creation of a control board with a member of the U.S. Employment Service, the St. Thomas Labor Union, the Immigration and Naturalization Service, and a representative of employers and businesses. The control board would determine when an actual shortage of labor existed, investigate the validity of requests made by employers for foreign labor, ascertain whether the requesting employer had made proper provision for adequate housing and transportation, assure that the alien worker would be paid the prevailing rate of pay and would possess health certificates certifying that they were free from communicable diseases.[16] In retrospect, these recommendations would have been cumbersome administratively, but would have prevented the development of the problems which subsequently resulted from the implementation of the foreign labor program in the Virgin Islands.

Despite the strong concerns of organized labor, the subcommittee recommended a more realistic and expeditious application of the H–2 provision for the natives of the British Island of Tortola only for seasonal employment in agriculture or the tourist industry. It was the sense of the subcommittee that the Immigration and Naturalization Service's present classification of these hotel and agricultural workers as permanent workers was too restrictive. They also recommended that an effective solution of the whole problem might be achieved through a locally applicable British-American agreement, such as the Mexican-American agreement.[17]

These recommendations of the subcommittee of the House Committee on the Judiciary received a favorable response from the Immigration and Naturalization Service, which proceeded to reverse its strict interpretation of temporary alien workers and set in place a more liberalized policy on the importation of foreign labor from the British Virgin Islands to the U.S. Virgin Islands.

On March 19, 1956, special procedures which limited the program geographically and occupationally were instituted. This 1956 agreement went beyond the subcommittee's recommendation. This disregard of intent, and misinterpretation of the laws and regulations, was to be a hallmark of the foreign labor program in the Virgin Islands.

Prospective employers were required to file a separate petition for each worker with the Immigration and Naturalization Service, and the consultation required by Section 214 (c) before a petition could be approved was held with appropriate agencies of the government on a continuing basis. The employer was then required to post a bond guaran-

teeing that the worker would not become a public charge, that he would maintain his status and depart at the expiration of his authorized stay.[18] This requirement gave birth to the term "bonded aliens."

By 1959, the program was extended to include foreign labor from the British, French, Dutch West Indies, reportedly by administrative error. By the early 1960s, the program's original occupational restrictions had been abandoned.

The laissez faire approach to the importation of foreign labor to the Virgin Islands on the national and local level, and the rapid economic development of the islands, created a phenomenal growth in the foreign labor population. A comparison of the 1960 and the 1970 population figures clearly illustrates this point:[19]

Total Population	Number of Aliens	Percentage of Aliens
1960—32,099	3,826	12%
1970—62,468	18,929	30%

Such a tremendous population explosion in a ten-year period would create dire effects in any community. In a small geographic area with limited resources, the results were even more severe.

A 1968 report highlighted some of the major consequences of this growth for the Virgin Islands which it characterized as being one of the most rapidly growing segments of the United States:

(1) The average annual increase in population is at a phenomenal rate of about 6.9% (as against approximately 2.0% for Puerto Rico), with a significant share of this increase attributable to the growth in the bonded alien population (nearly 45% of the labor force and climbing steadily) and illegal aliens and the children of bonded aliens in the Virgin Islands.

(2) Aliens are a sizable minority. In 1966, 16,887 persons were eligible to vote and the bonded alien population is estimated to be nearly that large.

(3) There is not one single agency or group in the Virgin Islands that represents the needs and problems of aliens, therefore, their health, housing, welfare, and educational needs get little attention.

(4) The processing of people from bonded alien status into permanent resident or immigrant status is not a viable alternative because the basic immigration laws of the country are changing.[20]

It is clear little attention was paid to the consequences of this mass migration into the Virgin Islands. The concept of temporary workers, who would leave the islands once their services were no longer needed, enabled the society to totally disregard the needs of this group. Since eligibility for available social services was contingent on citizenship, the noncitizen was left to fend for himself and his family. The consequences of this situation were that the foreign laborer and his family lived in the most deplorable housing conditions, were denied minimal job protections, were paid substandard wages, and were denied access to certain health and welfare programs. The foreign laborer was forced to live apart from his family. When he was able to bring his family with him, his children were denied access to the public school system.

By the mid 1960s, the conditions under which alien workers lived in the Virgin Islands became the subject of mounting criticism in the national news media, the Department of the Interior, the U.S. Congress, the U.S. Department of Labor, and other circles. A report included the following observation on the role or nonrole of the various government agencies involved:

Federal agencies almost totally ignore the problem. The Department of Interior, which has Federal responsibility, claims its role in the Virgin Islands is "advisory and that we take initiative only when requested to do so."

Other agencies such as the Department of Health, Education and Welfare and the Department of Labor also eschew any responsibility. Virgin Islands agencies generally conclude that most problems are "Federal."[21]

By the early 1970s, the foreign labor program had been redefined as the alien labor problem and a number of events resulted in major changes in the foreign labor program, in the treatment of alien workers' families, and in access to public social services. The three major events were (1) extensive review of the alien labor programs in the Virgin Islands by the U.S. Department of Labor; (2) Public Law 91–225; and (3) the decision in *Hosier* v. *Evans*.

In May 1970, the U.S. Department of Labor opened a Manpower Administration Office in St. Thomas to administer new procedures which would establish a free labor market in the Virgin Islands. The new procedures were aimed at integrating nonimmigrant workers into a permanent labor force and at curtailing the entry of new workers.[22]

This step also symbolized the reentry of a federal agency into the Virgin Islands' affairs in an attempt to improve the chaos that had occurred during the years of the department's indifference.

Identification and certification of the original group of eligible nonimmigrants was completed in July 1971. They totaled 12,500. Since 1971, there have been between 200 and 300 new certifications annually. By the end of fiscal year 1973, the number of nonimmigrant aliens had decreased to 11,200. The decrease was the result of nonresidents attaining permanent resident status and of death, deportation, and the expiration of the sixty-day grace period in which the alien worker could secure new employment. Due to the low annual quotas of the dependencies,[23] nearly 10,000 of the nonimmigrant aliens will be unable to secure permanent resident status without congressional action.

The new U.S. Department of Labor program has been viewed as a success in terms of integrating the nonimmigrant alien worker into the permanent work force. Dissatisfaction with the program remains, however, and has focused on the continued presence of the nonimmigrant aliens in the face of a comparatively high unemployment rate on the Islands.[24]

The second major event was the enactment of Public Law 91–225 on April 7, 1970, by the Congress of the United States. This legislation was designed to facilitate the entry of certain nonimmigrants by the establishment of a new H–4 visa classification for the dependents of aliens entering under the three "H" classifications. Although there was some discussion about the Virgin Islands while the bill was under consideration, it is questionable whether the Judiciary Committee was fully informed about the probable impact of the H–4 provision on the Virgin Islands.

Public Law 91–225 promoted family reunifications in the Virgin Islands on a massive scale. Estimates of the number of H–4 aliens on the U.S. Virgin Islands range from 20,000 to 30,000. This was an unforeseen effect of the legislation.[25] The entry of large numbers of dependents of foreign workers came at a time of economic downturn, further aggravated a worsening situation, and placed additional demands on the society when it was least able to deal with them.

The third major event was the decision in the *Hosier* v. *Evans* case. At the time that Public Law 91–225 was enacted, a large number of alien children were not allowed to attend public schools due to the regulations of the Virgin Islands Department of Education. On June 26, 1970, the regulation was declared null and void by a U.S. District Court. This action cleared the way for the H–4 children of temporary alien workers to attend the public schools of the Virgin Islands.[26] The decision was not appealed because the last appointed governor had promised the U.S. Congress to admit alien children into the public school system.

There was an immediate impact on the Virgin Islands public schools, since 80 percent of the new enrollees were alien children. By December 1974, 32.5 percent of the total public school enrollment was that of noncitizen children.[27] The Virgin Islands government has been hard pressed to meet the demands generated by this increase, even though the largest percentage of the total Virgin Islands budget is spent on education. Split sessions, overcrowded classrooms, and shortages of equipment and supplies have further eroded the quality of education in the Virgin Islands.

In the years of economic prosperity, the Virgin Islands government ignored the plight of its large alien labor force. By 1970, when the Virgin Islands government was forced to address the needs of the alien workers, the economy was in a severe recession. This has aggravated the resentments engendered during the many years of the mass migration of foreign labor. More critical, however, is the islands' lessened ability to provide an adequate

level of necessary social services. The expectations of the foreign labor population, and the government's inability to adequately provide social services to foreign workers, native Virgin Islanders, and/or American citizens, will increase the tensions, resentments, and hostilities currently evident in the Islands.

Twenty years after the initiation of the foreign labor program, the alien problem remains unresolved. Lewis describes the essence of the problem as a rapidly increasing population accompanied by very little planned effort to accelerate welfare facilities and services to meet the explosion.[28] The lack of appropriate planning has been pervasive on the local and national levels and has further exacerbated the problems. Current attempts to deal with the problems oversimplify the issues and fail to deal with the ramifications of the proposed actions.

During the past year, Congressmen Eilberg and Hutchinson have introduced two bills relating to the alien labor problems in the Virgin Islands. Under the Eilberg Bill, H.R. 11261, a Virgin Islands Immigration Commission would be established and charged with the responsibility of developing procedures for the granting of permanent residence to certain nonimmigrant aliens in the Virgin Islands. The commission would have the responsibility of reviewing, on a case-by-case basis, the status, circumstances, and character of those aliens residing in the U.S. Virgin Islands on or before May 12, 1970. Seven of the seventeen presidential and congressional appointments to the committee would be Virgin Islands residents. Ten criteria would be used to determine the extent to which permanent residence would be granted:

(1) such aliens who have relatives in the United States who are United States citizens or permanent resident aliens;

(2) the length of residence in the U.S. Virgin Islands of such aliens;

(3) the extent to which such aliens have relatives who are residing in the country of their nationality;

(4) the economic and political conditions in the country to which such aliens are returning;

(5) the business, occupational, financial, and

marital status of such aliens;

(6) the age and condition of health of such aliens;

(7) the employment record of such aliens while working in the U.S. Virgin Islands;

(8) the immigration history of such aliens and the extent to which other means of adjustment of status are available;

(9) such aliens' contributions to and positions in the community, and such aliens' desire to reside permanently in the Virgin Islands;

(10) the extent to which such aliens' deportation would result in unusual hardship;

The local response to this bill has been mixed. The Virgin Islands' Delegate to the U.S. Congress has endorsed it as precedent setting, in that it would give citizens of a local area a chance to participate in immigration decisions and would take into account the impact of federal immigration policy on the Virgin Islands' economic, social, and political life. The Virgin Islands' governor was more cautious in his support, noting that the bill proposed to alter the status of nonimmigrant aliens without providing any mechanism or standard for making a decision as to whether the status changes would adversely affect wages and working conditions of U.S. citizens. The governor also recommended greater Virgin Islands' representation on the commission, as he contended that Virgin Islanders would be more familiar with some of the problems inherent in a compressed insular setting. Also questioned was the relative weight that would be given to each of the criteria. The governor endorsed the overall thrust of the legislation, but argued that any action to alter the immigration status of a significant number of individuals in a small community with a depressed economy should be gradual, properly phased, and well-planned to mitigate any possible adverse impact.[29]

The Hutchinson Bill, H.R. 10323, would amend the Immigration and Nationality Act Amendments of 1975 by enabling nonimmigrants to adjust their status without regard to numerical limitations. The authority for screening aliens for status adjustments would be vested in the Attorney General of the United States.

This bill would create even more serious consequences for the Virgin Islands, since the legislation does not consider the impact of integrating large numbers of nonimmigrants into the community in terms of the additional social services to which they would be entitled once their status was adjusted.

A third bill, H.R. 11557, which was also introduced by Congressman Eilberg, would establish a Select Committee on Territorial Immigration Policy. This Committee would conduct a study to analyze the extent to which the territories required special treatment under the immigration and naturalization laws of the United States. This legislation would be a major step towards the recognition of the special needs of the territories and the development of policies that would best meet their needs. Unfortunately, the chances for action on this bill are small during this session of Congress.

There are no easy answers to the dilemmas posed in this presentation. Perhaps it is too late to search for answers or solutions given the current context of the Virgin Islands situation. As a Virgin Islander, one

> has to labor under great difficulties in his search for identity. He finds himself in a dilemma. Culturally he is a West Indian, but politically and economically, he is attached to the United States. While he shares with other West Indians the problem of personal and national identity, he has to labor under a dual loyalty. His emotional and political ties with the American people are strong on the one hand, and on the other his cultural ties with his fellow West Indians, with whom he shares a common origin and heritage, tug at his heart strings.[30]

Further complicating this dilemma is the fact that the majority position once enjoyed by Virgin Islanders has been seriously eroded. Compared with the total population, the native population declined from 73.6 percent in 1950 to 63.4 percent in 1960 and 46.5 percent in 1970.[31] This shift has occurred as a result of the extensive economic development which took place in the Virgin Islands during the past twenty years.

Although we have concentrated on foreign labor in this paper, there were two major migrations of American citizens into the Virgin Islands. The first group to arrive was the Puerto Ricans, who began migrating in the late 1920s. They now number 4,014 and represent 6.4 percent of the total population. Like the Virgin Islanders, their 1970 percentage of the total population declined from 12.1 percent in 1950 to 10.8 percent in 1960.[32] One suspects that these figures do not accurately reflect the first, second, and third generations of Puerto Ricans in the Islands. The cultural and language differences between the native and the Puerto Rican population have already had an effect on the life style and culture of the St. Croix community.

The second group were the United States citizens born and raised on the mainland. Their numbers have increased significantly. In 1950, they represented 4.1 percent of the total population but, by 1960, this percent had been increased to 8.1 percent. By 1970, they represented 12.9 percent of the total population. This large mainland population has played an important role in reinforcing the impact of American culture, values, economy, and way of life on the Islands' population.

The largest increase, however, has been in the foreign labor population. In 1950, they represented 9.7 percent of the total population. By 1960, this figure had increased to 13.4 percent and, by 1970, it had further increased to 28.2 percent.[34] Even with the stabilization of the nonimmigrant program, their high birth rate and the built-in stimulus of immigration will increase their percentage of the total population. One can only speculate on the societal impact if this group had also come as American citizens.

Today the Virgin Islander finds himself a minority in his own land. The economic prosperity which his political leaders envisioned has occurred. The process, however, has unleashed forces over which the Virgin Islanders have no control. As an unincorporated territory of the United States, the Virgin Islands have no clear guideposts of what that status entails. Decisions regarding the Islands' future are made in Washington by a Congress that has little real knowledge or understanding of the peculiar problems of the Virgin Islands' situation. The Organic Act, which spells out the constitutional relationship between the United States and the Virgin Islands, fails to provide sufficient autonomy to the Virgin Islanders to enable them to chart their

own destinies. The lack of a clearly stated dialogue, and the effects of the current constitutional relationship on local autonomy and local decision making, have meant that this very important issue has not been adequately addressed. Consequently, the forces unleashed by the economic development have been allowed unrestrained growth and development.

This is most evident as one views the consequences of the foreign labor program in the Virgin Islands. The outside capital, that had been encouraged to develop the Islands, needed a source of cheap labor. Through their power and influence, they were able to overcome local objections and secure the necessary policy reversals which set into motion the large scale migration of foreign labor into the territory. It was unlikely that a governor, appointed by the president of the United States and not subject to local control, would have any great concerns for the demographic implications of that migration. The rapidity with which prosperity came to the Islands lulled local leaders into feeling that all of the long-standing problems created by an underdeveloped economy would eventually be solved. Low unemployment and economic prosperity soon came to be accepted as "givens," and little attention was paid to the socioeconomic consequences of the large migration of alien labor.

The influence of status was most evident when concerns about the foreign labor program increased locally and nationally. Since the program was operated by the Immigration and Naturalization Service, policy changes had to be generated in Washington. Needless to say, there was little concern in Washington for the peculiar problems caused by the extension of the foreign labor program in the Virgin Islands, and changes, when they occurred, were in response to national concerns rather than local Virgin Islands' concerns. By then, however, outside capital, in the form of the local business community, had secured sufficient power and influence to continue to play a role in maintaining the foreign labor program in some form. Changes in the federal immigration laws created changes in the status of the foreign labor population, and the former foreign laborer secured permanent residence prior to securing citizenship. Prior to the extension of permanent residence privileges to this group, the Virgin Islands government had ignored the problems of providing social services to this group, limiting public housing facilities, health services, public schools, and social services to citizens. The change in status required that the Virgin Islands government respond to the change by providing services to this group of new and potential citizens.

The economic prosperity and the tourist trade opened the Virgin Islands to the outside world and, as a United States territory, the Virgin Islands provided free ingress and egress to American citizens who wanted to remain on the Islands. This group, because of citizenship, could not be treated as second class citizens, and established homes and businesses and began to play an influential role in the political and economic life of the territory. This further shaped the territory and the thinking that the Virgin Islands was only an extension of the United States. Concerns about the peculiar local conditions or nationality were thus ignored. In a twenty-year period, these trends have created a major shift in the Islands' population. The once dominant native majority is now a minority in his own land. The dominance of the United States system has surpressed any nationalistic concerns that might have existed, and the improved standard of living of the native population has been, despite the tensions, hostilities, and pressures of the rapid development, accepted as the price paid for entry into the consumer oriented society.

The displacement of the native population has helped to strengthen its resentments against the West Indian migrant, who now competes with the natives for jobs, housing, social services, and public education. In the past, the private sector has been primarily the domain of the mainland born United States citizen and the foreign laborer, and public employment primarily the domain of the native population. As public financial resources have shrunk, the government has not been able to continue the role as the employer of last resort, and today large numbers of young people are unemployed and totally alienated from society. Their restlessness, the increasing crime rate, the general discontent created by the government's inability to adequately address the many social problems

existing in the community, and the disparity existing between the majority black native and West Indian population and the white controlled economy are issues that the society cannot ignore indefinitely.

The critical issues for the native population are best stated in the following comment from one of the younger native politicians:

> It is a fact that the Virgin Islander—the indigenous population, as some people like to say—feels a stranger in his own land.
>
> It has been said that the problem is racial. I think it goes beyond that. First, if it is racial, who do we find strife between—Black native and Black immigrant, and Black native and Black mainlander? It is a fact that the Virgin Islander who has deep historical roots in the Virgin Islands, whose predecessors struggled through the hard years . . . yet every time something good happens to somebody, it happens to somebody who just got here.
>
> We find a way to deal with the Virgin Islander–alien structure by having a law which says the native must get the job before the alien. But then we get ourselves in a situation where we find we must make a choice between the native Virgin Islander and the American citizen from the mainland. We cannot deal with that because there is a constitution which prevents us from dealing with this. So, it seems as if we have to deal with our political system and perhaps nationality, if we are going to deal with that problem.[35]

But the more critical issue is that the majority population of the Virgin Islands will remain black and culturally West Indian, thus maintaining the unique and peculiar situation of the Virgin Islands with regard to American society. Failure to deal with this fact could lead to the development of a strong national consciousness that will some day echo the position of the Hawaiian Youth Congress which states:

> We, the Youth Congress family, see that secession from the United States of America will be a catalyst to the preservation of Hawaii's land, culture and people. The Westernization, Americanization and colonization of Hawaii has left in its wake pollution, congestion, ugliness on our land, has inflicted economic slavery upon our people, and has disrupted our culture through the domination of American culture.[36]

NOTES

1. Whitney T. Perkins, *Denial of Empire—The United States and Its Dependencies* (Leyden, Netherlands: A. W. Sythoff, 1962), p.342.
2. Ibid., p.13.
3. Ibid., pp.348, 349 and 352.
4. See Perkins, op. cit., p.342–43.
5. Roy Preiswerk, ed., *Documents on International Relations in the Caribbean* (Rio Piedras: Institute of Caribbean Studies, 1970), pp.552–53.
6. *The Daily News,* St. Thomas, Virgin Islands, 25 August 1973, pp.1 and 12.
7. *The St. Croix Avis,* St. Croix, Virgin Islands, 25 August 1973, p.9.
8. Gordon K. Lewis, *The Virgin Islands: A Caribbean Lilliput,* (Evanston, Illinois: Northwestern University Press, 1972), p.344.
9. James A. Bough and Roy C. Macridis, ed., *Virgin Islands—America's Caribbean Outpost—The Evolution of Self-Government* (Wakefield, Massachusetts: The Walter F. Williams Publishing Company, 1970), p.186.
10. Mario C. Moorhead, *Mammon–vs–History (American Paradise or Virgin Islands Home)* (St. Croix: Square Deal Printer, 1973), p.88.
11. Ibid., p.89.
12. Lewis, op. cit., p.104.
13. Bough and Macridis, op. cit., p.125.
14. Lewis, op. cit., p.104.
15. U.S. Congress, House, *Non-Immigrant Alien Labor Program on the Virgin Islands of the United States,* a Special Study of the Subcommittee on Immigration, Citizenship, and International Law of the Committee on the Judiciary, ninety-fourth Congress, First Session, 1975, pp.59–60.
16. U.S. Congress, House, *Report on the Administration of the Immigration and Nationality Act,* Report of a Special Subcommittee of the Committee on the Judiciary, Part 11, February 28, 1955, pp.117–23.
17. U.S. Congress, House, *Non-Immigrant Alien Labor Program on the Virgin Islands of the United States,* p.11.
18. Ibid., pp.11–13.
19. Ibid., p.15.
20. Social, Educational Research and Development, Inc., *Aliens in the United States Virgin Islands: Temporary Workers in a Permanent Economy,* (Silver Springs, Maryland, January 1968), pp.iii–iv.
21. U.S. Congress, House, *Non-immigrant Alien Labor Program on the Virgin Islands of the United States,* p.30.
22. Ibid., pp.36–37.
23. Dependencies are defined as not fully independent nation states, such as the British Associated States of St. Kitts, Nevis, Dominica, and Antigua. Most of the down island population in the Virgin Islands are drawn from these areas.
24. U.S. Congress, Non-Immigrant Alien Labor Program on the Virgin Islands of the United States, pp.37, 39–40.
25. Ibid., pp.31–32.
26. Ibid., pp.33–34.
27. Ibid., p.34.
28. Lewis, op. cit., p.225.
29. *Facts You Should Know About the Proposed Virgin Islands Immigration Commission,* Document prepared by the staff of the Virgin Islands Delegate in consultation with the staff of the House Subcommittee on Immigration, Citizenship, and International Law, mimeographed (1976), and *The Daily News,* St. Thomas, Virgin Islands, 5 February 1976, pp.3 and 18.
30. Valdemar A. Hill, Sr., *Rise to Recognition* (Printed in the United States by the author, 1971), p.120.
31. Jerome L. McElroy, *The Virgin Islands Economy: Past Performance, Future Projections, Planning Alternatives.* (Prepared for the Virgin Islands Planning Office; Office of the Governor, Charlotte Amilié, St. Thomas, Virgin Islands, July 1, 1974, Thomas R. Blake, Director of Planning). This study was financed in part with a Planning Assistance Grant from the Department of Housing and Urban Development under the provisions of Section 701 of the Housing Act as amended. Offset printed, Bureau of Libraries and Museums, p. 47.
32. Ibid.
33. Ibid.
34. Ibid.
35. *The Daily News,* St. Thomas, Virgin Islands, 21 October 1976, p.19.
36. Francine Du Plessix Gray, *Hawaii: The Sugar Coated Fortress* (New York: Random House, 1972), p.6.

Part 6

Adjustment Implications for the Immigrants Themselves I: Adaptations

THE RETURN OF THE CLANDESTINE WORKER AND THE END OF THE GOLDEN EXILE: RECENT MEXICAN AND CUBAN IMMIGRANTS IN THE UNITED STATES

Reynaldo A. Cué and Robert L. Bach

Just as a nascent social science responded to the influx of masses of Europeans at the turn of the century, the contemporary U.S. scientific community has turned its interests to the relatively large and sustained immigration from the Third World. While this "new immigration" involves several nationalities, Mexico and Cuba hold a primary position, representing 14 percent and 11 percent of the total immigration between 1960 and 1975, respectively.[1] The present paper attempts to conceptualize the underlying dynamic of these recent flows of Mexicans and Cubans within a general analytical framework. Starting at the macrolevel, we compare and contrast these seemingly diverse migrations in terms of their structural conditions. At the individual level, we attempt to relate how the macrostructural relations are reflected by the characteristics of the migrants. Our concluding discussion focuses upon the implications of the previous analysis for potential assimilation of the "new" immigrants in U.S. society.

Illustrative data are presented from an ongoing study which investigates the conditions and experiences of two samples of Mexican and Cuban immigrants. Data were collected during the fall of 1973 and the spring of 1974 on documented Mexican immigrants entering the U.S. through El Paso and Laredo, and on Cuban immigrants arriving in Miami. For both samples, eligible respondents included those between eighteen and sixty who could be identified as economically self-supporting males. The Mexicans (N=822) were interviewed in Spanish at the point of entry while the Cubans (N=590) were interviewed, also in Spanish, at their immediate residences in Miami.[2]

BACKGROUND

The well-known massive immigrations to the United States at the turn of the century reflected a rearrangement of the international economic order. The immigrants, displaced from central and southeastern Europe by the expansion of European capitalism, came to the newly expanding center of industrial capitalism in the United States. The well-publicized low wages and minimal living conditions combined with the increasing application of technology to maximize the rate of surplus value extracted from these workers. Consequently, the U.S. experienced rapid capital accumulation and industrial expansion. The industrial surpluses provided the sources of investment under which a new international division of labor was created. Under the power and dictates of U.S. capital, Latin American nation states became specialized producers of agricultural products and raw minerals for the benefit of foreign investors. This international division of "core" and "periphery"[3] was founded upon a structure of unequal exchange between the periphery and core, and established the basis of their uneven development. The core states, the U.S. and Western Europe, expanded their initial competitive edge upon the exploitation of the land, labor, and capital of the peripheral nations.

The expansion of the United States economy and, thus, the demand for labor was not without fluctuation, however. The introduction of labor-saving technologies and the rapid rate of technological innovation reduced the need for immigrant labor. As the capitalist system reached its cyclical turn of overaccumulation, investment opportunities dropped, production faltered, and many native and immigrant workers were thrust out of the labor market. The cyclical crisis and accompanying increased unemployment led to concerns over the presence and assimilation of these "foreigners" in American life. These concerns were expressed in terms of the competition of foreign and native workers in a tight labor market and the cultural and psychological obstacles to assimilation into the

Anglo-Saxon culture and social order. As a result of this crisis and nativist fear, the first systematic application of selective national immigration policy was adopted in 1921 and 1924. National quotas were established for the European countries but, interestingly, exemptions were offered to immigrants from Mexico and Cuba, and were later extended to the Western Hemisphere as a whole.

Two significant trends occurred after these early laws and the cessation of massive European immigration to the U.S. labor market. Firstly, in the period following World War II, the introduction of capital-intensive technology into the most productive sectors of the U.S. economy, plus the increasing strength of labor unions, curtailed the labor absorptive capacities of these sectors. The demand for "cheap" labor still remained, but the character of the demand shifted to newly developing regions, and to the less dynamic sectors for which capital investment was too expensive and the average rate of profit quite modest. The availability of an abundant, flexible and politically weak labor force in new areas of the world economy precluded a complete curtailment of the need for immigrant labor. Secondly, during the same period, the increasing rationalization of international industrial production added a new dimension to the old international division of labor based on agromineral exports. Instead of importing unskilled manual labor to the centers of production, the productive units themselves could be transported to the periphery. In this way, capital could still seek out cheap sources of labor without the cost-rendering immigration. The spread of multinational corporation to the periphery, thus, had an important impact on the potentiality of international migration. In sum, these two post–World War II trends indicate that migration acts as a response to the spatial organization of capital in its quest for labor which can be utilized to a profitable end.

THE FUNCTIONS OF IMMIGRANT LABOR

Castells has identified several of the uses of immigrant labor in advanced, capitalist societies.[4] International migration is seen as a product of two principles inherent in the capitalist mode of produc-

tion: the submission of the worker to the dictates of the owners of the means of production, and the law of uneven development. From the point of view of capital in the advanced societies, immigrants not only represent the internationalized "reserve army" which cushions the effects of cyclical trends in capitalist expansion, but also a permanent mechanism to counter the tendencies toward a declining rate of profit. These functions of migrant labor are evident in the companion, but contradictory, long-term trends of increased immigration and increased unemployment in western Europe[5] and in the United States.[6] Migrant labor can satisfy these needs of monopoly capital because of the intensified exploitation of the immigrant, given his alien politico-legal status. This reinforced exploitation takes two forms: an increase in the intensity and duration of work, and the ability to pay a proportionately smaller value for the reproduction of the labor force.

The fact that migrants tend to work longer hours and under worse conditions than native workers is fairly well-established.[7] There is much discussion as to the reason why immigrants accept such conditions. Contrary to conventional assertions that immigrants are forced to take such jobs because of extreme need or submissiveness, Castells argues that "the utility of immigrant labour to capital derives primarily from the fact that [capital] can act towards [immigrant labor] as though the labour movement did not exist."[8] That is, the very fact that immigrants are not native citizens and, hence, are politically weak enables capital to utilize migrants in such a way as to extract maximum surplus value.

The second function of immigrant labor is to lower the costs of productivity for capital as a whole through minimizing the cost of social reproduction. Most migrants are unmarried or forced bachelors (many leaving their children at home with grandparents), which means that the advanced society does not have to provide social overhead for entire families. Furthermore, after the migrants' productive years have been spent, the majority return to their countries of origin, again relieving the host country of costly social services. Finally, those services which are made available are below the standards for the native population. All three mechanisms "cheapen" the cost of immigrant labor relative to native labor and, thus, create a structural need for continued immigration.

Burawoy has extended Castells' argument in his analysis of immigrant labor in the United States and South Africa.[9] Burawoy has noted that U.S. capital has been able to externalize the costs of reproducing labor by separating the place of production from the place of residence along political boundaries. The costs of rearing immigrant Mexican labor to the U.S. is borne largely by the immigrants' families in Mexico, while only minimum maintenance by U.S. standards is provided for the workers during their stay in the U.S. Furthermore, legal and illegal migration, with substantial circular movement, provides the mechanism through which a cheap labor force may be exploited for production but ignored when outside the market place.

A crucial aspect of this separation of production and reproduction is the involvement of the state. By placing a politico-legal framework upon these structural linkages, the state provides the mechanism for preserving the subordination of immigrant workers. Rendering many of the migrants illegal through "restricted" immigration policies and imposing conditions on the stay of temporary documented immigrants, the state ensures the political weakness of the immigrants. Moreover, by casting clandestine immigration as a social problem, the state has successfully diverted the attention of the native working class from attempts to change the structural conditions of exploitation.[10]

The continuation of the structural need for immigrant laborers and, thus, the immigration, expresses the persevering hegemony of U.S. capital in the international division of labor. Immigration is only one mechanism in the dependent relations between the U.S. and peripheral nations; just as crucial is the spread of U.S. corporations into the economies of Third World nations.[11] These multinational corporations have secured control over native sources of labor and have affected the spatial organizations of production, thus conditioning the migration flows of the native population. The resulting structure of control includes linkages between the local, peripheral bourgeoisies and dominant interests in the U.S. While these economic and political interests have remained entrenched in most areas of Latin America, they have also produced significant challenges to these relations of dependence. National liberation movements and extensive national reforms have disrupted the conditions of subordination which have dictated the geographical distribution of the native population. As these national efforts are successful in transforming the existing structures of dependence, sectors of the population whose interests are tied to foreign economic concerns and to the dominant social classes respond by leaving the country. More often than not, this emigration proceeds to those hegemonic centers, like the U.S., that have the resources to offer humanitarian aid as well as the ideological commitment to provide for these emigres.

The contrasting imageries presented above inform our analysis of immigration to the United States from Mexico and Cuba. On the one hand, Mexico continues to maintain its dependent relations to U.S. capital. The flow of migrants, both legal and illegal, reflects the penetration of the Mexican economy by U.S.–controlled, capital-intensive industries, and the continued need for cheap labor in certain sectors of the U.S. On the other hand, Cuba has broken successfully her historically dependent ties to the U.S. economy. The rearrangement of her economic and social structure under relative national autonomy sparked a significant "flight" of individuals representing groups who were linked to and benefited from former ties with the U.S. As the social structure underwent extensive transformation with the deepening of the revolution, the character of the Cuban emigration changed accordingly. As these transformations became irreversible, the function of these immigrants for international capital also changed.

THE MEXICAN IMMIGRANTS

Given the historical development of internal migration to areas of northern Mexico, and the resulting high rates of urban growth, a greater proportion of Mexican immigrants, both legal and clandestine, have come to originate in northern urban centers. Table 1 demonstrates this residential pattern for our sampled immigrants. Starting with place of birth

TABLE 1

States and Cities of Prior Residence by Selected History of Previous Residence, Total (N=822)

	(1) Father's Comm. of Birth	(2) R's Place of Birth	(3) R's Place of Origin	(4) Next to Last Place of Residence	(5) Last Place of Residence	(6) Father's Present Place of Residence
States						
Southern Mexico[1]	.8	.5	.4	.3	.2	--
Central Mexico	31.6	25.5	20.0	14.3	7.3	21.1
Northern Mexico	27.6	17.4	14.0	7.9	2.3	9.3
Border States	35.2	56.6	65.6	59.7	50.3	51.1
Southwest U.S.	.5	--	--	11.5	27.4	15.6
Illinois	--	--	--	3.7	8.9	2.0
Other U.S.	.3	--	--	2.6	3.6	.9
Other Country	.1	--	--	--	--	--
Total	100.0	100.0	100.0	100.0	100.0	100.0
N. D. or	--	4.7	1.1	7.5	.01	11.0
Doesn't know	6.7	--	--	--	--	22.1
(deceased)	(N=762)	(N=783)	(N=813)	(N=760)	(N=821)	(N=537)
Cities						
9,999 or less	66.0	53.2	37.3	25.9	17.5	34.3
10,000-19,000	8.9	8.2	7.1	5.3	2.6	4.3
20,000-49,999	6.8	8.0	5.9	3.4	3.9	6.0
50,000-99,999	8.7	11.4	14.5	3.8	2.3	5.4
100,000-499,999	6.8	15.2	27.7	41.1	41.6	35.1
500,000-999,999	.5	.7	4.7	8.9	12.5	5.7
1 million or more	2.3	3.3	2.8	11.6	19.6	9.2
Total	100.0	100.0	100.0	100.0	100.0	100.0
Doesn't know	7.4	--	--	--	--	13.1
No Answer	3.4	3.9	.9	8.7	.5	--
Deceased	--	--	--	--	--	21.7

[1]States are collapsed by region in the following manner:

a) Southern Mexico: States of Oaxaca, Chiapas, Campeche, Yucatan, and Quintana Roo

b) Central Mexico: Federal District and States of Mexico, Puebla, Veracruz, Guanajuato, Michoacán, Jalisco, Guererro, Hidalgo, Zacatecas, Nayarit, Morelos, Queritaro, Tlaxcala

c) Northern Mexico: San Luis Potosi, Sinaloa, Durango, Aguascalientes, Baja California (Sur

d) Border States: Chihuahua, Nuevo Leon, Tamaulipas, Coahuila, Sonora, Baja California

e) Southwest U.S.: Texas, New Mexico, Arizona, California, Colorado

and moving to place of last residence, Table 1 reflects the spatial distribution within Mexico. Over 65 percent of the respondents lived in the border states (defined in the footnote to the table) as compared to 35.2 percent of their fathers. Central Mexico, an area of historical significance for emigration,[12] shows a steady decline of importance as individuals move from their place of birth to other regions. Samora and North[14] have also found a similar dispersion of spatial origins of recent undocumented immigrants.[13] The bottom half of Table 1 indicates the residential shifts to large urban areas. By size of respondents' place of birth, 53.2 percent lived in cities of 9,999 population or less. The rural concentration diminishes to 37.3 percent by respondents' place of origin. Concomitantly, there is an increased concentration in places with over 100,000 to 999,999 people. Clearly, our sampled immigrants come from those regional sectors which have the greatest links to the U.S. economy.

As the expansion of capital-intensive industries in these large urban centers has created and maintained the process of urban marginalization, a high proportion of emigrants have their origins in the sectors and occupations of the urban economy which are subject to the greatest fluctuation and highest rates of unemployment. In the 1973–74 sample of Mexican immigrants, 33.4 percent of all the respondents were employed in the service sectors, while an additional 25.7 percent came from the manufacturing sector. Construction activities employed the third largest subgroup in the sample (16.2 percent). This sectoral distribution takes on greater meaning when we note that over half (50.3 percent) of all the respondents were employed in low-skilled occupations, minor urban service workers, and unskilled and semiskilled laborers. These low-skilled occupations place the sampled immigrants well within the structural conditions of marginalization that create a pool of potential emigrants. These potential emigrants become active in response to the continuing demand for Mexican labor in the U.S. economy. That is, there exists a structural channel for them to enter the U.S. and satisfy important needs of advanced capitalism.

The insertion of Mexican immigrants into U.S. society is shaped by the functions which immigrant labor performs. We noted previously that the economic sectors in the U.S. which continue to require "cheapened" labor are those with low average rates of productivity and profit. While agriculture has been a focal point for much immigrant labor, Frisbie notes that the increased involvement of capital-intensive techniques in U.S. agricultural sectors of low productivity have taken over control of the destinations of immigrants.[14] These sectors (for example, construction, service, and commerce) require cheap labor in order to survive the competition of large-scale companies. The immigrants on which we have data clearly reflect a concentration in the low-paying occupations and low-productivity sectors. Table 2 shows the occupational distributions for the total U.S. population, those of Mexican origin, and the present sample of immigrants. Undoubtedly, the sampled immigrants have an overall lower occupational status than either of the other two groups. More important, however, is the concentration and overrepresentation of the immigrants as operatives, nonfarm laborers, and service workers. The concentration in low-productivity jobs is suggested when we examine sectors of employment. Over 56 percent of all the sampled immigrants were located in service (31.3 percent), construction (20.9 percent), or commerce (4.4 percent). An additional significant proportion (30.4 percent) were in the manufacturing sector; however, the heterogeneity of this sector makes difficult any conclusion about the concentration of these respondents in the low-productivity manufacturing enterprises.

Besides providing labor for those sectors of the U.S. economy with low average rates of profit, the Mexican immigration has provided a labor force which was reared at no cost to U.S. capital and is cheaper to maintain than a native labor force. Although the age range of our sample artificially identifies workers in the most productive years of the life cycle, it is interesting to note that almost 90 percent of the sampled immigrants are between the ages of eighteen and forty-four. These individuals are old enough to be productive but young enough to offer a flexible labor force to meet the constantly changing structure of demand in the U.S. The cost of this Mexican labor is less than native labor because of the minimal amount of social overhead required to maintain the immigrants. Unlike permanent labor-

TABLE 2
Occupational Distribution of the Total and
Mexican-Origin U.S. Population (males, age 16 and
over),[1] and of Sampled Immigrants,[2] First U.S.
Occupation (in percent)

Occupation	Total U.S.	Mexican-Origin	First U.S. Occupation of Sampled Immigrants
Professional, Technical and Kindred Workers	14.1	5.2	.8
Manager and Administrators, except Farm	14.1	5.7	.8
Sales and Clerical Workers	12.7	7.6	2.8
Craft and Kindred Workers	20.9	19.2	19.5
Operatives	17.9	26.9	28.6
Non-Farm Laborers	7.3	14.2	23.4
Farmers and Farm Managers	3.0	0.4	--
Farm Laborers and Supervisors	1.8	11.5	9.8
Service Workers	8.2	9.3	14.3
Total	100.0	100.0	100.0

[1]Sources: U.S. Bureau of the Census, Current Population Reports: Persons of Spanish-Origin in the U.S. March 1974, Series P-20, No. 280 (April 1975).

[2]Original survey categories adjusted for comparability with CPR categories.

ers who require services for an entire family, most Mexican immigrants, especially undocumented ones, enter the U.S. alone. This is true for our sample of legal immigrants. Almost 33 percent had no children while among those immigrants who reported having children, only one-third said their children were accompanying them.

Finally, the circular movement of Mexican labor is an important characteristic of this immigration. Circular movement creates the possibility of legitimizing de facto residence by establishing the social contacts necessary for meeting the provisions of the immigration law. Previous research has shown that clandestine immigration may be the normative path for achieving legal residency in the U.S.[15] Returning to Table 1, column 5 shows that almost 40 percent of the respondents to our interview gave the U.S. as their last place *before* entering the U.S. legally. These respondents are evi-

dently previous undocumented immigrants. Moreover, when the entire sample was asked specifically if they had lived in the United States, three out of five (61.5 percent) reported they had. The majority of these respondents (78 percent) had spent longer than a year in the U.S. Even though this is a large percentage of respondents experiencing prior undocumented U.S. residence, there is even some question about the remaining 38.5 percent. Many of these latter respondents, who reported no prior U.S. residence, entered legally under the preference status for spouses of U.S. citizens. While a number of explanations could account for how Mexican citizens could marry U.S. citizens,[16] there is reason to believe that these 313 individuals (38.5 percent of those answering the question) were reluctant to admit prior undocumented residence.

Clearly, the sampled legal immigrants have experienced an initial, clandestine move to the U.S.

where they acquired the qualifications, either a spouse or a job, which permitted legal entry. This legitimizing process demonstrates that the legal flow of Mexican immigrants cannot be separated from the undocumented movement. Indeed, the possibility of legal entry may act as a "carrot" in encouraging continued "willingness" among the clandestine immigrants to accept the conditions of their work and pay in the U.S. Our sampled immigrants are among those who have been "successful" in their clandestine pursuit. We must not forget, however, the apparently large numbers of those Mexicans who circulate between the U.S. and home without ever achieving legal status. It is these migrants that provide the bulk of cheapened and politically weak workers for the U.S. economy. Their alien status, plus the ideological battles waged in the southwest United States against these "intruders," perpetuate their subordinate position in the U.S. social structure.[17]

The history of the Mexican migration to the U.S. is undoubtedly a tale of the two principles of the capitalist mode of production cited earlier: the submission of labor to monopoly capital and the process of uneven development. We have seen how the insertion of Mexico into the new international division of labor has created a structure of dependence within which the international exchange of labor is merely an additional mechanism. The volume and nature of Mexican migration, therefore, rests upon the nature and preservation of the unequal relations between the U.S. and Mexico, and the perpetuation of the politico-legal situation of "alien" workers in the U.S. In contrast, the Cuban "exodus" represents the consequences of a successful national challenge to these dependent relations.

THE CUBAN IMMIGRANTS

Immediately following the Castro Revolution, the challenges to United States involvement in Cuba stimulated the emigration of a substantial portion of the upper socioeconomic strata.[18] These "political refugees" came from the land-owning and managerial sectors of the population as well as from the state bureaucratic and professional sectors. Many of these early emigrés expressed strong convictions that the "true" nature of the revolution had been betrayed after agrarian and urban reforms were enacted which threatened their positions of power and privilege.[19] This ideological character of the migration has led many analysts to view the Cuban exodus purely as a reaction to the socialist aims of the revolutionary leadership. This view was certainly supported by the activities of the emigrants as they resettled in the United States. Many of the emigrants believed they would be able to return shortly to the island. Indeed, by 1962, 55 percent of the total emigrés arriving in this initial period had not changed their status to "parolees" or "permanent residents," and were remaining in the U.S. as tourists under special permission for extended stay.[20]

The United States government, in its battle to prevent secession from its hegemony over Latin America, utilized these *declasse* immigrants in fomenting the aggression against Cuba in the Playa Giron (Bay of Pigs) invasion of 1961. Despite the invasion's failure, the military and paramilitary recruitment of Cuban immigrants against the Cuban revolution continued under the auspices of the Central Intelligence Agency. Furthermore, the C.I.A. extended its efforts beyond Cuba to support "covert" activities in other nations of the Latin American periphery which were perceived as a threat to the continuation of U.S. dominance.

Within Miami, substantial funds were directed to establish a base of operations, thus creating an appendaged informal economy within the immigrant community. At the same time, early capital transfers by farsighted and wealthier immigrants, business loans provided by federal and private agencies, and the reemployment of some immigrants by old U.S. employers contributed to the origins of the partial reproduction of the Cuban class structure within the social microcosm of urban Dade County. Downwardly-mobile immigrants began forming the new working class in the Cuban community.

Unlike the Mexican immigration which reflects the intensification of structures of dependency, the function of this early Cuban immigration was to counteract those movements which threatened the preservation of the international division of labor. This reactionary political and ideological process gave an initial advantage to the early Cuban immigrants which later Cuban immigrants, as well as

Mexican immigrants, would not have.

Direct emigration from Cuba to the U.S. was interrupted during the October crisis of 1962, itself an expanded consequence of the challenges to the Cuban revolutionary process. Commercial flights were stopped and all traffic was halted until the Cuban government offered, in 1965, to permit any person (except those eligible for the military and in strategic economic positions) who wished to leave Cuba to do so. This offer initiated the creation of the "aerial bridge" which would bring about 40 percent of all Cuban immigrants in the U.S. The characteristics of these immigrants were still overrepresentative of the prerevolutionary, upper socioeconomic strata of Cuban society. As one journalist expressed it: "To a great extent these people represent the professional and business class of Cuba; the able, the educated, the successful. The struggle in most Latin American countries is to build a stable middle class; that of Cuba has been gutted. This exodus is the biggest brain drain the Western Hemisphere has known."[21] While certainly expressive of a journalistic glamour, this observation contains much truth. However, over the course of the entire airlift (1965–73), the character of the emigration flow changed. For example, Casal and Hernandez have noted the declining level of education for successive waves of immigrants.[22] Although such tendencies may be due simply to higher proportions of old and female immigrants, or to statistical regression, since the early migrants were so heavily representative of the upper strata, there is little reason to doubt that significant changes in the Cuban social structure had created new groups of potential emigrants.

The Cuban revolution was still in tenuous existence during the early stages of the emigration. By the late 1960s, however, the structural changes had advanced far enough that the state could initiate more thorough socialist reforms designed to consolidate the economy through the elimination of the middle and small private sectors. Small entrepreneurial and urban service sectors were socialized. This restructuring of the middle sectors during the late sixties provided the push for the most recent wave of Cuban emigrants.

Our 1973–74 sample of Cuban immigrants captures much of this later flow. The majority of the respondents left Cuba between 1969 and 1974. Their socioeconomic background clearly reflects the changing sectoral origins. Table 3 compares the educational levels of the present sample with those of earlier groups of Cubans. Compared to other emigrés, these later immigrants are less educated. However, compared to the Cuban population before the revolution, our sample remains relatively select. Of course, there have been significant changes in educational opportunities in Cuba since the revolution, and it seems likely that the educational levels of the 1973–74 immigrants correspond to average levels of educational achievement in Cuba today.

The occupations of the recent sample also reflect the consequences of efforts to socialize the remaining urban private sectors. The new emigrés represent, for the most part, the middle sectors. Three occupational categories predominate: artisans and skilled workers (22.2 percent), intermediate service workers (19.7 percent), and white-collar and minor professionals (24.4 percent). Much of this middle sector was created by and linked to the expansion of the secondary and tertiary sectors during the prerevolutionary period of dependent development. The fact that approximately a third (32.5 percent) of our respondents received the largest portion of their income from the public bureaucracy, which was such an important employer before the revolution, suggests that these immigrants formed part of a labor aristocracy which the socialist reforms of the revolution are just beginning to penetrate.

Informal social networks also play an important role in the occupational character of the airlift emigration. The process of obtaining permission to leave on the airlift flights required a family member in the U.S. to declare this intention. For those leaving through Spain or Mexico, family members also had to purchase the airplane tickets. The result was a mediation of the consequences of those macro-structural relations representing the deepening of the revolution and resulting "selectivity" of individual migrants. It was, therefore, those Cubans who already had families in the U.S. that would react to potential changes in their relatively privileged social positions, and would take advantage of the opportunities to emigrate. This was so in spite of the temporary hardship that the application for emigration entailed.

TABLE 3
Respondents' Years of Education in Cuba

Years of Education	(1) Miami 1973-74 (N=587)* %	(2) Miami 1973-1974 categorized (N=587)* %	(3) West New York 1968a (N=155) %	(4) Miami 1962b (N=1,085) %	(5) Cuba 1953b (N=5,829,029) %
0	0				
2	0				
3	2	9	11.6**	4	52
4	7				
5	5				
6	26				
7	5				
8	17	69	50.8	60	44
9	7				
10	6				
11	3				
12	7				
13	3	13	21.6	23.5	3
14	1				
15	1				
16	1				
17	7	9	16.0	12.5	1
20	1				

a Source: Rogg (1974)
b Source: Fagen *et. al.* (1968)

*Percentages based on this figure. Three cases are missing.
**Cell figure includes respondents with five years of education.

Finally, these changes in the character of the migration have even been noted in the motivations of the individual immigrants. Several authors have found that Cubans arriving during later stages of the immigration are more like "traditional" economically-motivated migrants.[23] Of course, these findings have been linked to the changing occupational composition of the flow.

Interestingly enough, the changing view of the causes of Cuban emigration has been accompanied by similar changes in the perceptions of its consequences for both the individual immigrant and the social order of destination. From the study of Cuban immigrants in a "golden exile"[24] and journalistic Horatio Alger stories, attention has shifted to the emergence of Cubans as a discriminated minority,[25] and journalistic reports on the "curious intrigues" of Cubans in the United States[26] and of "Little Havana's Reign of Terror."[27] Although little systematic evidence is available to examine such shifts, there is little doubt that changes in the opportunities open to recent immigrants have occurred. Part of the change may be due to the reduction of available aid to the Miami community. By 1974, a total of $935

TABLE 4
Occupations of Cuban Refugees in the Miami Area

Occupation	(1) 1974 Cuban Minority Survey* %	(2) Miami, 1970 Census Data* %	(3) University of Miami Study, 1966* %	(4) Sample of New Arrivals Currently Employed, 1973–74 %
Professionals, Managers and Technicians	13.5	14.1	12.7	4.8
Clerical and Sales	24.6	23.8	27.3	9.6
Skilled Labor	17.3	18.0	17.3	47.6
Unskilled Labor	44.6	43.8	32.3	38.0

*Source: Hernandez (1974).

million had been spent by the Cuban Refugee Program in finding jobs, in resettlement, and in other welfare-related activities. About 35 percent of the immigrants had registered at some point for assistance.[28] Recently, however, budgets have been cut and the machinery for providing such aid has even begun to be dismantled.

Additional changes may be due to the structural transformations that have occurred within the Cuban community in Miami. After efforts to reestablish the early immigrants in relatively privileged subsectors of the U.S. economy had been successful, recent immigrants were left to face an existing socioeconomic structure without the government aid to help establish themselves independently. The consequence is that the insertion of the later immigrants, drawn from less privileged sectors of the Cuban economy, has tended to reproduce the social structure of prerevolutionary Cuba (albeit changed) within the context of the Miami community.

This process of insertion into U.S. society is illustrated in Table 4, which shows the occupational distributions for four groups of Cuban immigrants in the Miami area. The most recent group shows an overwhelming concentration in the laborer categories (85.6 percent). This proportion compares to only 49.6 percent of the immigrants in the earliest study. The 1973–74 sample has a correspondingly low proportion of respondents in the professional, managerial, and technical categories (4.8 percent). The greater concentration in the laboring sectors of the economy is further reflected in income levels. The median monthly income of these respondents is approximately $320, or $4,000 per year. This 50 percent of our respondents with incomes below $4,000 compares to only 14 percent of those earlier immigrants sampled in Miami by the Cuban National Planning Council.[29] Although the short period of exposure to the U.S. labor market may depress their income levels, it seems clear that the recent immigrants are occupying relatively subordinate positions in the socioeconomic structure of the U.S.

The insertion of the recent immigrants into the working class of a "Cuban economy" in Miami, and their low socioeconomic status, will most likely have great consequences for their future living opportunities. Moreover, this may be true whether the immigrants become assimilated into an "Anglo-Saxon" culture and social order or not. It is the relationship between the immigrants' structural position within an emerging ethnic community and the larger social structure that the final section of our paper addresses.

FINAL CONSIDERATIONS

Now that we have our immigrants inserted into the structure of U.S. society, the question is naturally what are their chances for assimilation? The thrust of conventional perspectives is to regard immigrant assimilation as an individual process of adjustment and adaptation to a static and homogeneous social structure or culture.[30] Therefore, the problem of immigration to the place of destination is reduced to individual socioeconomic or sociopsychological adjustment. Unlike these limited views, the perspective contained in this paper is that the experiences of immigrants in their new society are the consequences of the functions performed by the *system* of immigrant labor for the dominant interests of capital. That is, the theory that accounts for the relations between immigrant or ethnic groups and the possibility of changing these relations ("assimilation") is, to quote Burawoy, "first and foremost a theory of empty places in the structures of production and reproduction and only secondarily a theory of the allocation of individuals to those places."[31] Such traditional "determinants" of assimilation as color, sex, modernity, achievement motivation, and so forth, are thus rendered inconsequential relative to the structural positions in which the immigrant *group* finds itself. It is with this structural perspective in mind that we turn to a consolidation of our analysis and a brief look at the current structural positions of the Mexican and Cuban immigrant groups.

We have attempted to show that the Cuban and Mexican emigration derives from internal sociopolitical reactions to international relations of economic and social dependence. These reactions are reflected in the characteristics of the migrants and their insertion into the U.S. social structure.

In the Mexican case, the contradictions of dependent capitalist development have intensified. As a result of continued capital-intensive industrialization, high rates of rural and urban unemployment and income inequality have widened the spatial and social origins of Mexican emigrants and increased the volume of that flow. The characteristics of the emigrants have changed accordingly. Drawn from the urban centers of the North as well as the backward, low-productivity sectors of the urban economy, the emigrants have continued to move to areas of the U.S. where the functions satisfied by a *system* of migrant labor are needed.

These specific functions have changed over time with changes in the social formations of advanced capitalism in the U.S. Early Mexican immigration was important for the *renewal* processes involved in the reproduction of labor, particularly in the areas of agricultural production in the southwest United States. Large proportions of these immigrants were permanently inserted into the early processes of class formation in the region. Their structurally subordinate position and politico-legal status placed them among the most vulnerable and exploited fractions of the working class. Contemporary Mexican immigration, on the other hand, has become increasingly important for preserving relatively low costs of labor *maintenance*. Circular movement of Mexican labor is facilitated by the proximity of northern border cities, the relative ease of crossing back and forth, and the comparative advantages to spending U.S. wages in Mexico. At the same time, increased costs of social reproduction in the U.S. make residential stability in the U.S. more difficult, even for the returning "successful" clandestine worker.

The continuation of these relations creates a situation of increased polarization between the system of migrant labor and the dominant structure of U.S. capital. That is, it is to U.S. capital's advantage to maintain this circular movement of labor. Under these conditions, assimilation at the macrostructural level is deemed impossible. If this is true, then individual adaptation will become increasingly difficult, and contradictory antagonisms within the U.S. working class will increase.

In the case of the Cuban immigrants, the challenge to the international relations of U.S. dominance sparked the "flight" of particular sectors of the Cuban society. These early propertied groups came to Miami, serving the function of reproducing the hegemony of U.S. capital in Latin America. Within this function, the early immigrants benefited. However, as the irreversibility of the revolution became evident, and the sources of humanitarian aid to the Miami community were strained, the later immigrants were inserted into the working class of an emergent ethnic community. Unlike the earlier migrants, the function served by these immigrants was to reproduce the positions of domination of Cuban immigrant capital. This process of consolidation of the class structure within a rapidly emerging "ethno-nation"[32] serves to condition the opportunities of individual Cuban immigrants. Their prospects for assimilation into the dominant U.S. social order thus become similar to the Mexican immigrant, although the sources of this similarity are quite different. For both groups, the prospects for assimilation depend upon the continuation or transformation of existing relations which perpetuate the submission of the worker to the dictates of capital.

Since the forces of social transformation are currently fragmented and contradictory, our expectation for the immediate future is the continuation of "nonassimilation" for these new immigrants. Long-term forces are, of course, particularly difficult to predict. However, just as recent history has shown throughout the world, the obstacles to the unification of the working class are under siege. It is with the elimination of these obstacles that the opportunities for full participation in the structure of U.S. society will become a reality.

NOTES

1. U.S. Department of Justice, Immigration and Naturalization Service, *Annual Report: Immigration and Naturalization Service* (Washington, D.C.: 1960-75 inclusive).
2. See Reynaldo A. Cué, "Men from an Underdeveloped Society: The Socioeconomic and Spatial Origins and Initial Destination of Documented Mexican Immigrants" (master's thesis, University of Texas at Austin, 1976); and Alejandro Portes, Juan M. Clark, and Robert L. Bach, "The New Wave: A Statistical Profile of Recent Cuban Exiles to the United States," *Cuban Studies* 7 (1977): 1-32.
3. Immanuel Wallerstein, *The Modern World-System: Capitalist Agriculture and the Origins of the European World-Economy in the Sixteenth Century* (New York: Academic Press, 1974).
4. Manuel Castells, "Immigrant Workers—Class Struggles in Advanced Capitalism: The Western European Experience," *Politics and Society* 5 (1975): 33-66.
5. Castells, ibid.
6. Alejandro Portes, "Why Illegal Migration? A Structural Perspective," Latin American Immigration Project Occasional Papers, Department of Sociology, Duke University, Durham, North Carolina, November 1977.
7. S. Castles and G. Kosack, *Immigrant Workers and Class Structure in Western Europe* (London: Oxford University Press, 1973); and David North, *The Characteristics and Role of Illegal Aliens in the U.S. Labor Market: An Exploratory Study* (Washington, D.C.: Linton and Company, 1976).
8. Castells, op. cit., p.52.
9. Michael Burawoy, "The Functions and Reproduction of Migrant Labor: Comparative Material from Southern Africa and the United States," *American Journal of Sociology* 81 (March 1976): 1050-87.
10. Jorge Bustamante, "Structural and Ideological Conditions of Undocumented Mexican Immigration to the United States," in W. Boyd Littrell and Gideon Sjoberg, eds., *Current Issues in Social Policy* (Beverly Hills: Sage Publications, 1976).
11. Theotonio Dos Santos, "The Structure of Dependence," *American Economic Review* 60 (May 1970):   231-36; and F. Cardoso and E. Faletto, *Dependence y Desarrollo en America Latina* (Mexico: Siglo XXI, 1970).
12. Manuel Famio, *Mexican Immigration to the United States* (Chicago: University of Chicago Press, 1930).
13. Julian Samora, Jorge Bustamante, and Gilbert Cardenas, *Los Mojados: The Wetback Story* (South Bend, Indiana: University of Notre Dame Press, 1971); and North, op. cit.
14. Parker W. Frisbee, "Illegal Migration from Mexico to the United States: A Longitudinal Analysis," *International Migration Review* (1975): 3-15.
15. Alejandro Portes, "Return of the Wetback," *Society* 11 (March-April 1974): 40-46; and Cué, op. cit.
16. Charles Hirschman, "The Effect of Prior U.S. Residence upon the Socioeconomic Status of Mexican Immigrants," Duke University, Durham, North Carolina, 1976.
17. Bustamante, op. cit.
18. Lourdes Casal and Andres R. Hernandez, "Cubans in the U.S.: A Survey of the Literature," *Cuban Studies* 5 (July 1975): 25-31.
19. Richard R. Fagen, Richard A. Brody, and Thomas J. O'Leary, *Cubans in Exile* (Stanford: Stanford University Press, 1968).
20. Juan M. Clark, "The Exodus from Revolutionary Cuba (1959-1974): A Sociological Analysis" (doctoral dissertation, University of Florida, Gainesville, 1975).
21. Quoted in John F. Thomas, "Cuban Refugees in the United States," *International Migration Review* 1 (Spring 1967): 46-57.
22. Casal and Hernandez, op. cit.
23. Nelson Amaro and Alejandro Portes, "Una Sociologia del Exilio: Situacion de los Grupos Cubanos en Estados Unidos," *Aportes* 23 (January 1972: 6-24; and Francisco Wong, "Political Orientations and Participation of Cuban Migrants: A Preliminary Analysis," paper presented at meeting of the American Political Science Association, New Orleans, September 1973.
24. Alejandro Portes, "Dilemmas of a Golden Exile: Integration of Cuban Refugee Families in Milwaukee," *American*

Sociological Review 34 (August 1969): 505-18.

25. Rafael J. Prohias and Lourdes Casal, *The Cuban Minority in the U.S.: Preliminary Report on Need Identification and Program Evaluation* (Boca Raton: Florida Atlantic University, 1973).

26. Horace Sutton, "The Curious Intrigues of Cuban Miami," *Saturday Review/Worlds* 11 (September 1973): 24-31.

27. Dick Russell, "Little Havana's Reign of Terror," *New Times*, 29 October 1976, pp.36-45.

28. Clark, op. cit.

29. Andres R. Hernandez, ed., *The Cuban Minority in the U.S.: Final Report on Need Identification and Program Evaluation* (Washington, D.C.: Cuban National Planning Council, Inc., 1974).

30. For example, see S. N. Eisenstadt, *The Absorption of Immigrants* (London: Routledge and Keegan, 1954); and Milton Gordon, *Assimilation in American Life: The Role of Race, Religion, and National Origins* (New York: Oxford University Press, 1964).

31. Burawoy, op. cit., p.1084.

32. Immanuel Wallerstein, "Class-Formation in the Capitalist World-Economy," *Politics and Society* 5 (1975): 367-75.

AN EXAMINATION OF ROTATING CREDIT ASSOCIATIONS AMONG BLACK WEST INDIAN IMMIGRANTS IN BROOKLYN

Aubrey W. Bonnett

Under the changed United States immigration policy, preference is given to professional and skilled workers thereby attracting migrants from the West Indies with generally more education and training.[1] In general now, it is not the unemployed, unskilled West Indian who migrates to the United States but one who is likely to have some skill and to have been employed.[2] Yet, this high status of the black immigrant to the U.S. was not always the case. In the West Indian migration to the U.S. that commenced around 1900 and continued until around the 1930s, many were low status immigrants of rural origins and it was they who attracted attention because of their extraordinary frugality.[3] It was these immigrants who aggressively used rotating credit associations to improve their status and it is these associations we shall concern ourselves with in more detail. In several studies of these black minority communities, increasing concern has been focused on *rotating credit associations* and the way in which they may have contributed to the economic improvement in the black minority community.[4]

Thought to have originated in South China, Japan, and West Africa, these associations frequently differed with regard to membership, size and criteria of membership, type of funds, sanctions imposed on members, and so forth. Despite this element of variability, they have been regarded as a genuine type of cooperative financial institution.

In many parts of the nonwestern world, this type of association served the functions of western banks and, more importantly, served to assist in "small-scale capital formation" among immigrants.[5] Immigrants to the United States from Southern China and Japan employed traditional rotating credit associations as their principal device for capitalizing small businesses. West Indian black immigrants brought the West African trait, which has survived in their native lands, to the United States and England where they used it to finance small businesses, to buy houses, to operate grocery stores, tailor shops, jewelry stores, and real estate operations. In some instances they undertook direct competition with whites doing business in the ghetto.[6] Bryce-Laporte states that some of these black immigrants of the first generation believed that within a decade or two, if they were enterprising and willing to engage in some form of self-denial, they would move from their lowly stratum to reasonable prominence as professional local leaders, small property owners, small businessmen, or landlords.[7] So, it was reported, these immigrants used rotating credit associations as a means to amass the capital to realize their dreams.[8] The rotating credit association can thus be seen as a functional and instrumental institution serving socioeconomic functions in this immigrant community.

PURPOSE OF THE STUDY AND RESEARCH DESIGN

So far as can be determined, there has been no research on the adaptation of black West Indian immigrants to rotating credit associations. This study is not of black immigrants but rather a study of a specific institution, found in the countries of origin, which has been transplanted. It is a study of the survival capacity of these associations and their transformation in a new environmental situation.

It is proposed to examine the current importance of rotating credit associations of a segment of black West Indian immigrants in Brooklyn, New York. Brooklyn has the highest number of first and second generation black West Indian immigrants and this weighed heavily on the choice of Brooklyn as the area for study.[9] Rotating credit associations are informal voluntary associations. They are not formally listed or registered anywhere, nor are they advertised publicly, but are known on the basis of primary group contact. In short, there is no way of gauging how many associations there are in a given area nor of determining the total membership.

West Indian beauty parlors, some social clubs with West Indian clientele, barber shops owned by West Indians, and food markets catering to West Indians were contacted in order to try to ascertain who were some of the organizers of these associations. Of the ten organizers named, all were contacted in order to ascertain past and current members. From these organizers a list of one hundred names were compiled, each of whom was contacted and fifty-five responded to a mailed questionnaire or answered questions from an interview schedule.

In order to have some basis for comparison, we also drew a random sample from West Indian social clubs in the area to get a pool of nonusers. Of the ninety persons contacted, forty-eight responded. For each individual selected, available socio-economic data and information about association memberships were recorded.[10] In-depth interviews were also done with the ten organizers of rotating credit associations.

The methodology employed involved a number of techniques: published material, a mailed survey, and, finally, some unstructured in-depth interviews.[11] Some of the data are quantitative in nature and some qualitative. In total, it is felt that this several-pronged approach yielded substantial information which met the specified purposes of the study.

DEFINITION OF TERMS

In this study, first generation West Indian immigrant refers to natives of the Commonwealth Caribbean, that is, the English-speaking islands of the Caribbean, including the mainland nation of Guyana. For easy identification the first generation is called foreign born. Second generation refers to native born American children of foreign or mixed parentage.

Rotating credit associations are here defined as "associations formed upon a core of participants who agree to make *regular* contributions to a fund which is given, in whole or in part, to each contributor in *rotation*."[12] Rotation and regularity are, therefore, the two essential criteria used to differentiate these associations from similar associations like lodges, mutual benefit clubs, and so forth.

Associations in which contributions are held by an official or bank and are not distributed on a rotary principle are, by this definition, excluded.[13] Rotating credit associations are also referred to throughout this study as *boxes, partners,* and *susus,* the names by which they are familiarly known to black immigrants. Individual contributions of members in these associations are called *hands. Fund* refers to the total amount of individual hands.

ROTATING CREDIT ASSOCIATIONS IN THE WEST INDIES

Under slavery, West Indian blacks had direct responsibility for an important part of their own well-being, and also acquired experience in economic activity on their own, since they cultivated their own individual plots without supervision and were usually allowed to sell any surplus in the market.[14] The great population imbalance in the West Indies—90 percent black, 10 percent white—also forced the slaveholder to allow the slave some measure of economic autonomy in order to achieve plantation self-sufficiency in food.[15] West Indian slaves could possibly gain freedom apparently more often than their counterparts in the American South, for the West Indies needed non-white men in occupational niches that whites preempted in the United States.[16] This self-reliance of blacks in the West Indies, deriving from the economic necessities of the plantation combined with greater prospects of permanent escape and survival away from the plantation, made resistance and rebellion more feasible. Thus, it is likely, Sowell contends, that the West Indian setting may have permitted and fostered more self-reliance, more economic experience, and more defiance of whites.[17]

The freedmen, the self-reliant West Indian blacks, were invariably the mixed blood mulatto class and not the African descended black population from which the bulk of early black migrants to the United States came. Most blacks in the West Indies faced dire poverty combined with discrimination by both whites and mulattoes. Partly, however, because of the inability of the few whites and mulattoes there to man all responsible positions, there was less often the completely closed door to improvement which so many black Americans faced in so many occupations.[18]

It was the black element of the population who used the rotating credit associations in their various islands to purchase consumer goods which they could not get on credit and, in some instances, to help them run small petty trade. Feelings of self-sufficiency and independence were of the highest importance to a people just released from the wretched institution of slavery; every effort was made by the black former slaves to avoid working for any master or providing services which were considered to be menial. They avoided plantation labor, and some acquired their own plot of land, gained skill in trades, engaged in self-employment, and worked to rise through education. Social mobility for blacks in the postemancipation era meant obtaining positions which the mulatto and white members of the society occupied and trying to live in the style that they did.[19] Since, however, the immigrant groups that entered the West Indies after the slave system had formally ended (East Indians, Chinese, Syrians, Lebanese) engaged in business enterprises at a conspicuously higher level than was the case for local blacks,[20] they soon monopolized the ordinary commercial life of the West Indies. Many in the black population began to feel the effects of poverty as they experienced an inability to make ends meet and, as a result, rotating credit associations began to grow in importance among them.

Generally, blacks used the *susus, boxes,* or *partners* as they were called, to help them adapt to a poverty syndrome. Money from these associations was used to purchase consumer goods, to pay for important festivities such as weddings, to provide money for burial, and, in some instances, to set up small businesses, *cake shops*[21] as they were called. Numerous persons engaged in these associations to send their children to the best schools in the country in an endeavor to help them achieve greater social mobility.[22] Some social scientists of the Melville J. Herskovits School even contend that the persistence in the West Indies of the same customs of the descendants of African slaves accounts for the presence of these associations.[23]

In the Trinidad Village studied by Herskovits, residents referred to their rotating credit associations as *susu*.[24] The Trinidadian susu takes the form of a cooperative pooling of earnings by those in the group so that each member may benefit by obtaining, in turn and at one time, all the money paid in by the entire group on a given date. The total of the weekly contribution is called a *hand,* and care is taken to ensure that the contributors are all permanent employees of some organization, most often the government. Most rural Trinidadians appeared to have used the fund for consumption purposes.[25] Levin, in a more recent study, finds the *hui* still existing among the Chinese immigrant but the *chitty* (the East Indian rotating credit association) seems to have become anachronistic around the 1940s.[26] The hui among Chinese in Trinidad differs from the African susu in that the order for receiving the fund is decided by competitive bidding, the proceeds of which are redistributed to members as interest payments.[27]

Jamaicans refer to their rotating credit associations as *partners*. The organizations in Jamaica are headed by "bankers" and the members are called *throwers*. The number of throwers can be of any size but invariably range from ten to twenty members. Both bankers and throwers may be either men or women. Katzin describes the partners in this way:

> A partner is initiated by the banker, who must be financially able to see the mutual savings group to a successful conclusion. He must be a trustworthy person with real property, such as a home, and he must have a permanent address where he can always be found. A banker will try to include throwers who work at different occupations as a means of avoiding the possibility of a significant number of throwers simultaneously suffering a sudden reduction of income, and consequent inability to continue in the partners to its conclusion.[28]

Normally, the partners last the same number of weeks as there are throwers, with the amount of the throw varying in different partners but identical for all the members of a given group. It is also common for a thrower to request a hand at a time when he or she must meet some unusually large financial obligation, such as tuition fees for a child in school or a payment on land or a house.[29] Further, many petty traders use their hands to restock their stalls with imported goods for which they must pay cash. At times, the banker may get a portion of the hand as a gratuity because the system does not provide any compensation to the banker for the responsibility which he assumes and for his time. However, the banker does receive psychic income because to be a banker is a mark of prestige and a validation of economic status.[30]

In the Bahamas, rotating credit associations are also known as *esu*. Membership is often limited to employees of one's business, members of one's lodge or church, or to close friends of relatives so as to ensure both a minimum of defaulting members and strong social pressure on the holder of the money not to abscond.[31] In the event the holder does abscond, he or she may be prosecuted by the government as a thief. Wealthier Bahamians tend to put their savings in banks or in postal savings. However, poorer people on New Providence Island who fear involvement with the law prefer the esu, where they can be arrears a few weeks without difficulty and where they can get ready money for any emergency. In the Out Islands of the Bahamas, where there are no savings facilities except esu, the institution is highly important as a means of buying a share of a fishing boat, building a house, or getting married.[32] Crowley describes the esu in this manner:

> The originator of the *esu* takes a small cut out of the funds each week. When a member falls in arrears, the originator is expected to make up the difference from his own resources until the arrears is paid up. If the member falls in arrears before he has received his esu, the amount he owes will be subtracted from his esu. If he defaults, after having received the esu, it is up to the originator to put pressure on him to pay up or return all the money he has received beyond what he has paid in.[33]

At times a member who realizes he cannot continue to make weekly payments or who moves away may sell his membership for what it will bring, on the condition that the originator of the esu approves his replacement. It is also reported that a group of Catholics have founded the St. Francis Credit Union in hopes of adding earned interest to the accumulated capital of esu.[34]

Rotating credit associations are also found in Barbados, Guyana, Montserrat, Antigua, and other islands in the West Indies. In these societies they are normally called *boxes*. In Guyana, R. T. Smith found "throwing a box" to be an extremely widespread system of individual savings.[35] The capital thus accumulated was usually spent on consumer goods, including household furnishings and clothes, both of which were generally renewed or renovated for the big festive season of Christmas. Chronic indebtedness was as rare as affluence among black villagers.[36] In Guyana, Smith also found that the practice of "throwing a box" was also widespread among East Indians, particularly those who earned a monthly or weekly income. It is not known whether this is a result of cultural borrowing from the blacks or a persistence of a trait already existing in parts of India from whence the indentured immigrants came.[37] Finally, in the Dominican Republic, there are two distinct systems of credit, each serving a different social stratum. More affluent groups utilize commercial banks and personal savings, while low income groups turn to moneylenders and *san* which is a traditional Dominican rotating credit association.[38] San, it is said, exists as a savings institution or a capital mobilizing apparatus in the Dominican Republic because it satisfies economic, social, and psychological needs among the lower classes.[39] Workers and small entrepreneurial enclaves, such as shopkeepers or petty speculators, have neither the economic nor the social power to gain access to commercial banks and, hence, they play san.[40]

ROTATING CREDIT ASSOCIATIONS AMONG BLACK IMMIGRANTS IN BROOKLYN

Long before coming to the United States, the migrant often goes through various preparatory steps, desperate investment measures, and personal involvements in efforts to pass the consular requirements. Some in the kin network must "chip in" to make the trip to the United States a reality. The immigrants, thus, feel on arrival here that they must create opportunities not only for themselves but for the loved ones left behind. They must acquire money, build up experience or secure knowledge, and return home a success.[41] It matters little that the immigrant may never return; the important factor is that he or she has defined the situation in this manner and so consequences are indeed very real for the individual.

Aside from the unusually sophisticated and those who may have visited the country before, a sizable number of black immigrants are likely to experience shock and anguish upon first reaching the United States.[42] In the 1920s, the majority of immigrants came with skills in carpentry, brickmasonry, baking, tailoring, and so forth, jobs to which they had easy access back home. Once in the United States, they discovered these jobs were more difficult to secure, and they came into a system where the positions they must accept were in the lowest brackets of economic security and prestige.[43]

Except for the black middle class immigrant, most newcomers had not been imbued with the distinctively American penchant for conspicuous consumption. They were accustomed to unemployment without welfare, hard work or underemployment and low pay, and thus relative deprivation of many of the things black and white Americans consider basic necessities.[44] The usually agrarian-based status system from which they came to the United States led them to want to own land and other immovable properties, and to dislike being kept in a state of perpetual debt. Hence, the average black immigrant, even before he arrives in this country, is usually highly disposed to be an ardent practitioner of what Americans call the Protestant Ethic and a true tester of the American dream.[45] It was in this context that the rotating credit associations became important to the black immigrants. The money was used to bury the dead and to help form burial societies, for their pride would not allow them to let one of theirs be buried in ''potter's fields'' (public burial grounds). Money was sent as remittances to relatives, especially at Christmas, and it was also used to augment family finances, and to help form the nucleus of the benevolent societies which have become so popular today. By far, however, the most important use of ''susu'' money was to buy houses, set up businesses, and to accumulate relatively large amounts in savings banks.

West Indians would also combine to buy a house. Of the several corporations organized for this purpose the Antillean Realty Company had holdings in excess of $750,000.[46] Haynes states that, out of the 309 business enterprises he surveyed in 1909, about 19.7 percent had owners who were born in the West Indies, or a percentage that was about 103 percent larger than the West Indian proportion in the total population at the time.[47] Haynes also stated that conversations with many of them elicited the information that they had come to this country with the idea of saving money and entering business for themselves.[48] As they made themselves into stable members of society and began to be known for their frugality and thrift, they became more reluctant to accept the overt discrimination practiced upon nonwhites.

Rotating credit associations among black immigrants in New York City have been around for at least fifty years. Among West Indian blacks, their use is surrounded with a certain ambivalence. Some have commented on the manner in which they have been used to help some West Indian immigrants validate their middle class aspirations through initial down payments of homes, purchases of businesses, and so forth.[49] However, others have seen them as a relic of the past, an anachronistic institution that would surely disappear with the passage of time, especially in a highly urbanized, impersonal environment.[50] Our position is that these associations are used by the immigrant as a generational adaptive mechanism to cope with the urban complexities of New York. Consequently, we believe their use would be important among first generation immigrants and less so among their second generation.

ROTATING CREDIT ASSOCIATIONS: A GENERATIONAL ADAPTIVE MECHANISM OR EMBLEM OF WEST INDIAN IDENTITY

What follows is based on in-depth interviews with ten organizers of these associations, and numerous informants who volunteered the information on the condition of anonymity. We also attempted to increase our comprehension of this phenomenon by sending questionnaires to one hundred immigrants reported to have been users and ninety persons reported to be nonusers. Fifty-five users and forty-eight nonusers responded.

Almost half a century of inquiry and discussion of American immigrant groups have given currency to the idea that the erosion of ethnicity and ethnic identity experienced by most (but not all) American ethnic groups takes place in the course of three generations. It has been stated that this process involves the immigrant parents, their children, and their grandchildren.[51]

It has also been thought that the generational conflict between immigrant parents and their children represents the first major blow to the continuity of the ethnic groups and their culture in the United States. On the one hand, most of the children of the immigrant parents were found determined to forget everything—the mother tongue that left so many traces in their speech, the "strange" customs that they were forced to practice at home, in church, or even in public places.[52]

On close examination, however, it has been perceived that the process of acculturation is by no means a clear-cut one. Hence, there have arisen important questions concerning the meaning of acculturation and eventual assimilation. Parenti states that on the surface the immigrants may seem to have lost all behavioral and cultural distinctiveness but, on closer examination, manifestations of ethnic identity continue to appear.[53] In short, the process of acculturation itself is a very multifaceted one and, even as American life styles, practices, languages, and values are adopted, certain ethnic values and attitudes may persist as a vital influence. The question then arises: What of the first and second generation black West Indian immigrants in New York City? How do these various approaches illuminate their condition?

One commentator describes the tendency of West Indians—new immigrants and descendants of the old—to refer to other West Indians as "one of us" or "one of them," although very often "one of us" has never seen the West Indies and has no accent.[54] These first and second generation immigrants, Coombs further states, still eat their meat patties and drink ginger beer while identifying with some aspect of the native American culture.[55] Bryce-Laporte sees the second generation as having melted rapidly in the black pots and white pots of the United States, leaving only slight residues.[56] Ira De A.

Reid, as early as the 1930s, supported Bryce-Laporte's view. Reid stated that the second generation black West Indian immigrant reacted against the attitudes, traditions, and institutions of their immigrant parents.[57] In short, it was felt by some that the black West Indian immigrants faced the same problem as some white ethnic immigrants whose second generation children sought to become more acculturated and to depart from the ways of their parents.[58]

What then have these migrants transported to Brooklyn? Are the rotating credit associations still an integral part of the immigrants' cultural baggage, or are they confined to the first generation as the second becomes more Americanized? The results of our survey indicate that the usage of these associations is strongly tied to the first generation with very little participation by the second generation immigrant. Seventy-two of the first generation immigrants surveyed use rotating credit associations while only 25 percent of the second generation immigrants do so (N=92; significant at 0.00001 level). Even when length of time spent in the United States is controlled, being first generation is still positively related to participation.

Our second major finding indicates that not only is the rotating credit association a generational mechanism, but its pattern of use is strongly influenced by parental use. This finding illustrates the simultaneous effect of two independent factors (generation and parental usage) on participation. Among the first generation, if one or both parents participated, then the likelihood of the immigrant participating is very strong. If neither parent participated, then participation among the immigrants decreased. By the second generation there is less participation, completely disappearing if parents had not participated (N=84; Tables for both generations significant at 0.01 level).

This finding supports the theoretical position that members of groups to which the individual belongs, and who are important to him or her, may indirectly influence or even compel participation in these associations. In this instance we believe the parents may have acted as role models and so these associations became part of the socializing process. Some 80 percent of the users felt closer to West Indian culture as compared with 35 percent of nonusers (not significant at 0.10 level). However, when we control for generation, we find that it is still the generational tie and not the cultural one that is the critical variable. Further, when we control for other indices of West Indian cultural identification, such as reading West Indian newspapers, preferring West Indian music, or planning to transmit West Indian culture to children, the generational tie continues to persist as the crucial variable (none of these tables were significant at the 0.10 level).

The survey results indicate that the second generation immigrant prefers banks and, consequently, there is a sharp decline in usage of the rotating credit association. Among the first generation there is a split. There is a strong preference for the rotating credit association. Even among those immigrants oriented toward the use of banks there is still a residual generational tie manifested through participation in the rotating credit association with 14 percent of those immigrants who prefer banks still using the associations (N=21; significant at the 0.05 level). This, we believe, arises among the first generation from the lingering distrust of banks because of their impersonality. This consequently limits self-selection. Among the second generation there is more familiarity with banks, less of a fear to use them, and so he or she can be more discriminating.

At the same time, 61 percent of the first generation users had savings accounts and still participated in the rotating credit associations (N=56). Among the second generation there is no such generational overlap between the savings institution and these associations for there is a marked tendency to participate only in savings institutions (N=29).

Further, even though 17 percent of the first generation have the requisite collateral to use the credit system solely, the overlap still persists. Fifty-two percent would have to utilize the rotating credit to augment whatever they might get from the credit facilities in the larger society (N=54). Among the second generation the overlap decreases considerably, and there is a marked preference for the use of credit facilities rather than for the rotating credit association since 45 percent of the immigrants use bank credit facilities only (N=29). The second generation immigrant is obviously more immersed in the credit institutions of the host society.

Finally, there seems to be a different pattern of how these associations are used among generations. The first generation uses the money for basic urban necessities, such as buying furniture, clothing, and other consumer goods. There is little surplus capital for investment. Among the second generation there is a tendency to invest either in a small business or in the purchase of one's home. A possible explanation for this phenomenon may be that the first generation immigrant is still in the process of adapting to the financial stringencies of a large urban milieu and, cut off as he is from the larger credit system, he cannot afford to use his meager resources for capital outlays. The second generation immigrant, however, is more deeply involved with the credit system and consequently can use the rotating credit to "top off" investments.

ORGANIZATION OF THE ROTATING CREDIT ASSOCIATION IN BROOKLYN

There exist no specific criteria for membership except that the members be "working people." In most instances an organizer would decide that he or she has some specific goal to accomplish and that the association is the best way of reaching this goal. The individual then chooses among various friends those considered to be reliable, trustworthy, and who have regular, steady incomes.

Membership is not limited to black immigrants, either first generation or their second generation offspring among whom there has been some element of cultural assimilation. Native black and white Americans have participated in these associations. In some instances primary relationships on the job, the "informal aspects of bureaucracy," were often the compelling factor in an outsider such as a white American or native black American seeking membership. We even came across some instances where black Americans from the South are not only participating but have begun to organize these associations on slightly different lines than the black immigrants.[59] A process of indirect membership is also noticeable when, for instance, a hand is thrown by a working adult for a younger member.

In the West Indies, government workers tended to predominate as the government service was seen as very secure employment. In Brooklyn, members' occupations vary, although in quite a number of associations nurses seem to predominate.[60]

The total number of members may vary from approximately ten to fifty in the larger associations. The number of members is, however, contingent on the size of the ''hand.'' For example, if the organizer decides that a person needs $500 and that such a sum should be spread over twenty weeks, then he or she would need twenty members throwing twenty-five dollars a week. One organizer stated that she tried to get enough members so that the amount would not prove too difficult for anyone, hence lessening the possibility of default. Friends of the organizer can also recommend persons for membership, hence using their friendship as collateral for others.

There are no elaborate lists of rules and regulations, and no written constitution, contract, or other paraphernalia that characterize the associations in other countries. There is no advertisement in newspapers, on television, or on radio. The only advertisement is by word of mouth and emanates from the informal social relationship that ensues from the social network these immigrants form. This factor limited the researcher's ability to track down how many of these associations are operating in any one block or area of Brooklyn where the fieldwork was done.

The organizers normally stipulate when payment of the ''throw'' or ''hand'' is to be made, and then pass on this information to the participants. The throw or hand is normally paid weekly on Sunday, although in some instances allowances are made for monthly employees who pay at the end of the month. No receipts are given when payments are made as there is a large amount of trust involved among the participants. However, records are kept indicating when money was received and who is the recipient.

The associations have no branches; however, in one instance an informant stated an interesting case of members organized into subgroups. This particular ''box'' (synonym for rotating credit association) had a total of twenty members at forty dollars a week. One member, however, was unable to meet the forty dollar throw and subdivided it with three other persons, each person throwing ten dollars to him and, thus, sharing in the final hand that he received.

All contributions are made in cash and, in most instances, this requirement is the same for all members. There were a few instances where informants reported that some organizers did not throw any cash but rather were merely responsible for seeing that the associations were properly administered. In these instances the organizers were noncontributing members. The amount of money a member contributes remains constant, and members pay the same contribution after, as well as before, receiving their hand.

The organizer normally determines the amount of the hand but may take into account the ability of the members to make large or small hands. Some form of consensus, however, is necessary for, if the amount is excessive, then there would be difficulty in attracting members and, at times, in their meeting payments. Doubling (where one member throws two hands) and tripling (where one member throws three hands) does occur. In the case of doubling or tripling, the member does not get the total amount of all the hands simultaneously or even consecutively. Rather, an attempt is made to space the receipt of funds. In the case of doubling a member may receive an early hand and a late hand.

Payment is normally made at the organizer's home or place of work, but it may be collected at a member's place of work or home. The norm, however, is for the member to take the money to the organzier. Only after some delay in receiving the money does the organizer initiate attempts to get same.

The average amounts of a fund ranges between five hundred and six hundred dollars. There have been instances reported of funds approximating two thousand to four thousand dollars. Depending upon the size of membership, this could necessitate a weekly hand of sixty dollars and the association would run for the whole year. In those with five hundred dollars, the amount of time to complete the fund is approximately twenty weeks. There are no restrictions of the use of the money by a member. Some individuals use it for an initial downpayment on a home, while others may apply it to the purchase of clothing for their children, or to meet other basic necessities. There are also other interesting uses of the fund. One member reported that some persons would use the money to open fixed deposit accounts in savings banks, where they accumulate interest. Another informant, referring to the practice, described it this way: "My son, when you're really hard up and you need money, it is best to be able to say here it is than where is it, you know."

In another instance, it was reported that some participants would use the fund to deposit in their checking accounts at the commercial banks. This would, of course, reflect large balances on their bank statements, which can then be used to send to the immigration authorities as an indication of their financial status. The whole process ultimately leads to immigration to the United States of immediate family and other relatives. It should be noted that the amount of the fund is predetermined and the money is not transferable.

Ideally, the order of rotation is determined by general agreement among the members. What happens, in fact, is that the members make their requests known to the organizer who then ultimately makes the determination as to the order of rotation. If, for instance, the organizer is dubious about the reliability of a new member (even though he or she may have been vouched for), then invariably that member gets a hand very near the end of the association.

Further, some organizers have devised an equitable way of ordering the rotation so that over a period of time each member would have an equal chance of drawing an early hand in the rotation schedule. We have called this the "normalizing process."

In most instances no interest is paid. One informant responded to the question of interest payments in this way: "My son, I think it is mean to take out interest. God! is poor people using this 'box' you know. I have seen members take that money—all of it—and go right to purchase something they really need. Look, as far as I'm concerned I'm doing this to help these people and I'm not looking out for nothing."

The organizer in this case saw herself as performing an altruistic service for members of her ethnic community who needed it. However, in several instances the organizer, despite not charging interest, expected the member to give a small token and most members complied. The responses of an organizer and member are illustrative. The organizer: "Well, you know it is up to them and their conscience. They know you keep their money safe and that you are helping them save money they would otherwise throw away on cigarettes or women. It's up to their conscience to give you a small piece." The member: "Well, I usually give the organizer ten to fifteen dollars depending on the hand. After all, she is performing a service." Thus, we see in effect that, though no interest is paid, most members do give a small portion of their fund to their organizer as a form of appreciation for his altruistic service. It should be stated that, among some native black Americans who now organize these associations, members are required to give to the organizer a part of their hand. This is stipulated at the beginning of the association.

Organizers reported no instance of default by members. So rare was default that when queried, most organizers did not know how they would have dealt with such a situation. However, despite its practical nonoccurrence, most organizers tend to safeguard themselves by taking precautions.

First, if a member is suspect, the organizer makes certain that that person gets his or her money very near the end of the association. In this manner, the possibility of that member getting the money early and then failing to continue contributing is minimized. Also, some organizers try to limit membership to people whom they know very well, mainly those who are members of their social network. The strong sense of cohesiveness and group solidarity that results tends to militate against default. Finally, some organizers keep a hand as a security in the event of any contingency arising which would result in lateness of payment.

Very great importance is placed upon meeting one's payment. In some associations based on kin, default may be prevented by the acknowledged social obligations between relatives. In other associations recruitment is on the basis of island ties. Here the main point is that members who fail to keep up payments are traceable unless those members have left the city. Further, a major implicit sanction lies in the fact that the news of such a misdemeanor would be quickly communicated among black immigrants in New York, London, as well as the home island. This would, undoubtedly, give the offenders a bad name and would possibly adversely affect their future relations in the community. Reputation and respectability are important elements in the black community and, at times, a defaulting member can find both severely tested. Finally, in some instances, the organizer would visit the home of the defaulting member. Once there, he or she would proceed to announce to all and sundry in the vicinity what the defaulting member had done. This ''cussing out,'' as it is colloquially called, can keep a member in check, for no one likes a public intrusion into one's privacy.

ROTATING CREDIT ASSOCIATIONS: A SOCIOLOGICAL APPROACH

These informal voluntary associations are sociologically relevant in various ways.

A major manifest function is the adaptive role they play for the first generation immigrants in helping members meet the demands of the core society by providing services that facilitate group and individual activities. These adaptive and facilitative functions are manifested in varied ways.

One adaptive function is that these associations encourage savings or small capital formation. Many first generation members had accounts at local savings institutions but, despite this, continued to be involved in many of these associations each year. They reportedly saw them as providing short-term savings to help purchase clothing or meet the other basic necessities of urban life in New York. In a sense, this is almost a compulsory form of savings for, unlike the voluntary contribution in savings and loan institutions, the contribution to the rotating credit association has to be met. As was mentioned earlier, some organizers felt that, by socializing members in the process of compulsory savings, they were helping the members to avoid spending on nonnecessities.

Further, these associations provide credit on the sort of small-scale sums, such as one hundred dollars, in which banks are not normally interested. Moreover, the rates of interest are extremely high at banks and finance companies, whereas in these associations no interest is charged. This easy availability of credit goes a long way toward helping the immigrant cope.

Another adaptive function of these agencies is the service they provide for the newly arrived first generation black immigrant, especially the illegal alien. These people are not allowed to work in the United States yet most of them do so, thereby incurring the displeasure of citizens in Brooklyn and elsewhere. These aliens are often afraid to open savings accounts at banks where, in many instances, they have to provide social security numbers, which are becoming increasingly difficult for them to obtain.[61] Moreover, some illegal aliens need large and ready sums of money to pay their attorneys and for American brides to help them ''get straight.'' Through the rotating credit associations, they can both save their money and receive credit without fear of their illegality being discovered. One organizer of these associations even reported that on a few occasions she had helped arrange marriages between a few of her members and southern black Americans whom she knew as friends.

Of the latent functions, it was detected that they are value-expressive where they serve as a means of bringing people together and ultimately increasing their sociability. For some members these associations are seen as social networks which provide mutuality, group cohesion, and intense bonds of friendships. Some individuals come to regard themselves as part of a family, hence an altruistic feeling is engendered where members are concerned about the welfare of others.

Another latent function is their integrative function, since they act to bring together in the same organization immigrant group members with genuine value differences and, at times, outright animosities. Further, black immigrants from the islands are often perceived and treated by Americans as monoliths—West Indians. This generic categorization often may result in a homogenizing trend among these immigrants, causing them to stress the things that are common to them.

Another facilitative function of these associations for some black immigrants is apparent in their use to provide ''show money'' to immigration officials for the later migration of relatives. Some first generation immigrant users complained of the impersonal anonymous nature of New York and that the need to have their relatives near them was paramount. To the extent that the rotating credit association helped meet this need, it helped facilitate the adjustment process.

Finally, another latent function of these associations that we detected is that the organizers grew in social stature, since they were regarded as highly reliable, trustworthy persons to whom one's money could be entrusted. One informant aptly described them as "people who, given a chance, can make a buck work."

ROTATING CREDIT ASSOCIATIONS AS COMPARED WITH THE CREDIT AND BANKING SYSTEM OF THE HOST SOCIETY

We had also determined to ascertain what, if any, relationship exists between the rotating credit association and the credit and banking systems. To what extent is there any overlap between participation in rotating credit associations and having savings accounts? Are there any similar organizations within the financial institutions of the larger society, and how do rotating credit associations compare?

By its title, a rotating credit association is known as a credit association, that is, a group consisting of borrowers and lenders. The borrowers receive their money (fund) in the first half of the round and the lenders receive theirs in the second. In effect, the lenders do not charge interest and are transferring their potential interest earnings to other members. Economically speaking, had the "lenders" drawn their fund early in the round, their money would have been worth more. In a sense, they have foregone the opportunity costs of using their money in alternative ways.[62]

The members' "definition of the situation" with regard to rotating credit associations is that they are mainly *savings associations*.[63] Rotating credit associations are regarded as the poor man's bank. They act as a form of compulsory savings by providing a repository for small amounts of money that would otherwise be spent.[64]

In effect, some black immigrants do not have the initiative to systematically put aside some money, to deposit and leave it untouched until their goal has been reached. The rotating credit associations help to overcome this impediment. There are no forms to

fill out, no lines in which to wait. Moreover, the organizer is in close proximity to the members and, thus, no one has to go long distances to deposit money. Thus, the important feature of rotating credit associations is their ability to exert pressure and release reservoirs of potential savings.[65]

Despite the strong feelings that these associations are more savings associations than credit, there were a few instances in which some members regarded them as credit institutions. One individual summed up the sentiment of the latter group when she stated: "Look, box is like a loan, interest free, to meet short-term commitments. Getting small sums from a bank is a hassle. All 'dem damn questions they ask you!" Thus, the rotating credit associations are an uncomplicated way to obtain credit for some immigrants, especially the recently arrived first generation whose credit references in the United States would not be extensive.

Rotating credit associations are similar in some regard to the Christmas Club savings plans of the various banks. In each, a predetermined amount of money is set as a goal, a specific amount is deposited at regular intervals, the propensity for saving is encouraged, and ultimately one is assured of receiving back all that one has contributed. However, there are some differences. The rotating credit associations are informal structures with no interest payments or officially binding, fixed rules, only those decided upon by members who are normally friends, relatives, or fellow workers. In rotating credit associations the money can be received at anytime between the beginning and end of the association. Finally, while in both contributions are voluntary, or, in some banks, there is a process whereby compulsory deductions (savings) can be made at a specified time from a member's checking account and applied to his or her savings, in the rotating credit associations group pressure exerted to save regularly is strong.

FINAL COMMENTS

We have found rotating credit associations to be still viable in Brooklyn among black West Indian immigrants. These associations are a generational adaptive mechanism for the first generational immigrant and their use is not related to their being a symbol of ethnic identity. This is a major finding for it shows that, even though value-expressive and cultural factors are important, it is the instrumental functions that become paramount for immigrants exposed to the complexities of a highly developed urban society. They are in effect "structural shields" for these migrants in the metropolitan milieu.[66]

So far, rotating credit associations have little, if any, effect on the overall U.S. economic system. As presently constituted, these associations tend to give the member drawing the first hand an undue advantage over the member who draws the last hand, in that the former can deposit his hand in a bank and accrue a financial advantage. We assert that, if these associations are to be made meaningful for the "small man" in American society, they must be modified to take the maximum advantage of U.S. financial institutions while simultaneously passing on more benefits to members than they currently enjoy.

One such approach would be for organizers to prevail on each member to receive his hand at the end of the association rather than at the end of each period as presently constituted. The organizer could then put the money collected at each period in one of many special funds available for this purpose in U.S. financial banking institutions. At the end of the association each member would generate interest on his money and would receive much more than he now does.

As to the future role of these associations we are not entirely sure. It would seem that in the countries from which these black immigrants come, some effort is being made to make these associations an integral part of the financial community and an aid to the small man. In the U.S., the future role of these associations is cloudy. The effect of the Immigration Act of 1965 has been to cause an upsurge in the migration of West Indian nationals from countries such as Jamaica, Haiti, Trinidad, the Dominican Republic, to mention only a few. With the worsening of the economic conditions in these countries, the pull will continue to be towards the United States. However, unless these associations become less exclusive through massive publicity, and unless they are modified to make more use of existing financial institutions, they will remain limited to

exclusive use among the first generation black immigrants.

NOTES

1. Ransford W. Palmer, "A Decade of West Indian Migration to the United States, 1962–1972: An Economic Analysis," *Social and Economic Studies*, XXIII, No.4 (September 1974), p.572.
2. Ibid., p.573.
3. Ivan H. Light, *Ethnic Enterprise in America: Business and Welfare among Chinese, Japanese and Blacks* (Berkeley: University of California Press, 1972), p.33; George E. Haynes, *The Negro at Work in New York City* (New York: Arno Press and *The New York Times*, 1968), pp.100–102; Ira De A. Reid, *The Negro Immigrant: His Background, Characteristics and Social Adjustment, 1899–1937* (New York: Arno Press and *The New York Times*, 1969), pp.118–19.
4. The best description of this is found in Ivan H. Light, *Ethnic Enterprise in America*.
5. R. Firth and B. S. Yamey, *Capital, Savings and Credit in Peasant Societies* (Chicago: Aldine Publishing Co., 1964); M. Herskovits and M. Harwitz, *Economic Transition in Africa* (Evanston: Northwestern University Press, 1964); M. F. Katzin, "Partners: An Informal Savings Institution in Jamaica," *Social and Economic Studies*, VIII (December 1969), pp.436–40.
6. Light, op. cit., p.33; G. Haynes, pp.100–104; H. Robinson, "The Negro Immigrant in New York," (W/A research paper, Schomburg Collection), p.9.
7. R. S. Bryce-Laporte, "Black Immigrants: The Experience of Invisibility and Inequality," *Journal of Black Studies*, III, No. 1 (September 1972), p.135.
8. Light, op. cit.
9. The traditional research techniques of the social sciences cannot be used with much success in the study of immigrant social patterns. The compounded difficulties of sampling and interviewing immigrant populations means that research must be based on more indirect methods of data collection. The researcher found that second generation black immigrants could not be easily traced from New York census tracts. The category which listed the foreign stock of native Americans did not specifically list the English-speaking countries of the Caribbean. The researcher was forced to deduce that these countries were listed under the category "Other America."
10. The information for the interview schedule was extrapolated from an earlier study on these associations by S. Ardener, "The Comparative Study of Rotating Credit Associations," *Journal of the Royal Anthropological Institute*, XLIV, Pt.2 (July 1964).
11. Aaron V. Cicourel, *Method and Measurement in Sociology* (London: Collier-Macmillan Ltd., 1966), pp.142–43; also see Quentin Gibson, *The Logic of Social Enquiry* (London: Routledge and Kegan Paul, 1960), especially chap. 7, "The Study of History"; May Brodbeck, *Readings in the Philosophy of the Social Sciences* (New York: The Macmillan Co., 1968), especially chaps. 17, 19 and 20; G. Sjoberg et al., *A Methodology for Social Research* (New York: Harper and Row, 1968), especially chap. 9; L. Festinger et. al., *Research Methods in the Behavioral Sciences* (New York:

Holt, Rinehart and Winston, 1953); and finally , D. Cartey, "How Black Enterprises Do Their Thing: An Odyssey Through Ghetto Capitalism," in G. Jacobs, *The Participant Observer* (New York: George Braziller, Inc., 1970), pp.19–47.

12. Ardener, op. cit., p.201–204.

13. Ibid.

14. T. Sowell, *Race and Economics* (New York: David McKay & Co., Inc., 1975), p.98.

15. Ibid., p.99; R. Farley, "The Rise of Village Settlements in British Guiana," *Caribbean Quarterly*, X, No.1 (March 1964), p.54.

16. D. Lowenthal, *West Indian Societies* (New York: Oxford University Press, 1972), p.45.

17. Sowell, op. cit., p.100.

18. Ibid., p.101.

19. F. Nunes, "Social Structure, Values and Business Policy in the Caribbean," *Caribbean Quarterly*, XIX, No.3 (September 1973), pp.62–76.

20. Lowenthal, op. cit., p.193–96, and Nunes, ibid., p.63.

21. Cake shops are the West Indian equivalent of Mom and Pop Stores and Bodegas in New York City.

22. The top high schools in these countries—Queens College in Guyana, Queen's Royal College in Trinidad, Harrison College in Barbados, and the numerous boarding schools in Jamaica—all provided free places or scholarships to those of exceptional merit. Other students had to pay fees to attend these schools and, since they were the best in their respective countries, parents made exceptional sacrifices to send their "chosen" to these schools.

23. Melville and Frances Herskovits, *Trinidad Village* (New York: Octagon Books, 1964).

24. Ibid., and D. Levin, "Susu," *Caribbean Review*, VII, No.1 (January 1975), pp.19–23. This is a more recent account of susu and its effect in a developing society.

25. Levin, ibid., p.20.

26. Ibid.

27. Katzin, op. cit., p.436–40.

28. Ibid.

29. Ibid., p.437.

30. D. Crowley, "American Credit Institutions of Yoruba Type," *Man*, Art. 123 (May 1953), p.80.

31. Ibid.

32. Ibid.

33. Ibid.

34. R. T. Smith, "Ethnic Difference and Peasant Economy in British Guiana," in *Capital, Savings and Credit in Peasant Societies*, R. Firth, ed. (Chicago: Aldine Publishing Co., 1964), p.376.

35. Ibid.

36. Levin, op. cit., states that in Trinidad, which is ethnically similar to Guyana, the strength of this association derives from its cultural roots in all three of the largest ethnic groups in Trinidad: the Negroes, the East Indians, and the Chinese.

37. J. Wehrly and D. Norvell, "A Rotative Credit Association in the Dominican Republic," *Caribean Studies*, IX, No.1 (April 1969), pp.45–52.

38. Wehrly, ibid., p.52.

39. Ibid.

40. Smith, op. cit.; Levin, op. cit.; and Crowley, op. cit., among others.

41. Bryce-Laporte, op. cit., p.42.

42. Bryce-Laporte, ibid., p.34.

43. Reid, op. cit., p.119.

44. Bryce-Laporte, op. cit., p.44.

45. Ibid.

46. Reid, op. cit. p.121.

47. Haynes, op. cit., p.101.

48. Ibid.

49. Light, op. cit.; and Albert Hyndman, "The West Indian in London," in *The West Indian Comes to England*, S. K. Ruck, ed. (London: Routledge and Kegan Paul, 1960).

50. R. B. Davison, *West Indian Migrants,* (London: Oxford University Press, 1962); and S. Patterson, *Dark Strangers: A Study of West Indians in London* (London: Pelican Books, 1965).

51. V. C. Nahirny and J. Fishman, "American Immigrant Groups: Ethnic Identification and the Problem of Generations," *Sociological Review* (November 1965), p.311.

52. Ibid., p.313.

53. M. Parenti, "Ethnic Politics and the Persistence of Ethnic Identification," *American Political Science Review*, 61, No.3 (September 1967), pp.717–26.

54. O. Coombs, "Moving Beyond the Limbo Pole," in *Do You See My Love for You Growing* (New York: Dobb, Mead and Co., 1972), p.113.

55. Ibid.

56. Bryce-Laporte, op. cit., p. 51.

57. Reid, op. cit.

58. Ibid.

59. A true sense of cultural diffusion for these native black Americans has modified these associations to the extent that they charge interest to the members who participate. Moreover, most of the black Americans who use these associations were born in the South, especially in the Carolinas.

60. This trend was very common in the 1960s, especially after 1965 when large numbers of nurses migrated to the United States. See R. W. Palmer, op. cit., pp.571–87.

61. Recent innovations by the Social Security Administration, as a result of prompting from the Immigration and Naturalization Service, now call for the presentation of an alien card or passport before an immigrant is given a social security card. Since the illegal alien would have neither, he would be in a dilemma, for the use of a fictitious number might some day work to his detriment.

62. N. Barish, *Economic Analysis for Engineering and Managerial Decisionmaking* (New York: McGraw Hill, 1962).

63. Levin, op. cit., p.20.

64. Levin also found this to be true in Trinidad and we would suggest that this factor accounts for its success in developing societies.

65. Levin, op. cit., p.20.

66. L. Best, "Sou-sou Banking," *TAPIA*, XX (August 29, 1971), p.10.

COLOMBIANS IN NEW YORK CITY: THEORETICAL AND POLICY ISSUES

Elsa M. Chaney

Afro-Caribbean and Latin American migration to the United States—today rapidly replacing the large-scale European migrations of earlier decades—poses urgent new policy issues for inter-American relations, a complex set of economic, political, and legal problems for the sending societies and the host country alike. Many similar issues have surfaced in other industrialized metropolitan centers which are receiving their former colonials and other Third World nationals to undertake the menial tasks which persons born in the host societies no longer wish to do.

Colombians in the United States are a crucial population group to study, not only because they exhibit many of the same characteristics as other Latin American and Afro-Caribbean migrant groups, but also because Colombia is considered by many experts to be second only to Mexico and the Dominican Republic in the numbers of its citizens who are here without proper residence documents.

Apparently, toleration of these new immigrant groups in the host societies has come about because these persons are necessary to continued capitalist accumulation and economic growth in the industrialized centers. Piore suggests that "a continuous stream of migrants from economically backward areas is crucial to the process of economic growth, at least as it has occurred in the Western World."[1] For the most part, these workers cluster in the low-paid, low-prestige jobs nobody else will do, but they, nevertheless, are often resented because they are viewed as "taking jobs away from Americans."

Thus, the outcry against the new immigrants often has a spurious ring; for example, several of my panel members[2] in the Colombian Colony of Jackson Heights, Queens, believe that a great deal of the U.S. Immigration and Naturalization Service's (INS) effort to round up persons without the requisite green card is *puro teatro,* playacting by the Service which is intensified in periods of economic contraction to satisfy U.S. labor unions. Getting caught is not much fun, but so far the statistical danger is slight. Indeed, some believe U.S. officials must have informal agreements with several governments to permit the migrations to continue. Colombia, for example, is a "friendly, democratic government" which the United States has no wish to offend.

Such toleration certainly does not lessen the problems the migrants will experience on their arrival in the U.S., nor the tensions not only between themselves and host society nationals, but among the different migrant groups. In the long run, however, the most important fact about the migration may be its distinct character and the implications this poses for both the host country and the sending societies. The new immigrants apparently differ from the settlers of another era who left their homelands definitively; today's Third World migrants form part of a new international reserve army of labor. Industrialized nations no longer import only primary products from the developing countries but also (like some new kind of raw material) laboring hands. In some cases, the hands simply go home in periods when they are no longer needed, and host countries thus entirely avoid paying the social costs of the new, flexible labor reserve (in terms of social security and pensions, health and unemployment insurance, welfare provisions, and the like). Moreover, imported laboring hands are far less likely to organize in demand of such rights than domestic workers.[3]

Some have suggested that the only long-range solution (as to so many other urgent problems) may be the advanced nations' acknowledgment that the time has come finally to allow the Third World a truly autonomous development through the inauguration of a new world economic system of just prices for raw materials, generous transfer of technology (particularly intermediate scale), and political/material support for those societies attempting to attain a more equitable distribution of income and a better standard of living for their poor. To absorb their own surplus populations at home may be the only long-range, viable solution.

COLOMBIANS ON THE MOVE

In order to understand the dimensions of the problem, it is important to note that not all Colombian migrant streams flow to the United States; possibly, as Cruz and Castaño suggest,[4] there is more concern about this migration because, while it is not the largest, it is believed to be the most selective. Representing far greater numbers is the over-the-border migration of Colombian agricultural workers into Venezuela, adding perhaps a million persons to the neighboring republic. This migration apparently follows the classic step or fill-in pattern; as Venezuelan *campesinos* depart for the booming centers of their country, Colombians move in to take over their jobs in the agricultural sector. While the sheer numbers who cross the long, permeable border pose delicate political problems for the two nations, certainly the economic advantage of this escape valve to Colombia is enormous. We speculate that this migration functions in somewhat similar fashion to that over the U.S.–Mexican border, but exact information awaits a study being carried out by the Corporación Centro Regional de Población. Of course, many highly skilled persons also go to Venezuela; large display ads in the Bogotá newspapers invite, among others, technicians from Colombia's highly-developed textile industry to emigrate.

It is logical that steady, if not spectacular, numbers of Colombians have been going to their former territory of Panamá since the end of the 1920s.[5] More recently, perhaps 60,000 Colombians, with or without papers, have arrived in Ecuador because of the jobs created by the new petroleum enterprises. Although emigration to the U.S. began in the 1940s (we have exact figures on the numbers before 1965, since obtaining a permanent resident visa was as easy as getting a tourist document for Latin Americans before the Immigration Act of that year went into effect), the massive numbers of Colombians, totaling perhaps 150,000–250,000 in the greater New York City metropolitan area and smaller colonies in Chicago,[6] Miami, Los Angeles, and El Paso, have come since 1960—with total numbers reaching as many as 250,000–350,000 [?] in the U.S.

One dislikes playing a "numbers game" in what purports to be a social science enterprise. But it is difficult to evade entirely the question of "How many?" even though no one can say with any certainty what the total numbers may be of *any* of the new migrant groups. I compromise by giving the smallest and largest estimates of the panel experts involved in our study.

It is interesting to note that, in all but two of the past twenty-five years, Colombia has been first among South American countries in numbers admitted legally to the U.S., accounting for 34.7 percent of all migrants from the continent.[7] Many of these persons are highly qualified professionals; however, the panel of experts believes that the migration since 1960, while continuing to include some top professionals, many middle-level white collar and skilled blue collar workers, also contains many more unskilled persons of the "lower classes" than came earlier, and that perhaps 60 percent of these are without proper residence documents.[8]

Colombia has experienced minimal compensatory movements of immigrants to her territory; perhaps for that reason, it has remained one of the most thoroughly hispanicized, closed, and conservative societies in the Americas. Cruz and Castaño document[9] the countless laws, decrees, and thwarted attempts to attract Western and Northern Europeans to Colombia, beginning at Independence in 1810. This policy was pursued until recent times by officials who apparently believed that immigration was the best way to transfer to the territory not only industrious types who would, as the common Latin American expression has it, "mejorar la raza" (this means, as Cruz and Castaño point out, "whiten the skin" of Colombia's future generations), but would also bring knowledge and technology. An interesting sidelight, but, nevertheless, telling, is the fact that to the present day, this (perhaps unconsciously) racist body of legislation has mentioned the emigrant only twice: once in a 1922 decree specifying that contracts were to be required to protect Colombians hired to work outside the terriroty (never enforced) and, in 1972, a decree to facilitate the return of Colombian professionals, a project abandoned after only one year.[10]

Not only have massive numbers of Colombians been on the move beyond their country's borders, but this movement was preceded by a great deal of internal migration which has continued to the present day. In looking at both aspects, the Colombian and North American team members participating in our recent collaborative project concluded that the distinctions often made between internal and international migration probably are artificial, as Singer has suggested.[11] Because of the relatively short journey and cheap air fare (and the large number of Colombians clustered in Jackson Heights, Elmhurst, Corona, and Woodside), there is little reason now for migrants to hesitate to cross international borders. As Cruz and Castaño neatly put it, the migratory flow to the U.S. is analytically discernible but, nevertheless, fundamentally a part of the entire migratory process involving Colombians.[12] I have likened the Colombian colony with its center at Eighty-Second Street and Roosevelt Avenue in Jackson Heights (*Chapinerito,* named after a middleclass suburb in Bogota) to a distant province of Colombia,[13] and believe the migratory processes probably are more similar than different, whether the destination is inside or outside Colombia's borders.[14] From a structural perspective at least, the causes appear to be identical. Like most of the new immigrants to North America from the Afro- and Latin American Caribbean, most Colombians view themselves as ''economic exiles'' whether they are heading for the nearest Colombian provincial city, Bogota, or Queens.

MIGRATION: PERSPECTIVE FROM THE PERIPHERY

Whether we are talking about Colombians or other Latin American and Afro-Caribbean peoples on the move, we can no longer divide the fundamental mechanisms generating migration into those operating in the sending societies and those in the host countries. I am not speaking here of the ''push and pull'' framework—the set of precipitating factors common to many migration studies—but am attempting to identify the fundamental events in the international political-economic system which create the push and pull in the first place. Since around 1950, changes in the international system have generated a series of events of which massive movements of Third World peoples, often to their former mother countries, has been only one.

At the personal level (where most migration studies have concentrated), people almost always can ''explain'' their motives in leaving their home place. Not surprisingly, the cause often is perceived to be lack of economic opportunity in the place of origin and/or greater opportunity in the place of destination, rather than as the complex movement of political and economic forces now interconnected on a global scale.

A better explanation of the new migrations comes out of the theoretical framework of ''dependency,'' created by Latin American scholars and now diffused in an endless variety of modifications and mutations throughout the Third World. In this paradigm, patterns of capital-intensive, dependent development are spawning in Third World countries what might be termed a ''subuniverse'' of employment composed of persons who apparently may never be permanently integrated into productive work. Aníbal Quijano Obregón locates these persons at the ''polo marginal,'' that sector of the economy related so precariously to the means of production that it forms a new substratum of persons who may never enjoy stable, productive employment.[15] This paradox of a ''new strata of traditional economic activity is present in all three sectors of the economy,'' he notes,[16] a parallel development to the visible, scientific-technological system at the top. The artisan is not disappearing, nor is the small *comerciante.* Rather, to sum up the complex analysis of Quijano and others, a whole other level of activities (desperate people inventing jobs in the interstices of the dominant economy in order to stay alive) is growing and expanding.

An important part of Quijano's thesis is his insistence that these persons must now be viewed as a permanent level of economic activity. As he notes, such activities have always existed in Latin America, but it is only at the present time that they are tending not to disappear as conventional economic theory predicted, but to expand and to differentiate themselves as a separate level or strata: not a relic of the past, but a new sector produced paradoxically by the present patterns of economic development and the modern economic structures. This sector is intimately connected to the dominant economic system and profoundly affected by it; hence, the idea of a "marginal pole" has the advantage of expressing the margination of the workers without implying that they occupy a labor market completely separated, isolated, and discontinuous from the dominant forms of economic activity.

The complex factors generating the rising indices of worldwide un- and under employment have been analyzed by many scholars and need not detain us for long: capital-intensive techniques utilized in agriculture and mining push people out of primary production with no possibility of more than a fraction being absorbed either by the new mechanized agricultural enterprises or, alternatively, by the modernized manufacturing and service sectors.

In Colombia, the introduction of modern agricultural methods and machinery tended to exclude from the market all those who could not afford the new technology, contributing to an ever-accelerating movement of people towards the cities.[17] The agrarian reform program of the 1960s (much less radical than its public image) affected relatively few Colombian peasants. Moreover, most analysts now agree that even if it had succeeded, the effort would have had little effect in stemming cityward migration because there simply was not enough land to give sufficient numbers of peasants plots of viable size. An added ingredient was the high rate of population increase (3.6 to 3.2 annually) during the preceding two decades. As a consequence, some 25–30 percent of the work force in Colombia is un- or underemployed.[18]

Many of the experts in Queens share the common conception that "La Violencia" was the principal cause of the arrival of Colombians in the 1950s and early 1960s. During a period of about 10–12 years, the phenomenon of The Violence, widespread armed insurrection and guerrilla activity in the rural areas stemming from complex political and social roots,[19] precipitated large-scale movements of people within Colombia. Studies of internal migration in Colombia indicate that the rural population took refuge in the nearby towns (not only from The Violence, but from the poverty and misery of the countryside), while the residents of these smaller urban places headed for the cities and the capital. Thus, while it seems improbable that The Violence had any direct effect on Colombian migration to the U.S., there is strong evidence that the resultant uncertainty and malaise indirectly spurred migration during this period.

In the Third World, as is well documented by now, most of the rural population has moved *directly* from agriculture to the tertiary sector. Not all tertiary sector employment is marginal, but as Amin observes, only in developed countries does the service sector resemble the secondary (in terms of wages, working conditions, worker benefits, productivity).[20] In countries of the periphery, the tertiary sector has undergone a process of "hypertrophy," to use Amin's term, becoming swollen and distorted so that the proportion of the work force occupied in tertiary activity is much greater than in the secondary. On the periphery, the tertiary sector contains a much greater number of marginal occupations than in the center countries.

MIGRATION: VIEW FROM THE CENTER

Turning from the periphery to the center, we find a situation in some respects the mirror opposite to that in the developing countries. In later stages of capitalist development at the center, as Piore has noted, there is a paradoxical shortage of workers for low-level jobs. Industrial society, he adds, has always tended to generate a set of jobs unacceptable to the native born;[21] these have been filled in the U.S. first by immigrants, then by black labor from the South, and more lately, by rural Puerto Ricans (and in the Southwest by Mexicans). Many developed countries solve this problem by importing contract labor or tolerating illegal immigration. Once inside the center countries, these imported workers greatly resemble the marginal labor force of developing countries. Indeed, they are one and the same, and that is why it is important to link these questions of capital-intensive modernization (often exported by Western development planning experts), rapid urbanization without accompanying industrialization, and internal migration *within* Third World countries to the problem of international migration.

Even in the case of those relatively privileged migrant workers who do factory work, migrant labor is much more economic at times than the other option of opening a branch of a multinational concern (or locating an agribusiness) within the borders of a Third World country. In using migrants, the metropolitan economy can take up slack capacity already in place, rather than risk building and equipping new plants.

Just how complicated this can get is illustrated by Piore, who notes that in the Boston area, the employment of Puerto Rican immigrants, especially in the shoe, textile, and garment industries, indeed was seen by some of the employers he interviewed as the alternative to moving abroad. At the same time, agricultural interests in Puerto Rico were lobbying for the import of Colombian coffee workers to take the place of rural Puerto Ricans who no longer wanted to do this kind of work and had gone to Boston (and elsewhere) to work in factories![22]

But only a relative few of the new immigrants find work in factories; typically, they take on the residue of low-skilled, low-salaries jobs that defy automation (or simply are not worth automating because cheap laboring hands are available)—restaurant workers, day laborers, construction workers, street cleaners, janitors and custodians, parking lot attendants, baggage handlers, truck and gypsy cab drivers and, particularly for the women, domestic service. This is true regardless of qualifications; as North and Houstoun note, occupations of both the legals and illegals differ significantly from what they did in their homelands; the percentage doing white-collar work drops sharply, the percentage in skilled blue-collar increases slightly, but those in semiskilled operative jobs increase significantly.

> Respondents' concentration at the bottom of the U.S. labor market, with more than three-quarters employed in unskilled or semi-skilled jobs, contravened the heterogeneity of the study group . . . . Hence the American labor market apparently tends to homogenize at a low level an otherwise more heterogeneous but still predominatly low-skilled work force.[23]

Recent independent studies confirm that Hispanic migrants generally are grouped near the bottom of the prestige and earnings scale.[24]

So far as the Colombians are concerned, what-ever their qualifications (and there is the same phenomenon of downward mobility already noted), the majority apparently go to work in "factorias" or desire to do so. Not only are the salaries better, but factory work is viewed as *un poco mas decente,* a bit more decent, than washing dishes in a restaurant. Others work in a great variety of jobs—for example, there appear to be many mechanics, and the Colombian universally is considered to be highly skilled in this trade. Of course, some migrants prosper, and there are cases of successful entrepreneurs and professionals, some of them women, in the colony. (Interestingly, Colombian married women show higher indices of employment outside the home in the greater New York City metropolitan region than either married women in the general population or Puerto Rican women.[25] This poses interesting questions on the changing role of Colombian women.)[26] The travel agent and the real estate broker (mostly persons, again including women, who came in the years before the big influx of Colombians in the 1960s) are perhaps the best examples of the business and leadership élite; the few Colombians of any prominence in cultural, community, and political affairs (mostly Colombian politics) come principally from their ranks.

Mainly, the Colombians as well as all the new immigrants do perform needed and useful services which, however, bring low rewards and little prestige or recognition. Despite the fact that they often are viewed as competitors, it appears that relatively few "take jobs away" from North American workers. Admittedly, at a time when the unemployment rate in the U.S. hovers around 7 percent, resident workers might gladly take on some of these tasks temporarily. But, we are considering the long-run trends which have been working themselves out since the mid-1950s if we take the European experience into consideration. The evidence is somewhat contradictory. On the one hand, the INS may well inflate the number of migrants, especially the persons without documents and the dire implications of their presence—classic bureaucratic ploys for getting a larger budget. On the other hand, the North and Houstoun study, cited several times above, does appear to confirm that the majority of the illegals are not the drain on the welfare and tax systems that they so often are accused of being. The survey already described demonstrates the following:

- 51 percent earned less than $2.50 an hour.
- 77 percent had social security taxes withheld.
- 73 percent had Federal income taxes withheld.
- 44 percent paid hospitalization insurance.
- 31.5 percent filed U.S. income tax forms.
- 27.4 percent used U.S. hospitals or clinics.
- 7.6 percent had their children in U.S. schools.
- 3.9 percent collected one or more weeks of unemployment insurance.
- 1.3 percent secured food stamps.
- .5 percent received welfare payments.[27]

The survey authors note that the group was typically young male workers who would not make demands for transfer type payments.

Our observations and interviews among the Colombians confirm that they may fit the above profile—rather high on their contributions to the system, low in their claims upon it. For every person who avoids the withholding tax (either through working "off the books" or through claiming an excess of dependents), there are probably two others who do not file for their tax refunds because of their irregular status; the national, as well as the state and local governments, are net gainers. As well, a large proportion of social security taxes never will be collected in the form of pensions by those who work in the U.S. for a few years and then return to their home countries. Finally, the influx of Colombians and other Hispanics into Jackson Heights has not changed the low indices of persons on welfare; in Jackson Heights, welfare dependency remains minimal. It is higher in North Corona and East Elmhurst.

An important sidelight on the question of work: many of the experts are convinced that factory owners and other employers now are able to distinguish between Colombians and other Hispanics. It is their view—it is almost a mythology—that employers often *prefer* Colombians over Puerto Ricans as workers. This is so, they say, not only because they can be paid lower wages if they are without proper immigration documents, but also because Colombians are perceived as "harder workers," "more disciplined, they do not stay home from work," "more educated, more refined" than the Puerto Ricans, many of whom "have done nothing but cut

sugar cane," and even "Colombians are not troublemakers like the Puerto Ricans, they are more obedient, more respectful."

Part of this view of the docile Colombian as positive may stem from the fact that everyone realizes the necessity of shielding fellow workers without documents—many Colombians, say the panel, want to preserve a low profile and not make waves because of the large number of illegals in the colony.

None of the experts, even when challenged, thought that the passivity and deference of the Colombian worker might be negative qualities, even though in the short run such docility apparently leads to great exploitation of Colombian workers—*factoría* salaries sometimes are as low as $70 a week—and to resentment on the part of the Puerto Rican workers who have no reason not to be "troublemakers" over substandard working conditions and wages because they are citizens and cannot be deported. In the long run, the growing reputation of Colombians as passive (and the almost universal view of the panel that this is "good") poses serious questions in the new *ambiente* where conflict and hard bargaining are the normal tactics for extracting benefits from the political system.

Whatever kind of work she or he does, the Colombian will most probably need to go beyond Jackson Heights and the surrounding residential areas to find it. Only twelve firms (including LaGuardia Airport) within the three districts of Jackson Heights, North Corona, and East Elmhurst employ more than fifty workers, and several of these are firms that do not hire many Hispanics. Added to these are the retail trade and smaller manufacturing enterprises, many of which cater almost exclusively to Hispanics, and where many previous immigrant entrepreneurs have made their fortune. The Colombian perception is that most of these opportunities have been monopolized by Cubans, even in Jackson Heights; confirmation awaits an economic census we intend to take in the community as part of our next research effort.

Is there upward mobility for the Colombian through hard work as has been the case for immigrants in the past? From our very limited study, it is impossible to draw any firm conclusions. Yet, several of the panel believe that the more recent Colombian migrants lack aspirations. This is so, they say, not only because to rise from the dead end jobs in which most work (which permit them little time for study, even for the essential mastering of English upon which moving ahead depends) is extremely difficult, but also because Colombians are inclined to view their stay in the United States as provisional. Therefore, they do not exert themselves sufficiently, even after some years of residence, to find better employment. Of course, lack of achievement motivation is not the whole explanation. There are structural reasons for the lack of mobility from the lower echelons of the labor force as we already have indicated. And, a growing literature attests to the widening gap between the highly skilled, creative positions at the top and the residual "drone" work at the bottom of technological society.

GOING HOME: MYTH OR REALITY?

Do Colombians, in fact, go back? Our evidence on this question is inconclusive. Return for Puerto Rican migrants now is well established; Hendricks documents that some Dominicans returned to their village during the temporary economic recession of 1970, but his study was completed well before U.S. unemployment hit its peak in May 1975. (Interestingly, Hendricks thinks that any improvement in the economic situation of the Caribbean countries would increase rather than decrease the number of migrants since more would be able to afford the trip.)[28] Return of European contract laborers is well documented. In the final section of this paper, we consider the relationship of Colombians to their homeland, and speculate about the dimensions of the return.

There was one note of almost universal agreement among the panel of experts interviewed for this study: no Colombian would make a permanent change in residence if he or she were not forced to do so by circumstances. Since Colombians come to the United States against their will, they "will always be aliens," according to one expert. An official of the Colombian Consulate mentioned as other evidence the reluctance of Colombians to become U.S. citizens, an attitude which the Colombian government does not oppose, he said, because it does not wish them to sever their last ties to their homeland.

There was no single person among the panel who thought the Colombians in the colony were more interested in the local scene than in Colombia. "Colombians live *pegados*—glued—to the happenings in the homeland," "Colombians know much more about the (sports) (politics) (gossip) in Colombia than about similar events here," "Colombians are obsessive in their attachment to the homeland," are typical comments. This attachment is nurtured by the fact that Colombian daily newspapers—nine or ten of them from the capital and the principal provincial cities—can be bought in many places throughout the greater New York City area, with a lag of only a day or two. The most popular magazines from Colombia also are available, and there are at least two full-time correspondents based in New York City who report on the happenings in the colony to their newspapers in Bogotá.

It is routine for most Colombians to make a visit to the homeland at least every two or three years. The airfare offered by some of the non IATA–affiliated airlines puts such trips within the reach of nearly everyone (the fare at Christmas 1975, for example, was $288 for a round-trip journey). The fact that Colombians also receive visits from political figures and vote in their national elections (President López Michelsen, for example, visited as a candidate and made another visit in the fall of 1975, where he spoke to thousands of Colombians gathered at the Americana Hotel in New York City), and have Colombian beauty queens, sports stars, folkloric ballet groups, musical conjuntos, and singers keeps Colombians in constant touch with their own culture.

Yet, this does not mean that Colombians are entirely dissatisfied with their situation and prospects. The panel reiterated that many discover, upon arrival, that they must "work harder than they ever did in Colombia" to achieve their dreams; yet the dreams themselves suddenly become much more attainable. Relatively speaking, work of whatever type is better paid in the U.S. and enables families to join the society of consumers, that is, to own a television, refrigerator, stereo, even an auto. Moreover, they routinely do things that many would only rarely if ever have been able to do in Colombia: buy ready-made clothes in a store; go out to eat in a restaurant; take the children to the beach or theater; go off on a vacation or weekend trip in their car.

Some panel members speculated that the easy credit system, which enables consumers to use as you pay, contributes to the Colombian ambivalence about the work situation. With credit, it is possible to enjoy many amenities without waiting. Moreover, the fact that once a family has credit cards, it often remains in debt, adding new items before the previous purchases are entirely paid, means that the breadwinner(s) must keep on working. As several pointed out, this situation may be the reason that the return to Colombia is postponed and postponed again, always advancing to a more distant future when the family has acquired all the consumer durables it wishes to take back to Colombia, paid off the installments, and has the requisite nest egg, that is, the financial stake to invest in a small business enterprise and/or to purchase a home that was the whole point in coming to the U.S. in the first place.

The crucial question of whether or not the "transient" situation of Colombian (and other) migrants will continue may very well depend upon two variables: whether or not the influx of newcomers constantly reenforces the links to Colombia, and whether or not a second generation develops, socialized to the North American environment and more receptive to its values and attitudes. New immigrants keep the links fresh and immediate, but a second generation pulls in the opposite direction.

The intention to return and the actual return may not make such a great difference to the older generation; lacking requisite skills and never completely secure in English, they may not ever really adapt to their surroundings, yet not outwardly rebel—the harshness of life tempered always by the rainbow at the end of the trail: the real or mythical return to Colombia. The panel was almost universal in its perceptions that most Colombians, particularly the mass of migrants who have come in the 1960s and early 1970s, view their lives as hard; find the New York *ambiente* (if not the Jackson Heights neighborhood) inhospitable and alien; suffer from the rigors of a climate which perversely produces both artic winters and tropical summers; and come

to view their situation as exploitative when they realize that their wages, while high by Colombian standards, are low in relation to those prevailing in the U.S. The North and Houstoun study documents that the situation is general; at least the illegals not only are earning considerably less than similarly employed U.S. workers, but they also work considerably longer hours.[29]

Yet, it is only a second generation, as Piore points out in the same study of Puerto Ricans in Boston cited above, that may simply refuse to accept the kinds of work their parents have had to do. Indeed, Piore speculates that it is just to the extent that metropolitan countries succeed in preventing a second generation from growing up and being socialized to the host country's norms (as the second generation blacks and Puerto Ricans have been in the Northern cities of the U.S.) that they will avoid explosive class/racial clashes such as the United States experienced in the 1960s.[30]

It is here that some hard policy questions enter. In the year after the U.S. Bicentennial, those in whose competency it falls within the executive branch and the Congress may need to reexamine the basis for the current outcry against the "new immigrants" in our midst. Just as immigrant groups have always done, the vast majority are hard working people who have taken on the necessary, but disagreeable and low-paid tasks that the citizens do not want to do, except as Piore notes in periods of dire unemployment.[31] There are practical as well as idealistic considerations. For example, as many of those who cry out the loudest against the immigrants for political reasons must know very well, if the Hispanics who came to New York City in the past fifteen years suddenly were to depart tomorrow, the city would cease to function. Moreover, the scenario for the "round up" many call for conjures up truly ominous visions of martial law, the U.S. Marines occupying New York City for several weeks, low-flying helicopters spotting fleeing migrants with no place to hide, and similar scenes which at once render the whole prospect extremely unlikely.

Since the elimination of the kinds of jobs migrants do appears to be some time in the future, some now say that the U.S. should preserve the option of expanding and contracting the labor force as the host country's needs dictate. This might be done, some suggest, through careful regulation of migrants through labor contract on the European model (not allowing them to bring their families), or legislation such as the so-called ''Rodino law'' and similar bills introduced in the House of Representatives by Mario Biaggi, as well as in the New York State Assembly at Albany (which would make the employer liable to imprisonment and/or fine for hiring person without residence documents). But difficulties immediately arise; not only radicals are protesting such measures. Power outlines how exceedingly complex the whole issue of migrant workers has become in Western Europe as doubts arise on the whole project of making economically disadvantaged workers from other countries the coolies of the industrialized nations.[32]

What can be done? As far as short-range solutions are concerned, we need to rethink some of the current solutions being offered here in the host society. Can a nation of immigrants really tell those persons who come to do the ''shit work'' of the society that they cannot stay if they wish, so that their children at least may reap the benefits? What about those who have established their homes and families in this country—do we really wish to repeat scenes reminiscent of General Amin Dada's expulsion of the Indian population of Uganda? What of the fact that Latin America itself received so many of the now advanced nations' surplus populations in an earlier era? Is there not some kind of international quid pro quo? Perhaps some type of general amnesty, as the Carter Administration has proposed, may be a partial solution.

In the long run, so far as the U.S. is concerned, those entities both private and public in the U.S. which deal with development planning and related issues need to dedicate much more thought to the kinds of development strategies they have been exporting to Colombia and other countries with surplus labor. Employment is one of the great problems of the 1970s, and many analysts now attest to the fact that it must be dealt with directly and consciously; un- and underemployment do not automatically disappear with increased indices of economic growth. In terms of international justice, the U.S. needs to recognize that it helped create the high rates of un- and underemployment in the

Caribbean and South America with its exportation of labor-saving, highly capital-intensive technology, and that we are now reaping the consequences of our own errors of the 1960s. We need now to do something more creative than offer more population control programs, if that is only to give a more sympathetic hearing and response to what the Third World nations now are proposing in various international forums.

So far as Colombia is concerned, it would seem that the authorities there need to concern themselves not only with the long-range issues of economic development which will, of course, affect the high rates of out-migration, but also in the short run with the current problems of the emigrants. An Institute of Emigration, as outlined by President López Michelsen on several occasions, or some other mechanism designed to deal with emigration, is an urgent necessity, and this proposal has the added advantage of being the one suggested by leaders of the President's own Liberal Party in Queens. Those who plan to emigrate from Colombia need orientation and some manner of regularizing their status by work contracts or other legal arrangements which will assure them just wages for their years of labor abroad, and will relieve many of the necessity to migrate without proper documents. Those who already are abroad need some entity to defend their interests, in order to give a true picture of the contribution they are making in the host society (to counter the negative image projected by those few Colombians caught in the drug traffic), and to Colombia as well. Finally, those who wish to return to Colombia need assistance in making their arrangements and in reorientation to life in Colombia.

Because the adjustments to the Immigration Act of 1965 made in the last months of the Ford Administration may have had the effect of bringing more Hispanics to the eastern seaboard cities as legal migrants, and since at the present time, at least for some countries, there does not seem to be any real possibility of stemming the exodus of persons without proper documents, a rethinking of policy measures has become an urgent problem in inter-American relations.

NOTES

1. Michael J. Piore, ''The Role of Immigration in Industrial

Growth: A Case Study of the Origins and Character of the Puerto Rican Migration to Boston," Manpower Administration, U.S. Department of Labor (1973), p.1. (Mimeographed.)

2. Information is from a prior study carried out by U.S. and Colombian social scientists and directed by Ramiro Cardona, Corporación Centro Regional de Población, Bogotá (1976). The panel in the Colombian Colony included educators, clergy, entrepeneurs in ethnic and other business enterprises, politicians, real estate and travel agents, journalists, and members of the sports/social club network of Jackson Heights.

3. Celso Furtado, *The Economic Growth of Brazil: A Survey from Colonial Times to Modern Times* (Berkeley: University of California Press, 1971), p.140.

4. CarmenInés Cruz and Juanita Castaño, "Colombian Migration to the United States," in *The Dynamics of Migration: International Migration,* Occasional Monograph, 2, No.5 (Washington, D.C.: Interdisciplinary Communications Program of the Smithsonian Institution, 1976), p.77.

5. Jorge Villegas, "Condiciones del trabajador migrante," *Documentos de Trabajo,* No. 3 (Bogota: Organización Internacional de Trabajo, 1974), p.75, quoted in Cruz and Castaño, ibid.

6. Priscilla Walton, "Having It Both Ways: The Migration Experience of Colombian Professionals and Their Families in Chicago," master's thesis (University of Texas, 1973).

7. Cruz and Castaño, op. cit., p.98.

8. Elsa M. Chaney, "Latin America in the United States: Colombians in New York City," in *The Dynamics of Migration: International Migration,* Occasional Monograph, 2, No.5 (Washington, D.C.: Interdisciplinary Communications Program, 1976), p.28.

9. Cruz and Castaño, op. cit., pp.16–50.

10. Cruz and Castaño, ibid., pp.43–44.

11. Paulo Singer, "International Migration and Development," in *International Migration, World Population Year* (Paris: Committee for International Coordination of National Research in Demography, 1974), p.128.

12. Cruz and Castaño, op. cit., p.79.

13. Chaney, op. cit., pp.59–60.

14. At the time President Lyndon Johnson began new negotiations over the Panama Canal, there was a joke making the rounds in the colony that if Johnson would give Panama back to Columbia, then the Colombians would return Jackson Heights to the U.S. (I do not know if the joke was revived during later negotiations!)

15. Aníbal Quijano Obrégon, *Polo marginal de la economia y mano de obra marginada* (Lima: Taller Urbano Industrial, Universidad Católica, 1971), p.1.

16. Ibid., p.5.

17. Ramiro Cardona, "Migración, urbanización y marginalidad," in Ramiro Cardona, ed., *Urbanización y mar-*

ginalidad (Bogotá: Asociación Colombiana de Facultades de Medicina, 1969), pp.64–65, and William McGreevey, "Causas de la migración interna en Colombia," in *CEDE, Empleo y Desempleo en Colombia* (Bogotá: Ediciones de la Universidad de los Andes, 1963), pp.213–14.

18. Hernando Gómez Buendia, "El desempleo urbano: raices, tendencias e implicaciones," *Coyuntura Económica,* 5, No.1 (April 1975), and the following three articles in Hernando Gómez Otálora and Eduardo Wiesner Durán,eds., *Lecturas sobre desarrollo económico colombiano* (Bogota: Fundación para la Educación Superior y el Desarrollo, 1974); Roberto Jungito, "El sector agropecuario y el desarrollo económico colombiano," pp.577–98; Robert L. Slighton, "Desempleo urbano en Colombia: medición, caracteristicas y problemas de politica," pp.111; and Antonio Urdinola, "Empleo, desempleo en Colombia," pp.83–99.

19. See Orlando Fals Borda, *Subversion and Social Change in Colombia* (New York: Columbia University Press, 1969) for the best account of the period.

20. Samir Amin, *El capitalismo periférico,* trans. Gerardo Dávilla (Buenos Aires: Editorial Nuestro Tiempo, S.A., 1974), p.61.

21. Piore, op. cit., p.25, and Michael J. Piore, presentation at Fordham University Sociology Seminar, March 1976.

22. Piore, "Case Study," ibid., pp.18 and 35.

23. David S. North and Marion F. Houstoun, "The Characteristics and Role of Illegal Aliens in the U.S. Labor Market: An Exploratory Study," report prepared for the Employment and Training Administration, U.S. Department of Labor (1976), pp.152–53. (Mimeographed.)

24. See Lois S. Gray, "The Jobs Puerto Ricans Hold in New York City," *Monthly Labor Review,* 98, No.10 (October 1975), pp.12–16, and Glenn L. Hendricks, *The Dominican Diaspora: From the Dominican Republic to New York City—Villagers in Transition* (New York: Columbia University, Teachers College Press, 1974).

25. Mary G. Powers and John J. Macisco, Jr., "Colombians in New York City—1970: Some Socio-demographic Features," in Ramiro Cardona, *Elements for a Comprehensive Model of International Migration: The Case of Colombian Migration to the United States* (Bogotá: Corporación Centro Regional de Poblición, 1976), Table 5.

26. Chaney, op. cit., pp.40–43.

27. North and Houstoun, op. cit., pp.66, 118.

28. Hendricks, op. cit., pp.78–79.

29. North and Houstoun, op. cit., p.126.

30. Piore, op. cit., pp.25–31.

31. Piore, ibid., p.25.

32. Jonathan Power in collaboration with Anna Hardman, "Western Europe's Migrant Workers," *Minority Rights Group Report* 28 (London: Minority Rights Group, 1976).

CULTURAL AND SOCIAL ADJUSTMENT PATTERNS OF KOREAN IMMIGRANTS IN THE CHICAGO AREA[1]

Won Moo Hurh, Hei Chu Kim, Kwang Chung Kim

INTRODUCTION

The first wave of 7,226 Korean immigrants reached the Hawaiian shores during the period of 1903–05; however, the number of immigrants was relatively insignificant thereafter until 1958, when it increased more than twofold from the previous year (from 648 to 1,604 in 1958).[2] The Korean government's restriction on emigration (November 1905), the Japanese occupation of Korea (1910–45), the American immigration quotas levied against non-Europeans (1924–65), and the Korean War (1950–53) may account for this phenomenon. For the following ten years (1958–68), Korean immigration showed a steady growth rate of twofold, but then jumped to a phenomenal sevenfold rate during the next five-year period (1969–74).[3] In 1974 alone, 28,028 Koreans emigrated to the United States, and the trend may persist by virtue of the revised U.S. immigration legislation (PL 89–236 of 1965) that has had a similar effect on other Asian immigrants.

If the 1970 Census report on Korean population (70,000)[4] were correct, there would have been 126,100 Korean residents in 1973, an increase of 80 percent in three years. And, if the same trend continued for the following three years, there would now be 182,000 or well over 200,000 Korean residents in the United States in 1976, taking the other additive factors into consideration such as natural increase and the changes in visa statuses of nonimmigrants to that of permanent resident. As the recent Health, Education, and Welfare report predicts, there will be over a quarter of a million Korean residents in the United States by 1980 with the possibility of becoming the fourth largest Asian group in the country.[5] Furthermore, some drastic changes in the socioeconomic composition of recent immigrants over immigrants in previous years might be expected.

Although Korean immigrants seem to be more dispersed geographically than other Asian counterparts, the substantial majority of them are concentrated in metropolitan areas, such as Los Angeles, New York, Honolulu, and Chicago. In the metropolitan area of Chicago alone, some 25,000 Koreans establish their permanent homes today.[6] In the last several years, they have been moving into the old Japanese neighborhood (North Clark Street), effecting a new type of natural area and a new pattern of ecological succession. The similar trends can be observed in other metropolitan areas (for example, Olympic Boulevard in Los Angeles).

Until the early 1960s, the geographic and social mobilities of Korean residents in the United States (mostly in Hawaii and on the West Coast) were relatively insignificant compared to those of other minorities. However, the rapidly increasing number of Korean immigrants and their mobility seem to alter the fabric of interethnic relations in the major metropolitan areas.

The Korean immigrants share the common marginality with other Asian minorities; however, they seem to be subjected to a more severe sense of social marginality. Unlike the other recent Asian immigrants from Hong Kong, the Philippines, India, and Pakistan, the Korean immigrants are extremely handicapped by their unfamiliarity with Western culture, in general, and in the use of the English language, in particular, largely because Korea has never had any Anglo-American colonial experience. Moreover, they as an ethnic group seem to be accorded an extremely low social prestige by the Americans, in general, although the recent Korean immigrants are the most highly educated among Asian immigrants.[7] The past empirical studies on social distance repeatedly demonstrate that the American people want even less association with the Koreans than with other Asian groups.[8]

The problems of Korean immigrants are compounded by the fact that they are the latest arrivers among the Asian immigrants without a traditionally established ethnic foothold (for example, "China Town" or "Little Tokyo").[9] In addition to such objective marginality, the recent Korean immigrants also suffer the subjective marginality which other first-generation immigrants have suffered. As was mentioned earlier, approximately two-thirds of Korean residents in the United States today came from Korea after 1970! Cultural ambivalence, fear of social rejection, and identity crisis are the manifestation of the marginality. Their problem represents a typical case of "marginal man."

Of special note with regard to the recent Korean immigrants is their diversity. They include a large number of professionals (for example, nurses, physicians, engineers, and the like), as well as a significant number of Korean students in the United States, who, upon the completion of their training, change their visa status to immigrant status every year. Also joining the wave of immigration in increasing numbers is the group of semiskilled and skilled workers, who had been negligible as recent as the late 1960s. Then, there is the group of Korean wives of American servicemen and their children.

Given the circumstances described above, one may wonder how the Korean immigrants adjust themselves to the American society. More specifically, one might be curious about the various patterns of cultural and social adjustment among the recent Korean immigrants as related to such variables as sex, age, marital status, education, occupation, income, and duration of stay in the United States.

Unfortunately, very little research has been done of the Korean immigrants in the United States, although a number of sociologists have recently made some valuable contributions by publishing their studies on Japanese and Chinese Americans.[10] The present study hopes to meet such a need in the American minority studies, to promote interethnic understanding, and to generate social policy implications for solving ethnic community problems.

The main purpose of this study is, therefore, to examine the general living opportunities and life styles of the recent Korean immigrants in the Chicago area in terms of structural variables, and to survey the degree of cultural and social adjustment in terms of behavioral and attitudinal indices. Beyond the descriptive analysis, a series of hypotheses are tested in order to examine existing theories on acculturation and assimilation.

A condensed version of our findings is presented in the following order: (1) design of study; (2) descriptive overview; (3) analysis of data; and (4) implications.

DESIGN OF STUDY

Due to the paucity of previous studies on the Korean immigrants as noted earlier, the present study was meant to be primarily exploratory in nature, based mainly on the general typology of assimilation advanced by Milton Gordon,[11] and on the recent studies on the relationship between structural variables and acculturation rates by Alexander Weinstock, Ronald J. Silvers, and Erich Rosenthal.[12] For a comparative perspective, references were also made to other Asian minority studies.[13]

Based on the above theories and research on ethnic assimilation, the following five specific hypotheses were formulated:[14]

1. Among Korean immigrants, those who have achieved a high degree of social assimilation are the ones who also have achieved a high degree of cultural assimilation. However, the reverse is not true.
2. Among Korean immigrants, those with high SES (socioeconomic status) achieve a higher degree of cultural assimilation than those with low SES.
3. Social assimilation is *not* related to SES among the Korean immigrants.
4. Among Korean immigrants, status inconsistency affects the degree of both social and cultural assimilation.
5. There is no direct linear relationship between the length of sojourn in the United States and the degree of cultural and social assimilation among the Korean immigrants.

The data for this research were obtained from structured interviews with 283 individuals (169 males and 114 females), a sample randomly selected from the Korean population in the Chicago metropolitan area, which was estimated to be 15,000 in 1975. They were interviewed by trained interviewers using an interview schedule. The interview schedule was divided into four sections: (1) demographic and socioeconomic variables; (2) cultural assimilation questionnaire; (3) social assimilation questionnaire; and (4) status inconsistency and others.

Through the procedures of zero-order correlation matrix and factor analysis, two indices were constructed: one for cultural assimilation and the other for social assimilation. The collected data were tabulated according to four descriptive dimensions (demographic, sociocultural, attitudinal, and adjustmental), in terms of frequencies, means, and standard deviations. For hypothesis testing, the relationships between the assimilation indices and structural variables were established by Pearsonian correlation coefficients, analysis of variance (and covariance) and dummy-variable, multiple-regression equations (for status inconsistency variables). The variables of sex and length of sojourn in the United States were controlled in testing all five hypotheses.

DESCRIPTIVE OVERVIEW

The Korean immigrants in the Chicago area are relatively young (median age 36), most of them are married, highly educated (four years of college or more), and have been residing in Chicago less than six years (mean: 4.47 years). While 65 percent of our sample held white-collar occupations at the time of their emigration from Korea, only 37 percent currently hold the same level of occupation.

About half of our sample experience language difficulty and do not subscribe to any American printed media. For the majority of the respondents, the traditional Korean food is predominantly preferred over Western food, while the latter is occasionally used for convenience. Membership in voluntary organizations is largely limited to Korean ethnic organizations, with Korean churches dominating. Concerning social interaction with Americans, more than half of our sample do not

have any American friends. While approximately one-third of them have never been invited by Americans, almost half of them have never invited Americans, indicating more immigrants have been invited by Americans than vice versa.

From the above descriptive sketch of objective dimensions, one would infer that most of the immigrants in the Chicago area are in the very early stage of adaptation process, having the "usual" adjustment difficulties, such as language, underemployment, housing, social distance, marginality, etc. Feelings of ambivalence, status inconsistency, and identity problems among the immigrants are thus likely to be observed. The feelings of ambivalence are evident in their attitude toward their cultural and social identity: for instance, the majority of our sample agree that some Korean customs should be discarded, such as the burden of traditional family obligations, male-dominant marital roles, authoritarian treatment of children, ancestor worship, cumbersome Korean cookery, and expensive wedding and other traditional ceremonies. In contrast to the above, however, the vast majority of our sample indicated that the Korean language, history, morals, and general customs should be taught to their children. These seemingly contradictory findings reveal the immigrants' ambivalence between their desire to discard some specific aspects of traditional culture and the desire to preserve their general ethnic heritage through generations. The immigrants' ambivalent feelings are also manifest in other areas. Although the majority of our sample are reserved or negative about living with Americans as their neighbors, making friends with Americans, and interracial marriage, the overwhelming majority indicate their wish for their children to associate with American children and feel favorable toward the anglicization of their first names.

Furthermore, despite objectively apparent status inconsistency (the preimmigration educational attainment versus low postimmigration occupational status), nearly half of our sample perceive little status inconsistency, about half of them feel most Americans accept them as their equals, and the majority of them think that they are not discriminated against in terms of monetary remuneration for their work. A plausible explanation for the attitudinal ambivalence and perceptual incongruency seems to be that the respondents, being newcomers, are not yet able to grasp the reality which belies them: the relatively high standard of living they enjoy in the United States in comparison to that in Korea may tend to prevent any sense of relative deprivation from entering their consciousness in the early years of their immigrant life. This would mean the recent Korean immigrants have not yet transferred their reference groups from Korean peers to WASP peers. This may be why only a small portion of our sample (6.2 percent) cited inadequate income as the most important problem. Our respondents' perception of their adjustment problems in order of importance is language, busy routine, concern for children, social isolation, job-related areas, inadequate income, and racial discrimination.

Whether this unrealistic perception of reality ("false consciousness") will continue is a moot question. As the immigrants' living conditions generally improve, accompanied by raised level of aspirations, they may tend to transfer their reference groups from Korean peers to WASP peers. When and if these phenomena occur, the immigrants may begin to experience feelings of relative deprivation and social marginality. Through our study such a conjecture cannot be verified. Our sample was inadequate to test the above proposition due to the fact that the majority of them arrived in the United States after 1970. It can be best tested in Hawaii, Los Angeles, or New York, where a substantial number of Korean immigrants have resided for a longer period.

ANALYSIS OF DATA

Beyond the descriptive study, we tested five hypotheses in order to examine existing theories and propositions through inductive generalizations. The first hypothesis dealt with Milton Gordon's proposition that, while cultural assimilation may take place *without* social assimilation, social assimilation occurs concomitantly with or subsequent to cultural assimilation. In other words, social assimilation is dependent upon cultural assimilation but not vice versa; that is, "acculturation only" is possible. Analysis of our data revealed mixed find-

ings: while the degree of social assimilation generally predicts the degree of cultural assimilation, the reverse is also found to be partly true. "Partly true" in the sense that some dimensions of cultural assimilation predict differentially certain dimensions of social assimilation. For instance, English proficiency (cultural assimilation) is found to be a strong predictor for the frequency of invitations extended by Americans and the Korean female immigrants (social assimilation). This would mean the causal relationship between cultural assimilation and social assimilation is not always unidirectional.

The relationships among the assimilation variables depend upon the assimilation dimensions and control variables. We found time and sex variables to be the most important control variables throughout our analysis. The problem of causal relationships among assimilation variables will be explicated later when we deal with theoretical implications.

The second hypothesis was derived from Weinstock's and Silvers' proposition that the higher the socioeconomic status, the higher the degree of cultural assimilation will be. The above proposition is generally confirmed for both sexes. The third hypothesis was again mainly based on Gordon's "acculturation only" typology that socioeconomic status may have little or no direct effect upon the degree of social assimilation, although it may be related to cultural assimilation (as was confirmed in our second hypothesis). This hypothesis is generally confirmed for the male respondents, but *partly* for the female respondents. This difference in the strength of confirmation of the above hypothesis generates an interesting question: Are Korean males less socially accepted by Americans than Korean females regardless of the level of socioeconomic status?

The fourth hypothesis was derived from our imporession of the unique characteristics of the recent Korean "elite immigrants" (high preimmigration educational and occupational status). Using the existing theories of status inconsistency (for example, Lenski, Treiman, Olsen and Tully),[15] we hypothesized that pre- and postimmigration inconsistency affects the degree of social and cultural assimilation. Implied in this proposition is an assumption that the feelings of relative deprivation would hinder the immigrants' rapid assimilation into American culture and society. Our data, however, generally do not give strong support to the hypothesis. Moreover, the immigrants' subjectively perceived status inconsistency does not closely correspond to objectively apparent status inconsistency (for example, those with high education and low occupation generally show low scores of perceived status inconsistency). Is this a manifestation of "false consciousness," mentioned earlier? We must again defer the discussion on this question until later.

Our last hypothesis was formulated upon the following assumption: although the process of assimilation may progress to a point, in parallel with the initial adjustment period and subsequent upward occupational mobility with increased desire for Anglo-conformity, such progress may not continue beyond a certain temporal point when the "successful" immigrant starts to compare his living opportunities to those of his WASP peers. We hypothesized, therefore, that the relationship between the length of sojourn and the degree of cultural and social assimilation may not be linear. Contrary to our expectation, the above hypothesis is rejected for the male respondents. For the female respondents, however, the hypothesis is confirmed, only for certain dimensions of assimilation (English proficiency, invitation by immigrants, and willingness to discard native customs). These findings clearly demonstrate the existence of sex differences in the assimilation dimensions as related to the length of residence in the United States.

The most plausible interpretation of the findings for the male respondents would be that either the male immigrants are making real progress toward total structural assimilation ("the keystone of the arch of assimilation" in Gordon's terms) into American culture and society as time lapses, or they are just passing through a temporary adaptation stage with a "false" or "naive" definition of their situation. Such a situation may lead to an indentification crisis sooner or later when the immigrants begin to "discover" an immutable barrier ("race") that would block their way toward structural assimilation.[16]

As mentioned earlier, it is impossible to justify either of the above interpretations of the Korean immigrants in the Chicago area without a longitudinal study in the future. The present study, however, has some theoretical, methodological, and practical implications.

IMPLICATIONS

Theoretically, the most significant implications of this study concern the following: (1) relationships among assimilation variables; and (2) cognitive ambivalence or incongruency in adaptation processes. Although Milton Gordon's classic model of assimilation, especially the relationships between cultural and social (structural) assimilation, is generally reaffirmed by the present study, the relationship between the two is found to be dependent upon the assimilation *dimensions* (or indices) and, more crucially, on control variables of time and sex. For instance, such a seemingly important cultural assimilation index (willingness to discard native customs) is consistently found to be unrelated to other assimilation indices, structural variables (SES), and the time variable, but significantly related to two social assimilation indices (invitation by Americans and perceived equal treatment) only for the male respondents. Another cultural assimilation index (English proficiency) is not related to the time variable, but significantly related to the frequency of invitations (social assimilation index) only for the female respondents.

At this point, the theoretical and methodological implications are clear: the relationships among the assimilation variables cannot be ascertained unless the dimensions of assimilation are specified and the time and sex variables are controlled. This simply means differential assimilation patterns emerge due to the multidimensional indices of various types of assimilation; for example, one can be assimilated in certain dimensions of social assimilation but may not necessarily be assimilated in other dimensions of cultural and/or social assimilation. In this sense, beyond Gordon's assimilation typology (cultural, structural, marital, identificational, attitudinal, behavioral, and civic types of assimilation), there is an urgent need to construct adequate indices that would faithfully reflect the most significant dimensions of *each* type of assimilation. The neglected control variables in the past assimilation studies—sex and time—also need to be considered most seriously.

There are also some additional problems involved in assimilation studies: the problems of linguistic-conceptual discrepancy and attitudinal-behavioral inconsistency. Even though the interviews for this research were conducted by native-born Korean interviewers, some misunderstanding occurred (for example, the confusion between individual and family incomes). Also, for the investigators, some seemingly important attitudinal indices (such as willingness to discard native customs, anglicization of names, pro or con about interracial marriage, and so forth) turned out to be generally meaningless for measuring the degree of cultural and/or social assimilation. These methodological problems, however, may derive not only from the interviewers' miscommunication and the investigators' oversight, but also from the respondents' cognitive ambivalence toward their existential conditions in their newly adopted country.

As discussed earlier, our respondents revealed their seemingly mixed feelings on many crucial assimilation items, such as discarding native traditional customs versus preservation of ethnic identity, reservation about making friends with Americans versus favorable attitudes toward their children associating with American children, and objectively apparent underemployment versus little subjective perception of relative deprivation. Since these various dimensions of the respondents' cognitive inconsistency might have seeped in their responses in various ways, the relationships among the assimilation variables have become extremely complicated. Nevertheless, such ambivalence reflected in our data is very significant for a processual analysis of the immigrants' adaptation process.

Our theoretical contention is that the immigrants' cognitive ambivalence is closely related to the time variable. In other words, our respondents may be going through one of several critical phases or stages in the adaptation process. A hypothetical model for the adaptation process is constructed to explicate our contention (see Figure 1).

Our respondents may be going through the "resolution stage"—between exigency and optimum states—in our processual model shown in Figure 1. At this stage, most of the immigrants' initial exigent conditions (for example, cultural shock, unemployment, language barrier, social isolation, and so forth) may have already been redressed through their familiarity with American culture, employment (even though some of them may be underemployed), improvement in English proficiency, and relatively stable incomes. Although some of their initial adjustment difficulties may still linger on, the immigrants may now have developed a taste for material affluence (purchasing a color T.V., a new car, a house, and so forth), their interaction with Americans may increase, the desire for Anglo-conformity may also increase (conversion to Christianity and anglicization of names) and, thus, a degree of cultural assimilation may progress as time goes on.

Despite this progressive acculturation and relatively improved living conditions, the immigrants seem to find themselves psychologically in the middle between Korea and America. Their reference groups still seem to be the Koreans "back home" and/or Korean Americans in the United States. No wonder most of our respondents perceive little sense of relative deprivation, in spite of their objectively apparent status inconsistency. To put it simply, the immigrants, at this stage of the adaptation process, would feel more comfortable by identifying themselves with Korean peers than with WASP peers. Although their aspirations for further "success" in the United States may become accentuated, the immigrants may still perceive themselves as "guests" who cannot possibly enter the intimate social circle (*Gemeinschaft*) of their "hosts." Moreover, the idea of competing against the dominant groups of their host society would be unrealistic—at least in their own generation.

The above interpretation may explain the immigrants' cognitive ambivalence which affects their differential adjustment patterns. How would the immigrants resolve their cognitive ambivalence? Our hypothetical processual model may be able to answer the question and to predict the direction and intensity of the immigrants' comfort and plight;

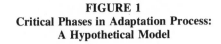

FIGURE 1
Critical Phases in Adaptation Process:
A Hypothetical Model

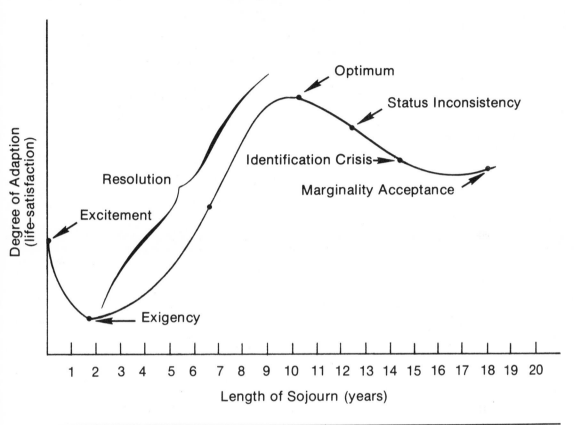

however, that is beyond the scope of the present research.[17]

Finally, the practical implications concern the possible application of our findings to the improvement of Korean immigrants' living conditions in particular, and the interethnic relations in the United States in general. The results of our study reveal that most of the Korean immigrants in the Chicago area seem to adjust themselves to American culture progressively, mainly due to their high levels of education and achievement motive. On the other hand, however, they are undergoing cognitive ambivalence, mainly due to their limited range of social (or structural) assimilation. As in the case of other immigrants, the Korean immigrants' adaptation to their host society is a dialectical process: the interplay between the structure of their host society and the subjective definition of the immigrants' situation in a temporal nexus.

The above notion implies that the immigrants' "comfort and plight" ambivalence may eventually lead to a severe identity crisis, which in turn would result in voluntary segregation when and if the majority members of American society maintain social distance from the immigrants. Under this condition, any governmental policies based on "Anglo-conformity" and "melting pot," or even "assimilation" would be meaningless, unless they are directed toward reducing or eliminating *social (structural) barriers* between the WASP and the immigrants, especially nonwhite immigrants.

NOTES

1. This is a condensed version of our final report, ''Cultural and Social Adjustment Patterns of Immigrants in the United States: A Case Study of Korean Residents in the Chicago Area,'' submitted to the Department of Health, Education, and Welfare, July 1976. This research was supported by a grant from the National Institute of Mental Health (#R03 MH 27004).

2. For details, see Warren K. Kim, *Koreans in America* (Seoul: Po Chin Chai, 1971), and Hyung-Chan Kim, ''Some Aspects of Social Demography of Korean Americans,'' *International Migration Review* 8 (1974), pp.23–42.

3. Number of Korean immigrants to the United States, 1964–74 from U.S. Department of Justice, Immigration, and Naturalization Service, *Annual Reports 1964–1974:*

1964 - 2,362	1968 - 3,811	1972 - 18,876
1965 - 2,165	1969 - 6,045	1973 - 22,930
1966 - 2,492	1970 - 9,314	1974 - 28,028
1967 - 2,956	1971 - 14,297	

4. The 1970 Census represents the first time that Koreans were enumerated as a separate ethnic group. Compare with U.S. Department of Health, Education, and Welfare. *A Study of Selected Socio-Economic Characteristics of Ethnic Minorities Based on the 1970 Census,* II, *Asian Americans,* p.132, and Hyung-Chan Kim, op. cit., p.36.

5. U.S. Department of Health, Education, and Welfare, op. cit., p.32.

6. ''Chicago Haninun 25,000 Myong?'' *The Hankook Ilbo Miju News,* 14 August 1975, p.1.

7. Compare with U.S. Department of Health, Education, and Welfare, op. cit., pp.25, 70, 105, 134.

8. Emory S. Bogardus, ''Comparing Racial Distance in Ethiopia, South Africa, and the United States,'' *Sociology and Social Research* 52 (1968), pp.149–56, and Hurh, Kim, and Kim, op. cit.

9. Although some Korean ethnic enclaves are emerging, such as ''the Second Seoul'' in Los Angeles and ''Korea Town'' in Chicago, they are still in the formative stage. Compare with Nancy Yoshihara, ''Koreans Find Riches, Faded Dreams in Los Angeles,'' *Los Angeles Times,* 1 February 1976, part IV; ''Bonnyong hanun jeiui Seoul,'' *The Joongang Daily News,* 6 February 1976; and ''Korean Influx,'' *Jade,* December 1975, pp.22–23.

10. Harry L. Kitano, *Japanese Americans: The Evolution of a Subculture* (Englewood Cliffs, New Jersey: Prentice-Hall, 1976); William Petersen, *Japanese Americans* (New York:

Random House, 1961). Very recently Kim and Condon conducted extensive research on Asian Americans in Chicago in terms of social service needs, but from social work and welfare perspectives: Bok-lim C. Kim and Margaret E. Condon, ''A Study of Asian Americans in Chicago: Their Socio-Economic Characteristics, Problems, and Service Needs,'' *Interim Report to the National Institute of Mental Health,* U.S. Department of Health, Education, and Welfare, 1975. Marn J. Cha's study on the Koreans in Los Angeles offers a valuable insight for reexamining Milton Gordon's assimilation typology; however, it suffers from an inadequate sample and the lack of intensive sociological analyses: ''Ethnic Political Orientation as Function of Assimilation With Reference to Koreans in Los Angeles,'' *Journal of Korean Affairs* 5 (1975), pp.14–25. Hyung-Chan Kim's study, op. cit., may be considered one of the most extensive studies on Korean immigrants but, again, is limited only to the demographic dimension.

11. Milton Gordon, *Assimilation in American Life* (New York: Oxford, 1964).

12. S. Alexander Weinstock, ''Role Elements: A Link Between Acculturation and Occupational Status,'' *British Journal of Sociology* 14 (1963), pp.144–49; Ronald J. Silvers, ''Structure and Values in the Explanation of Acculturation Rates,'' *British Journal of Sociology* 16 (March 1965), pp.68–79; and Erich Rosenthal, ''Acculturation Without Assimilation,'' *American Journal of Sociology* 66 (1960), pp.275–88.

13. Compare with Kitano, op. cit., Harry L. Kitano and Sue Stanley, ''The Model Minorities,'' *The Journal of Social Issues* 29 (1973), pp.1–9; Francis L. K. Hsu, *The Challenge of the American Dream: The Chinese in the United States* (Belmont, California: Wadsworth, 1971); and Lyman, op. cit.

14. For details, see Hurh, Kim, and Kim, op. cit.

15. For example, Gerhard Lenski, ''Status Crystalization: A Nonvertical Dimension of Social Status,'' *American Sociological Review* 19 (August 1954), pp.405–13; Donald J. Trieiman, ''Status Discrepency and Prejudice,'' *American Journal of Sociology* 71 (May 1966), pp.651–64; and Marvin E. Olsen and Judy C. Tully, ''Socioeconomic-Ethnic Status Inconsistency and Preference for Political Change,'' *American Sociological Review* 37 (October 1972), pp.560–74.

16. Compare with Won M. Hurh, ''Comparative Study of Korean Immigrants in the United States: A Typological Approach'' (San Francisco: R & E Research Associates, 1977).

17. Compare with Hurh, op. cit.

NEW ETHNICS: THE CASE OF THE
EAST INDIANS IN NEW YORK CITY

Parmatma Saran

INTRODUCTION

Some of the most moving documents in American history are those based upon immigrants' descriptions of their experiences after arriving in the United States. These documents were derived from an earlier wave of migration, primarily from Europe. However, migration is not only a historical process, no longer relevant to the United States. With recent changes in the immigration laws, and political and economic difficulties in many parts of the world, the flow of migrants to the United States and, in particular, to the New York metropolitan area, has reemerged as a major social process. To allow this process to go unnoticed is to disregard a major event in contemporary American society. Subsequent historians may disinter some of this information in the future, but it would seem to be incumbent upon us at this time to develop research projects which would focus our attention on migration as a continuing process and provide information about this phenomenon.

Another factor which has stimulated the development of our research interest is the lack of ethnographic and survey data available about recent immigrants. There is an established body of theoretical and substantive writing about "older" immigrant groups, such as Italians, Jews, and the Irish,[1] but there are few readily available discussions of the newer immigrants, especially East Indians. While some work has been done on Indian immigrants in Great Britain, the West Indies and Africa,[2] there is none so far in the United States. It is hoped that our research will add to this literature and provide additional insights into migration as a continuing process in American society.

Such a study has relevance not only for scholars but is equally important for policymakers in the host society. It would certainly be beneficial for the population studied, and would help them develop better perspectives for dealing with problems that confront them.

EMERGENCE OF A NEW COMMUNITY

New York City has always had a small population of Indians (graduate students at various universities, people working for the Indian consulate and other official agencies, Air India, the United Nations, and similar organizations). However, this population has been transitory. Now, for the first time, there is evidence suggesting that a permanent Indian residential community is developing in the city.

As indicated above, the small Indian population in the city was transitory, scattered, and did not constitute a community in the functional sense. Starting in 1969 or 1970, because of the change in the immigration laws (passage of Public Law 89–236, 1965), scores of Indians came with their families to live and earn a living in this country. A large number of these immigrants live in and around New York City. They generally live in certain localities which allows close contact and constant interaction, with the largest numbers concentrated in Queens. It is estimated that close to 30,000 Indians are living in the tristate area.

In the last two years, a clear trend has been evidenced among Indian immigrants. A good proportion of these immigrants are buying houses and moving to different areas generally within fifty miles of New York City. The largest portion of those who have moved have settled in New Jersey, Westchester, and Long Island. However, the majority of this population still remains in Queens.

The Literary Guild of India (a local cultural and literary organization) recently published *India Guide* which gives a good deal of information about Indians and their activities in Manhattan. According to this guide, there are close to fifty Indian artists such as painters, dancers, and musicians. An Indian art gallery, more than thirty insurance agents, some tax consultants, quite a few medical practitioners, two weekly newspapers, one monthly and one biweekly magazine, more than one hundred businessmen (a large number in the export-import business), twenty travel agents, twenty-five cultural and social centers, at least thirty-five grocery stores, ten radio programs, two television shows (begun in September, 1976), eight to ten movies shown during weekends, two temples, one Gurudwara (for Sikhs), and more than one hundred formal organizations. All these enterprises flourish because of the large Indian community—which is still growing.

Another important indication of the growing Indian community is a directory of Indian immigrants published in New York in 1975. Even though this directory includes Indians from all over the United States and Canada, it shows clearly that the heaviest concentration of Indians is in the New York metropolitan area. The directory also lists Indian stores and businesses, and generally gives the same figures as that of *India Guide*.

PURPOSE OF THE STUDY

The act of migration is one of the most significant changes which can take place during an individual's life experience. The decision to leave one's home environment and start a new life in a completely different sociocultural setting may be based upon a multitude of factors, but the very act of migrating must have a number of major consequences for those who actually move.

The purpose of the proposed research is to investigate the consequences of migration for those East Indians who have recently migrated to the New York area. Further, the purpose of this study can be viewed as an attempt to describe, analyze, and understand the pattern of adaptation of Indians living in the New York metropolitan area, and to determine emerging community patterns. More specifically, the focus is upon six important areas:

(1) What is the profile of Indian immigrants? In view of the fact that they easily fit into the occupational structure, how do they adapt themselves to a new cultural setting?[3]

(2) What are the patterns of social and psychobiological adaptation among Indian immigrants residing in the New York metropolitan area?

(3) What are the emerging patterns of leisure time activities for the community?

(4) Is the hypothesis that East Indians in New York tend to develop subcommunities based upon region, language, and caste correct?[4]

(5) What is the institutional mechanism and social network that helps this community to maintain a separate identity?[5]

(6) What is the function of formal organization and informal activities in the maintenance of boundaries and identities?

RESEARCH METHODS

In terms of techniques, the major emphasis in this study is on participant observation. However, some formal and informal interviews have also been conducted.

A pilot study (directed by me) is underway to obtain a background and behavioral profile of Indian immigrants living in the New York City area. Some data from this survey has been used for this paper.

During the last two years, I have met many Indians who came here as immigrants. Most of the new arrivals stay in a hotel called the Clinton Arms, situated on West End Avenue. I have had occasion to visit this place several times, and feel that this hotel acts as an entry point for many Indians coming to the city. Most of the men are married and have left family members behind, hoping to bring them here at the earliest opportunity. In this hotel, men live together in groups of three or four persons, like families, and have a common kitchen. Two of my relatives who stayed with me for a few days when they first arrived, discovered this place, then moved there. One of them said, "Clinton is the most comfortable and friendly place in the whole city." As soon as they get settled and have saved enough money to get their families here, they move to private quarters. A good number of these people are presently living in the Bronx (near the former New York University uptown campus) and in Queens

(Flushing, Rego Park). There are about twenty families living within a five-square block area in the Bronx—mostly coming from the same caste and region in India. There is also a more heterogeneous group of about sixty families living in one apartment building in Rego Park, Queens. We have used these three entry points (the Clinton Arms Hotel, the five-square block area in the Bronx, and the apartment house in Rego Park, Queens), and then spread out our contacts from these geographic foci.

Participant observation has been centered upon (1) formal organizations such as the Association of Indians in America; (2) special events (such as the India summer festival in Central Park), and (3) weekly film showings and Sunday religious services at the Hindu temple and the Sikh Gurudwara. In addition, I have also participated in a variety of activities, formal and informal, which bring together members of the community.

The ethnographic method has been used to obtain insights into some of the more significant areas related to adaptation and the survey method to obtain demographic and behavioral data. This feedback system between sociological and anthropological research methods is a major thrust of recent urban studies.[6]

PROFILE OF INDIAN IMMIGRANTS: OCCUPATIONAL STRUCTURE AND ASSIMILATION

The East Indians who came to the United States as immigrants, starting in 1968–69, tended to be between the ages of thirty and forty. Those who came as students, and then changed their status to permanent residents, were in most cases below thirty years of age. The majority of them came from middleclass backgrounds and lived in urban sectors. At least ninety percent had college degrees or professional diplomas. While wives tend not to have the same educational background, they do have some college education, in most cases.

It must be pointed out that, because of the immigration laws, Indians who come here are professionals or at least skilled people. The largest number of these immigrants are engineers and physicians; among other professionals are professors, accountants, and businessmen. In many cases, wives and adult children also work. Some Indians are in skilled or semiskilled jobs. By these occupational indices, the Indian community can be distinguished from many other ethnic groups in New York City. The average family income is above fifteen thousand dollars per annum.

The profile of Indian immigrants provides an interesting phenomenon in the context of their structural assimilation. Perhaps, because of their educational background, it was much easier for them to fit into the structural part of American society. For example, their earnings are high, they own property, live well and, gradually, through their organizational strength, are also trying to exert themselves politically.

However, their cultural assimilation is minimal. A look at the Indian community clearly suggests that there is a strong desire to maintain their cultural heritage. The notion of ethnicity remains strong and is also perceived as desirable.

Based upon preliminary investigation, we can put Indians into three categories with respect to their cultural assimilation into American society:

(1) those who claim to have become completely Americanized (a very small portion, though);
(2) those who carefully maintain their Indian heritage, and at the same time accept new values and consider themselves as part of the mainstream of American life (a reasonably large portion); and
(3) those who are highly conscious of their Indian heritage and want to keep it intact; they generally resist new values and live as marginals in this society (the largest portion).

Adaptation Patterns of Indian Immigrants

At this point we shall examine patterns of adaptation in the areas of family, religion, economics, education, and politics in light of data gathered primarily through participant observation (often supplemented with interviews and questionnaires).

Family. A large number of the Indians who migrated to the United States did not belong to joint families. Even those who belonged to a joint family in most cases lived independently in India. Therefore, coming to the United States and living in a nuclear family did not pose any serious problems for Indians. However, the lack of primary group relationship and community support did create a sense of alienation for them.

In order to examine patterns of adaptation of Indians in the context of the family, we would focus on (a) patterns of relationship between spouses and (b) patterns of relationship between children and parents.

In a traditional society like India, where family structure is essentially patriarchal, marriages are arranged and the husband is the bread winner; the supremacy of husbands generally prevailed. The wife remained contented with supervising household activities and maintaining close ties with the husband's family and relatives as well as her own relatives, and also found herself busy with neighbors and friends within the community. This, in most cases, contributed to a loving and stable relationship between husbands and wives.

After coming to the United States, both husbands and wives, especially wives, found themselves in a different environment. Many things which had kept wives busy and contented in India were simply not present in the new environment. This led to a search for jobs on the part of wives, most of whom found some sort of employment, for example, as salespersons, bookkeepers, or secretaries.

As a result of change in the status of wives, their roles also changed. They simply were not able to keep up with the household work and care for husbands as they had done in India.

Husbands on their part found their jobs were more taxing and demanding, coupled with long hours of commuting. At the same time, there was no community and social support for them. Their wives' economic independence also posed some concern and threat. These are some of the factors responsible for creating strains in the relationship patterns of husbands and wives. However, their early socialization, very strong commitment to marriage and the family, and greater tolerance have greatly helped them to deal with the new realities of life. Aside from some almost negligible exceptions,

we found that the relationships between husbands and wives remained amicable, and that there has been reasonable success in maintaining stability.

As we look into the patterns of relationships between children and parents, we find that it is not as smooth as those between spouses and often creates serious confrontations. This is more apparent in those families where children have attained the age of fourteen or fifteen.

Parents want to maintain the traditional authority structure in their families and often ignore the fact that the child's socialization is highly influenced by the enviornment outside the family. Children are generally more reasonable in that they recognize that their parents come from a different social and cultural background. However, they do not always understand why they should act as their parents want them to rather than as their peers do. In this case, peer group influence is more dominant than the family influence. Children also face a major identity crisis and find it very difficult to preserve their "Indianness." As a result, the relationship between parents and children deteriorates. Because of the excessive love and affection for their children, and perhaps better understanding on the part of mothers, and also the fact that in most of the families children are less than ten years of age, the situation remains under control. However, there are some incidents which have resulted in complete breakdown of relationships and remain explosive.

Religion. One of the questions raised in the study of Indian immigrants is what happens to Hinduism and religiosity of Hindus as they migrate to this country. There are many ways of looking at this phenomenon. We chose to focus on both formal and informal religious behavior of Hindu migrants.

There are at least five temples in the Queens, New York area. One of them, Hindu Temple, has a large membership and has been able to raise over one million dollars for the construction of a new temple.

Many social and cultural organizations are very particular about observing religious festivals and see it as good strategy to attract more people and increase their membership. There is a committee based in New York which draws more than 10,000 people to celebrate Durga-puja (the festival of the goddess Durga). The Sikh Gurudwara also draws large numbers of people during their annual feast.

Also, on the individual level, Indians remain religious. Their religiosity has not declined in any way because of Western influences. On the contrary, I find that there are more religious activities in many families than in India. In certain communities, organizing private services at homes by inviting a priest and friends to participate is more frequent than in India. Priests are at a premium. Recently I had an occasion to invite a priest to perform a wedding for a friend's daughter. It was not easy. Two priests were out of town and others had previous engagements. Only after frantic efforts was I able to locate one for the wedding.

It seems that religion and religious activity are perceived as very important aspects of life for Indian immigrants, and it is likely they will grow even stronger.

Economics. We have already seen that the majority of Indians are professionals, or at least skilled. Consequently, they have been able to find reasonably good jobs in their respective professions and have good incomes.

In terms of their economic behavior, they retain their traditional values and greatly emphasize saving. Patterns of leisure activities center around family and friends; the standard of living is good but comparatively low when gauged against the American counterparts. They are also property-oriented, which has resulted in the purchase of property (houses, land, and stores). It is very clear that, economically, the Indian immigrants are rather successful. However, because of their value system, in many ways they are in an advantageous position which places them in a unique economic status. This population, in terms of economic behavior and its economic strength, is comparable to Jewish immigrants.

Education. In the sphere of education, Indians find themselves in an advantageous position. Although the majority of them come with college degrees or professional qualifications, as soon as they settle down they go to American schools to enhance their qualifications. Because there is no language problem, they do not face any serious handicap in the educational system here. They do face some difficulties though, because of their British educational background and their cultural values which are quite distinct from those of the American system. One gentleman told me that at the end of a semester his teacher called him into his office and said, "You know, I am very pleased you got an 'A' for the course. I was a little concerned about you since you did not say much in the class." Another friend said that after his comprehensive examination he was informed by his committee that his performance was exceptionally good.

Children of these immigrants are also doing well in schools. Some of them have received Regents' awards and various other scholarships. However, in some quarters there is some doubt about their continued success because of the influence of external factors. As they assimilate in the new society, they become more independent and act more in terms of their own values rather than the family tradition which is very strong in India. However, there is not yet sufficient data to give a clear picture at this time.

Politics. Considering the total Indian population in the United States, the number of Indian organizations is overwhelming. In the New York area, there are more than one hundred organizations. The majority are regional organizations, but a few represent the larger community in that they are based neither on language, region, nor religion. All of them claim to be nonpolitical. However, a close look at these organizations indicates that there is clear recognition on the part of the leadership that these organizations are vital in order to have some political influence in this country.

The Association of Indians in America, which is considered to be broad based and professionally oriented, was recently successful in obtaining a reclassification of Indians as "Asian Indians" for the 1980 Census. Presently, Indians are classified as "Caucasians." The implication of this reclassification is that Indians will be eligible for "minority status" and also qualify for equal opportunity employment.

While many Indians privately concede that they

would feel somewhat uncomfortable with the new "minority status," they also agree that the practical advantages outweigh this disadvantage. It is clear, then, that Indians are quite aware of the politics within a pluralistic society, are quite eager to exert strength as a pressure group and, increasingly, they are proving it by their deeds. However, it should be noted that only about ten to fifteen percent of the Indian immigrants have become American citizens. In many informal interviews, respondents have revealed that they are faced with the dilemma of changing citizenship. However, since barely fifty percent of them qualify to become citizens, it would be premature to make any judgment on this issue at this time.

Psychobiological Adaptation

Now we shall direct our attention to the psychobiological adaptation of Indian immigrants, and focus our discussion on the areas of mental health, health-related issues, child-rearing practices, and food habits.

Mental Health. Various studies have shown that there is some relationship between migration and mental disorder. H.B.M. Murphy[7] suggests that, with all the variables controlled, we find that the phenomenon of migration itself is not a primary causative determinant.

Compared to the previous immigrant groups studies,[8] such as Norwegians in Minnesota, Puerto Ricans in New York, West Indians in the United Kingdom, and various European groups, the case of the East Indians is very different because of their distinct sociocultural background, coupled with their educational and economic status.

In an earlier study,[9] the question of whether Indians felt more tense and irritable since coming to the United States was used to gain information on psychosomatic illnesses. It was felt that change in environment might lead to a greater number of these diseases. However, only a small percentage of the sample reported such illnesses.

It is clear that Indians too have felt the strain of a highly competitive and impersonal way of life, even though they have close contacts within the Indian community. There are a few cases of divorce, mental illness, suicide, and similar pathologies.

In the present study, almost ninety percent of the respondents said that they feel more mental tension in the United States than in India. However, none indicated that they had ever consulted a psychiatrist.

As we have noted earlier, even though the Indian community is recent and small, it is very well-organized and has developed organizations, institutional mechanisms, and a social network which provides tremendous social support and helps its members meet the crises that they confront in a new cultural setting.

Yet, it should be pointed out that, while the level of tolerance is also very high, the Indian community attaches a strong stigma to those who have psychological problems. As a result of this, the incidence of psychological problems reported by Indians is very small or nonexistent.

The time factor involved is short and it does not provide substantial data at this stage to suggest any future trends.

Health-Related Issues. A study was conducted[10] to see the change of ecology and social environment and its effect on a small population of Indian students and physicians working in the New York City area. One of the most significant findings from an ecological point of view was an increase in the number of episodes of upper respiratory tract diseases associated with urban as well as congested neighborhoods.

In terms of change in social environment, it was found that eighty percent sought help from non-professional sources. Sixty-four percent indicated that they visited American physicians in case they needed professional help. There was also an increase in this sample of usage of various patent drugs. In response to a question concerning whether or not it was "worthwhile to pray for someone who was ill," there were no favorable responses. However, the respondents seemed to agree that illness could be a punishment for bad deeds.

In the study presently underway, we find that a large number of Indian immigrants are satisfied with the medical care they receive in the United States. However, they are divided as far as preference for a doctor is concerned. About fifty percent feel that they have cultural and communication problems with American doctors. Almost eighty percent indicated that they would consult an Indian medical friend before seeking professional help in case of illness. An overwhelming majority (almost ninety percent) of the respondents indicated that they are more health conscious here than they were in India. They also go for periodic medical check-ups.

Child-Rearing Practices. As we look at the profile of Indian immigrants, we find that there is some variation in terms of their patterns of adaptation and assimilation into American society.

Observation of Indian families reveals that, to a great extent, parents translate their own values in raising their children. The most prevalent assumption among Indian immigrants is that the first six or seven years of a human being's life are the most important in the making of the personality. Therefore, if the child-rearing practices center around traditional Indian values, the child is more likely to identify with those elements and maintain his Indian identity. However, we find that while early experience does have a great impact on the child presonality and self-image, environmental factors outside the family have an equally important influence.

We have already indicated that children are often faced with this dilemma and sometimes reject those values which are transmitted by their parents. We believe that this area warrants closer observation to test certain hypotheses in the area of child-rearing practices of Indian immigrants. One thing is clear though: it is not easy for the parents to find a middle ground which is satisfactory to them and acceptable or desirable from the point of view of their children.

Food Habits. Like their American counterparts, Indians also eat three meals a day. However, they do not eat as much for breakfast and lunch, but generally eat an elaborate, large dinner. A good number of the immigrants still have their evening tea with snacks, and therefore eat dinner usually after 8 p.m.

The majority of these Indians are nonvegetarians but some, especially among the women, do not eat beef. Even those who are not vegetarians do not eat large portions of meat, and in some cases do not eat meat on a daily basis. For the most part, they eat little for breakfast (for example, juice, toast, eggs, and tea or coffee), and lunch is generally eaten out, usually consisting of a sandwich, a hamburger, or a pizza. Dinner is the most important meal and includes rice, bread, vegetables, meat, and salad. There is some variation due to regional backgrounds, but the main difference is that those who are vegetarians have additional items such as some yogurt preparation, lentils, etc. Tea remains the most popular beverage, but some prefer coffee. Most of the Indians drink alcohol socially, but their consumption of alcoholic beverages, even on social occasions, is very small. A friend told me that at his Indian parties consumption of alcohol is less than half of what it is at parties to which he invites mainly American friends. Indians however eat more for dinner and like many varieties of foods. If someone cooks only four items for a party it is considered "cheap." Generally, eight to ten items are prepared for parties.

Recently, a friend visiting from India remarked, "Indians have adapted well here. They've learned many American attitudes, but in one area, the area of food habits, they have not changed. They still do a lot of cooking at home, especially for parties, and they keep their tradition."

On the whole, the food habits of Indian immigrants have not changed much. Those who have come since 1969 have not found any difficulty in buying Indian groceries or spices, and they have therefore maintained their eating patterns. Children, however, are more exposed to American food and often prefer it.

Emerging Patterns of Leisure Time Activities

Patterns of leisure-time activities for the Indian community centers around friends and family. The pattern of visiting friends on weekends, without prior engagement, was common during the earlier phase of immigration (1969–72). In January, 1972, I visited a family one Sunday afternoon (as the result of a last-minute telephone conversation), and was told that I was the sixth or seventh visitor and hopefully not the last. My host was right. Later in the

evening there were more visitors, and it was proposed by the host that "all stay for dinner." They
did not have enough cooking pots (this family was a
new arrival and had just moved to the apartment), so
others brought some from their homes (all lived
within a six-to-eight block area), and at about 10
p.m. there was a "bhoj" (community eating).

However, this phenomenon is no longer very
common. People now generally make plans for the
weekend and invite friends specifically for dinner or
lunch. Meeting friends along with family for dinner
or lunch remains the most important leisure activity.

Shopping on weekends also takes a good portion
of leisure time. Even if they do not have much necessary shopping to do, wives often look for bar-
gains.

In recent times, going to Indian movies on weekends is perhaps the most popular thing to do. Many
Indian singers, dancers, and comedians are frequently visiting cities in the United States, and this
seems to be catching the fancy of the Indian immigrants.

Eating out and going to Broadway plays or to
concerts is prevalent only among a very small proportion of the Indian immigrants.

Participation in the activities of various organizations seems to be growing and is prevalent among
most Indians irrespective of level of assimilation in
American society.

The Role of Subethnic Factors

It is interesting to note that religious, regional,
linguistic, and caste factors still play an important
role in the lives of the Indians living here. There are
subcommunities along these lines. An illustration of
this, based upon an informal interview, is shown by
the comments of an insurance agent:

> When I started as an agent back in 1969 my Indian
> identity did help me to do business among Indians.
> Later I found out that as the Indian community grew it
> was not enough to be an Indian, business was done
> now on a regional basis, then I discovered that coming
> from the same region did not matter much, that the
> caste factor became more important.

As the community grew in size and complexity, Indians were associating more and more with people
of their own region, caste, and language, as my insurance friend observed. Thus, the larger social
network, also to a great extent, evolves along these
lines.

The emergence of regional associations strongly
suggests that the regional associations serve the
purpose of maintaining a separate Indian identity,
plus providing a setting for meeting people coming
from the same region who also speak the same language.

Recently, one friend invited me for dinner, but
since he comes from another part of India than we
do he cautioned us, "You see, all our friends who
are coming are from our part of the country. Hope
you won't mind it." I naturally had no reservations
about it and gladly accepted the invitation. However, some of the invitees at my friend's place did
not feel very comfortable since I did not speak their
language.

On another occasion, some people started talking
to me in their regional language, taking it for
granted that I too must be from the same region as
they.

Some of my friends, who come from the same
part of India as I do, have politely indicated that they
did not enjoy my party because there were many
people from another part of the country who did not
speak the same language.

Social Network and Identity Maintenance

Studies of ethnic groups in most cases clearly involve the study of networks. The emergence of a
large number of organizations, grocery stores, restaurants, movie showings, centers of cultural activities, temples, and similar activities, and its relationship and meaning to the Indian community
provide an interesting example of how these networks operate and serve as a means of identity
maintenance.

Members of a given organization very often become personal friends and develop social contacts
with one another. As a result, they establish a pattern of relationships with one another and develop a
network system. Upon examination of many activities, both formal and informal, within the Indian
community, we find that there exists a social network. Not all members would be necessarily part of

a network but most of them are. Especially we find that, in regional associations, networks are stronger and more prevalent.

These networks also develop informally. The owner of a grocery store or a travel agent or an insurance agent has direct contact with many members of the community, and often serves as a link between those who themselves lack direct contact, and hence can support and maintain their identities through such networks.

Maintenance of Boundaries and Identities

Beyond the problem of finding jobs and settling down, members of any immigrant group face a psychological crisis as a consequence of migrating, and that is the identity crisis.

On the surface, it appears that various organizations within the Indian community have come into being for the purpose of organizing social, cultural, and religious functions. In fact, this is quite true. However, it goes beyond this and results in the maintenance of boundaries and identities.

As we have indicated earlier, there is a large number of organizations within the Indian community. When members of these organizations meet formally they are, of course, very conscious of their heritage and have a sense of pride in being part of these groups, which perhaps gives them great psychological satisfaction. Even when they meet informally, very often conversations center around these organizations.

Recently, a new regional organization was formed. Members of this group had had some contact with each other even before this organization, but now this community is much closer. Interestingly enough, some wives remarked at a private party that "now the men only talk about this association and its activities." It is quite apparent that the organization has become very important in the lives of its members.

Some young people attending college, whose parents emigrated much earlier, observed that, "We always identified with blacks and Spanish groups; that was our identity. We never participated in any Indian activities at all." These young people are very correct; there were none when they were growing up. As a result, they do not necessarily identify with Indians.

THE NEW IMMIGRATION: IMPLICATIONS FOR AMERICAN SOCIETY

This exploratory study of Indian immigrants in New York City suggests many hypotheses to be tested and to establish a body of theoretical and substantive data on the new immigration.

An examination of the Indian community in New York City gives many insights and provides a new direction in the study of ethnics, their patterns of adaptation, and processes of assimilation. Unlike older immigrant groups, we find that structural assimilation for Indians is relatively smooth. Their behavior patterns and attitudes also suggest a strong sense of ethnicity and its desirability, and a growing support for cultural pluralism. A comparative study of the new immigrants—that is, East Indians, West Indians, Pakistanis, Philippinos, Vietnamese—is warranted to help scholars and administrators understand the implications of the new immigration and provide guidelines for policy making.

NOTES

1. See Oscar Handlin, *The Uprooted* (Boston: Little, Brown, and Co., 1973), and Nathan Glazer and Daniel Patrick Moynihan, *Beyond the Melting Pot* (Cambridge, Mass.: The M.I.T. Press, 1963).

2. W. Elkan, *Migrants and Proletarians* (New York: Oxford University Press, 1960); M. Kuper, *Indian People in Natal;* H. S. Morris, "Indians in East Africa," *British Journal of Sociology* VII, No.3 (1956), pp.194–211; Morton Klass, *East Indians in Trinidad: A Study of Cultural Persistence* (New York: Columbia University Press, 1961); R. Desai, *Immigrants in Britain* (New York: Oxford University Press, 1963); G. S. Aurora, *The New Frontiersmen: Indians in Great Britain* (Bombay: Popular Prakashan Press, 1967); and A. K. Singh, *Indian Students in Britain: A Study of Their Adjustment and Attitudes* (New York: Asia Publishing House, 1963).

3. Milton Gordon, *Assimilation in American Life* (New York: Oxford University Press, 1964).

4. E. J. B. Rose et al., *Color and Citizenship* (London: Oxford University Press, 1969).

5. Elizabeth Bott, *Family and Social Network* (New York: Free Press, 1974).

6. See Edwin Eames and J. Goode, *Man on the Urban Scene* (Englewood Cliffs, N.J.: Prentice-Hall, forthcoming).

7. H. B. M. Murphy, "Migration and the Major Mental Disorders: A Reprisal," in M. B. Cantor, ed., *Mobility and Mental Health* (Springfield, Illinois: Charles C. Thomas, 1965), pp.5–29.

8. O. Odegaard, "Emigration and Insanity," *Acta Psychiatrica Neurologica,* Supplement 4 (1932).

9. Parmatma Saran and A. V. N. Sarma, "Ecological and Sociological Influences on Patterns of Illness and Treatment," *Indian Journal of Social Research* XI, No. 1 (1970), pp. 31–41.

PATTERNS OF FRIENDSHIP AMONG
SOUTH ASIAN WOMEN

Lorna Rhodes AmaraSingham

This paper is about alternative ways in which women from South Asia form friendships in the United States. It is proposed that there is a discontinuity between the values which are associated with friendship in India and the perception which immigrant women have of the potential for friendship in the United States. George Coelho has outlined the following values for friendship in India: (1) interdependence—friends are seen to have mutually dependent interests; (2) nonnegotiated reciprocity—friends do not have to be concerned about time in expecting favors of each other; and (3) permanence—relationships are not believed to change over time.[1]

The friendships discussed in this paper are all among women and occur in the context of the home and family. Two questions are raised: What aspect of the circumstances of Indian women immigrants influence friendship formation? What are the implications of different kinds of friendship for perception of self?

This study is based on research among immigrant women from India and Sri Lanka in the Boston and New York areas. In the course of interviews with these women, it was discovered that the topic of friendship was of major importance to them. Two of these women have been chosen to illustrate two different styles of friendship which are called here "boundary emphasizing" and "outward reaching." These two ways of approaching friendship are indicative of the way in which women who are restricted to the home and family use the mundane experience of daily life to express a translation of the ideal of friendship into actual experience.

I shall call the first woman "Mrs. A." She describes herself in the first months here as "very homesick," and much of this homesickness consisted of the contrast between her isolation here and her recollection of her friends in India. Her college friends formed a close group of about twelve girls,

with various subgroups of closer friends within it. They got together everyday, meeting at a favorite outdoor spot or visiting each other. She says of their "informality": "It's nice to know that you can just go and knock on the door and be comfortable they won't mistake [misunderstand] you." Mrs. A recognizes a connection between these friendships and the restrictive life she led in India. In the context of these relationships it was possible for friends to keep each other's secrets, talk about boyfriends (especially when parents disapproved), and help to set up trysts or carry letters. She stresses the mutual dependence of these relationships—in one case, all the friends contributed to help one who was in financial difficulty. She says that "we used to help each other in every way."

At times this group of college friends regarded their association as a refuge from the restrictive demands of their families. But the form of the relationships within the group was nevertheless modeled on the expectations pertaining among family members. The friends were incorporated into each other's families, visiting, staying overnight, and helping each other. They expected a kind of openness of each other that paralleled the openness within the family. For instance, in the family they were expected to be always ready for callers, always prepared to be cheerfully hospitable with visiting relatives. "Every other day someone would come and just ring the bell, and sometimes you might be in the middle of a family argument, or somebody might be sick or something, but most women put up a happy face." This expectation was extended to friends. Mrs. A particularly remembers an incident from her visit to India. On her first night back, her family and friends all gathered at one house, and there were so many of them that they all slept together on the floor in one room, talking and laughing all night.

For Mrs. A, the image of the friends and family

together all night stands for the closeness and permanence of these relationships. Like her, many of
my informants use "family" as a metaphor for what
should happen between friends. They say, for instance:

"Friends are like an extension of your family."

"*Relatives* do not break up, why should
friends?"

"Friends are more like family than family."

By this they mean, I think, what Coelho means in
his description of the values inherent in friendship.
The kinds of things that cause dissension or es-
trangement among relatives are not important to this
metaphor; rather, the element of permanence, the
lack of bargaining, and the assumption of mutuality
of interest are the aspects of kinship which are
perceived to be salient to friendship also. This
equivalence not only upgrades friendship to that of
"almost kin," but it also provides a guideline for
expectations within the relationship.

For Mrs. A, these relationships are mostly in the
past, and talking about them provokes a kind of
nostalgia. Yet, because they are permanent, they
have not disappeared from her life. Several of these
old friends from college now live in the United
States, and she sometimes has a chance to visit them
or have them visit her. At these times, she says, "I
can be so free, I don't have to worry about anything.
I can talk without having a second thought." During
their visits the two women sleep together in one
room, and the husbands in another, so that they can
talk all night. Mrs. A feels she can take over any of
the cooking or housework or childcare for one of
these friends; as in India, "I wouldn't mind doing
anything for them," and this included lending them
money or putting them up for an extended visit. She
feels that these relationships will always be the
same. In this context of talking about "old" and
"family" friends, all of my informants had great
difficulty in thinking of anything that would cause
them to "lose" this kind of friend. As one said,
"Friendship and love do not change."

The freedom which is felt with these friends involves a perceived similarity of style which precludes misunderstandings over such daily events as
childcare and cooking. Mrs. A and the other
women I talked with speak of being able to "just
be" with their old friends and family. In such

phrases as "you know what to expect," "you don't
have to say anything to them," "you can just sit,"
they seem to be indicating an acceptance which is
not based on any deliberate attempt to create an
interesting social persona. They expect to be always
prepared for this kind of friend. There is no boundary around their "private" lives which could be
intruded on by either a family member or friend. For
example, I asked all the women whether they were
not afraid that they would "drop in" on a friend
who was in the middle of an argument with her
husband, or a nap. Sometimes they were simply
puzzled by this question; the ones who understood it
said that they would not regard the visitor as an
intruder, but would expect to "cheer up" or wake
up in response. This kind of companionship is felt to
be effortless.

While Mrs. A experiences these relationships
based on permanence and merged interests largely
as remnants of her past, the second woman, called
Mrs. R, is involved in an effort to construct such
relationships in her new environment. When she
arrived, she was immediately drawn into the life of a
small enclave of immigrants in the city. She and her
husband were taken care of at first by a family they
already knew from home. This family taught them
how to get along in the new environment—how to
go shopping, look for an apartment, buy a car, and
so on.

Their initial dependence on this family was rapidly expanded to a circle of immigrants from the
same area who form a community. This community
of, at times, fifty people provides a facsimile of
home for Mrs. R and is her only source of friends.
Most of her information about American life comes
from these people. As she was invited to parties and
met people through her original friends, this group
of immigrants soon resolved itself into six or seven
couples who are "good friends," and three who are
"very good friends." Mrs. R describes good
friends as those who can be visited "whenever we
feel lonely" but who must be called slightly ahead;
they are also the people with whom parties are
arranged. She exchanges recipes with these women,
gossips about home, and maintains, through them,
wider networks of acquaintances who provide information about home. The "very good" friends
are those with whom a more complete reciprocity is

maintained. One important kind of exchange within these friendships is babysitting—they can leave their children at each other's house in order to go shopping or to a movie. They can borrow from each other, including money. Transportation is often shared. These reciprocal gestures do not require negotiation over "paying back." Close friends can talk about their problems with husband or children, usually without fear of gossip. They do not need to call ahead, but can "just go" whenever they feel like visiting. When I asked Mrs. R whether she was ever worried about "dropping in" on someone who was tired or busy, she simply said, "No, at any moment it's OK." Another woman who had a similar community of friends says that "we formed a close community, anyone could just walk into the other person's house. If it hadn't been for that, I think I really would have wanted to go back."

Mrs. R and other women in her situation perceive the major danger to these relationships to be gossip. Mrs. R considers "talking behind someone's back" as the one thing likely to make her lose a friend; this is far more important to her than such breaches of reciprocity as borrowing money and not paying it back, or failing to provide equal babysitting time. Friends will "split up" and stop talking to each other if one discovers something that has been said about her by the other. For this to happen, of course, implies a closed community in which all the friends are known to each other and gossip travels a closed circle. This, says Mrs. R, is "just like home." Because of the assumed permanence of these relationships, moving away is a lesser danger; Mrs. R frequently calls a friend who has moved "just to chat," but she expressed some concern about the distance.

Mrs. R does not have any American friends. She describes her neighbors as "friendly," but says that "we don't go to their place; we only talk to them outside [in passing]." Her husband's colleagues are also "friendly" at the annual party, but she does not know them and never socializes with them. She says about all Americans that "you just can't talk to them." In this she contrasts herself with one of her own "good friends" who lives nearby in very similar circumstances but who has become friendly with her American neighbors. They are "very good friends, they invite each other, and go out for shows together." Although talking about this relationship causes Mrs. R to say that "there are some people [Americans] who are very nice," she reiterates her own feeling of not knowing what to say to Americans.

When Mrs. R and her friends talk about life in this country, they emphasize several kinds of dangers which justify, they feel, their decision to remain as aloof as possible. Of primary importance to them are the bad influences which they feel surround their children here, and which, as the children get older, they feel more and more powerless to keep at bay. Disrespect is mentioned most often; two of Mrs. R's friends, noting that American children do not address adults as "aunt and uncle," say that "they have no respect." Mrs. R mentions the American children she sees who are out late at night, and she expresses a great deal of apprehension about drug taking and drinking. She fears her children will "turn against her" or "forget her" as they get older. Like most of the women in this community, she is reluctant to leave her children with hired babysitters; as one woman said: "If you leave them, how will they know who their parents are?" Mrs. R says that her husband frequently laments that Americans seem to have "no family life." He believes that most Americans are heavily in debt as a result of buying on credit.

Another frequent theme for Mrs. R is the danger of violence which she feels surrounds her at all times. She does not go out alone, use the subway, or walk alone even from her building to a nearby car. She does not distinguish clearly between the news and the other programs on television, and accepts the level of violence she sees as directly representative of the streets outside her own home. Her husband emphasizes the dangers and is insistent that she does not make herself vulnerable in any way.

Although Mrs. R does not particularly dwell on it, other women like her mention the threats to stable marriage which they perceive in the new environment. They say that people here [Americans or "Americanized" Indians] "change all the time" and do not take any responsibility toward their families. They fear that their husbands are exposed to temptation at work and they feel that, in a world where the maintenance of family ties does not have the same importance which it has for them, they must make an extra effort to protect their families from the intrusion of outsiders.

The network of friends—the "closed circle" within which Mrs. R lives—superficially resembles the network of family and "family friends" she had at home. Yet this resemblance rests, in fact, on an exaggeration of certain aspects of her previous life. For one thing, in order to create such a network, some of the selectivity which would operate in the choice of friends at home must be compromised—some members of her inner circle are people she would not have become friendly with in her own country (for reasons of community, education, and class). She says that if they all went back tomorrow, they would probably remain friends; this is an example, I think, of the strength which the idea of permanence has even when the context for it has changed.

There are other ways in which this network involves a kind of exaggeration. Another woman in similar circumstances says, "We become *more* friendly here." Loneliness produces more visiting and more dependence among a smaller and less homogeneous group of people. There is considerably more exchange of meals, and gossip has an intensity not present in the larger circles of home. The exchanges of babysitting, and the constant need to take the children everywhere involve a more explicit merging of family and friendship than occurs at home, where children can be left with servants. The emphasis on danger and intrusion from the outside increases the importance of "known" people, and frequent contact and mutual reciprocity intensify their dependence on each other.

I think it would be a misapprehension of this kind of boundary emphasizing to consider it simply a passive resistance to change; instead, the value of sameness—the protection of the stability of social life which is perceived to be threatened by change—is defended by actually perpetuating as much as possible the qualities which permanent relationships are felt to have. Mrs. R tightens the inner circle of friends and family by drawing a sharp boundary around it and preventing, as much as possible, the intrusion of the outside world.

Like Mrs. R, Mrs. A was also initially a guest in the home of a known person, a cousin in her case. But unlike Mrs. R, who is not prepared to perceive change in her friends here, Mrs. A noticed from the beginning that "Indians change after coming here." Through her cousin, she and her husband were introduced to other Indians and, like Mrs. R, they went to parties and small get-togethers where they met people from their area at home. But she lived further from the center of an already established network, and her dependence on other Indians was from the beginning somewhat different in her own perception from the situation she had left behind. Two or three of the people she met have become "very close" to her. This closeness is indicated more clearly by her freedom in feeling that she can call them up and say, "Oh, I'm bored, why don't you come over and we'll talk." But although she feels free to just sit with these friends, some of the rules have changed. She finds the Indians "more formal" about reciprocity, and she does not involve herself in intense exchanges of babysitting or other favors. She feels that they have changed in the direction of "more independence," and that she cannot expect the same stability of relationship from them. Only with her family and old friends from India can the "merging" kind of relationship be perpetuated. She does not feel that her new friendships with Indians depend on a shutting out of outside influences.

In summary, then, one of the two women presented as a case study is a housewife, in this country for five years, who lives in an urban enclave with other immigrants of similar background. She has formed friendships only within this group and does not have American friends. Within her group of friends there is an emphasis on sharing, dependency, and permanence of relationships. Danger from outside forces is stressed. The greatest danger to friendship is perceived to be gossip. The metaphor, "friends are like family," is used to underscore the aspects of friendship which are felt to provide the greatest protection to traditional values.

The other woman had friendships in India which followed Coelho's model of friendship values, and which are still valued by her as "true friendship." However, she now lives in a suburb outside a U.S. city and has begun to "reach out" to make friends outside the circle of immigrants. This reaching out process involves a reassessment of the qualities which are demanded of friends. She has ceased to expect complete reciprocity or similarity of concerns from her friends, and has begun to make changes in her behavior to increase her participation in the life of American friends. Part of this process was aided by an initial American friend who acted as a "local guide." She now perceives "change," both in circumstances and in self-perception, to be potentially undermining to the permanence of friendship. "Reaching out" has also begun to involve changes in her perception of herself, and an increasing tendency to contrast "submissive" with "independent" behavior both within and outside the family.

Thus, there seem to be three ways of approaching friendship formations, which constitute dimensions among which immigrant women move as they make choices about their lives in the United States. The first alternative is intense, mutually dependent relationships with co-migrants, which are assumed to be permanent. These involve an exaggeration of the values placed on friendship in India. The second option involves a further alternative of redefinition which allows more people to be "friends." There is greater flexibility in choice and less expectation of mutuality; more categories for friendship are created. Finally, there is the possibility of a change toward separation from family and a redefinition of what friendship itself is—it becomes less dependent and less merged with kinship.

The differences betwen the two women are felt to be partly a result of their different living circumstances. The urban woman is closer to her co-migrants and more aware of danger and intrusiveness from the environment, while the suburban woman has more opportunity to meet Americans and more occasions for independent action. Further, the two women differ in their orientation toward returning to the home country. The first woman has not committed herself to staying in the United States, while the second women, by, for example, buying a house, has indicated a greater investment in a future in this country.

I have tried to show that choices about friendship have certain consequences for the world views of the women who make them. If they try to reduce the discontinuity between India and America by creating a community modeled on the one they left, they must exaggerate certain features to maintain its integrity. If they develop new definitions for relationships in order to include new experience, they must work out ways of reconciling their primary values with the new categories. And if, as seems possible within the third alternative, they dwell on the discontinuity and begin to perceive themselves faced with either/or choices, they must work out some kind of compromise which will allow them to maintain their former relationships.

NOTE

1. George W. Coelho, "Changing Patterns of Friendship in Modern India," in *Studies of Friendship*, Cora DuBois ed. (unpublished manuscript, Harvard University, 1955).

Part 7

Adjustment Implications for the Immigrants Themselves II: Conflict

IDENTITY PROBLEMS IN MIGRANT MINORITIES: A PSYCHOCULTURAL COMPARATIVE APPROACH APPLIED TO KOREAN JAPANESE

George A. DeVos

A salient feature of the American ideology is its emphasis on democratic participation and equal access to political and economic power. The "American dilemma" in Myrdal's words is an inconsistency or a "cognitive dissonance," caused by a strongly shared belief in equality conflicting with the stubbornly held belief in racial segregation.[1]

We note a shift from the belief in the melting pot toward one which views American society as ethnically pluralistic. This is an attempt to resolve dissonance. If racial minorities can be viewed simply as "ethnic minorities," then the dilemma between racial visibility and political equality is partially resolved. A self-consciously evolved ethnic identity on the part of all the racial minorities allows them to take a more equal position among other "ethnic groups" of more recent arrival. Their political struggle against the majority can then be viewed at least as "equal" competition within an ethnically plural society.

I have discussed elsewhere my contention that, in fact, the African-American minority, as well as the Mexican-American, have reactively adopted an attitude of "ethnic distinctiveness" about themselves with a strong intention to remain a separate part of the pluralistic American society.[2] For a number of economic as well as political reasons, Jews and Italians in New York are reasserting symbols of separate ethnic cohesiveness. Even the majority of Americans are seemingly no longer opposed to an ideal of nonassimilation.

This trend in the United States suggests that social science theory with regard to assimilation needs serious reexamination, not only in the case of American society but with regard to what happens to migrants elsewhere. Are the processes which are occurring similar or different? The essential issue is how and under what conditions ethnic identity is maintained against pressures toward assimilation in migrating individuals or groups.

For the past two years I have been studying, with Korean colleagues, the plight of the Korean minority in Japan. The purpose of this research is not simply to describe the difficult social and psychological situation of Japanese Koreans. Ultimately, it is a study done in a psychocultural comparative perspective using our knowledge of immigrant conditions in Japan, compared with societies in Europe and the United States, to arrive at more definitive conclusions about the social and psychological forces involved.

Research at the subjective, experiential level, which includes Germani's "normative" level[3] as well as the "psycho-social" level, is obviously of donor community attitudes on relative individual readiness to migrate, given contexts of economic, social, and political inducements toward migration. Moreover, the cultural factors embedded in community attitudes not only differentially influence the social attitudes of those migrating, but also the social attitudes of members of the host society. The social adaptation of migrants is a mutual process taking place between members of donor and host cultures which varies specifically in the forms of conflict, accommodation, or assimilation that result.

In our ongoing study, besides eliciting attitudes in direct interview material, we find that the TAT (Thematic Apperception Test) and the CPI (California Psychological Inventory) elicit social attitudes which, we hope to demonstrate, are not directly related to the conscious attitudes of Koreans about their minority status in Japan. Moreover, our results will be concerned not only with the migrants themselves but with their progeny. The psychological effects of migration are most apparent in subsequent generations. Indeed, it is our contention that, from a psychological standpoint, the migrants themselves are already immunized from certain forms of psychological problems by the ability to maintain a stable personality structure after attaining adulthood. It is the children of migrants who are most susceptible to the effects of migration as far as consequent personality difficulties are concerned. The study of migration psychoculturally, therefore, becomes more than the study of the adaptive capacity of the migrants themselves. It becomes a longitudinal study of various processes of acculturation and assimilation that involve more than a single generation.

In this paper I take a look at the maintenance of a Korean identity as part of the very large picture of the psychocultural problems which ensued in postcolonial situations within Japan. A situation in which Japanese, on the one hand, assimilate Koreans, but on the other hand so discriminate against anyone of Korean origin that the individual must capitulate psychologically when it is possible for him in some circumstances to attain Japanese citizenship. Implicitly throughout the following analysis, there is a comparative concern with the similarities and differences in the social forces at work contrasting and comparing the American and the Japanese situation.

PSYCHOCULTURAL DETERMINANTS OF ETHNIC MAINTENANCE AMONG JAPANESE KOREANS

The Korean situation in Japan graphically illustrates that the problem of assimilation, in this instance, is more Japanese than Korean.[4] Despite archaeological and linguistic findings that point to the common origin of the Japanese and the Korean people, more Japanese are still firmly convinced of their unique genesis. Up to the end of World War I, the sense of origin was embedded in a mythology that affirmed an autochthonous origin, and they thought they were the descendants of indigenous gods. In the postwar period there is still reluctance to examine evidence that suggests that the Japanese nobility at least were identical to, and the people close in language and culture with, at least part of the Korean peninsula.

The problem of Korean minority status in Japan, therefore, is still the problem of a deep-set conviction that Japanese ''are and should remain ethnically homogenous.'' Almost unique among modern industrial states, the Japanese pride themselves on this homogeneity and resist the idea of assimilating or accommodating any outsiders fully within their concept of citizenship. The Japanese concept of citizen, therefore, is almost identical to a concept of racial purity. This emphasis on uniqueness is apparent if we contrast the situation which exists in all other modern industrial states, with perhaps the exception to some degree of Germany.

Admittedly, none of the large pluralistic states of the present world have achieved a level of accommodation without continuing ongoing social problems. Supposedly, during the colonial occupation of Korea for over forty years, the Koreans were considered citizens of the Japanese empire. Theirs was, in act, a secondary nationality. In the postwar situation, those Koreans remaining in Japan are still under constraint, if they are to be absorbed, to pass by denying Korean parentage.

As a consequence of an inner sense of integrity, as well as the result of continuing discriminatory attitudes, the Koreans insist on maintaining for themselves a separate ethnic identity. Most do not choose to pass. They do not choose simply to perpetuate the Japanese myth of homogeneity. Japanese racialist thought is so strong, it cannot consciously assimilate even those who offer no physiological visibility. Whether they avow it openly or not, the Japanese tend to consider the Koreans biologically inferior to themselves. They do not consider behavioral differences solely due to differences in cultural heritage. The Koreans are, therefore, faced with an unsolvable dilemma. On the one hand, the Japanese suggest silent assimilation; on the other hand, they continue to evidence a profound disparagement that suggests the Koreans can never become true Japanese. Overall, just as the black problem in the United States or that of Mexican Americans, the Korean problem in Japan is really a problem of total Japanese identity. As long as racial attitudes continue and remain inherent in the fabric of Japanese society, it remains socially, as well as legally, difficult to take the simple steps that would extend citizenship, at least to those who are born in Japan, without restrictions which are personally demeaning to those made eligible for naturalization.

Although presently torn by a seemingly irreconcilable ideological split into North and South Koreans, as a total people, Koreans are equal in population to either Italy or France. Both North and South Korea have demonstrated amazing industrial growth and an increased standard of living. Why can't the remaining minority Koreans in Japan return? The reasons for remaining in Japan are not difficult to find. The "Koreans" in Japan are not simply Koreans who may choose to go back to Korea should it become economically feasible. They are, in most instances, now third generation inhabitants of Japan who speak no Korean and, despite their continuing Korean identity, are only familiar with life in Japan. Why, then, do they maintain any Korean identity? The processes at work among the Korean minority are, in effect, little different from what contributes to the persistence of distinct ethnic enclaves elsewhere, where they remain separate despite discrimination on the one hand and, on the other, inducements to disappear by assimilation.

INSTRUMENTAL AND EXPRESSIVE CONSTITUENTS OF THE KOREAN JAPANESE MINORITY

Elsewhere for expository purposes we have related the maintenance of an ethnic identity from a psychocultural point of view to ten basic concerns in interpersonal relationships.[5] These interpersonal concerns are broadly divided into those that are prevailingly "instrumental," that is, goal oriented, in contrast to those concerns that are "expressive," or are emotional states universal to man as a social animal. Let us first consider the Korean persistence of a social self-identity with regard to instrumental concerns; then, we shall consider the expressive needs that are involved in an ethnic identity.

Achievement vs. alienation

Social definitions of social, occupational, economic, and political success or achievement are found in every society. In any pluralistic society that emphasizes the ascendency of one group, the achievement of social success may well require one to disguise one's origins. "Passing" is not limited to cases of racial invisibility. Passing is practiced in movement from one class position to another or by moving out of an ethnic minority. In racial situations, passing depends on physiological acceptability as well as assumption of "proper behavior patterns." In passing from one class to another, the individual must disguise behavior patterns, or linguistic usages that would betray his past social affiliations.

To be known to be "Korean" in Japan is to court possible failure in most business and professional careers. It is dangerous economically to "surface" even after gaining occupational recognition. The situation in Japan is somewhat more excruciating because the Japanese are not accustomed to according citizenship to non-Japanese. A Korean Japanese, therefore, remains a social anomaly; whether he or she is or is not technically a foreigner makes little difference. Third generation youth growing up in Japan who know no other social atmosphere than the Japanese one, gain little acceptance as Korean Japanese. To avoid the perplexity and partial withdrawal that would be accorded if known to be Korean, many, who by some circumstance achieve success in public life, either as entertainers or as members of some professional business occupation, when they can pass, choose to pass.

Many instances of discrimination interfere with achievement. Patterns of social and economic discrimination cut very deeply, and the need to consider passing is very pressing. There is a continuing ambivalence among Koreans about their mutual awareness of the need to pass. At the same time, there are strong group pressures on the individual who is passing to somehow maintain, at least covertly, some allegiance with Korean causes. There is a great deal of mutual distrust, however, that fellow Koreans will desert, and there is deep bitterness toward those who totally have turned their backs on their Korean origin.

Robert Merton, in his seminal volume,[6] first discussed Durkheim's concept of anomie from the standpoint that deviant criminal careers are actually very often alternative patterns of achievement for the socially marginal. One finds a strong support for this in the fact that Koreans in Japan have in large numbers resorted to criminal careers since the ordinary avenues of advancement in society are not open to them. Some Koreans of an intelligent, energetic nature have found that they can only actualize themselves in marginal occupations since they are looked upon with such animosity by the majority. In a situation of mutual hatred, many find themselves psychologically free from the constraints and restrictions that ordinary Japanese would feel over entering criminal activity.

We have no firm criminal statistics of any kind, but those on delinquency that are available attest to the fact that many Koreans respond to discrimination with delinquent behavior during their youth. In the statistics of the city of Kobe that we examined some time past, the arrest rate of Korean youth was seven times that of the Japanese majority.[7]

There is also a more passive form of alienation which, in our psychological evidence, is experienced by the majority of Korean Japanese. A lack of projection into the future demonstrates the degree of alienation that Korean Japanese of all ages experience. Even those who at the surface have at least very successful university careers manifest this sense of alienation from the success goals common to Japanese society.

We have been unsuccessful thus far in gathering any evidence of the relative amount of mental illness and forms of anergic withdrawal among Koreans. We do know impressionistically, however, that there are various observable forms of social apathy and a very large unemployment rate as a consequence. The degree to which this represents individuals who have given up seeking out meaningful occupations, or the degree that this represents the actual refusal of jobs above the level of the simple day laborer or construction worker, is hard to fathom. Probably both determinants are at work. In sum, to look at how achievement motivation of a minority such as the Koreans is inhibited, one must examine how many forms of deviant behavior, either active or passive, are symptomatic of existing social discrimination.

Competence

Ethnic identity may determine to a large extent the varieties or nuances of self-confidence or self-doubt found among various groups in a competitive, achievement-oriented society. Readily available negative attitudes of the majority are easily used to explain failure, because the individual is vulnerable to disparagement and will often act in such a way that he manifests for the witnessing majority the negative stereotypes directed toward his group. With family cohesiveness, the individual can be inoculated against such social disparagement. A close cohesive family will bolster the self-esteem of its members. Many Koreans are not so blessed. Their families are subject to internal divisiveness.

It is psychologically easier, therefore, for many Japanese Koreans to experience failure than to witness success. They do not share group expectations of competence. To the contrary, they see before themselves, even selectively, continuing examples of failure and degradation.

Responsibility and Obligation

Part of being socialized within any group is the internalization of a moral code. In addition to proscriptions surrounding acceptable behavior, a moral code includes obligations and expectations. In Japan, this internalization about what to do and what not to do is put in terms of assuming obligations for repayment to parents, as well as responsibility to the nation viewed in megafamilial terms. For the Korean minority, there is ambivalence about being governed in good conscience by standards and moral proscriptions while, in effect, they are already considered as innately inferior to Japanese. They are presumed to be not capable of being "responsible" on the one hand, and on the other hand, they are not accorded the social acceptance which makes any assumption of obligations a reward by positive acceptance and appreciation. Maintained as outsiders, they can only assume the moral proscriptions of Japanese society, despite social rejection.

Animosity and resentment over discrimination in one sense, therefore, may free the individual from assuming the internal standards of the majority. One dilemma of identity for Koreans has to do with whether or not they feel compelled without reward to meet the social obligations assumed by ordinary Japanese.

For some Koreans, therefore, maintaining a Korean identity suggests maintaining some antagonistic posture toward the rules of the majority society. Implicitly, this animosity condones illegal or deviant marginal activity. Becoming ''Japanese'' implies accepting social criticism and assuming a sense of social obligation that may not be acceptable to many peers in the Korean group. That is, to identify with the Japanese majority is to assume, partially at least, their depreciatory attitudes and a sense of self-righteousness toward those who fail to live up to expectations. Therefore, the individual is caught in a dilemma of integrity.

There is also possible a concerted reaffirmation of a Korean identity, either individually or collectively, in some form of group movement. But here we find another dilemma for the Koreans in Japan. Severe political cleavages are present in the contemporary Korean communities, and the individual senses the fact that much of what is done by some of the political factions is for selfish benefit. He is caught by the fact that, on the one hand, he should espouse a political cause that would enhance his Korean identity, but, on the other hand, he cannot identify with some of the extraneous political purposes that are advocated. What does this individual do in this circumstance?

Furthermore, splitting into smaller factions may occur in a minority group as individuals seek to define gradations of political involvement from the far right to the far left. The individual may feel that this is part, in this instance, of being Korean, that he should assume some civic and political responsibility, but he may not find his convictions well-represented in the leaders available. It is easier to unite in protest than to pursue a sustained, affirmative program of action.

Self-control, dominance and submission

Being a Korean in Japan is to come in conflict with a well-defined system of social hierarchy in Japanese society. One is placed outside and in a subordinate position without social reward. Koreans are not bestowed with some of the patterns of emotional gratification through dependency that Japanese in subordinate positions find as payment for participation in social hierarchy. Koreans are not brought in to ''belong''; they are not treated in a positive sense with the paternalistic care that

Japanese exercise toward one another. The emotional gratification that makes power controlled relationships tolerable is not forthcoming. Therefore, Koreans can only resent subordination.

Koreans are Confucianists within their own family. They expect the exercise of paternal authority. They avow male dominance in the family as part of the value of family life. Authority is more apt to be reinforced by physical punishment. Also, by and large, we note that Korean women are less long-suffering and constrained by submissive role behavior than Japanese women; although ideally as dutiful and responsible, they are also perceived as capable of aggressive, even violent, remonstration.

The use of physical punishment or control of children by both parents seems to be more accepted among Koreans than Japanese. They are, therefore, more prone to their being perceived among the Japanese as more aggressive in their interpersonal relationships. One finds that, generally speaking, one of the problems in ethnic relationships is the degree to which physical aggression is permitted within particular minorities. A great deal of minority alienation of groups and mutual dislike is derivative of different attitudes toward childhood aggression permitted in groups.

Koreans finding themselves in a subordinate minority status do not, by and large, use long-range devious submissive tactics in relating; they are more apt to lose patience and let the superior know what their attitudes are. This contributes to a confrontational atmosphere which discomforts Japanese. They are, therefore, reluctant to maintain continuing relationships with Koreans and avoid them.

Cooperation and Competition

Koreans can work together but in many respects seem to be much more individualistically inclined than Japanese. One does not find collective team work and a sense of loyalty as strong as one finds in Japanese groups. Koreans are not apt to subordinate themselves to group causes with the same degree of altruism. They are more apt to be distrustful of one another. While distrust is not lacking among Japanese, Koreans operate within institutional networks that are not as binding on the individual's behavior so that it remains highly predictable.

Japanese can afford to trust others in their group operations because the constrictions placed on behavior are very severe. Koreans, in contrast, have a greater sense of unpredictability about the possible behavior of others.

It has often been reported how Japanese clique behavior depends on school ties and other intricate networks that are not easily broken without jeopardizing future activities. Japanese are age-graded within organizations to avoid competition. Koreans, in contrast, are less comfortable in finding vicarious satisfaction in group membership. They do not seek to lose themselves in a group identification. Koreans expect to reach their goals without dependence on groups or without identification with group goals as substitutes for individual accomplishments.

EXPRESSIVE BEHAVIOR IN KOREAN IDENTITY

Harmony vs. discord

Maintenance of one's ethnic loyalty is a very deep emotional need for most Koreans. The psychological rewards of remaining Korean in a Korean family are, in most instances, much more direct and sustaining than are the instrumental advantages of leaving or changing behavior to gain occupational or social advantage within an alien majority society. A variety of expressive factors are involved in the overall strength of one's ethnic identity. "Harmony" is a virtue strongly advanced by the Confucian heritage. Koreans place great stress on family harmony as the ideal of all group relationships. Ideally, one should mute feelings of conflict and tension within the group. Hostilities, when they exist, are best displaced outside rather than within the immediate family or group.

It is unfortunate among Koreans and among many other minority groups, however, that whereas the ideal may be harmony, circumstances of history have resulted in traditions of within-group discord, hostility, and resentment which even split families and sever long friendships. Koreans find their capacities for harmony dissipated by deep discords and inherited hostilities and traditions of political and social divisiveness: witness the ongoing splits

between North and South Korea and between the pro- and antigovernment forces, between Christians and non-Christians in their contemporary Korean communities.

It is, indeed, an unfortunate destiny for many groups to embody in their traditions forms of discord that are more internally than externally directed. Social movements arising from within a minority group, such as the Koreans, are often attempts to unite the group to achieve a sense of harmony within. The most expedient mechanism for achieving internal harmony is to find some means of deflecting socially disruptive behavior onto an outside individual or group. It is not surprising then, that Koreans, in turn, in order to maintain some form of internal harmony, used the Japanese as the enemy. It is easier to deflect hatred on all Japanese than to distinguish between those who are, indeed, prejudiced from those accepting and potentially helpful. Hence, many Koreans would behave with anger and hostility toward all Japanese, contributing to the continual animosity that separates Koreans and Japanese in Japan.

Also, there tends to be considerable discord within families. The maintenance of Confucianist values in which the wife subordinates herself to the head, and sees to it that the children are obedient in their relationships with parents, is not too well-actualized in many homes. External influences undermine parental roles. Lack of family cohesion is sometimes expressed in delinquent behavior of Korean youth. The reasons for this are to be found in a variety of determinants. But uppermost is the devalued status of the father. His lack of occupational security, and the fact that often women will be the economic breadwinners in the family, turn the father into an embattled figure who may take to drunkenness. He may strike out ineffectually periodically, creating an atmosphere of inconsistency and strain on children who see the father as some type of ogre given to violent outbursts. The Korean male is devalued both outside and within his own family. This destruction of the male occupational role occurs in many minority groups. There are, of course, differential cultural traditions which may counteract the force of discrimination on parental roles. However, in the case of Koreans, it has to be noted that many do not survive the degradation of the role of family head as well.

Affiliation

Being alone is intolerable for most human beings. Being without some sense of group membership produces a sense of agony and malaise. An ethnic group provides a mutual sense of contact and affiliation; however, some individuals are of sufficiently independent character that they have less trouble maintaining themselves daily in sustained social contact. Individuals in groups vary in this regard.

One cannot maintain one's ethnic identity and leave the group without some sense of tension and animosity. There are various sanctions applied to those who are attempting to leave. The group that feels themselves rejected can become destructive towards a deserter. At the very least, there is a mutual rejection and enforced isolation. For some individuals such an ostracism can be heavy sanctioning.

In questions of marriage, Koreans follow the Confucian tradition, emphasizing the expected role patterns in a marriage rather than the possibilities of intimacy or companionship. We have noted with younger Koreans that there is a sense of closeness and intimacy in marital bonds. Sometimes the sense of individual love transcends the barrier between the majority and minority. There are mixed marriages occurring between Koreans and Japanese. These can compound a sense of identity on the part of the Korean pattern and, suffice it to say, the children of such marriages have great difficulties in sorting out their ultimate loyalty, given the obvious conflict between the Japanese and Koreans. A child must choose sides whether he is to become Japanese or to become Korean. In many instances, where his ancestry is known, he is given no choice but forced to maintain the more pejorative identity, very similar to the mixed racial situation in the United States.

Appreciation vs. degradation

The pejorative attitudes Japanese hold toward Koreans are pervasive and Koreans living in Japan cannot avoid being influenced by them. To identify with being Korean is to contend with problems of self-degradation and self-hate. The issues are as severe as any experienced by African Americans. Life history material parallels self-revealtions of African Americans such as Malcolm X. Evidence discloses how racist attitudes do not depend on actual physiological differences for their effect. Many Koreans learn to devalue themselves. Others, with great difficulty, maintain their sense of self-respect.

The Japanese depreciation is not simply towards cultural differences of Koreans, although much issue is made of Koreans being personally dirty and having "unpleasant" eating habits. Few Japanese can tolerate garlic, although Korean restaurants in Japan are now on the increase. Few Japanese appreciate the freer expression that Koreans manifest in their interpersonal relationships. The constraints that Japanese place on themselves force them to derogate Korean openness, especially in the expression of aggression.

The essential crux of majority/minority prejudice is that it is difficult for a majority group to accord acceptance to patterns that are in themselves a source of personal tension and disavowal. Only a very open individual who arrives at his behavior with the sense of choice rather than inner constraint can freely accord to others the possibility of behaving differently without making any adverse judgements. Koreans in Japan are, in effect, scapegoats, as are the *burkumin*. They bear upon themselves all that is disavowed, all that is criminal and reprehensible. Koreans are depreciated: they are vunerable objects of a projection of the disavowed.

Nurturance vs. deprivation

Maintaining one's ethnic identity often implies that one expects to receive as well as to give care, help, and comfort to others. One expects to receive dependent gratification from one's group in time of need. A member of an ethnic group may, however, find that he is disappointed because others in his group are not equipped financially or attitudinally to come to his aid. He himself, desperately seeking whatever advantage he can obtain as a minority member disguised and passing, may avoid any responsibility or obligation to care for others in worse plight. As a matter of integrity, however, he may join some form of mutual help organization, both for political strength and for emotional nurturance.

Many cultural traditions have voluntary organizations which can serve as supportive networks in minority settings. There is, for example, a cultural tradition among Koreans to form an economic group which, in turn, provides capital without interest to each of its members to aid in financial ventures. Many cultural traditions have such forms of voluntary organization. These groups can serve as supportive networks in minority settings.

A sense of nurturance is intergenerational. In some instances the older generation supports the younger, with the explicit anticipation that older people will be supported when they have reached a more helpless state. In some instances of poverty in minority settings, the aged are sadly neglected. Many older Koreans are forced to work despite advanced age and ill health.

Japanese society is highly paternalistic. Younger individuals receive mentorship and assistance from their superiors. It is here again where one also must note how Koreans are subjects of discrimination. In many instances they do not receive such benefits of paternalistic attention. Younger Koreans are not fostered as they would be were they considered "truly Japanese."

Minority groups, with a strong sense of social deprivation, may consider their just due whatever welfare is extended to them. Having a hostile attitude toward the majority allows some individuals to "rip off" welfare agencies when they can get away with it. Today, the Japanese *burakumin*, or former outcastes, are well aware of the fact that they can pressure government agencies to ameliorate problems of housing, schooling, sanitary facilities, etc. But the Koreans in Japan, technically aliens, have no such leverage. Whatever aid is accorded them is given with sufferance, as a charity not as a right. Welfare is extended in an atmosphere of social degradation. The animosity and distrust of the minority toward the majority made it difficult to achieve communication.

Satisfaction vs. *suffering*

Finally, without a sense of oneself, whatever the price paid in suffering in maintaining an ethnic identity, there can be no satisfaction in social life. It is one's affirmative identity that gives life meaning. A commitment to any social group, profession, occupation, or ideology is a commitment to endure the consequences. Conversely, avoidance of consequences can lead to what is described variously as identity diffusion, alienation, a sense of normlessness. In short, when there is a lack of regulation, one is faced with a loss of meaning. Each individual who becomes self-conscious about his minority status is faced with the necessity to suffer as a means toward achievement of any sense of personal "satisfaction" which combines the various instrumental and expressive concerns discussed.

Koreans in Japan are faced with a particular historical instance of general processes in play where individuals are accorded minority status in a multiethnic society. The intensity of suffering may differ but the processes involved are universal, viewed either in their subjective experiential dimension or delineated objectively in an analysis of a multiethnic social structure.

NOTES

1. Margaret Mead, "Ethnicity in Anthropology," *Ethnic Identity*, in DeVos and Ross, eds. (Palo Alto: Mayfield Publishing Company, 1975), chapter VII.
2. George A. DeVos, "Social Stratification and Ethnic Pluralism," *Race*, 14, No. 4 (April 1972), pp.435–60.
3. Gino Germani, "Migration and Acculturation," in *Handbook for Social Research in Urban Areas*, Philipp Hauser, ed. (UNESCO, 1964).
4. R. C. Taylor, "Migration and Motivation," in *Migration*, G. A. Jackson, ed. (London: Cambridge University Press, 1969).
5. George A. DeVos and Lola Romanucci-Ross, eds., *Ethnic Identity, Cultural Continuities and Change* (Palo Alto: Mayfield Publishing Company, 1975).
6. Robert Merton, *Social Theory and Social Structure* (Glencoe, Ill.: Free Press, 1949).
7. DeVos and Romanucci-Ross, op. cit.

DIVERSITY AND CONFLICT BETWEEN OLD AND NEW CHINESE IMMIGRANTS IN THE UNITED STATES

Frank Wen-hui Tsai

INTRODUCTION

Studies on Chinese Americans in recent years have produced two seemingly conflicting reports. One group of scholars has portrayed Chinese Americans as a "model minority" by virtue of their high socioeconomic achievement, hard work, thrift, family cohesion, and community. They are usually stereotyped in such favorable terms as being courteous, clean, patient, intelligent, crime-free, and faithful.[1]

There are other studies, however, which have pointed to the many problems of acculturation and assimilation among the Chinese in the larger American industrial society. They argue that a closer analysis of the status of Chinese Americans would not support an unadulterated success story, and that the Chinese are being discriminated against by the majority of Americans. As a matter of fact, the Chinatowns in San Francisco, Chicago, Los Angeles, Boston, and New York represent ghetto areas where unemployment, poverty, poor health, and juvenile delinquency are prevalent.[2]

A recent report by Dr. Yuan-li Wu of the University of San Francisco has found that both of the above descriptions are one-sided and narrow-minded. Based upon an analysis of the United States census data, Dr. Wu shows that Chinese Americans appear to be concentrated mainly at the two extreme ends of the income and occupational scale. He indicates that, in the occupational pattern of male Chinese employment, the dichotomy falls between service and clerical workers on the one hand, and professional and technical workers on the other. In the distribution of income, while Chinese Americans have a higher than average family income in comparison with most other ethnic groups in the United States, the income of individual persons among Chinese Americans is lower than the U.S. national average.[3] He further suggests that the apparent discrepancy shown in the two conflicting theories we mentioned earlier might be the result of the differences between the old and new Chinese immigrants in the United States today.

In general, Chinese Americans in the United States today can be divided into two major groups, each with its distinctive socioeconomic characteristics. The great majority of Chinese Americans are those who migrated to this country in the late nineteenth and early twentieth centuries, and their descendents. There is a strong feeling of regionalism among members of this group. They came from the same geographical region in southeastern Chinese provinces; they shared similar language, value, and cultural orientation; and they stay together, often within the boundary of Chinatowns in few metropolitan areas. Their outlook is conservative as well as traditionally oriented and, most importantly, they resist change and assimilation. Often, their descendants are called ABC by other groups of Chinese, that is, American-born Chinese.

The other group of Chinese Americans is comprised of those new arrivals from diverse geographical backgrounds who moved into this country after World War II. They are highly educated, professionally trained, and relatively liberal. They seldom stay together and, instead, are dispersed throughout the country. And, they see Chinatown as a marketplace for food and recreational activities, not as an identity symbol. They accept the American way of life with great enthusiasm and are accepted by the majority of American people. There is little interaction among the members within the group, and there is almost no interaction at all between them and the ABCs. As a matter of fact, there exists a certain degree of tension between these two groups of Chinese Americans.

The main purpose of the present paper, then, is to describe the differences between these two groups of Chinese immigrants, with special emphasis on their respective attitudes toward assimilation. The paper will be divided into two major sections. The first section will be devoted to the socioeconomic profile of the old Chinese immigrants. Discussion will include a history of early Chinese immigration into the United States, major anti-Chinese discriminational legislation, the life in Chinatown, and the problem of integration. The second section of the paper will examine the socioeconomic characteristics of the new Chinese immigrants, and their successful integration into the larger American society.

SOCIOECONOMIC STRUCTURE OF THE OLD CHINESE IMMIGRANTS IN THE UNITED STATES

The early immigrants

Three principal factors contributed to Chinese migration to the United States in the nineteenth century. First, internal turmoil and economic breakdown in nineteenth-century China, as a result of ceaseless civil wars and of frequent defeats suffered by China at the hands of major western countries, supplied many Chinese with a powerful incentive to leave the country of their birth for a better life. Second, the discovery of gold in California provided additional attraction to Chinese peasants to move to America in the hope that it would help to improve their economic status. Third, the establishment of the "coolie" trade enabled Chinese peasants to work in California mines by selling their services as contract laborers for a certain period of time in exchange for deferred payment of their passage across the Pacific.[4]

To the early Chinese immigrants, America was a dreamland full of opportunities and gold. The first group of Chinese "coolies" went to the mines directly after their arrival. In the 1850s and 1860s, the Chinese population in the United States was concentrated almost entirely in California, with approximately 80 percent of them in the mining areas.[5] Later, however, many migrants paid their own passage over, or were aided by relatives and friends already in America who paid for their travel to California. Unlike the early coolies, this latter group was able to enter other occupations immediately. Unrestricted by prior contractual obligations as in the case of the coolies, they entered the fishing

and shrimp industries, canning, construction, sewing trades, farming, restaurants, laundries, and domestic services.[6]

The arrival of the Chinese was looked upon by Californians very favorably at first, for they were considered desirable, industrious, and dependable. In his report to the president of the United States on October 10, 1865, California Governor Leland Stanford praised the Chinese for their clean living, diligence, and steadiness. He reported: "As a class they are quiet, peaceable, patient, industrious and economical. Ready and apt to learn all the different kinds of work required in railroad building, they soon became as efficient as the white laborers."[7]

Similar observations of satisfaction were reported in almost every field in which the Chinese were engaged.[8] In a period of labor shortage at the time in California and other western regions of the United States, the efficient and industrious Chinese hands were understandably highly welcomed. As a consequence, the Chinese population increased sharply from 758 in 1850 to 107,488 in 1890.

However, the attitudes of the majority of Americans changed gradually from an early welcome to a subsequent hostility as a result of labor competition, cultural differences, and suspicions about their shipping California gold back to China.[9] Numerous anti-Chinese legislations awere passed, and evictions from various occupations were carried out by labor unions against the Chinese, culminating in the near disappearance of Chinese workers from the labor market by 1910.

"California for Americans" was the central theme of all anti-Chinese legislation passed in California and by the federal government. For example, a law taxing Chinese miners was passed by the state of California in 1853; a law prohibiting the "incompetent" Chinese from entering the state of California was passed in 1858; and the California Supreme Court ruled in 1854 that "Chinese shall not be witness in an action or proceeding wherein a white person is a part."[10] Within the federal government, several laws, commonly known as the Chinese Exclusion Acts, were passed by the United States Congress to suspend the immigration of Chinese laborers. Not until the end of World War II were these discriminating laws relaxed.

An analysis of Table 1 will show the effect of

TABLE 1
Chinese Population of the United States by Sex, 1860-1970

Year	Total	Male	Female	Excess of Males
1860	34,933	33,149	1,784	31,365
1870	63,199	58,633	4,566	54,067
1880	105,464	100,685	4,799	95,906
1890	107,488	103,620	3,838	99,752
1900	89,863	85,341	4,522	80,819
1910	71,531	66,856	4,675	62,181
1920	61,639	53,981	7,748	46,143
1930	73,954	59,802	15,152	44,650
1940	77,504	57,389	20,115	37,274
1950	117,140	76,725	40,415	36,310
1960	236,084	135,430	100,654	34,771
1970	431,583	226,733	204,850	21,883

Sources: Census of Population, United States of America.

anti-Chinese legislation on the distribution of Chinese population in the United States from 1860 to 1970. The table shows that there was a decrease of Chinese population in the United States during the period of anti-Chinese movement between 1890 and 1950, on the one hand, and an unbalanced sex ratio distribution among the Chinese in the United States in the years before World War II, on the other.

Chinatown and the old Chinese immigrants

There is considerable statistical evidence that a large proportion of Chinese Americans are still to be found today in the remaining Chinatowns in such large cities as Los Angeles, New York, Chicago, and Boston, as well as San Francisco. Although the census data do not permit a precise identification of the Chinatown population in these cities, an indirect indication can nevertheless be obtained from Table 2.

From the data, which include nearly 70 percent of the total Chinese population then in the United States, it can be seen that Chinese in this country were heavily concentrated in the five selected cities of the four selected states, each of which has a Chinatown. This heavy concentration becomes even more impressive if we bear in mind that these five cities alone accounted for 40 percent, and the five corresponding SMSAs more than half (53.6 percent), of the total Chinese population in the United States in 1970.

Table 3 shows further that a great majority of the Chinese living in these four states are to be found in

TABLE 2

Chinese Population in Five Selected Cities and the Corresponding Standard Metropolitan Statistical Areas (SMSA), 1970

(Number of Persons)

	City	SMSA	Total in State
Boston, Mass	7.163	12,157	14,018
Chicago, Ill.	8,876	11,995	14,077
New York, N.Y.	70,182	77,099	81,904
Los Angeles, Calif	27,279	41,500	170,419
San Francisco, Calif.	59,079	88,402	
Total	172,579	231,153	280,417

Source: Betty Lee Sung, *Racial and Ethnic Group Population by Census Tract*, Asian Studies Monograph I, II, III published by Department of Asian Studies, The City College of the City University of New York, 1970.

TABLE 3

Distribution of the Chinese Population in Five Selected Cities and the Corresponding Standard Metropolitan Statistical Areas (SMSA), 1970

(In Percent)

	I	II	III
Boston, Mass	58.92	51.10	86.72
Chicago, Ill.	74.00	63.05	85.21
New York, N.Y.	91.10	85.69	94.14
Los Angeles, Calif.	65.73	62.51	82.36
San Francisco, Calif.	80.38		

Note: I: City population as % of SMSA
II: City population as of the state
III: SMSA population as % of the state

Source: Same as Table 2

the respective SMSAs, and that more than one-half of the Chinese in each of the four states live in the five selected cities with Chinatowns. It is, therefore, safe to say that Chinatown is the core of this particular urban residential pattern among Chinese Americans.

Chinatowns have become a symbol of the existence of many Chinese immigrants in the late nineteenth century, whose search for a common physical environment in the west led to the establishment of Chinatowns as a separate settlement in the larger white world. Historically, three important factors have contributed greatly to the emergence and development of Chinatowns in the United States. To every new Chinese arrival America was, and still is, a strange country with a different culture, language, and way of life. In Chinatown, however, he could feel at home. There he could relax away from a sense of alienation and hostility he felt directed at him from the outside world. His contacts with his fellow Chinese could be freer and more intimate. He could also converse with his own kind in familiar tongues which the rest of the world could not understand. More importantly, perhaps, he was one among equals within his own community. It is not surprising, therefore, that almost every

new Chinese immigrant tried to stay close to or live together with his own countrymen, particularly since many of the new immigrants not only came from the same geographical region in China but also some were actually kinsmen.

Another important factor which has contributed to the emergence and development of separate Chinese communities in the United States, particularly in the west, is the lack of an established social order among the white population in the so-called "wild, wild west" of the nineteenth century. Lawlessness and the absence of a distinct and established society in the west gave the Chinese room to maintain their own way of living and culture, particularly since the Chinese were proud of their own heritage and traditions. As a group of "marginal men" the Chinese were left alone to practice their own culture in their separate ghettoes where they also worked.

The third factor is related to the great pressures which the anti-Chinese movement created for the Chinese at the turn of the present century. As Professor Stanford M. Lyman has indicated, the anti-Chinese movement has had two important consequences: (1) the concentration of the Chinese population in big cities, and (2) the increased power of control by traditional associations over Chinese immigrants living in Chinatowns. In Lyman's words:

> The anti-Chinese Movement had certain unintended consequences. It encouraged the Chinese to restrict their lives to the ghetto in which they had only resided in their off hours. . . . It strengthened the control of Chinese traditional associations over their members. And, finally, it forced the settlement of Chinese in cities where Chinatown businesses could realize a ready market for their special goods and services.[11]

Chinatowns provided not only physical refuge for early Chinese immigrants, they also represented a vehicle of judicial dispensation and a foil against institutionalized discrimination. The Chinese Six Companies came into being as the natural answer to the need for an overall organization to administer justice among the Chinese in the United States. Since the Supreme Court of the state of California had ruled that Chinese might not testify either for or against a white person, the Chinese Six Companies served practically as the Supreme Court of the Chinese in California. The Chinese Historical Society of America described the main functions of the Chinese Six Companies as follows:

> By general agreement it was empowered to speak and act for all the California Chinese in problems and affairs which affected the majority of them. It also became the official board of arbitration for disputes which arose between the various district groups, as well as other social groups. It was given the power to initiate and promote programs for the general welfare of the California Chinese. Then, too, before the establishment of any Chinese consular or other diplomatic agency in America, the Chinese Six Companies acted as spokesman for the Imperial Manchus government in its relations with the American Chinese.[12]

To a large degree, therefore, the emergence of Chinatowns at the turn of the current century could be said to be a result of the unwitting crystallization of both internal needs for ethnic practice and external threat of racial discrimination. It is not the outcome of a single fact, as some have suggested. Given the existence of Chinatowns, it is conceivable for a Chinese immigrant to stay behind this cultural and sociological wall all his life without

ever coming into contact with the outside world. To many Chinese, especially those who are poor and illiterate, Chinatown means everything.

Today, Chinatowns are still very much separate communities, both geographically and culturally within the larger American society. To many non-Chinese tourists, Chinatown is a mysteriously attractive place to visit. Yet, to the Chinese living and/or working there, it is a ghetto-like troublesome settlement separated from the rest of the world.

Residents of Chinatown today are mostly poor and have little education. A 1960 study puts the average educational level for Chinatown residents in California at below the fifth grade. A later study of San Francisco's Chinatown shows that 85 percent of its residents have never gone to high school, and 60 percent are "poor" by federal OEO standard.[13] A 1970 report on Chinatown in Boston shows that in 1969 the average income of the Chinese in Boston Chinatown was "significantly lower than those of blacks or of the major white ethnic groups."[14] Sixty-three percent of the Chinese families interviewed had an annual income of less than $6,000. None of the other ethnic groups in Boston had a larger proportion of families in these lower income categories than the Chinese. The report also noted that "the level of education attained by Chinese heads of households was, on the whole, extremely low. More than two-thirds of those surveyed had obtained less than an eighth grade education."[15]

Businesses in the Chinatowns have tended to be limited in size, being both traditional and family oriented. Much of the commercial business in Chinatowns today finds its market primarily in Chinatowns, and is related to supplying the needs of its inhabitants with food and produce for home use, together with traditional recreational facilities and services. As shown in Table 4, most of the businesses in both San Francisco and New York Chinatowns are related to food, clothing making, and tourist trade.

The main economic function of Chinatowns, therefore, is to serve their local Chinese residents. By their very nature, most of the commercial businesses in Chinatowns are small in capital investment and employment, and their services are traditionally oriented and restricted, while their market consists largely of regular customers, except

TABLE 4
Distribution of Businesses in San Francisco and New York Chinatowns, 1960

(In Percent)

Types of Business	Number of Business Establishments			
	San Francisco		New York	
	N	%	N	%
Food-related Businesses	254	35.1	158	45.4
Clothes-making & Retail Stores	138	19.1	28	8.0
Gift Shops	136	18.8	21	6.0
Insurance & Travel Agencies	50	6.8	39	11.2
Laundries	29	4.0	8	2.3
Druggists	29	4.0	4	1.2
Beauty & Barber Shops	25	3.5	5	1.4
Jewelry	12	1.7	5	1.4
Miscellaneous	51	6.9	80	23.1
TOTAL	724	99.9*	348	100.0

Sources: S. W. Kung, *Chinese in American Life* (Seattle: University of Washington Press), 1962. Table 31, p. 185.
Introduction to the *Report of San Francisco Chinese Community Citizens' Survey and Fact-Finding Committee*, April 1969. Table 4, p. 722.

---

of course tourists. Most businesses are run by members of the family, not by hired hands.

Unemployment and substandard wages go hand in hand in Chinatown today. Because many of the Chinese residents in Chinatown do not speak English well, they are forced to work in Chinatown where jobs are scarce and pay is low. Indeed, life in Chinatown is not easy. Today, the old immigrants and their descendents are trapped in the Chinatowns in search of psychological security while hopelessly economically poor and humble.

SOCIOECONOMIC CHARACTERISTICS OF NEW CHINESE IMMIGRANTS IN THE UNITED STATES

As China became one of the United States' major allies during the war against Japan, some anti-Chinese legislation was rescinded, and the Chinese Exclusion Acts were also relaxed. As a consequence, the number of Chinese immigrants have increased steadily ever since. In Table 5, we see Chinese immigration jumping from 4,928 persons

TABLE 5
Number of Chinese Immigrants From 1931 to 1970

Year	Number of Chinese Immigrants
1931–1940	4,928
1941–1950	16,709
1951–1960	35,858
1961–1970	120,622

Source: U.S. Bureau of the Census, *1970 Census of Population, General Population Characteristics: Final Report, United States Summary*, PC (1)-(3).

---

in the ten-year period before the war, to 16,709 persons in the first decade after World War II, and rapid growth to 120,622 in the years between 1961 and 1970.[16]

Although there are no systematic reports on the status of these new Chinese immigrants, it is no secret that they are quite different from the early Chinese immigrants. The most striking difference lies, perhaps, in the fact that this new group of Chinese immigrants consists largely of well-educated and highly trained intellectuals and professionals.

The United States Immigration and Naturalization Service *Annual Report* showed that, among the Chinese admitted to the United States in the years of 1969 and 1970, professional, technical, and kindred workers comprised the largest group: 36.9 percent in 1969 and 28 percent in 1970.[17]

Another report indicated that, during the year of 1970, about 19 percent of a total of 6,783 Chinese male and female aliens adjusted to the status of permanent resident were professionals and technical workers.[18]

Several factors have been responsible for the migration of Chinese intellectuals and high professionals into the United States in the post–World War II period.

First, the rapid industrial expansion in the United States economy during and after the war opened the door for many foreign skilled and technical workers around the world (including the Chinese) to move into this country for better paid jobs and working environments. The United States was the only ideal country for many of these intellectuals and professionals to utilize their knowledge and skills due to the fact that the economy in Europe was in a stage of disruption and chaos, and that civil war was at its height in China and many other eastern European nations.

Second, the United States immigration policy in recent years has also tended to be in favor of alien professionals whose knowledge and skills the United States most needed; these immigrants are allowed to stay in this country as permanent residents at first, and eventually become citizens of this country.

Third, the Chinese Communists' takeover of mainland China in 1949 resulted in the migration of a large number of political refugees into the United States. This particular group of Chinese consisted largely of the well-educated and professionally trained Nationalist government officials and their immediate families. Many of them, as a matter of fact, were the graduates of U.S. colleges and universities.

Fourth, the outbreak of the Korean War in the early 1950s had forced the United States government to take action to prohibit any Chinese student to leave this country. These students were then allowed to accept employment and change their student visa to become a legal alien resident of the United States.

Unlike the old immigrants, this new group of Chinese immigrants does not come from the southeast coast of China, where the great majority of old Chinese immigrants came from; they represent almost every region of Chinese territory. Moreover, they do not have any kinship relation with one another and/or with the old immigrants, and they speak completely different dialects from the old Cantonese which is the major language in Chinatowns.

Since geographical regionalism and kinship tie are two of the most important elements in Chinese daily interactional network, the new immigrants share no similar identity with the old immigrants, and at the same time, they are not welcomed by the residents of Chinatowns. To the people of Chinatown, the new immigrants are, in fact, ''non-Chinese.''

Armed with high education and professional skills, however, this new group of Chinese has found no difficulty in moving right into the large American society. As the country needs the skilled laborers, they are welcomed by American industries. Employment is no problem among these new Chinese immigrants, at least before the great economic depression of the early 1970s.

This new group of Chinese immigrants scattered around the country, with large concentrations in major northern industrial states. As most of the middle class Americans do, they live in the suburbs and commute by car to work daily, and they send their children to the prestigeous schools in the district. They are enjoying the fulfillment of what most Americans have called "the middle class American dream."

There is very little interaction among the members of these new Chinese immigrants for they share little common background with each other, on the one hand, and no similar political ideology about the fate of China, on the other hand. As Chinese intellectuals themselves, they still care about China, but they know there is almost nothing they can do to change the course of China's history. Since the hope to go back to China is extremely slim, the United States is now their home, and they are here to stay. Consequently, they are not only willing but also eager to accept the American way of life and integration.

There is almost no communication between this new group of Chinese immigrants and the old immigrants. To the new immigrants, Chinatown is a marketplace, not an identity symbol. Trips to Chinatown once a month, or once a week, or even daily, are out of necessity, for many of them still enjoy food and recreational facilities provided in Chinatown. As a matter of fact, they tend to look down upon the old immigrants in Chinatown, for the latter group is poor and uneducated. Professor John T. Ma observed that "most of the people in Chinatown were businessmen, storekeepers, service workers, and manual laborers, while intellectuals from China were mainly government officials, academicians, students and professionals. These differences between them sometimes caused mutual distrust or even resentment."[19] Professor Rose Hum Lee also has a similar observation as he pointed out that Chinese Americans were regarded by China-born intellectuals as cultural hybrids or marginal men, and that they were backward.[20]

The new immigrant Chinese are proud of the fact that they are successful in the large American society. There is not much identity crisis among the members of this new group, for they always take pride in their Chinese tradition and cultural heritage which they received in China or Taiwan before they came to the United States and, at the same time, they know that they are the "permanent guests" of the people of the United States and that they would never become "real Americans." The question whether they are Chinese or Americans never bothers them, because in their deep heart they are Chinese by every definition. They look down on the old Chinese immigrants living in Chinatown, for this latter group knows neither Chinese nor American culture.

Consequently, the new immigrant Chinese offer almost no help to the rising problems in Chinatowns throughout the country. Crimes, youth problems, poverty, poor housing, and gang wars in Chinatowns are not their problems, for they share no identity or common interest with the people of Chinatown.

CONCLUSION

In this brief essay, I have described the diverse socioeconomic characteristics of the two distinctive groups of Chinese immigrants in the United States today. The old Chinese immigrants, who moved into this country before World War II, are characterized by a homogeneous regional identity and by their relatively poor socioeconomic attainment in the American society. The new Chinese immigrants in contrast show an overall higher socioeconomic status.

In general, the differences between the two groups of Chinese immigrants in the United States today can be roughly said to be differences between life "within" and life "without" Chinatown. I have demonstrated in this essay that old Chinese immigrants seem to take Chinatown as an end in itself, that is, they tend to settle down in Chinatown for good, instead of taking it as a transitory stop for the preparation of moving into the larger American society.

The new immigrants are scattered around the whole country. They are knowledgeable and relatively successful. But there is little interaction between the new and old Chinese immigrants due to the existence of a strong regionalism in Chinatown, and the lack of respect for the people of Chinatown among the new intellectuals. To the old immigrants, the new arrivals are non-Chinese because the latter do not come from their geographical region in mainland China. To the new immigrants, however, the old immigrants are not really Chinese because the latter know nothing about Chinese culture and cannot even speak the Chinese official language, the Mandarin.

As one can easily see here, a mutual understanding between the two groups of Chinese immigrants is urgently needed. Rising problems in Chinatown today cannot be solved by the residents of Chinatown alone, for they lack resources, both technically and financially. Since the majority of the new Chinese immigrants are intellectuals and professionals, a helping hand from them in cooperation with leaders of Chinatown would certainly provide some necessary expertise and incentive for problem solving in Chinatown.

But before we could hope for a mutual understanding and assistance between the old and new Chinese immigrants, we must be able to identify the characteristics of each of these two groups and the nature of their tension and conflict. Systematic analysis of the relationships between these two groups of Chinese immigrants is thus greatly needed. I hope my short paper would serve as a beginning for such an inquiry.[21]

NOTES

1. Harry H. L. Kitano and Stanley Sue, "The Model Minorities," *Journal of Social Issues*, 29, No. 2 (1973), pp.1–9.

2. Harry H. L. Kitano and Stanley Sue, "Stereotypes as A Measure of Success," *Journal of Social Issues*, 29, No. 2 (1973), pp.83–98.

3. Yuan-li Wu, "Income, Employment and Occupational Patterns: Three Decades of Change," unpublished manuscript (1976).

4. Cf., Rose Hum Lee, *The Chinese in the United States of America* (Hong Kong: Hong Kong University Press, 1960). S. W. Kong, *Chinese in American Life* (Seattle: University of Washington Press, 1962).

5. Stanford M. Lyman, *Chinese Americans* (New York: Random House, 1974), pp.56–58. Kung, op. cit., p.66.

6. Thomas W. Chinn, ed., *A History of the Chinese in California: A Syllabus* (San Francisco: Chinese Historical Society of America, 1969), pp.30–31.

7. Ibid., p.45.

8. Ibid., pp. 43–65.

9. Ibid., pp.23–24.

10. Cheng-tsu Wu, ed., *"CHINK!"* (New York: Meridian Books, 1972), p.22.

11. Lyman, op. cit., p.80.

12. Chinn, op. cit., p.65.

13. *Introduction to the Report of San Francisco Chinese Community Citizens' Survey and Fact-Finding Committee*, April 1969, p.721.

14. Charles Sullivan and Kathlyn Hatch, *The Chinese in Boston*, 1970 (Boston: Planning and Evaluation Department, Action for Boston Community Development, 1970), p.45.

15. Ibid., p.55.

16. U.S. Bureau of the Census, *1970 Census of Population, General Population Characteristics: Final Report, United States Summary*, PC(1)–(3).

17. U.S. Immigration and Naturalization Service, *Annual Reports (1965–1973)* (Washington, D.C.: U.S. Government Printing Office).

18. John T. Ma, "The Educated, Professional, and the Technical Workers Among Chinese-Americans," unpublished manuscript (1976), p.12. Will be published as a chapter in a forthcoming book on Chinese Americans edited by Dr. Yuan-li Wu of the University of San Francisco.

19. Ibid., p.13.

20. This paper is based, in part, on my earlier paper entitled, "The Chinese-American Poor," which will be published as a chapter in the forthcoming book edited by Dr. Yuan-li Wu.

21. Rose Hum Lee, op. cit.

LOWELL, AN IMMIGRANT CITY:
THE OLD AND THE NEW

Shirley Kolack

HISTORICAL BACKGROUND

Lowell, Massachusetts, and the Merrimack Valley region of which it is a part, represents in microcosm the intertwining of the industrialization process and immigration in the United States. The Valley's history, its patterns of settlement and development, provide a laboratory setting for an investigation and analysis of ethnic and religious group relations.

The historical significance of Lowell lies in its unique experience as the first American city founded expressly for the production of cotton textiles. Lowell became America's first great industrial city due to the harnessing of the Merrimack River. The mills which brought prosperity to early Lowell depended on the water power delivered by a complex system of river canals.

From 1826 to 1836, Lowell's population grew from 2,500 to 18,000 inhabitants. As the output of the mills expanded, immigrant labor from Europe began to replace the work force supplied by local Protestant farm girls who were the initial factory workers. With the flood of immigrant families from Europe, the new town grew at an accelerated rate. By 1840, Lowell was the second largest city in the Commonwealth, population, 21,000.[1]

By 1912, the population had grown to over 100,000, and 40 percent of the community was non-English speaking.[2] In *Immigrant City,* Donald Cole indicated that nowhere in the country was the proportion of foreign born to the total population higher than in the Merrimack Valley.[3]

The immigrants came in three waves. Before the American Civil War, the Irish, fleeing famine at home, settled along the Merrimack River. They continued to come after the war and were joined by French Canadians, English, and Germans. Between 1890 and 1912, the earlier immigrations slowed as Italians, Austrians, Lithuanians, Poles, and Syrians arrived. Smaller groups, such as Scots, Armenians, Greeks, Jews, Franco-Belgians, Portuguese, and Chinese, rounded out the many subcultures of the area. All came to escape some form of felt oppression in their countries of origin.

Today, new immigrants and migrants are arriving. They are Spanish-speaking Puerto Ricans, Cubans, and Latin Americans. The lure is the same as for the earlier arrivals—the hope of finding jobs in the industrial plants of the area. However, the major source of employment, the textile mills, moved south years ago.

Newcomers appear to follow patterns similar to the earlier immigrants. They settle in ethnic enclaves and start at the bottom of the occupational ladder. The influx of the Spanish population is a clear indication that immigration continues as an ongoing process in Lowell.

These recent arrivals, as did the ethnic groups before them, provide a cheap source of labor for the industrial factories in the city and its environs. It should be noted, however, that the wealth created by Lowell industry for more than 100 years flowed out of the city in the form of dividends to the mill owners of English Puritan background, and to the high salaried managerial elite. Cardinal O'Connell, writing of his early youth in Lowell, states: "Lowell and its population, which began to increase year by year by the thousands, got all the hard work and almost nothing else—certainly not compassion, pity or understanding of the almost insupportable conditions of labor at that time.

"These newcomers, first entirely Irish, later French Canadian Catholics from the Provinces, were treated precisely as if they were part of the machinery which ground out the millions being produced for the rich managers and millowners who spent the money not in Lowell, but in New York, Boston, Paris and London."[4]

The observations of the Cardinal have relevance today. Against the background of thriving industrialization, followed by a period of decline and a most recent modest revival of manufacturing pursuits, the immigration process continues to unfold. The relations of ethnic groups to one another and the tenacity of survival itself is interlaced with the competition for work. The ethnic enclaves that continually dominate the city disproves the theoretical myth of the melting pot.

One of the overall assumptions of this paper is that religion and ethnicity remain independent variables that influence and determine the dependent variables of values, attitudes, and behavior patterns. The past plays a part in present day ethnic identification. Some aspects of ethnic identification that survive are undoubtedly a reaction to the initial harsh treatment and threats to survival of each group posed by overt bigotry and discrimination. It is particularly interesting to probe what elements of ethnic separatism survive based on past experiences, and what factors reflect a true desire to maintain cultural pluralism. Group cohesiveness continues to be automatically reinforced by language barriers and different life styles, which still reinforce a network of closed subcultures.

From the outset, each ethnic group lived in segregated quarters. The immigrant cycle inevitably brought the newest immigrants into the least desirable dwelling areas of the city. The Irish, replacing the local farm girls, settled in the Acre, the section along the canals which they helped build. The French Canadians followed, replacing many of the Irish in the mills. These French-speaking workers settled in "Little Canada" and, by the 1880s, built a thriving community which published the first French daily newspaper in the United States, the L'abeille.[5] After 1890, labor was increasingly supplied by immigrants from Greece, Poland, Italy, and Portugal. They occupied the more central areas of Lowell near the factories while many of the more settled population moved to the suburbs.[6]

The Greeks established the first Greek-American day school in the United States in 1901, and established a bilingual curriculum to serve the residents of the Greek neighborhoods.

Thus, there was a juxtaposition of many cultural groups, but the residents of each more or less remained self-segregated and mingled with those from other groups only at the workplace. Although there is some blurring of the sharp lines of residential division today, observers will note that these population patterns generally remain intact.

The living patterns of the nationality groups is an indication that immediate assimilation did not take place. There was always a flood of antiimmigrant feeling that greeted the arrival of each new group. The fear of the newcomer revolved partly around the struggle over jobs and the concern that the new arrivals would provide a cheaper supply of labor. Later, this factor became a major consequence when violence errupted over the press for unionization.

From the time that the earliest immigrants started to arrive in Lowell, the fear of unrestricted immigration was reinforced by religious intolerance. In the neighboring city of Lawrence in 1893–94, a series of meetings and lectures sponsored by the American Protective Association (APA) took place. The dominant theme of these lectures was the threat of the Catholic Church to America.[7]

The APA lecturers alleged dual loyalty on the part of Catholics. They charged that Catholics could not remain loyal to the United States and the Pope in Rome at the same time. The speakers spread rumors of disloyalty and suggested the existence of a Catholic conspiracy.

Cardinal O'Connell, writing about the conditions that prevailed in Lowell, chronicles the bitterness of feelings expressed against Catholicism. He discusses the rise of the Know-Nothing Movement and its vicious attack on Catholics. He reports that the movement was led by fanatical ministers who preached hatred from their pulpits. In the streets Catholics were met by taunts and gibes, summed up in these two epithets--Paddy and Papist. "As for myself, both in school and out of school, in fact, everywhere except in church and home, I was clearly conscious of this sentiment of petty animosity."[8]

The development of the Know-Nothing Movement all over New England increased the antipathy of the native born Yankees towards the incoming Irish and French Canadians. The citation "No Irish need apply" frequently appeared in the help wanted advertisements in the daily papers. The newcomers were not allowed to occupy any civic posts, and were totally excluded from major economic activities such as banking and insurance.[9]

By the turn of the century, the Irish in Lowell, Lawrence, and other Merrimack Valley Communities began to gain status. The increase in numbers, and the acceptance of the Protestant Ethic expressed in their willingness to do the hardest and dirtiest work, spurred their movement up the ladder.

Later on, however, the Irish took on the role of oppressor as a new wave of immigration made up of French Canadians spread over the Merrimack Valley. They had by now achieved a foothold and some economic power which appeared threatened by this mass of newcomers. Having gained higher status, the Irish in turn displayed the same antipathy toward the French that they had experienced at the hands of the native Americans.

Between 1899 and 1906, the French newspaper *Le Progres* carried at least thirty articles which voiced complaints about the Irish, many of which related to religious antagonism; political friction is also noted. The basis for the religious conflict was the issue of whether bishops in predominantly French Canadian districts should be French Canadians or Irish. The Irish clergy were also accused of suppressing the use of the French language and downgrading French culture. It was assumed that errors made by Irish city officials in the pronunciation of French names were intentional.[10]

On the political level, the French newspaper accused the Irish of bribing French Canadian leaders in order to obtain Canadian votes. In addition, *Le Progres* expressed dissatisfaction over the Irish domination of all Catholic societies.

It is interesting to note that, in this struggle, the emphasis on exclusive ethnic identity produced antagonisms which were much stronger than the common religious ties which might have bound these groups together.

Just as the arrival of the French Canadians made the position of the Irish stronger, so the arrival of the southeastern Europeans increased the security of the Canadians. The Italians, who were also part of a common religious pool, were viewed as cheap foreign labor. *Le Progres* bluntly stated that these immigrants belonged to a less desirable class.[11] Blatant prejudice went so far that many plant foremen, recognizing the bitterness felt against the new Italian arrivals, placed them in separate departments from the other employees.

Only today is accommodation in evidence with regard to the common bond of Catholicism, manifested in Irish, French Canadians, Italians, and Poles occasionally crossing ethnic lines to marry. It is not unlikely though that, even in the present, a significant symbol of rising social status is for an Italian boy to marry a girl of Irish descent. But it is likely that separate ethnic identities are gradually becoming muted into one common identity for American Catholics of European descent. In this new alliance, the Irish represent the older American society, much as Protestants of British ancestry did in the past. Resentment is still expressed though against the domination of the church by Catholics of Irish background, and over Irish monopoly of politics.

A study of Lowell in 1940 outlines a pattern where each immigrant group within its neighborhood contained a national church, parochial schools, and a business section. There were considerable numbers of French in Lowell near the church and school of Notre Dame de Lourdes, and near the church and school of Sainte Marie. In the French section there were French names on the streets and French names on the shops. The Polish colony was served by the Polish National Church; the Greek, Armenian, and Portuguese colonies each had their own quarters with their own separate church. Jews tended to congregate near the northern end of Chelmsford Street where there were three Jewish synagogues.[12]

The Boston Catholic Directory (1969) lists all of the Catholic churches in the Greater Boston area. For Lowell, Catholic churches are identified with these designated headings: German, Italo-American, Polish, French, Lithuanian, Byzantine-Melkite, Portuguese, and Franco-American.[13] This is an indication that ethnic divisions remain within the church, and that mixing occurs only when there is a felt threat to the entire religious community.

After 1890, the labor force was increasingly supplied by population from southeastern Europe: Greeks, Poles, Russians, Lithuanians, and Italians.

Represented among the new arrivals at about the same time were Jewish immigrants. Although some Jews worked in the mills, they largely made their livelihood as peddlers and small shop keepers. Just as the arrival of the French Canadians served to solidify the position of the Irish, so now the arrival of the southeastern Europeans increased the security of the French Canadians.

The French singled out the Jews for particularly vicious attacks. The basis for the conflict appeared economic. *Le Progres* insisted that the dirty Jewish junk shops were the source of spotted fever, and attacked Jewish peddlers for taking over Canadian sections.[14] The French Canadians referred to Jews as "Sheenies," and the Catholic Literary Society held up Shylock at the typical Jew.

In *The Record of A City*, written by George Kenngott to commemorate the seventy-fifth anniversary of Lowell, the author is critical of most of the ethnic groups living in the city. The Jewish community is not excluded from his attacks. Kenngott states: "The Hebrews can hardly be placed in the working class of Lowell, and they seldom have more than one family in a tenement, but their surroundings are kept none too clean."[15]

Kenngott reports that in 1912 there were four synagogues in the city and two Jewish papers were published, *Star of Bethlehem* and *Zion's Banner*.[16] In the practice of their religion, the Jewish community found refuge from attack. Orthodox and largely Yiddish speaking, Judaism provided them with a way of life in a strange and largely hostile milieu. As soon as a handful of Jews arrived, their first collective effort was to establish an organized Jewish life; religious survival was as vital a concern as life itself.

This brief history of the settlement patterns and relations that developed between the diverse part of the population of Lowell provides a background for assessing present day conditions. A common system of education and communication has not wiped out group differences. To a large extent, ethnic groups still behave as interest groups, and the ascribed status of ethnicity remains a viable force.

A current profile of the French Canadians, Greek Orthodox, Irish, Jews, Polish-Lithuanians, Portuguese, and Spanish communities reveals that each group still maintains some institutional completeness. There are professional, fraternal, social, business, welfare, literary, church, and school associations associated with each ethnic segment. Some members of each group still live within prescribed physical boundaries which contain stores, parks,

clubs, churches, and schools perceived as belonging to a designated population. Many local stores provide services and products for specific ethnic groups. In addition, many residents maintain their ethnic ties by participating in ethnic-oriented activities and traditions.[17]

National churches are still operative for most groups. French, Irish, Polish, Portuguese, and Spanish—all Catholic—still attend separate churches. This is an indication that religion has not yet replaced ethnicity as a source of identity. Interviews with clergymen made clear that many church festivals and celebrations revolve around the celebration of the homeland. In many cases, church bulletins have replaced foreign language newspapers as the primary source of community activities and events of note.[18]

Many groups still maintain their own schools where the language of origin is still taught. Most notable are the Hellenic, French, Portuguese, and Hebrew day schools.

Functioning ethnic associations run the gamut from Greek coffee houses and restaurants to special bars where the Polish and Lithuanians congregate. There are barber shops, grocery stores, and bakeries that serve as social centers. An example of an existing ethnic club is the Richelieu Club, whose purpose is to preserve the French language and culture. Business is conducted entirely in French and members are fined $.25 for each lapse into English.

Each group still supports an elaborate structured framework of churches, schools, neighborhood clubs, and relief societies which reinforce the distinctive group patterns and life styles of the region. The most meaningful breakdown of barriers occurs only in the world of work.

The occupational distribution of the groups varies. The Irish, French, Greeks, and Jews are well-represented in the professions. The Irish have taken over political control of the area. There are many French represented in real estate and local insurance companies. The Portuguese, Polish, and Spanish are still predominant in work roles in factories. In general, the longer the group has been around the higher it has moved in economic and social class.[19]

Using intermarriage as an indicator of assimilation, the French Candians are the most assimilated, freely intermarrying; the Spanish and the Greeks, the least. In general, a high level of group endogamy prevails. Although a segment of each group expresses a willingness to live in the same neighborhoods with others, work at the same jobs, and join the same clubs, most still draw the line at marrying outside their group.

CONTEMPORARY STATUS OF ETHNIC GROUPS

Ethnic survival remains a potent force in the dynamics of the city of Lowell. It is therefore legitimate to question why this is so.

The 1970 Census Tract data for Lowell provides part of the answer.[20] The overall population is now 94,280. Represented in this total are 31,842 people who are foreign born or of foreign born parentage. Thus, roughly one-third of the population is still of "foreign stock." Included in the population segment of those who are foreign born are 2,251 persons of Spanish heritage, 243 Cubans, 71 Latin Americans, and 1,000 Portuguese recently arrived from Madeira.

Thus, the population of Lowell represents a decidedly heterogeneous mix. The population figures prepared by the Lowell City Development Authority indicates the expectation of continued growth for the Spanish groups. It is estimated that the Spanish speaking will comprise over 10 percent of the population by the end of 1977.[21]

With the arrival of the Spanish, the cycle of prejudice and discrimination against the newcomer is again repeated. *The Minority Group Housing Study* reports that the Spanish speaking find it difficult to locate standard housing at an affordable cost. They are concentrated in neighborhoods where there is overcrowding, exorbitant cost, and substandard housing. The study concludes that the Spanish speaking paid a higher rent per room than did white families, while on the whole living in units of poorer quality.[22]

It should be noted that the Spanish do not view themselves as one group. Each segment, the Cubans, Latin Americans, and Puerto Ricans, seeks to exert their individual identity. However, the general community does not recognize these distinctions and lumps them all together in much the same way that earlier European immigrants were collectively viewed as foreigners. Currently, most of the

Spanish people are in low-paying, unskilled factory jobs with little hope for advancement.

Another parallel to the struggles of the earlier immigrants for acceptance is reflected in the hostility expressed against the Spanish for their willingness to work for lower wages in a tight labor market.

Similar to the experience of previous groups, the Spanish are struggling to gain a foothold in the community and are beginning to set down roots. A striking difference between them and the earlier ethnics is their conscious desire to cling boldly to their heritage.

They have fought for and demanded the creation of bilingual programs in the public schools. There are approximately four hundred students enrolled in the bilingual education program in the city of Lowell—the majority of these students are Spanish, with some Portuguese students as well.

The Lowell Sun, a daily newspaper read widely in the region, expressed its opposition to the bilingual program in an editorial stating, "Before this law (Bilingual Education) was written onto the state's books, there was no responsibility on the part of cities such as Lowell to provide instruction in French to the French-speaking people who came from Canada, in Greek to the Greek-speaking people who came here from Greece, or in any other language to any other foreign group that might have chosen to immigrate to Lowell. The French-speaking people, therefore, established their own schools and the Greek-speaking people did likewise, but never did either of these groups feel it was the responsibility of Lowell to educate their young people in any other language but English."[23]

The paper, in general, has not been sympathetic or sensitive to the special needs of the Spanish group. The attitude that comes across is that other groups have made it on their own, let us not coddle the Spanish.

There has developed a network of social service agencies to help the Spanish through the difficult transition period. A local community based, weekly newspaper, the *Communicator*, features a Spanish page where all items are written in Spanish. This newspaper serves as a conduit for passing on information about housing, jobs, and so forth, that is of special interest to the Spanish.

The two social service agencies that have the

greatest impact on the community are UNITAS and the Spanish American Center. Both are private agencies whose funds come from religious sources, foundations, and donations. Though sometimes rivals for funds, both institutions represent a response to a felt need of the Spanish people. They provide counselling, credit unions, job banks, summer camp programs, and day care centers.

The Catholic church is influential in both these organizations due to the fact that the Spanish population is overwhelmingly Catholic. Local priests, working with the people in their parishes, have begun to respond to their needs.

An interesting development, in terms of the impact of religion on the lives of the Puerto Ricans, is that many have turned away from Catholicism and joined Pentecostal churches. There are several storefront Pentecostal congregations in the area. The local parish has not provided the strong base for identity for the Puerto Ricans as it did for the earlier immigrants. Therefore, the Pentecostal church is often turned to in order to serve this function of providing an exclusive intimate circle in which the Puerto Ricans can feel at home.[24]

The Catholic church has begun to provide special masses and services in Spanish and has brought several Spanish priests into the area, in an effort to retain the loyalty of the Spanish population.

The Spanish community, within its neighborhood boundaries, has taken on a special cultural flavor. There are special food and variety stores providing a wide assortment of items imported from Puerto Rico. Special festivals and national holidays of the island are observed. All in all, the Spanish continue to tenaciously cling to their cultural heritage. They appear to say that, if the price of acceptance is the loss of their ethnic past, then this is too high a price to pay.

In recognition of the endurance of the Spanish traditions in the community, the Lowell City Library recently opened a Spanish room. It is staffed by a Spanish-speaking librarian. All of the books and record albums in the collection are in Spanish. As a result of this new facility, the use of the library on the part of the Spanish people has greatly increased.[25]

Thus, in the Merrimack Valley evidence is crystal clear that, for the newest immigrants as well as for the old, cultural pluralism remains alive. The traditions and values of each group still plays an important part in their lives. A great diversity of values, lifestyles, and needs are still expressed. Undoubtedly, part of the self-segregation of each group is a protection against the real or perceived manifestations of hostility on the part of others. Certainly, this is true for the Spanish.

The empty mills still dominate the city and unemployment is high. The Spanish who have come to work in the small plants that remain are often viewed with suspicion and alarm.

Some members of each of the European immigrant groups escaped the mills and moved up into professional, political, and business roles. It is unlikely that few, if any, of the Spanish community will find the American dream of unlimited mobility a reality.

CONCLUSIONS

None of the ethnic groups were ever completely absorbed into the dominant English Protestant way of life that prevailed in Lowell for over a hundred years. Though somewhat transformed and their cultural traditions altered, the immigrant groups still have not emerged into a new American type.

It is not likely that complete ethnic assimilation will occur, nor will complete ethnic pluralism remain. Ethnic ties have weakened during periods when groups did not feel threatened, only to resurface when threats to a group's existence reappeared. As each ethnic group experiences less pressure to conform, it may, in turn, voluntarily strive to protect its identity. The striving to maintain cultural diversity is far from over.

A common system of education and communication has not wiped out group differences. Indeed, for many of the first generation, all of life can be lived within the confines of an ethnic community: for them church, family, and work remain intertwined.

As had been commonly assumed in the post–World War II years, religion has not replaced ethnicity[26] as the most important determinant for placement in Lowell. National churches are still operative for most groups. Within the confine of the religious group itself, there is a network of organizations and informal social relationships which permit and encourage the members of the religious group to remain within the group for all of their primary relationships, as well as for some of their secondary relationships throughout the life cycle.

Religion and ethnicity still provide barriers to social interaction. It is only in the world of work that any meaningful interaction takes place between individuals from different backgrounds.

Membership in a social class does not supersede religious and ethnic ties as repositories for shared values and lifestyles. There appears a need for placement based on identifying symbols that transcend class position. It is apparent that ethnicity cannot be shed in the same way as social class.

Groups in Lowell have made varying rates of progress towards adaptation and assimilation; some have made no progress at all. With new groups continually entering the city, there is the prospect of the indefinite prolonging of structurally separate ethnic groups. There is likely to be recurring conflict between the new immigrants and the old as they compete for access to the limited economic rewards available in the area.

There is currently a proposal submitted to the U.S. Congress to make Lowell a national urban park, based on its varied ethnic heritage and its historical importance as the birthplace of the Industrial Revolution in the United States. This development will have impact on preserving the multigroup character of the city. Thus, even outside forces may be brought to bear on preserving the city's cultural heritage. The greatest resource for the revitalization of the city lies in maintaining the ethnic, religious, and racial communities to complement the restructuring of the architectural history of the city. Paradoxically, the newest immigrants, the Spanish and the Portuguese, who have been treated so badly, will play a vital role in keeping the city's heritage alive.

This paper represents an initial probe in understanding the dynamics of the absorption process taking place in Lowell. There is a need for a definitive study to be undertaken to assess the current status of relations between the diverse groups, and to pinpoint the various stages in the adaptation process. What is clear at this juncture is that the process of absorption is extremely complicated. Perhaps

groups generate power and influence only at the point at which they stop accepting the model of the melting pot.

NOTES

1. Human Services Corporation, Lowell, Massachusetts, *Lowell Urban Park Report, 1973-74*.
2. Ibid., p.16.
3. Donald B. Cole, *Immigrant City* (Chapel Hill: University of North Carolina Press, 1963), p.1.
4. Cardinal William O'Connell, *Reflections of Seventy Years* (Boston: Houghton, Mifflin, 1934) p.12.
5. Human Services Corporation, op.cit., p.16.
6. Margaret Terrell Parker, *Lowell, A Study of Industrial Development* (New York: MacMillan, 1940), pp.89–91.
7. Cole, op. cit., p.84.
8. O'Connell, op. cit., pp.15–16.
9. Ibid., p.22.
10. Cole, op. cit., p.89.
11. Ibid., p.90.
12. Parker, op. cit., pp.14–20.
13. Boston Catholic Directory, Boston, Massachusetts, XXI (1969), pp.69, 73, 75, 77, 79, 81, 83. The assumption can be made that the churches, such as St. Patrick, which do not have ethnic listings are predominantly Irish.
14. *Le Progres*, 7 Feb. 1902, 14 May 1903, 5 April 1906.
15. George Kenngott, *The Record of a City*, (New York: MacMillan, 1912), pp.192–201.
16. Ibid., pp.192–201.
17. Shirley Kolack, "A Course in Ethnic Studies," *Teaching Sociology*, 3, No.1 (October 1975), pp.60–73. In this course, my students and I canvassed each ethnic community. Organization leaders and representative members, young, middle-aged, and elderly, were interviewed. Wherever possible three generations of the same family were questioned. Much of the material that follows is based on our participant observation.
18. Ibid., p.67.
19. Ibid., p.67.
20. U.S. Department of Commerce, Bureau of the Census, *1970 Census of Population and Housing, Lowell, Massachusetts*, PHC (1), No. 119, p. 5.
21. Lowell City Development Authority, *Minority Group Housing Study* (January 1972). It should be noted that this housing study deals also with the black population of Lowell which is expected to increase in size over the next few years. I have not singled the blacks out for discussion due to the fact of their small numbers, 786. It should be noted, however, that they suffer the effects of prejudice and discrimination and, for the most part, live in segregated substandard housing. There have been tensions between the black and Puerto Rican communities in recent years.
22. Ibid.
23. *Lowell Sun*, 15 February 1973.
24. Based on an interview with a local priest who served the Spanish community.
25. Interview with librarian of the Spanish Room.
26. Will Herberg, *Protestant-Catholic-Jew* (New York: Doubleday, 1955).

NEW STRUCTURES, NEW IMMIGRANTS:
THE CASE OF THE PILIPINOS

Antonio J. A. Pido

THE IMMIGRATION EXPERIENCE IN THE CONTEXT OF MAJORITY-MINORITY RELATIONS

Traditionally, the immigration process was and is commonly perceived as a transnational or crosscultural phenomenon affecting peoples from two nations and cultures. Recent "brain drain" studies indicate that the process has become an international phenomenon involving more than two nations and cultures. And, that professional networks and/or universal outlooks, attitudes, and life styles become the linkages in interpersonal associations, rather than ethnicity, national or political origins, and affiliations. If some of the immigrants to the U.S. in the last two decades have the "brain drain" characteristics, then it can be assumed that their immigration experience as well as their status in the U.S. will take on an additional or different dimension.[1]

Unlike the earlier or traditional immigrants who have to straddle two cultural or national identities, the new immigrants may already have preimmigration crosscultural, nonnational, and apolitical outlooks and orientations. The "intellectual" or "modern" characteristics of the new immigrants should link them to Americans with similar characteristics, and who may feel closer to these immigrants than they are with fellow Americans with more traditional characteristics. Furthermore, the new immigrants' "brain drain" educational and occupational credentials may no longer place them at a disadvantage in dealing with the host (U.S.) society and institutions. Their credentials could provide them with wider international options for employment and professional advancement. In other words, culturally and/or ethnically, they may see no need to "Americanize" in order to maximize their economic and occupational participation in the system, and search for meaningful lives.[2] On the other hand, a theoretical as well as empirical question that may be posited is to what extent have these "brain drain" credentials and presumably "modern" or "intellectual" outlooks affected the new immigrants' ethnocentricity towards their own traditional values, norms, social institutions, and patterns of interpersonal behavior? Gordon contends that intellectuals who may find professional, occupational, and/or intellectual networks as alternative ways to pursue their goals, will in the long run find more comfort with those with whom they culturally identify and share a common country of origin.[3]

SCOPE AND DIRECTION OF THE STUDY

This study took the position that a conflict and change model is a more realistic approach in understanding race and ethnic relations in general and in the immigration process in particular. It posited that, although the immigrants in voluntary immigration are the ultimate actors in the immigration process at the micro level, this action is precipitated by structural factors at the macro level over which the immigrants may have no control; moreover, these structures at the macro level also determine the contact and interaction between the immigrants and the host peoples at the micro level.

Therefore, it used a conflict and change model of society and a multilevel analysis in examining Pilipino immigration to the United States. It examined the historically-developed macro structures that may have precipitated the immigration of Pilipinos to the U.S., and how these impinged upon their interaction with the host society at the micro level. The study focused attention on the new Pilipino immigrants who may have higher education and/or and/or occupational credentials and middle to upper class backgrounds compared to their earlier predecessors.

An open-ended or exploratory approach was used. It made extensive use of historical and census data and other reports on Pilipino immigration to the United States. It likewise secured field data from a sample of fifty-one Pilipino adults eighteen years and older residing in a medium-sized midwestern U.S. urban area, which shall be referred to in this paper as "Midwest City." This sample represented 66 percent of a possible universe of seventy-seven Pilipino adults in the field site during 1974 and the middle of 1975. Field data were gathered by a combination questionnaire and interview schedule administered to the respondents. Aside from demographic or biographical data, the instrument provided leads which were then pursued in the ethnographic portion of the field work.

THE PILIPINOS IN AMERICA AND STRUCTURAL CONDITIONS RELATED TO THEIR IMMIGRATION

The United States Census of Population for 1970 reported that the Pilipinos comprised the smallest ethnic-racial group in the U.S., from among the minority groups that were separately and distinctly counted as racial or ethnic groups. However, the U.S. Immigration and Naturalization Service (INS) reported that, next to Mexicans, Pilipinos have been the largest group of immigrants admitted to the U.S. during the last two years via the "normal" procedures, that is, exclusive of such massive movements of refugees such as the South Vietnamese and Cambodians. Undoubtedly, most if not all of this immigration was brought about by the decisions and actions of the immigrants themselves at the micro level. The immediate cause for this large number of Pilipino immigration to the U.S. was the change in the U.S. Immigration Laws in 1965. However, the Philippines is not theoretically favored by the 1965 Immigration Act, nor is it the largest country-source of immigrants from Asia.

From an historical perspective, it was determined that the Pilipino immigrants to the U.S. came from a country with a long colonial experience. The Philippines was a colony of Spain for three centuries, and later of the U.S. for more than fifty years. This colonial status has linked the Philippines and Pilipinos into a position of dependency in an international network and a prolonged state of underdevelopment. The status of dependency and underdevelopment, combined with years of wars of independence, the world economic depression of the 1930s, and the destruction brought about by World War II, led to the development of structures in the country that precipitated the emigration of Pilipinos from the first decade of this century until the 1970s.

Towards the end of the nineteenth and start of the twentieth centuries, structural changes were occuring in U.S. agriculture, particularly on the west coast and in Hawaii, that precipitated the need for agricultural workers. This need was initially met by native Americans, Spanish-speaking, and some poor, unskilled, highly mobile, white males, the "hobo." They were later supplanted by the Chinese and Japanese, although mostly the latter since the Chinese were primarily in low-level service work, mines, and railroads. However, shortages of these Asian workers became acute when the anti-Oriental atmosphere ("yellow peril") led to the passage of immigration laws stopping and limiting their immigration.[4]

The acquisition of the Philippines by the United States from Spain, resulting from the Spanish American War of 1896, helped solve some of the U.S. agricultural labor shortage. A large number of Pilipinos were willing and able to immigrate to the U.S. to fill this gap in the U.S. labor market. The alternative to immigrating to the U.S. was resignation to economic, social, and cultural deprivation.

It was under American control that the Pilipinos were exposed to massive public education, albeit the "American way." There was a short interim during World War II. However, at the end of the war, the American system of public education was resumed, in addition to which secondary schools and higher educational institutions (public and private) had increased. By 1956, the Philippines had the second highest number of students at 1,560 per one hundred thousand of its population in the world.[5] The country was, therefore, producing college graduates faster than the economy could absorb, most of whom were having different and higher outlooks and life styles than their parents.[6]

Thus, upon promulgation of the U.S. 1965 Immigration and Naturalization Act, the Philippines had a surplus of college trained labor. This partially explains why, among the Asian countries, the Philippines became the largest supplier of "brain drain" type immigrants.

IMPLICATIONS OF THE 1965 ACT

The 1965 Immigration and Naturalization Act was designed to meet three goals: (1) to facilitate the unification of families, (2) to allow admission of workers needed by the economy, and (3) to permit the entry of a limited number of carefully defined refugees. Theoretically the racial-origin quotas have been replaced by quotas from the Western and Eastern Hemisphere. But, practically, the Immigration Act of 1965 tended to favor immigrants from certain nations, as well as certain types of immigrants over others. For instance, by nationality the act tended to favor immigrants from Italy, Mexico, and the Philippines where there are more applicants for immigration than slots alloted. The Italians and Pilipinos always fill up their annual 20,000 quotas. The former are favored by the Fifth Preference (siblings of U.S. citizens, their spouses, and their children), while immigration of Pilipinos is facilitated by the Third Preference (professionals, spouses, and children). Also, the excess of immigrant applicants with high qualifications over the available slots tended to be very selective of those with the highest qualifications. Thus, of the 46,151 admitted as professionals in 1970, the majority came from Asia, and the largest single group came from the Philippines. In general, the qualificational selectivity of potential immigrants from the Eastern Hemisphere tended to make the immigrants from this area professionals and from more affluent backgrounds. Keely reported that the 1965 Immigration Act had shifted the main sources and number of immigrants from Western Europe to Southern Europe, Asia, and Oceania, particularly the underdeveloped areas of these regions.[7] The 1965 Immigration Act not only radically increased the number of Pilipino immigrants to the U.S., but also the social, economic, and educational backgrounds of the immigrants.

In addition, the total number of immigrants classified as "Professional, Technical, and Kindred Workers" increased significantly from 1960 through the 1970s. The percentage coming from Asia and the Philippines even increased more dramatically. By 1969, or four years after the Immigration Act took effect, India and the Philippines had replaced all of the European countries as the leading source of scientists, engineers, and physicians for the U.S., with the Philippines as the main source of physicians.[8] Gupta reports that the leading professional or occupational groups admitted as immigrants to the U.S. from the Philippines were doctors, surgeons, dentists, and those classified as "technologists and related fields." The latter include natural and social scientists, nurses and student nurses, paramedical occupations, technicians, journalists, lawyers, judges, professors, instructors, teachers (elementary and secondary), religious workers, social workers, and other unclassified professional, technical, and kindred workers.[9]

The 1965 Immigration Act has likewise affected the age and sex composition of the new Pilipino immigrants. The prospects of better employment in the U.S., coupled with easier credit for fares, has also had an impact. Whereas earlier immigrants barely had passage money for themselves, it is now possible for the new immigrants to take their families with them or join them in the U.S. in a short period of time. From 1960 to 1973, the category, "Housewives, Children, and Others with no Reported Occupations," has constantly composed about half of the Pilipino immigrants admitted to the U.S. And, except for the age group nine years and younger, there were more women admitted in 1973 than men. The preponderance of women among the new Pilipino immigrants may be due to the operation of the 1965 Immigration Act and/or a combination of the preimmigration qualifications of the immigrants themselves. Since the act favors the immigration of whole families, male immigrants can also bring in their wives and children and, if unmarried, their parents (mothers) and siblings. Secondly, since there are more college-trained women in the professions in the Philippines compared with other immigrants, it is most likely that a good number of

Pilipino women were admitted as immigrants on their own qualifications. Moreover, the greatest demands are in medicine and health-related professions, such as physicians, nurses, pharmacists, medical technologists, and institutional food professionals (food technologists, dieticians, and nutritionists). Except for physicians, where females almost equal the males, all of these professions are dominated by women in the Philippines. Married women carry the primary immigrant status, with their husbands and children entering the U.S. as "dependents," particularly if the husband's profession is low on the preferred reference lists.[10]

Although not all of the Pilipinos in midwest cities immigrated after 1965, those who did not cannot be classified as early immigrants in a strict sense, since those who came before 1965 came during the 1950s. Furthermore, their educational credentials are indicative of their being part of the brain drain.

THE BRAIN DRAIN

As used in this essay, the term "brain drain" refers to those persons of high educational credentials and/or skills from one country, but whose services are being utilized elsewhere. Another narrower economic definition of the term refers to those persons whose education and training have been possible through the efforts and resources of one country, but whose services are being utilized by another.[11]

Until the promulgation of the U.S. 1965 Immigration and Naturalization Act, the brain drain was mostly a European problem and, to a certain extent, some of the former European colonies. For instance, one of the major political issues in Britain in the 1960s was the emigration of the highly educated from Britain to the American continent (U.S. and Canada), Australia, and New Zealand. At the same time, Britain was making full use of doctors and nurses from former colonies (principally India and Pakistan) who were willing to work for less in Britain's National Health Service than the British doctors and nurses would.

By the late 1960s, Philippine authorities began to be concerned with the outflow of skilled manpower from the country. However, other than outright curtailment of foreign travel, which at the time would have been considered an infringement of civil liberties, there was nothing the Philippine government could do to directly stop or minimize the brain drain. In view thereof, certain segments of the population and the leadership began to rationalize the "benefits" of the brain drain. For instance, it was argued that a Pilipino scientist would contribute more to the world, and to the Philippines in the long run, if he or she was adequately compensated and working under favorable conditions elsewhere than being underpaid in the Philippines and working under limited and frustrating conditions. It was also argued (although not adequately substantiated) that the remittances of Pilipinos working abroad contribute to the country's dollar reserve. Another rationalization was that the emigration of Pilipinos (skilled and unskilled) relieves the pressure on the country's unemployment, especially for the educated unemployed (or underemployed) who were perceived to be more dangerous.[12]

IMPLICATIONS OF MACRO STRUCTURES IN THE IMMIGRATION EXPERIENCE AT THE MICRO LEVEL

The macro structures that precipitate immigration (or constraints under which immigration occurs) to a great extent also determine the level and extent of the interaction between the immigrants and the host peoples, and the former's participation in the latter's institutions. From the beginning of this century to the early 1970s, the major factor that precipitated emigration was the actual or perceived deprivation of the Pilipino immigrants, had they not opted to leave their country. Whereas the state of deprivation (actual or perceived) of the early immigrants may have been absolute, for the new immigrants it may be more relative. Immigration was perceived as the most viable means of resolving the conflicts that they were confronting in their own country.

The structural "brain drain" characteristics of the new immigrants, coupled with the changes in the macro structures (political, social, and economic) in the U.S. at the time of their immigration, made the process at the micro level less difficult compared with the early Pilipino immigrants with low educational/occupational credentials and who immigrated to the U.S. at a different period in the latter's history.

The new immigrants had a more realistic perception of what their new environment was most likely to be. They were aware that immigration itself would present new conflicts (that is, racial prejudice and discrimination). However, these were preferred to the conflicts that they were confronting. And/or they perceived that the structures (economic, social, and political) of the new country would allow them more and better options and alternatives in their search for meaningful lives.

This study supports other studies on the Philippine "brain drain" which show that knowledge of conditions in the Philippines is a better predictor of Pilipino international migration than the immigrants' experiences and/or attitudes about the U.S. and the world.

EMPLOYMENT AND INCOME

In general, the new immigrants are competitive on the labor market over a period of time after their arrival in the U.S., which is usually two years or more. The general pattern of initial entry into the labor market was in a lower, different, or parallel occupation with the one previously held in the Philippines, and then movement upwards either in the same occupation or diagonally in a different occupation.

Since the media of instruction in the Philippines from high school to higher education is English, the language problem is minimized. The major barrier to getting employed in a parallel occupation from the Philippines is the licensing regulations. Other than law, this is not an insurmountable problem, since licensing examinations can be taken (and prepared for through self-study and review) in addition to residence requirements. By and large, regardless of whether they get a lower, parallel, or different occupation in the U.S. than the ones they had in the Philippines, their incomes and standards of living in the U.S. are relatively higher. Except for those who have preimmigration prearranged employment, the manner by which jobs are acquired varies. It ranges from person-to-person contacts (usually for the first

job), who may be Pilipinos or colleagues and friends, and direct applications, to response to announcements and a few direct offers of employment.

In areas where there is a large concentration of Pilipinos (for example, California), discrimination, albeit more covert, continues to persist. At lower level positions, the Pilipinos have to compete with other minorities as well as with whites. However, since the new immigrants usually have higher education than the minorities, they usually have the advantage, except when citizenship is a requirement for employment. It is, therefore, not unusual to have highly qualified Pilipinos occupying jobs for which they are overqualified.

The mean individual income for midwest city Pilipinos for 1973 was $8,909 ($10,111 for the men and $7,467 for the women). Table 1 shows a comparison of the median individual and family incomes for whites and blacks compared with all races in the midwest and midwest city Pilipinos.

On the surface, the data indicate that midwest city Pilipinos have a much higher income than either blacks or the white majority. It must be noted, however, that the respondents are a highly select group in terms of their educational and occupational qualifications. The income information for the U.S. and midwest state were computed from the general population which included those with high and low occupations and incomes. It would be more realistic to compare the incomes of the whites and blacks having the same educational and occupational attributes as the respondents.

It can, therefore, be posited that the individual median income ($8,337) for this highly educated group is, in fact, low. The median family income of $14,249 is even lower when one considers the high educational and occupational qualifications of the women, and who are wives and who are also employed. In short, the individual and family incomes of midwest city Pilipinos is not commensurate with their educational and occupational credentials.

The more the economic security, the better the chances for individual preferences, among which is the opportunity to maintain a cultural integrity or acquire a different one, whichever the case may be. All the Pilipino immigrants to the U.S. across time

TABLE 1
Individual and Family Incomes of Whites and
Blacks in the U.S., All Races in "Midwest"
Region, and "Midwest City" Pilipinos in 1973

	Individual[a] Incomes	Family Incomes
U.S. Whites	$ 4,270	$ 12,595
Blacks	3,191	7,596
"Midwest" Region (All Races)	5,439	11,947
Midwest City Pilipinos	8,333	14,249

Source: U.S. Department of Commerce. *Statistical Abstracts of the United States.* July 1974: 380–385.

[a]Figures for U.S. and Midwest are for related individuals sixteen years or older.

have had to face racial discrimination and prejudice in one form or another. However, the early immigrants were at a disadvantage. First of all, their low socioeconomic backgrounds, and lack of educational and professional credentials, made it more compelling for them to emigrate. Once in the U.S., these educational, economic, and social disadvantages exacerbated their problems of adjusting to a new environment. In addition, they were also immigrating to the U.S. at a time when prejudice and discrimination were more overt and virulent.

Another factor that has to be considered is the structural relationships between the immigrants and the host country (bilaterally as well as in the international network of relationships). The Philippines' subordinate relations with the U.S. exacerbated the subordinate status of the Pilipinos in the U.S. From the time Pilipinos immigrating to the U.S. from the turn of the twentieth century until the late 1960s to occupy the back seat in its "special relations" with the U.S. If the Philippines was subordinate to the U.S. (even to the extent where Americans had more advantages *in the Philippines* than the average Pilipinos), it is hardly to be expected that Pilipino immigrants in the U.S. would be treated any better.[13]

The Philippines has become more independent of the U.S. during the last two decades, partly due to the more nationalistic and Third-World (rather than pro-American) outlook of a new generation of Pilipinos. However, it takes more than just attitudes to be independent of such a country as the United States, especially after generations of economic, social, political, and cultural domination. It is also necessary to have some power, or at least a bargaining position in international power politics. Part of the independent stature of the Philippines is made possible by its association with the Third World which is emerging as an international power block. In addition, the emergence of China as a political, economic, and military power in Asia, and the withdrawal of the U.S. military presence in Southeast Asia, except in the Philippines and Thailand where it is now being questioned by the Pilipinos and the leadership, has placed the Philippines in a better bargaining position with the U.S. in international politics, at least in that part of the world.

Thus, the more independent the Philippines is of the U.S., and/or the better its bargaining position at the macro level, the more likely this will affect the status of Pilipino immigrants for the better. Protests by the Pilipino nation and its leadership against the mistreatment of Pilipino immigrants to the U.S., today, are less likely to be ignored as they were during the earlier history of Pilipino immigration to the United States.[14]

OTHER SELECTED PATTERNS OF PARTICIPATION OF NEW PILIPINO IMMIGRANTS AND THEIR IMPLICATIONS

Until recently, most Pilipinos did not associate themselves with the other nonwhite minority groups in the U.S. racial conflict. First of all, this is partly due to a Pilipino personality cultural trait of avoiding interpersonal conflicts. Hence, they tend to avoid potential situations where open racial confrontation at the personal level is most likely to occur. Secondly, the Pilipinos are not a homogeneous group. They are differentiated, intergenerationally, by social class and by ethnolinguistic origins. Thirdly, they perceive that their immigrant status puts them in a different category than other nonwhite minority groups, such as blacks, Spanish-speaking, and native Americans, within the context of U.S. majority-minority relations. Whereas the latter may have the *right* to make demands on the U.S. social, political, and economic systems, the Pilipino immigrants perceive their being in the U.S. as a *privilege*, which can be unilaterally or bilaterally voided if they are unsatisfied with the treatment accorded them by the host society. In other words, being allowed to immigrate is preferred to being right on the racial issue. This does not mean that they are less critical of certain issues in the U.S. In fact, they are just as critical of their own country. Whether it is the Philippines or the U.S., "My country right or wrong" is no longer a viable concept either for most of the new immigrants or for other people in the U.S.

Each society assumes the position that its culture, values, norms, and social structures are more desirable than others. Deviations from this position or assumption are perceived as threats to the existence of that society. The deviations can come from inside the society or externally, for example through the influx of large immigrant groups. The tendency to make deviants conform to what the society values most is a legitimate concern, especially as it is practiced by most, if not all, societies. The issue, therefore, is what are the most effective means of inducing people (immigrants) to appreciate what the host culture values most and to effect some degree of conformity.

The findings of this study support the sociological definition of culture as a viable and dynamic phenomenon. The new Pilipino immigrants to the U.S., as exemplified by the respondents of this study, were neither traditional nor modern, Pilipino nor American. Their perception and behavior were dictated by perceived and real situations which they had to confront. When all basic necessities of life and comforts needed for physical survival are met, or when the conflicts that precipitated migration are fully or partially resolved, human beings will look to those aspects of life that give it some meaning. More likely than not, this will be identification with fellow human beings who can give them the maximum psychological, social, and emotional security. These are most likely to be their families and other people, and the culture that shaped them into the kind of human beings that they are.

In a broadest sense, the concept of a Pilipino-American heritage may be a viable one, which would include the sum of the Pilipino experience in America for about three-quarters of a century. However, the concept of a Pilipino-American culture has to be a limited one. It would be more realistic to posit an early with regard to a new (and different) Pilipino-American culture, since different types of Pilipinos have been immigrating to America during different periods of the latter's history. In effect, there were several or at least two preimmigration Philippine "subcultures" moving into the U.S. One would be typical of a more traditional and rural-based Pilipino culture which most of the early immigrants came from, and another may be exemplified by the new immigrants who came from an educated and cosmopolitan culture, and who may, in fact, feel more comfortable with Americans and other peoples coming from a similar cultural milieu, than with their more traditional countrymen.

In fact, it was not until recently that the early and new immigrants began to have a more meaningful interaction, especially on the U.S. west coast. The early immigrants perceived the new immigrants as upstarts and snobs who were now reaping the benefits of what the early immigrants had sown at a great cost in anguish and deprivation. The new immigrants look upon and treat the old immigrants patronizingly (or even with disdain as equivalent to "hillbillies"). Although no Pilipino term has yet been developed to identify the new immigrants, the early immigrants are referred to both in the U.S. and the Philippines as "old timers," or simply "OTs," and "Penoys." As far as can be determined, the last term is derived from "Pilipinos in the U.S." but it always means the early immigrants.

The patterns of immigration by the early and new immigrants prevented the development of Pilipino geographical settlements in the U.S., such as the Chinatowns and Little Tokyos. First of all, the early immigrants were mostly males, who lived on the plantation camps or worked at low-service occupations in the cities. Between agricultural seasons they moved to the cities for low-skilled employment or went to work in the fish canneries in Alaska. Furthermore, most of the early Pilipino immigrants did not intend to settle in the U.S. They believed (or were made to believe) that, after some years in the U.S., they would be able to make enough money to return to the Philippines to get a fresh start in life by acquiring their own small farms or businesses, or getting better employment by dint of their experience and training while in the U.S. The high educational and occupational credentials and higher social economic status of the new immigrants, allow them to bring their families with them and pursue their employment and professional opportunities throughout the U.S., so family or ethnic based preimmigration networks are no longer necessary. While Pilipinos do not form any particular neighborhood groupings, they are concentrated in a few areas in the United States, such as California.

Hence, since the turn of the century when Pilipinos started immigrating to the U.S., and up to the 1970s, the Pilipino community in the U.S. has been more a community of consciousness, located in social space, rather than a definite locality-based physical phenomenon. The closest concrete manifestation of a Pilipino community is the formal organizations, which range from social clubs to professional groups, and the U.S. (or Canadian) based Pilipino media.

Thus, for almost three-quarters of a century, wittingly or unwittingly the immigration of Pilipinos to the U.S. resulted in a symbiotic relationship between, and beneficial to, certain interests in both countries. The emigration of Pilipinos relieved the pressure from Philippines' economic and political interests from undertaking economic, social, and political reforms, thereby maintaining the status quo to their advantage. At the same time, certain interests in the U.S. were provided with a reserve pool of cheap surplus labor to draw upon.

IMPLICATIONS OF THE BRAIN DRAIN

The brain drain immigration benefits the host society as well as the immigrants themselves. It provides the former with cheap skilled labor and the latter with opportunities for a more meaningful life. However, the phenomenon could have its undesirable effects on certain segments among the "native" nonwhite minorities. The brain drain credentials of the new immigrants give them an advantage over other U.S. citizens (white and nonwhite) in employment who may have lower qualifications. Also, with a pool of highly qualified immigrants who are willing to work for less, and who may be less demanding, what would be the point in training and increasing the job opportunities of less fortunate U.S. citizens?

The hiring of immigrants at lower positions (and lower compensation) than U.S. citizens or whites could also have its implications on the issue of majority-minority relations in the U.S. A case in point are the health-related occupations. One alleged reason for the restrictions placed on foreign doctors to set up private practices or be connected to better institutions is their alleged inferior training. Therefore, they are relegated as interns and junior-level residents in lower quality hospitals, clinics, and health centers in inner cities and rural areas. We are not competent to comment on these contentions. However, for the sake of argument, accepting (without conceding) the inferiority of the foreign-trained doctors, then it can be argued on moral and perhaps even legal grounds that, if they are not competent enough to treat middle and upper class (mostly white) patients, then they should not be competent to treat any patients at all—rich or poor, white or nonwhite.

The implications of permitting foreign-trained (and presumably inferior) doctors to treat the poor tend to support criticisms of the U.S. health delivery services. Namely, that it is a commercial commodity and that good health is available to the highest bidder, while low-quality health service is what the poor can afford to bid or be provided with.[15] Consequently, foreign-trained, that is, second-class, doctors are only good for treating second-class citizens. On the other hand, would the poor get treated by doctors at all if there weren't foreign-trained doctors that were willing to treat them for less pay? There is also the possibility that wittingly or unwittingly the poor may, in fact, be treated by excellent physicians who could be treating the rich (and making more money), had they been allowed to by the system.

Another implication of the brain-drain type of international migration is its effects on the "contributing" countries. The developing countries were and are losing the people they need most for their development, and those that are left (who are barred from emigrating and immigrating elsewhere because of their low qualifications or skills) are those that cannot help themselves, much less their countries' developments. The net effect of the international migration of the talented and skilled, or brain drain, is an additional loss to the countries of origin and gain for the developed countries (particularly the U.S.), the international organizations, and the multinational corporations that engage their services.

CONCLUSION: TOWARDS A FUTURIST PERSPECTIVE

As anyone who has had some exposure to international agencies and institutions can attest, the worldwide (no longer just to the U.S.) migration of Pilipinos is not unique. This calls for a truly *international* perspective on migration, rather than the traditional transnational perspective involving two nations and cultures. The macro structures that are and will precipitate the migration of the brain-drain immigrants may no longer be nationally and politically based, but rather international or regional in character, such as the international agencies and

multinational corporations. Will new immigrants be international civil servants or employees of multinational corporations, rather than citizens of one country? Would they, in fact, be willing to be citizens of any one country and committed to a political ideology? (In such a case they would not be immigrants in the traditional meaning of the term, but sojourners who move and live in many parts of the world for periods of time.)

The term underdeveloped (or developing), developed, industrial, and technological have been used to define stages of a country's or region's development. The term "Third World peoples," designating peoples that are poor, oppressed, and discriminated, has gained acceptance during the last few years. Would the term "technocratic peoples" (or something similar) also be a viable appellation in the near future, just as "Eurocrats" is now used to designate people working in European agencies, such as the European Common Market? Would it be too Orwellian to conceive of a world where the fate and destinies of the poor and uneducated will be decided upon by an international technocratic elite, whose structural affiliations and commitments are not based on national affiliation and political ideologies?

NOTES

1. Walter Adams, ed., *The Brain Drain* (New York: Macmillan Company, 1968), and Daniel Lerner and Morton Gorden, *Euratlantica* (Cambridge: Massachusetts Institute of Technology Press, 1969).

2. Milton Gordon, "Social Class and American Intellectuals," *American Association of University Professors Bulletin* 40, No. 4 (Winter, 1954–55), pp.517–28; Melvin Seeman, "The Intellectual and the Language of Minorities," *American Journal of Sociology* 64, No. 1 (July, 1958), pp.25–35; and Seymour Martin Lipset, "American Intellectuals: Their Politics and Status," *Daedalus* 88, No. 3 (Summer, 1959), pp.460–86.

3. Milton Gordon, *Assimilation in America* (New York: Oxford University Press, 1964), pp.224–32.

4. Carey MacWilliams has addressed this topic in two books: *Factories in the Fields* (Boston: Little, Brown, and Company, 1939), and *Brothers Under the Skin* (Boston: Little, Brown, and Company, 1964).

5. United Nations, Educational Scientific and Cultural Organization (UNESCO), *UNESCO Statistical Yearbook 1968* (Paris: UNESCO, 1969).

6. Sixro K. Roxas, "Investments in Education," *The Philippine Economic Bulletin* II, No. 1 (1963), pp.32–39, and Edita A. Tan, "Philippine Market for Educated Labor," report to the National Science Development Board (NSDB),

Bicutan, Rizal, Philippines, 1970. (Mimeographed.)

7. Charles B. Keely, "Effects of the Immigration Act of 1965 on Selected Characteristics of Immigrants to the United States," *Demography* 8, No. 2 (May 1971), pp.157–69.

8. Royal F. Morales, *Makibaka: The Pilipino American Struggle* (Los Angeles: Mountainview Publishers, Inc., 1974), p.71.

9. M. L. Gupta, "Outflow of High-Level Manpower from the Philippines," *International Labor Review* 8 (February 1973), p.172.

10. Keely, op. cit., pp. 157–59; Charles B. Keely, "Philippine Migration: International Movements and the Emigration to the United States," *International Migration Review* (Summer 1972), pp.177–87; Purita F. Asperilla, "The Mobility of Filipino Nurses," paper presented at the Conference on International Migration from the Philippines, East-West Center, Honolulu, Hawaii, June 10–14, 1974; and Christina P. Parel, "A Survey of Foreign-Trained Professionals in the Philippines," paper presented at the Conference on International Migration from the Philippines, East-West Center,

Honolulu, Hawaii, June 10–14, 1974.

11. Walden F. Bello, Frank Lynch, and Perla Q. Makil, "Brain Drain in the Philippines," in *Modernization: Its Impact on the Philippines* IV, IPC Papers No. 7 (Quezon City, Philippines: Ateneo de Manila University, 1969), pp.93-100, and Gupta, op. cit., pp.167–91.

12. Adams, op. cit.; Bello, Lunch, and Makil; and Gupta, ibid.

13. MacWilliams, op. cit., pp.244–46; Jose W. Diokno, "The Issue with the Americans," *Solidarity* III, No. 10 (October 1968), pp.11–19; and William J. Pomeroy, *An American Made Tragedy* (New York: International Publishers, 1974).

14. Burno Lasker, *Filipino Immigration to Continental United States and to Hawaii* (Chicago: University of Chicago Press, 1931), pp.273–88, and Garel A. Grunder and William E. Livezey, *The Philippines and the United States* (Norman, Oklahoma: University of Oklahoma Press, 1951), pp.248–75.

15. William Ryan, *Blaming the Victim* (New York: Random House, 1971), pp.142–70.

THE IMPACT OF EMIGRATION ON PUERTO RICANS[1]

Luis Nieves-Falcón

Puerto Rico is a country with a veneer of material prosperity and a socioeconomic infrastructure of endemic poverty. Penury is the permanent condition of the many while continued affluence is the monopoly of the few. This is evidenced in the widening economic distance between the privileged classes on the one end and the proletariat and rural masses on the other. Contrary to what frequent official statements would have us believe, the prevailing situation in the island owes less to the lack of natural resources than to the working of a system characterized by the unequal distribution of social and economic gains, and the flight of profits which are generated in the island and ploughed elsewhere for the benefit of corporation stockholders based in the United States. It is a system whereby the monied groups of the island perform the function of an intermediary bourgeoisie, serving the interests of the continental corporations with one hand, and keeping the mass of Puerto Ricans in perpetual exploitation with the other.

In an effort to justify this lopsidedly onerous condition, the regime and its retainers have emitted explanation often betraying a vicious racism and a utilitarian class prejudice. Most of such statements are, at bottom, racist appraisals whose intent is to justify white North American ascendancy and Puerto Rican subordination. They are typical rationalizations of the racial relationship inherent in all situations of exploitation.

Class-biased justifications put the blame on the working class for its social state. The social phenomenon with which the Puerto Rican worker has come to be associated during this century of American colonization is population increase. Since the worker was the decreed cause, he was to be the principal target of instituted control systems. These of necessity bear the stamp of the political and intellectual elites which have controlled the country. These groups never conceal their fear of population expansion and its possible diluting effects on their gains. Thus, they have been quick to endorse, support, and carry out measures, the full weight of which bear on the working classes. They have had particular success in the formulation of the emigration policy, as well as the sterilization program and the stimulation of foreign immigration to a supposedly over-populated Puerto Rico. Many persons think that these elements are the main components of a population policy aimed at the gradual dissolution of the cultural and psychological supports of the Puerto Rican nation. I will deal here with some aspects related to emigration.

Emigration is a vital part of the life of all Puerto Ricans. The importance of this process may be gauged from the fact that around 30 percent of the island's population in the age group eighteen years old and over has had some emigratory experience. The Census Bureau of the United States reported an aggregate of more than one million Puerto Ricans residing in the United States during the year 1970. These figures all too well attest to the significance of mainland bound migration in the lives of the islanders. It is a process which not only has impinged upon considerable numbers of them but also promises to affect many more of their kind. This process started the same year in which the island was militarily conquered by the United States in 1898 and continues today. Although some of its early history has been difficult to trace, there were, as there are now, recognizable ingredients to show that the mainspring of the process is exploitation. Through it, a manpower resource would be made available to fill jobs whose position in the socioeconomic scale was the lowest, since they were residual occupations left behind by a rapidly mobile and affluent society. The central economic proposition behind migrant labor was that it was cheap and abundant, and as such guaranteed employers a wide margin of profits.

The displacement of Puerto Ricans to the United States has had a diverse impact. On the matter of national identification Puerto Ricans seem not only to perceive cultural differences between North Americans and themselves, but overwhelmingly identify as Puerto Ricans rather than Americans. They keep track of goings on in Puerto Rico, prefer to speak Spanish rather than English, choose Puerto Rican neighborhoods above others and, more often than not, plan to go back to the island. Significant differences emerge with regard to language among second and third generation Puerto Ricans. Most of them are aware of the effects of migration on the inherited family structure, particularly on the roles of the female and of children. The proportion of them backing independence for Puerto Rico is larger than that found among voting population on the island. The picture which emerges of the migrant is one of a person closely identified with the land, both in national and cultural terms.

In a study in which about 200 Puerto Rican immigrants were asked to appraise their objective conditions as individuals within the adopted society, 23.5 percent thought that they were better off than on the island, 32.8 perceived the reverse, 19.5 saw their situation to be the same, 16.6 did not know, and 1.6 refused to answer.[2] How does this pattern of verbal response correspond to actual reality as measured by available aggregate data? How does it relate to the publicized promise of opportunity and material plenty as an animating force behind their migration?

It appears that the dream of individual betterment in the new environment had remained an unattainable one for the majority of the group in question. Contrary to what social scientists of the North American establishment have given us to believe, the Puerto Ricans have not made it, nor are they making it, nor will they ever make it in the forseeable future. Indeed, collected data indicate that the situation of Puerto Ricans here in the United States is getting worse. As part of the poor in this country, their social distance from the haves of the society is increasing rather than diminishing. As an ethnic poor they are even further behind, as evidenced in the following findings: (1) the majority of them are employed in low-skill occupations and lowest-paying jobs; (2) they have the highest recorded rate of unemployment; (3) their median income is the lowest; (4) the rate of dependents (persons outside the labor force) per employed individual is highest among them; (5) their housing conditions are the worst.

The educational variable correlates highly with the economic. Thus, we find Puerto Ricans having (1) the lowest level of educational attainment among their adult population; (2) a minimal number of college graduates; (3) the highest dropout rate in the public school system; (4) the weakest holding power in college.

In a society where education is the principal escalator for social mobility, the position of Puerto Ricans in the American educational system appears more disadvantaged when current performance standards are applied, that is, when the efficiency of the system is tested. In New York City specifically, where the highest concentration of Puerto Ricans in the whole United States is found, available data show that the average reading score among Puerto Rican students was lower at each grade level than that of either blacks or whites. Furthermore, the higher the grade level, the higher the proportion of Puerto Ricans reading below grade standard. Data for other cities show the same trends. In other words, "the longer a Puerto Rican child attends school the less he learns." The precarious position of that child within the school system remains still, as described by the Coleman Report which showed his standing in verbal ability, reading comprehension, and mathematics to be the poorest compared to that of blacks and whites.

With these highly negative findings in view, we wonder if there can really exist a viable alternative which will help Puerto Ricans break the cycle of subordination and poverty they have long been riveted to. The prospects appear very dim indeed from testimonies of recently arrived Puerto Rican migrants, and from community perception of their situation.

On the matter of problems supposedly faced by Puerto Rican children, language is the principal reason mentioned. But an examination of the whole listing of factors reveals that the weight of the blame and responsibility for such problems is almost wholly thrust on the individual, while the institutional setting which originates and nourishes his condition is absolved. In all these areas, Puerto Rican residents tend to show a low level of consciousness regarding their own situation. This unawareness reflects the working of a socioeconomic order nourished on the inequalities of its constituents, and imbued with the ruling purpose of the dominant group. Through organization and control of the societal processes, the ideas and attitudes of that group are pumped into the social psyche of the other groups, shaping the view which the latter are to take about prevailing conditions. The Puerto Rican thus sees himself as the controlling groups see him. Poverty is partly if not entirely his own making. Similarly, when he views the education made available to his children, he sees the poor and discriminatory education received as normative. The wellspring of this unawareness is the repeated pattern of suffering, abuse, and disparagement which underlies his life experience and has become normative before his eyes. His experience has a corrosive effect on his sensibilities, leaving him for the most desensitized to his own condition and unable to establish causal relationship between the environment and his personal condition. But, there are other aspects of the Puerto Rican's situation other than the socioeconomic ones. As a child he is an unwary victim of a systematic process of cultural erosion, as reflected in the limited opportunities which the school system gives him to learn his own language and culture and to identify himself positively as a Puerto Rican. Thus, in New York City, although Puerto Rican children comprise 22.8 percent of the public school enrollment, only a small percentage are getting assistance through bilingual programs. Moreover, these programs, which are intended to strengthen specific cultural components, are, in fact, geared to increase their rate of assimilation in another culture, namely, the American.

The negative implications of the institutional assault on the culture of the Puerto Ricans are reflected in the following findings. Firstly, data show that cases of social pathology, specifically drug abuse and juvenile delinquency, are more prevalent among Puerto Ricans farther removed from their cultural roots. Secondly, a study in 1965 on mental illness shows a higher rate of hospitals' first admissions among second generation New York–Puerto Ricans than among other large ethnic groups.[3] Thirdly, a 1972 study of college students reveals "a significantly greater degree of psychiatric impairment . . . among mainland born Puerto Ricans than among island born Puerto Ricans." The author's concluding observation was that there seems to be an inverse relationship for the Puerto Rican between acculturation and mental health.[4] Finally, a recent study of dropouts among Puerto Ricans results in the following observations:

> One gets the impression that those who eventually drop out from school drop in spirit long before they actually leave. It also seems as if the dropouts are not as close to the Puerto Rican culture as the stay ins. There is evidence that the dropouts do not identify with Spanish terms and that their parents and grandparents have been in the United States longer. This could mean that what they experience in school is not a culture conflict but a sense of cultural loss because they do not have a heritage they can identify with readily. This would mean that they are not bi-cultural or culturally different but that they are marginal mainstreamers.[5]

Thus, the second mentioned studies point to one singular fact about the Puerto Rican in the United States, which is, the more assimilated he is the lesser are his chances of achieving personality integration and, therefore, the greater is his susceptibility to social maladjustment. In other words, the price which a Puerto Rican pays for his assimilation is his own emotional impairment. From those studies, however, we cannot gauge the personal agony which inheres in the loss of one's identity through cultural erosion. We can partially capture the desperate gropings for such an identity on the part of those who are obviously in search of one. A Puerto Rican college student, born and raised in New York City and who had never been to Puerto Rico, puts it this way: "I am not American, that I know. I am Puerto Rican but I do not know why." In the same vein, another Puerto Rican, a poet, pours out his feelings in the following verses.[6]

who i am/who i touch
who touches me

:i am a Puerto Rican/
although i speak in the language of my oppressor.

although my thoughts are blends of
my oppression.
:i am Puerto Rican.
although/most time/
i cannot clearly understand what words my
people use to voice their pain/
I am felt by that pain.
& that/to me/ is love.

who i am. who i touch
who touches me
. . . .
the oppressor's language/i speak
the oppression's pain/i feel.
who i am/who i touch.
who touches me

i am Puerto Rican. Borinqueno/mind &
soul. & that no chains can hold.

That's the life of every Puerto Rican in the United
States. It is one of continuous personal and cultural crisis. The instruments by which he can be helped to cope with that crisis apparently have not emerged. For many of us, it is doubtful whether they can emerge at all, without the liberation of our country.

NOTES

1. This work is based on a recently published book, *El Emigrante Puertorriqueño* (Rio Piedras: Ediciones Edil, 1975).
2. Ibid.
3. B. Malzberg, *Mental Disease Among the Puerto Rican Population of New York State*, 1960, 61 (Albany research Foundation for Mental Hygiene, Inc., 1965). Quoted by Josephine Bustamante, "The Relationship Between Acculturation and Mental Health among Puerto Rican College Students in New York City: A Comparative Study," Ms. (December 1972), p.10, Malzberg's standardized rate for hospitalized mental illness among Puerto Rican born males was 266.8, and among Puerto Rican born females was 179.3. The rates for the second generation, or United States born, were 429.7 for males and 220.3 for females.
4. Josephine Bustamante, Ibid., pp.16-20.
5. Puerto Rican Research and Resources Center, "Results of First Pilot Study (Drop Out Study)," ms., p.4.
6. A poem by Papoleto.

SOCIALIZATION AND THE PROCESS OF MIGRATION: THE CASE OF THE INTERNATIONAL STUDENT IN THE U.S.

Phillip Carey and Alemayehu G. Mariam

INTRODUCTION

The migration of international students to the U.S. is an event that dates back to the nineteenth century.[1] Although the experiment in educating international students continued until the turn of the century, it was, however, limited in scope and remained largely in the sphere of private sponsorship. The importance of expanding and facilitating international student education was formally recognized by the U.S. government in 1924[2] and 1948,[3] when Congress enacted special legislation exempting international students from certain immigration restrictions by providing special legal classification and status. Thus, in the past several decades, hundreds of thousands of government and privately financed international students have received technical and academic training in American educational institutions.

A SELECTED REVIEW OF THE LITERATURE

The ensuing literature review intends to show that the education of international students in American educational institutions has been of special interest to administrators, educators, governments, international organizations, and social scientists for quite some time. Only recently, however, has interest been expressed in the unique problems associated with the socialization process of migration for education. Interestingly, problems and questions associated with binationalism and cultural pluralism within the context of educational acquisition are no longer limited to students from abroad. They have emerged as critical issues in American higher education. Although much of the early research in this area tends to be noncumulative and diverse, the more recent literature shows a systematic effort to accumulate more knowledge about the broader issues of international education, and the salient factors affecting international students' adjustment within the academic setting.

The early research and studies on international students in the U.S. have been carefully reviewed by Cormack,[4] Cussler,[5] and Walton.[6] Cormack's survey of the literature shows two themes dominating the early investigations of international students: first, she finds there has been a preoccupation with international students' attitudes toward the U.S.; and second, there has been an emphasis on the examination of the various aspects of international exchange programs, with the view to effecting improvements and making policy recommendations. Cormack notes the inadequacy of the previous research, both in terms of substantive and salient knowledge regarding international students, as well as the application of certain methodological procedures that are "superficial" and "harmful" since they fail to give adequate consideration of social conditions and "deeper aspects of psychological effect," while purporting to generate empirical knowledge. Cussler's survey of the early research provides a rigorous review of the underlying assumptions that propelled international student exchange programs in the U.S., and certain aspects of social acculturation that need to be fostered for better communication between students and the society at large. She makes an effort to distill some of the tentative generalizations that had been advanced in terms of the class origins of international students, the various types of "orientation programs," the effects of length of stay and language competence as principal variables in adjustment, and as factors that affect a student's perception and interaction beyond the academic milieu.

Walton's evaluation of the early literature is designed as a systematic summary of two decades of research on international students, and provides a perspective on the general trend in the early research and suggests shifts in scholarly foci. She suggests that international students tend to view their sojourn in the U.S. favorably, although they may be disapproving of certain American practices and foreign policies. Further, the process of image and attitude formation by international students transcends simplistic and impulsive judgments, and results from a consideration of positive and negative attitudes toward certain manifestations in American society. According to this analysis, there has been undue emphasis on a narrow area of research focusing on specific attitudes of foreign students, "brain drain" phenomena, and schematic studies purporting to test hypotheses. Consequently, Walton suggests that future research should focus broadly on the impact of exchange programs on American society, and the effects of social and technological change on international students.

Generally, a review of the early literature on international students tends to show an overemphasis and concentration of research in a relatively few areas. Many of these studies have tended to be insufficiently focused on the actual processes of culture conflict and patterns of adaptation by international students. Research efforts to vigorously explore the dynamics between the divergent cultural values of international students and the effects of American values on these students has been grossly lacking. The research orientation has therefore tended to be limited in scope by largely focusing on formation and change of attitudes by international students. The lack of a theoretical framework to systematically examine the wide-ranging issues that attend to international exchange programs and patterns of adaptation by students appears to have been an important factor in the divergent nature of the early studies. On the other hand, the emphasis on research with policy orientations has tended to limit the development of cumulative knowledge on international students, since the effort to improve and facilitate exchange programs was of primary consideration.

The methodological problems in the early studies have also tended to be inhibiting factors in research on international students. Opinion surveys and loosely structured interviews have been employed to investigate student attitudes and changes in attitude over a limited period of time. The undue reliance on verbal responses has tended to render much systematic inquiry to a level of superficiality,

since consideration of fundamental social and cultural conditions of the students were lacking. Thus, the tendency has been to measure attitudes on the basis of student opinions, which for a variety of reasons fails to adequately reflect the beliefs and actions of these students. On another dimension, limitations in acquiring reliable data and the absence of vigorous methodologics have been salient factors in inhibiting the construction of systematic research designs that may be replicated for further research.

The recent literature on international students shows a pervading consciousness for higher levels of explanation and accumulation of basic knowledge on various aspects of their sojourn in the U.S. Although there is still a notable lack of interdisciplinary effort toward theory building, numerous systematic studies investigating specific aspects of international students' sojourn in the U.S. have been completed. Similarly, despite the absence of a standardized or replicable methodology, considerable improvements have been made in the application of measurement techniques and analysis of data. The trend broadly shows that researchers are acquiring greater sensitivity both to the cultural backgrounds of the students as well as to the effects of American culture on the perceptions, attitude formation, and change of these students.

Recent studies and research efforts that particularly focus on international student attitudes and their social adjustment in the U.S. have revealed certain interesting generalizations and findings. A good many of these studies employ well-constructed research designs with relatively sophisticated methodological procedures for data collection and analysis. Although a number of these studies rely on tabulations of average and gross comparisons of pertinent data, criteria for the selection and identification of variables show qualitative improvements over earlier studies.

The most pertinent studies on the social and educational adjustment of international students in the U.S. fall along three categories: studies of the differential rate of socialization and adjustment of students by national origin; studies on international students' social interactions during their stay in the U.S.; and studies on factors that contribute to adjustment problems of these students in the host country. Consequently, research in these three general areas has led to a number of significant findings that are relevant both in gaining greater understanding of the adjustment patterns of foreign students, as well as in determining the crucial sociocultural factors that are operative among the diverse international student community. Although a considerable number of these studies examine international students of a specific geographical area or national origin, they nevertheless address the broad social and psychological dimensions that characterize the patterns of student adaptation in general.

Studies that specifically examine the process of socialization of international students show that geographic and national origin are salient factors in adjustment and communication. For example, Antler,[7] investigating social contacts among medical residents in university affiliated hospitals, found greater interaction between students of the same national origin than with host country representatives. The tendency of international students to limit their range of social interaction to their compatriots is further supported by studies on cultural patterns and sentiments of nationalism. Becker[8] suggests that international students who have been in the U.S. for more than two years still tend to associate more with their compatriots than any other groups. The factors that appear to be crucial in this syndrome of withdrawal from meaningful social interaction were identified as attachment to cultural values, and varying sentiments of nationalism.

Further explanations of the adaptation process of foreign students have been advanced by Klein, et. al.[9] In their study on Asian students, they were able to ascertain that most of these students sought to explain their alienated disposition in terms of American's tendency to be insincere, superficial, and ephemeral about matters of friendship. With regards to the Asian students themselves, Klein, et. al. suggest that perceived role conflict and self-esteem are crucial factors in determining their mode of social adaptation. However, it should be noted that different categories of Asian students may show contrasting patterns of adaptation and attitudes. In fact, Wakita[10] found that students from mainland Asia tended to show feelings of superiority to Asian Americans and others who did not speak the Asian languages. Furthermore, their reaction to racial prejudice and discrimination in American society

was relatively less intense. On the other hand, Hawaiian born Asian Americans showed closer association among themselves and manifested greater sensitivity to factors of racial prejudice. They felt that Asian students were generally shy, especially in situations of close interactions.

The tendency of international student groups to socialize among their own co-nationals is further supported by Kang.[11] He found that 80 percent of the Chinese students at the University of Minnesota associated with their compatriots, maintaining their own organizations and activities without much participation in outside events. In a similar study, Kang[12] finds that those Chinese students that had anglicized their names had greater social interaction and communication with other Americans. Their increased level of communication appears to have contributed substantially to a relatively varied set of social and economic expectations and adjustment patterns.

Other studies on Indian and African students show similar patterns of social interaction among international students. Gandhi,[13] studying Indian students at the University of Minnesota, found that 90 percent of the students lived together or within close proximity to each other. He finds linguistic, religious, or regional differences to be of limited importance in their interactions. Although their commitments to cultural sentiments and life styles tended to vary, this appears to be a consequence of prolonged sojourn rather than a relegation of traditional life styles. Hegazy,[14] in a comparative study of British and Egyptian students, finds a similar tendency of restricted social interaction by the Egyptians. He found that the British students had a better knowledge of American society, while the Egyptian students appeared to manifest stereotypic views of American culture and society. Thus, Hegazy found British students to associate more with other Americans than the Egyptian students who tended to congregate together and lead their own community life. The factors that appeared to inhibit greater social communication by the Egyptian students were attributed to discrepancies in religious values, sexual morals, and types of eating and drinking habits.

The social, psychological, and financial problems that aggravate international student adjustment to American society have been enduring topics of investigation. Although a comprehensive inventory of these student problems is lacking, factors related to language ability, availability of financial resources, and sociocultural attitudes of the students seem to be of major importance. Johnson[15] found that, among the students he surveyed, 60 percent reported problems with the English language and financial resources. Mishler[16] broadly identifies problems in adjustment as stemming from an experience of national status deprivation, the quality of an individual relationship with home country and class origins of the individual. Melby,[17] (1966) testifying at a Congressional hearing, suggests that social and political problems extant in the U.S. are important factors in the adjustment problems of international students. Yankelovich[18] finds further support for the contention that problems internal to American society hinder student adjustment. He found that, although the international students and faculty he surveyed tended to be apolitical with regards to domestic American politics, they nevertheless expressed strong disapproval of U.S. foreign policy toward underdeveloped countries and immigration policies regulating international student employment.

The literature review on international student adjustment and adaptation to life in the U.S. shows the dominant pattern to be one of withdrawal, and formation of small communities with limited interaction with the society at large. The factors that contribute to such a pattern of adaptation are broadly identified to include elements internal to American society as well as sociocultural factors unique to the international students. The ability of culturally different students to effectively participate and communicate with the larger American society, and their academic success, is shown to have been hampered by such problems as language facility and limited financial resources. International students' attitudes are also shown to have been affected by U.S. government policies toward the so-called Third World countries, and racial practices in American society. On the other hand, the literature review significantly points to the lack of theoretical and methodological sophistication in the accumulation of substantive knowledge on the behavior of international students sojourning in the U.S. The cumulative research effort has thus far

provided useful insights and a constellation of partial, tentative, and quasi-explanations to discrete aspects of international students' behavior. However, the trend in the acquisition of systematic knowledge on international students has been marked by broad diversity and discontinuity in research topics, and inability of researchers to build upon previous research. Such a trend has tended to counteract the effort to systematize and standardize approaches and methodologies crucial to the development of substantive knowledge regarding international student behavior. Thus, the existing trend in the direction of individual scholarly judgment in determining research topics and areas, and the application of diverse measurement techniques, necessitates a reevaluation among the scholarly community with the view to greater agreement on relevant approaches and methodological techniques.

In this regard, the literature survey shows only a limited effort in terms of the construction of organizing concepts and theoretical frameworks that take into consideration the broad systemic factors that condition the behavior of international students in either American educational institutions or the society at large. Unfortunately, this trend has persisted in spite of the more recent and innovative approaches to isolate the crucial factors and variables and quantify their salience. The lack of a theoretical framework appears to be one of the major contributing factors to the existing confusion. The conceptual and theoretical problems are related to problems of both levels and units of analysis. Existing research shows confusion and lack of specification in these two crucial areas.

Research on international students has been dominated by case studies. Numerous studies have been undertaken with the view of identifying certain characteristics and adaptation modes of specific groups of international students. However, the usefulness of these studies other than identifying the critical features of a selected group is limited. Attempts to generate propositions and generalizations on the basis of case studies is particularly problematic due to the diversity in cultural backgrounds, nationality, family, and so forth, of each group in the international student community. On the other hand, the maldistribution of the case studies to students of certain regions and geographical areas has led to the neglect of others, thereby limiting the scope of any generalization that might be formulated. This problem is particularly manifest when generalizations are sought merely on the basis of speculative connections. Although some aspects of the behavior of international students manifest overt similarities conceivably engendered by certain shared experiences in the U.S., there is, however, little systematic effort made to identify systemic variables that operate as conditioning factors.

Methodological problems pose another dilemma in research on international students. While the application of certain testing instruments and measurement techniques is of crucial importance, the particular uses of these instruments can sometimes prove to be misleading and inappropriate. A review of questions designed for interviews and opinion surveys tend to show a broad and rigid format giving the impression to the interviewed that a specific answer must be given. Questions regarding affect, satisfaction, acceptance, disposition, and so forth, do not effectively isolate the particular concerns of the students under investigation. Another set of problems associated with survey techniques is the apparent mistrust by international students that their responses might be used for purposes other than those stated by the researcher. These uncertainties are supported by experiences such as those in which certain social scientists have conducted studies on particular groups or nations and have tended to report unfavorably or in a way that can be construed as demeaning. Thus, in such circumstances careful consideration is needed.

Finally, the factor of international student adjustment to life in the U.S. may be regarded as disparate phenomena and examined in terms of unique characteristics. However, in the following discussion we seek to suggest that it can be productively studied from a broader systemic perspective, that is, in terms of the dynamic interaction between international students and factors in American society. While recognizing the merits and functional value of diverse scholarly preferences in studying segments of the international student community, we also feel strongly about the need in the scholarly community to show a consciousness for paradigms to guide further research. The following endeavour

does not pretend to undertake all the major tasks in theory building. However, it does seek to bridge some existing gaps and interconnect some of the islands of explanation by providing a sharper theoretical focus.

In the following presentation, we shall attempt to provide an outline of a theoretical orientation on international student adjustment within the general theoretical framework of the socialization process. Although the employment of socialization models in the analysis of international student adjustment is limited, we believe that the general theoretical framework of socialization can be used to provide the analytical and conceptual tools useful to the examination of the patterns of adaptation and adjustment among foreign born students. Particularly, the socialization model that we are proposing derives from conceptual schemes applicable to studies of the socialization of racial/cultural minorities. Empirical findings and observations strongly suggest an interesting parallel between the pattern of international student adaptation to life in the U.S. and the socialization of certain minorities into the American society. Implicit in this proposition is the assumption that the typical American institution of higher education is for the most part a microcosm of the society at large. Even though our focus tends to emphasize the experiences of Afro-Americans in conjunction with the adjustment process of international students, it is presumed that, with proper qualifications, the experiences of other minorities can lend greater conceptual clarity to the issues in question.

TOWARD A THEORY OF FOREIGN STUDENTS ADJUSTMENT

Socialization as a social-psychological concept can be employed to delineate the lifelong process by which an individual is indoctrinated into a particular culture. Socialization is, therefore, a ubiquitous process by which an individual learns and cultivates behaviors, attitudes, beliefs, values, and expectations of a given society. In most industrialized societies, education, administered through organized institutions and structured curricula, operates as a principal agency in supplementing the family in the ongoing process of socialization. In such institutional contexts the individual acquires not only knowledge of his physical environment but also his social environment by learning about the functions of social institutions, roles of different individuals and groups in society, and the particular ways in which he communicates and relates to other members of society. Education also occurs in a less structured form through family and peer associations, from which the individual gains particular knowledge of his personal identity and his relationship to other groups within society. Thus, through the formal/informal educational process, cultural and social beliefs are transmitted and legitimized.

The relationship between formal education and socialization can be jointly considered in terms of social functions. The function of formal education can be seen in terms of its unique role in social mobility, class identification, role-status allocation, development of skills and knowledge, and as a key mechanism through which ideas and cumulative knowledge are disseminated in society. Thus, it can be argued that the socialization of international students into the American society through formal educational institutions lends itself to the propagation of cultural values and norms that are prevalent in the society at large. Obviously, the acquisition of these cultural values is a necessary tool in the educational process.

From a sociological perspective, foreign students constitute a minority both in terms of their numerical presence as well as their diverse national, cultural, and racial backgrounds. Proper adjustment during their sojourn in the U.S., therefore, requires a certain measure of reconciliation between factors in their sociocultural identity and ethnocentric norms, and those factors present in the larger society. This process of adjustment and accomodation is understandably a difficult one. The complex values of an advanced industrial society frequently come into sharp conflict with the cultural orientation of the less industrialized societies from which most international students migrate. Unfortunately, the accomodation of new values and belief systems are usually made at the expense of the student from abroad. This observation implies the presence of a progressive erosion of one's cultural and national identity, thereby creating cognitive dissonance and an imbalance in one's belief system and attitude structure. Indeed, the tendency of international students to withdraw into their own small communities and associate with their own compatriots can be partially attributed to this constant conflict (real and perceived) of values and beliefs.

Limited participation in the general process of social and educational activities leads to inadequate adjustment, *a fortiori*. It also signifies an ongoing process of alienation. Needless to say, this detachment from active participation and communication is further aggravated by confrontations with practices of racial/cultural discrimination inherent in the American society. The effects of such practices on the students tend to be cumulative, and evolve as salient events in their experiences during their sojourn in America. The intensity of their experiences and the perceived gravity of the event can sometimes operate as decisive factors in the total adjustment of these students. As a result, they might tend to perceive a higher incidence of such occurrences and conclude that further attempts to communicate would only lead to greater frustrations. These experiences are structurally interdependent to varying degrees, and new experiences can be predicted from the structure of others. Hence, alienation and avoidance become an adaptation mode in an environment perceived to be hostile. Withdrawal into compatriot communities, therefore, serves as an effective countermeasure to such disappointments. Since the impact of these types of experiences tends to be felt by most members of the group, the experiences gained from these events are transmitted into the informal socialization processes. Such useful knowledge about their common circumstances are shared and stored as ego defence weapons.

To be sure, the socialization of international students in American society involves consideration of diverse factors. Specifically, the process of socialization involves a complex set of internalization processes through which the foreign born student must assimilate new and different values, attitudes, and roles that are often contradictory. In this regard, the sociological process of assimilating international students into the American society through educational institutions is identical to the minoritization process of Afro-Americans and other racial and cultural minority groups. The framework suggested in the following discussion seeks to provide rudiments of a theoretical framework on the adjustment pattern and socialization of international students to life in American society.

MINORITIZATION AS A SOCIALIZATION PROCESS

The minoritization of international students in the U.S. is formulated to outline the process by which international students are introduced to life in American society and acquire adaptive skills during their educational sojourn. Broadly, therefore, minoritization as one type of socialization process encompasses a series of social interactions that occur between international students and segments of American society. These social interactions evolve along two main processes. First, the students are resocialized into the mainstream of American society and culture by learning new values, beliefs, and modes of behavior. Second, the students selectively pursue modes of behavior that maximize their adjustment in American society as they find it appropriate and beneficial to the attainment of their projected goals in education.

The literature on race relations and the status of minorities in the American society suggests that there are at least three phases in the minoritization process involving separation (real/symbolic), labeling, and treatment. Minorities, *ipso facto,* are regarded as a people apart from the mainstream of social processes and institutions. For the most part they are perceived to be politically, socially, economically, and educationally distinct. Distinguished from the dominant group by physical or cultural characteristics, or both, they are conveniently excluded from full participation in the institutions and social activities of the broader society. Thus, an important consideration in the functioning of minorities in society is the fact that "they are treated as members of a category, irrespective of their individual merits."[19] Consequently, when members of two or more external groups begin to compete for status, rights, and privileges within a dominant group's stratification or institutional systems, and are debarred categorically, then a minority-majority situation is articulated. It is within this context that we suggest that the acculturation of international students as they pursue higher education in American institutions is identical to the general minoritization phenomena of indigenous peoples.

Since the identification of the characteristic features of minority groups in the context of the larger society may lend some useful insights into understanding the range of adaptation modes available to and employed by international students, we shall briefly summarize them. Wagley and Harris[20] identify five descriptive features that characterize a minority group. Essentially, a minority group appears as a subordinate social group whose members experience disadvantages resulting from prejudice and discrimination; they have particular physical or cultural characteristics which the dominant group holds in low esteem; minority members manifest sensitivity to their minority status; membership in a minority group is proscribed and nonvoluntary; and lastly, minority group members, because of their status, tend to be endogamous and directed toward their own communities. In a peculiar manner, these factors seem to characterize both the status and adaptation patterns of international students. The social practices that foster the maintenance of such a pattern of social relations affect international students in an ascriptive process of separation, labeling, and treatment which structures a chasm that is difficult to bridge. Thus, an important dimension of the minoritization process of international students is the categorical treatment they receive either as foreign students in general, or as particular members of a "foreign" race or nationality.

In many respects, such a process of categorical treatment constitutes a unique aspect of the international students' socialization as minority groups. The ramifications of minority status for the international student in American society have multiple dimensions that pose severe social and personal dilemmas for the student. In most instances, the international students come from a somewhat socially generic-based culture in which they are regarded as elites. And, although their elitist status in their own societies makes them a "minority" (numerically), their positions of influence and dominance often desensitizes them to their minority status. However, this pattern of social dominance and participation is hardly reproducible in American society. The general tendency therefore becomes one of resignation in the face of divergent expectations, beliefs, and values, and adaptation to complex organizations. Thus, the crucial and pivotal factors in the minoritization process appear to be labeling and differential treatment that engender marginality and frustration among foreign students. The intensity of these experiences ultimately characterizes the antagonism of the students toward the larger American society before and after they return home.

The process of minoritization or categorical treatment also triggers a set of psychological reactions that tend to hamper the international student's adjustment. The experience of minoritization is first of all most likely to affect the individual's sense of self-esteem and status. The general lack of overt recognition of the individual's status and distinction that he enjoys in his home country engenders a basic trauma in the student's sense of self-esteem. The initial reaction to the perceived loss of self-esteem generally fosters regression to primitive modes of behavior and rationalization of the events that confront him. These tend to be manifested in the student's view that most Americans lack a good appreciation of his own country and consequently treat him with disrespect or "benign neglect." The student in such circumstances might venture to marshal the cultural and historical achievements of his own society and view Americans as a people without cultural continuity and long-standing history. However, the recourse to compensatory chauvinism does not mute an expression of open and/or abiding hostility to the larger American society. In fact, such a tendency seems to be accentuated by the length of the student's sojourn. Nonetheless, other forms of rationalization and modes of behavior tend to be simultaneously present, oftentimes resulting in processes of intellectualization and philosophical abstractions as coping mechanisms against their socialization as minorities.

The international student's negative emotional reactions toward his American educational and social experience gradually but surely shape his outlook on the total American society. He tends to employ a stereotype view of American society as mechanical, materialistic, superficial, and hypocritical. Interestingly, such stereotypic views are reinforced by American students who are themselves disturbed or dissatisfied with aspects of American society. Such selective interactions serve both the international and the disaffected American students to reflect upon their predicaments through mutual understanding.

It is somewhat interesting to note that the socialization of international students as minorities may be viewed as a set of complex processes that generally occur in patterns. Wolf[21] observed that, upon entrance into a new social/cultural system, immigrants tend to follow a tridimensional pattern of acculturation or cultural adaptation. Although the three dimensions appear to be characteristic of all immigrants' mode of adaptation, particularly the international student, we propose a fourth dimension that is equally relevant to the understanding of the pattern of adjustment in migration.

The first phase in the minoritization of the international student is generally characterized by a dualism that involves the possession of at least two sets of cultural orientations that serve to facilitate the student's initial experience and perception of his new environment. The possession of two or more cultural experiences is an important mechanism in the improvement of the student's life chances, since the uncertainties and disorienting factors present in the new environment can be conveniently cushioned by interchanging cultural orientations. This phase marks an important point in the student's perception of his new environment, and overshadows his future experiences during his sojourn. There is a general tendency to formulate a broad view of his new environment and the salient differences that are present between his own personal and background factors and those in his new setting. Thus, the student seeks to sharpen his skills to successfully maneuver for a better balance of chances and risks.

The second pattern of social-cultural adjustment takes the form of "cultural straddling." This phase signals the beginning of the student's conscious attempt to employ some of his learned social skills to circumstances in his new environment. It is generally manifested in the student's tendency to alternate cultural forms with which identification is made for the sake of social and/or economic motives. Thus, the student given a set of circumstances may resort to a pattern of behavior by activating distinctive "foreign" cultural traits in the form of language and speech patterns, dress, and so forth. On the other hand, the same individual may deny his "foreign" cultural heritage if and when the situation changes.

The third pattern of socialization as a minority occurs in the form of multiple adaptations involving a conscious and determined attempt by the student to strike a balance between the cultural experiences that one possesses. There is limited intentional vacilation for the sake of convenience, and the student simply selects cultural forms that are desirable from the range of his experiences and charts a consistent course in the attainment of his future goals. Such a pattern of adaptation generally confronts the student in a complex and traumatic fashion since it requires a resolution of a set of acute contraditions present in the student's personal and social life, and a crystalization of goals and objectives to be pursued. However, once this is decided, the student's sojourn is characterized by a state of relative calm in the natural dynamics of life in the host society.

The fourth and final pattern of socialization as a minority generally tends to lead into a fatal immersion in the host country's culture and social activities. The student may feel overwhelmed by the attractiveness and relative advances of the host society, and consequently may attempt to totally embrace the culture of his host society by consciously trying to be a part of it. The student may develop contempt for his own culture and even hostility towards certain practices and cultural values of his own society. Rejection of one's own cultural background usually entails severe psychological scars and social problems for the student. The student may be exorcised from the compatriot community as a "foreigner" and shunned with polite greetings. On the other hand, the inability of the student to gain full acceptance in the host society elicits a set of emotional reactions that interchange between condemnation of the host society and self-indulgence. This experience is akin to the marginal man phenomenon.

CONCLUSION

In the foregoing discussion we have sought to make some contributions to the theory-building effort in international student adaptation behavior. An attempt has been made to construct and explore, albeit briefly, a framework of analysis. Our effort has primarily been concerned with a presentation of a framework useful in the examination of those determining factors that promote or inhibit international student adjustment to life in the U.S. Nonetheless, the effort has been a limited one and no doubt the preliminary model requires further refinement and specification.

Most importantly, we believe that, in the context of the minoritization process, two basic processes can be adequately studied. First, the proposed framework facilitates an examination of those factors that gravitate the international student to the minority situation, that is, in terms of effects on self-concept, expectations, role conflict, and perception of others. Second, it facilitates an investigation of the dynamic process of social interaction in the broader societal context, that is, in terms of the cultural factors and particular organizational setting that define the purpose of the interaction, the normative expectations and rules that govern the interaction, and the range of options that are available. The focus on interaction processes provides greater insight if it is explored as a function of the dispositions of the participants and the organizational context within which they are consummated. Thus, greater understanding of the processes in which social institutions shape the behavior of individuals can be gained. Although minoritization represents a level of analysis that is primarily sociopsychological, the major concern is the process in which the relationships of the individual student to the various components of the host's social system are mediated through processes of social interaction. The framework of minoritization can provide a broad perspective to examine these dynamic transformations.

NOTES

1. The first such educational experiment was fostered by the Rev. Samuel, who brought three Chinese students to the U.S. in 1847. The first of these students, Yung Wing, became the first known graduate of an American university, completing his studies at Yale in 1854. For a brief historical overview, see Forrest Moore, "Factors Affecting the

Academic Success of Foreign Students in American Universities," PhD thesis, unpublished (Minneapolis: University of Minnesota, December 1953), pp.13–22.

2. In 1924, Congress enacted a special immigration classification applicable to international students. This classification, known as a 4(e) nonquota student status, for the first time defined the legal status of international students pursuing education at American educational institutions, and further provided exemptions from quota restrictions.

3. The enactment of the Educational Exchange Act in 1948 further redefined the legal status of international students, and provided for a new legal status known as the 3(2) exchange visitor classification.

4. Margaret L. Cormack, *An Evaluation of Research on Educational Exchange* (Washington: U.S. Department of State, Bureau of Educational and Cultural Affairs, 1962).

5. Margaret T. Cussler, *Review of Selected Studies Affecting International and Cultural Affairs* (College Park: University of Maryland Press, 1962).

6. Barbara J. Walton, *Foreign Student Exchange in Perspective* (Washington: U.S. Department of State and Office of External Research, 1967).

7. Lawrence Antler, "Correlates of Home and Host Country Acquaintanceship Among Foreign Medical Residents in the United States," *The Journal of Social Psychology*, 73 (1968), pp.431–42.

8. Tamar Becker, "Patterns of Attitudinal Change Among Foreign Students," *American Journal of Sociology*, 73 (1968), pp.431–42.

9. Marjorie Klein, et al., "The Foreign Student Adaptation Program: Social Experiences of Asian Students," *Exchange*, 6, No.3 (1971), pp.77–90.

10. Kayoko Wakita, "Asian Studies Survey—Spring 1970" (Los Angeles City College, October 1971).

11. Tai Kang, "A Foreign Student Group As an Ethnic Community," *International Review of Modern Sociology*, 2 (1972), pp.72–82.

12. Tai Kang, "Name Change and Acculturation: Chinese Students on an American Campus," *Pacific Sociological Review* (1971), pp.403–12.

13. Rajnikant Gandhi, "Conflict and Cohesion in an Indian Student Community," *Human Organization*, 29 (1970), pp.95–102.

14. Mohammed E. Hegazy, "Cross-Cultural Experience and Social Change: The Case of Foreign Study," PhD dissertation (University of Minnesota, 1968).

15. Dixon Johnson, "Problems of Foreign Students," *Exchange*, 7 (1971), pp.61–68.

16. Anita Mishler, "Personal Contact in International Exchanges," in *International Behavior*, ed. Herbert Kelman (New York: Holt, Rinehart and Winston, 1965), pp.550–60.

17. John Melby, "The Foreign Student in America," in *International Education: Past, Present, Problems and Prospects*. Prepared for the House Committee on Education and Labor by the Task Force on International Education (Washington, D.C.: U.S. Government Printing Office, 1966), pp.319–26.

18. U.S. Department of State, *A Preliminary Study on Foreign Students in America: The Effect of Today's Campus Environment on Their Attitudes Toward America* by Daniel Yankelovich, Inc. (Washington, D.C. 1971).

19. Judith Kramer, *The American Minority Community* (New York: Thomas Y. Cromwell, 1970), pp.1–25.

20. Charles Wagley and Marie Harris, *Minorities in the World* (New York: Columbia University Press, 1964), pp.4–11.

21. Eric Wolf, "Specific Aspects of Plantations Systems in the New World: Community Sub-Cultures and Social Classes," *Peoples and Cultures of the Carribean*, ed. Michael Horolwitz (New York: National History Press, 1971), pp.163–78.

Part 8
Theoretical and Methodological Considerations

THE ILLEGAL MIGRANT:
SOME RESEARCH STRATEGIES

Glenn L. Hendricks

For the past several years the American public has become increasingly aware of the presence of considerable numbers of improperly documented aliens in the United States. The casual reader of the press would probably assume that their presence constitutes a social phenomenon, if not problem, of quite recent origin. However, their discovery is, undoubtedly, more a matter of bureaucratic management of the news than the sudden emergence of a tidal wave of a new kind of alien in our midst. One indication of their long-time prevalence might be found in the fact that the term ''wetback,'' defined as an illegal Mexican farmworker, is a word to be found in any standard American dictionary.

My introductory skeptical perspective is deliberate. It stems from research carried out beginning almost a decade ago among immigrants from the Dominican Republic who reside in New York City. From the first it was apparent that a large number of aliens were present in various illegal statuses. However, any attempts made to discuss this issue with Immigration and Naturalization authorities met with a denial (on the official level at least) that it was a problem of significant proportions. Subsequently, however, we have witnessed a barrage of public pronouncements, in Congressional hearings, speeches, and press releases, admitting the presence of unknown numbers of persons without proper documentation (perhaps more than eight million) who constitute a major threat to our economic and social order. These undocumented persons are said to exacerbate the unemployment problem by occupying positions in the work force that rightfully belong to citizens and legally present aliens. They are said to burden our public health, welfare, and educational facilities with their demands for equal services. Our law enforcement system is said to be strained to the breaking point in coping with their presence.

Whether in Miami, New York, San Francisco, El Paso, Chicago, or even Duluth, Minnesota, anyone conversant with the present U.S. immigration scene recognizes the existence of large numbers of immigrants with varying degrees of illegality. Observers of global migration activities are aware of similar situations in a number of other countries. In South America, Venezuela is reported to contain more than half a million illegal Colombianos; thousands of Brazilians work illegally in French Guiana; and Argentina faces problems with illegal workers from Chile, Uruguay, and Italy. Several years ago, when visiting the southern Mexican state of Chiapas, I was surprised to be told of the problems caused by illegal plantation workers crossing the border from Guatemala to work in Mexico. Northern European industrial countries face similar kinds of problems with Greeks and Turks in West Germany, for example, or Portuguese in France. In South Africa, political as well as economic vicissitudes have placed millions in similar legal circumstances. Koreans live illegally in Japan, occupying very much the same vicissitudes of existence as illegal Haitians in the U.S. The problem, then, is not to identify or to justify the phenomenon of illegal migration but rather to accurately describe it.

First, if it is to be labeled a problem, then we must ask the question, a problem for whom: the government, the alien, or the researcher? Obviously, in this game of international cops and robbers, it is as much a problem for the would-be catcher as the catchee. However, we must be careful in remembering who defines the problem. Citizenship and alienship are surrounded by a morass of legal definitions which largely represent cultural categories. United States immigration law is represented in a nearly 200-page basic document, but elaborated in volumes of administrative and judicial decisions. Because it is specifically stated that preference is given to actions which maintain the integrity of the family, a husband can gain preference for his spouse and children. But, at least in the case of the immigrants I know, those from the Dominican Republic, within their social norms a spouse constitutes what Americans call a common-law wife, and the legitimacy of children, on a social level at least, is defined by the relationship between parent and child, not by the legal status of the relationship of the procreating parents. Consequently, attempts to circumvent the U.S. definition in order to gain entrance into the U.S. are often not seen by them as an act of illegality but rather overcoming the North Americans' cultural blindness. In a similar vein, legal marriages may be contracted solely for the purpose of fulfilling the U.S. law in order to gain immigrant visa status. Since a sharp distinction exists between civil and ecclesiastical acts, a civil marriage contracted solely for the purpose of gaining a visa constitutes no moral dilemma whatever.

For the researcher, the problem is of a different order. What is it we need to know, or even what can we know about the illegal migrant? Obviously, one of the great problems of dealing with this population is that it is illegal and almost by definition hidden. If our question involves demographic description, then some questions can only be answered tenuously. A basic problem is one of finding boundaries around what constitutes illegal alienship. Even if we use a broadly based definition, including all those with improper documentation, we are still faced with the problem of what constitutes *proper* documentation. Some hold papers which have been blatantly falsified. During my stay in the Dominican Republic, the American authorities were able to break a ring of falsifiers whose excellent counterfeits were detectable only because they used a single "p" in the word application (probably a result of the similarity to the Spanish word *aplicación*). But many more applications, supported by either blatant lies or subtle fuzzing of the truth, were passed upon unnoticed by the consular officials. I shall return later to the impact of this circumstance in accounting for the social behavior of alien groups, but for now I note it because it serves to alert us that what initially appears as a seemingly clear-cut category begins to fuzz as the boundaries are approached.

Even without this definitional problem, the social and legal position of illegal alienship does not lend itself to easy description of salient variables which usually make up demographic descriptors, such as how many, what kind, and where. A recent study by North and Houston entitled "The Characteristics and Role of Illegal Aliens in the U.S. Labor Market" was based upon 793 apprehended aliens.[1] While the authors specifically disclaim any pretense that it is a random sample of all illegal aliens, the press's coverage of these findings did so in a manner that led one to believe it described all aliens. If those in the ultimate position of gatekeepers of the United States, the Immigration and Naturalization Service, are unable to give more than approximations ranging from three to eight million illegal aliens, it seems unlikely that an outside researcher can do even as well. Even if such information were available as to exact quantities, the question remains as to what degree illegal aliens share any other attributes besides their common status of illegality.

I would propose, then, that we could more usefully examine subsets of this category. One approach might be to build typologies of categories of illegal migrants, not as an intellectual exercise or as an end in itself, but rather to distinguish salient differences that exist within that grouping loosely labeled as illegal aliens. Among possible distinguishing characteristics I would include: type of visa violation; an individual's socioeconomic characteristics within the home society; degree of cultural distinctiveness from mainstream U.S. culture; area of residence in the U.S.; and the concentration of fellow countrymen or ethnic grouping in the individual's area of U.S. residence. The patterns of existence for an illegal Mexican farmworker are in many ways quite different if he settles in a Texas border area than if he follows the migrant worker stream northward and then subsequently remains to work in the beet fields of northwestern Minnesota. The Dominican *campesino* living in New York City, sheltered within ghettos of a hundred thousand or more of his countrymen, further tucked within several million other Spanish speakers, carries out a quite different social existence than an English-speaking Canadian living and working in Buffalo, New York. Based upon my knowledge of the New York Dominican population, I know that quite different patterns of existence can be found between the illiterate *campesino* who has little if any previous contact with urban living, and his urban counterpart. This might well hold true even if they both worked side by side as assemblers in a Brooklyn light bulb factory.

An ethnographic approach may be the most productive means to ascertain the information necessary to make socially useful statements about many illegal alien groups. To do so often requires intimate knowledge of both the sending as well as the receiving society. In my own field work I found that often inexplicable, if not irrational, behavior could only be understood in the total context of what was going on concurrently in the home village or country and in New York City. I came to see the necessity of examining the total social field in which individuals operated, and how much this social field intimately included events, persons, and conditions in the sending society, even for persons who had lived in New York for years. Most immigration research has continued to focus on only the receiving end (an approach which was more defensible in the prejet, preelectronic age).

The villagers on whom I focused my work came from a seemingly isolated interior area of the Dominican Republic some 125 kilometers from Santo Domingo. Yet, it was less than six hours from New York, one and a half of these hours taken up by the taxi ride from the airport to the village. A constant daily trickle of arrivals and returnees flowed between New York and the village. The impact of this constant circular migration was enormous. One household I came to know in the Bronx made at least two telephone calls a month to a relative in Santiago, (the second city of the Republic located some 15 kilometers from the village). Through both personal visitations as well as telephonic exchange, business transactions were carried out and information flowed back and forth. The gossip in the *parque* of Aldea continued to exercise as much social restraint on many of the villagers in New York as had they never left home. Among other things, the immediacy of this contact served to effectively mitigate many of the expected normal processes of acculturation to the new host society. It provided current information to would-be migrants, both legal and illegal, on a whole variety of essential facts, such as job openings or available housing.

That this situation is not unique to Dominicans was later demonstrated to me when I found that the Hong Kong Student Association at the University of Minnesota gathered lists of newly admitted Hong Kong students and organized summer seminars in Hong Kong for the purpose of providing them with information about life in the United States. Part of the information imparted included details of books and supplies they could buy cheaper at home and bring with them, and also details on job possibilities and ways to circumvent IRS regulations about student employment. Since most of these individuals are products of a limited number of academic high schools and are connected through links of friendship, family, and business ties, in many ways the social linkage of the Hong Kong students at Minnesota are directly comparable to my Dominican *campesino* friends in New York. In addition to utilizing the concept of social field, one comes to perceive the networks of social relations and how these linkages cross and crisscross vast physical distances. In the case of either Dominicans or residents of Hong Kong, few arrive as social isolates but rather, especially in the case of my Dominican friends, continue social linkages established long before their arrival. In fact, some of my informants among the Dominicans expressed no comprehension of my questions about the lifestyles of those who know no one. For them such a situation did not exist.

Another conceptual tool useful in understanding the ongoing process of social action among the immigrant group I studied was the discernment of the brokerage role occupied by certain individuals. These culture brokers occupy key positions in mediating between the individual alien and the wider American society, and stand in a position to "guard the synapses of social relations." In a society which places primary emphasis on familial ties, this brokerage role often falls to kinsmen, both real and fictive, who have had longer experience in the United States and are able to assist the newcomer or the circumscribed illegal alien in dealing with the wider society. This brokerage role can be played by institutions such as the church or a social club, although at least among the group I focused upon which places great emphasis on *personalismo*, this brokerage role still centered about individuals such as the priest or an officer of an organization. A key individual for many Dominicans, as well as other Latin Americans in New York, is the travel agent who in many cases performs a whole host of services which may range from the most simple translation of a postal address change card to elaborate and perhaps illegal assistance in arranging for the visas of family members a client wishes to bring to

New York. It is in the activities of those occupying brokerage roles that power and influence begin to emerge, whether within the family setting or the wider Dominican colony. (Note the use of the word colony rather than community because the latter connotes a good deal more interaction among all its constituents than does the former.)

All immigrants have been deliberately included rather than singling out the illegal alien. Within this population the illegal and legally present aliens are thoroughly intertwined within established sets of social relations. This obviously has repercussions for the entire group. The repercussions of this can be significant in terms of both the group's internal relations as well as its relations with the wider society. The illegal migrant can make no firm commitment to his new situation. Among my Dominican friends, few individuals, legal or illegal, arrive with the assumption that the move to New York is a permanent commitment to immigrate. Rather, the migration is looked upon as an opportunity to accumulate capital, to return to the Republic, and either retire comfortably or to invest in some enterprise in the homeland. For the illegal immigrant, it is imperative that he make the most of his opportunity, for he is well aware that at any time some event could precipitate his detection and return to the Republic. Thus, what is interpreted by some outsiders as an inordinate concern for industry and making money is in reality a response to the tentative nature of their position.

Employers are well aware of the tenuous position of the immigrant job seeker, and examples of flagrant intimidation and illegal substandard pay rates are common. During the course of my fieldwork, a large restuarant chain which hired many Spanish-speaking immigrants as kitchen helpers and dishwashers was faced with the threat of unionization. They successfully intimidated a number of workers, including some of my informants, by threatening to have agents of the Immigration and Naturalization Service examine their worker's visas if they voted for the union. Since the alien, legal or illegal, often does not understand his lawful rights or even how to negotiate for information about them, all were easily cowed regardless of their status.

A frequent comment by police officials was that there was far less fighting and brawling among Dominicans. "Thirty years of Trujillo taught them to respect law and order," commented one precinct officer in an area of mixed Puerto Ricans and Dominicans. What he failed to realize was the basis of the norm system operating to settle disputes internally: the fear that someone within the circle of those involved would be detected as illegally present in this country.

While for the most part the shared desire to avoid scrutiny from outsiders operates rather consistently, this same situation creates areas of possible friction. The illegal individual is open to intimidation by those within his social network who are aware of his status. Of necessity, he must at times accept subordinate and submissive roles because he fears to carry out any activity publicly.

Direct daily flights between New York and Santo Domingo make it possible for the immigrant to return frequently to his homeland. But the illegal resident does not have this option since, once he returns, his visa usually becomes invalid and he must apply for another. The consequence of this is that the individual often feels "trapped" in a land that was to have been his golden opportunity.

One of the functional results of this tentativeness about settlement in New York is that there is no attempt to acculturate, even to the larger Hispanic society of New York. The social network into which the new arrival is introduced tends to be quite closed and, rather than provide him or her with a stable platform from which to launch new social relationships and experiences, it more frequently operates to prevent the widening of it. Outsiders from the Anglo world, street workers, and welfare workers who attempt to break into it are met with great suspicion for fear they may somehow be agents of the Immigration and Naturalization Service. One well-meaning church group decided to offer English lessons. At the end of the first meeting a paper was passed around on which the students were to write their names and addresses. Of the ten present, three (whom I knew to be illegal) failed to sign the sheet and two gave false names and addresses. These five never returned for the second session.

One further response to an illegal status is that it provides additional reasons for the individual to remain in close proximity to the social network. A move to a less urban area makes for far greater visibility. It was my observation that only those persons who were entirely free of financial, familial, and legal obligations (that is, completely certain of their immigrant visa status) ventured to move outside the confines of their New York ghetto enclaves.

Marriage patterns are influenced by illegality. Marriages arranged strictly for the purpose of acquiring resident visa status are common enough that consular officials seriously question each request for a change in status based upon conjugal ties acquired after arrival in the U.S. An open market exists in major American cities for such liaisons. Thus, data the field worker collects about household and family relationships are not always congruent with legal marriage patterns. Among my informants, such arranged marriages to outsiders tended to be rare. Rather the marital tie was most often made endogamously to others from the extended kin unit, or those known to possess that much sought-after quality of *confianza*. Since endogamy was common in the village, and marriages of first cousins frequent, it is not possible to know to what degree the selection of mates in New York was a reflection of persistent traditional practices or that it was simply functional behavior reinforced by the circumstances of the individual's visa status.

Obviously, for the field worker, the situation presents problems and limitations. One is perceived in several roles, including that of a potential threat, possibly an agent of the immigration authorities. As one informant remarked, "Why else would the Americans pay attention to us?" On the other hand, as there is a constant search for someone from whom help might be received, much of the researcher's time is spent in answering questions about how to gain a legal visa. This also creates difficulties, as too much knowledge reinforces the belief that one is an agent, and too little willingness to impart knowledge of possible options is interpreted as an equally justifiable reason to believe one is an agent who might betray them. Thus, even events over which the field worker has no control are often imputed to his or her presence. This was most vividly brought home to me in one case when I

had knowledge which was potentially damaging to an applicant. When the individual was turned down for a visa, it was assumed that my knowledge was responsible for the consulate's action.

Some traditional methodological techniques of social anthropology, such as household censuses, genealogies, and land tenure, are rendered ineffective because seldom is it possible to interview or even gain complete information about given sets or subsets of family, household, or social networks. "What do I have to gain by spilling my guts to the Americans?" was the reply carried back to me when I attempted to meet one individual I considered key to the recruitment of a large number of his kinsmen headed for New York. An outright threat of violence was passed on to me if I pursued my inquiry into another kinship-based unit.

None of these problems is unique to research among illegal migrants. However, the situation exacerbates some of the typical problems of role perception with which almost any researcher is confronted. For persons who have much to lose in the disclosure of their actions, violence is not an improbable possibility. While working in the village, one of my chief informants always insisted upon escorting me home in the evening when I stayed past nightfall. At the time, I inferred this to be his concern over the possibility of my being harmed by the wandering spirits within the night air, a romantic notion gleaned from reading Latin American ethnographies. In reality, (I was to learn much later) it was his concern over potential injury inflicted by individuals involved in a visa falsification ring in the area that was being uncovered by American officials in Santo Domingo.

This paper has suggested some viable research strategies in investigating aspects of the illegal alien population in the U.S. I have suggested that an ethnographic approach may yield the most socially useful information, while acknowledging that it does not lend itself to supplying answers to some of the persistent questions of even gross demographic statistics. The concepts of social field and social networks which encompass elements within both the sending and the receiving societies can be successfully employed to explain immigrant behavior, whether legal or illegal. In the Dominican case at least, the relationships between legal and illegal migrants were shown to be crucial to the nature of the total group's interaction with the larger host society. Delineating the role of culture broker, whether it is held by an institution or by an individual, is seen as explanatory of how key influential persons emerge within a seemingly amorphous social category. The task I outline is not easy, but from my own personal experience these approaches have been most rewarding.

NOTE

1. David North and Marion Houstman, *The Characteristics and Role of Illegal Aliens in the U.S. Labor Market* (Washington, D.C.: Linton & Co., 1976).

A PRELIMINARY LOOK AT AN
ALTERNATIVE APPROACH TO THE STUDY OF IMMIGRANTS

Reyes Ramos

Like my father, my mother was an immigrant from Mexico. We were a large family, nine children, and we were poor. Yet, my mother raised us believing we were very fortunate. According to her, we were lucky because the people in helping services such as welfare workers and school teachers treated us as if they knew everything about us when in actuality they knew nothing about us. The people who dealt with us knew about Mexican immigrants in general and, because of that, assumed that they knew about the Ramos family. My mother defined this state of affairs as good fortune. In fact, she would get after us whenever we tried to enlighten school teachers about how it actually was with us. I remember quite clearly hearing her say, ''Don't tell those people about what we are doing. If you do, then they will be able to interfere with our lives more efficiently. Let them keep on thinking that they know what we are like. That way we will always be able to do whatever we please without much interference from them.'' The point here is that we know very little about immigrants as particular persons, and that we need to learn how immigrants, as particular persons, structure and manage their practical circumstances.

Practically all studies on immigrants are written from the perspective of assimilation.[1] From this perspective, immigrants are described and discussed in terms of their group specific culture, and the immigrants' cultural values are contrasted with American cultural values. Moreover, the conflicts immigrants experience are seen as cultural conflicts which are taken as evidence of the immigrants' undergoing an assimilation process, and it is assumed that, once immigrants take on the cultural values of the host society, they experience less cultural conflict because they have assimilated into the host society.

By viewing the immigrant only in terms of his group specific culture, as specified in a perspective of assimilation, we do not address how the immigrant uses what he knows about the world in which he lives (that is, his common-sense knowledge) to interpret how he is to manage his practical circumstances. If we are to learn how immigrants manage their practical circumstances in ways other than those determined by their group specific culture and Anglo middle-class norms, we need an alternative perspective. I recommend an ethnomethodological perspective. Ethnomethodology is not the study of ethnic groups. It is a perspective in which attention is given to the ways people, as particular persons with personal histories, use their common-sense reasoning to develop methods for structuring and managing their everyday lives.

The world of everyday life for most people consists ordinarily of familiar people, places, things, and events which they expect to encounter. To any given person there tends to be nothing mysterious about his daily life: it is an ongoing world that was here before he was born and is expected to be here when he dies. It is not only held in common with others, but it is a world that is taken for granted. Schutz refers to the fact that people know about or have a sense of the larger world in which they live, and he points to the fact that most of the time people live out their everyday lives in a particular world or common place setting.[2] A person comes to think of his daily life as being organized and self-evident. This process of awareness occurs through what Husserl calls the ''natural attitude.''[3]

Because of a natural attitude towards daily life, a person tends to have few major doubts about the workings of his daily life. He simply takes it for granted. He does so because his daily life consists of the daily activities he creates to manage his affairs, and because of the knowledge he has of the ever encountered world he holds in common with specific others. Therefore, a person assumes that those other people he interacts with not only perceive the world as he does, but in the process of interpreting it, also ''fill in'' or use the knowledge that they hold in common to make sense of what they are doing or saying. This knowledge held in common is what ethnomethodologists call common-sense knowledge.

In the ethnomethodological literature, common-sense knowledge is referred to as shared background knowledge because it is shared and embedded in the ongoing activities of the people under study. It provides people with the cues and nuances of situations which enable them not only to make sense of their daily activities, but to manage their daily lives in ways they consider reasonable and effective.[4] Shared background knowledge has three essential features to it: 1) it is possessed and sanctioned by a more or less inclusive population members; 2) it is known in a particular mode of relevance; and 3) it has a sociotemporal locus of relevance.[5]

METHODOLOGY

Since shared knowledge is taken for granted, and thus not readily available to a nonmember of a particular group of people, it needs to be uncovered or revealed. In the ethnomethodological literature, it has been suggested by some that this can be done by making the familiar strange.[6] Accordingly, when a person is shocked or caused to doubt his everyday world, he then makes visible the background expectancies he uses as a scheme of interpretation.

Garfinkel's idea for unmasking the taken-for-granted world is to "make" trouble.[7] Indeed, sociologists (in this case ethnomethodologists) need to expose the taken-for-granted world the people under study take into account. However, it is not necessary to "make" trouble. Trouble already exists. It is constantly being generated by people in the process of managing their practical circumstances. Trouble happens naturally.

Trouble is caused when people, in carrying out daily activities they have created to help them cope with their affairs, fail to take into account that there are some people whom they may encounter who are working under a different definition of social reality, and who occupy positions or are found in different environments than their own.

I suggest, then, that the task of sociologists is to take advantage of naturally occurring trouble and use it as an investigative procedure. The notion of using naturally occurring trouble as an investigative device can be further extended to include any unexpected events, whether troublesome or not, which reveal the taken-for-granted world which underlies people's behavior.[8] By unexpected events, I mean any event which is not planned or expected by a person and which conflicts with the person's original idea of what is to happen. I suggest that, when unexpected events occur, opportunities are created for field researchers.

MEXICAN IMMIGRANTS

In most studies on Mexican immigrants,[9] researchers first locate their topic within a cultural explanation. It does not matter what the topic might be—education, employment, health, or some other aspect of the immigrant's life—the researcher proceeds to tell the reader that Mexican culture, which is always typified as being rural or folk, stresses the celebration of such values as present-time orientation, immediate gratification, nonintellectual pursuits, nongoal orientation, nonsuccess orientation, fatalism, dependency, and traditionalism. These cultural values are then contrasted with those that are attributed to the Anglo culture, which is also described as being representative of an urban culture. The cultural values attributed to the dominant Anglo culture are always the opposite of those attributed to Mexican American cultures. For example, Anglos are typified as being future oriented, independent, and modern. In making these sorts of assertions, some researchers point to the family as the culprit.[10] Mexican immigrants are also said to be unable to deal with bureaucratic organizations.[11] Finally, upward mobility is said to be a trait Mexican immigrants as a group lack. Upwardly mobile Mexican immigrants are usually said to be the exception to the rule. Generally, two things are said about upwardly mobile Mexican Americans· they are upwardly mobile because they are attempting assimilation into Anglo society, and the attempt at cultural transfer is said to place them in psychosocial situations which produce extreme stress and anxiety. The lives of these people are often described as being fraught with cultural conflict.

Social scientists define the conflict in the everyday lives of Mexican Americans as cultural.[12] In so doing, social scientists describe the conflict Mexican immigrants experience as a perpetual clash between Mexican rural culture and Anglo American urban culture. (Never does the social scientist consider the possibility that a given Mexican American urban migrant's conflict may be the result of his being fat and having a big red nose.) It is with little wonder, then, that in most urban migration studies, social scientists recommend that Mexicans assimilate in order to conform to the dominant Anglo culture. Implied in this recommendation is the idea that Anglos do not experience any cultural conflict. Indeed they do! Psychiatrists and psychologists make their living from it. However, before I discuss in detail the weaknesses of the existing cultural explanation of Mexican American behavior, it is important to discuss a basic aspect of assimilation.

Although it is suggested in practically all studies that Mexican immigrants assimilate, the assimilation process is never clearly defined. What we have in the literature are examples of who is and who is not assimilated, and examples of what tends to happen to those who succeed and to those who fail in assimilation. We are never told *when* and *how* those Mexican immigrants who are labeled "assimilated" become so. We are only told in a generalized way that assimilation creates more cultural conflict for the Mexican immigrant. That is, it is suggested that the Mexican immigrant must abandon his culture to gain entry into Anglo culture. Furthermore, it is suggested that if he does this, he is in trouble with the members of his ethnic group, in particular with his relatives. In the literature, it is suggested that this trouble would be worthwhile because the migrant would be on his way to becoming assimilated.

However, as most researchers are quick to point out, not all Mexican immigrants who reject their ethnic culture are accepted by the dominant culture. These Mexican immigrants, then, are said to be caught between two cultural worlds and they are labeled marginal by social scientists. In addition, most social scientists claim that marginal Mexican immigrants often engage in deviant social acts to cope with their marginal existence.[13]

By typifying Mexican immigrants in the ways discussed above, one can see why most researchers conclude that there is "no exit" for the Mexican immigrant from his social condition. If he stays, as social scientists claim he is, "hanging tenaciously to his cultural values," he will remain forever at the bottom of the social hierarchy which exists in the United States. And if he attempts to leave his ethnic culture for Anglo culture, he ends up being rejected by both, doomed to spend the rest of his life in some marginal state between the two cultural worlds.

Is this really the case for the Mexican immigrant? Are so-called assimilated Mexican immigrants the childlike, simplistic fools typified in the literature? And, are upwardly mobile Mexican immigrants leading the life of the marginal man or woman? Indeed not! The everyday life of the Mexican immigrant is complex and dynamic. It cannot be described solely in terms of the cultural values social scientists attribute to Mexican culture in their abstract models of Mexican American society.

To assume that it would be, one would have to imagine a very strange world. For example, it is difficult to imagine a world in which Mexican immigrants are present-time oriented and nongoal oriented *all* the time. It is even much more difficult to imagine Anglo Americans as being future and goal oriented *all* the time, as typified in the literature. It would be nice if Anglo Americans and Mexican immigrants behaved as typified. Then I, as a university professor, could expect Anglo students to hand in their term papers on time, if not before, and Mexican students to hand in their papers late, if at all. But, it does not happen that way. Members of both groups hand in papers both early and late. To assume that the early papers belong to the Anglos and to assimilated Mexicans, I would also have to assume the late papers belong to Mexicans and to Anglos who had acculturated into Mexican culture. To many people, my assumption would not seem plausible. Therefore, I conclude that the assumptions found in the literature on Mexican immigrants are not plausible either.

Researchers do not consider what Mexican immigrants take into account while managing their routine affairs. Researchers assume that immigrants manage their routine affairs solely in terms of the cultural values (that is, norms) social scientists attribute to Mexican culture. No effort is made in the normative explanations to document what the Mexican immigrant takes into account when he makes decisions. For example, to help him cope with whatever problem is before him, does the Mexican immigrant take into account past, present, or future events which may or may not be readily visible to a researcher? It is in this sense that I suggest an ethnomethodological explanation of the conflict Mexican immigrants experience. From an ethnomethodological perspective, Mexican immigrants are, in at least one important sense, like any other people in the United States. They encounter, know, and see the world in which they live consisting of normal courses of action that are dealt with in routine ways. Furthermore, Mexican immigrants see the world of everyday life in common with others, and with others take it for granted, and use their common knowledge of everyday scenes as schemes of interpretation to manage their everyday affairs. Mexican immigrants, then, like other members of society, not only engage in what Garfinkel calls "judgmental works,"[14] but in doing so constantly rely upon the background knowledge of commonplace settings which they presume they share with others. That is, Mexican immigrants tend to rely upon their common-sense understandings of social structures about which we have little knowledge, and not upon the idealized norms that have been attributed to their culture or social status in the larger society by social scientists. True, the idealized norms of the social order form part of their common-sense knowledge, but they do not fully explain how Mexican immigrants go about interpreting the norms to make sense of the many situations they find themselves in, and which may not have anything to do with their cultural heritage.

By looking at the Mexican immigrant from an ethnomethodological perspective, we can get a better sense of how Mexican immigrants, in conjunction with others (recent arrivals from Mexico, Mexican Americans as well as nonimmigrants), participate in the social construction of reality. I suggest that, by looking at how Mexican immigrants and others participate not only in the social construction of reality, but in the construction of multiple realities, we can talk about the conflict Mexican immigrants experience in terms of the clashing of different definitions of social reality and not of cultures. I am *not* suggesting that there is a Mexican American reality or an Anglo American reality. I am only suggesting that different definitions of social reality exist simultaneously in the social order, and that conflict occurs when the different definitions clash. Moreover, the different definitions that exist should not be labeled either Anglo or Mexican American because different definitions exist within each community (or between persons). Also, I suggest we do not know or cannot tell what an Anglo or Mexican immigrant reality might be or appear to be.

Multiple realities exist simultaneously in the social order because of two basic reasons. People operate under different assumptions because they occupy different positions in different environments. People occupying one social position have common-sense knowledge which is different than the knowledge which is found in other positions and environments. And, as Schutz put it: "The popular mind conceives of all these subworlds more or less disconnectedly, and when dealing with one of them forgets for the time being the relations to the rest."[15]

Schutz is not talking about a middle class reality, or a lower class reality, or even a Mexican immigrant and Anglo American reality. He is talking about the different realities which exist simultaneously between different small groups of people regardless of social class or ethnicity. He is also saying that people get so caught up in managing their practical circumstances that they tend to forget the relationship between one another until people discover they are not operating on the same wave length.[16] A person tends to assume that the sorts of things that he takes into account in the management of his affairs are the same for others, and that others use the relevant background features of everyday scenes in the same way that he does. A person tends to work under this assumption until he discovers that others are not operating under the same assumption.

Two important and interrelated aspects of Mexican immigrant everyday life are implied in the above discussion. One is that Mexican immigrants do not see their lives in a strictly Anglo–Mexican American relationship. And the other is that Mexican immigrants are more concerned with the practical circumstances of their everyday lives than with being Anglo or Mexican.

It is in this sense (the one just discussed) that I suggest that Mexican immigrants do not see the conflict in their everyday lives as stemming from their "hanging tenaciously to their cultural values" as suggested in the literature. That most social scientists make this assumption is a verification of how many social scientists overlook in a gross fashion how Mexican immigrants use their common-sense knowledge to make sense out of the world in which they operate. Most social scientists simply assume that Mexican immigrants are as typified in social scientific literature. And when they find a Mexican immigrant "out of character" (that is, as typified in the literature), social scientists label him either assimilated or marginal.

ASSIMILATION AND MARGINALIZATION

This labeling is done without specifying in concrete terms the process of assimilation or marginalization. I suggest these two concepts are not very useful for explaining behavior. If we are not told, we cannot tell who is assimilated. Moreover, we cannot tell when assimilation starts and when it stops, or how we might measure it. And suppose what might happen when we mislabel someone assimilated when they are not? This brings up the question, "Are people assimilated all the time?" The same thing can be said about the concept of marginality. I have been looking for a marginal person for the last ten years. I have yet to find one. Every time I think I have found one of these "confused and between two cultural world" types my marginal person quickly documents for me how he is very much within the world and how he wishes he could get out of it.

To document further how the concept of marginality is rather useless, I will relate the following account. Last year a Mexican student, whose family had immigrated to the U.S., came up after class to talk. The conversation went something like this:

S: I'm having trouble with the assignment.

R: How is that?

S: I'm marginal, you know.

R: Well, no I don't know. How do you know you're marginal? (At this point I wanted to run and get my tape recorder to get on tape this self-proclaimed marginal man.)

D: Well, you see, my mother is Chicano and my father is Italian.

R: How does that make you marginal?

S: Well, it's not that really. It's . . . well, when I left high school. You know, graduated. The counselor told me I'd have trouble here because I'd become marginal. You know, the school here is Anglo oriented. And we (Mexican Americans) are not. The Anglos are oriented to doing their papers. Because of our culture we are not, you know. We are not prepared and we find ourselves out here in this Anglo world. You know, Anglos are oriented for all this. We are not.

R: I don't understand what all of this has to do with the assignment.

S: I can't write my paper because I'm marginal. You know, I'm not Anglo oriented.

R: Let me ask you two things: are you marginal with your girl friend?

S: No man, I really groove with my woman. I know how to handle that.

R: Okay, you know how to handle your girl friend. This brings me to the second question: is your definition of marginality based on whether or not you have the ability to do something?

S: Yeah, like the paper. Anglos are oriented for writing.

R: What does knowing how to write have to do with Angloness or Mexicanness?

S: Everything. My counselor said we're not oriented for writing stuff.

R: Lets leave this marginal, Anglo-Mexican orientation stuff aside for awhile. I would like to propose the following: interview ten Anglos and ten Chicanos in the class on how they do their term paper. After you've done that, bring your data to me, and I'll help you write the paper which we'll base on your findings.

To make a long story short, my "marginal man" found that knowing how to write a term paper had nothing to do with ethnicity. The Anglos he interviewed were in the same boat he was in; they did not know how to write a term paper either, while seven out of ten Chicanos did.

I should point out that this particular student was serious in his belief that he was marginal. In my teaching career, I have had Chicano students use this "marginal routine" as a coping strategy to get out of writing their term paper.

UNEXPECTED EVENTS

An important question to ask at this point is, "How can a field researcher distinguish a coping strategy from normative behavior?" An ethnomethodological perspective provides an answer to this question by suggesting that field researchers use as methodological devices the trouble produced naturally by immigrants and the people they interact with. These naturally occurring troubles are referred to as unexpected events by ethnomethodologists.[17] The immigrants' way of coping with an unexpected event provides the researcher with data to contrast with what the researcher and the immigrants under the study themselves expected to go on, if the unexpected event had not occurred.

What I am suggesting here is that we need to collect at least two types of data. One can be baseline data. These are data which researchers accumulate as they go about their field research in "standard" ways.[18] The other is "unexpected event data." These are the data which are provided and produced by people's ways of managing an unexpected event. When we collect and compare these types of data, we can be in a better position to discern what behavior may constitute normative behavior.

Unexpected events also reveal interactional, or coping, strategems. We know that interactional strategems exist, and we are told about their complex features in the literature.[19] But we are rarely told in the literature how we may find or recognize a strategy in use. Unexpected events can help us find them. Strategems can be "found" when we collect unexpected event data and compare them with baseline data.

A third aspect which the occurrence of unexpected events reveals is the different social contexts in which the people under study operate. When people manage an unexpected event, they expose what they take into account (that is, their common-sense knowledge), which in turn reveals how they structure and manage a specific situation in terms of past and probable future situations they know about. I suggest that the common-sense knowledge people use to structure and manage a particular situation can be seen as the linkage between the different situations that make up a person's everyday life. Thus, in managing unexpected events, the people under study reveal not only the immediate social context in which they operate, but the "larger" social context in which the immediate context is embedded.

As unexpected events reveal the broader social context in which the people under study operate, they also make visible the parameters of the research setting for the researcher. In a sense, it can be said that the discovery of the broader social context in which the people under study operate is synonymous with the discovery of the parameters of the research setting. Researchers indeed start a field research project with some definite ideas of the types of people, places, and activities to be studied, but it takes something like an unexpected event to reveal the other relevant aspects of people's lives, places, and activities which are not visible or readily available to us. And if such things are visible, we as researchers may not take them to be relevant or related to what we may be studying until the people under study, in coping with an unexpected event, reveal for us the linkages that exist between the immediate context and the "larger" world in which they operate.

A virtue in discovering the parameters of the

research setting is not only that we are able to discover what else needs to be studied, but also that we are able to collect data on the same people in different settings. Thus, we have data which we can compare. What the people under study tell us at one point or situation can be compared with how they perform at other times and in other places. This is important in terms of verifications of ethnographic data.

SOCIAL POLICY

Two basic features of an ethnomethodological perspective are the notions of common-sense knowledge and trouble. These two notions are also the reasons why an ethnomethodological perspective can lend itself to the construction of more useful social policies on immigrants. To illustrate why this is the case, and to show in a concrete fashion the theoretical points made in the body of the paper, I will present an example where we can see how a teacher of a bilingual class makes trouble for a family of immigrants by trying to help them. Once again I draw upon the case of the Mexican immigrant.

Consider now how Carlos, a bilingual teacher in a Southern California elementary school, makes trouble for the family of one of his students. In talking with the father of one of his students, Carlos learned that the family was having financial difficulties. Carlos told the father that he would see what he could do for the family, and the father expressed appreciation for any help Carlos might get for the family. In search for help, Carlos went to a local community church that had a reputation for giving financial aid to needy families. The minister of the church agreed to help the family, and asked Carlos to have the father sign a form which he gave to Carlos to give to the father. Knowing the urgency of the situation, Carlos rushed the form over to the family the first chance he had. When he arrived at the home, the parents were not at home and he left the form. Carlos assumed that the father would sign the form as soon as he got home, and would rush it over to him so that Carlos would be able to get some money for the family. It did not happen that way.

After a day went by, Carlos went to visit the family to see what had happened to the form. The family members, in particular the father, were not interested in pursuing the matter any further, even though they still needed financial aid. This turn of events was confusing for Carlos, and he thought he would try to get them to change their minds about receiving help from the church. He worked on the assumption that he had misread their cues and that they really wanted him to help them, so he persisted in trying to get the father of the family to sign the form. He simply assumed that the father did not want to impose upon him.

It was not until the family had kept the student in Carlos' class out of school for a week and had refused to talk with Carlos that Carlos realized that something was wrong. To cope with the situation, Carlos solicited the help of a relative of the family in question. From the relative Carlos learned that he, unbeknownst to him, was making trouble for the family.

As it happened, the trouble revealed to Carlos that he did not know the family as well as he had thought. They were illegal aliens, and he had assumed all along that they were not only local Mexican Americans, but citizens of the United States.

According to the relative, trouble occurred when Carlos' initial step in the helping process had been misinterpreted by the father. Carlos had mentioned to the father that he has to sign some papers (the application form) before he would get any financial help from the church. The father saw the suggestion to sign "papers" as problematic. He feared that the act of signing his name might lead to someone discovering that he was an illegal alien. In addition, he took Carlos' zeal to get him to sign the papers as evidence that Carlos might be working with the United States Department of Immigration.

It might be argued here that the trouble created could have been avoided if Carlos had not assumed that the family were locals as well as citizens. But, the truth of the matter is that Carlos, like any other societal member, could not know he had mislabeled the family until some form of trouble occurred. The occurrence of trouble, then, is what gives people "hindsight."

In addition, it is not only a matter of mislabeling the family, but family members performing to convince Carlos as well as others that they were locals. Their part cannot be overlooked in the production of the dilemma. Moreover, it is certainly plausible to assume that illegal aliens such as the family in question work very hard to appear as if they are local Mexican Americans. And, when events such as the one described here are presented, the role that family members play in defining who they are needs to be addressed. If we do not, we will imply that illegal aliens, as well as legal immigrants, are passive people who do not participate in the social construction of the events that make up their everyday lives, and we will overlook how people socially organize themselves.

In terms of social policy, I am saying several things. First, quantitative data should not be used as primary data for the formulation of social policy. They should be used as secondary data. Quantitative data do not lend themselves to the discovery of how specific immigrants structure and manage their practical circumstances in terms of their common-sense knowledge. Thus, a great deal of what an immigrant takes into account gets glossed over or overlooked. Secondly, if social policy is to be written to help immigrants and to help people in public service do a better job, it must be suggested that the helpers discover the common-sense knowledge the specific immigrants who are to be helped take into account. In making this discovery, the helper is then able to give a service in a manner that is acceptable and seen as a help by the immigrant because it meshes with what the immigrant thinks is required or to be done. If this does not occur, it may be that the help becomes a hindrance or, as one immigrant told me, "just one more damn thing to deal with." Finally, by using an ethnomethodological perspective, we can address simultaneously the micro and macro aspects of an immigrant's life. As I suggested earlier, the common-sense knowledge an immigrant uses to structure and manage a particular situation can be seen as the linkage between the different situations that make up an immigrant's everyday life. By focusing on what constitutes the common-sense knowledge an immigrant takes into account, we are also able to address how others (members of the immigrant's immediate environment as well as members of the larger society), in interaction with

the immigrant, participate in the construction of the immigrant's social reality. An ethnomethodological perspective, then, provides us with a theoretical framework that helps us to understand concretely how the micro and macro aspects of the social order influence how immigrants and the helping services make sense out of what they are doing.

NOTES

1. For example, see B. Barry, *Race and Ethnic Relations* (Boston: Houghton Mifflin, 1965); A. Dworkin and R. Dworkin, eds., *The Minority Report* (New York: Praeger Publishing Company, 1976); Nathan Glazer and Daniel Patrick Moynihan, *Beyond the Melting Pot* (Cambridge, Mass.: MIT Press, 1963); Milton Gordon, *Assimilation in American Life* (New York: Oxford University Press, 1964); Harry L. Kitano, *Japanese Americans* (Englewood Cliffs, N.J.: Prentice-Hall Inc., 1969); and Robert E. Park, *Race and Culture* (Glencoe, Ill.: Free Press, 1950).
2. Alfred Schutz, *Collected Papers: The Problem of Social Reality*, vol. 1 (The Hague: Martinus Nijhoff, 1967), p.7.
3. Edward Husserl, *Cartesian Meditation: An Introduction to Phenomenology* (The Hague: Martinus Nijhoff, 1960), pp.33–37.
4. Herbert Garfinkel, *Studies in Ethnomethodology* (Englewood Cliffs, N.J.: Prentice-Hall, Inc., 1967), pp.36–37.
5. R. Kjolseth, "Making Sense: Natural Language and Shared Knowledge in Understanding," in Joshua A. Fishman, ed., *Advances in the Sociology of Language* (The Hague: Mouton and Company, 1971), p.15.
6. Garfinkel, op. cit., and Schutz, op. cit.
7. Garfinkel, op. cit.
8. Reyes Ramos, "The Production of Social Reality: An Ethnomethodological Study of the Making of Trouble," (doctoral dissertation, University of Colorado, Boulder, Colorado, 1973).
9. See L. Grebler, et. al., *The Mexican American People* (New York: The Free Press, 1970), and N. D. Humphrey, "On Assimilation and Acculturation," *Psychiatry* 6 (November 1943), pp.343–54.
10. C. Heller, *Mexican American Youth* (New York: Random House, 1968), and M. Ramirez, et. al., "Mexican American Cultural Membership and Adjustment to School," *Developmental Psychology* 4 (1971), p.141.
11. See W. Madsen, "The Alcoholic Agringado," *American Anthropologist* 66 (April 1964), pp.355–61, and A. Rubel, *Across the Tracks* (Austin: University of Texas Press, 1966).
12. For example, Heller, op. cit.; W. Madsen; and Rubel, op. cit.
13. Heller, op. cit., and Madsen.
14. Garfinkel, op. cit.
15. Schutz, op. cit., pp.222, 247.
16. Schutz, ibid.
17. A. V. Cicourel, *Method and Measurement in Sociology* (New York: The Free Press, 1964), and Reyes Ramos, "Data Everywhere," unpublished paper, 1977.
18. Norman K. Denzin, *The Research Act: A Theoretical Intro-*

duction to Sociological Methods (Chicago: Aldine Publishing Company, 1970), and Paul Lazarsfeld, *Qualitative Analysis: Historical and Critical Essays* (Boston: Alyn and Bacon, Inc., 1972).

19. M. Davis, *Intimate Relations* (New York: The Free Press, 1973), and many works by Erving Goffman: *The Presentation of Self in Everyday Life* (New York: Doubleday and Company, Inc., 1959); *Encounters* (Indianapolis: The Bobbs-Merrill Company, 1961); *Asylums* (New York: Anchor Books, 1961); *Behavior in Public Places* (New York: The Free Press, 1963); *Where the Action Is* (London: The Penguin Press, 1969); *Strategic Interaction* (Philadelphia: University of Pennsylvania Press, 1969); and *Relations in Public: Microstudies of the Public Order* (New York: Basic Books, 1971).

ALTERNATIVE INTELLECTUAL FRAMEWORKS FOR STUDYING THE NEW IMMIGRANTS

Eva E. Sandis

This paper considers the implications of two alternative intellectual approaches to the study of immigration and immigrants: the traditional intellectual framework within which this subject matter has been conceptualized, taught, and investigated in the United States; and an alternative model which is only now being introduced at the intellectual periphery, mainly by immigrant intellectuals themselves.

The traditional framework is one which reveals a continuing heavy reliance on the "assimilation" approach to immigration and immigrants. The latter are viewed from the standpoint of their relationship to the receiving society, and analyzed in terms of their motivations for the move, their selective characteristics in relation to those remaining at home, and their assimilation into American society. On the other hand, the newer framework stresses the conditions of underdevelopment in colonial possessions which have produced unemployment, overpopulation, and emigration from the sending countries.

This paper examines the main themes of the traditional framework and the extent to which this approach still appears to have a hold in the sociological literature. In this paper the traditional approach is contrasted with themes characterizing an emergent framework of the, as yet, peripheral immigrant intellectuals. After a brief content analysis of the general literature, the paper focuses on one specific migrant group, the Puerto Ricans, who have been analyzed from both points of view. The implications of the two approaches will be considered in the final section.

TEXTBOOK SURVEY

The following introductory sociology textbooks were examined to note current sociological approaches to the treatment of immigrants and immigration:

Berger, Peter L. and Brigitte Berger. *Sociology: A Biographical Approach,* Second Edition. New York: Basic Books, 1975.

Broom, Leonard and Philip Selznick. *Sociology*, Fifth Edition. New York: Harper and Row, 1973.

Chinoy Ely. *Society: An Introduction to Sociology*, Second Edition. New York: Random House, 1967.

Fichter, Joseph H. *Sociology*. Chicago: University of Chicago Press, 1957.

Horton, Paul B., and Chester L. Hunt. *Sociology*, Second Edition. New York: McGraw-Hill, 1968.

Light, Donald Jr., and Suzanne Keller. *Sociology*. New York: Alfred A. Knopf, 1975.

Lowry, Ritchie P. and Robert P. Rankin. *Sociology: Social Science and Social Concern*. New York: Charles Scribner's Sons, 1972.

Lundberg, George A., Clarence C. Schrag, Otto N. Larsen and William R. Catton, Jr. *Sociology*, Fourth Edition. New York: Harper and Row, 1968.

Rose, Arnold M. and Caroline B. Rose. *Sociology: The Study of Human Relations,* Third Edition. New York: Alfred A. Knopf, 1969.

The criteria for selection included such considerations as recency of publication, authored rather than edited texts, reflection of diversity of sociological schools of thought, and publishing firms with a wide distribution network.

The main impression left by a review of the introductory texts is that there is little systematic attention to immigration and immigrants at all. The material tends to be scattered throughout the texts under a variety of topics: chapters on population devoted mainly to fertility, and chapters on American ethnic groups largely concentrating on the situation of American Indians and American blacks. Information can be found, here and there, in chapters on social process, social change, and social deviance.

Three topics recur in the treatment of immigration and immigrants in these sociology texts: the causes and the effects of immigration, and the responses of both the receiving society and of the migrants themselves.

The causes of migration are conceptualized in terms of the "push and pull" factors affecting the motivation of migrants. Some mention is made that these factors have operated on potential migrants selectively: males versus females, those in the productive age groups as against the old and the young, and so forth.

Occasionally, the statements go beyond the motivations of the migrants and relate the migrant streams to certain structural characteristics of the sending and receiving societies. According to these generalizations, one can expect high rates of emigration-immigration when (1) population growth outstrips economic development; and (2) economic opportunity in the receiving country outstrips economic opportunity in the sending country.

Textbook discussions of the *effects* of migration deal mainly with the impact immigrants have had on this country, and their own experiences regarding socioeconomic mobility and assimilation.

Only one text deals with the impact of emigrants on the sending society, describing them historically as agents of social change in the cultural diffusion of metropolitan ideals. Broom and Selznick also mention the recent emergence of the brain drain problem.[2]

Sociologists describing the impact of immigrants on American society mention their contributions to ethnic diversity, cultural diffusion, and the provision of needed skills on the labor market. Another effect noted by Fichter and Rose is that the immigrants, who have always moved in as a body at the level of the lower classes, have therefore "pushed up" the native born.[3]

In discussing the effect of immigration on the immigrants, the texts' authors concentrate on the extent of their social mobility and assimilation into society. The Lundberg text, for instance, describes Rosen's study on race, ethnicity, and the achievement syndrome, noting different rates of social mobility displayed by six different ethnic groups. Light and Keller emphasize the role of the school system in enforcing "Anglo-conformity."[4]

Several authors discuss problems of deviance in immigrant groups, especially in the second generation, as arising from conflicts between norms of their immigrant parents and the norms of American society.[5]

Virtually all texts conclude that the past reaction of American society to the immigrants has been one of prejudice of the earlier arrivals towards the later ones, in addition to fears about their potential economic competitiveness and political alignments. Some maintain that the shift now is to a concern with conditions of our environment, such as depletion of our resources.[7]

As for the migrants themselves, according to Fichter, in the past they have tended to show more concern with assimilation than with confrontation.[8] At the present time, Light and Keller suggest, closeness to the homeland tends to reduce the incentive of migrants to assimilate.[9]

THE APPROACH OF THIRD WORLD INTELLECTUALS

Although the views of Third World intellectuals have not yet penetrated the academic establishment through such media as sociology texts, one can find expressions of these views in conference papers, statements delivered before congressional committees, and newspaper articles.

The main theme of the new immigrant intellectuals is that the immigrant streams are the result of the "crisis of underdevelopment" in the home countries, and that a major factor in that crisis is foreign domination of their economies. To these intellectuals, the motivations of the migrants, while important, are secondary to the "material basis" of the migration. "In Puerto Rico, the Dominican Republic, Haiti, the Virgin Islands, and the entire English speaking Caribbean, the crisis of underdevelopment (i.e., the use of Caribbean resources to the disadvantage of the region) is reflected in widespread unemployment, high levels of inflation, and balance of payments problems."[10]

Watson maintains that foreign ownership of wealth, and the foreign control and use of resources, have been main contributing factors to the crisis.

In a similar vein, Bryce-Laporte observes that the "stagnated colonial status" in which many of the islands were found until recently has resulted from the fact that many of the policies and attitudes of the United States toward the Caribbean have been based largely "on the simple, clear objective of protecting and advancing U.S. interests."[11]

Third World intellectuals take issue with the notion of overpopulation as accounting for the immigration streams. They argue that it is the capitalistic mode of production in their countries which is producing "surplus" populations, both by encouraging population growth and by restricting employment opportunities. "So-called 'surplus labor' and unlimited supplies of labor do not just happen to exist. None of this can be understood outside the context of the nature and operation of the mode of production."[12]

They also note that, through draining capital resources from the Third World countries and channeling them to the metropolitan countries, this mode of production creates labor mobility. They are concerned with the general drain of human resources, and specifically, the brain drain problem. Bryce-Laporte notes that "in fact, the impressive leadership and success of first-generation black West Indians (in the U.S.) suggest that emigration had a projected loss of human resources built into it for the societies from which they came."[13]

While it is agreed that there is "no guarantee" that in their homelands these talents would have been utilized, this is attributed to the condition of socioeconomic underdevelopment which has to be eradicated so that the cycle does not perpetually repeat itself.[14]

Less attention is directed to the immigrant stream in the receiving country. When the focus shifts to this topic, it is on the benefits of the immigrant stream to the market of the receiving society as a source of trained, cheap labor. As Bryce-Laporte observes, many middle class immigrants may settle for jobs for which they are overtrained because they receive higher salaries than they would receive at home as professionals.[15] According to Watson, given the level of emigration of trained personnel from Jamaica, her "gift of labor to the imperialist economies" from 1970 to 1975 was about nine million Jamaican dollars.[16]

THE PUERTO RICAN MIGRATION: CONTRASTING INTELLECTUAL APPROACHES

The Puerto Rican migration presents an interesting case study, since it has been analyzed from both the traditional sociological point of view and, more recently, from the perspective of the mainland Puerto Rican sociologists themselves. Technically speaking, it constitutes an "internal" migration, since Puerto Ricans are United States citizens and U.S. immigration laws do not apply to them. But just as those sociologists employing the traditional model have emphasized the common problems of Puerto Ricans and earlier European immigrants regarding their cultural and social assimilation into the American mainstream, so do the sociologists who are utilizing the newer model stress the similarities of Puerto Ricans and other Third World immigrant streams regarding their common fate as a colonized, economically and culturally dispossessed peoples.

Both groups of sociologists recognize the conditions which motivate Puerto Ricans to migrate. They agree that these conditions are to be found in the relationship between population growth and economic growth on the island. But they differ in their assessment of the nature of that relationship.

In perhaps the most extreme expression of the traditional thesis, Glazer, noting that Puerto Rico's birthrate "has remained among the highest in the world," argues that Puerto Rico was "too crowded" to think in terms of prosperous family-type farms, and needed sugar as a cash crop, high mechanization involving "less" labor, the stimulation of mainland investment, and the connection with the American market. Nevertheless, he maintains, Puerto Ricans were "not happy" to stay at home because "the reconstruction of the island destroyed almost as many jobs" as it made, and the wage rates of the remaining jobs were low in contrast to the wage rates on the mainland. For Glazer, the growth rate of the Puerto Rican population largely accounts not only for the economic situation on the island but also for that on the mainland.[17] His emphasis on the negative consequences of rapid population growth in Third World societies reflects the thinking of sociological academics generally, as already noted.

Other mainland students[18] of the Puerto Rican migration have also noted the uneven race between population growth and economic development.

An analysis of various works shows that some sociologists are less concerned with the matter of unchecked growth of population than with the meaning of the loss of human resources to the sending countries when persons have to emigrate because of economic conditions. However, the condition of economic underdevelopment in these societies, while recognized, is not tied to a particular mode of production which creates and increases the gap between population and employment opportunities. On the contrary, the "Fomento" program of stimulating American private investment in the Puerto Rican market is praised as a development model for other Third World countries. Senior and Watkins applaud "the fantastically successful record of 'Fomento' in getting factories established in Puerto Rico in the past 15 years or so. Its work deservedly attracted the attention of the world. . . . The direct and indirect results of the Fomento program and related private investment projects have furnished some 128,000 new jobs, in round numbers, during the past 20 years."[19]

It will be recalled that the Industrial Development Company, popularly known as "Fomento," established in 1942, systematically tried to promote private investment in industry through such incentives as tax holidays for United States corporations and the "Operation Bootstrap" campaign. As part of the latter, Fomento undertook an Aid to Industrial Development program through which it provided free technical advice on plant location and design, advance recruitment and training of workers for new factories, the construction of industrial buildings for lease or sale on liberal terms, and loans and subsidies to businessmen for financing new industries.[20]

The Puerto Rican intellectuals' assessment of Fomento is in stark contrast to that of the North American group:

> Finally, the increased capital labor ratios required to sustain productivity as wage levels crept upward transformed the Fomento sector into an extension of the mainland economy. By 1960 only about ten percent of Fomento firms represented local investment. The critical facts, however, were not the source of investment or control over production, but that the prices of labor and other commodities as well as profit ratios were being determined by market relationships and economic policies in the U.S. rather than by the relationships among local firms, producers, and workers. By the 1960's it was already unclear in what sense one could continue to talk about a Puerto Rican "economy."[21]

To these sociologists the foreign absorption of the Puerto Rican economy into that of the mainland, and the loss of local decision-making control, is the main explanatory variable for the uneven race between population and economic growth. This is so, first, because the capitalistic, free enterprise system produces "surplus" populations, and second, because American economic decisions are made with reference to U.S. interests rather than to those of the local population.

About the effect of the mode of production on the relationship between population growth and employment opportunities, the authors of the CENTRO study maintain: "The specific characteristic of the capitalist mode of production is rooted in the fact that the development of the productive forces itself constitutes the generative cause of relative overpopulation."[22]

The authors add that, since capital must be in constant motion, migration is also a continual process. But they point out that migration only transfers the problem from one geographic zone to another, where once again the process of the "excess" workers come into being.[23] The entire study then seeks to trace the development of Puerto Rico as a dependent economy whose employment opportunities could not keep up with its population growth because of its reliance on a profit-oriented, mainland-dominated productive system which relied on capital-intensive means of agricultural and industrial development, with a resultant movement of capital and labor resources to the mainland.

Echoing Bryce-Laporte's earlier quoted statements about the Caribbean in general, López[24] maintains that United States policies toward Puerto Rico have been motivated by advancing and protecting American interests, and that whatever benefits accrued to Puerto Rico were incidental. According to López, after the United States acquired Puerto Rico in 1898, roads and bridges were built "to facilitate the transportation of commodities" of American companies; the university was established to train "a class of intermediaries and managers;" and health and sanitation facilities were established "to create a better living environment for metropolitan investors and colonial officialdom."[25] The present exodus of Puerto Ricans is similarly viewed by López, Rodriguez,[26] and others, as a response to the self-interested demands of mainland corporate interests for cheap labor.

Since the motivational factor is secondary to the material basis of the migration according to this group of scholars, motivation receives virtually no attention from them. North American scholars tend to refer to the pull of economic opportunity on the mainland. They also note that this pull has tended to operate selectively on Puerto Ricans in the economically productive age groups and in the middle range educational categories. While the interest of North American sociologists in selectivity has been mainly from the standpoint of the impact on socioeconomic integration of the migrants into the receiving society, Puerto Rican intellectuals have been concerned from the standpoint of the impact on the sending society.

North American scholars recognize the "debits" of emigration for Puerto Rico, as Senior and Watkins put it, the costs of raising persons who are then relinquished to another economy, the loss of initiative and skills possessed by the migrants, and the effect of migration in increasing the dependency ratio.[27] On the other hand, they also point to the benefits of remittances to family and friends. And, additionally, they also suggest that the migration has removed persons from Puerto Rico who would otherwise have been a "strain" on the job market, on per capita income, and on school, health, and welfare services. The economic benefits from social

security and unemployment insurance benefits, according to Senior and Watkins, "might be considered as repayment on the 'cost of production of a man.'" Finally, the mainland economy has served "as a vast training school" for many return migrants.

Discussing the impact of the migration on mainland society, Fitzpatrick notes the contribution of the Puerto Rican migrants to the New York economy. He maintains that the hotel and restaurant trades "would be helpless without them."[28] Glazer, however, does not share this appraisal of the overall advantages of the Puerto Rican migration on economic grounds; he asserts that the abundance of cheap labor in New York City also accounted for overcrowding, scarcity of housing, and increased welfare costs.[29]

Rodríguez has sharply rebutted the argument that Puerto Ricans make heavy demands on welfare. First, she argues that the conditions of the American market today tend to keep the Puerto Ricans down, and second, that the welfare system, which exists for the benefits of its own bureaucracy, tends to track the poor, and therefore the Puerto Ricans, into it.

According to Rodríquez, the conditions which account for the Puerto Rican migrants' malintegration into the New York labor market are as follows: "Automation, sectoral decline, blue collar structural unemployment, racial and ethnic prejudice, restrictive union policies, inadequate educational opportunities and the restriction of Puerto Ricans from government employment."[30]

Rodríguez underscores the "migration dividends to the economy" which, she insists, is the obverse side of the "exploited, yet crucial position" of Puerto Ricans in the economy.

After noting the high proportion of self-supporting Puerto Rican families "given the low-income, high unemployment and insecure jobs held by Puerto Ricans," Rodríquez declares:

> Welfare can be seen to be a contracting economy's response to structural and sectoral unemployment. In addition to taking up the slack in the economy, it also provides jobs for the clerical and higher skilled workers—the welfare establishment—while it cools out what may otherwise be an unbearable and explosive situation for the unemployed. At the same time, it

tends to subsidize the low wage industry sector and the landlord class, which is a direct beneficiary of welfare rent payments.[31]

North American students of the Puerto Rican migration have also commented on the low occupational and educational position of first generation Puerto Rican migrants, but find reasons for optimism both in their "higher real earnings."[32] and in the "impressive improvement" in occupational levels of second generation Puerto Ricans.[33]

The mainland Puerto Ricans' assessment of their people's future on the continent is less optimistic in tone and more radical in its goals. Among the effects of the migration on the immigrants, López has noted that "most tragically of all," many Puerto Ricans have "internalized the prejudices of the very society that was exploiting and humiliating them. White Puerto Ricans who on the island had lived next to black Puerto Ricans now avoided black Americans and often referred to them as 'niggers'; black Puerto Ricans often did their best to emphasize their Puerto Rican-ness so as not to be confused with American blacks."[34]

Bryce-Laporte[35] has reported the same tendency for some West Indian immigrants to emphasize their cultural distinctiveness in the "pathetic hope" that in this way they would escape the stigma and mistreatment directed at native blacks by the larger society.

The mainland Puerto Rican sociologists see the future of the continental Puerto Rican community as the responsibility of the second and third generation Puerto Ricans on the mainland. These must look forward, not backward to the island, for the achievement of their goals. The goals set forth by the authors of the CENTRO study, and by Rodríguez, López, and others like them, are not assimilation into the American mainstream or any kind of pluralism. Not even socioeconomic integration through the acquisition and manipulation of political power—the road North American sociologists like Fitzpatrick see ahead for the Puerto Ricans[36]—holds any programmatic appeal for this group. To them the only hope lies in a complete social transformation of American (and with it, Puerto Rican) society. In the words of López, only when socialism, a system which is "truly concerned

about human needs," will replace capitalism, will the causes of the problems affecting blacks, Indians, Chicanos, Puerto Ricans, and other groups disappear. He calls for the establishment of "linkages" with these groups, "for the problems of those minorities are almost identical to the problems of the Puerto Ricans."[37] This call for unity among the "colonized minorities"[38] is simliar to the sentiments expressed by Bryce-Laporte, who notes the beauty and necessity of West Indians and American blacks finally "getting together."[39]

IMPLICATIONS

The traditional sociological approach to immigrants and immigration, with its emphasis on social and cultural assimilation into the American mainstream, implies social policies designed to accomplish the socioeconomic integration of the immigrants into American society. The institutions involved in this integrating process are the schools, the labor market, political organizations and unions, religious, community, and recreational organizations, health, welfare, and other service institutions.

On the other hand, the newer model, with its emphasis on the crisis of underdevelopment in the sending societies, and on the unending process of drainage of capital and human resources as the process of their underdevelopment becomes exacerbated, shifts the focus away from the *end* of that chain of events—the adaptation of migrants in the receiving country—to its *origins*.

The newer approach calls attention to the *structural* causes of emigration streams from the home countries, rather than to the individual motivations of migrants which determine their choices to move. Furthermore, these structural causes are seen as intimately tied to the economic and political policies of the very countries to which the streams migrate. What these intellectuals are increasingly calling for is that these policies be changed, to be more in accordance with their own national interests, including the conservation of their human resources. Adoption of this framework also implies that since the economics of the sending and receiving societies are so intimately linked, a fundamental change in the situation of the immigrants in the receiving country, as well as of the population in the sending country, may require basic structural changes involving the mode of production in the United States. Another implication is that since the position of Third World peoples in the United States, regardless of their particular origins, is basically the same, they constitute appropriate groups for the establishment of mutual linkages in order to achieve their common goals.

NOTES

1. Broom and Selznick, p.296; Rose and Rose, p.432; Fichter, p.316.
2. Broom and Selznick, p.296.
3. Fichter, p.335; Rose and Rose, p.352.
4. Light and Keller, p.241.
5. Berger and Berger, p.312; Chinoy, p.470.
6. Chinoy, p.230; Fichter, p.81; Light and Keller, p.231; Lowry and Rankin, p.70.
7. Broom and Selznick, p.297.
8. Fichter, p.102.
9. Light and Keller, p.231.
10. Hilbourne A. Watson, "West Indians in the U.S.—Why So Many?" *Amsterdam News,* 2 October 1976. See also his paper, "Migration and the Political Economy of Underdevelopment: Notes on the Commonwealth Caribbean Situation," presented to the Panel on International Migration as a Policy Issue: The Western Hemisphere, at the International Studies Association Conference held in Toronto, Canada, February 25–28, 1976.
11. Roy S. Bryce-Laporte, "Dreams and Destinations: The Caribbean Immigrant in the United States." Remarks delivered before the United States House of Representatives, Subcommittee on Inter-American Affairs, September 10 and 21, 1973, and reprinted in *Continuities* (New York: CUNY, Black Studies Department, Spring 1975).
12. Watson, op. cit., p.9.
13. Bryce-Laporte, p.8.
14. Cf., Bryce-Laporte, op. cit., p.8, and Wason, op. cit., p.12.
15. Bryce-Laporte, loc. cit.
16. Watson, op. cit., p.11.
17. Nathan Glazer, "The Puerto Ricans," in Nathan Glazer and Daniel Moynihan, *Beyond the Melting Pot* (Cambridge, Mass.: M.I.T. Press and Harvard University Press, 1963). See pp.86, 95, 96, 117, 118.
18. See Clarence Senior and Donald O. Watkins, "Toward a Balance Sheet of Puerto Rican Migration," in *Selected Background Studies,* prepared for the United States-Puerto Rico Commission on the Status of Puerto Rico, 1966, and Joseph P. Fitzpatrick, *Puerto Rican Americans: The Meaning of Migration to the Mainland* (Englewood Cliffs, New Jersey: Prentice-Hall, Inc., 1971).
19. Senior and Watkins, op. cit., p.739.
20. Henry Wells, *The Modernization of Puerto Rico* (Cambridge, Mass.: Harvard University Press, 1969), p.150.
21. CENTRO, *Taller de Migracion, Conferencia de Historiografia: Abril 1974* Centro de Estudios Puertorriqueños: CUNY, 1975), p.162.
22. CENTRO, ibid., p.24.
23. CENTRO, pp.38-40.
24. Adalberto López, "The Puerto Rican Diaspora: A Survey," in Adalberto López and James Petras, eds., *Puerto Rico and Puerto Ricans* (Cambridge, Mass.: Schenkman Publishing Co., 1974).
25. Ibid., p.317.
26. Clara E. Rodríguez, "Economic Factors Affecting Puerto Ricans in New York," Unit three of the CENTRO Study, and previously delivered as a paper under the title, "Puerto Ricans in the New York Economy."
27. Senior and Watkins, op. cit., p.748.
28. Fitzpatrick, op. cit., p.60.
29. Glazer, in Glazer and Moynihan, op. cit., p.131.
30. Rodríguez, op. cit., p.20.
31. Ibid., p.40.
32. Senior and Watkins, p.753.
33. Fitzpatrick, p.60.
34. López, op. cit., p.327.
35. Roy S. Bryce-Laporte, "Black Immigrants, The Experience of Invisibility and Inequality," in *Journal of Black Studies,* 3, No.1 (September 1972), pp.29–56.
36. Fitzpatrick, op. cit., p.180 ff.
37. López, op. cit., p.344.
38. Robert Blauner, "Colonized and Immigrant Minorities," in *Racial Oppression in America* (New York: Harper and Row, 1972).
39. Bryce-Laporte, "Black Immigrants," p.53.

IMMIGRATION THEORY: A REVIEW OF THEMATIC STRATEGIES

Paul Meadows

INTRODUCTION

Concerning matters of theory

Karl Mannheim's "perspectivism" is a useful way of introducing this paper on immigration theory. He held that reality tends to be a function of the observer's perspective, itself a product of his position, training, and interests. His perspective not only selects those aspects of reality to which he attends, but also informs and organizes them. Theory, which in its most general form is a statement of relationships among and between facts, is a perspective organization of facts. Perspective provides themes by which such organization can and does occur. "Thematic strategies" here refers to the various modes of organizing facts.

This paper proposes to review some of the thematic strategies which appear in immigration theory literature. It is primarily a taxonomic review, that is, it selects studies which illustrate certain modes of organizing data; the data on immigration as a form of territorial mobility, on migrants in terms of donor and host societies. These modes are identified in terms of the major orientation of these studies: theories of immigration in terms of the international system; mechanistic metaphors of forces, fields, and flows; and semiotic and structural interpretations of immigrant behavior.

It is a taxonomic review of theories. It is not an effort at theory explication.[1] Such an effort may very well be undertaken at some time in the future; it is well beyond the scope and capacity of this study. What is being attempted here is, first, the identification of theoretical statements about some properties and relationships of migration as they have been formulated by various writers with different professional backgrounds; second, the placement of these statements in the characterizing contexts named above; and third, the determination of relationships among variables and properties which

may be found in the contexts of these placements. The focus of the selection and review is on the theoretical constructs which have been used in empirical and, to a lesser extent, in formal analyses of immigration. The paper may be said to be a very preliminary form of abduction, whose purpose is the identification and formulation of theoretical statements for replication and for explanation.[2]

Immigration literature is not noted for its abundance of postulational statements of relationships, though some notable formulations have indeed been made. Much of this literature is historical, or descriptive, or evaluative (often in a filio-pietistic way), or reportorial (in some common form, such as journalistic or case history). Some of the literature has been able to formulate variables and has developed some middle-range statements. Very little of it approaches the stage of formal theory development. A huge problem-orientation, either of the ordinary "social problems" kind or of policy-relevant problem-contexts, pervades the literature. Reductionism abounds. And yet, as will be discussed below, a slowly enlarging body of studies has been concerned with the formulation of some sort of stable structures of actions and relationships, which may very well prove to be the developmental background of formal theory.

It requires only a slight acquaintance with the field of immigration studies to understand quickly why theory construction does not predominate. Immigration is a subject which, for various reasons, has not excited a great deal of scholarly interest, certainly not of the sort we are considering here. Data have been and are being collected but, for the most part, they lack the precision and the detail, the comparability and the reliability, which are elementary necessities of significant theory construction. The levels of analysis reflect sheer variety of perspectives: some studies are macrocosmic, others microscopic; the whole and the parts, the general and the specific, the highly abstract and the very empirical, and above all the national and some crosscultural mingle in vast profusion. Research models are rare.

Theory construction[3] is not the same thing as theory-work.[4] Of the latter we have a good supply in immigration literature. This taxonomic review does not propose to sort out immigration theory into either the theory-work or the theory-construction typology. What is assumed here is a much less ambitious but very preliminary task—the identification of thematic strategies which may be said to characterize immigration literature as it has been developed in different disciplines. The more mature and more useful task of theory construction must yet be done. It is hoped that this review may help set the stage for such work.

Pattern of presentation

This review of thematic strategies in the literature on immigration theory does not pretend to be comprehensive, except in the sense of a sampling of studies which illustrate a certain range of perspectives. For purposes of this review, certain assumptions were made by the present writer. First, the core aspect of immigration is, of course, territorial mobility. The second assumption of this paper is that the perspective of the theorist determines his topic, his definitions and premises, his data, and to a large extent his findings. A third assumption holds that, because the area of inquiry has attracted a number of scholars from several professional disciplines, a review of immigration theory is necessarily interdisciplinary. The fourth assumption of the study is that theorizing done in any area of migration study can, at least in suggestive form, be transposed to other areas. This is indeed a risk. This writer is well aware, for example, that internal and international mobility are not the same phenomenon; but he also holds that an examination of the structure of definitions, premises, and constructs does warrant some limited empirical or formal generalizations. A fifth assumption is that the literature on immigration theory, which is by no means as extensive as that which may be found on other social phenomena which have attracted social scientists, can hardly be expected to be as mature and as definitive as that of these other areas. There is only

the beginning of a body of formal theory, mainly in spatial interaction inquiry. Most of the theoretical literature is concerned with empirical generalizations, many of which have to await the retesting and validation which they invite. In terms of the Mertonian paradigm, the bulge of the literature is of the first order of generalization. Some, in fact, a surprising amount, represent middle-range propositions. The third order of formal theory is scarce.

What is attempted is a review which uses the following classificatory principles: presence of "system" as an interpretive construct, and the differential attention paid to externalistic as against internalistic properties. Some writers, reflecting perhaps an older tradition in the philosophy of science, are interested in migration and the migrant as objects in a field of forces. Other writers, expressing another tradition in the philosophy of science, think of the field (system) and the migrant in subjectivistic and internalistic terms. Thus, the theories reviewed in these pages form a continuum of perspectives, roughly from action theory to behavior theory. In the same manner, these theories express the same awareness of and devotion to a structuralist mode of interpretation, from the *external structuralism* of the Atlantic economy, world industrialization, the mechanistic metaphors of pushes and pulls, to the psychologistic, psychocultural, culturalistic, and social system categories couched in the language of a *subjective structuralism* of some sort.

Finally, this study does not essay a coverage of the literature of *normative* immigration theory, that which concerns itself with national and international policy, for example. The issues and themes which mark the debate on pluralism, or assimilation, or the dual economy, or segregation are present in the literature reviewed here only in a very indirect way. Analytical theory precedes, or ought to precede, normative theory, thereby making a contribution in no small measure to the ultimate cogency of normative theory itself.

The taxonomic perspective of the present study suggests a conceptual model for the consideration of immigration theory. As such it may be useful as a preliminary to the development of formal immigration theory, which is without question both lacking and needed.

SHIFTS IN TAXONOMIC PERSPECTIVE

The historical perspective

In migration theory, as elsewhere, it is important to maintain an historical perspective. Policy and other current concerns with the volume, selectivity, and problems of modern mass migration often overshadow basic historical facts about human movement itself. This fact was well understood by the anthrogeographers who founded the field of migration theory; that is, Friedrich Ratzel, Jean Brunhes, Camille Vallaux, F. von Richthofen, E. F. Gautier, J. Blache, and more recently E. Huntington and G. Taylor in cultural geography. These scholars established both the antiquity, universality as well as variety of human migrations. Other typologies have dealt with the dimensions of frontiers, continental and intercontinental patterns of migration, all attesting to the extent and variety of human movements. Each great age of European history was characterized by waves of human movement. Similarily, the Woytinskys have noted that, since the 16th century, seven major currents of movement have taken place, five between and two within nation-states: from Europe to North America; to South America and the Caribbean, to South Africa, Australia, and Australasia; slave importations to the New World from Africa; from China and India to neighboring countries; intracontinental migration in North America; and internal migration in Russia eastward. These movements total well over 120 million persons, approximately half of this number since the mid-nineteenth century in the familiar European movement.[5] Movements of such volume and variety invite the taxonomic curiosity as a necessary preliminary to the work of theory.

The taxonomic perspective

Classification of human movements reflect not only the analytical concerns of the theorist but his dimensional perceptions as well. Any phenomenon can be observed from different perspectives, with consequent shifts in the process of classification, for phenomena have different determinable properties, each property or set of properties serving the taxonomic cause. Each dimension or set of dimensions will generate its own taxonomic orientation.

In the United States, migration taxonomy seems to have begun with Henry Pratt Fairchild's pioneering albeit simplistic differentiation of types: invasion, conquest, colonization, free, and compulsory.[6] This basic classification appears also in the work of M. R. Davie, J. Issac, Davis, and Taft and Robbins.[7]

William Petersen, starting with a critical revision of the familiar push-pull polarity which distinguished between innovating and conserving migration, as well as migrants' level of aspiration, developed "an improved typology of migration."[8] A decade later, Petersen suggested another taxonomy, this time emphasizing migratory selection as the basis of his classification.[9]

The Scandinavian geographer Edgar Kant has greatly enriched the field of migration taxonomy in a study published in the middle 1950s.[10] His classification is repeated here because of its useful chorographical emphasis, even though his immediate reference is to continental migrations only.

I. *Intralocal or intraregional migrations*
   A. *Intraurban migrations*
   B. *Intrarural migrations*

II. *Interlocal or interregional migrations*
   A. *Migrations by change of environment or milieu*
   B. *Migrations between similar parts of a country*

In a novel approach to the problem of migration taxonomy, Israeli sociologist J. Matras starts from a distinction between "the population balancing equation" approach of more traditional research and the "mobility status" approach, which he suggests.[11] The first incorporates the familiar differentiations in the formula,

$$P_1 = P_0 + B - D + 1 - 0,$$
where,
P_0 = population at the beginning of an interval
B = the number of births in the interval
D = the number of deaths in the interval
I = the number of in-migrants in the interval
O = the number of out-migrants in the interval
P_1 = population at the close of the interval

Noting the well-known unreliability of data from reporting agencies, he suggests the use of the "migrant status" or "mobility status" approach which reconstructs past movements on the basis of information returned by individuals in census or survey inquiries. The data which this procedure yields specify what kinds of moves actually constitute migration, or who is or who is not a migrant. Both procedures, of course, reflect the possibilities of a demographically generated typology of migration, limited in all probability to national situations with more sophisticated reporting devices.

A theme common in anthrogeographic discussions (but not well-developed there) is the presence of distinguishable geographic mobility patterns within different populations and societies.[12] Thus, Textor's crosscultural survey, which classified some 332 cultures by pattern of settlement, distinguished settlements as nonpermanent and permanent. And, in its ecological orientation, the fascinating thing about Textor's tabulation is the way it portrays human settlement in terms of the variable of human movement.[13]

It is possible on this basis to work out certain useful empirical generalizations concerning the nature of human movements, as Goldscheider has done.[14] Thus, both small-scale, low-density populations as well as those having higher population density (but with no food-cultivating technology) are characterized by movements, either permanent or temporary. The property institutions of larger agrarian societies inhibit much movement. Goldscheider has characterized migration in traditional societies as a function of the development of new territories or new sources of sustenance, of marriage, of warfare, conquest, or other political causes.

Industrialization and modernization obviously represent polar contrast to these conditions. Thus, Goldscheider has noted specifically the relationship of economic changes generated by trade and production, repressive taxation, new labor recruitment practices, and changing attitudes toward migration as some of the factors important in the stimulation of mobility in industrializing societies. Clearly, the technological orientation represents another series of possibilities for migration taxonomy.

Petersen has observed that the value of typology is, of course, in its utility beyond that of satisfying the classificatory impulse itself.[15] It is, of course, apparent that the type of movement has a major bearing on the type of analysis used, unless the analytic approach can devise some cross-type uniformities, at least in terms of some level or phase of migration, which can be said to exist among the varieties which have been observed. Can we develop thematic strategies and research models by which we can generalize from internal to international migration, from continental to intercontinental movements, from free to compulsory, from individual to mass, from preindustrial to industrial migrations?

INTERNATIONAL STRATEGIES OF INTERPRETATION

International interpretive strategies as a structural approach to immigration theory

For the last century and a half, the most impressive form of migration has been the mass movement of people across the nation-state boundaries, continental or intercontinental. Therefore, in terms of sheer number and socioeconomic as well as political implications and consequences, the international context of approach is appropriately the first context to be considered here. Generally, however, this context is treated in the literature (1) demographically, (2) politically, in terms of policy and administration, and (3) very secondarily, in terms of psychocultural or socioeconomic consequences for migrants as persons and nations as sending and receiving entities. Such interests tend to be largely reportorial and evaluative; they do not primarily induce or encourage analytical theory.

Analytical theory on such a macroscopic scale must necessarily be structural; that is, it must be concerned with the identification of structural elements and structural relationships. This section of this paper will review three such approaches to the international context of immigration theory as examples of the possibilities for immigration theory and research. These three represent a widening pattern of analysis: first, Brinley Thomas's study of the

Atlantic economy; second, Walter Zelinsky's mobility transition model; and third, a comparative consideration of industrialism as a world socio-economic system, a consideration which utilizes the work of Gunnar Myrdal, Immanuel Wallerstein, and Richard Rubinson.[16] The three represent a gradient of increasing abstractness and generality, literally from emphasis on empirical structural variables to system-wide structural variables seen here as having immediate relevance to immigration theory.

The concept of the Atlantic economy

Each of these approaches utilizes the concept of system, seen as an operational totality. For Brinley Thomas, the system vantage point is "the Atlantic economy" during the 19th-century period of heavy migration to North America. His work starts with the notion of population and capital as expressions of international economic growth, with migration regarded as integral to the process of economic expansion. Searching for "structural turning points," Thomas rejects the static classical dichotomy of "international trade and a long period of emigration," and utilizes a more dynamic concept of development. His suggestive reference point is John Stuart Mill's concept of "the larger community" of countries, in this case the Atlantic community as the economy "in which the international movements of labor, capital, and commodities" are thought of "as if they were interregional." Migration, he writes, "not only induces but is itself partly determined by changes in the structure of the international community."

Noting that, in the case of sending countries, "industrialization inhibits emigration," but in receiving countries it stimulates it, he identifies the condition in the Atlantic economy which would maximize growth:

> At the outset in the eastern sector of the economy—the Old World—labor and capital were plentiful relative to land and natural resources; in the western sector—the New World—labor and capital were scarce, relative to land and natural resources. Given freedom to move and the means of transport, units of the plentiful

factors would migrate from east to west. As long as the marginal social net product of labor in the New World was greater than in the Old World, east-west migration of workers would promote the economic efficiency of the Atlantic economy.[17]

Migration and the hypothesis of the mobility transition

The system approach may be made along another line of inquiry, one which relates the concept of the world demographic transition, so well-known in demography, to human mobility. This relationship has been developed in an outstanding study by Walter Zelinsky.[18]

Demographic transition theory asserts that, at certain thresholds of socioeconomic development, countries "will pass from a premodern near-equilibrium, in which high levels of mortality tend to cancel out high levels of fertility, to a modern near-equilibrium, in which low fertility almost matches low mortality, but with the decline in births lagging far enough behind during the decline in deaths to ensure a substantial growth in numbers during the transition phase."[19] Using Everett Lee's eighteen hypotheses of mobility,[20] Zelinsky summarizes them as generally being "explicitly migrational cases of the principle of least effort," and then formulates "the hypothesis of the mobility transition."

To this proposal, he adds a number of related statements which further elucidates his hypothesis:

(1) A transition from relatively sessile condition of severely limited physical and social mobility toward much higher rates of such movement always occurs as a community experiences the process of modernization.

(2) For any specific community the course of the mobility transition closely parallels that of the demographic transition and that of other transitional sequences not yet adequately described. A high degree of interaction may exist among all the processes in question.

(3) There are major, orderly changes in the form as well as in the intensity of spatial mobility at various stages of the transition—changes in

function, frequency, duration, periodicity, distance, routing, categories of migrants, and classes of origin and destination.

(4) There are concurrent changes in both form and intensity of social mobility and in the movement of information, and under certain conditions the potential migrant may exercise the option of changing his locus in social space or of exploiting a superior flow of information rather than in engaging in a territorial shift.

(5) At a fairly high level of generalization, which dampens out minor spatial and temporal irregularities, we can recognize in mobility conditions coherent patterns that propagate themselves onward through time as successive periods and outward through space as concentric zones emanating from successful growth points.

(6) The processes in question tend to accelerate in spatial and temporal pace with time, apparently because of the steady accumulation and intensification of causative factors within any given community and because of information and effects transferred from more advanced to less advanced regions.

(7) Thus, the basic spatiotemporal scenario of change may be preserved, yet be noticeably modified when a region initiates its mobility transition at a late date, so that absolute dating is a significant consideration.

(8) Such evidence as we have indicates an irreversible progression of stages.[21]

The transitional sequences which Zelinsky has specified are accompanied, he notes, by a number of other parallel transitions. Zelinsky then proposes a five-stage mobility transition sequence characterized by the following stages: (1) the premodern transitional society; (2) the early transitional society; (3) the late transitional society; (4) the advanced society; and (5) a future superadvanced society. Each phase is portrayed as having its own distinctive patterns of "territorial mobility." The phases are depicted as having a fatalistic inevitability, with some pervasive developmental crisis inherent in the overall sequence; but relativity within the pattern is stipulated.

Migration and world industrialization

In the last three decades, the idea of global industrialization has become widespread. Stimulated by the notion of development, of modernization, and of the Third World theme, the conception of a world economic system has firmly established the international context as a major desideratum for a great variety of theoretical topics. Without pursuing here the useful distinction between "industrialization" and "convergence," a distinction which emphasizes a universal process having many variable national cultural embodiments as Daniel Bell has pointed out, the idea of a world economic system, industrial in nature, will be utilized here as another system-structure thematic strategy for immigration theory.[22]

In most structural approaches, the concern is with the relationships of the whole and the parts. System structuralism expresses the idea of determination, or at least of influence, by the whole or its parts: the properties of the whole are significant, causally or otherwise, for the properties of the parts.

Two models have been very popular in the postwar literature: the development model, as against what we may, following Rubinson, describe as the world-economy model.[23] The latter name is not especially fortunate because both models assume an international economy. The difference lies in the major value premise. The liberal development model, as Gunnar Myrdal has shown, assumed the desirability and the urgency of an international economic integration;[24] the other does not, certainly not in the familiar manner of traditional liberal statements.

The developmental model is in many ways an extrapolation from the historical conditions of 19th and early 20th century international economic growth. The themes of this model stipulated an open international economy, with a dynamic international market system, with flows of labor, capital, and technology across nation-state boundaries. This was the period of great mass migration. To be sure, as Myrdal points out, "the First World War demarcates an abrupt end to this great era of relatively free mobility."[25] Although several million people during the decade following the Second World War entered the main receiving countries, despite statutory and administrative barriers, and although the flow has continued, the anticipated *international* economic integration of the liberal development model has not occurred. Indeed, politically, we have seen the emergence of sizeable *national* economic integration everywhere, a circumstance which has multiplied the problems of the sending countries in which "surplus labor" has mounted.

In fact, the consequences for the industrially less advanced nations have been monumental. To quote Myrdal: "the problems of the tremendous, and growing, disparities between the industrially advanced nations and the underdeveloped areas" are "the main and dominant problem of international integration."[26] In the meantime, the drive for development among the less industrially advanced countries involves "a tendency to skip the stage of capital accumulation," with the result that the "underdeveloped countries," unlike "the now advanced countries in the time of their early industrialization," do not have "an international capital market providing them with a cheap and plentiful capital inflow."

Wallerstein presents evidence for the argument that the success of the liberal developmental model derived from the fact that the industrial economy has been and is, in fact, a capitalist world-system, with an interdependence pattern of "core," "semiperipheral" and "peripheral" areas of the globe, each making its own unique and essential contribution to the operations of the system, with differential political, social, and economic effects for each.[27]

The prospect seems to be that the movements of labor and capital will continue within this structure of the world-system, with proponents of the developmental model urging greater and greater movements of capital and credits as well as technology into the semiperipheral and peripheral areas, but not of people. If so, the pressures for social restructuring within the member states, particularly among the semiperipheral and peripheral states, will intensify, with heightening pressures for continuing entry into the historically receiving "core" countries.

Recently, in a very significant article, Richard Rubinson has presented an analysis which lends little strength to the expectations of the liberal developmental model. Noting that many studies show "that increasing economic growth does not necessarily lead to the expansion of structural differentiation and economic diversification which are assumed to be mechanisms leading to greater equality" within the less developed countries, he formulates three conclusions which have grave implications for traditionally sending countries: "the greater the strength of the state, the more *equal* the income distribution; the greater the degree of direct foreign control over production, the more *unequal* the distribution of income; and the greater the reliance of a state's production on external resources, the more *unequal* the distribution of income."[28]

The social structure of the international economy is as Myrdal observed in the middle of the 'fifties, "an international class society" in which cohesion among countries can develop along class structure lines, at least in the noncommunist world, with the dominant policies in each case reflecting the pursuit of national economic integration. Myrdal did project, somewhat weakly, a concept of a "welfare world" as a possible alternative to the historic Marxian projection. Whatever the ultimate outcome of that hope may be, the theory of mass migration in the foreseeable future will surely have to come to terms in some ways with the implications and consequences of the world-system model sketched here.

APPROACHES THROUGH FORCES, FIELDS, AND FLOWS

On some implications of "movement"

The distinctive theme in immigration literature is that of "movement"—mobility of people over space and time. Different disciplines emphasize different perspectives. Certain matters unify these different emphases. The movements of people are seen within a "system" of structural elements and relationships. Such relationships are characterized as "mobility streams" attributable to "forces" acting within a "field" whose inherent trend toward equilibrium is disrupted. This interpretation of human movement has been the most common form of analysis of migration: aggregates in motion described in the purely determinative language of vectors and volumes, that is, the kinetic model. A supplementary version has been the approach which, with more empirical specification, has delineated the forces as "pushes" and "pulls" acting upon mobile aggregates of human beings. However, there emerged during the postwar period another modality of interpretation, a somewhat subjectively oriented model, which has concerned itself with some limited motivational aspects of human aggregates in motion.

Basically premised in a Smithian economic man orientation, these interpretative approaches to immigration have found the dynamics of migration in certain motivational properties of (a) the sending or receiving countries, or (b) the composition of the mobile aggregates, or (c) migration as a type of social action. These different modes of interpretation have generated three different thematic options for the understanding and explanation of migration: (1) the mechanistic model of forces, of "pushes and pulls"; (2) the "stocks and flows" model of the volume and vectors of mobile aggregates; and (3) varieties of action theory which view migration as a particular form of social action.

Fields: approach through mechanistic metaphor

The Newtonian conception of forces, according to which every particle tends to approach every other particle in the universe, was formally expressed in the law of gravitation, which held that every body or portion of matter attracts or is attracted directly as to the quantity of matter, and inversely as the square of its distance from the attracting body. This conception of action at a distance was transliterated from Newtonian physics to the social sciences, which developed a vision of the social universe on which human beings as objects are impacted by forces in a field acting upon them at a distance. The gravitational model became a social physics.

Even the famous Ravenstein "laws" of migration echo the Newtonian laws of motion. Thus, movement was seen as occurring inversely to the distance from the great centers of population, and directly to the size of the "giant centers of commerce and industry." Ravenstein, in a manner suggestive of the third law of motion, stipulated "currents" and "compensatory counter-currents" of population.

Generally familiar to readers of immigration literature in its popular form of "pushes" and "pulls" on potential migrants, the older mechanical model was given a sophisticated form by astronomer John Q. Stewart, among others.[29] Holding that the Newtonian equations have relevance "to the average interrelations of people," Stewart made them applicable by substituting N, the number of people involved, whenever the quantity *mass* appears in the original equations. He then derived measures of "demographic flow," "demographic energy," "demographic potential."

Developments since Stewart's work have been along the lines of "dimensional analysis" of spatial interaction, according to which relationships are shaped by the basic units of measurement.[30] Cases in point are the "interactional" and the "negative exponential distance decay" models.

Fields: approach through stocks and flows

The Newtonian scheme represented a relational point of view, or field theory of causation.[31] Gravitation is not contained in some essence but occurs in terms of the relationship between the falling body and the earth. In later work, equilibrium came to be understood in terms of opposed processes moving at an equal rate, constituting thus a unity of the whole which was seen as a system of balanced processes, and which was characterized by mutual penetration of opposites. Action and reaction are so nearly simultaneous they cannot be described separately. This condition is sometimes conceived of as a pattern of interdependent effects, a conception so essential to the characterization of systems or fields. It is no great analogical leap to think of origin and destination as constituting such a field.

It is just such considerations which have prompted attempts to theorize about human movements in terms of "stocks and flows" of people.[32] Developed for data on internal migration, this approach has been shown by O'Rouke to be useful in the study of the Irish migration, and thus for immigration data generally.[33]

Fields: approach through action theory

The origin and destination countries constitute a migration field in the Newtonian sense, a field of attraction over distance, creating action at a distance. Therefore, it is not unexpected that distance appears as a major dimension on some approaches to migration theory. Except for the early Ravenstein formulation, however, distance does not appear alone but in a mix of variables, including such items as labor supply, wages, information, and migrants' contacts with the destination country.

Students of economic theory have long been attracted to labor mobility. Thus, the classical competitive model of factor mobility stipulated that migration from area i to area j will occur so long as the average wage in j is greater than in i, with volume of responding migration increasing provided that (a) migrants desire to maximize income; (b) information about employment opportunities is perfect; (c) workers are equal and homogeneous in skills and taste; and (d) there are no barriers to mobility.

Focussing as it does on the individual's maximizing the money gains of movement, the money-income model has produced a number of generalizations which have been explored in the mobility literature: the inverse relationships between distance and migration (because of the costs of transportation), the positive relationship between migration and measures of industrial similarity (that is, income is maximized by movement to areas where the worker can work at his old job), the role of information in the distribution of migration, the "multiplicative" relationship between information and other independent variables, and so on.[34]

Distance as a major dimension of mobility was tackled by Stouffer in another way. The migrant stream from region i to region j was assumed to be inversely related to the number of opportunities between i and j. Social distance, as thus defined, is superior to physical distance in explaining geographic mobility.[35]

The mechanistic metaphor which has dominated the migration theories reviewed thus far in this section has created a paramount interest in the specifications of the field of migrant action. Some attention has been paid to the migrant as an economic actor in the migration field; as such, however, he has been endowed with properties which make it possible for him to be fitted into the mechanistic interpretive mode of action, properties which largely conform to the classical economic concept of the human being, such as rationality, desire to maximize gain (benefits over disbenefits), and so on. One such property, stipulated in more recent labor mobility theories, is that of "information-processing," a property which reflects the influence in recent years of the cybernetic metaphor.[36]

There is no dearth of such formulations of mobility. Thus, in a series of outstanding presentations, Hagerstrand has formulated a model of spatial interactions in terms of what he calls the "mean information field."[37] This approach is anchored in the highly popular contemporary emphasis on the decision-making process. It also underlines the strategic role of information about costs, expected income, competitive labor supply, and so on.[38]

In a brief but valuable paper, Berry and Schwind have summarized the major elements and problems of the resort to information and entropy in migrant flows. Migration is viewed as "an equilibrating mechanism, redistributing population (labor, human capital) in response to inequalities in the distribution of social and economic opportunities."[39]

There are two sources of deviation from the model: lack of parity and aggregate flow differential. These determine that distance is the principal source of the regularity in the gravity model. But they find that migrant origins show greater entropy than predicted by the gravity model; they are led to "presume that there is some level of excitation present that produces migrants, with only weak size and distance effects operating. The picture is thus one of a broadly-operating, general level of propensities to migrate, but with substantial concentration in the destinations of the migrant flows." Because there are many systematic elements operating, and since they are based upon residuals from the gravity model, they represent "systematic regularities over and above the ordering effects of size and distance. Clearly, one is dealing with a situation of organized complexity in which many are interacting simultaneously in subtle ways."[40]

BEHAVIORAL APPROACHES TO IMMIGRATION THEORY

Shift to behavioral analysis

The review of migration theory, operating in terms of the mechanistic metaphor, started with theoretical formulations which treat the migrant as an object in a field of forces having impact values as the field is described, with increasing emphasis on the behavioral properties of the migrant as an actor. The shift in emphasis enables us to turn to theories in which the migrant appears not as an object but as a person.

In this section, I shall start with some traditional theoretical formulations which still evoke the older imagery of field determination of action, and shall then turn to those theoretical strategies which assume behavioral properties of action. Some of those theories are concerned with the properties and dimensions of migrant behavior with increasing explicitness. These theoretical perspectives can be sorted into those concerned with the semiotic dimensions of immigrant behavior and those concerned with the structural dimensions. These formulations accent the structural properties of the social field. The review will, however, note other formulations which are not so completely structural, having regard in their premises for more dramatistic interactional properties of action. In a sense, the transition which I have been denoting may be described as a shift from action theory to behavioral theory.

Some transitional thematic strategies

Some theoretical perspectives on immigrant behavior in the new society retain the older concern with forces and fields. Two such perspectives will be selected here for review; a third, which sketches out the possibilities of complete and exclusive commitment to explicit behavioral strategies of interpretation, will be considered.

Recently, in an article which focuses entirely on a type of immigrant situation, refugee movements, E. F. Kunz has displayed an awareness of the significance of the shift in interpretation from the "kinetic" to the "motivational" mode. Although he is interested entirely in a kinetic presentation, his taxonomic and suggestive skills produce a valuable mode of theorizing. Distinguishing between "anticipatory" and "acute" refugee movements, he notes that the former conform largely to the push-pull pattern of free migration analysis, with "pull" being less important than "push": he talks about a "push-permit" model. In acute refugee movements, the "push" factors are overwhelming. "Refugee kinetics" display a variety of possible adjustment patterns in the situations of temporary refuge: (1) "push-press-plunge"; (2) "push-pressure-stay"; (3) "push-pressure-return." Refugees move in time-clusters of departure which Kunz calls "vintages"; these also have different times of arrival which he calls "waves." Vintages also differ in the circumstances of their departure: he distinguishes these as "displacement by flight," "displacement by force," and "displacement by absence." Throughout, Kunz underlines the variable perceptual world of the refugees.[41]

The refugee case is not only a reminder that free migration, to which the bulk of our immigration theory refers, is only one of a number of types of migration situations, but it also serves to underscore the semiotic dimensions of migrating behavior. Human behavior is action with meaning.[42]

After reviewing Ravenstein's famous "laws" of migration (which actually are empirical generalizations rather than laws), Lee formulates a series of eighteen hypotheses sorted into three groups, concerned with (a) the volume of migration, (b) "stream and counter-stream" of migration, and (c) characteristics of migrants.[43] The last group of hypotheses suggests, in reference to selectivity, intervening obstacles, life cycle stages, and resemblance to populations of origin and destination, the presence of semiotic factors.

In an article which is not directly devoted to immigration, Johann Galtung poses a problem which all behavioral strategies of immigration theory are ultimately concerned with—the problem of integration. With its double emphasis on values and structures, it sets the stage for our consideration of semiotic and structural strategies of interpretation. Although Galtung is primarily concerned in his structural theory of integration with territorial, organizational, and societal units of sociality, his thematic strategy of integration theory—so important in so much immigration writing—not only highlights the multidimensionality of migratory behavior, but also the inevitable importance of the perceptual world of "original" and "new" actors in the development of integration in the society of destination. His observation about the necessity of avoiding the confusion between definition of integration and the conditions producing and the consequences resulting from integration, needs to be remembered in any discussion of the behavioral problems of migrants in a new culture.[44]

Semiotic strategies of behavioral interpretation

Behavioral approaches to immigration theory accent, first of all, the interior world of the migrant—the perceptual, motivational, valuational, and attitudinal aspects of the migrant as a person.[45] The centrality of this theme is borne out in an important set of contributions by a group of European observers interested in the problems of "uprooting."

Among her interviewees, Maria Pfister-Ammende distinguishes between "firmly rooted" individuals who were able to retain unimpaired ties with the society of origins, and the "uprooted" who did not possess this ability. Among the latter she found the following types: (1) "isolated individuals from groups in need of leadership," (2) "deeply traumatized individuals, not dependent on groups," (3) "those who identified themselves with their social class or profession," (4) "drifting individuals and escapists," (5) *problematiker*. She also noted different aspects of rootlessness: (1) individuals, dependent on their immediate environment, who were uprooted through outside forces; (2) loss of identification with, and clinging to, the previous social levels; (3) being rootless due to inherited traits or faulty childhood development.[46]

Considerations of rootlessness, which may embrace the usual continuum of psychological strategies of interpretation extending from "normality" to psychosis, point to the importance not only of the epidemiological aspects of migratory behavior, but also to the role of social psychological phases of adjustment processes generated by the movement from country of origin to country of destination. Such considerations also make it clear that the investigations of migrant behavior problems by professionals in psychology and psychiatry are so very important to the development of immigration theory.

J. J. Mangalam and H. K. Schwarzweller conceive of migration as a social process, having some aspects located within the culture system, some within the social system, and some within the personality system of the migrants. Their formal definition states: "Migration is a relatively permanent moving away of a collectivity, called migrants, from one geographical location to another, preceded by decision-making on the part of the migrants on the basis of a hierarchically ordered set of values or valued ends and resulting in changes in the inter-related system of the migrants."[47] Each component of their definition enters into their proposed "middle-range" approach to analysis. What the authors formulate is a set of "theoretical guidelines," which actually function as a set of "sensitizing" concepts, in Herbert Blumer's language.[48]

This same observation may be made of an important contribution by Stephen Golant. His approach focuses on the fact that spatial movements are goal-oriented and involve individuals contemplating and making decisions to move,[49] decisions which tend to be what H. A. Simon has called "subjectively rational"[50] and not necessarily the most correct in terms of the information potential afforded by the sociocultural system. Utilizing current systems theory,[51] Golant utilizes in an ingenious and attractive manner the concepts of "meaning," "variable stress," "resultant of flow variable stress," "flow stress values," and "flow stress thresholds" in a model of migrant individual decision making. It is a sophisticated improvement over earlier presentations: "behavior" replaces traditional "action" theory, even though his constructs retain the older action frame of reference.

Bibliographies of immigrant behavior adjustment, such as that by Meadows, Lagory, Leue, and Meadows,[52] make it clear that theorists of migrant behavior have been attracted to a wide range of aspects of migrant behavior phenomena.[52] The constructs utilized reflect the basic language orientation of the observer's professional discipline. Australian psychologist Alan Richardson deals with what he calls the "satisfaction-dissatisfaction-acculturation" sequence of migrant adjustment. His identifying constructs include patterns of "elation," "depression," "identification," and "acculturation." The latter pattern he utilizes in formulating a "structural model for the general process of assimilation."[53] His formulation of the psychological phases of migrant adjustment serves to reinforce the strategic character of the semiotics of migrant adjustment, whether the latter is viewed in the more general framework of cultural or of psychocultural interpretation.

Structural strategies of behavioral interpretation

Structuralist theories are highly variable, mainly because they have been developed in response to the interests and data, and have been shaped by the special analytical language of particular disciplines. Even finding a core of common agreement on definition is difficult. In general—and very general at that—structural theory of any variety is concerned with the discovery of stable and determinative connections among social variables. Such suggested connections are many: rules and meanings, roles and statuses, needs and functions, culture and personality; and to these one might add the long list of demographic and other properties: age, sex, class, ethnicity, religion, education, and so on. Two kinds of structural theory can be distinguished in terms of these connections: empirical varieties which regard social structure as a system of social relations among differentiated parts normatively and functionally interrelated, and formal varieties which identify social structure as a system of logical relations among general principles; this latter is usually

the distinguishing interest of writers generally grouped under the heading of "structuralism."

Clearly, immigration theory at its best is largely of the empirical sort. However, the empirical bent of structural theory in immigration research has had a valuable practical significance, for it has focused on the familiar fact that migrants to a new society are entering into a differentiated status and role system, with hierarchical patterns of authority and power that find expression in many normative and functional ways. The structuralist theme accents the presence of differentials—in skills, capacities, resources, authority, power, statuses, roles. The net societal outcome is a group and individual differential in access to valued means and conditions of social existence. Each society has its own structure, and the migrant moves from one differentiated system to another, with differentials in all the respects that make a difference. This structural fact has an obvious bearing on the viability, the directions, the problems of migrant adaptation to the new society. By means of a brief sampling of relevant literature, the final section of this review of immigration theory will sketch some of the thematic strategies which characterize structural approaches to immigrant behavioral interpretation.

By and large, structural approaches all call attention to multiple factors which enter into immigrant adaptation. A case in point is Goldlust and Richmond's proposed "multivariate model" which sounds this distinctive theme.[54]

One popular thematic strategy concerns itself with the properties of the immigrant and of the system, as does, for example, a study by Lyle Shannon who reports a bidirectional thrust in his findings.[55] Another thematic strategy is interested in the role of donor and host system properties in the migrant adaptation process.[56] A third thematic strategy attends to the structural variables which are contained in the labor market. Thus, in an important article, Edna Bonacich has developed a theory of ethnic antagonisms which result from price differentials of labor stemming from differences in resources and motives, themselves correlates of ethnicity. The ethnic antagonisms which this situation entails take two forms, exclusive movement and caste systems. Societies which are high on ethnic antagonisms "all have a powerful white, or more generally, higher paid working class.''[57]

Deriving from a concept of "middleman minorities" which Blalock developed,[58] two recent studies by Bonacich and Zenner have examined the roles of such minorities, seen as status and role categories, in a variety of cultural settings, with a major stress on the reactive patterns of host hostility and conflict and the adjustment impact these have had on these migratory minorities.[59] Zenner's presentation, which includes an examination of Bonacich's "sojourner" dimension, attends to other aspects of host-middleman interaction. Of special interest is Zenner's establishment of relationships between group visibility and solidarity and host hostility.[60]

Problems of superordination and subordination, an inherent aspect of structural analysis, loom large in structural theories of immigrant behavioral adjustment. Typical of these studies is Stanley Leiberson's.[61] He develops a major thesis that, in societies where a migrant population imposes its social order, "the ethnic relations cycle" differs sharply from the cycle in societies where the indigenous population is superordinate.

Structural studies are concerned with the many status and role entailments in a social system, covering an extensive spectrum of analytic possibilities: status differentiations, group cohesion, status legitimacy, group power, group access to resources, and international adjustments between and among newcomer and host ethnics. The structuralization of these possibilities has been described by the present writer in a study which summarizes a considerable historical and sociological literature.[61] One aspect of this structuralization refers to the varieties of ethnic status systems which have been evolved in different social systems. Another aspect of this structuralization involves the interactions of self and system. A third aspect deals with the variable status and role involvements of newcomers and hosts, as in the following table:

	Host Ethnic Status	
Role System	Dominant	Ascendant

Relatively open	Situation A	Situation B
Relatively closed	Situation C	Situation D

This preliminary cross-cultural taxonomy suggests a possible natural history of the sociopolitical existence of ethnic newcomers, somewhat as follows:

Situation A
  Host ethnic status dominant;
  ethnic newcomers accepted;
  newcomer insiderness (re: power access)
    declining.
Situation B
  Host ethnic status dominant;
  ethnic newcomers increasingly restricted;
  newcomer outsiderness increasing.
Situation C
  Host ethnic status exclusiveness;
  ethnic newcomers increasingly subordinated;
  newcomer outsiderness intensifying.
Situation D
  Host ethnic status paramount;
  ethnic newcomers' exclusion virtually complete;
  host insiderness (re: power access) high.

It should be pointed out that this tableau of status situations is derived largely from accounts of post-colonial societies.

A fourth and final structuralization may be seen in the manner in which "the role system" of a society and "the role price" which it exacts appear in a variable pattern of options.[62]

CONCLUSION

Theoretical formulations reviewed in this paper dwell on the relevance, indeed, on the utter necessity of the semiotic dimension. However, it would be a distortion of reality to assert that there is here, or anywhere else for that matter, a general theory of migrant behavior. On the contrary, what we find in the semiotic presentations is an array of constructs, definitions, emphases, stipulated relationships among variables, and an insistence on a multivariate approach, with a rich variety of disciplinary vocabularies of description and explanation. Empirical generalizations abound, as do hypotheses and propositions; formal theory is scarce, though formal schemata as typologies and paradigms are readily available. One cannot repress the thought that, for the most part, approaches are utilized as part of the explanatory factors in a general recognizance of migrant adjustment behavior. At the level of formal theory and prediction, cultural and psychocultural formulations are probably most useful and productive as adjunctive and reportorial constructions. Structural theories are, or so it is projected in this paper at least, in all likelihood going to prove to be far more prolific and determinative in the development of an acceptable body of migrant behavior theory.

NOTES

1. R. G. Dumont and W. J. Walker, "Aspects of Concept Formation, Explication, and Theory Construction in Sociology," *American Sociological Review* vol. 32 (December 1967), pp.985-95.
2. D. Willer and M. Webster, "Theoretical Concepts and Observables," *American Sociological Review* vol. 35 (August 1970), pp.748-57.
3. R. K. Merton, *Social Theory and Social Structure* (New York: Free Press, 1968).
4. T. Parsons and E. Shils, *Toward a General Theory of Action* (New York: Basic Books, 1957).
5. W. S. Woytinsky and E. S. Woytinsky, "World Immigration Patterns," in their *World Population and Production* (New York: Twentieth Century Fund, 1953).
6. Henry Pratt Fairchild, *Immigration* (New York: Macmillan, 1925), chapter 1.
7. M. R. Davie, *World Immigration* (New York: Macmillan, 1949); J. Issac, *Economics of Migration* (London: Kegan Paul, Trench, Trubner, 1947); K. Davis, "The Theory of Change and Response in Modern Demographic History," *Population Index*, vol. 29 (October 1973); and D. R. Taft and P. Robbins, *International Migrations* (New York: Ronald Press, 1955).
8. William Petersen, "A General Typology of Migration," *American Sociological Review* 23 (June 1958): 256-66.
9. Idem., *Population* (New York: Macmillan, 1969).
10. Edgar Kant, "Classification and Problems of Migrations," in P. L. Wagner and M. M. Mikesell, eds., *Readings in Cultural Geography* (University of Chicago Press, 1962), pp.342-54.
11. J. Matras, *Population and Societies* (New York: Prentice-Hall, 1976).
12. See ibid., p.364.
13. R. B. Textor, *A Cross Cultural Survey* (New Haven: RRAF Press, 1967).
14. C. Goldscheider, *Population, Modernization and Social Structure* (Boston: Little, Brown, 1971).
15. William Petersen, "Migration: Social Effects," *International Encyclopedia of Social Science*, vol. 10 (1968), p.286.
16. Brinley Thomas' works: "International Migration," in Hauser and Duncan, eds., *The Study of Population* (Chicago: University of Chicago Press, 1959); and *Migration and Economic Growth* (Cambridge: Cambridge University Press, 1973); Walter Zelinsky, "The Hypothesis of the Mobility Transition," *Geographic Review* vol. 61 (April 1971), pp.221-49; Gunnar Myrdal, *The International Economy* (New York: Harper, 1956); Immanuel Wallerstein, "The Rise and the Future Demise of the World Capitalist System: Concepts for Comparative Analysis," *Comparative Studies in Society and History* vol. 16 (1974), pp.387-415; and Richard Robinson, "The World Economy and the Distribution of Income among Status: A Cross-National Study," *American Sociological Review* vol. 41 (August 1976), pp.638-76.
17. Thomas, "International Migration," p.531.
18. Zelinsky, op. cit.
19. Ibid., p.227.
20. Everett W. Lee, "A Theory of Migration," *Demography* 3 (1966): 47-57.
21. Zelinsky, op. cit., p.227.
22. Daniel Bell, *The Coming of Post-Industrial Society*, 2nd ed. (New York: Basic Books, 1976).
23. Rubinson, op. cit.
24. Myrdal, op. cit.
25. Ibid., p.90.
26. Ibid., p.312.
27. Wallerstein, op. cit.
28. Rubinson, op. cit., p.647.
29. John Q. Stewart, "Demographic Gravitation: Evidence and Applications," *Sociometry* 11 (1948): 31-58.
30. R. M. Haynes, "Dimensional Analysis: Some Applications in Human Geography," *Geographic Analysis* (January 1975): 51-68.
31. R. L. Schanck, *The Permanent Revolution in Science* (New York: Philosophical Library, 1954).
32. T. P. Lianos, "A Stocks and Flows Approach to Migration," *Journal of American Agricultural Economics* 52 (August 1970): 442-43.
33. D. O'Rourke, "A Stocks and Flows Approach to a Theory of Human Migration in the Examples from Past Irish Migration," *Demography* 9 (May 1972): 243-44.
34. P. Nelson, "Migration, Real Income and Information," *Journal of Regional Science* 1 (Spring 1959): 43-74.
35. S. A. Stouffer, "Intervening Opportunities: A Theory of Relating Mobility and Distance," *American Sociological Review* 5 (1940): 845-67. See also O. R. Galle and K. E. Taeuber, "Metropolitan Migration and Intervening Opportunities," *American Sociological Review* 31 (1966): 5-13, and Wadycki, "Stouffer's Model of Migration: A Comparison of Interstate and Metropolitan Flows," *Demography* 12 (February 1975): 121-28.
36. S. Gale, "Some Formal Properties of Nagerstrand's Model of Spatial Interaction," *Journal of Regional Science* 12 (1972): 199-218; "Specifying an Econometric Model of Irish Migration," *Journal of Regional Science* 14 (1974): 107-10; and V. J. L. Berry and P. J. Schwind, "Information and Entropy in Migrant Flows," *Geographic Analysis* 1

(January 1969), pp.5-15.

37. Gale, ibid.

38. Walsh, op. cit.

39. Berry and Schwind, op. cit., p.13.

40. Ibid.

41. E. F. Kunz, "The Refugee in Flight: Kinetic Models and Forms of Displacement," *International Migration Review* 7 (Summer 1963): 125-45.

42. Lee, op. cit.

43. Ibid.

44. Johann Galtung, "A Structural Theory of Integration," *Journal of Peace Research* (1968): 375-85.

45. C. Senior, "Migration as a Process and Migrant as a Person," *Population Review* 6 (1962): 30-41.

46. C. Zwingman and Maria Pfister-Ammende, (eds.) *Uprooting and After . . .* (New York: Springer-Verlay, 1973), pp.7-18.

47. J. J. Mangalam and H. K. Schwarzweller, "Some Theoretical Guidelines: Toward a Sociology of Migration," *International Migration Review* 4 (Spring 1970): p.8.

48. Ibid., pp.5-19.

49. S. M. Golant, "Adjustment Process in a System: A Behavior Model of Human Movement," *Geographic Analysis* 3 (July 1971): 203-19.

50. H. A. Simon, *Administrative Behavior* (New York: Macmillan, 1947).

51. J. C. Miller, "Toward a General Theory for the Behavioral Sciences," *American Psychologist* 10 (1955): 513-31.

52. Paul Meadows et. al., *Recent Immigration to the United Staes: The Literature of the Social Sciences* (Washington, D.C.: Smithsonian Institution Research Institute on Immigration and Ethnic Studies, 1976).

53. Richardson, op. cit.

54. J. Goldlust and A. H. Richmond, "A Multivariate Model of Immigrant Population," *International Migration Review* 8 (Summer 1974): 193-224.

55. Lyle W. Shannon, "The Economic Absorption and Cultural Integration of Immigrant Workers," in E. B. Brody, ed., *Behavior in New Environments: Adaptation of Migrant Population* (Beverly Hills: Sage, 1970), p. 183.

56. Brody, op. cit., pp.16-17.

57. Edna Bonacich, "A Theory of Middleman Minorities," *American Sociological Review* 37 (October 1972): 547-59.

58. H. M. Blalock, Jr., *Toward a Theory of Minority Group Relations* (New York: Wiley, 1967), pp.79-84.

59. Edna Bonacich, "A Theory of Middleman Minorities," *American Sociological Review* 38 (October 1973): pp.583-95 and Walter P. Zenner, "Middleman Minority Theories," unpublished manuscript, 1976.

60. Zenner, ibid.

61. S. Lieberson, "A Societal Theory of Race and Ethnic Relations," *American Sociological Review* 26 (December 1961): 902-10.

62. Paul Meadows, "Insiders and Outsiders: Towards a Theory of Overseas Cultural Groups," *Social Forces* 46 (September 1967): 61-71.

MIDDLEMAN MINORITY THEORIES:
A CRITICAL REVIEW[1]

Walter P. Zenner

INTRODUCTION

In recent years, social scientists have given much attention to interethnic relations and the problem of racism as it refers to dominant Europeans, and conquered or otherwise subordinated nonwhite proletarians and peasants. Much less stress has been given to that subtler racism which affects stigmatized groups of middle economic position. Yet these ethnic groups have been the objects of some of the most violent attempts at "final solutions" of conflicts in this century. The question of the relationship of economic class to ethnicity is crucial to an understanding of the precarious social position of these "middle-level" groups.

Here, a review of various theories and other explanations of this phenomenon will be made. It will draw on social and economic history, sociology, and anthropology. Since many of the theories started as explanations of anti-Semitism, attention must be given to Jewish history, although these theories have a much broader relevance than the sociology and ethnology of Jewish groups. For a long time, analogies have been drawn between the socioeconomic roles of the Jews in Europe and other groups, notably East Asians in East and South Africa, Lebanese in West Africa, and the Chinese in Southeast Asia.[2] This analogy forms the basis of the "middleman minorities theory" which generally seeks to explain the economic specialization of certain minorities who occupy strategic niches in the commercial and industrial life of certain countries, and the hostility these minorities evoke. Explanations are sought for anti-Semitism and similar prejudices in cultural and structural features of the minorities' situation, with particular emphasis on the economic roles which the minorities occupy. (While "middleman minority theories" are discussed here without special reference to the problems of American immigration, the various theories reviewed are relevant to the American context. The theories do pertain to any discussion of economic competition between new immigrants and veteran residents in general, and in the context of a capitalist job market or business situation in particular. They also have something to say about the problems of middle class professionals.)

Proof that such prejudices are caused by the economic position of the victims would affirm middleman minority theories, just as affirmation of similar consequences among other middleman groups throughout the world would strengthen the plausibility of this kind of explanation of anti-Semitism. Systematic data retrieval on trading and similar groups is in its infancy. Thus, while the different middleman minority theories suffer from weaknesses and inadequacies which will be pointed out in this review, they are still useful as propositions for use in further study.

In defining these ethnic minorities, the term "middleman" is derived from the roles of trader and broker in commerce. Voltaire, in 1761, referred to the Jews as "these wandering brokers," while Kant conceived of the Jews as "a whole nation of merchants"; both epitomized the "middleman" or "marginal trading" minority-type.[3] But even the Polish and German Jews of the eighteenth century were not merely traders. In addition to trade and commerce, one finds that members of the "middleman minorities" include labor contractors, rent collectors, moneylenders, craftsmen, government officials, and even truck farmers.

This lack of clarity is no different from that of other areas of comparative research in which there should be applied hypotheses and theories which have been developed to various minorities, rather than try to develop a "synthetic" definition to cover all cases.[4]

There are, of course, several examples of "trading minorities" which are cited by the "middleman minority theorists,'' and which may be seen as ''proto-typical.'' Besides the Jews, these include Parsis in India, Armenians and Greeks in the Balkans and Asia Minor, overseas Chinese and Indians, the Syro-Lebanese in West Africa and Latin America, and Scots in subarctic Canada and southern Africa. All of these groups have had their successful traders, although some have not faced persecution. Two other groups are the Japanese Americans[5] and mixed-bloods (for example, mestizos in Middle America; mulattos in the West Indies). The main characteristics which these minorities share include involvement in a money economy and occupying a position between the dominant elite and the poor. The economic position alone does not suffice to explain host hostility against the minority. In this paper, most of the examples will be drawn from groups within which trade is a major occupation.

ECONOMIC POSITION: STATUS GAP AND COMPLEMENTARITY

The specialization of these groups as ''middlemen'' can be explained as an adaptation to particular economic conditions. Many have pointed to circumstances where a dominant elite, whether conquerers, colonists, or feudal lords, is disinclined to enter the commercial sphere, and the indigenous peasantry does not possess the skills necessary to undertake such activities.[7]

This condition has been labeled a ''status gap'' in which the other status holders do not challenge those who come to occupy these roles and which is a state of complementarity rather than competition.[8]

The situations which bring about such a status gap are several. Blalock's label of ''peasant-feudal'' for this setting is simplistic and misleading,[9] but he has specified the kinds of situations which produce such complementarity. These include the needs by a conquering or colonist elite for intermediaries with the native population, the introduction of a new technology, and the incorporation of a territory into the world market economy. The same type of situation may arise if those who have previously fulfilled these tasks have either been expelled or have removed themselves.

Several ''strategies'' may be followed in filling the ''status gap.'' Outside skillholders may be ''imported'' or the skills may be ''adopted'' by training members of the society in the new skills.[10] ''Importation'' takes various forms, such as slaves and indentured labor, contract labor, and the encouragement of outside entrepreneurship, either individual or corporate. While individual enterprise is most commonly associated with the ''middleman minorities,'' all of these imported skillholders share a common characteristic, in that all segment the economy along ''insider-outsider'' lines, whether it is the ''split-labor'' market created by low-paid foreign workers,[11] or a monopoly on the sale of imported goods.

Importation of skillholders in the short run has advantages, such as far fewer prerequisites for training and demands for fewer accommodations. Since the imported skillholder is relatively isolated, the host society and its rulers appear free to decide to what degree they wish to accommodate to him.[12] While Hirsch concentrates his attention on groups employed by the ruling elite, his statements have wider application. Examples include the medieval and Renaissance Jewish merchants and moneylenders invited to immigrate to such communities as the cities on the Rhine in the eleventh century, or Mantua and Venice in the fifteenth and sixteenth centuries.

In ''adopting'' skills, societies often turn to those elements which are either *declassé* or otherwise degraded. Displaced from their warrior trade, the samurai are an example of this type, having helped Japan acquire modern skills in the nineteenth century. These groups have ''little to lose and much to gain.''

In the case of commercial middlemen, there are political implications to their group membership. If they are ''indigenous,'' it is presumed that their loyalties lie within the boundaries of the state and with the dominant ethnic group. They would reinvest their capital locally and add to local power. If they are foreign, it is assumed that ''their interests were linked primarily to those of the emerging poles of development, what in time would be called metropoles.''[13]

In dealing with the ''importing'' or ''adopting'' strategies, the filling of the gap is viewed from the ruler's outlook, but it can be seen as well from the perspective of "native" and "foreign" skillholders, where the situation may be one of competition rather than complementarity. In the creation of a money economy, such as that of medieval Europe, Jews may first fill intermediary roles, only to be displaced by a new native bourgeoisie.[14] Conversely, foreign and minority middlemen may displace native traders, as a national economy is encapsulated into the "world economy" in a dependent position. "Minority" traders with extensive foreign ties may have competitive advantages over the natives.[15]

STRANGERS AND TRADE

Questions of determination of stranger, pariah, or sojourner status or advantage, and others at a more basic level, cannot be answered without examining the relationships of economics to questions of group and self-identity.

Even in the beginnings of craft specialization, there is a connection between "strangeness" and dealing with outgroups.[16]

In the fairly simple horticultural societies of the African East Horn, it has been suggested that itinerant craftsmen have a low status because (a) they depend on trade and bargaining for their living rather than agriculture or herding; (b) varying demand for their products forces a higher degree of mobility on them than on others; (c) they "socialize" natural products (cotton into cloth; iron ore into iron objects);[17] (d) they are a symbolic reflection of landlessness in a landed society.[18] This is so, despite a lack of major linguistic or cultural differences in other aspects.

In the transformation of simple agrarian societies into complex urban-agrarian ones, trade is often associated with the appearance of foreign merchants; thus, the alien may symbolize the replacement of monetary exchange for reciprocal transactions.[19]

The outsider has advantages in monetary dealings precisely because he does not face the same kinds of demands for reciprocity which confront the members of the insider group. This reduces the stress of commerce which threatens the "folk" moral order and which, in turn, is threatened by the moral demands of traditional society. His "opportunism" and mobility aid him in keeping "objectivity." "The ethnic difference has the effect of reducing the conflict inherent in face-to-face commercial transactions."[20]

But, as Foster writes of Thailand: "Tension and conflict arising from commerce are not eliminated by traders belonging to a different ethnic group from the people surrounding them. The tension is simply shifted from the interpersonal level to another level of social structure on which there are mechanisms for dealing with it. Shifting the conflict to the level of interethnic relations is made possible by the police power of the state."[21]

The "stranger" is attractive in certain intimate roles (from moneylender to courtier) precisely because he is socially distant. He treats loans and transactions as purely commercial. He is not as likely to enter the competition for authority and prestige because as a stigmatized stranger he is excluded.[22]

CULTURAL ATTRIBUTES OF MIDDLEMEN

There is agreement that the success of certain groups in trade and other middleman roles is not simply a function of being strangers to their clients, but a product of their special aptitudes, residues of past experiences, and present ways of life. It is noteworthy that the groups most generally cited as "middleman minorities" have had their origins in the "old civilizations" of Asia and the Middle East, namely Indians, Chinese, Armenians, Syrians, Jews, and Greeks, even though some of these groups had been predominantly peasant prior to migration.[23] These special characteristics are viewed as independent variables.

The two opposing views of Sombart and Weber represent two poles in the consideration of the economic role of middleman minorities. Sombart sees the Jews as rational capitalists par excellence, while Weber sees Judaism as supporting a nonmodern "pariah capitalism."[24]

Most authors follow Weber's opinion that Jews and other minority middlemen were not the foremost "midwives" of modern capitalism, although they do so for different reasons.[25] However, even those who accept Weber's basic reasoning

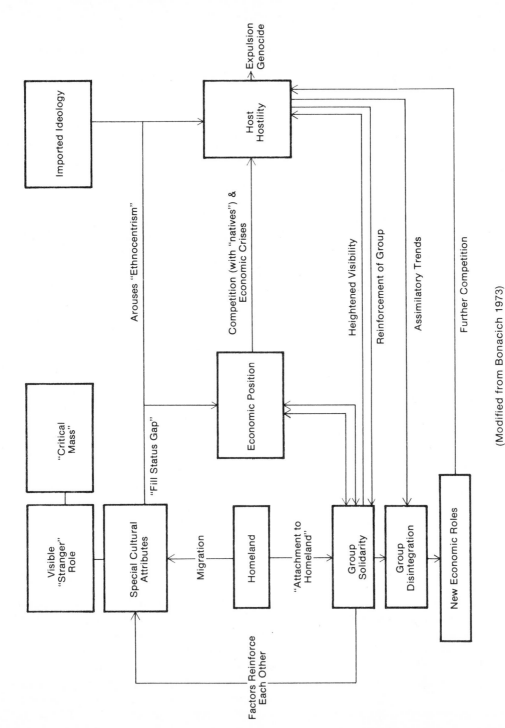

FIGURE 1
Inter-Relationships of Major Factors in
"Middleman Man" Theories

(Modified from Bonacich 1973)

may be close to some of Sombart's interpretations; for instance, Bonacich[26] accepts Weber on the limits of pariah capitalism, but attributes a rational future-time orientation to these minority members. Thus, the following listing of elements and patterns attributed to middleman minorities is not internally consistent.

Social scientists have claimed that middleman minorities have the following traits:

(a) rational "economizing" behavior, including price cutting and frugality;[27]

(b) future-time orientation[28] and high achievement motivation;[29]

(c) intellectual, rational orientation to religion and life, marked by restraint and self-control;[30]

(d) economic activity viewed as necessity, not as means to salvation;[31]

(e) "ritualistic" segregation of group, including ban on outgroup marriage and restrictions on eating with outsiders;[32]

(f) a double standard of morality towards ingroup and outgroup members (as opposed to scrupulous fairness to all), including over- and under-pricing;[33]

(g) high group morale and self-esteem, as well as sublimation of feelings of vengeance in the face of rejection by others;[34]

(h) tendency towards frequent migration (Sombart's "Saharaism");[35]

(i) strong attachment to former homeland;[36]

(j) perpetuation of "separatist complex," including continued teaching of a foreign language and/or religion.[37]

Various authors have stressed that the separate culture of the minority is reinforced by the minority situation, either because it has an economic payoff,[38] or because it is reinforced by host hostility.[39] Leon[40] very strongly maintains that the occupational ethos to which the group adapts may become a crucial part of its culture. In his Marxist view, the Jewish "people-class" became so adapted to being moneymen during the feudal period that, if a Jew became a feudal landlord or peasant, he would be forced to convert to Christianity. In modern times, when the niche to which the Jews had accommo-dated became obsolescent, they either tended to assimilate or were squeezed out.

STRANGERS, ENTREPRENEURSHIP AND THE STATE

Weber and Sombart were primarily concerned with a problem which is only touched on here—the role of various ethnic groups and religious groups in facilitating the " 'take-off' of a society into the developed world." Weber's view that the Jew could not provide the model for the society can be accepted by looking at the culture of the host society, rather than the minority.

Eisenstadt[41] argues that, if a group like the Puritans or the samurai is viewed as a secondary elite, it is more likely to be integrated into the society and will have much greater influence in transforming the society. On the other hand, if a large part of the capitalist class in society is composed of members of a despised "strange" minority, this may make trade and commercial enterprize a despised occupation and prevent the development of capitalism, as occurred in Poland.[42] This suggests again that it is the host society rather than the minority alone which determines the influence of the minority.

Related to this are the services which the middleman minority provides the ruling elite. Minority members are likely to serve the elite as taxpayers, farmers, personal retainers, and the like; in turn, the state provides minority members with protection, except when the service which the elite requires is that of scapegoat.[43]

The state may encourage the "separatism" of the minority. This was certainly true of the medieval and early modern Christian and Muslim states which treated religious minorities differently from members of the majority religion.[44] In West Africa, European colonial governments created split-labor from outside, and they controlled "stranger groups" through designated "tribal" leaders. Such policies often gave "stranger" groups a sense of extraterritoriality.[45]

One recent theory, known as the "sojourner hypothesis," strives to explain the economic success of these minorities, their persistence in modern industrial as well as agrarian societies, and the hostility towards them in terms of their own attributes and relationships to both emigrant community and host society.[46] According to Bonacich, the "stranger" quality of those groups which become "middleman" minorities is derived from their continued attachment to their homeland and their desire to return to it.

To Bonacich, middleman minorities start as immigrants who do not plan to settle permanently in the host country, thus contrasting strongly with both natives and permanent settlers. The economic effects of this strong attachment to the homeland are (1) thrift and a future-time orientation, since they need to plan their return, and (2) the selection of occupations which provide them with liquid resources and do not tie them to the place of sojourn. In fact, liquidity and the attachment to the homeland are the defining attributes of this minority type, rather than trade or any other particular occupation.

Since the sojourner remains attached to his homeland, he maintains a high degree of ethnic solidarity, which gives him economic advantages over natives and permanent settlers against whom he discriminates. For instance, the fellow ethnic is favored as an employee. The economic success and refusal to assimilate also arouse host hostility which, because of the high morale of the sojourning minority, further reinforces group solidarity.

Bonacich has extended the range of middleman minority theory from preindustrial to industrial societies, much as Sombart tried to do, but by using a Weberian framework. While she has framed reasonably clear, usable hypotheses, her thesis is weakened by the essential vagueness of her terms, several of which must be refined.

Still, while her definition of "middleman minorities" stretches out very far, and while her hypotheses do not necessarily apply to all such groups, they are operational and can form part of our armory of propositions in studying minorities, whether Gypsies or Jerbans. However, Bonacich's effort to find an objective definition and correlatives for "sojourning" do demonstrate the difficulties for finding cross-cultural and cross-national definitions of "alienness."

ETHNIC SOLIDARITY AND "OBJECTIVE" VISIBILITY

Edna Bonacich is not alone in seeing the social networks and ethnocentrism of the minority as a factor in its success. Still, it is the task of the social scientist to specify the level and form of social organization.[47]

Middlemen minorities do not simply favor all "coethnics" equally in the network of jobs. Generally, family, kin, and compatriots from the same locale are favored over those farther removed. The *Mans* who have been successful in the Chinese restaurants of London are all members of one Hong Kong single lineage village,[48] and various varieties of local and language and ritual groupings of Jews;[49] all served a similar purpose in providing the basis for patronage in obtaining job placement or business contacts.

While favoritism towards kinsmen and compatriots is viewed as a form of precapitalist particularism, it is evident at the upper reaches of high finance and multinational corporations.[50]

Of course, some ethnic groups have greater solidarity in maintaining monopolies over lines of trade or particular occupations than others.[51] In general, however, the informal organization and ethnic solidarity of a group, whether an elite or a middle-status group, helps it maintain morale and may aid its members' economic success.

Groups which exhibit extreme "sojourning" behavior, like the Ibadi Jerbans, will maintain such separation. Their families are completely segregated from the host environment.[52] The often celibate Chinese laundrymen,[53] and the London Chinese restaurant workers, left their families at home,[54] although in the latter case, the British immigration laws forced these "sojourners" to become immigrants and thus become subject to acculturation.

One would expect that such a "separatist complex would be manifested mainly by first-generation immigrants. Later descendants of immigrants would be more likely to show signs of assimilation and acculturation, unless there were institutional and situational bars.

Variations may occur, however; even among first-generation immigrants, one may find breaks with the "sojourning" pattern, such as individuals who intermarry. For instance, an immigrant or sojourning group of males is more likely to intermarry or carry on sexual contacts with local women than those importing brides. This would provide the stage for considerable offspring identifying with the local population. Whether or not this occurs depends on how distant the immigrants are from the homeland. In an age where the trip from Hong Kong to London is less than twenty-four hours, absolute distance is less relevant than during an earlier period.[55]

Ideological bars (for example, religious, caste, or racial prohibitions) to contact and assimilation should be examined. Some groups, like orthodox Jews or Hindus, may have more of these in the tradition than other groups. Learning the *lingua franca* of the country is necessitated by the nature of commercial activity, although many in the immigrant group can escape this. Related to the very phenomenon of perceived alienness, avoidance of involvement in local politics may or may not be related to occupation.

In general, Bonacich and her predecessors exaggerate the middleman group's exclusivity and overstress its unity. They often fail to note the importance of assimilation, self-hatred, and similar phenomena. While "middleman minorities" appear to be more unified and less downtrodden than other minorities, they also are affected by low esteem. In addition, changes in the general political environment may require a strategy of imitation rather than separation.

Bonacich implies that the ethnic solidarity and failure to assimilate is a factor in arousing host hostility, while others[56] see visibility as preventing assimilation and arousing hostility. In fact, it is difficult to disentangle these factors. It is important to realize that what matters is perception of the separateness, whether in terms of visibility or of group solidarity, rather than the actual behavior of the minority. "Elite," "middle-status," and "low-status" groups may all utilize strategies which heighten their visibility or lower it, and others may try to heighten the perception of separation as well.[57] In light of this, whether we consider a particular group of traders as "strangers" or as "native bourgeoisie" must be investigated in terms of the mutual perceptions of those participating in the social field.

HOST HOSTILITY

The economic position of middleman minorities, and their visibility and presumed solidarity, are all seen as factors in arousing the hostility of others towards them over and above simple xenophobia. There is general agreement that here we have a case of "class conflict reinforced by ethnocentrism."[58] Two motifs which appear in various combinations in models explaining host hostility are the "scapegoat" explanation and the "rational kernel of truth" hypothesis. The different theories may also emphasize a generalized host hostility, the "resentment of the clientele" or the "competition of native middlemen."

Blalock presents a series of propositions which see the middleman group as used by the elite to displace the attacks of the masses and to stabilize the society:

(a) A foreign or visible group filling the "status gap" is more suited to fulfill the scapegoat role than are former peasants or mixed bloods.

(b) Since the distinctive group is less assimilable, it serves the elite as a buffer and preserves the triadic relationship of elite, minority, and masses.

(c) In times of prosperity and tranquility, there is an economic coalition between elite and middleman minority, with the latter group enjoying high economic status without political power; in times of stress, the elite will form a coalition with the masses and blame the minority for troubles.[59]

(d) The middleman group serves as an ideal scapegoat during time of stress because it is the apparent source of frustration; it is politically impotent and yet visible, and sufficiently similar to the elite in position and function to serve as its stand-in. Its visibility is perpetuated through its own solidarity, adaptive skills, and the reinforcement given to these through host hostility.[60]

Blalock presents a rather static picture of elite-minority-mass relations. He writes as if political power can be separated from economic power, which is overly simple. He also does not give sufficient weight to the service which the minority may serve as a source of income, in the form of taxes or even bribes, for the elite. One may argue that the elite will support the minority in times of prosperity, when it gains monetarily from such support, but will abandon the minority when it becomes impoverished.[61]

Applying her "sojourning hypothesis" to industrial, as well as feudal and colonial societies, Bonacich also stresses hostility coming from the clientele of the minority. Whereas Blalock focuses on the "scapegoating" function, she sees the conflict between the minority and the masses as realistic. In her analysis, she does not distinguish situations where the conflict is primarily between clients and shopkeeper from those stressing labor or commercial rivals, but sees them as operating simultaneously.

Bonacich also perceives kernels of truth in the charges that these minorities either refuse citizenship in the host country or have "dual loyalties," and that they "drain the host country of its resources" by sending remittances home, not building the productive capacity of the host country. The latter charge of extracting profits is made against multinational companies and native bourgoisie, as well as minority traders.

The nationalism which underlies such charges is considered by Stryker[62] to be an important "political motif" that distinguishes situations where minorities which maintain a separate culture face much hostility from those where they do not.

Skinner[63] suggests that nationalism in Africa played a similar role in heightening hostility to the "strangers" (Africans from other regions), but that it was primarily a reaction to the separatism which was encouraged during the colonial period. However, he does make it clear that competition between the "strangers" and the locals for jobs has been an important factor in this hostility.

Because of the synthetic nature of her article, Bonacich obscures the differences which exist between situations where the leading opponents of the minority are clientele from those where they are competitors. She assumes that it is the more "efficient organization" of the minority which establishes and maintains a monopoly, when, in circumstances such as absolutist Germany of the eighteenth century, minority entrepreneurs may be brought in to break the monopolistic powers of native bourgeois guilds.[64] Similarly, native guildsmen in sixteenth-century Padua wished to oust the Jewish craftsmen, but the University of Padua opposed this, preferring competition to monopoly.[65]

Bonacich correctly sees rational motivation behind much of the host hostility, but she leans toward an acceptance of the hostile views of the opponents of the middleman minorities. For her, the commercial competitors are only one of several factors in the conflict between the minority and the majority; for others, they are the "prime opponents."[66]

The potential rivals may be members of other ethnic groups, as between Christians and Jews in Syria,[67] and Scots, Jews, and Indians in the Central African "kaffir trade."[68] Thus, the Roscher distinction[69] between "native" and "foreign" traders must be examined carefully in each situation.

The Marxist interpretations emphasize the rivalry between different types of producers. To Leon[70] anti-Semitism originates in the "antagonism toward the merchant in every society based principally on use-value." In feudal society, it is the hostility of the landowner to the moneyman who "exploits" the modes of production but does not "create" them. The landowner is the client of the merchant for luxury goods, for which he must yield part of his surplus. While remaining hostile, merchants and lord develop a bond of necessity, a situation of complementarity, and antagonistic cooperation.[71]

Leon does not assume that it is the unassimilable nature of the middleman minority which produces antagonism; rather he lays stress on a change from complementarity to competition.

Andreski's[72] interpretation presents a quite sophisticated analysis of one instance when competition replaced complementarity and created mass anti-Semitism. His analysis allows for such sociopsychological features as prejudice and perception of group difference as playing significant causal roles. When Andreski speaks of a movement, he does not necessarily deny the preexistence of the prejudice on which the movement is based, but only that the prejudice has become active.

Andreski's thesis is as follows:

Strong popular movements against a nondominant minority are stimulated by (a) "the conspicuousness and indelibility of the distinguishing marks"; (b) "the coincidence of cultural and religious and racial dividing lines"; (c) "general poverty, and particularly, the process of impoverishment"; (d) "the ratio of the minority to the majority, and particularly, the process of increase of this ratio"; (e) "the minority's share of the total wealth, and particularly, the process of growth of this share"; (f) "the extent to which economic complementarity is absent"; and (g) "the absence of common foes." Andreski's introduction of demographic factors is significant. The larger the ratio of the minority to the majority of the total population, the more the points of friction. The proportion of minority members to majority members that is needed to stimulate the animosity of the majority is about ten percent, he writes.

Andreski does not indicate if this ratio is for key urban centers and the capital city or the country as a whole. Considerations of proportions of minority members should take the location of the minority into account. For instance, a concentration of a minority population in the capital city may give rise to an antiminority mass movement in the capital and credence to such sentiment elsewhere.

The factor of control of wealth in a constricting economy relates with particular sharpness to the situation of middleman minorities in general.[73] Andreski's concern with the direction of control of wealth, impoverishment, and enrichment is acute. He suggests that the minority must achieve some economic success, since a "mass movement aiming

at spoilation needs prospect of booty of some size." He does not deny the possibility that at this crisis the minority may be on the wane.

Andreski's effort at stating elegant propositions, including relatively precise ratios of minority to majority, involves him in a somewhat garrulous effort to differentiate Polish anti-Semitism from Hitlerite anti-Semitism. It is also noteworthy that Andreski makes no assumptions about the actual solidarity of the minority group or its failure to assimilate. In fact, his stress on increasing competition between the two groups would support Duker's suggestion that anti-Semitism thrived on assimilation. One would suppose that, as members of the majority and the minority seek similar positions in the socioeconomic hierarchy, they would compete more with each other than before. Thus, a "final solution" is more desired than the assimilation of minority members.[74] With the modifications indicated, Andreski's interpretation should be applied to cases of host hostility besides pre-World War II Poland.

In a recent exchange between Stryker and Bonacich,[75] the factors accounting for the absence of host hostility were briefly reviewed. Both reemphasized the situation of complementarity, as it may have existed in pre-British India with its "emphasis on the small scale locality group" as one where there was absence of conflict. In turn, Bonacich suggests that these minorities "indeed arouse the hostility" of competing classes, but these classes must have sufficient power for such hostility to surface. She denies that there was an absence of hostility towards the Parsis, but only that such hostility did not surface.

The degree of separateness is another variable in determining host hostility. Stryker[76] suggests that, after their emigration to Protestant countries, the Huguenots did not face intense anti-Huguenotism because they lacked a "separatist complex" despite their economic position. But Protestant refugees did face opposition from local residents who resented their competition.[77] However, Portuguese immigrants in Brazil did go through a period of acute host hostility during the 1890s, including instances of violence. This campaign did peter out, in part, because Portuguese origin is hardly an indelible stigma in a Portuguese-speaking country where many claim such an origin.[78]

In dealing with host hostility, one must examine whether particular hostile acts are channeled towards the minority alone (for example, the Tsarist pogroms of prerevolutionary Russia; Amin's expulsion of Asians from Uganda), or towards all the "haves" (for example, the October Revolution; the Cambodian evacuation of cities in 1975). While Marxist class conflict would obviously have a crippling effect on a prosperous middleman minority, it may involve different imagery and activity. This, of course, should not be assumed since ethnocentrism may be disguised.

OTHER SOURCES OF ANTIMINORITY IDEOLOGY

So far, in considering this set of socioeconomic theories, one cannot fail to notice some repeated criticisms. The categories by which the minority is distinguished from majority members, as found in social scientific writing, are often vague. These theories do not answer questions of why particular groups have been singled out for genocide and expulsion. The concepts of "stranger" and "sojourner" and "native bourgeoisie" are too vague to help us. While the "middleman minority" theories tend to focus on the minorities, the sources of this distinction lie in the majority, with certain groups playing a major role.

In the previous sections, the clientele and labor and business competitors were seen as possible sources of hostility. Competitors, particularly commercial ones, are often those most hostile to the minority. Since the banner of antiminority sentiment is often outspokenly anticommercial, its origin must be sought in groups other than rival trandesmen. Lenski[79] suggests that the priests in agrarian societies may be such a group. Groups among the priests often were the main social critics in those societies.

In modern societies, intellectuals often take over this function, especially that alienated segment of the intelligensia which is likely to become the leadership of revolutionary cadres and who provide revolutions with a counter-ideology. To overthrow a regime, they must form coalitions with others, since by themselves they are too weak.[80] In any case, whether clergy or intelligensia are advocates of an old tradition of reciprocity, that is, an ethos of *noblesse oblige,* or are opponents of bourgeois Philistinism or exponents of a radical egalitarianism, they are antagonistic to the moneymen.

The degree to which the minority becomes the "scapegoat of revolution,"[81] of course, will depend upon the needs of coalition-building, the proportional position of the minority, and the type of revolution which the particular ideologists advocate. If xenophobia, however, is added to the vulnerability of a minority and to hatred of the "worshippers of Mammon," a potent mixture indeed has been created. Attacks against the minorities may be either sincere or cynical. A controversy has arisen as to whether the Portuguese Inquisition was a "cynical" instrument of power, designed to eliminate members of a class and to enrich itself, or a sincerely "fanatical" court ferreting out "judaizers" and other heretics.[82]

Opposition to the middleman minorities could develop independently. Indeed, much of the socioeconomic interpretation of antiminority sentiment which has been discussed here is written *as if* antiminority ideology is developed independently. That this is not always the case has been demonstrated amply with regard to European anti-Semitism.[83] The anti-Jewish ideology, which included a villainous stereotype of the Jew as a devil and/or moneyman, persisted in European countries even after Jews had been expelled. In England and France, certain economic roles have been identified with Jews, including the second-hand clothing trade and usury; thus, anyone involved in these was identified as a "Jew" of sorts.

European "anti-Semitism in the pure state" has been carried by non-European traders or by Asian intellectuals who have studied abroad. A sobriquet such as "Jews of the East" applied to the Chinese in Southeast Asia is such a transfer. A pamphlet entitled "The Jews of the East," allegedly written by King Rama VI of Thailand, was written during a period when the Thais and other non-Europeans were undergoing extensive westernization, including the beginning of studies abroad and mission school education. It was also a period when anti-Semitism was endemic in most European countries, including the colonial powers. Anti-Semitism is not the only ideology which is imported for use against middleman minorities. The "Yellow Peril," anti-Communism, or antiwesternism can all serve this purpose.

Obviously, the hostility between these minorities and their hosts is the product of particular social conditions. If it were only a stereotype it would be shortlived, as was the anti-Semitic outbreak against the fripiers of Paris.[84] Nevertheless, Bonacich's query as to why host hostility against "sojourning" middleman minorities is often so intense must be answered by an examination of both the stereotypes which are projected onto the minority in question, and the objective conditions. If the label used carries with it overtones of conspiracy and diabolism, it will be more potent than without such connotations.

THE STATE OF MIDDLEMAN MINORITY THEORY

So far, the theories reviewed here present a useful set of hypotheses which are of value in comparing minorities cross-culturally and cross-nationally, including ethnic groups whose specialties are not strictly in trade, such as the Japanese–Americans, one of Bonacich's key examples. One could further extend many of the hypotheses to groups which are not "middlemen" in any sense of the word. Bonacich's "sojourning" concept could be applied to "guest workers" in Europe who are "sojourners" of a very proletarian variety. One could even use her formulation in contrasting dissimilar groups such as Gypsies and Jews.

Such stretching of a theory has the effect of vitiating other aspects. Weber's interest in discovering the link between modern capitalism and the "economic ethic" of particular religions is lost when one substitutes abstractions such as "liquid occupation" for specific occupations like peddler and shopkeeper. There is a difference between a truck farmer and a merchant. We must be careful to ground our abstractions in ethnographic and historical detail, of the type provided by Waterbury and A. Cohen.[85]

At present, minority theory in general, and middleman minority theory in particular, provides useful questions and tentative answers. In my view, this type of socioeconomic explanation is insufficient to explain all aspects of the situation of these groups. As many exponents of these theories realize, attention must be paid to the specific historical circumstances of each group. The symbols used in uniting subgroups for effective economic activity and for mobilizing masses of people for antiminority action are often grounded in a long history.

In this evolution, the mythical Jew is often as important as the real Jew. This applies as well to those who become "Jews" by extension. Even the descriptions of Jews and others by Sombart (and to a lesser extent Weber and Becker) seem imbedded in the imagery of the myth.[86] Thus, even the sociologist must pay attention to the phenomenology of the stereotype. And, comparativists must deal more sensitively with internal variation within the minority in terms of occupation, subgroup organization, and tendencies towards assimilation and separation, as well as majority group perceptions of the minority.

Much more systematic comparison must be done. Some can be "controlled comparisons" like Skinner's contrast of Thai and Indonesian Chinese, or Eitzen's comparison of Philippine Chinese with Polish Jews,[87] even though the latter did not use the middleman minority framework explicitly. Stryker[88] has attempted a more ambitious comparison of three groups, although his published article is reduced from a longer manuscript. Not only must we compare whole minority groups with each other, but particular role types, such as the moneylender, the courtier, and the artisan, must be compared across cultural lines. Coser, Cahnman, and Zenner[89] have discussed the role of the Court Jew in a comparative perspective.

Systematic comparison which makes use of recent ethnographic and historical data can help steer us away from the stereotypes which have pervaded social scientific writing on this subject from the days of Marx and Weber. This effort at review of previously published work is only the beginning.

NOTES

1. The research for this paper was done with the aid of Faculty Research Fellowship 020–725A from the Research Foundation of the State University of New York. I would like to thank Thomas A. Barker, Maurice N. Richter, Jr., Werner Cahnman, George Gmelch, Robert Jarvenpa, and the participants in the Culture, Ethnicity, and Class Seminar at the University of Albany, as well as anonymous reviewers for their comments and encouragement.
2. Howard Becker, *Through Values to Social Interpretation* (Durham: Duke University Press, 1950); Max Weber, trans. *Ancient Judaism* (Glencoe: The Fall Press, 1952); and W.F. Wertheim, *East-West Parallels* (The Hague: Mouton, 1964).
3. See two articles in Jacob Katz, (ed.) *The Role of Religion in Modern Jewish History* (Cambridge, Massachusetts: Association for Jewish Studies, 1975): Jacob Katz, "Religion as a Uniting and Dividing Force in Modern Jewish History," and Lewis Feuer, "Response."
4. Igor Kopytoff, "Types of Religious Movements," in *Symposium on New Approaches in the Study of Religion* (Seattle: American Ethnological Society and University of Washington Press, 1964).
5. See Ivan Light, *Ethnic Enterprise in America* (Berkeley and Los Angeles: University of California Press, 1972) and Edna Bonacich, "A Theory of Middleman Minorities," *American Sociological Review* vol. 38 (1973), pp. 583-94.
6. Hubert Blalock, *Toward a Theory of Minority Group Relations* (New York: John Wiley, 1967).
7. W. Roscher, "Die Stellung der Juden in Mittelatter vom Standpunkt fuer die allgemeine Handelspolitik," *Zeitschrift fuer gesamte Staatswirtshaft* xxxi (1975), pp. 503-26; Abram Leon, *The Jewish Question: A Marxist Interpretation,* 3rd ed., (New York: Pathfinder Press, 1970); Becker, *op. cit.;* Irwin Rinder, "Strangers in the Land," *Social Problems* vol. 6 (1958), pp. 253-60; S. Andreski, "An Economic Interpretation of Anti-Semitism," *Jewish Journal of Sociology* vol. V (1963), pp. 201-13 [Reprinted in *Elements of Comparative Sociology* (London: 1964)]; T. Shibutani and K. Kwan, *Ethnic Stratification* (New York: Macmillan, 1965); R.A. Schermerhorn, *Comparative Ethnic Relations* (New York: Random House, 1970); and Blalock, *op. cit.*
8. Andreski, *op. cit.*
9. Blalock, *op. cit.,* p. 82.
10. Abraham Hirsch, " 'Importing' and 'Adopting' Skills," *Human Organization* vol. 24 (1965), pp.124-27.
11. Edna Bonacich, "A Theory of Ethnic Antagonism: The Split-Labor Market," *American Sociological Review* vol. 37 (1962), pp.547-59.
12. Hirsch, *op. cit.*
13. Immanuel Wallerstein, *The Modern World System* (New York and London: Academic Press, 1974), vol. 1, p. 151.
14. See Roscher, *op. cit.;* W. Roscher, "The Status of Jews in the Middle Ages from the Standpoint of Commercial Policy," trans. by Howard Becker *Historia Judaica* vol. 6 (1944); and Wertheim, *op. cit.,* p.84.
15. Wallerstein, *op. cit.,* p.151.
16. W. Cahnman, "Socio-Economic Causes of Anti-Semitism," *Social Problems* vol. 5 (1957), pp. 21-29; and Brian Foster, "Ethnicity and Commerce," *American Ethnologist* vol. 1 (1974), pp.437-48.
17. C.R. Hallpike, "Some Problems in Cross-Cultural Comparison,": in T. Beidelman, (ed.) *The Translation of Culture* (London: Tavistock, 1971).
18. R.A. Reminick, "The Evil Eye Belief among the Amhara of Ethiopia," *Ethnology* vol. 13 (1974), pp. 270-92.
19. Leon, *op. cit.,* pp. 134-35; and Elliott P. Skinner, "Strangers in West African Societies,": in *Africa* vol. 33 no. 4 (1963), pp. 307-320.
20. Foster, *op. cit.,* p. 442. See also Shibutani and Kwan, *op. cit.,* p. 191 and Georg Simmel, *Soziologie* (Leipzig: Drucker and Humblot, 1908), pp. 685-91.
21. Foster, *op. cit.,* p.443.
22. Simmel, *op. cit.,* pp.685-91; W. Cahnman, "Pariahs, Strangers and Court Jews - A Conceptual Classification," *Sociological Analysis* vol. 35 (1974), pp.155-66; L. Rosen, "Muslim-Jewish Relations in a Moroccan City" *International Journal of Middle East Studies* vol. 3 (1972), pp.435-49; and Foster, *op. cit.*
23. Bonacich, "Middleman Minorities."
24. W. Sombart, *The Jews and Modern Capitalism,* trans. (1951), and Weber, *op. cit.*
25. For example, see Leon, *op. cit.,* p.182.
26. Bonacich, "Middleman Minorities."
27. Sombart, *op. cit.,* pp.148, 206-07.
28. Bonacich, "Middleman Minorities."
29. David C. McClelland, *The Achievement Motive* (New York: Appleton-Century-Crofts, 1953).
30. Sombart, *op. cit.,* pp.222-38.
31. Weber, *op. cit.,* p.345.
32. Weber, *ibid.,* pp.336-55.
33. Weber, *ibid.,* p.344 and Becker, *op.cit.,* p.110.
34. Bonacich, "Middlemen Minorities," and Weber, *op.cit.,* pp.403-04.
35. Sombart's "Saharaism," *op. cit.,* p.328.
36. Bonacich, "Middleman Minorities."
37. Weber, *op. cit.,* p.353; Cahnman, *op. cit.;* Bonacich, *ibid.;* and Sheldon Stryker, "Social Structures and Prejudice," *Social Problems* vol. 6 (1958), pp.340-54.
38. Abner Cohen, *Customs and Politics in Urban Africa* (Berkeley and Los Angeles: University of California Press, 1969), pp.141-60 and Walter P. Zenner, *Syrian Jewish Identification in Israel* (Ann Arbor: University Microfilms, 1965).
39. Edna Bonacich, "Reply to Stryker," *American Sociological Review* vol. 39 (1974), p.282.
40. Leon, *op. cit.,* pp.82-7, 139-40.
41. S. N. Eisenstadt, *The Protestant Ethnic and Modernization* (New York: Basic Books, 1968), p. 15.
42. This viewpoint is expressed by S. Andreski in two articles: "Methods and Substantive Theory in Max Weber," in S.N. Eisenstadt, (ed.) *The Protestant Ethnic and Modernization* (New York: Basic Books, 1968), p. 60 and Andreski, *op. cit.*
43. Blalock, *op. cit.;* Lewis Coser, "The Alien as a Servant of Power: Court Jews and Christian Renegades," *American Sociological Review* vol. 37 (1972), pp.547-59; Cahnman, "Pariahs,"; and Foster, *op. cit.*
44. Stryker, "Social Structure"; S.W. Baron, *Social and Religious History of the Jews,* 2nd ed. (New York: Columbia University Press, 1967), XII; and Leon, *op. cit.,* pp.133-93.
45. Skinner, *op. cit.;* and Cohen, *op. cit.,* pp.9, 141-50.
46. Bonacich, "Middleman Minorities."

47. Cohen, *op. cit.;* James L. Watson, *Emigration and the Chinese Lineage* (Berkeley and Los Angeles: University of California Press, 1975); and John North, *North for the Trade* (Berkeley and Los Angeles: University of California Press, 1972).

48. Watson, *op. cit.*

49. See two articles by Walter P. Zenner: *op. cit.,* and "Syrian Jews in Three Social Settings," *Jewish Journal of Sociology* vol. X (1968), pp. 101-20.

50. Abner Cohen, *Two Dimensional Man* (Berkeley and Los Angeles: University of California Press, 1974), p. 99 and Pierre Michel Fontaine, "Multinational Corporation and Relations of Race and Color in Brazil: The Case of Sao Paulo," *International Studies Notes* vol. 2 no. 4 (1975), pp. 1-10.

51. Abner Cohen has presented this thesis in two publications: *Custom and Politics,* and *Two-Dimensional Man,* pp.94-98.

52. Russell Stone, "Religious Ethic and the Spirit of Capitalism," *International Journal of Middle Eastern Studies* vol. 5 (1974).

53. Paul C.P. Siu, "The Sojourner," *American Journal of Sociology* vol. 58 (1952), pp.34-44.

54. Watson, *op. cit.*

55. Watson, *ibid.,* p. 144.

56. D. Stanley Eitzen, "Two Minorities: Jews of Poland and Chinese of the Philippines," *Jewish Journal of Sociology* vol. X (1968), pp.221-40; Andreski, "Economic Interpretation," and Stryker, "Social Structure."

57. Cohen, *Two-Dimensional Man,* pp. 90-118.

58. Shibutani and Kwan, *op. cit.,* p.196.

59. See also G. Lenski, *Power and Privilege* (New York: McGraw Hill, 1966), pp.243-48; Foster, *op. cit.;* Ellis Rivkin, *The Shaping of Jewish History* (New York: Scribners, 1971); and W.F. Wertheim, *East-West Parallels* (The Hague: Mouton, 1964), pp.53-57.

60. Blalock, *op. cit.,* pp.82-83.

61. Leon, *op. cit.,* pp.159-60 and Baron, *op. cit.,* pp.198-202.

62. Stryker, "Social Structures."

63. Skinner, *op. cit.*

64. Selma Stern, *The Court Jew* (Philadelphia: Jewish Publication Society of America, 1950); F.A. Norwood, *The Reformation Refugee as an Economic Force* (Chicago: American Society of Church History, 1942); and Coser, *op. cit.*

65. Brian Pullan, *Rich and Poor in Renaissance Venice* (Oxford: Blackwell's, 1971), p.528.

66. Andreski, "Economic Interpretation"; Ber Borochov, *Nationalism and the Class Struggle* (New York: Young Poale Zion Alliance of America, 1937), pp.184-85; Leon, *op. cit.;*

and Mordecai Lahav, *Sotziologia shel Toldot HaGolah HaYehudit Le'Or HaMarxism* (Marhiva: Sifriat Poalim, 1951), pp.57-59.

67. Waterbury, *op. cit.,* p.69.

68. F. Dotson and L. O Dotson, *The Indian Minority of Zambia, Rhodesia and Malawi* (New Haven: Yale University Press, 1968), pp.78-86.

69. Roscher, *op.cit.*

70. Leon, *op. cit.,* p.71.

71. See also Rivkin, *op. cit.,* and Lahav, *op. cit.,* p.46.

72. Andreski, "Economic Interpretation," pp.201-13.

73. Rivkin, *op.cit.*

74. Abraham G. Duker, "Agriculture and Integration: A Jewish Survivalist View," in J.L. Teller, (ed.) *Acculturation and Integration: A Symposium* (New York: American Histadrut Cultural Exchange, 1965); and Wertheim, *op. cit.*

75. Sheldon Stryker, "A Theory of Middleman Minorities: A Comment," *American Sociological Review* vol. 39 (1974), p.281; and Bonacich, "Middleman Minorities."

76. *Idem,* "Social Structure."

77. Norwood, *op. cit.*

78. June E. Hahner, "Jacobinos vs. Galegos: Urban Radicals vs. Portuguese Immigrants in Rio de Janeiro in the 1890s," *Journal of Interamerican Studies and World Affairs* vol. 18, pp.125-34.

79. Lenski, *op. cit.,* pp.264-66.

80. *Ibid.,* pp.70-71.

81. Judd Teller, *Scapegoat of Revolution* (New York: Scribner, 1954).

82. Herman P. Salomon, "The Portuguese Inquisition in the Light of Recent Polemics," *Journal of the American Portuguese Cultural Society* vol. V (1971), pp. 19-28, 50-55 and Wertheim, *op. cit.,* pp. 79-82.

83. Norman Cohn, *Warrant for Genocide* (London: Harper, 1967), and L. Poliakov, *The History of Anti-Semitism* (New York: Schoken Books, 1974).

84. Poliakov, *op. cit.,* pp.196-97.

85. Waterbury, *op. cit.,* and Cohen, *Custom and Politics.*

86. *Sombart, op. cit.;* Weber, *op. cit.;* Becker, *op. cit.;* and E. Shmueli, " 'The Pariah People' and Its 'Charismatic Leadership' ";*Proceedings of the American Academy for Jewish Research* vol. 36 (1968), pp.167-247.

87. G. William Skinner, *op. cit.* and Eitzen, *op. cit.*

88. Stryker, "Social Structure."

89. Coser, *op. cit.;* Cahnman, "Pariahs"; and Walter P. Zenner, "Jewish Retainers as Power Brokers in Traditional Societies," paper presented at the Annual Meeting of the American Anthropological Association, San Francisco, 1975.

THE ECONOMIC ROLE OF MIGRANTS IN THE U.S. LABOR MARKET

Michael J. Piore

This paper is addressed to the question of the role of the new immigrants in the productive structure of the United States economy. Beginning with the proposition that the migrants are coming to take a distinct set of jobs, the first part of the paper summarizes the characteristics of these jobs and explains why it appears that immigrant workers are a particularly attractive source of labor to fill them. Subsequent sections then go on to identify and explore a series of alternative hypotheses about the role of this type of work in industrial economies. The hypotheses are tentative and the discussion does not lend itself to definitive conclusions.

It should be mentioned that the point of departure for this paper is the view that the new immigration is occurring in response to certain quite specific requirements of the U.S. economic structure, and the problem is to identify what those requirements are. This view implies that while it is true that immigration has escaped the bounds of administrative controls, there have also been decided limits upon its spread, imposed by the demand of the U.S. economic and social structure. This view is in direct conflict to that implicit in much of the recent commentary, which focuses upon the population growth and income levels in the countries of Latin America and the Caribbean from which the new immigration is coming. Such a focus implies that the controlling factors in the process lie in those other economies instead of our own. To be interested in this paper, the reader who subscribes to that view must temporarily suspend his commitment.

THE CHARACTERISTICS OF IMMIGRANT EMPLOYMENT

My own view of the nature of immigrant jobs derives from recent research efforts to identify the particular establishments in which immigrant employment is concentrated, to attempt to under-

stand the distinguishing features of those establishments and/or the jobs which immigrants hold within them, and to determine why migrants are concentrated there and not in other parts of the economy. That research suggests that the jobs held by migrants exhibit the characteristics attributed to jobs in the secondary sector by the dual labor market hypothesis. They tend to be unskilled, to pay low wages, to require low status work under poor working conditions, to offer little in the way of job security or advancement, and to involve a highly personalized relationship between supervisor and subordinate without the web of formal work rules, and without a more or less institutionalized grievance procedure which mediates the relationship between labor and management in more attractive job opportunities. In all of these respects, they present a sharp contrast to work in what the dual labor market hypothesis terms the primary sector. This characterization of migrant jobs is consistent with what quantitative evidence is available from the Immigration and Naturalization Service and the North-Houstoun study.[1] The characterization is also consistent with available data about the role which migrants play in the industrial economies of Western Europe. However, it is to be emphasized that even for purposes of theorization and generalization, it would be highly misleading to suggest that all of the jobs exhibit all of the characteristics. There are exceptions, the most outstanding of which are the jobs on the automobile assembly lines of Western Europe. If one were forced to specify one single factor which characterizes *all* migrant jobs, it would be simply that the work is distained by native workers.

The basic reason why the migrants find the work acceptable whereas the natives do not appears to be that most migrants view their stay in the industrialized country or region as decidedly temporary. Migrants are target earners whose plans are to accumulate funds quickly, which they can then utilize to finance upward social mobility at home. The temporary nature of the commitment makes certain job characteristics a lot more tolerable than they would be if the commitment were permanent. For example, temporary workers tend to be indifferent to career opportunities offered by a job because they do not plan to remain long enough to profit from them. They are also less concerned about job security since their own attachment to the job is very insecure. Temporary migrants are also less concerned with the social status which the job confers because they are essentially strangers, or outsiders, to the society in which that status is defined. Their own status is defined instead by their position in their native community: the physical and social distance separating that community from the work enables them to divorce the job from the earnings and use the latter to finance advancement. As one Puerto Rican put it: "If I am going to do that kind of work, I would rather do it over there."

This is not to denigrate the importance of the wage itself, which obviously looks higher in the context of the migrant's home community than it does to natives of the place where he works. But the critical factor does appear to be his status, in his own eyes, as outsider or stranger, which enables him to work in purely instrumental terms. And the jobs held by migrants are shared by other sociodemographic groups who, like the migrants, define themselves and their identity independently of the work they perform. Two such groups are native women, who define themselves by the roles as wives and mothers, and adolescents, who are looking for money to finance education or leisure pursuits.

The manning of secondary jobs with temporary migrants appears to be an ideal solution. It meets the needs of the industrial society for this kind of labor and the needs of the migrants for income. But it is not as facile as it appears on the surface. The migrants, although they may plan to stay only temporarily, often stay longer than expected. As they do so, their own aspirations change somewhat. More importantly, they tend to form families and have children. The children are essentially native workers with a native's perspective on the labor market, a distain for the work of their parents and desires for

upward mobility within the society where they grew up. There is nothing in the migration process which assures that higher level job opportunities will be available to meet these aspirations. Therefore, one is led to examine the issue of what role the jobs of migrants play in the productive structure and whether, and at what cost, such work could be curtailed or eliminated. This is not a trivial question. It appears that efforts to restrict the flow of migrant labor for certain jobs are repeatedly frustrated. The United States may be the most glaring case of a rhetoric of official policy and legislative intent far afield of the practices which the society actually is willing to fund and administer. But in most European countries a similar gap between policy and practice has emerged whenever policy has become excessively restrictive. The jobs seem to be playing some sort of social or economic function which industrial societies find difficult to do without. On the other hand, that function appears to be relatively circumscribed and limited. There seems to be no want of migrants willing to come and, if official immigration policy is not a constraint upon entry, the capacity of the society to absorb them must be. The following pages explore four basic hypotheses about the jobs which migrants hold which might explain this situation.

HYPOTHESIS I: THE JOBS EMPLOY MIGRANTS

The simplest hypothesis is that what is really common to the industries which employ immigrants is simply that they employ immigrants. That fact alone is enough to impart to the work environment certain distinguishing characteristics. For example, it would explain the low social status of immigrants, who clearly carry low social status in most industrial societies in and of themselves, and if that status does not already adhere to the work which they perform, they quickly confer it to the work when they take it on. To the extent that the immigrants are temporary workers, an immigrant labor force will have a high turnover. This forestalls the development of strong social groupings in the work place and produces more individualistic, and possibly personalistic, relations between labor and management. To the extent that the immigrants are target earners, they will have backward-bending supply curves, and this will affect compensation systems and the way in which they respond to economic pressures, and so on. The legal status of immigrants may also affect their willingness and ability to join trade unions. All of this will give a distinguishing caste to the immigrant labor market; the caste, however, derives from the labor force and not from the jobs.

Under this hypothesis, one might imagine the process through which immigrants are attracted to industrial economies as being one which is governed by the process of economic expansion. As economic expansion proceeds from some relatively low level (the United States in the Great Depression on the eve of World War II; Europe beginning its recovery after the war came to an end), it absorbs the native labor force. It then begins to experience labor shortages. Those labor shortages naturally concentrate in the low paying, low status jobs because natives gravitate toward better paying, more prestigious positions. The labor-short jobs must then compete for labor. They might do so by offering higher wages, better working conditions, and the like. Or they might substitute capital for labor. But under these circumstances, the amount of employment would clearly have to be reduced. Either the labor-short jobs would themselves be eliminated or they would transfer their labor shortages to other jobs, which would be eliminated. The alternative is to recruit foreign workers. In this view it is not necessarily critical that immigrants are unskilled and come from underdeveloped regions. When the migration is an internal one, this could easily be explained by a theory in which jobs are allocated among workers on the basis of their productivity. The rural workers are seemingly the least productive and hence are the last in line. They are absorbed only when labor shortages begin to emerge. However, when the workers are foreign, one may also think of nationality as conferring a kind of monopoly power upon the native labor force. In other words, nationality is like union membership, but a national group is a much more powerful, cohesive unit than a union. Hence, national restrictions are used to reserve good jobs for natives and to exclude foreigners, even when the foreigners are more skilled and more productive.

This view of the demand for migrants does not provide a very clear idea of what might be involved in curtailing the migrant labor force. Presumably, it would involve a decline in the national standard of living, since one supposes the resort to migrants to be a kind of "least cost" alternative. If it were cheaper to substitute capital for labor or to raise wages and attract native workers, employers would have chosen that course of action on their own. It would also affect certain economic indexes which are of interest in the formulation of national policy, independently of their impact upon the standard of living. The index most prominent in discussions of migration in Europe is the balance of payments. It is clear from even a cursory glance at the industries where migrants are concentrated that some of them are under very intense competitive pressure from abroad; that is why they cannot pay the wages required to attract native labor. And, if migration were curtailed, they could no longer survive domestically and the goods they produced would be imported. An attempt to curtail the demand for migrant workers would also presumably require the limitation of the rate of economic expansion to that which could be sustained by native labor. In the short run, this would undoubtedly imply slower rates of economic growth and quite possibly higher rates of unemployment.

Beyond these general remarks, one can only say that the elimination of migrants would involve certain structural adjustments in production, in which some native workers would lose their jobs and have to find others. In general, immigrants are employed in businesses owned by natives and managed by native supervisors. The equipment is often built and repaired by native craftsmen, and the productive process is frequently integrated in such a way that the work of immigrants utilizes goods and services produced by native workers or services as inputs into the productive activities of natives. All of these native workers would be affected by elimination of the immigrants and the consequently increasing costs of the things which they produce. All of this is perhaps obvious, but it is just such effects which are generally neglected by proposals to curtail immigration. Such effects must be partly responsible for resistance to immigration laws, and they would have to be dealt with if such laws are to be effective. The kinds of structural adjustments which would be required would depend upon which industries and occupations were affected and how the economy reacted to changes in castes. As we have seen, there is no general pattern among countries and, so, one would have to look at the specific nations involved. Even then, it is probably very difficult to predict exactly what adjustments in the productive structure would follow. There would also have to be corresponding adjustments in the structure of consumption.

It is no doubt more useful to try to envisage the effects of immigration in these terms than simply as an overall decline in native living standards. Again, however, the diversity of national patterns makes it difficult to generalize, except to say that in all countries there would be less household help; hotels and restaurants would either be more expensive or less sanitary; in France, the streets would be dirtier; in England, there would be less public transportation.

HYPOTHESIS II: LOW STATUS JOBS ARE SUSTAINED BY INERTIA

The preceding discussion of the demand for migrant labor is built essentially upon conventional economic reasoning. It explains the politics of migration policy—in particular, the difficulties of halting migration and the very limited tendency of the market for migrants to spread—by stressing something which conventional economic models almost never stress: the *inertia* of the structure of economic activity, especially in the short run. If this view is correct, then it is clear that people do not like to change either their consumption patterns or their production patterns, and, when there is great pressure to make changes, they seek ways to avoid making them, such as the recruitment of migrants.

The inertia of existing patterns is critical here, and not simply the availability of low wage workers. One needs to explain not only why we resist attempts to curtail migration but also why we do not use migrants more intensively. The wage differential between the United States and the underdeveloped world is such that every American family could have a foreign maid.

The importance of inertia in governing the processes involved makes these particular hypotheses about the role of migration in the economy very unsatisfactory. Policy must deal with this "inertia" if it is to successfully moderate the demand for migrants. But there is no theory of the inertia in economics; nor, for that matter, is there much of a theory of inertia in other disciplines. This makes the hypotheses discussed in the remainder of this paper both more attractive and more plausible. However, it is important to consider one extention of the hypothesis about inertia: that *inertia* affects not only the structure of production and consumption, but also the structure of wages.

Conventional economic theory treats the wage structure as an instrument which varies so as to distribute labor to various different sectors of the economy. However, the wage also plays a social function by confering status and prestige. Since status and prestige are also generally assumed to adhere to the job to which the wage is attached, people have very distinct notions about what the appropriate wage relationships are among different kinds of work. They expect the wage structure and the hierarchy of status and prestige to coincide. The existence of these two distinct functions of the wage—the economic and the social—creates a variety of analytical problems.

Economists do not always recognize the social function of the wage, as distinct from the economic. They generally *assume* that the economic function dominates. This is by no means clear: the social function could be such that the economic function is not allowed to function at all. But even if the economic function dominates, one needs to specify how the relationship between these two functions is worked out. The specification which is least troublesome from the point of view of conventional economic theory is that the social wage follows the economic. The status and prestige which adhere to the job are *determined* by and reflect the wage which is attached to it. If this is true it is clearly true only in the long run. In the short run, the two are distinct, and the distinction creates the possibility that changes in wage relationships generated by economic pressures—such as cutting off immigration—will be resisted by the native work force and that, as the wage of migrant jobs are driven up, the native labor force will exert pressure to restore the original wage differentials. In the long run, the efforts to change the wage structure might be successful, but in the short run they will be inflationary.

The inflation is important for two reasons. For the economy as a whole, this suggests that as a consequence of curtailing migration, we must anticipate not simply a decline in living standards, adjustments in the balance of payments, slower growth and higher native unemployment, but we probably must anticipate a certain amount of additional inflationary pressure as well. On the microeconomic level, it is clearly the fear of the leverage which wage increases at the bottom would impose on internal wage structure which leads employers to seek out and encourage foreign migration. It is simply inconceivable to a restauranteur that he can raise the wage of the dishwasher and the busboy without paying more to the waiter and the cook. The hospital administrator cannot envisage paying more to orderlies without paying more to nurses. If the warehouse man gets more in a shoe plant, the production workers will get more as well. And you cannot pay stitchers a higher wage than you pay cutters. Even if these traditional relationships will yield in the long run, the employer is unwilling or unable to absorb the short-run costs, and his resistance is the genesis both of the initial migration streams and of evasion of the law. However, it is in no sense clear that these social forces, which conventional economic analysis generally ignore, can be integrated into the theory as easily as the foregoing suggests.

HYPOTHESIS III: HIERARCHY AS A MOTIVATING FORCE

A third explanation of the role of migration in the economic structure revolves around the notion of a hierarchy of jobs, or of employment opportunities. In conventional theory, the existence of such a hierarchy is viewed as an accidental result of differences in the productivity of individual workers or, possibly, of the nature of technology. However, it is

possible that such a hierarchy is critical to the motivation of the labor force, that is, that it is basically the accumulation and maintenance of social status, and not income, which induces people to work. In this view, people work either to advance up the hierarchy of jobs (and, hence, of social status) or to maintain the position they have already achieved. This suggests that there will be acute motivational problems in two kinds of jobs. The first are jobs at the very bottom of the social hierarchy, since in effect there is no position to be maintained. The second are jobs which, whatever position in the hierarchy, are basically dead-end and provide no opportunities for advancement.

Recruitment for both types of jobs is a basic problem for the economy. The problem in the case of dead-end jobs is not fundamental. Such jobs could be placed high enough in the social hierarchy so that people would be motivated to work *toward* them and would fear losing them once the positions had been obtained. Or the society could simply dispense with the jobs through substitution, technological change, or other adjustments in its patterns of consumption and production. However, jobs at the bottom of the hierarchy create a fundamental dilemma because, in a very real sense, the bottom of the hierarchy can never be eliminated. If the bottom jobs were somehow cut off, the jobs directly above them would be at the bottom. The locus of the problem would be changed, but the problem itself would remain.

Migrants provide a solution to the problem because they come from outside and remain apart from the social structure in which the jobs are located. The exact sense in which this is true cannot be explored here. There would appear to be at least two factors involved. First, the jobs may actually stand in a very different position in the social structure of the migrant community from the position which they hold in the host society. Second, even when that is not the case, the migrant's position as a stranger in the host country enables him to view his work in purely instrumental terms. For him, the work really is nothing more than a provider of income, a means to some other end. In this sense, he is a true *homo economicus*, divorced from the sociological restrictions which prevent the variation in wages and response of workers which economic theory assumes.

This is a much richer theory of the distinction between migrant and native jobs. It begins to explain not only why migrants are attractive to industrial societies, but why the correspondence between the needs of the industrial society and the migrant stream might diverge over time. It also embeds the whole migrant process in something fundamental to the nature of the economic structure and makes the resistance to efforts to cut off the migrant stream and eliminate their jobs endogenous to the nature of the economic system and the way in which it motivates the labor force. It suggests that such efforts are threatening to the underlying structure of the system itself.

This view does not necessarily imply that all of the jobs which migrants hold are fundamental to the basic motivational forces. But it does suggest that some core jobs are, and that efforts to reduce that core are likely to threaten the system itself. Given the present economic system, to reduce migration below that core level, it is necessary to attack the problem not through the elimination of jobs but through the substitution of other kinds of workers. To go beyond this and dispense with migrants altogether, we would have to devise a social system which relied upon a very different kind of motivation. The question of whether or not it would be possible to do so lies beyond the scope of this paper.

It may be noted that this view of the migration process does not necessarily exclude the more conventional view that migration results from a tendency for demand to outrun supply. The migrants may also be recruited under these circumstances to fill vacancies, possibly vacancies fairly high up in the job structure. The hypothesis suggests that many of these vacancies could be eliminated without touching the underlying socioeconomic system. But it is a hypothesis which grows out of a conception of man which suggests why efforts to eliminate even these jobs are likely to meet considerable resistance. The core of that view is that economic activity is generally embedded in a wider social system. It is only the relatively rare case of the temporary migrant where work is simply a means to an end and where most jobs can be reduced to the

level of income and, at that level, are interchangeable. For the rest of us, our roles in the productive structure and our patterns of consumption are much more fundamental to the way in which we conceive of ourselves and understand the world. Changes in the productive structure thus seem to threaten the core of what we think we are, and it is for this reason that they are resisted. The impact of changes in these things is not adequately measured by the income gained or lost. Even is assured, compensation will not relieve our basic fears and hence cannot overcome the underlying resistance to change.

One can also understand the reason why migrants generally remain in essentially unskilled, menial jobs in social terms. The jobs directly above them in the hierarchy involve skills which are acquired on the job in the process of production and tend to be relatively specific to a particular work environment. Such skills are essentially social. This process of skill acquisition involves the integration into a work community and the assumption of roles which the community defines. The individual tends to understand his skills in terms of the particular social context in which he can learn. Advancement up the skill ladder thus tends to require that the worker abandon the instrumental detachment which characterizes the migrant initially and that he begin to take on the kind of roles in the work place that root one in the society.

HYPOTHESIS IV: ECONOMIC DUALITY

A fourth perspective upon the role of migrants in developed, industrial economies is suggested by the dual labor market hypothesis. In that hypothesis, two distinct parts of the labor market can be identified—a primary sector and a secondary sector. Migrants are found in the secondary sector, and the jobs in the primary sector are largely reserved for natives. Thus, there is a fundamental dichotomy between the jobs of migrants and the jobs of natives, and the role of migrants in industrial economies can be traced to the factors which generate the distinction initially, to the role and function of the secondary sector in which migrants are found, and to the evolution of its labor requirements.

A certain tendency toward dualism resides in the

flux and uncertainty which inheres in all economic activity. Variations in economic activity are created by a whole host of factors ranging from the natural variations introduced by the seasons and the weather to the social variability of trends in fashion and taste, the economic fluctuations of boom and depression, and the human successes and failures which dominate the fate of individual enterprises, speculation, invention, and bankruptcy. All of these fluctuations alternately absorb resources into a given productive activity and then discharge them to find employment elsewhere. A fundamental problem in social organization is how that process is to be handled and who precisely is to bear its costs.

In this regard, the organization of capitalist economies creates a fundamental distinction between capital and labor. Capital is the fixed factor of production. It can be idled by fluctuations in demand, but it cannot be laid off. The owners of capital are always forced to bear the cost of its "employment." Labor is the variable factor. When demand declines, it is simply released. In the sense that workers can be said to own their own labor power, the owners of labor are like the capitalist. They each bear the cost of unemployment for the factor which they own. But there is a fundamental difference between the owners of capital and those of labor. In a capitalist system it is the latter who organize and control the productive process. The effect of this difference is that labor is forced to bear a disproportionate share of the cost of economic flux and uncertainty. Whenever possible, the capitalist will try to seek out the more stable and certain portions of demand and reserve it for the employment of his own equipment.

The clearest case of this distinction is one where there are two distinct technologies of production, one which is intensive in capital and employs relatively little labor, the other which is labor intensive and utilizes less capital. When demand can be divided into stable and variable portions, as for example in any industry with a stable basic demand and a high seasonal component, the capital intensive technique will be used to meet basic demand and the labor intensive one for the seasonal portion. In this sense, the most basic dichotomy in the economy is between capital and labor.

However, the duality between capital and labor inevitably creates certain distinctions *among* workers. Where there are two distinct technologies, for example, it is clear that if the capital intensive method of production utilizes a fundamentally different group of workers than the labor intensive technique, the one will *perforce* have secure jobs and the other will not. But there are also cases where the employer is forced to invest in labor in very much the same way in which he invests in capital in order, for example, to have a skilled labor force when workers cannot or will not invest in training themselves, or to recruit laborers and house them at an isolated and remote location. The nature of the system creates incentives to organize production so that these workers too have more stable, secure employment opportunities and, in this way, extends the dichotomy inherent in the distinction between capital and labor to a distinction within the labor market itself.

This distinction which emerges naturally within a capitalist mode of production appears to have been immensely exaggerated in modern economies by organized efforts on the part of the labor force to escape the role which the logic of the system assigns to them. The form which these efforts have taken varies substantially from country to country, and within any given country it also varies over time.

Since the late 1960s Italy and France have evolved severe restrictions upon the layoff or discharge of any workers in the strongly organized sectors for economic reasons. In Italy, those restrictions seem, in fact, to amount to an outright prohibition. In the United States, the restrictions are somewhat less severe. In particular firms and industries certain workers may have virtual job guarantees, and one can argue that the thrust of guaranteed income demands in auto and steel industries is moving the whole economy in that direction. But in most of U.S. industry, employers can still discharge workers so long as they do so in accord with certain basic procedures. Nonetheless, the effect is similar to the more restrictive provisions in France and Italy. Layoffs become more expensive, and the workers subject to these provisions begin to take on some of the aura of capital as factors of production in the eyes of those who organize and control production. Their employment ought to, if possible, be avoided.

The difficulty with these efforts of organized workers to deal with their own unemployment in this way is that it attacks a symptom of the problem and not the problem itself. The problem is the flux and uncertainty which adheres to economic activity. So long as the flux and uncertainty remain, the specific prohibitions create an incentive for employers to look for some way to evade the rigidity which workers' organizations introduce into the system. The secondary sector constitutes a means of evasion. It is a sector of the labor market which is not subject to restrictions upon layoffs and discharges and to which the unstable portion of demand can be transferred. The precise institutions through which that transfer occurs vary from one country to another, following the variations in the way in which restrictions upon layoffs and discharges are imposed. In Italy, the distinction is between small and large enterprises; in France, it depends upon subcontracting and temporary help services; in the United States, it seems to depend upon all three institutions. But in each country, the institutional distinctions appear to correspond to the distinctions between the jobs of migrants and the jobs of natives.

In its extreme forms, these distinctions between secured and unsecured job opportunities create a dual labor market, but the tendencies which they express are present even when it fails to achieve the kind of uniform expression throughout the national economy. Because of their temporary attachment to the labor market, migrants will always be more adaptable to these employment opportunities than permanently attached native workers. And, indeed, one can identify particular cases where migrants were clearly recruited for these purposes in historical periods where the distinctions were nowhere near as clearly drawn as they seem to have become today. The chief difference is that under current circumstances, the institutional arrangements and hence the politics of both job security and of migration are more clearly national in scope.

This explanation of the role of migrants in the labor market is not necessarily exclusive of the two preceding ones. The unsecured jobs in the sec-ondary sector generally do lie at the bottom of the job hierarchy. The existence of these jobs may serve to motivate the work of natives as well as to secure their employment opportunities. Having created a set of institutional distinctions for one purpose, the economy may utilize it for other purposes as well. And a secondary sector, whose institutional history is dominated by the politics of employment security, may house all of the low status, menial jobs.

A dual labor market is not exclusive of the conventional explanation either. Indeed, one might well argue that when the demand for labor outruns supply, the last jobs created in an employment expansion are likely to be the least secure jobs. If a dual labor market exists, these jobs will therefore be disproportionately concentrated in the secondary, or unsecured, sector and, in the sense that migrants are recruited for one purpose, they will be recruited for the second purpose as well.

This particular version of the dual labor market hypothesis adds several factors to our understanding of the demand for migrants which the other explanations ignore. First, it links that demand to the flux and uncertainty of the economy itself. Second, it moves the focus away from particular industries and occupations to other characteristics of employment, and it suggests that migrants may be required in all industries and occupations. That this is not in fact true has less to do with the underlying structure of the problem than with other complications, such as the fact that not all jobs are unskilled and, hence, readily filled by migrants, and that, in the case of skilled work, there are incentives inherent in the skill acquisition process to stabilize employment, or at least handle the instability in a different way. Third, this view points to the connection between migrants' jobs and the characteristics of the jobs of native workers and suggests a reason why workers, as well as their employers, might have an interest in the continuation of the migration process. Moreover, that interest is not open-ended, such as their interest in the standard of living or the productive structure under the first hypothesis. It would explain not only why the demand for migrants is as large as it is, but also why it is not larger.

Finally, in the form which we have developed it here, the dual labor market hypothesis places the politics of worker organization at the very center of the way in which the society utilizes migrant workers and the way in which that utilization evolves over time. At root, it suggests that the migrants provide a way in which the native labor force is able to escape the role which the system assigns. To a certain extent, this is a Marxist perspective upon the problem. It places at the center of the whole migrant issue the nature of the economic system and the struggle of various different groups and classes within it. However, because the analysis resembles so closely a Marxist perspective, it is in danger of being submerged in one or another Marxist interpretation, and it is therefore worth distinguishing clearly the various features of the theory which are being put forward.

The term "capitalist system" has a very specific meaning here, and it is properly used in this context instead of other terms of reference used elsewhere in the text to refer to the economy of the recipient country, such as, for example, industrial economy. The meaning of the term "capitalist system" is one in which, from the point of view of those who organize and control the productive process, capital is fixed and labor is the variable factor of production. To the extent that labor succeeds in imposing upon the system the obligation to treat it in one respect or another, the system becomes less capitalistic. One might call it instead a *quasi*-capitalist or a *quasi*-socialist system. Somewhat paradoxically, in terms of the conventional Marxist wisdom, the migrants are called upon not because the system is capitalistic but because it has become quasi-capitalistic. However, it is not simply the quasi-capitalistic nature of the system which is important in creating the need for migrants. Another feature is also critical: the flux and uncertainty which inheres in economic activity. Presumably, this feature has no necessary connection to the relationship between those who control the productive process and the factors of production. It is something to which all industrial economies are subject whether capitalist or socialist. Possibly it is something which affects all economies, period. Also, it is easy, and essentially within the spirit of the analysis, to see in the process a struggle among socioeconomic classes, a struggle first between capital (in the sense of both

those who organize production and of those who own capital and bear the cost of its unemployment) and labor, and then among different groups of workers, in particular natives and migrants. It is also essentially within the spirit of the analysis to describe migration as a way in which capital is able to stave off the pressures from the labor force by dividing the working class. However, this characterization of the process is incomplete without some subsidiary points not present in most Marxian analyses. One such point is that in the case of migration, the capitalists do not seem to create the distinctions among members of the working class. It would be more accurate to say they find and exploit distinctions which are already there. However, this statement of the problem fails to give sufficient weight to the complicity of the native labor force in the process. In the conventional Marxists analyses such complicity is misguided. Divisions within the working class serve to postpone the revolution which would otherwise be inevitable. But nothing in the analysis here assures that the alternative would not be a return to a more purely capitalist system in which native labor bore flux and uncertainty.

This leads to another point: it is not completely accurate—and analytically not very helpful—to describe the role of migrants in industrial society as necessarily one of exploitation. As has been suggested earlier, the motivation of the migrants differs fundamentally from that of native workers and there is a real sense in which the migration, at least initially, may be described as mutually beneficial. The character and motivation of the migrants shift systematically over time. The migrants begin to want the same things which natives want and to aspire to their positions in the society. As this happens, the migrants begin to *feel* exploited, and it seems more natural to reserve the term "exploitation" for those feelings. More conventional Marxist analyses might prefer to use the term exploitation to characterize the whole migration experience and term the migrants' feelings in the beginning before those feelings were felt as "false consciousness." To this terminology, I have two objections. First, it seems to imply that the old consciousness is unreal whereas it can be understood as rooted in the objective conditions of the migrants themselves and to change systematically in response to changes in the objective conditions. Second, it suggests that such feelings can be created and maintained independently of the objective conditions themselves, whereas nothing in the analysis here implies that this is the case.

Perhaps the most important point to emerge from casting the problem of migration in terms of the dual labor market analysis is that one is able to interpret much of the shifting history of worker movements in terms of successive waves of migration and the conjuncture of motivational changes within each wave, which follows more or less automatically and independently of the economic forces which start the migration in the first place. This is too complex a point to be developed here, but it is perhaps possible to convey the basic idea. As migration streams age, two things occur. First, the motivation of the individual migrants shifts from one where work in the industrial society is purely instrumental and the uncertainty and insecurity of employment are relatively unimportant, to one in which industrial work is seen as central to their social roles and any uncertainty or insecurity seems fundamentally threatening. It is this shift which gives rise to the feelings of exploitation.

At the same time, it tends to be accompanied by a change in the structure of the migrant community in the industrial society. Initially this community is overwhelmingly populated by temporary migrants. Its size and physical location may be stable, and thus it may be perceived as permanent by outsiders. But its membership is subject to very rapid turnover, and under these circumstances it is very difficult to organize. However, over time the membership of the community begins to stabilize and, as it does so, organization becomes feasible. These two processes are distinct, although they respond to similar forces and tend to coincide. Thus there comes a point in the history of each migrant community where it wants to change the character of employment opportunities and is capable of organizing to do so. The stage is then set for a new organizational drive. Of course, other factors may enter to affect the precise timing and actual evolution of these events, but it is easy to see this process

in the great waves of worker militancy such as the 1936 sit-down strikes in the United States. The changing political activities of the migrants must, of course, affect the whole structure of working class organizations. To the extent that the job security of the organized sector is predicated upon the acquiescence of the migrants' community, any attempt by the latter to organize requires adjustments in the former.

The basic point about these organization bursts, which the dual labor market interpretation underscores, is that while they may be successful from the point of view of the migrants, they are only a temporary solution to the social tensions from which they spring. So long as the system continues to exhibit flux and uncertainty and those who organize and control production are unable or unwilling to deal with it in other ways, some new labor force must be found to restore the flexibility which the system requires and sustain the new organizational arrangements. Typically, that new labor force has been another stream of migrants from another as yet undeveloped area.

While it is a mistake to apply to this process too much of the orthodox Marxist vocabulary, there is a basic truth in the Marxian notion that the migration process enables the society to avoid a confrontation with the underlying nature of the social system. In the midst of the organizational crisis that accompanies the maturation of a migrant community, it has seemed as if they might precipitate the revolution. In fact, that has seldom occurred. And, in fact, so long as there remain underdeveloped areas from which to draw migrants, there is no necessary reason why such a revolution should occur. Perhaps as world industrialization continues, and the presently underdeveloped regions disappear one by one as a source of migrant labor and add their own demands to those of the rest of the developed world, migration as a solution to the problem of flux and uncertainty will become increasingly untenable, and capitalism or quasi-capitalism will indeed break down. But it may be that what is at stake is relative development, and that as long as the industrial world is not homogeneous, the kind of migration I am describing can continue indefinitely. Or perhaps there will be substitutes for migrants in people who see, or can be induced to see, their work in similar ways.

SUMMARY

This paper examines four basic hypotheses. The first is that the call for immigrants is simply a result of the tendency of the demand for labor to outrun supply. The shortages are felt at the bottom of the labor market in menial, unstable jobs either because natives are genuinely more productive than migrants, and hence are nationally preferred to them, or because natives are able to use nationality to monopolize the better job opportunities and confine foreign access to the residual. The simplest version of this hypothesis is completely consistent with the spirit of conventional economic analysis and is built out of elementary economic tools. However, it fails to explain several aspects of the underlying social process. In particular, it does not provide an explanation for the resistance of the economic structure to efforts to do without migrant workers. It predicts that such efforts will lead to increases in the wages and working conditions of the jobs at the bottom of the employment hierarchy, and a redistribution of the native labor force in response to these wage changes and adjustments in the structure of consumption and production. In fact, these adjustments might occur in the long run if the process were actually allowed to work itself out. But there appears to be tremendous inertia in the distribution of workers, in the structure of production and consumption, and in the wage structure itself. The second hypothesis is an extention of the first, and emphasizes these types of inertia. It suggests that the inertia is such that efforts to cut off migration and generate adjustments are most often aborted by evasion or outright defiance of legal restrictions. To cut off migration, policy would have to overcome the resistance to change. It is here that conventional theory fails, for it provides no basic explanation of what generates the inertia and what determines its strength relative to the pressures for change. It cannot say when and how long it will prevail. Nor does it provide a clue as to possible policy measures which might be taken to overcome the resistance.

A third explanation of the role of the migration is in the economic structure and revolves around the notion of a job or employment hierarchy. It suggests that such a hierarchy may be critical to the motivation and control of the existing labor force; that worker motivation is critically dependent upon aspirations towards moving up into the job hierarchy and an underlying fear of downward mobility. Given this view of the world, it is critically necessary for society to have someone to man the bottom rungs of the job hierarchy, particularly in an economic expansion. This is so because if economic shortages during periods of expansion are dealt with by eliminating the jobs at the bottom of the hierarchy, motivational problems will be created further up the job hierarchy. This view suggests that the society does not have the alternative of eliminating the jobs at the bottom of the hierarchy and is forced to find someone to fill the bottom-level jobs. Migrants serve this function very well.

The fourth perspective is suggested by the dual labor market hypothesis. It argues that there is an essential dichotomy in the structure of all capitalist societies between capital and labor. That dichotomy results from the fact that there is a tremendous need in the nature of the economy for flexibility. Capital is by definition more rigid than labor and, therefore, labor must be relied upon to provide the flexibility needed by the economy. Moreover, the duality between capital and labor inevitably creates distinctions among markets and workers so that, for example, labor in the primary market is generally supplied by natives, while migrants are located in the secondary market; further, those workers in capital intensive industries have more stable employment than those in labor intensive areas. Also, labor periodically resists its role as the flexible factor of production, and large groups of the labor force achieve, through struggle, something resembling the job security or preferred position which capital has in the primitive structure of the economy. Those periods are usually major periods of labor unrest. Under such circumstances, the economy becomes very rigid and it is forced to attempt to find new sources of flexibility. It appears that one of the major sources of this flexibility is found in migrant labor.

So, under this view of the process, there is an economic function for migrants in the secondary labor market which is central to the operation of a capitalist (and possibly any industrial) economic system. While it may be possible to reduce, curtail, or refine the role of the jobs migrants fill in the economy, it is probably not possible to eliminate them. To the extent that migrants are performing these jobs, and given the essential role they play in the economy, the only alternative is to attempt to find substitutes for migrant workers.

NOTE

1. See U.S. Department of Justice, Immigration and Naturalization Service, *Annual Report: Immigration and Naturalization Service* (Washington D.C.: 1960-1975, inclusive) and David S. North and Marion F. Houstoun, *The Characteristics and Role of Illegal Aliens in the U.S. Labor Market: An Exploratory Study* (Washington, D.C.: Linton & Co., Inc., 1976).

TOWARDS A THEORY OF INTERNATIONAL MIGRATION: THE NEW DIVISION OF LABOR

Elizabeth McLean Petras

INTERNATIONAL MIGRATION WITHIN A WORLD ECONOMIC SYSTEM

Without the availability of a surplus laboring population, the process of accumulation which presupposes the expansion of production cannot proceed.[1] During periods of rapid capital accumulation, when the demand for labor power is great, three sources of labor reserves[2] are traditionally considered. One is the floating reserve, which is repelled and attracted through cyclical and technological unemployment and employment patterns. The second source concerns the latent reserve generated by the setting loose of agricultural workers displaced by the introduction of large scale machinery into commercial production, and therefore reduced to earning wages at an unlivable minimum. And, the final source comes from the stagnant reserve composed of the ever-present group of irregularly employed working poor.

The accessibility of this surplus is structurally necessary for the expansion of capital, just as it is structurally produced by the contraction of the same accumulation process.[3] At certain conjunctures these traditional sources of labor *appear* to no longer exist. But the accumulation of capital cannot ultimately have its drive restricted by spatial barriers. Therefore, when local developments such as the momentary depletion of an adequate labor source within geographic and national boundaries appear to have halted the growth and survival of capitalism, capital moves, through the process of trial and error, toward other means of satisfying its labor energy. Accumulation thus continues its process by turning to a source of labor outside the traditional endogenous surplus population.

International migration is governed by much the same group of conditions which set in motion internal migration, especially the rural to urban movements associated with the process of urbanization. Within the framework of a modern world economy, bound together into one world capitalist system, the driving tendency towards capital accumulation is realized internationally as a single division of labor existing within a multiplicity of polities and cultures.[4] Within a late stage of capitalist development, surplus or reserve labor is drawn across national barriers toward the most flourishing and healthy centers of accumulation. Cross-national labor flows are at times hindered and at times abetted by policies and economic cycles within the various nation states involved. The general pattern, however, is based on the attraction of free labor from those nations located in the peripheral and semiperipheral areas of production, to the core, or metropolitan centers.

Structurally, the relationship between the core and peripheral regions, and the countries which they encompass, is defined by uneven development. Development disparities exist between the economic sectors, and within the structure of production of specific economic sectors as well. Uneven development is born of the natural drive of capital toward concentration and centralization, and is nurtured by intercapitalist competition and political relationships between the core, or advanced capitalist countries, and the periphery and semiperiphery, or less advanced, although not necessarily dependent, capitalist countries. Viewing the separate nations as regional aggregates, some regions appear as major importers of labor, while others are major labor exporters. Through the exchange of population, as well as in a variety of other relations, the periphery, the semiperiphery, and the core regions are locked together in much the same manner as are labor and capital. Although they are at opposite poles, the status of each is determined by the status of the other: they are linked through the bond of combined and uneven development.[5] Thus linked, the expansion of the whole proceeds on the basis of disharmonious rates of growth among (and within) the regional aggregates. Major migration patterns tend to correspond to the global relations among regional aggregates, while more subtle shifts in population occur in response to cyclical economic rhythms within individual countries.

Orthodox economists and demographers focus on the homogenizing and harmonizing effects of immigration, but do not test their theories within a larger ongoing historical and international trend toward the concentration and centralization of capital. Consequently, they commonly fail to account for the social and economic disadvantages incurred by the labor dispatching countries which often deepen the already unequal relations between the poles. Additional insight is lost into the broader relations involved when population movements are classified only by occupations (for example, farm workers, and brain drain of trained technicians and professionals), instead of also locating them within the subsuming category of "labor," be it skilled, technically trained, or unskilled.

Historically, the internationalization of production took the form of moving capital out of the advanced capitalist countries into the labor-rich colonies or dependencies where it was invested in extraction of raw materials or production of goods. Transportation costs of moving raw materials or durables to market locations were offset by the utilization of inexpensive, unorganized labor. So far as the spatial relocation of labor is concerned, this arrangement involves only the small number of managers, technicians, supervisors, and bureaucrats who accompany capital and technology to the "poor country" in order to supervise production there. Where the technical complexities of production are not prohibitive, there remain two other disadvantages. First, transportation costs of moving the product to the market location where surplus value can be realized through consumption may be prohibitive.[6] Second, political struggles inevitably emerge as these populations begin to resist the exploitation of their labor and raw materials. Thus, by *importing labor* to the location of capital and capital plant, capitalists in the core not only cut circulation costs, but also make a spatial adaptation which reduces the political and social costs of production. In this sense, the recruitment and importation of labor may be seen as a new variant of colonialism or imperialism.

THE ROLE OF FOREIGN LABOR IN THE CAPITAL ACCUMULATION PROCESS

Since the phenomenon we are considering is the large-scale shift of labor toward capital growth poles, it follows that gains and advantages are anticipated by those who move. Given higher wage and living standards in the regions to which they move, some relative betterment may be realized. Yet, to concentrate on potential relative advantages to the immigrant or their countries of origin is usually to ignore the disadvantages incurred by both. In addition, it is often to gloss over the special advantages to capital in the receiving countries which are realized from the employment of foreign workers. Generally, this theory concerns itself with a classical theory of economic evolution involving gradual and relative changes in wages, working conditions, and economic development for underlying and governing economic laws by which the social organization and social relations of production, and the structural relations between the core and the periphery—all of which also lead to the process of immigration—are maintained.[7] For this reason, I wish to direct this discussion away from an examination of the differential advantages of immigration experienced by those who immigrate, and focus instead on the impact on the political, economic, and class structure in both labor receiving and labor dispatching countries, and on the specific influences on capital accumulation in the core.

Within the core states, the use of an imported labor force offers many advantages. These benefits can be identified regarding several aspects of the accumulation process.

USE OF IMPORTED LABOR IN CORE NATIONS: ADVANTAGES

The rate of exploitation, or alternatively, the rate of surplus value, refers to the amount of profit received by an employer from the products of a worker's labor over and above the actual wages and benefits which the employer must pay that worker. It is determined by three factors: (1) the length of the working day; (2) the real wages paid for the performance of a specific task; and (3) the productiveness of the worker. The amount of profits an employer can derive from the labor of an individual worker can be increased if the rate of exploitation can be intensified. In simple terms, this may involve extension of the working day, a lowering of the real wage, the increase of productivity of labor through speedups or introduction of technology and automation, or some combination of these three factors. Additional profits may be produced by lowering the amount of constant capital invested in the methods and machinery of production, as in the case of labor intensive rather than capital intensive production. Intensification of exploitation is particularly critical in the production areas of (1) the less efficient, less productive competitive sector; (2) sectors in the process of moving *toward* economies of scale and dominance in the monopoly sector; and (3) some locations at the bottom of the job hierarchy within the monopoly sector during periods of *especially rapid* expansion.

To the extent that cross-national reserves of labor have been concentrated in those sectors of production which are lowest paying, least skilled, irregular, and less desirable jobs, but which are nevertheless *essential* to the continued functioning of the economic system, capital has been able to extract a higher rate of surplus value from these workers. Newly arrived waves of immigrants and migrant workers, temporary and permanent, clandestine or legal, often form the most exploited, least privileged stratum of the working class. Construction, public works and services, hotel and restaurant industries, agriculture, and industries in the least rationalized or competitive sector of production have traditionally been open to immigrants.

Immigrant workers in labor intensive and inefficient sectors of production have permitted production to expand without investment of profits in mechanization and automation of capital plant. This is critical in production areas not easily rationalized or where the costs of better organized, technical methods are prohibitive. This is especially true in construction, hotel, and restaurant industries or services, in which economies of scale are difficult to organize because of the necessarily small units of production.

Also, foreign workers have frequently been important in the early stages of the capital accumula-

tion process, or in individual areas of production which are dominated by small, less efficient firms which may be undergoing a process of rationalization. Lacking political rights, and fleeing from poverty and unemployment, their vulnerability renders them more docile and, therefore, dependable at a time when capital is attempting to increase control over all aspects of production and marketing. Large-scale dependence of U.S. capital on immigrant workers from the midnineteenth to the midtwentieth centuries is a case without parallel. Important structural changes in which production moved from the sphere of individual enterprises to production controlled by a large-scale corporate sector marked this period. Without the mass of low paid foreign workers recruited from the surplus populations of Europe where they had been displaced or unabsorbed as productive labor, the emergence of monopoly capitalism in the United States could not have proceeded at the rate it did. Indeed, it is quite likely that this stage might never have been completed at all.

The period of rapid capital accumulation following World War II in Western Europe shows striking similarities with this previous situation, the main difference being in the stages of the development of capitalism represented. The European case involves an advanced stage of capitalist development, while the U.S. case represents the period of monopoly emergence. Large intra-European migrations are not new to that continent, but they take on special dimensions during the post-War period, in part because of their massiveness, but more importantly because of (1) the particular role they play in facilitating the rapid capital growth of Western European capital during this period, and (2) because of the particular core-periphery relations within which this labor flow occurs.[8]

Stimulated by large amounts of international public capital plus substantial investment of private capital, both primarily from the United States, the Western European region underwent a remarkable development surge between 1945 and 1952.[9] At the same time, the decimation of the labor force because of the war was exacerbated by continuing low birth rates. By the 1960s, the capital accumulation process had become so rapid as to necessitate an expanded labor force to maintain its pace. West

Germany provides one example. Between 1953 and 1961, the volume of industrial production rose by one-third, almost entirely from immigration. By 1972, an intricate recruitment system in the Mediterranean area provided for about two-fifths of Germany's annual inflow of foreigners, and among all those emigrating from the Mediterranean region, Germany absorbed between 50 percent and 90 percent.[10]

The majority of these foreign workers absorbed the slack in the bottom ranks of the labor market. At the same time, however, production was undergoing rapid technological alterations. These same immigrant workers in the less efficient competitive sector of industry contributed directly to the increasing rationalization and domination of the monopoly sector. Firstly, the high rate of surplus value extracted from foreign workers provided capital necessary for the scientific and technological reorganization toward which many industries were moving. Ironically, the very automation and technology which permits a rise in productivity also produces a counter force which decreases the demand for active labor. Thus, the capital produced by labor, which permits increasing rationalization of production, at the same time tends to create unemployment and redundancy among the very labor which produced it. Secondly, the influx of a cross-national reserve army of unemployed during a period of rapid economic growth helps prevent the uncontrolled rise of domestic workers' wages. Willing to work for lower pay at longer hours and under worse conditions, immigrants provide a competitive element in the labor market which prevents indigenous workers from continuing to accelerate their pay and benefit demands. At the same time, as they perform jobs which free domestic workers for some degree of mobility, the presence of foreign workers also serves as a check on the wages and working conditions of that mobility.

SOCIAL COSTS OF PRODUCTION AND LABOR FORCE REPRODUCTION

Social costs of production refer to those individual and collective expenditures and investments in the education, health, housing, and general welfare necessary for the production, maintenance, and reproduction of a work force. Social costs can be greatly reduced through the use of immigrant labor. To begin with, since foreign workers are predominantly young males (frequently single) having recently reached the age of entering the labor market, the costs of rearing and educating this potential worker have been already absorbed by his country of origin. In addition to providing the receiving countries with the potential source of surplus value to be realized from the labor of an immigrant worker, the peripheral countries are also providing social capital stored up in the form of each person who leaves.

Magnifying the social costs borne by the labor exporting regions is the selective nature of migration, which constitutes a skill drain as well as a capital drain. Those who leave are typically among the more vigorous and ambitious young workers. For example, in the case of Turkish emigrants, it is those with the greater technical training and literacy levels who have moved to West Germany.[12] One Turkish survey (1963) found that 74 percent of the emigrants had backgrounds in industry while, contrary to the popular image, only 11 percent had come directly from agricultural production.

General good health among those who emigrate adds to further selectivity. Careful medical screening required by the nations in the core network insures that those who enter legally will not have serious health problems, and in some locations, they are probably more healthy as a group than comparable national workers. Ironically, however, precisely because they are forced into jobs in which the health and safety conditions are the most treacherous, immigrant workers suffer a disproportionate rate of occupation-related mental and physical ailments.

To add a further twist to the original selective labor talent drain, plus the habit of deporting bad health and accidents, studies in Western Europe report that among those who *do* return home, the unskilled form a disproportionately large group. In addition to the savings in the social costs of producing an immigrant worker, the labor importing country also benefits from savings in the social maintenance of a foreign work force. This is illustrated by the dependency ratios and economic activity rates among immigrants, by the standards and availability of housing and schooling, and in the payment of social welfare coverage.

ACTIVITY RATES AND DEPENDENCY RATIOS

Among the unmarried males of prime work age who are predominate among immigrant groups, somewhere between two-thirds and three-quarters fall between the ages of 15 and 40, with propensity to migrate being highest among the 20 to 25 age group.[13] The result is a rise in the activity rate and a lowering of the dependency rate in the receiving country. Frequent restrictions on family immigration produces a high rate of involuntary bachelorhood among certain groups of immigrants. At the other pole, the result is often a disruption of sex ratios and marriage rates.

Although the activity rate is high among foreigners during their tenure in the metropolitan countries, this does not mean that they are unaffected by unemployment. Indeed, recent recessionary unemployment figures among immigrant workers in Western Europe indicate that they are apt to be hit as a group even harder than domestic workers. Upon being unemployed any length of time, most return to their country of origin, either voluntarily, or because they no longer possess the work status which permits them to remain legally. Likewise, during the successive economic recessions in the United States from 1884 through 1914, immigration statistics indicate substantial waves of return migration as the depression-related unemployment was deported back to the countries of origin.[14]

The counterpart of this high activity rate is to be found among the labor exporting countries where the elderly, the (potential) wives and children of migrants, and the unemployable who remain behind all add to the social costs created by dependency. Without attempting any calculations as to the human capital contribution of the periphery and semiperiphery to the core nations in the form of an immigrant labor force, the low dependency, high activity rates alone confirm the fact that the social costs of production are lowered to the recipient nation. The costs are borne by the dispatching states, and incorporated into the general level of poverty and misery reproduced among those who remain in the periphery.

The shameful standards of health, education, and welfare to which foreign workers are often subjected have been the topics of many compassionate accounts.[15] Immigrant workers tend to live in poorer housing, experience worse health care, and receive inferior education for their children when they are accompanied by their families. However inferior the poor living standards may be to those of native workers, the relative rise in the standard of living experienced through the act of migration offsets these poor standards. The fact that so many foreign workers report that they expect their work tenure to be only a temporary interlude until they accumulate savings with which to return home, may make their lives in bare rented rooms and bunkhouses more tolerable. On the other hand, evidence points to the fact that where these conditions are rejected as unacceptable, the absence of political rights and representation prevents migrants from availing themselves of organized political pressure for protection. When disenfranchised immigrants do organize over living conditions, action by the state is often swift and irrevocable.

Direct and indirect benefits to capital through low social costs have two aspects. First, the low investment in schooling, the cheap and inadequate housing, and the paucity of demands from workers for a higher standard, of living all combine to permit a lowering of labor force maintenance. Secondly, the low living standards, combined with the low level of consumption resulting from self-enforced savings, mean that productive foreign workers do not add much to the inflationary trend of capital expansion periods.[16]

Finally, the reduced social welfare benefits which foreign workers receive is an additional source of social cost cutting. Many foreign laborers and their families do not qualify, or are not aware that they qualify, for the common social welfare coverage available to the domestic workers of most industrialized nations. Add to this the number who are ineligible because of their illegal status within the country, the number who return precisely at such time as they might receive coverage such as unemployment or disability insurance, and the large numbers of dependents who have not accompanied workers during their employment abroad and therefore are not covered by social welfare legislation, and the savings, both relative and absolute, become substantial.

If foreign labor reserves are drawn in to fill the gaps in production during periods of capital expansion, capital is equally as eager to have them disappear during periods of capital contraction. Structurally, they play a unique role in helping maintain an equilibrium for capital during periods of economic fluctuation. Increased attempts this past year to locate and deport aliens working without legal status in New York State suggest the manner in which an excess work force is "gotten rid of" legally at a time when the economic pressures of recession contain within them potential social and political pressures as well. Conversations with certain taxi drivers in Buenos Aires or Athens allow the story to be pieced together from the other side. Usually the essential elements of the story involve a long-hoped-for move to the U.S., a period of irregular work at low pay and long hours, a final loss of job combined with the realization that no fortune was being accumulated, and a disillusioned return home.

In Western Europe today, most countries have provisions which restrict the length of stay for foreign workers to such time as they maintain legitimate employment, often with a specific employer with whom they have signed a contract. Although most foreign employees are required to pay unemployment as well as social security contributions while working, only a few ever draw their benefits. These payments are lost if a worker loses his or her job and therefore must leave the country. Retention of the legal right to deport any worker who is unemployed permits the importing state to maintain a flexible labor force which can be recruited and expelled according to the demands of the accumulation momentum. This is particularly useful in seasonal production, such as agriculture or construction, where capital can slough off the cost of unemployment and readmit workers when production resumes on a regulated basis.

Subtle advantages accrue from the fact that immigrants, concentrated in unskilled jobs which are more heavily hit by unemployment, suffer disproportionately from cyclical unemployment. Therefore, a proportionately greater part of the cost of supporting unemployment can be transferred to the periphery, where, incidentally, such costs are magnified, given the already high unemployment rates and lack of public capital available for maintenance of unemployment and welfare programs. What emerges is a contradiction between the drive for maximizing private profit in one instance, and the adequate provision for social security and welfare protection for labor, specifically immigrant labor, in another. When recession, industrial accidents, or bad health hit, the migrant often discovers he has all of the disadvantages of working in the metropolitan country and none of the advantages.

Fluctuations in the economic cycle are also expressed in the amount of inflow of workers seeking employment, as well as in the proportion of return migration. The relationship established by Jerome for prerestriction immigration to the U.S. revealed certain governing principles for which we have a variety of examples: the industrial growth period of Argentina, contemporary oil-boom Venezuela, post–World War II capital growth in Western Europe, World War II expansion of agri-business in California.[17] Essentially, Jerome demonstrated that migratory movements correspond to fluctuations in available employment stemming from contraction and expansion of the internal business cycle. A slight lag of anywhere from a few months to a full year will occur in both the accelerating and decelerating process. Specific conditions such as agricultural failure or industrial depression within the labor dispatching country do influence the lag, but conditions in the receiving country essentially dominate the rhythm and location of the migratory flow. In the main, this is because of the ability of the receiving state to formally regulate the movement of workers into its labor market. As a supplement to labor contracting and recruiting stations abroad, a variety of incentives to immigrate are offered during high demand periods. During low demand periods, the state ceases replenishment of the foreign work force by denying new admittances or reentry of workers among those who are constantly returning to their home countries, or by placing formal restrictions on specific immigration. The most outstanding example of the latter was the gradual closing of the gates to foreign immigration to the U.S. culminating in the final establishment of quotas in the 1922 Immigration Act.

It is frequently observed that, in order to see the slums of Berlin or Paris, one must travel to the outskirts of Athens or look to the impoverished villages of Andalusia. By the same token, in order to fully comprehend the magnitude of the current economic crisis of monopoly capitalism, and therefore the levels of unemployment suffered by its working classes, one must look beyond the official unemployment statistics of the core nations and turn also to the agricultural villages and urban slums of the periphery and semiperiphery. One might go so far as to argue that the great international movements of labor constitute something akin to a form of development aid given by the poor countries to the rich.[18]

THE POLITICS OF CLASS STRUGGLE: A METROPOLITAN WORKING CLASS AND ITS RESERVE ARMY FROM THE PERIPHERY

The advantages in the use of foreign labor may vary for different sectors of capital. For small capital, or the competitive sector, its need for ready cheap labor is satisfied. For big capital, or the monopoly sector, the need for a degree of planning and regulation of production may force the regularization of immigration through some minor economic and social security measures. Both sectors have common political needs, however, which grow out of the contradictions between labor and capital, that is, the withholding of political and trade union rights for immigrants, in order to thwart their capacity to participate in class struggles. A cleavage is thus created between immigrant workers and the political organizations of domestic workers, and the historic role traditionally played in democratic politics by the working class is thus effectively denied. Just as employers' governments deport industrial accidents or unemployment, they also retain the power to deport political dissidence. Any protest or overt political activity can potentially result in the loss of jobs and subsequent deportation. The absence of active political support from the trade unions leaves few alternatives between acquiescence and passivity, or semispontaneous actions aimed at securing concrete political rights. The situation is summed up succinctly by a foreign worker in a French Citroen plant, "If we open our mouths

to protest (about anything), we are threatened with being fired and thrown out of the country."[19]

It seems that no phrase ever written by Marx has been so trivialized and abused as his call for international workers of the world to unite. But it is difficult to imagine a situation in which it would be more appropriate than in the case of the metropolitan working classes and their reserve labor armies from the periphery and semiperiphery. Nonetheless, a schism remains, maintained by economist self-interest and racist and national-chauvenist ignorance, and aggravated by the fear that the foreigners might be invading to take their jobs and eat their bread.

Union policies toward immigrant workers reflect a series of contradictions. Many explanations have been offered for their ineffectuality, including xenophobia and racist attitudes among indigenous workers and their leaders, hostility toward the competitive role of foreign workers in the labor market, and the potential for strikebreaking. In addition, divisions and lack of contact are encouraged because foreign workers are isolated in cerain categories of the occupational structure (often occupations which have not been traditionally represented by strong unions), because of the transitory, seasonal work patterns to which many immigrants are bound, and because of cultural and language differences. Furthermore, the work experience of immigrants in their home countries has not typically involved contact or commitment to workers' unions and organizations. This is complicated by the sense on the part of the immigrants themselves that the union policies and struggles do not usually focus on the immediate difficulties they face as a semimarginal work force or subproletariat, and hence there is low motivation for them to subject themselves to the regulations and dues of the unions.

Finally, of equal importance, is the strategic interest of trade union bureaucrats in maintaining their relationship with capital as labor elites. This causes them to sacrifice one sector of the working class (foreign workers) in order not to disrupt that arrangement. For example, the International Ladies Garment Workers' Union has a close working relationship with employers in the industry. But, at the same time, the union does not put up any real fight over the conditions and wages under which Puerto Rican and Caribbean workers are laboring, since the organizational interests of the bureaucracy frequently take precedence over the real needs of the workers.

Performance of low paying jobs by foreigners contributes not only directly to capital's accumulation, but indirectly to the mobility within the occupational hierarchy which is thus made available to domestic workers, benefits from the employment of a foreign labor reserve. Just as labor in a sense "belongs" to capital, so do its reserve armies "belong" to a working class. However, the exploitative relationship of the first to the second is qualitatively different from the relationship of the working class to its reserve armies. In fact, by serving as a wage check, a foreign reserve periodically and ultimately becomes a disadvantage to that working class within the labor market.

One final insight into the lack of active organizing among foreign workers by trade unions involves the politics of prolabor and leftist political parties where they exist. Tactically, both unions and the parties which represent them concentrate their energies on certain crucial points of production in their struggles with bourgeoisie over power. Production in key areas relies on a large organized urban proletariat. The unity of this proletariat in militant strike actions is a vital source of power for both unions and political parties, especially those of the left. When machines halt in major industries, the accumulation process is impeded not only in that industry, but in other productive facilities and areas of the economy as well.

In contrast, since they control no stable and vital means of production, the combined power at the point of production of those at the bottom ranks of labor—the service workers, the small groups of workers employed in backward, nonunionized shops, the irregularly and seasonally employed—is greatly diminished in comparison to that of the organized industrial worker. Politically, their potential is weak in matters relating to struggles over control of the means of production, and thus they are less likely to be counted by labor unions and labor parties, However, voting allegiance of these marginal workers can be extremely significant to labor and left parties, especially when this sector is numerically large. But foreigners carry no weight in parliamentary or electoral challenges because they have no voting rights. Thus, the degree to which left and labor parties have failed to use their base within the trade unions to develop policies aimed at the specific problems of immigrant workers may be a function of the fact that they are not viewed as "important," neither for their strength over production related struggles, nor for the electoral support they embody.

A seemingly logical reaction from the trade unions and the parties oriented toward the working class would be an immediate demand for full political rights for all workers, foreign and domestic. The relative absence of such demands seems to return us to the question of whether the unions are operating essentially to protect one section of the working class which represents a privileged stratum. So long as foreign workers can be deported or kept out during contractions of the business cycle, they are reduced as a potential threat not only to capital, but to the indigenous working class as well. The highly competitive character of a reserve army is always intensified during economic downswings. But this role diminishes when the reserve army contains large numbers of foreign workers who can simply be removed from the labor market. This diminishes the imperative for incorporating reserve labor into workers' organizations, an imperative which is logically heightened during economic crises.

One political dimension which becomes operative in the periphery as a result of large outmigration should be considered. For those countries with their high birth and unemployment rates, and their low standards of living and sharp class divisions, migration may siphon off latent social disturbances and rebellions which are always a potential possibility under the oppressive conditions of underdevelopment. A safety valve is opened by outmigration which draws off precisely those active young males who are just at the point of seeing their life's aspirations blocked, and who as a result could provide that energetic mass which has traditionally been in revolt against backward and repressive regimes. The draining off of this vital sector from the periphery, and the corresponding reduction in unemployment and frustration, may contribute to the control maintained by many reactionary, repressive, and often fascist governments. The existence of such regimes is in the interests of monopoly capital in the advanced capitalist states, since it helps maintain that precarious fulcrum on which the world capitalist system balances.

PERIPHERY-CORE MIGRATIONS: SOME PRECONDITIONS

The flow of labor is primarily at the expense of the impoverishment of the working class, and coincides with some combination of certain general preconditions. Within the core nations, several preconditions for labor importation appear as mirror images of the preconditions for labor export from the periphery and semiperiphery. Both sets of preconditions constitute aspects of the structure of dependency and uneven development into which these areas are interlocked.

Preconditions for labor export

(1) high displacement or unemployment among the rural working class either because of stagnation of the agricultural sector, or because of a shift in the organization of production from labor intensive to capital intensive, based on the introduction of large-scale machine technology;

(2) lack of capital investment in a viable industrial center which would generate the creation of badly needed jobs;

(3) low rate of economic growth as an ongoing condition;

(4) persistence of high birth rates combined with low rates of economic growth;

(5) generally low standards of living of the mass of the population compounded by a low level of essential welfare and social service provisions guaranteed by the state;

(6) political regimes ranging from conservative to extreme right to military dictatorships;

(7) economic dependence upon the metropole;

(8) "misdevelopment" or no development strategies.

Preconditions for labor import

(1) private and public policies designed to recruit and regulate the movement and location of migratory flows;

(2) high rate of economic growth and capital accumulation;

(3) highly rationalized agricultural production, which eliminated this sector as a source for surplus labor;

(4) high employment rates plus low demographic increases, based on low birth rates and/or population decimation such as that which occurs during massive wars;

(5) production based upon, or moving toward, advanced technology;

(6) control of scientific and technological knowledge and techniques by the core states.

Presence or absence of some combination of these preconditions should be studied within the larger context of power and inequality within a modern world system. To the degree that migration patterns exhibit a certain kind of hierarchy in which labor from the poorest nations tends to move on to work in the less poor nations, and emigrants from that region migrate to the wealthier and wealthiest nations, international migration takes on the characteristics of an international division of labor which is reproduced by inter-regional and international inequalities.

Cross-national labor movements cannot be predicted on a linear supply and demand basis without first considering business cycles and other fluctuations in the rates of capital accumulation within a world economy. Supply and demand interpretations assume a harmonious relationship between the movement of labor and the location of production. Logically and historically, this relation is one of contradictions, not of harmony. It is integral to the polarization of development at the international level between the centers of capital growth and the regions where large amounts of "human capital" remain unintegrated into production relations.

Traditional studies of international migration have been organized about the identification of specific push or pull factors operating within the supply and demands pressures of a free market. The role assigned the migrant, or groups of migrants, is that of a rational actor, making his decision to move in accordance with these pressures and constraints as a strategy to better his group or individual status. Further studies are apt to concentrate on the consequences and behavior of the immigrant within his or her target location. While these studies do much to illuminate and expose the conditions of life and work to which the immigrant laborers must adapt, they shed less light on why these conditions and these push-pull factors repeat themselves historically again and again. A number of interesting problems arise out of aspects of immigration, which may extend an understanding of the structural features of the internationalization of labor:

(1) an examination of the role of national state mechanisms which facilitate or regulate the entrance of foreign labor, and the availability and manner in which such controls are utilized to the advantage or disadvantage of both the labor importing and the labor exporting nations;

(2) the degree to which state capitalist planning is facilitated by the exercising of such regulatory controls within the labor importing nations;

(3) the manner in which national trade unions are implicated in the low job status to which immigrants within the various occupational categories tend to be confined;

(4) study of the theory that unions perpetuate the political disenfranchisement of immigrant workers through exclusionary policies, and that union policies in labor importing nations are generally economist in nature, and must necessarily lend themselves to dividing rather than uniting foreign and indigenous workers;

(5) an examination of the conflicts between an indigenous working class and immigrant workers in terms of competition between an active labor army and an (international) reserve labor army (which represents the potential for depressing wages and working conditions), and the extent to which discrimination and racial hostility against foreign workers are better understood in this context rather than in the context of race relations;

(6) determination of the predominant class composition of international migration, and of whether the brain drain of trained professionals and skilled technicians can be understood

within the same set of laws which apply to wage labor migration;

(7) study of the degree to which the differential impact of economic crisis is intensified between the core and the peripheral nations as a result of emigration/immigration relations;

(8) a careful quantitative and sectoral analysis of the home flow of emigrants' remittances as a component of a viable development strategy;

(9) the primary and secondary demographic consequences of emigration as a deterent to the development process;

(10) identification of the specific social costs incurred in the production, maintenance, and reproduction of immigrant labor;

(11) the number of instances where tourist economies, especially within the semiperipheral nations, actually involve a population exchange based on the structural relations in which a portion of surplus labor moves to the location of capital growth, at the same time as national populations from these centers travel to the underdeveloped countries to enjoy the pleasures of tourism made attractive by the availability of a large service sector, the low prices (relative to the metropolitan countries), the channeling of investment into the hotel and restaurant sector rather than manufacturing, and the more leisurely pace and unspoiled natural beauty of a nonindustrialized, nonurbanized society;

(12) identification of hierarchical patterns among labor movements which coincide with hierarchical patterns of power and inequality among nations;

(13) a search for historical evidence which supports or disproves the notion that "out-migration is a substitute for revolution," and that it therefore serves to support or weaken the political and economic relations among nations within a world economic system.

NOTES

1. Karl Marx, *Capital*, Vol. 1 (New York: International Publishers, 1967), p.632.
2. Ibid., p.635.
3. On this component of capital accumulation, see Paul Sweezy, *The Theory of Capitalist Development* (New York: Monthly Review Press, 1968), pp.83–94.

4. For an elaboration of this theoretical framework, see I. Wallerstein, "The Rise and Future Demise of the World Capitalist System: Concepts for Comparative Analysis," *Comparative Studies in Society and History*, 16, No.4 (1974).

5. Ernest Mandel, "The Laws of Uneven Development," *New Left Review*, No.59 (December 1969), p.22.

6. See David Harvey, "The Geography of Capitalist Accumulation: A Reconstruction of the Marxian Theory," *Antipode*, 7, No.2 (September 1975) for a thorough discussion of the costs of circulation.

7. Sweezy, op. cit., ch. VI., P.1.

8. For example, by the mid–1880s, the number of Irish immigrants in Britain was pushing three-quarters of a million. E. P. Thompson, *The Making of the English Working Class*, ch. IX (New York: Random House, 1963), and J. A. Jackson, *The Irish in Britain* (London: Routledge and Kegan Paul, 1963). For useful discussion of migrants and the European labor market, see Manuel Castells, "Immigrant Workers and Class Struggles in Advance Capitalism," *Politics and Society*, 5, No.1 (1975); Stephen Castles and Godula Kosack, *Immigrant Workers and Class Structure in Western Europe* (London: Oxford University Press, 1973); John Berger, *A Seventh Man: Migrant Workers in Europe*, (New York: The Viking Press, 1975); and Marios Nikolinkos, "Notes Toward a General Theory of Migration in Late Capitalism," *Race and Class*, XVLL, No.1 (1975).

9. The net inflow of some $22,800 million in public capital from the U.S. alone to Western Europe during the ten years following the war created a tremendous expansion in productive capacity. Brinley Thomas, *International Migration and Economic Development* (UNESCO, 1961), pp.35–38.

10. In 1961, Italians alone comprised over 40 percent of the foreign work force; by 1972, both Yugoslavs and Turks outnumbered Italians. W. R. Böhning, *The Migration of Workers in the United Kingdom and the European Community* (London: Oxford University Press, 1972).

11. Suzanne Paine, *Exporting Workers: The Turkish Case* (Cambridge, England: Cambridge University Press, 1974); and Castells, op. cit., p.47.

12. Paine, op. cit.

13. Brinley Thomas, "International Migration," in Hauser and O. D. Duncan, eds., *The Study of Population* (Chicago: University of Chicago Press, 1959), p.524.

14. See, for example, the accounts in Gerald Rosenblum, *Immigrant Workers* (New York: Basic Books, 1973), and the Immigration Commission, *Abstract of Statistical Review of Immigration to the U.S., 1820–1911* (Washington, D.C. U.S. Government Printing Office, 1911), plus the annual *Report of the Commissioner General of Immigration* published from 1900 to 1930.

15. One of the most graphic and poignant recent accounts is that of John Berger, *A Seventh Man*, which is in the best of the reform tradition established by Jacob Riis in his classic, *How the Other Half Lives*.

16. Castells, op. cit., p.56. There is by no means uniform agreement on the contribution of immigration to deflationary trends, however. See, for example, the arguments with regard to contemporary Europe between Böhning (summarized in Paine, op. cit.), C. P. Kindleberger, *Europe's Postwar Growth and the Role of Labour Supply* (Oxford University Press, 1967); and Castles and Kosack, op. cit., vs. the opposing views that immigration does not tend to have a deflationary impact, which is proposed by E. J. Mishan and L. Needleman writing on Britain, for example, their article, "Immigration: Some Economic Effects," *Lloyds Bank Review*, No.81 (July 1966).

17. Harry Jerome, *Migration and Business Cycles*, (New York: National Bureau of Economic Research, 1973). This relation seems to hold true not only for economic short cycles which Jerome analyzed, but for the long cycles as well. On the latter, see B. Thomas, *Migration and Urban Development: A Reappraisal of British and American Long Cycles* (London: Metheun and Co., 1972).

18. See Castles and Kosack, op. cit., for further discussion of this concept.

19. Schofield Caryell, "New Grapes of Wrath," *Ramparts*, 12, No.8 (March 1974), p.17.

AFTERWORD

WHERE DO WE GO FROM HERE?
"THE NEW IMMIGRATION" AND IMPLICATIONS FOR RESEARCH

Stephen R. Couch

While the recent rise in interest in contemporary immigration has attracted scholars and researchers from all disciplines of social science and from many differing perspectives, there remains the fact that many questions are yet to be answered at all levels of investigation. The papers which comprise this volume point to some of the major implications which flow from ongoing immigration research. The present article has been limited to focusing upon certain specific research areas. By no means is it intended to be, nor should it be viewed as, a "shopping list" of research topics. There are many of those to be found within the papers themselves, and many more which a researcher with a reasonable amount of imagination could devise. The thrust here is on what seem to be the major foci around which research projects can most fruitfully be built. I will begin by discussing the three interrelated levels at which research might proceed: macro, midrange, and micro. This is followed by a consideration of various methodological approaches and their usefulness.[1]

MACROLEVEL RESEARCH

Three papers point out an important shift in emphasis in recent research on immigration. In his paper on immigration theory, Paul Meadows concludes that there is an increasing trend toward viewing immigration in a worldwide context. Eva Sandis discusses the emergence of a new group of scholars who emphasize the role of structural conditions of international inequality on the volume and characteristics of immigration. And the paper by Elizabeth Petras provides an example of these trends by conceiving immigration as one element within a modern world capitalist system. While international economic inequality has long been seen as a critical "push-pull" factor which motivates a person to migrate, recent work such as that of Petras represents a much more advanced attempt to place immigration within the context of an international political economy. Many of the papers show the influence of this change in emphasis in varying degrees (for example, Bustamante, Maldonado-Denis, Pido, Campos, Cue and Bach, Nieves-Falcón). While not yet possessing a developed comprehensive theory or, especially, methodology, this emergent perspective is extremely interesting, challenging, and holds great promise to help us further understand immigration at all levels of analysis.

This new approach is particularly important in two ways. First, it emphasizes the fact that we live in a world characterized by inequality at an international level. This is not merely in terms of some countries being richer than others. The real insight is the knowledge that these countries are not isolated but are linked (often intimately) with other countries in a system of dominance/dependency relations. "Underdevelopment" is not caused simply by the characteristics of a country, but also by the relations and linkages of that country with others in a world system structurally characterized by the exploitation of some classes and countries by others. Similarly, "development" has proceeded because of the ability of some classes and countries to exploit others within the structure of a world system. Immigration has been and still remains a part of this process. To understand immigration fully, and to understand the past, present, and future development of the world system, it is critical to further elucidate upon the role of immigration within this world structure.

This brings up a second and related point. At the macrolevel, it is important to see immigration not only as the movement of people from one country to another, but as part of a worldwide exchange of people who are both caught up in and at the same time producing an international division of labor.

Moreover, viewing international migration as simply ''people exchange'' is still insufficient. Migration must also be seen in relation to international exchanges of capital and commodities, that is, as part of international factors of production and consumption which ultimately produce, maintain, and change the structure of the world capitalist system. At this level, research should focus on discovering the relationships between and among these various factors, their correlative effects upon one another, and the way in which various configurations of them influence the system as a whole.

To do this, scholars must elaborate upon and refine the theoretical framework which is being developed. Before this can be done in detail, much more attention must be given to the development of a methodology which not only allows for broad description of these processes but which can be used in empirical verification.[2] The theoretical perspective is new and the task enormous, but the time has come to try. Empirical indicators and methodological techniques must be developed which would allow us to move beyond broad outlines to a more detailed understanding of this system and its interrelations.

In line with this reorientation of research at the macrolevel, two additional questions strike me as particularly interesting. One is the question of the usefulness of separating the study of ''international'' migration from that of ''internal'' migration. To the extent that there are inequalities between nations as well as between classes, and to the extent that national policies influence the international movement of peoples, this analytical separation is important. Yet, it is also important to ask what processes internal and international migrations have in common. To what extent are internal migrations also a part of a worldwide system of structural relations which cut across national boundaries? And in terms of migration, what do national boundaries and policies mean? The whole issue of the role of the state in international migration needs to be explored in depth at this level of analysis.

Finally, research is needed on the linkages between migration, economics, social structure, and culture. In both the new emergent theories and the more traditional ones, it is often argued that the causes of international migration are primarily economic. For example, in terms of a ''world systems'' approach, migration is seen to occur in response to the needs of a world economic system. Assuming for the moment the correctness of the argument that economics is a determinant of migration ''in the last analysis,'' one must still be very careful not to fall into a mechanistic view of migration, a view which sees the world as a large, self-regulating system of socioeconomic interactions. Even at a macrolevel, we must not lose sight of the fact that history is made by real-life people operating within social structures, and not by the machinations of an animate, omnipotent ''system.'' Further, we should investigate the conditions under which political and/or ideological considerations override economic ones, and with what consequences. To cite but one example, what has been the role of racism in limiting or encouraging migrations? A study on this and other similar subjects would do much to fill the lacunae which now exist in theories of migration at the macrolevel.

RESEARCH AT THE MIDDLE RANGE LEVEL

Historically, most research at this level of analysis has dealt with the adaptability or assimilation to the host society of specific immigrant groups. A number of papers presented in this volume focus on this question (for example, Nair, Bonacich, et. al., Sung, Chaney, Bonnett, Saran, Hurh et. al., AmaraSingham, Kolack, Tsai, Pido). Indeed, some of these studies go beyond the specific subject matter of immigrant adaptability and attempt to link this variable with macrolevel developments and/or compare the adaptations of various immigrant groups (Cue and Bach, DeVos). Such studies are particularly enlightening in that they move beyond considering immigrant adaptation out of the sociohistorical context in which it evolves. Many more need to be done with these linkages in mind.

Related to the notion of linking adaptability to macrolevel forces are the factors of ethnicity and social class. To what extent do these variables influence immigrant adaptability, and how do they interrelate with each other? These questions were at least implicit in many of the conference papers (for example, Bonacich, et. al., Zenner). While much work has been done on the subject, the nature of the relations between class and ethnicity has yet to be worked out adequately. I strongly suggest studies be undertaken which attempt to spell out these relations, and their causally interactive relation with immigration. Such research is not only essential to the ultimate construction of more adequate theories of immigrant adaptability, but it is also critical for an understanding of class and ethnic group relations as well. Moreover, studies of class, ethnicity, and immigration could provide the key link to research at the macrolevel of analysis.

As in the case of Mexican- and Cuban-Americans, while understanding the adaptation of all immigrant groups cannot be complete without analysis of the large-scale sociohistorical forces which have impacted upon those groups and influenced their migration (Cue and Bach), one must also analyze the history and conditions of specific immigrant groups in order to give full substance and refinement to macrolevel generalizations. Work at one level complements work at the other, with class development and ethnicity providing the key linking concepts.[3]

Keeping the above remarks in mind, a number of areas stand out as particularly important and in need of further research. First, studies on the labor market impact and experience of immigrants should be continued. A number of such studies have been carried out, most having been centered on fairly narrow areas and pursued as policy research, often at the instigation of policy makers or implementers. Problems of data and methodology are great, and yet something has been learned about the subject from this type of research. At the same time, attempts should be made to move beyond what narrowly can be defined as "policy research" (which tends to be basically descriptive and carried out with a minimum of social scientific theory), and broaden labor market research so that it is informed by and impacts on theory (for example, Piore). This is surely desirable from the point of view of social scientists. It would also be of long-run value to policy makers, for, if policy is to be informed and effective, it must be based on an understanding of human behavior, not only on knowing what is going on, but why.

Related to labor market research is the need to study more fully the migration of professionals, particularly from less to more developed countries (Glaser, Pido, Jones-Hendrickson, Carey; and Goodman). The causes and consequences of this phenomenon need to be explored more fully, not only from the point of view of labor market impact, but also for its effects on development. Furthermore, the migration of professionals to and from developed countries has implications for work at the macrolevel as well. Strong arguments have been advanced that, notwithstanding such factors as ethnicity, an international working class has been produced as a result of the development of capitalism. To what extent does the migration of professionals constitute the development of an international elite? And with what implications for future class development (Pido)?

There is one further area where middle range research would be especially fruitful. This is the area of relating economic and structural factors to the culture and consciousness of immigrant groups. Under what structural conditions is the sense of ethnic group consciousness strong or weak, and with what consequences? Under what conditions are immigrant cultural traits assimilated and/or lost, or under what conditions do they remain distinct, and with what consequences? A number of papers in this volume approach these questions at least indirectly, and generally on a case study basis (Maldonado-Denis, AmaraSingham, Monteiro, Nieves-Falcón, DeVos, Bonacich, et. al.). Again, I would suggest that comparative work is especially important here, and also that explicit attempts should be made to develop general working hypotheses about the interrelations between structure and culture. Without implying that work in this area is not theoretically informed, I contend that the theories used tend not to spell out hypotheses on this particular relationship. At the same time, the relationship between structure and culture is still regarded generally as one of the major theoretical distinctions in social scientific work, and yet, one the nature of which is particularly elusive. What better place is there to explore this relationship than at the point of contact of both established and new cultures and structures, where the alterations and conflicts tend to be intense and the changes can be well-documented?

SOCIAL PSYCHOLOGICAL AND INDIVIDUAL LEVEL RESEARCH

Finally, at the microlevel, how do the factors involved in migration affect the individual? Papers in this volume represent a number of approaches to this question. Some emphasize the individual's problems of adjustment to a new environment (for example, AmaraSingham); others call for an orientation which emphasizes research on the individual experience or viewpoint of the immigrant (Ramos); and some seek to explicate linkages between psychology and other levels of analysis (DeVos).

While further work needs to be done in all these areas, the most pressing area is again that of discovering linkages between the individual and the other analytic levels. Such work is needed in order to answer adequately some of the more important questions brought out at the conference with reference to migration and the individual, such as the conditions under which various forms of individual coping responses occur; under what conditions individuals decide to migrate, remain or return home; under what conditions migrants wish to assimilate or remain distinctive; and under what conditions happiness and mental health are fostered. In addition to these questions, there seems to be an overarching one, recognized by some of the conference participants: To what extent are individual immigrants "passive victims" or "active creators?" Put another way, under what conditions are immigrants able to gain a fairly high measure of control over their lives? By using this as a guiding question, research could be done which would not only explicate psychological and linkage factors involved in immigrant decisions and action, but also would be of help to those who wish to aid immigrant adjustment through policy formation or social service.

In the above discussion, much emphasis has been placed on exploring linkages between various levels of analysis. It might be argued that such work runs the risk of seeing compatibility where it may not exist; that the differences in levels represent real differences in theoretical approaches which cannot be reconciled. Of course it should be realized that there are real and sometimes fundamental differences presented by the theoretical approaches of the papers in this volume. Nevertheless, I think that the various levels of analysis are not incompatible in themselves, and that research at more than one level simultaneously is necessary if order to avoid an overly narrow and unbalanced view of immigration. On the one hand, for instance, are studies which emphasize the motives of immigrants for moving, staying, and/or returning. On the other is work emphasizing structural and demographic factors. An overemphasis on the first type results in the ignoring of critical questions of international, national, and local stratification, of economics, and of social structure. An overemphasis on the second can lead to an overdeterministic view of the immigration process. Neither result needs to occur if the linkages between social, psychological, and structural forces are explored. Certain differences which now appear to be theoretically fundamental may instead turn out to be differences only in levels of analysis and vocabulary. At the same time, research which explicitly crosses these boundaries would demarcate those differences which *are* fundamental.

METHODOLOGICAL THRUSTS

Shifting to a consideration of research strategies employed by the conference participants, they ran the gamut from quantitative to qualitative. As would be expected, most quantitative studies were in the areas of demography and economics (for example, Warren and Jones-Hendrickson). The qualitative studies were wide-ranging, including anthropological studies, work on ideology, and a call for increased emphasis on the subjective meaning of immigration to the immigrants themselves (Hendricks, Maldonado-Denis, Ramos).

From a methodological view, a number of recommendations can be made. First, there is a need for closer systematic, multilevel analyses. As with the question of multilevel theoretical studies, there is no reason why multiple methodological strategies cannot be used to study immigration and immigrants. Perhaps because of the tendency for scholars to be oriented toward one kind of methodological approach, the systematic use of multiple methodologies is seldom carried out. Even in cases where multiple methodologies are used, improvements usually can be made. In some cases, these improvements would involve further integration of the various methodologies, while in others it seems that, with some extra effort spent on rigorous use of each chosen methodological strategy, the conclusions reached could be less preliminary, more open to generalization, and more refined in detail. Rigorous use of multiple methodologies could not help but greatly aid in the verification of theoretical hypotheses in most areas of the study of immigration and immigrants.

Secondly, there should be additional historical studies of international, national, and local migration. Only when immigration is viewed historically can we begin to understand it as a continuing process, a continuation based on historically produced and changing economic, social, and cultural forces. Such studies act as necessary correctives to our tendency to view our contemporary situation as totally unique rather than as having differences, but also important similarities, with past migrations and circumstances. With regards to immigration as a phenomenon, as a research topic, and as a public issue, we must constantly guard against myopia.[4]

Related to this is the need for additional comparative work, especially at an international level, with a view to identifying divergencies and parallels between migrations across time and space. Such work is badly needed so as to understand the similarities, differences, and linkages between, for instance, Mexican migration to the United States, Yugoslavian migration to Western Europe, and Egyptian migration to oil-producing states. All are similar in that they are intimately linked to an international labor market, illustrating the tendency of labor to move relatively freely across national boundaries under various conditions, seemingly regardless of the political nature of the governments involved. Yet, there are limits to this "freedom," and certainly there are differences in the social and cultural consequences of these migrations. Only through use of a comparative perspective can we begin to understand the nature of any one migration in any detail.

Concerning quantitative studies, data are hard to come by and the data that do exist are often unreliable. Also, the need for data on return migration is great. At the same time, it is possible to do more with the existing data than has been done to date.

First, an inventory and evaluation of existing data sources need to be undertaken, both to alert researchers to the existence and condition of the data as they presently exist, and to call attention to the inadequacies in the quality and availability of much of the data.[5] Second, efforts should be undertaken to improve both the data and the manner in which they are made available to researchers. The goal of improving communication and coordination among data holders and between data holders and users should receive high priority. Emphasis should be given to the development of some form of interagency consortium of those who are responsible for immigration data, both in order to improve the data and to provide a central link with immigration researchers. Finally, researchers should be encouraged to use data which do exist in more imaginative ways, emphasizing where possible longitudinal studies in the case of immigrants, and comparative studies concerning both immigrants and the process of immigration. The condition of the data is bad, but if the proper qualifiers are used concerning the significance and generalizability of studies, and if the data are approached sensibly and sensitively, there is no reason why quantitative studies cannot add significantly to our understanding of immigration and immigrants.

FINAL COMMENTS

This paper has given only the briefest idea of the magnitude and variety of research presented in this volume and of the myriad of further research topics suggested by the contributors or implied in their papers. One must read the papers in order to appreciate this fact fully. I do hope that this paper has focused attention on some of the more important general areas in need of social scientific research as suggested by the conference, and that work will proceed apace.

Where do we go from here? In very broad terms, the major recommendation I have is that explicit attention be paid to linking the three levels of analysis as discussed above, to being careful to apply methodological rigor to research, and to using multiple research strategies wherever appropriate. This emphasis on multiple levels of analysis and research strategies should not be construed to mean that worthwhile studies must always have an equal emphasis on these levels and strategies; indeed, this is often impossible if one is to avoid losing focus and discussing huge topics in little detail. What I do mean is that researchers should always be cognizant of all levels and possible strategies, even when focusing on only one in detail. It is apparent to me that increasing numbers of researchers are recognizing the benefits of such an approach. If the papers presented in this volume are any indication of the direction future research on immigration will take, we are assured of continued progress in our attempts to better understand the continuing phenomenon of immigration and its many and varied implications.

NOTES

1. Notes appearing in the text refer to the papers located elsewhere in this volume. I wish to thank Roy Bryce-Laporte for helping me to flesh out many of the ideas presented in this paper. Many of the points discussed here are elaborations on ideas appearing in a paper entitled, ''Research Suggested by the Smithsonian Bicentennial Conference on 'The New Immigration': Some Preliminary Considerations,'' presented at the Workshop on U.S. Immigration: Research Perspectives, sponsored by the Center for Population Research, National Institute of Health, at the Belmont Conference Center, Elkridge, Maryland, 16–18 May 1977.

2. See Elizabeth McLean Petras, ''Some Thoughts on the Study of Immigration Patterns within the Modern World Economy: Established Alternative Data Sources,'' in Stephen R. Couch and Roy S. Bryce-Laporte, eds., *Quantitative Data and Immigration Research,* RIIES Research Notes No. 2 (Washington, D.C.: Smithsonian Institution, Research Institute on Immigration and Ethnic Studies, forthcoming 1979).

3. An additional key linking concept is sex. See Delores M. Mortimer and Roy S. Bryce-Laporte, eds., *Contemporary Studies of the Black Female and the Migratory Experience in the United States,* RIIES Occasional Papers No. 2 (Washington, D.C.: Smithsonian Institution, Research Institute on Immigration and Ethnic Studies, forthcoming 1979).

4. Akin to this would be studies of the studies of immigrants over time. See Shirley Hune, *Pacific Migration to the United States: Trends and Themes in Historical and Sociological Literature,* RIIES Bibliographic Studies No. 2 (Washington, D.C.: Smithsonian Institution (Research Institute on Immigration and Ethnic Studies), 1977).

5. Fortunately, work along these lines is finally proceeding. See Couch and Bryce-Laporte, op. cit.

THE NEW IMMIGRATION: A CHALLENGE TO OUR SOCIOLOGICAL IMAGINATION

Roy Simón Bryce-Laporte

A PERSONAL EXPERIENCE

I am an immigrant to the United States of (North) America. Born in the Republic of Panama, of a varied West Indian (Caribbean) ancestry, I lived, studied, and worked much of my younger life in the Canal Zone. My departure from Panama, however, was not simply a personal decision and it was not without input (both push and pull) from the United States.

Since the 1840s—the times of the California Gold Rush and the Westward Expansion—the major foreign investor, intervener, and recruiter of immigrant labor into Central America has been the United States.[1] I pertain to a significant group of West Indians who began to migrate to Panama and other Latin American mainland countries in the middle of the last century as the mainstay of the labor force used in constructing and maintaining railroads, canals, colonial communities, lumber and labor camps, military and port installations, fruit plantations, oil fields, and business or industry complexes of North American companies and government. As a result of canal operations, Panama, and more particularly the Canal Zone, became the unrivalled sites of Caribbean immigration, employment opportunities, per capita income, and even living facilities in the circum-Caribbean region for about one hundred years.

By the 1950s, however, the Canal Zone was to begin to suffer serious declines in its socio-economic role, vitality, prestige, and gradually its clear hegemony over other places in the region. This was due to changes in transportation, other forms of technology, world geo-political and economic relations, and in the United States business interests and military strategies. Also, shifts in fiscal and civil policies by the United States Federal government, canal treaty negotiations between this country and Panama, and the implementation of all these changes by Zonian authorities resulted in (1) bureaucratic streamlining of Canal operations along a more self-sufficient revenue-producing rationale, (2) reducing or retaining a high proportion of the labor force which indirectly depressed employment and business opportunities in adjacent Panamanian cities, and (3) Hispanizing Zone schools for non-whites on the basis of national and ethnic terms rather than race in order to solvent the anticipated Supreme Court ruling on school desegregation. The demographic consequences of such restructuring were the beginning of a massive displacement of Canal workers and their families (a considerable proportion being of West Indian birth or origin), and their subsequent migrations from the Zone into Panama, and from Panama to the United States. While a minor stream of retired West Indian workers repatriated to the islands, the major movement from Panama to the United States also includes a wide range of Hispanic-colonial types and continues at a steady but moderate pace today. Depending on implementation and effects of the recent Carter-Torrijos treaty, new movements can be anticipated in either or both directions.

Specific times, personal motives, and the manner of entry may vary but the decisions to go and the preconditions for having to leave are commonly shared among the Isthmian immigrants. The push is largely based on United States stimulated socio-economic dislocation and insecurity; the pull is the hope that in the metropole itself the people would find employment, living standards, and a economic-political structure that would provide opportunity to realize ambitions and gain firmer anchorage for their offspring (even if we or our offspring should choose to return to Panama).

Black and reasonably bilingual from an early age, I petitioned leave from the threatened school system where I was teaching in order to come to this country. I was already the head of a family which would join me over a period of two years and would live with me in almost every geographical region of this country, including Puerto Rico. In order to do so I drew upon personal savings, drew loans, and departed with a sense of reliance that my family was part of a larger, then stable support system of networks and that I would find employment in the United States. I came as an advanced undergraduate foreign student with intentions of completing my degree while doing part-time work (all of which I did) in two years, and returning home immediately after, if necessary. But I also intended to explore possibilities of obtaining more secure support or employment in order to pursue advanced education not available in Panama, which I believed would have enhanced my status and ability to be helpful and influential in my country or the general Caribbean region. However, the lack of funds and other extenuating circumstances requiring expedient decisions resulted in my continued stay in the United States. I have never returned home for any extended period of time or engaged in any self-fulfilling or consequential professional role in the country or region of my birth.

Not being immune to the objective or subjective marginality of my presence in this society as an alien, black, critical scholar, I have suffered the underside of the brain drain. I still have a sense of uprooting from past and persons. I still experience racial, socio-cultural and political alienation, and therefore, dilemmas of identity. As I assess the "progress" attributed to and sometimes envied of me by others, I constantly ponder as well the relative loss and gain of my presence here to me, my family, country, people, and region. And when through disenchantment or for the "better" education, stabilization, or sanity of my children I conceive of repatriation, I am confronted by mitigating commitments, powerful attractions, and constraints

or attachments which I have accumulated over twenty years of residence in this country.

The "mobility" trap is dual and far more real, complex, and painful for immigrants. The demands made on our imagination, our imaginativeness, is much more taxing and intricate. Thus, it is with purpose and apparently psychological causes that I dedicate my scholarly efforts to educating the world about the connections between history, plight, and potential of those exploited, subordinate alien minorities and small source countries or regions with whom I identify. This I do not without price and penalty; I am concerned that crucial gaps do not remain in the understanding of the connections between world processes, population movements, national developments, and human experiences. In the face of increasingly complex and interrelated challenges of human migration, it is only with fuller and more sensitive understandings that more appropriate policies can be pursued and more adequate political actions can be taken.

Today quite a few Panamanians of West Indian origins are resettled in the United States. This includes all of my family of orientation. Our "roots" are drawn from a multiple-stop, multiple-generational background, and as is my case, can involve transfer, rupture, and reconstruction of extended families. Our "routes" provide us with a wide transnational network of kin ties, linkages, and identities but with several historical, geographic, and cultural gaps, and with unusual cosmopolitan views of the world and high ambitions but little institutional anchorage or political-economic power. Our history is a legacy of persistent victimization in many levels of unequal arrangements as well as of envy, resentment, and suspicion even by competing black populations of host societies. Our legend is one of an impressive hardworking—adaptive—competitive ethos, striving for achievement and equality in our places of sojourn or eventual settlement.

In the United States we have been less cohesive, visible, and effective on the level of group politics or business, yet there are among us those individuals who have acquired extraordinary prominence (generally as "blacks" rather than as "first-generation immigrants") and made outstanding contributions in both national and ethnic domains. Among them are Drs. Herrington Bryce and Lloyd Hogan, economists; Billy Cobhan, Carlos Garnet, and Mauricio Smith, jazz musicians; Panama Al Brown, Rodney Carew, Rene Stennet, Lloyd LaBeach, and George Steward, athletes; Kenneth B. Clark, social psychologist; insurance expert and banker Cirilo McSween, civil rights activist; Elio Pomare, choreographer; Dr. James Haughton, Cook County public health administrator; Dr. Alfred Gerald, executive public health administrator with the World Health Organization in Washington, D.C.; Dr. Orville Goodin, repatriated economist now of sub-cabinet rank in Panama's government; and repatriated Monsignor Carlos A. Lewis, one of the first black bishops consecrated in the Roman Catholic Church in recent epoch, and now Associate Bishop of Panama City. There is an unusually high number of educators, a wide range of professionals and bureaucrats. There are also politicans, labor leaders, and a few small businessmen among us as well. Ordinarily proliferated by rivalling social clubs and personalist leadership, the Panamanian-West Indian community in the larger cities of the United States engaged intensely in supporting or criticizing the negotiations of Carter-Torrijos treaty before authorities of both Panamanian and North American governments. Concerns were expressed about Panamanian sovereignty, canal security, future form of government, international ties, politics of Panama, socio-economic development plans for the Zone, and the consequences they would have on the communities and labor forces traditionally dominated by the West Indian element.

Not unlike many other circum-Caribbean immigrant groups in the United States, many of us are of working class background with experience as urban residents and ethnic minorities in North America. We are accustomed to sufferings, making sacrifices and struggling, even though we seem to be less pressed and more prepared than most of the other new immigrants, legal and illegal, from Latin America, Asia, and some Southern Europeans. Even those of us who have not achieved such impressive achievement patterns encourage, support, and aspire for our offspring to acquire higher edu-

cation and better paying, quality, or consequential positions in the United States (or at home if they should return). Much is and can be expected of our young people; we expect them to serve, achieve, prepare themselves, and participate in shaping and sharing the benefits of their societies of residence, birth or ancestry. And, we expect them to be treated equally and hope they contribute to making their world more equal than ours.

In summary, while labor-induced immigration—as really is much of the "new" immigration to the United States—ultimately derives from a moral or practical decision made by the adults involved, that decision emerges out of an actual, structural, or perceived situation of insecurity or dissatisfaction and doubt that such a situation can be resolved adequately or quickly by remaining in the country of residence, compared to going to the country of intended migration. It requires appropriate wit, assurances, faith, and resources for travel. Yet, even in practical terms it is not usually an easy decision. Neither are its consequences easy—achievement is balanced by alienation, optimistic projections by unanticipated frustrations, pursuit by failure. Old relationships and early dreams are never fully escaped or often satisfactorily realized while new ones emerge. Labor-inspired immigrations—indeed labor immigrants—are symptoms of economic inequality, signals of an ongoing struggle for equality of opportunity and at least shifts towards balancing out economic inequality, and symbols of change and yet of continuity, on the personal, cultural, and socio-historical levels.

A PHENOMENON IGNORED:
A POPULATION MADE INVISIBLE

At the risk of being premature, I concur with those who view the decades of the 1950s and 1960s as among the most eventful and significant periods in the second century of republican existence of the nation. The period was characterized by massive demonstrations, heightened activism, idiosyncratic happenings, communal movements, and major political crises. As a consequence it witnessed the most significant legislations, rulings, and policies in the area of Civil Rights. These were decades of decisive efforts to redress problems of inequality in and of the American society. Most likely future historians and social scientists will view the period also as a baseline of the most serious shifts in ethnic composition and status, cultural configuration, and international linkages for the United States.

The important role played by various kinds of human migration in some of the occurrences of these past two decades has now become clear. However, the rise to saliency of immigration, itself, as a subject of popular concern has been slow and late in arriving. Immigration has been overshadowed in the 1950s and 1960s by other events, which were viewed to be of higher priority or more sensational and appealing in character. Some of these very events, such as the Freedom Rides, Vietnam War, and self imposed exiles involved sizeable population movements in, out, and around the United States. Yet unless perceived as discrete events in themselves, as was the Cuban refugee movement, their immigration components were often treated secondarily, if not ignored altogether.

The series of legislative and policy reforms instituted since 1952, received only limited attention by the public media or academia. Even the New Immigration and Nationality Act of 1965, was ignored for all practical purposes. Yet, it revolutionized American traditional restrictive and racist positions on immigration and resulted in the sharp increase in immigration as well as significant shifts in types and origins of immigrants to the country. For more than five years after its passage, the New Act and the new immigrants were the subjects of concern of only a very small faithful group of scholars, service and pressure groups, and policymakers.

It is especially appalling (to me as a sociologist), that among those academic groups who ignored or underestimated the New Immigration was a large majority of the legitimate social scientists, including sociologists. The latter group represents a particular kind of irony since its inception as a legitimate discipline in the United States was intimately associated with existent defaults and gaps in the academic study of American society. One of the principally ignored areas of concern which

sociologists sought to fill in the early stages of their discipline was the study of the movement and adaptations of "new" immigrants to this country, especially in the cities. In turn, through default on their own part the more general works on American immigration had become the pasttime of historians by the 1950s. When considered together with the seemingly stabilized, low immigration figures of the period, this replacement by historians must have suggested to the public mind a general sense of finality or past tense to the process of immigration, instilled a false sense of settledness, and reinforced the myth of closedness of the country as a frontier.

The 1950s and 1960s produced few general sociologies whether historical, comparative, theoretical, or projective on American immigration. Despite a repertoire of pioneering empirical works of earlier periods such as *The Polish Peasants*, by Znaniecki; *The Negro Immigrants*, by Reid; *The Puerto Rican Journey*, by Mills, *et. al.;* and *Mexican Immigration to the United States*, by Gamio; the most outstanding sociological works of the period in question were still specialized; namely, on Mexicans, Puerto Ricans and more recently, Cubans. During this time sociologists and anthropologists directed much of their attention to urban, ethnic, sub-cultural, poverty, and related policy studies; demographers and economists focused on problems of population control, internal migration, comparative urbanization and development; and political scientists concentrated on voting patterns and ethnic concentrations in the public arenas. Yet, none of these groups seemed to have perceived the interrelationship between their on-going interests and the ensuing changes in immigration, population, or culture of the United States whether on the level of phenomenon or policy.

This abdication of the study of immigration extended beyond the social sciences to government, private foundations, and popular media as well. By the 1960s the pattern had become clear and entrenched that social scientists had developed increasing dependence on these external sources for research support and direction. The prestige of their research was to rest on the massiveness of its data, the intricacies of its processing, and the visibility, relevance, urgency, and saleability of its results.

Financing and functions exceeded the purview of most academic institutions or individual researchers. The value of a research problem had become increasingly tied up with real or created public *issues* and less with sociologically defined significant social phenomena or priorities, *per se*. That is, while some issues genuinely merited the relevance and primacy associated with them, others acquired such status mostly as a result of successful mass action, militant activism, or sophisticated advocacy. For still others, their ascendancy or the form it took was the handiwork of professional opportunists and interventionists.

The impact of this kind of exogenous influence affected every level of the academy. Its sub-unit personnel and programs all came to rely upon such sources for sustenance, promotion, and even for direction. Throughout the two decades it became increasingly difficult for serious academic social scientists to obtain support for research or training on current immigration, save for the specialized cases mentioned before. Scholarly efforts to influence the early study of the impacts of the Immigration Act as a policy issue or research problem were generally futile; efforts to publish scholarly work on the subject in the major professional or national media met with success mostly in very specialized journals, or as special issues of other periodicals, but not as a regular subject of dissemination.

Thus, it generally can be said that through the early 1970s, not only foreign Blacks but almost all new immigrants (except for massive refugee populations) suffered varying degrees of social "invisibility."[2] Part of that invisibility was in the form of sociological disregard, notwithstanding their sudden, massive influx into the country as of the 1960's. Another part was due to the generally collective passiveness, cautious behavior, and indefensive status of immigrants themselves. They tend to be disoriented, disinclined, and at best marginal in open politics. This is particularly true, of course, in the case of illegals, students, parolees, and some dependents in temporary status. Even alien residents suffer certain limitations insofar as suffrage, campaigning, and officeholding are concerned. Although they may support or affiliate with the affairs of special interest or pressure groups, they

become involved only indirectly in the collective influencing of government and politics.

Recently we have observed very sporadic, aggressive, mass and persuasive politics by immigrants and ethnics in the United States pertaining to international or internal crises of their countries of origin. Another set of recent observations include efforts to unionize agricultural and temporary workers from the Caribbean in the Southeast and collective protests and strikes by illegal farm workers in the Southwest. Generally, however, unless pressure organizations are rather specific in their ethnic, neighborhood, racial, labor, or international concerns, the participation of these aliens may be unwelcome, minor, exploitative, or viewed as illegal. On the whole, immigrants—as a new, alien population—are either ignored, used as objects rather than subjects or as causes rather than constituents in politics. They themselves tend not to have access to or control of agencies for communicating and politicing in their group or self-interest. And, in hostile situations or critical times they provide very convenient targets for opportunistic politicians and desperate publics.

In summary, the period of abandonment of the study of immigration has been costly and adverse for the country as a whole. Both immigration and immigrants have been rendered "invisible." Much of the lively details of their process, meaning, and consequences of their movement have not been registered, and the significance and lessons of their presence remain denied. The result is that there is a serious set of gaps in accumulated knowledge and systematic understanding of (1) immigration whether isolatedly or in conjunction with concomitant processes such as ethnification, development, international stratification, world economic-political structures, transnational linkages, and various levels of conflicts of interest; (2) psychological, socio-economic, or cultural characteristics of new immigrants and their changes, experiences, contributions, and activities in the host society; and (3) the various levels of reception or treatment which they receive from crucial sectors and institutions of American society. The New Immigration has occurred then in a vacuum of knowledge, theory, method, data, and expertise and in a context of underestimated or distorted importance.

A CONFUSION OF MISSION: ADVOCACY AND ANALYSIS

Among those filling the void created by the general abandonment of the study of immigration, after the passing of the 1965 Act, has been a very active group of anti-immigration advocates. The motley group is comprised of various special interest advocates, policy makers, entrepreneurial consultants of varying ranges of competence, and certain self-serving bureaucracies. Some scholars are involved in such activities on almost every level mentioned as well.

Not all, but many of these groups or individuals have been driven by an opportunistic ethos, reactionary emotions, or both. They have seen in the New Immigration a topic which can be exploited for their own or other narrow ends or they see it as a disastrous threat which has to be stopped at once and at the expense of the newest, most vulnerable, exploitable and defenseless segment of the American population and their source countries.

Their tactics include very desperate, sometimes illogical, erroneous, and ahistorical efforts. They attribute disproportionately to new immigrants a wide array and significant degree of social ills or societal fears. These attacks are often reminiscent of that version of the ideology of social pathology in which the victims are conceived as the causes of their own problems and blamed for society's as well. In some cases these advocates would skillfully employ Machiavellian tactics, turning their strategy around diametrically in order to appear to be pleading for the dignity and equality of the poor of other countries, immigrants, their native-born ethnic peers, or the American working class through the use of apparently liberal-sounding rhetoric. Such groups try daringly to co-opt useful government officials, minority group leaders and scholars, the political processes, and public media. Even more seriously, they utilize the image, jargon, paraphernalia and personnel of the social sciences to persuade the lay publics, policy-makers, and funding organizations of the legitimacy and urgency of their contentions over those of others.

The campaign by these advocates is a sociological reminder in itself of how public issues can be created and utilized for reasons other than the solution of the problem stated. This is often done with too little regard for the conflict of principles, empirical unreliability of ethical-professional discomforts that such moves create for more sincere or scholarly segments of their membership. But scholars are not to be absolved *carte blanche* for aside from those who cooperate naively or avariciously with the above practices, there are others among them who exploit the theme of immigration and the immigrants strictly as bases of their ambulatory career advancement. There are others, of course, who pursue a brave struggle toward the end of researching and disseminating the "whole truth" against odds and temptations—they and their non-academic peers deserve great commendations for their fortitude and commitment.

Recently, quite ugly and special problems are being exposed in this nation in terms of unbridled growth and control of public bureaucracies which counter the democratic tenets of clean efficient government, decentralization of power, and civil rights protection. This was particularly dramatized in the case of the recent revelations of dangerous tendencies among investigatory, police, and para-military agencies toward consolidation or collusion of power and the unscrupulous invasion of the privacy and civil rights of minorities or dissident groups. Nevertheless, there is a growing public record of:

1. Persecuting and molesting by such agencies of visible minorities or aliens suspected of being or supporting illegals.
2. Proposing of the intensification of controls, border patrols and threats to build extensive border fences.
3. Pressuring certain source-transit countries to absorb if they cannot prevent passage of illegals and refugees into the United States.
4. Obscuring the surreptitious character and meaning of certain statistics on foreign migrants (e.g. students and parolees) from certain countries and emigrants from the United States (e.g. military or technical personnel) into others.
5. Ignoring special needs of legitimate foreign stu-

dents, local and urban governance, and United States overseas territories.

6. Underplaying the alleged collusion between local industries and government representatives or rumors of investment of organized crime in the trafficking and use of illegal immigrant labor.

7. Failing to pursue openly the suggested relations between the United States immigration and other levels of its international and internal politics, especially as these involves commercial sectors and impacts on domestic minority and working populations.

Moreover, the anti-immigration reactions at play follow in close neo-conservative pattern the general backlash to other Civil Rights legislations, liberal racial policies, and legal gains of the previous two decades. Leaving menacing marches to the likes of the reemergent Klu Klux Klan, the more sophisticated neo-conservative advocates employ among their tactics the misuse of social science and the spurious drawing upon reasonable or traditional concerns in other areas to discredit or overturn such measures as school desegregation, sharing by minorities of public housing, economic opportunities and political power. Similarly, while there is a growing frequency of police assaults and violent crimes against illegals, the most sophisticated levels of attack against New Immigration involves tendencies to misrepresent new immigrants, their numbers, their nature and magnitude of threat. It is marked by pressures to (1) resist any institutional adaptation and economic or cultural concessions to immigrants, (2) deny illegal immigrants free education, welfare, and jobs, and (3) curtail legal entry or adjustments of status. Such pressures are aimed at effectively reducing chances for interested aliens to be absorbed as other than marginal parts of the national economy, population, or citizenry of this country, and for dissuading policies which may seek to reflect the structural and cultural presence of the new immigrant sub-populations.

There seems to be mutual reinforcement in attitude and advocacy of retrenchment in Civil Rights and against significant advancement among nonwhite minorities and the resistance to entry and participation of new nonwhite immigrants in the society. The tension between the economic exploitability and the social objectionality of both groups of nonwhites exemplifies the persistence of an underlying troublesome aspect of American society, which began from colonial times. Balancing the open door and melting pot myths have been the great efforts throughout American history to recruit and quarantine certain groups for their utility as providers of cheap, low status labor while at the same time restricting their entry or containing their localization because of the believed economic threat or aesthetic-socio-cultural contaminating force that they represent.

When viewed myopically and ahistorically as solely a present-time, demographic, or a domestic, political issue; when casted and exploited principally as a social *problem* of *only* the American society, the phenomenon of the "New Immigration" suffers both a skewed and limited treatment. It tends to be marked by premature upward estimates and panic-inspiring negative exaggerations about its over populating, competitive, alienating, disorganizing, and even subversive potential. Additionally, it suffers the absence of a broad, balanced, profound, and systematic debate. Finally, it lacks serious critical or scientific scrutiny toward the fuller understanding of the subject and social reality that it is, the levels of policies and presentations that it requires as a world phenomenon, and the actions and agencies that must become involved in its management if it is to link local concerns with global problems.

The anti-immigration campaign reaches the extreme of myopia, absurdity and insensitivity, however, when it utilizes the legitimate media to make some of the most irresponsible threats, impatient criticism, fear and hate instigations, or stereotypically-ridden scenarios about the immigrants, their native ethnic counterparts, and their countries of origin. There its limitedness becomes most obvious; it houses a conflict between blind, belligerent opportunistic advocacy and claims of objective authority in the pursuit of understanding immigration as either phenomenon or policy issue. This is especially evident in the international arena, which is becoming increasingly more complex and interdependent in itself and in relation to the arena of domestic affairs of each country or group involved.

In the case of Mexico—historically the major source and conduit of the most consistent and highest number of immigrants (legal and illegal) to the United States—we have witnessed misguided, reckless, and confused statements by the anti-immigration compaigners. Much of their statements ignore history, distort reality, and show little sophistication or sympathy for Mexico or the Mexican-American community. In their hysterical bandwagon they focus on stopping, by any means necessary, illegal immigration from or through Mexico; they have blinded themselves from what could be learned from the experience with the bracero and drug control programs, and have introduced through their unnecessary statements difficulties into the intricate, sensitive parlays of high level diplomatic negotiations and potential of intra or inter-ethnic (or class) confrontations. Such complex backfirings, conflicts of interests, and "unpredictable" developments ought to suggest the limitations of simplistic, one-sided, short-run but publicity-oriented approaches which characterize the campaign: bad scholarship, bad politics, and bad public relations; it may well have been bad intelligence as well—particularly as we enter into a period of ascendancy in influence by both Mexico and the Hispanic-American populations of the United States.[3]

Curiously, Iran, whose recent government reconstruction makes Mexican oil even more coveted by the U.S., was never focused upon as a source of illegal immigrants by the campaigners even when it figured prominently among such sources according to U.S. government reports. Many of these "illegal" Iranians allegedly were recruited by and entered as foreign "students" in educational institutions of varying levels of respectability. This is not unlike the practices of certain agricultural and marginal industries in the case of Mexican, Caribbean, Latin American, and Asian illegals. These Iranian "illegals" obviously represented a safety-valve for a beleaguered Iranian government and a source of sustaining revenue for a waning school industry and spontaneous crash programs in the United States.

Now that their political and financial functions have been nullified, and in punishment for their embarrassing political activities or technically illegal behavior, some legitimate Iranian students were being deported. Obviously, their fate and flux (as is true of many other immigrant and refugee groups) are reflected by changes in U.S. international situation as much as the lack of carefully consistent immigration policy.[4]

Hence, in a manner not very different or independent from the economic and Malthusian impulses expressed in the fanatical birth control campaigns of the past decade—which also had their ancillary apparatus obligated funds and provided jobs for field personnel and scholars—the present politics of immigration restriction have more than demographic implications. They seem tarnished with panic and blind, reactionary racism; committed to foster internal conflicts among ethnic minorities and laboring classes in the United States; and committed to maintaining national and international inequalities with its dependence-domination syndrome favoring the United States. They are pregnant with nefarious consequences for the future internal tranquility of the country and its status and relations with Third World countries. Those exaggerated statements and one-sided strategies avoid the forthright considerations of the most serious structural questions and challenges for correcting the dynamic persistence of national and international inequalities.

Eventually a political, democratic judgment must be made about immigration, inequality, and their appropriate alternatives or counter-balances. But the publics and governments deserve a knowledge of the wider range of adequate choices. This cannot be developed within the context of a bias-filled and panic-stricken campaign. For although crucial, this is not the case of an emergency situation; it is an urgent problem still amenable to legitimate, sophisticated, balanced, and careful study.[5]

Granted, politization of social (or even sociological) problems may sometimes result in exposing the need for data and support for study and training that can be useful in understanding or resolving such problems. However, the enactment of these research programs tends to lag behind the increasing complications and expanding magnitude of the problems; generally such politization also tends to cast the setting and introduce confusion, constraints, or premature priorities. In so doing the political takes primacy over the intellectual imperative; there is more preoccupation with stability than structural change and with control than institutional adaptation; legal-political expediencies override sociological-economic essentials; and dramatic, short-run national resolutions are sought over thorough long-lasting integrated, global, international solutions of the problem.[6]

It is unfortunate that there is an apparent necessity for sociological problems to be so politicized, publicized and made saleable before they can obtain serious attention in American society (even in the academic sector and policy circles). For this means heightening risks of reification or misplacing emphasis so that the crises themselves and the structures, statuses, or personalities they create become predominant ends in themselves. It also increases the possibility that the true meaning and the full messages of troublesome events (for example, Jonestown, Guyana) are either overlooked or suppressed—so too are the cues that could be learned from the unusual migrations which occur around them and other troubled countries.

Finally, such politicization can confound the fuller understanding of immigration by veiling or suppressing "sensitive" information on U.S. involvement and perhaps its responsibility for the rise in number of immigrants from certain countries. It is becoming increasingly clear, nevertheless, that most of the leading sources of illegal immigrants to this country are not simply countries with high population growth rates and intermediate stages of development. Generally, they are also countries (1) with large numbers of legal immigrants and non-immigrants coming to the United States; and (2) host a high presence of American personnel, capital investment, military or security aid. These characteristics are shared as well by countries now dominated by communist governments; from which large numbers of refugees are received. They are shared also with U.S. extra-territorial holdings which in addition to producing their own significant exodus of emigrants receive numerous immigrants as well.

Hence, the relative benefits of trade-offs and the manner of function, sufficiency, or adequacy of U.S. involvement or that of its Western allies in these leading source countries must enter into any thorough understanding of the problem of legal and illegal immigrants.[7] Here it may be fruitful to engage in analytical comparison of immigrants in socialist and other political-economic systems, as well as projective, anticipatory studies.

The fact is that until recently the scope, most serious questions, and most positive challenges about the New Immigration have been distorted, overlooked, masked, or classified. However, this is by no means limited to the matter of the New Immigration. Unfortunately, it is a general pattern in the United States toward any subject which is perceived as "troublesome." This whitewashing, paranoid, or expediency-oriented mentality and its subsequent whimsical, spontaneous, and exogenous influence on scholarly research tends to mitigate against truly historical, global, or comparative views which are required for a fuller understanding of the most basic sociological problems, phenomena, or processes involved. This inversion of role between advocacy or policy on one hand and analysis and technical solutions on the other is dangerous and inefficient. It leads to gaps and defaults not only in intelligence and policy studies but also in classical social analytical scholarship and public knowledge such as those which plague the field of immigration studies today. In turn the chaotic result of all this is being felt now by policy makers, service professionals, public bureaucrats, immigrant populations and the peoples and societies which they leave as well as those in which they now live. Therefore, the situation has become multiply vexing; it is contradicting, self-defeating, and frustrating.

THE MORE GENERAL STATE OF CRISIS: THE NEED FOR FULLER UNDERSTANDINGS AND SANGUINE SOLUTIONS

In the wake of the nation's bicentennial, approximately ten years after the passing of the 1965

Act, the broader patterns of the New Immigration have become clear and in some ways seem to have stablized. Yet crises—the sensing of threats of some self-cherished values[8]—have begun to emerge around the New Immigration in the society itself and also in the legitimate social scientific sector. Historically, immigration has given form, content, and direction to the United States, but now there is the struggle in the United States to formulate laws against further immigration. Too many Americans wish to do so without understanding, memory, or imagination of what immigration fully means for other individuals and societies, nor how much immigration is induced, relied upon, and engaged in by the United States itself. The traditional myth of the United States, "land of the free and home of the brave," an open door frontier, is still sold and bought abroad. But from within the United States it is being confronted by arguments regarding the stage of ecological, economic, and cultural incapacity at which the society has arrived and therefore the imprudence of its continued absorbtion of "additional" (often meaning "different") populations. On another level, American sociology which had emerged as an instrument to understand or explain society and meditate between inarticulate people and troubled government now is being employed, together with repressive, intruding police methods and a negative press, to defend *the* society, state, or *status quo* against unwanted aliens—the least vocal, defensible, adjusted, or understood group of individuals in the society.

Twenty or so years ago, a critical sociologist, C. Wright Mills, observed that the North American people often felt that their private lives were a series of crises and traps, many of them not aware of the ties between their personal experience and the historical changes, structural contradictions, and value conflicts taking place in their society. Ordinary people were outpaced by the shaping of history; unclear of the connection between themselves, their personal milieu and the world and public views around them; unaware of themselves as historical beings and of the roles they were playing in making the history of their particular moment, society, and world.[9]

Today we feel ourselves not only trapped in, but also that our roles, groups, nations, and world are caught up in complex interests and economic systems which create seemingly unresolvable problems. These preclude rather than promote the higher values we cherish or the conditions, life-chances, and statuses we seek. Hence, today we find ourselves located in an aura of crises, disillusionment, distrust, and alienating powerlessness.[10] Many people now wonder in light of the great wealth and advancement of this country, indeed of the great expanses and progressions in the world, if this entrapment is a necessary, temporary, or paradoxical price we pay for such progress and advancement? Many of us believe it not to be so.

It is obvious that not only are we all in structural crisis on a world level, but also to some extent we are in the midst of general confusion about and loss of control over much of what is going on around us in our immediate milieu. Many new immigrants soon find out, for instance, that a shift from one country to another need not resolve their political, economic, or ethnic difficulties as individuals or groups. But remaining at home in insecurity, frustration, or misery seems no better an alternative, short of revolution. Leaders of source countries do not find induced emigration, any more than local isolationists will find the cessation of immigration, satisfactory solutions to the economic problems of their respective communities and countries. With regard to the New Immigration, even we social scientists are confused about what to research, what position or direction to take on issues, or how to advise. Immigrants, minorities, academics, silent majorities—many of us are either not aware of and responsible for our roles in the making of history, or fear our powerlessness relative to those whom we think can and do make history. We lack that certain kind of imagination, really a kind of courage, which C. Wright Mills so eloquently called for at the start of the 1950s.

Criticizing the predominant trends in sociology for having departed from the classical roles of social analysts, Mills made an eloquent, historic, and still pertinent plea for the rededicated pursuit of a "sociological imagination."

. . . It is by means of the sociological imagination that

men now hope to grasp what is going on in the world, and to understand what is happening in themselves as minute points of the intersection of biography and history within society . . .[11]

this sociological imagination is the most fruitful form of the self consciousness . . .[12]

by such means the personal uneasiness of individuals is focused upon explicit troubles and the indifference of publics is transformed into involvement with issues . . .[13]

This sociological imagination is not confined to the special group of professionals who traditionally call themselves sociologists. It transcends the broad range of social and humanistic disciplines; it extends to the larger society and world. In the United States, it quite certainly must involve the opinion and policy-making sectors, various politicized publics, and the masses of ordinary people. All can benefit directly or indirectly from such imagination.

According to Mills, social scientists are faced by the moral dilemma of addressing the difference between what people are interested in and what is in people's interest.[14] Hence, it is not the addressing of issues or troubles, *per se*, which cripples the imaginativeness of social and humanistic scholars today, but our failure to (1) determine the validity, magnitude, and critical nature of these issues; (2) reformulate such issues and troubles into classical analysis of the interconnections of biography, history and society/world; and (3) educate ourselves and *all* segments of the society/world to the essentials and dynamics of such issues and troubles, as well as to the probability and merits of their solutions. Thus, as social scientists we have a political task to perform as well as to employ and promote this imagination (or fruits of it) through our research, teaching, and dissemination to other publics, other opinion-makers, other policy-advisers—to the widest possible range of audience provided by the society.

Therefore, contrary to the sense of accomplishment or finality that the Bicentennial too often connotes, we must see it as an event linking past to future, second to third centuries, and see it as a chronologically direct observation point in the trajectory of continuity and change which gives form and substance to this Nation—its people, the

world around it, and the relations with the two. In this context immigration is not only a universal role and special meaning in the continued formation of the United States—its peopling as well as its debts, ties, and contributions to the rest of the world. As such immigration is a matter to be understood seriously and a mode for the serious understanding of the United States.

THE THIRD CENTURY—A CASE FOR MORAL AND METHODOLOGICAL IMAGINITATIVENESS

Guided by such thinking and in conformity with our mission to diffuse knowledge and ideas, this research institute of the Smithsonian Institution engaged in the promotion of a series of research and dissemination projects culminating in the sponsorship of the nation's first and only major scholarly conference on the New Immigration, in observance of the Bicentennial of the American Revolution. In the pages of this volume, the *Supplement* which accompanies it, and other publications such as the September/October 1977 issue of *Society* on "The New Immigrant Wave," RIIES has sought to report on the larger involvement of the academic community in the debate on immigration, as an American and world topic. In so doing, we have sought to exhibit the works and thoughts of a wide range of our scholarly colleagues—their disciplines, ideologies, and methodologies—from various levels of abstraction, parts of the world, and on differing points and levels of the immigration stream.

Not all but certainly many of the most serious aspects of the New Immigration (and the new immigrants) have been addressed in these manuscripts. Perhaps we have even emphasized too much on structure and immigration at the expense of psychology, cultural change, second generation, and post-entry or return migration adaptations. Moreover, there still does not exist a comprehensive history, taxonomy, or theory of immigration (or of immigration policy). A cursory reading of them would show, however, that many of these topics have not been the subject of public interchange even among academic peers, and others had not been pursued in the context of a conference, nor resulted in publication. Even with the publication of this *Sourcebook,* many important questions remain unanswered, and others have been asked only implicitly. Together with the *Supplement,* this is an example of variety and range of potential academic input, an historical record of exchange in the study of immigration between scholars, bureaucrats, and interested publics. Finally, it is also a testimony to the categorical expansion of the nucleus of old and young, well-known and less-known scholars who dedicate themselves to the scientific study of the phenomenon of the New Immigration—with all the seriousness, dignity, and vision that it deserves.

For those of us located in research-museum complexes like the Smithsonian Institution, there is another special set of challenges to the manner in which we deal with history and culture—challenges which ongoing processes such as the New Immigration present to museums. Normally viewed as custodians of the past and celebrators of the great heritage and long dead heroes, museums are limited by design, perspective, methodology, and technique to holding culture and history still. Thereby they provide their spectators with a synchronic and selective past which emphasizes product or artifacts rather than production or process. But the present is history and history is process. In fact, in the case of the New Immigration, it is world process; it is world history-making. Also, it is different cultures; new culture-making, and more peopling; the appearance of different peoples. Our special challenge then is to transcend the limitation of our methodologies, extend our various perspectives, and capture for museological exhibit and other instructional media the complex reality of the New Immigration as a connection between learned aspirations and personal decisions; structured inequality and search for opportunity for advancement, freedom and security; sociological phenomena and social issues. It also requires a greater involvement of conventional social sciences and new technological media in the work of capturing cultural change and formation as processes—not simple products and artifacts as traditionally done in museums.

If, without much sociological imagination, we were to succumb to the wishful fancy of present campaigns, we could imagine that in the near future immigration as a phenomenon would be brought to an end, and the Statue of Liberty could be converted into a great museum or great museum collection signalling a closed period in American history. That is hardly likely to occur without changing the U.S. as we know it. On the other hand, with much museological imagination, great and local museums need not await such an unlikely doomsday. Instead, we should seek to capture and exhibit the living and the *new*—the New Immigration, the new immigrants, their homeland conditions, culture and contributions; the dreams, traps, crises, challenges that they experience; the causes and connections to which they give rise; the new homes they will build and new Americans they will bear; the institutional and cultural conversions that they are bringing and are bound to bring about.

CONCLUSION

Perhaps in concluding I may be equally premature compared to my opening statement in this essay. As the 1950s and 1960s have been among the most eventful decades of the second century of republican existence in the United States, the 1970s and 1980s could be among the most decisive for its third century. The new incoming elements in the American population and their relations with the rest of the nation and peoples of the world, the new United States they will form and its relations to other countries of the world are the new challenges which American scholarship will face. Such challenges require new surges of dedication, new levels of study and deliberation, and a broadening of our sociological imagination—to include terms of morality and policy, research and diffusion, knowledge and information, technology, ideas and criticism, and common sense and sentimentality. It does not call, however, for premature agitation, presumptive assertions, and prejudiced actions which, in the immediate or long run, are likely to be both embarrassing and injurious to the welfare of this country. It may not have to mean breaking the promise for which this country supposedly stands for its citizens and other peoples of the contemporary world.

The New Immigration is a challenge to our courage and imagination; it demands a reconsideration of very essential aspects of this country's past and future, its structure and actions, its image and reality. It demands a reconsideration of what the Republic supposedly stood for then and what it can stand for now; what we conclude it must stand for in the future against what we understood it to have stood for in the past: The Protestant Ethic? The American Dream? The postponement of gratification? The deferment but realization of dreams?

While the American-born John Kennedy found insights on American immigration in the thoughts of the French visitor, De Tocqueville, I, myself an immigrant, find identity in the words of American-born, Langston Hughes:

> A world I dream where black or white
> Whatever race you be
> Would share the boundaries of the earth
> And every man is free.[15]

Most new immigrants still identify with the views of John Kennedy, the dreams of Langston Hughes, the inscription on the Statue of Liberty, or the opening words of the Declaration of Independence.[16] This human search is historic; it preceeded and produced the colonial peopling of what is today the United States and the rest of the Americas. The spirit is continuous; that which today (U.S.) Americans call their own spirit is likely held and practiced more strongly by immigrants than natives. The continued presence of immigrants, then, is as much a reminder as it is a challenge; it promises revitalization as much as reconstruction of what is "American" about the United States. The New Immigration is part of a closely-held value and historical process without which a dynamic U.S.A. is unimaginable; it is also a complex problem that can only be resolved to the extent that North Americans are willing to do their share to make of this world a place of freedom, equality, opportunity, and basic satisfaction of human needs. Together we must strive and work to make it less necessary for human beings to have to migrate or remain sedentary because of economic/political constraints. But if they should want to do either for whatever reason, they should be free and able to do so. What we need today is an equitable redistribution of opportunity

for happiness, comfort, freedom, security, and the economic goods and profits benefits of progress— not of poverty, pathology, discrimination, institutional control, or imposed contraception. We need that kind of redistribution which from all available evidence is likely to be followed by a voluntary reduction of birth rate, family size, and (the need for) permanent migration. This is the challenge the New Immigration poses for us all as citizens, policy-makers, and scholars—irrespective of our status, class or origin—in the third century. And, hopefully, this volume takes us at least one significant step in that direction.

NOTES

1. Bryce-Laporte, R.S. "Crisis, contraculture and religion among West Indians in the Panama Canal Zone," in *Afro-American Anthropology: Contemporary Perspectives"* (Norman Whitten and John Szwed, eds.). New York: The Free Press, 1970, pp. 103-108. See also "Varias ideas sobre el significado de la experiencia del grupo de origen afro-antillano de Panama para los estudios afro-americanos," in *Actas del IV Simposium Nacional de Antropologia, Arqueologia y Etnohistoria de Panamá*. Panama: Universidad de Panama: Instituto Nacional de Cultura, (Octubre, 1973); "Religion Folklórica y Negros Antillanos en La Zona del Canal de Panamá: Estudio de un Incidente y su Contexto," in *Revista Nacional de Cultura*, Número Cinco, 1976.

2. Bryce-Laporte, R.S., "Black Immigrants: The experience of Invisibility and Inequality," *Journal of Black Studies*, Vol. 3, No. 1, September 1972; pp. 29-56. See also, "Black Immigrants," in *Through Different Eyes* (Peter I. Rose, Stanley Rothman, and William J. Wilson, eds.). New York: Oxford University Press, 1973, pp. 44-61. See also "Introduction," in *Caribbean Immigration to the United States*, RIIES Occasional Papers No. 1 (R.S. Bryce-Laporte and Delores M. Mortimer, eds.). Washington: Smithsonian Institution, Research Institute on Immigration and Ethnic Studies, 1976, pp. i-vi.

3. Lindsey, Robert, "U.S. Hispanic Populace Growing Faster than any Other Minority," *New York Times* (February 18, 1979), p. 1 and 16. See also Jackson, Jacquelyn J., "Illegal Aliens: Big Threat to Black Workers," in *Ebony*, Vol. XXXIV, No. 6 (April 1979). Chicago: Johnson Publishing Company, Inc., pp. 33-40; Huss, John D. and Melanie Wirken, "Illegal Immigration: The Hidden Population Bomb," and Downes, Richard, "The Future Consequences of Illegal Immigration," in *Futurist* (April 1977), pp. 114-127. See also various American comments in *Structural Factors in Mexican and Caribbean Basin Migration*, proceedings of a Brookings Institution-El Colegio de Mexico Symposium (June 28-30, 1978).

4. Allen, Henry, "Castillo's Border Problems," *The Washington Post* (April 18, 1979), p. B-1 and 4); Pess, Robert, "New U.S. Court Discovers Forty Percent More Iranian Students," *The Washington Star* (February 7, 1979), p. A-6; and Crittenden, Ann, "Iranians at U.S.

Embassy Charge Records Show Wide Corruption," *New York Times* (March 2, 1979), p. A-8.

5. Manus, Abul Kasim, "U.S. Must Heed Honest Reporting on Special Allies," *The Washington Star* (March 4, 1979), p. D-1; Bryce-Laporte, R.S., "The New Immigration and its Caribbean Component-An Overview," *Immigration to the United States* (hearings before the Select Committee on Population, House of Representatives). Washington, D.C.: U.S. Government Printing Office, pp. 335-378; and his statement in *Undocumented Workers: Implications for U.S. Policy in the Western Hemisphere* (hearings before the Subcommittee on Inter-American Affairs of the Committee on International Relations, House of Representatives). Washington, D.C.: U.S. Government Printing Office, pp. 70-84.

6. See Couch, Stephen R., "Where Do We Go From Here? The New Immigration and Implications for Research," in this volume.

7. During the course of the last few months, important thrusts and redirecting have been taken in the form of programs and public laws by the major private foundations (Ford, Rockefeller, etc.) and the Federal Government; i.e. Public Law 95-412, and NIH, to expand the scope and lift the level of studying immigration. We at the RIIES are heartened by such developments. They represent significant victories in the struggle we and our academic supporters have been waging since our inception for the treatment of the New Immigration as an historical, cultural socio-economic phenomenon and not simply a domestic, short-term political issue. However, we continue to press for serious opportunities to be given to legitimate, balanced, and independent scholarship in the hope that serious attention will be paid to their contribution toward the fuller study of the New Immigration, and the scientific formulation and more humane implementation of policies therein derived.

8. Mills, C. Wright, *The Sociological Imagination*. New York: Oxford University Press, 1969, pp. 11-14.

9. *Ibid.*, p. 3-5.

10. For various discussions on this theme, see *Alienation in Contemporary Society*, Roy S. Bryce-Laporte and Claudewell S. Thomas (eds.). New York: Praeger Publishing, Inc., 1976.

11. Mills, *op. cit.*, p. 7.

12. *Ibid.*, p. 7.

13. *Ibid.*, p. 5.

14. *Ibid.*, pp. 193-94.

15. Hughes, Langston, "I Dream a World," in *Hold Fast to Dreams*, Arna Bontemps (ed.). New York: Fullett Publishing Company, 1969, p. 29.

16. See for example, Williams, Katherine, *Where Else But America?* Annapolis, Maryland: Fishergate Publishing Company, 1977, p. iii. See also several articles in Bryce-Laporte and Mortimer, *op. cit.*, 1976; and Bryce-Laporte, R.S., "New York City and the New Caribbean Immigration—A Contextual Statement," in *The New Caribbean Migration to New York City* (a special issue of *International Migration Review*), Elsa Chaney and Constance Sutton, eds. New York: Center for Migration Studies (forthcoming).

APPENDICES

APPENDIX A

INTERNATIONAL COMMENTARY

John A. Rex, England:

When I was asked to come here, I thought that the role which I was asked to play would be a threefold one. Firstly, I realized that the new migration has already been a part of my life. And, during the period when I was living in Toronto, I became conscious of the need to conceptualize this and am very delighted that something like this is going on in the United States. I think there is clearly a different, and not just a chronological, cutoff point that Roy Bryce-Laporte has chosen. But, there is a very real empirical area of study which is the new migration.

Now, the second interest that I had is that I am interested in comparability and in trying to see what the relationship is between migration in this continent and migration in Europe (migration in Britain in particular). I am particularly torn, in a way, by the fact that the British system and situation has some parallels with the American situation, some parallels with the European situation, and some things which are uniquely British. Our situation is, of course, that we have our Deep South in the West Indies, and the fact that people who come from those stagnant economies to what used to be thought of as an advanced industrial country to look for jobs has some parallels clearly with the United States; the behavior of our West Indians, and the ideologies that they take over, are very much influenced by the blacks in the United States. Although, in Britain, our black people descended from the slave plantation culture and are immigrants, they were not part of the structured society. But, we also, of course, have the Asian immigrants who are so very different from the Asian minorities whom we heard about in New York, and who are very largely professional people. It is true that the Asian immigrants have found themselves downgraded in their occupations, but there are a lot of them. There are enormous numbers of them in England who are peasants from Pakistan, India, Kashmir, and Bangladesh. That is a kind of migration which hasn't really been dis-

cussed here.

The third thing that I wanted to discuss here, and to say something most seriously about, is the fact that there is a need for theoretical conceptualization in the field. I think that some of the papers which we have heard were professionally excellent—Won Moo Hurh on the Koreans, Edna Bonacich, Elsa Chaney—all were very interesting in themselves. They were very exciting for me because of my own gropings toward some sort of theoretical model in terms of which the whole thing could be understood and through which these things could be seen as parts of the whole. I think that, when it comes to theory, I really only heard two papers which worked with an attempt at a systematic theory, and they shared the same theory. That was the paper by Elizabeth Petras of Binghamton, and the one jointly authored by Cué and Bach of Duke University. That theory was the theory of political economy about the development of monopoly capitalism, and what happens at certain stages in its needs for ultraexploitable labor and to accumulate capital, and so on.

I think theory on that level is important, but there must be two qualifications. First, I am less than wholly convinced of the concepts which are used about the organic composition of capital, the falling rate of profit, and so on. And, so long as this theory is simply stated and not brought into some sort of mediated relationships with the events which actually occur, those things remain untested. But, the important thing is that the theory remains a theory of political economy and doesn't have a close explanatory bite on the events which actually occur. Having said that, I want to emphasize that this concept of a metropolitan economy and its periphery or its colonial outpost seems simple to me. The kind of sociological-structural theory that I want to see must give some account of the construction and the structure of colonial societies as dynamic entities which have to be viewed in terms of modes of production, exploitation, plantation peasant economies, and so forth. We have to look at the various groups which become marginal to the plantation or present system—the coloreds, the freed slaves, and other groups; we need to look at pariah groups of traders who exist in those territories; we need to look at the very important kind of settler-bourgeoisie, or the settlers who come to those territories and who actually constitute a privileged group whether they are workers, entrepreneurs, and so on, and who, in due course, take independence and responsibility for the society. We have to look at people like missionaries and administrators, and all of those things are combined in varying degrees in different kinds of societies. Equally, we have to look at the complexity of the metropolitan societies—I don't mean just urban metropolitan societies, but the countries like Britain, France, and the United States—to look at the class structure of those societies and to be prepared to recognize a great deal of diversity within them. The tendency on the one hand is to talk about monopoly capitalism as though it is a clear and distinct entity—but then, interestingly, someone like Edna Bonacich was talking about the operation of people within the interstices of capitalism. Well, the fact is that, whether it is monopoly capitalism or any other stage of capitalism, there are these things going on. There are these interstices where people may operate. It is also true that there is a complex relationship in these societies between class conflict and the status system in which groups move upwards in terms of social mobility. So, the metropolitan structures are themselves complicated. It seems to be that, against that background, we should be doing more studies of the sending societies—we need to know more about the social structures of Spain, Yugoslavia, Turkey, in Europe: of the Latin American territories; of the West Indies; and of the Asiatic continent. But, focusing on the migrants when they are here, it seems to me that there are a set of concepts—the colony, the immigrant colony, the ghetto—and we need to look at these.

What is quite crucial here is a distinction I feel we have to make between a colony which people move through during the process of social mobility, and colonies within which people stagnate and may, indeed, organize rebellion. Thirdly, there is the

groups, and this is particularly true of Asian groups, who live in a kind of international diaspora and may not become wholly committed to the societies that they are in. All of these possibilities are there. If one looks at them, then one begins to forge the kind of paper which Elsa Chaney gave on the Colombians. One of the things which occurred repeatedly which interested me was the margin between legal and illegal activity, and the role of brokers in the communities where complex relationships were at play. But, when I look at the Colombian community, I see a people who will find relatively easy absorption into the United States society compared with other groups.

At the other end, of course, are the native Americans. How glad I was that there were papers by Christina Brinkley-Carter and William Austin on the comparison of the native American minorities with the incoming immigrant minorities. It seems to me to be an extremely important precedent, and one of the discussants in a different session was arguing with the same thing in mind: that the whole immigration question should be thought of in terms of manpower policy as a whole. Those papers, it seems to me, were quite crucial to the understanding of the new migration.

When I think of these, I think also of the British situation in which we have West Indian and Asian groups suffering from increasing hostility and punitive policies from the native population, and the move within those communities to some sort of encapsulation, some sort of preparation from a sense of confrontation. I think a distinction has to be made in terms of the political sociology of these groups, between groups who face that sort of destiny and groups for whom the colony is, for a few generations, a place through which people will pass.

To end on a light note, it seems that one of the interesting questions is how well the Koreans will make it. Will they, in fact, have an easy passage into the United States mainstream population? Will they, through their commercial aptitude, be able to move from a relatively middleman role to a mainstream role? I personally think that a people who can corner the market in false eyelashes is probably well-fitted to survive in American society.

Francois Raveau, France:

I was surprised by one fact during the conference, and that was the absence of psychological approaches to migration. I have been wondering whether this was because you have killed all of your psychologists or whether the topic is not seen as "interesting" anymore. I know there is a recession for psychologists and psychoanalysts in the U.S., but I did not know it was that bad. But, perhaps, they are not interested in migration and that is what I am wondering about.

There is another aspect that has surprised me. That is, I did not find an industrial psychological approach or psychology of organization, inquiries which in some countries have taken the form of looking at the migrant at work.

Another thing has been interesting, and that is the way that migration has been approached by all the scholars who have delivered papers. I had the impression that from the beginning, minorities wanted to be studied by minorities. And that, of course, is relatively new in this country. But, I had the feeling that sometimes a few things were mixed up. To be brief and clear about it, I had the feeling that the purely empirical, the practical approach, trying to find answers to very acute crises through the minorities, involves the researchers so much that they are perhaps losing sight of the possibility of broadening the subject. I have read a lot of monographs about Puerto Ricans, Pilippinos, Chinese, and West Indians. But what is the use of all those studies? I understand that they could be brought up in front of your administration but, I have heard, like in other countries, you are not so optimistic about the administration listening to you.

But, after describing the states in which you find the minorities, what do you do? What are the possibilities of universalization of the concept? I think that, in a way, migration is a quasi-experimental approach to very deep psychosociological problems. And, that in the heat of the excitement of the day-to-day answers that you want to give to minority suffering, perhaps this view has been slightly fogged. That is my general feeling.

So, there is a slight confusion between what is the pragmatic approach and what is the purely theoretical approach which is enriched by the so-called pragmatic approach to the study of migration and minorities.

Another thing, interesting too, is the political implications of minorities. In Europe, we are very interested in our minorities because it is the "proof"—it gives to our society a very crude view (and societies are hiding, by all means sometimes, the contradictions, the class struggles, and so on) of the foreign workers who are revealing lots of things that the dominant classes are trying to hide. And so, the migrants are used by simple political groups as weapons—"Molotov cocktails" in a way—against some kinds of political power. And, even among the opposite, the minorities argue, against each other. I have a very interesting feeling that sometimes it was done that way here too, but I don't know for sure. So, I am asking you, Dr. Bryce-Laporte, if it was done consciously or unconsciously. I am sorry but I am a bit of a psychoanalyst, and I have to ask what is behind the appearance. That has been for me very interesting and very surprising. But, it still leaves me wondering about the ideas behind the minds of many of the people who have spoken here. Some were very clear, but I don't know if some were mystified or if they were trying to mystify their audience.

I should like to add another thing. And that is, this "new" immigration business is the proof that you are now an old country. A very old one. And, perhaps, the fact that you have the need to baptize things that are simply migration as the "new" migration is the proof that your society is really going through a readjustment that is very unique and which calls for longitudinal and comparative studies.

I will take back to my colleagues the diagnosis that America is a very old country which has new problems.

W. R. Böhning, Switzerland:

Listening to the proceedings brought home to me the peculiar characteristic of American immigration, old and new. Mainstream America views itself as hospitable, screens the newcomer on entry, but then ignores him for all practical purposes and leaves him to his own devices. In European eyes this lacks logic and coherence. In American eyes, there is a freedom price to be paid for European-type postmigration concern with migrants, because language training, housing, and other social services on the one hand, and identification and surveilance on the other, are inextricably linked. One is faced, therefore, with a trade-off between freedom and welfare, at least during the first ten years or so of immigration. However, the questions that come to my mind are: (1) whether this trade-off holds true for the illegal immigrant, and (2) will it be stable in future American politics.

Another observation I made was that immigration or international migration does not seem to figure very high on the list of priorities of U.S. social scientists, and what is happening as a result of this movement in countries of emigration seems to figure at a rock bottom position. The Research Institute itself is making a commendable effort to change this. My reason for mentioning this is to point out the banality of migration being selective. Since under "laissez-faire" circumstances it may produce even greater marginality since the poorest 20 or 40 percent of the rural population are rarely selected as much as they should be.[1] There are measures which national policy makers in the emigration country can take to fight impoverishing effects; that is, not to stop emigration but to change the pattern of emigration, and to counter remittance-induced inflation.[2] Here lies a whole range of urgent research topics that should, in my opinion, be explored by American scholars, too.

Finally, we arrive at the question of international cooperation. The selectivity of migration, the permanence of migration, and the productive use of remittance are among the key areas that lend themselves to international cooperation. Two provisions need to be fulfilled for *selection* to favor the socially most needy persons. Firstly, international labor movements should be organized bilaterally or multilaterally (as in Western Europe). And, secondly, preimmigration training should be given for the unskilled where they are recruited for given jobs (this was also beginning to happen on a large scale in Western Europe in the early 1970s on a cost-sharing basis), or where general labor market con-

siderations demand that this be the case. By *permanence* I refer to the malpractice of using migrant labor as a foreign "reserve army" and, additionally, to deprive it of social security benefits to which it should be properly entitled. Equity demands that this be changed. Foreigners should have a right to unemployment benefits or whatever takes their place. They should also have their entitlements to old age pensions transferred whenever they leave their country of last employment. That *remittances* (not used for consumption) can be used productively, and eventually provide employment for returned migrants or for family members staying in the home country, requires that (1) they be pooled; (2) the governments of either or both countries make feasibility and marketing studies available to migrant investors; and (3) either or both governments provide some financial support for the critical running-in period, for example, through development aid. This model is beginning to take shape in German-Turkish and Dutch-Turkish relations and would seem to be of wider applicability.

Frank Hernandez, Dominican Republic

I share with Mr. Raveau the sense of confusion that he said he had in the seminar. And, this is why my comments will be very naive. I want to share with you some questions which were raised during the seminar and the answers which I provided for myself.

One of the questions was why we are discussing immigration to the United States. What are the goals of the seminars? Perhaps, as Bryce-Laporte stated, the conference was necessary to draw attention to, share opinions about, and provide a beginning basis for responsible and well-thought-out actions on a pressing issue of national and international importance.

And, the focus on the "new" immigration provides the grounds for my second question: What is the new immigration? The question was raised more than once during the seminar. I took a few minutes to discuss it with Dr. Bryce-Laporte, along with the question of what the question meant to the host institute. According to him, it basically refers to the immigration that is taking place after 1965, the date of the New Immigration Act.

My third question was asked concerning the paper by Dr. Eva Sandis, in which she pointed out some valid ideas about two approaches to the study or understanding of immigration: (1) providing a forum for the voices of the host society, and (2) eliciting input from intellectuals who share the same origins as the immigrant groups.

For me, these approaches are valid. But, where can one find an expression of the nature of the dreams, hopes, and fears of immigrants within the living context? There may be yet another position in addition to the two approaches suggested by Dr. Sandis. Perhaps the gap can be closed using what Professor Reyes Ramos proposed as ethnomethodology to provide a way to understand and make a proper interpretation of what the people feel and think, how they live, and how they perform during their daily lives. In this sense perhaps we, the academicians, are acting in pursuit of our own scientific curiosity instead of moving toward solving the real human problems behind the subjects of our studies. Or, maybe, we are only acting as holders of our own research gains, using immigration as a research topic.

My fourth question is what does assimilation mean? Most of the problems of adjustment for the new immigrants have to deal with the process of acculturation or assimilation. As a Dominican, I think of New York City as part of this process. What does assimilation mean for the immigrant coming to New York? Assimilation to what? Where is this ubiquity called American society and how can the immigrant identify and use it as a model?

I am not an immigrant. I am just a visitor to the United States and I have visited New York many times. But, for me, it is really difficult to identify a cluster of houses, or a group of people, that I can say are typical of American society. Imagine what the impression must be of the immigrant coming from the *aldea* (in the Dominican Republic) almost illiterate and with no knowledge of the English language. Standing in the New York airport and even walking around and finally working, he will never be able to identify the unit known as the American Society.

In *The Literature of the Social Sciences* published by our host institute, I did not find Glenn Hendricks' *Dominican Diaspora* in the bibliography; I did not find Professor Nancie Gonzalez's *Progress, Persons or Dominicans in New York;* and I did not find my own modest contribution about the brain drain from Latin America, and especially from the Dominican Republic, to the United States that was published by Notre Dame University.

For the Dominican Republic, this is an important immigration because New York represents the most important and higher source of employment whenever comparisons are made with the rate of employment in the Dominican Republic. There is no other common source of menial employment than New York. But for people coming from the *aldea* or from other places, theoretical discussions, discourses on the structure of the societies, or comparative studies about immigration don't matter. Nothing matters but survival. They come here because they want to participate in and use the symbols of productive consumption in the same way that we use them. Therefore, in order to change those aspirations, we have to change the very nature of the structure of the Dominican society. But, if we are concerned only with the extremes of the continuums of the studies of the social nature of immigration, we have to understand that people come to the United States for betterment, even if they must initially live in a shanty town. It is better according to their own definition.

The more important framework, in terms of understanding and affording less confusion during the seminar, is to take into account the fields that defined every session of the conference. For example, session one dealt with theoretical and methodological considerations. We Dominicans made only one contribution in that field, and that was in terms of Professor Glenn Hendricks' position about the implications of the methodological approach to the study of illegal Dominican migrants. We have no research works done in the Dominican Republic by Dominicans to make a contribution in that field. (My own experience has been working with Haitians coming into Santo Domingo. And, most of them are illegal but the situation is not quite the same.)

And as regards the second session on immigration and U.S. policy, Dominican people as migrants, or as representatives of our country or government, have no achievements to influence the immigration or political policies of the United States toward immigration of other groups in the Caribbean.

In the third session we have diplomatic and political implications of the new immigration. In the diplomatic field, no Dominican-related presentations were made. However, it is in the realm of political considerations that Dominicans are more actively involved. Most of the political parties of the Dominican Republic (especially the left wing) have outlets in New York. In uptown New York (around 155th Street), you find posters and other signs about political activities in the Dominican Republic. That there is more liberty and more freedom to pursue such activities points out the possibility that perhaps on the mind of many Dominican immigrants is the idea of constructing and building an ideal political community. They have the opportunity to talk and to hold public meetings that they do not have in their own country. And, they have the protection of the police.

Finally, I must point out that we send many professionals. And that is the note I want to end on. According to the 1962 study, one-third of the civil engineers graduating from the Dominican university came to the United States. And, in the last few years, we have been sending the entire graduating class. Thus, if it is really important to have international cooperation, we hope you Americans take into account that these students are coming from a very poor and a very little country.

Dawn I. Marshall, Barbados:

Comments on the wide variety of papers on migration that we have heard here during the past three days, if they are diffuse and wide-ranging, could easily have little impact. In attempting, therefore, to give some coherence to my remarks, I work on the assumption that a gathering of migration scholars such as this should give some indication of the current "state" of migration studies. Instead of attempting a critique of individual papers, therefore, I hope to assess the state of migration studies,

as revealed not only by the presentations, but also by remarks and reactions from the floor. Thus, the themes selected by me are not necessarily the principal points made by the speakers and may even be completely incidental to their main lines of argument. Using the framework of the organizers, I assumed that session one, "Theoretical and Methodological Considerations" would indicate the important current themes or strands in the study of migration; and then, in the following sessions, I tried to see to what extent these themes were reflected in the more empirical papers.

THEORETICAL AND METHODOLOGICAL CONSIDERATIONS

Among the six papers presented in session one, there seemed to me to be three key papers; key because they introduced themes which were to recur in most of the sessions which I attended, and which, therefore, seemed to represent the main concerns of migration scholars. The first of these was the paper by Elizabeth Petras: "Toward a Theory of International Migration: The New Division of Labor," which took a global or macro approach, was mainly economic in orientation, and saw international migration as one of the major consequences of the unequal division of the capitalist world into developed and underdeveloped nations—a perspective which is very acceptable ideologically today. The second paper was by Eva Sandis: "Alternative Intellectual Frameworks for Studying the New Immigration," and it commented on the movement by "new" intellectuals away from the traditional assimilation, receiving-society oriented migration studies to an approach which saw migration as a loss of human resources to the sending society. And, finally, the paper by Reyes Ramos: "A Preliminary Look at an Alternative Approach to the Study of Immigrants," which also represented a move away from the usual assimilation framework by pleading the case for ethnomethodology, and the elevation of the concerns of the individual migrant to the realm of formal methodology.

My interpretation of the climate in which these three papers were received is a decidedly personal and subjective interpretation, but I think it has some merit—if only because it is mine! The Petras paper was presented with an easy assurance and received with an enthusiastic acceptance which I think was not only due to the fact that the presenter herself seemed confident and assured, but which seemed also indicative of the status of that kind of approach in migration studies. Whereas, again given the personality factor, the Sandis paper was presented with an apologetic diffidence and received with a tolerant indifference. The Ramos paper, on the other hand, was presented aggressively and received with impatient rejection. I am suggesting here that both the manner in which the presentations were made, and the responses to them went beyond the inherent quality of the presentations themselves (I stress presentations since no papers were available to me), and that to a large extent both indicate the status which the particular approach holds in migration theory and methodology. I would even stretch the point a little further and suggest that the acceptance of the macroeconomic approach and the almost total rejection of the individual approach indicate a polarization of these two into an either/or situation.

One comment from the floor also represented a concern which was to recur in a number of other sessions: Professor Rex's comment on the need for sociological variables to be inserted into Petras' economic framework.

Session one, then, seemed to be saying that the macroeconomic approach, with emphasis on the economic, has developed to the stage where it has gained almost universal acceptance; nevertheless, there was a nagging feeling that economic factors alone are not adequate to explain the complex phenomenon of migration. The marked reluctance to accept the possibility that the concerns of the individual migrant could contribute anything to the development of the migration theory, which I noted in the literature over six years ago, not only still exists but has developed to the stage where scholars seem to think that any acceptance of the possibility represents a rejection of the macro approach. Whereas I think they represent two different levels or scales of inquiry: one chooses one or the other, or both, depending on the types of questions one is asking about a particular migration. Sandis' observation seemed to be saying that the time was com-

ing, or had come, when scholars from the periphery, often-representative of the migrants themselves, were about to make an input into the theory of migration. The reaction to Sandis' paper is more difficult to assess—perhaps it was indicative of a feeling that only the obvious was being stated; perhaps indicative of a feeling of uncertainty—what does one say to such an observation when the participation in the very conference at which the paper is being presented is evidence enough?

I am not going to try to detail or document my observations in the short time allowed me, but shall merely try to present them under the main themes already identified.

GLOBAL OR MACROECONOMIC APPROACH

The general acceptance of the economic approach was implicit in many of the presentations but it was accompanied by an almost as general recognition of the need for the incorporation of other factors into the basic framework; or as one speaker from the floor put it: "It's a mistake to gross things up." For example, the presentation by Demetrious Papademetriou argued that account had to be taken of the differential between the sending countries since they were at different stages along the development continuum; and this argument was reinforced by various comments and observations from the floor, such as that which pointed out that sending countries in an undeveloped state could not really accommodate the returning migrant, neither for the benefit of the individuals nor of the country.

Attention seemed to be given mainly to a cost-benefit analysis approach to the study of the impact of migration on sending countries. I do not deny this need, and it is understandable that this concern should emerge at a time when economic development is a major concern of most underdeveloped countries. The concern has to be more comprehensive, but I think that this was recognized by most participants, if the explosive remark made in session five is any indication: "It is just that economic thinking which has got us into this mess."

One of the possible consequences of the new emigration from the sending countries is what I call compensatory migration: the immigration into the underdeveloped country of professional, managerial, and technical personnel into decision-making positions, thus perpetuating dependency. Another consequence is the disintegration of the social fabric of the sending societies, illustrated, for instance, by the desertion of old people. The social impact of migration on the sending country has been completely neglected. Thus, session five, perhaps because of its specific focus on the development implication for the sending societies, illustrated the underdeveloped state of research on the impact of migration on the sending countries, in contrast to the well-developed state of assimilation studies.

ASSIMILATION ORIENTATION

The fact that most migration studies are assimilation oriented, or written from the point of view of the receiving society, did not receive much specific attention during the conference; and I think that this lack is indicative of the extent to which this orientation has been accepted, albeit unconsciously, in the study of migration. This is why I think Sandis' paper is so important. Again in session five, which, in retrospect, seems to have been a key session for me, Juan Diez-Canedo observed that migration is seen as a one-way process to such an extent that the return migrant is seen as a failed migrant (See Supplement.) I would have expected this orientation to have been diluted, or at least questioned, at a conference in which a large number of the participating scholars are themselves migrants. But migrant scholars seem to have tended to accept both the assimilation orientation as well as the basic economic approach.

Given my cynical nature, I question whether the current great concern with loss of human resources is connected only with the need for development; or whether it has also been caused by the fact that many of the new immigrants, at least from the Caribbean, are now "respectable" migrants. Little concern was expressed previously when most migrants came from the less privileged groups of the sending societies. Manuel Maldonado-Denis' presentation in session three received little attention from the floor, but to a Caribbeanist it is significant because

it expressed concern about a situation which was once common in the Caribbean, when governments encouraged emigration because it was perceived as a political and economic escape valve for the society. In fact, in the Barbadian Development Plan for 1965/68, the policy is explicitly stated of training for emigration by encouraging skills which were scarce or sought after in other, more developed countries.

The main effect of the long supremacy of the assimilation orientation was seen in session nine, and apparently also in the simultaneous session eight. Actual factual knowledge seemed greater, especially among the participants from the floor; the conceptual tools were much better developed, yet still being refined; there was less tendency for speakers to be emotive; and, in general, the entire session emanated an air of greater sophistication than was evident in any of the other sessions which I attended.

THE INDIVIDUAL

Despite the strong reaction to Ramos' paper in session one, it was clear in session nine that the individual migrant is very much an integral part of assimilation studies. It seemed to me, then, that there is a sort of dichtomy in the study of migration, with theoretical and methodological considerations being discussed mainly in the context of motivation and the causes of migration which, together with the impact on the sending society, have a strong economic bias. Whereas, the study of assimilation has a strong sociopsychological bias and, therefore, the individual migrant comes into his own.

A question from the floor in session five demonstrated the definite need for these noneconomic aspects to be incorporated into all migration studies: how do you measure the success of a migration? Does the objective of the migrant himself have no place in the assessment?

Let me end by expressing my great thanks to the RIIES and to Dr. Bryce-Laporte for inviting me, both to the conference and to give these remarks, and by stressing again that they are very much my personal reactions to the presentations and are, therefore, colored by my own view of migration and its study.

Gordon K. Lewis, Puerto Rico:

The panels of this meeting have divided themselves, ideologically, between papers that have interpreted the "new" immigration into the United States since 1965 in cultural and psychological terms, and those that have interpreted it, in terms of Marxist sociology, in structural terms. I am basically disposed to prefer the latter interpretation. Granted, the importance of studying the conflict situations between the traditional culture carried by the immigrant and the modernizing culture of the industrialised societies; granted too, the importance of analysing how the immigrant person copes, psychologically, with those situations; but it remains true that those aspects at best are derivative only. The fundamental question must relate to the structural forms of economic organization that make some societies "sending" societies and other societies "receiving" societies. The answer lies in the growing need of contemporary industrial capitalism to find a new reserve army of mobile and easily exploited labor to do the less attractive work disdained by its own native labor force. In that sense, the "new" immigration to the U.S. is part and parcel of the postwar influx of foreign labor imported from Africa, the Caribbean, and the southern Mediterranean by the Western European capitalist economies. We witness a new international class war. The new mobility of global labor is a necessary consequence of the new mobility of global capital. The multinational corporation is matched by the new international labor force.

Having said that, let it be noted that there is a distinct tendency on the part of the structuralist argument to oversimplify the situation. It tends to abstract everything into global terms. But industrial capitalism is not the same everywhere. It still retains its distinctive national forms. That is evident in the different welcome that awaits, say, the West Indian immigrant in Britain and the Latin American immigrant in the U.S. It is a difference best summed up, perhaps, in the observation of the Chicago Irish-American wit, Mr. Dooley, that the difference between American sports and English sports is that the Americans defeat you, and the English disqualify you. So, the immigrant in England is met with a series of subtle disqualification acts, social, cultural, and linguistic; the immigrant in America is met with an institutionalized crypto-racism. The English kill you with kindness: be nice to dogs, cats, and immigrants. The Americans kill you with benign neglect: once you are in you have to make it on your own in the urban jungle. The immigrant in England must deal with the special kind of English politics of compromise: which means that the Englishman is prepared to meet you half way if you are prepared to meet him all the way. The immigrant in America must learn to live, on the other hand, with a more open, no holds barred politics: the murderous interethnic struggle to control City Hall. The English social structure is still impregnated with snobbish class prejudice, so that the worst offense of the immigrant is to seek social ascendance: it just isn't done. The American social structure, although almost equally rigid, at least theoretically allows that everybody can rise by exercise of the Puritan virtues, so that, at times, it seems that the only people who still take the American Dream seriously are, indeed, the "new" immigrants—Cubans, Southeast Asians, Haitians, Dominicans, Mexicans, and Puerto Ricans. And to all these differences, finally, there must be added the signal difference that whereas postwar England has been a capitalism in decline, postwar America has been an expansionist capitalism, which explains why English immigrant legislation since 1962 has been increasingly restrictive while, by comparison, American immigrant legislation since 1965 has been increasingly liberal. All of these differences, in sum, make a real difference to the quality of the immigrant experience.

From the immigrant viewpoint, of course, these differences may appear academic. For, in both cases, he and she, are the victims of an exploitative system, however much better it may seem from life back home. That is why I would like to insist, as a further point, that the only way in which we, as academic observers, can fully understand that experience is to let the victims speak for themselves. I am not sure if all of us are not engaged in a vast, erudite conspiracy of condescension in which we see the immigrant as an object to be studied rather than a subject to be sympathetically understood. It is only occasionally that we produce studies like Oscar Lewis' *La Vida,* or Sidney Mintz's *Worker in the Cane,* that allow the victims to speak for themselves. It is true that Mintz's book is more concerned with internal migration in Puerto Rico, and that Lewis' book tends, typically, to mistake pornography for anthropology. Even so, they both have the virtue of seeing things from the right perspective, the view from the dunghill, as we say in the West Indies. For immigrants are not abstract categories. They are people, with all of their rich oddity and individuality. What I am saying can best be expressed, perhaps, by quoting a remark of the late Professor Alfred Zimmerman, speaking of the early beginnings of British sociology. "The difference," he said, "between the Webbs and Graham Wallas is that whereas the Webbs are interested in town councils Graham Wallas is interested in town counselors." The remark is still an apt one, for there is a sort of modern scholarship that sees slavery but not the slave, and sees immigration but not the immigrant. If, then, we are to see the immigrant experience in its totality, we have to learn to combine the rich documentary of the personal experience along with the equally necessary construction of theoretical categories that places the individual within the collective experience.

One final note on the phenomenon of the "new immigration" with reference to the Caribbean region. Strictly speaking, of course, this is no "new immigration" at all. For, the five hundred year history of the region has been the history of the vast cyclical movements of its folk peoples, first with the involuntary immigration of slavery and then with the semivoluntary immigration of Asiatic indentured servants after the abolition of slavery; then the twentieth century movement of emigrants from the islands back to the metropolitan economies, most notably since 1945 with the twin movement of West Indians to Britain, and of French and Spanish speaking emigrants to the U.S. The outcome of this historic process has been that in all Caribbean people there exists a sort of diffuse immigrant-emigrant mentality; in the sharp phrase of Eric Williams, "We are all a bunch of transients." But, by the same token, it is clear that the vast majority of these people on the move are economic refugees. They are seeking relief from the cancerous scourge of mass unemployment, still the characteristic feature of all the Caribbean economies, Cuba excepted. There will always be the immigrant who is a political refugee, of course; the latest example is the Cuban refugee groups (although I must add that, from my own socialist perspective, that group, in the light of the social values and attitudes it has carried with it, might just as well have emigrated on the *Titanic*). If this line of anlaysis is correct, it follows that the only real solution to the mass exodus of the Caribbean peoples is the effective organization of a new economic order that will guarantee full employment in the region. That, admittedly, is an order for the long run. But, until we set about it, we shall still see a continuing emigration from the islands, with all of its consequent heartache, tragedy, frustration, and homesickness, as evidenced in the literature that is coming out of the Puerto Rican experience in New York and the West Indian experience in London. For who, after all, in his right senses, would prefer to live in Wolverhampton rather than Jamaica, or Buffalo rather than Puerto Rico?

NOTES

1. Cf. W. R. Böhning, "Migration from Developing to High-income Countries," in ILO, *Tripartite World Conference on Employment, Income Distribution and Social Progress* and *The International Division of Labour, Background Papers, Vol II* (Geneva, 1976), pp.119–38; and N. Abadan-Unat, et al., *Migration and Development: A Study of the Effects of International Labour Migration in Bogazliyan District* (Ankara: Ajans-Türk Press, 1976).
2. See also my "Migration and Policy: A Rejoinder to Keith Griffin," in W. R. Böhning, *Basic Aspects of Migration from Poor to Rich Countries: Facts, Problems, Policies,* ILO World Employment Programme Research Working Papers (Geneva, July 1976).

APPENDIX B

THE NEW IMMIGRANTS AND THE PEOPLING OF THE U.S.A.: VARIOUS PERSPECTIVES

Elliot P. Skinner

I should like to view and discuss immigration not only in personal terms but also, as an anthropologist, in terms of a longer and more dynamic process.

The human species has been moving ever since man crossed the Homo sapiens line somewhere in southeast or northeast Africa. As Homo sapiens emerged, they moved into all sorts of niches; changing, with raciation taking place as the human species adapted to various ecological systems and in the process more and more complex state systems were developed.

As one looks at the world from the fifteenth century on, one is struck by the gonadal activity of the European subspecies of humanity. And, indeed, as one looks back over the past three centuries, over and above the strength of technology and efficiency of weapons, one might say that the expansion of Europe was, in fact, a demographic expansion. Wherever the Europeans have found empty space they have filled these spaces. And, wherever they have encountered large local populations, they were able to dominate these populations. But now they are being assimilated or extruded from these areas. The United States was founded by Europeans who, by and large, saw the New World as the site for their New Jerusalem: there are New Spains, New Frances, New Amsterdams, New Swedens. But, ironically, not a single European nation-state (whether the English, the French, the Portuguese, the Danes) felt they could settle or colonize this land without Africans. In the process, then, my ancestors were taken from the West African coast. They had the fortitude and strength to survive the Middle Passage, and ended up in Barbados. But, I was born in Trinidad.

From Barbados people came to these United States. A man by the name of Barbados played a very important role in Boston at the time of the revolution. Another man, Prince Hall, also came from Barbados and may have been related to my ancestors. He moved into Boston, fought with the British and later fought with the Americans. He founded a Masonic order that was finally legitimized by the Scots, thus providing one of the very interesting voluntary associations that relieve the lives of the Black population in Boston and other parts of the United States.

Like Prince Hall and Barbados, Blacks from almost every part of the New World, whether they originally went to Barbados, Nevis, Bermuda, Haiti, Surinam, even Brazil and Jamaica, ended up in the United States. So, as the United States was in the process of aggregating the tired and the poor from Europe to become the most cosmopolitan white nation in the entire world, the United States was also in the process of becoming the most important and the most cosmopolitan Black nation in the world. Thus, as one looks at immigration to the United States, one finds a country which has become the successor to Europe, for after all, through the Monroe Doctrine, we did bar the Europeans from further involving themselves in the history of this country. And, having aggregated all of these different people and using their skills, America became the foremost society in the entire world. This was a very dynamic process. The Europeans who came here, including de Tocqueville (despite his attitudes towards the barbarians he found here), saw within the United States a dynamic process, a process in which people, probably because of their provenience, possibly because of the environment from which they came, were able to work together. They were able to lose a certain sense of their uniqueness—profiting sometimes from the myth of the melting pot and the Horatio Alger myth. They used and lent their skills to create the society we find ourselves in today.

The early laws were quite permissive and people entered with none of the problems of illegal immigrants. However, as society became more prosperous and as new interest groups emerged, laws were passed. Laws were passed in the hope that such legislation would stop the flow of immigration. One wonders about this problem. Despite the laws, America has millions of illegal immigrants. And, notwithstanding the Exclusion Acts and hostility to various groups and races because of wars, more Asians have immigrated to the U.S. Because of the independence of many of the colonial territories, new patterns of immigration have been encouraged.

Now, one of the things that has struck me, as I roam around the world, is that I have always been part of a larger movement of people as a function of dynamic forces in the history of the world. Clandestine people come and they are not caught and it is not because America does not have the police force to catch these people, but because there are more fundamental forces at work in the world. We are in the process of creating a worldwide civilization with a fantastic movement of people. Europe is much more cosmopolitan today at the end of the Empire than it was at the height of the Empire. My fellow West Indians run the transport system of London. And, it is very difficult to find an English person serving in the hotels on the Strand; the Germans find themselves host to Turks; the Swiss have problems as to whether or not to turn back the Portuguese; the Turks are found in Austria. There is movement of population, sometimes irrespective of the volition of the governments and of the people concerned. In other words, there are sociological processes, economically-based for sure, and these processes have a way of overcoming the laws and the moves which groups periodically enact in order to preserve the status quo.

We have talked about people moving from the so-called Third World or undeveloped world into the First World or the Second World. But what is equally intriguing is the movement of people from the First World to the Third World. The French have discovered, to their amazement that there are more French in the Ivory Coast, in Senegal, and Gabon than ever before in the history of the French colonial system. In other words, there has been an exchange. We talk about the brain drain. People who were trained in the best schools (very often here in Washington or in New York, Massachusetts or California) now live here. (You may have seen recent articles such as in the *New York Times* about the voluntary exile of Nigerians.) They are part of a new group of people. Not quite the jet-set, but people with a certain kind of training. They come here. But how about the Americans? The Peace Corps volunteer we find when we go to Ouagadougou, Nouakchott, Dar es Salaam, and Banjul is American. Americans, then, are going to these areas. Americans have flooded the West Indies trying to find the sun and the sea. And my problem is that I cannot go back to the plot owned by my grandmother because I cannot afford it. It is being occupied by Americans. In other words, what I am suggesting here, then, is that immigration is a very complex process. It is becoming more complex because of the growth of technology as people move, can move, and are moving. So, as you feel frustrated because of laws which cannot stop the clandestine migrant, recognize that behind the inability to control migration might be fundamental processes of change as human beings now move, as human beings are being "englobed," if you wish, by a whole new set of ideas. They are trying to find the kind of life that suits them.

As part of the Skinner clan I know that part of the family was located in Barbados, it moved to Trinidad and, at one time, we despaired of finding any Skinners in Trinidad because they were all located in the Bedford-Stuyvesant area of Brooklyn, New York. Some Skinners left Bedford-Stuyvesant and are now found on the West Coast—Los Angeles and San Francisco—but the most fascinating odyssey of the Trinidad clan was the return to Trinidad. A different generation of Trinidadians had come to the United States, has been trained, but they are going back. And, they are doing something that might solve part of the problem of the United States. They are taking back

Afro-Americans as spouses. Thus, the process of immigration is dynamic and, possibly, uncontrollable. Look at it, think about it, reflect upon it. But, recognize that human beings have always moved. And, perhaps will continue to move.

Charles Keely

I would like to say a few words about United States immigration policy currently and about the particular problem which, probably more than any other, has caused immigration to come to the public consciousness and that is the whole question of clandestine immigration also known by the pejorative term illegal immigration. I will start with what I think is axiomatic; that is that the U.S. has no integrated immigration policy. In fact, what de facto policy we do have is really a reflection of legislation and administrative practice. We do not have a policy that is well thought out, that is integrated with labor needs, with clear foreign policy decisions, with a clear set of priorities about what immigration to do or not do. In fact, we have a patchwork of laws that have been put together over the years. Most recently, in October of this year, a new piece of legislation was signed by the President which will have a major impact.

So, in terms of the field of immigration, in terms of the question of U.S. immigration policy, what it has done, continues to do, and may do, I think the first thing to note is that we really have not decided as a country what we want immigration to do. And, we do not have policy or administration of a policy to meet a set of goals. I'll go further and say we're not even sure what priorities we have in terms of immigration. We have stated on various occasions that we want immigration to do certain things depending on the mood of the moment. We have in our legislation now efforts to help reunite families, to be a haven for refugees, to meet our labor needs (temporary and permanent), to avoid the brain drain.

We have all of this pending legislation, but we are really not sure what we want to do first. And, even within these particular goals, we are not very sure about how to go about it. For example, on the question of refugees we end up with a situation where many of the refugees we accept into this country come, not under our immigration law, but at the suffrance of the attorney general who permits them to enter on a temporary basis. Thus new legislation has to be passed with each new set of immigrant groups (the Hungarians, the Cubans, and probably the Indochinese) to allow them after a while to change to an immigrant or permanent resident status. Because, in fact, we allow them in under what we call a parolee status which is really an administrative limbo. One the one hand, we want to be a haven for refugees, but we have a definition in the law that is so restricted that most of the refugees in the world whom we want to welcome to this country cannot come in under our immigration legislation as refugees. Part of our difficulty in looking at and assessing the future of immigration in this country is that we really don't know what we want immigration to do. I think a major challenge ahead of us, as a country, is to decide what we want immigration to be. What do we want our policies to be, where do we want immigration to fit in the national population policy, in the manpower policy? What role should we have in foreign policy? What role should we have in our image of ourself as, in fact, of a land of immigrants and a haven for refugees? We have a major task in front of us to formulate a policy and then to make sure that it is administered according to the goals we set down.

I would like to switch to the question of the clandestine migration because that is the topic or the dilemma that has really made immigration in the U.S. a hot issue. I would say that at this point the U.S. has only gone as far on the question of clandestine migration as to have raised it to our consciousness.

We are aware that there are people in the U.S. without documents. We have not really addressed seriously what we *want* to do about that, what we *should* do about that, or why, in fact, the situation even exists. Our response to this point has been pretty much (at least on an official level) akin to what I would think of as a somewhat naive and ''knee jerk'' reaction of law enforcement. Sanctions for employers have been proposed, and border patrols can be beefed up. But, the problem is much deeper and much more serious than that. What we have to start doing is assessing what it is about the

U.S. that draws people without documents here. They don't come to the U.S. only because there are pressures in underdevelopment countries. However, I think much discussion has been addressed to the question of how rapidly populations in developing countries (particularly to the south of the U.S.) are growing, what the potential for future growth is, what the problem of unemployment rates will be in the very near future. What all of that means is pressure on the U.S. from this population tide, this wave, this deluge and other sorts of pejorative terms that are used as metaphors that describe these people as enemies or threats—as if persons in countries in our hemisphere are a threat to us—not because of bombs, but because of babies. That is a naive approach. If it was purely push factors, then the U.S. would have many more people coming to it, both legally and clandestinely. If it is merely push factors it would seem to me that many more people would be taking much more drastic steps of cutting themselves off from home, from family, from familiar culture to come into a different culture and in an very ambiguous statement leaving themselves open daily to harrassment and to possible arrest and de facto deportation.

The other aspect of the equation we have to look at besides the push factors is what is it about the structure of the U.S. that still demands cheap labor, that still has to tap reserve industrial armies. Persons who, in fact, at this point, are not part of our population. They are not the Black population, and are not the previous legal immigrants who built the subways in New York, or who built the canals and the railroads that link this country. We now have to look for cheap labor and we have to look abroad for it. The question is, does our economy have to be structured this way and, if not, what can we do to change it, so that we do not draw people? It is not the push, it is not the pressure that is the real problem in terms of clandestine migration. It is that the United States demands, the United States wants, the United States uses, the United State benefits from the cheap labor. We benefit from it when we eat vegetables from our table, when we go to restaurants, when we go to hospitals, and in many other areas. I will say that on the whole question of clandestine migration we are at this point in terms of policy, discussion

and development only at the beginning. We have admitted to ourselves that there is a problem and we have admitted to ourselves that we are part of the problem. Our legislation or past administrative practices as well as the structure of our economy are important contributors not only to the clandestine migration, but also to the population developments in the countries that send clandestine migrants to our shores.

So we are indeed on the brink of the future in terms of our next century and perhaps this conference will contribute to our discussion about what we want immigration to do, and what we will do about the short-term problems that we face that seem to loom so large before us now. But, perhaps, this may be a passing phase in our immigration history and the building the peopling of this country.

Elsa Chaney

This presentation was basically an oral discussion for the public audience of the material presented in her "Columbians in New York City: Theoretical and Policy Issues." For a full transcription of her oral presentation, see Supplement.

Mohamed A. El-Khawas

Political refugees are a special type of immigrant. Departure from their home country is usually abrupt and their entry into a new country is often a matter of no other choices being available. Advance planning may be impossible for the refugees themselves and, significantly, may be impossible for the host country as well. A governmental decision to admit political refugees can be seen as an ad hoc measure, made on humanitarian grounds in the midst of an international emergency of some kind.

In the limited time I have available today, I would like to add a note of political realism to this generalized description of refugee situations, and to remind us of the often considerable extent to which political considerations influence a country's action toward refugees. The decision to grant political asylum is ''. . . a privilege conferred by the state . . .'' More often than we realize, the fate of people seeking asylum is left in the hands of individual governments who are influenced primarily by domestic or foreign policy considerations in determining whether or not to grant asylum. The recent history of the United States will provide my example, but the general point applies to other countries as well.

The United States is known as a "nation of immigrants" and as a "melting pot" in which peoples of different nationalities and ethnic backgrounds come together to live in one country. As we are all aware, this image of the U.S. as a potential "haven" for oppressed people has been severely limited in practice—particularly since the 1920s—by the restrictive immigration laws maintained by an isolationist U.S. foreign policy. In fact, it may be surprising to recall that, up until the early 1950s, there was no distinction made between the alien immigrant and the refugee seeking asylum. Up until that time, consequently, prospective refugees from certain countries for which there were tightly restrictive quotas encountered barriers more than they found assistance from the U.S.

The first special distinction made for refugees seeking political asylum was introduced only in the 1950s, beginning with the 1953 Refugee Relief Act, a measure which gave limited relief to "refugees, escapees, expellees, or displaced persons" in an international emergency. This special preference, which was made to relax the normal limitations and requirements for admission, developed out of the post-war concern of the United States to respond to new international events caused by the sudden expansion of Communist-controlled areas.

In the post-war period. U.S. foreign policy interests substantially influenced the adoption of this new policy. As the 1953 Report of the President's Commission on Immigration and Naturalization stated, "American immigration policy and law must be formulated in awareness of their international impact and must be designed to advance our policy." It also recommended that the national-origins quota system be replaced by a unified annual quota system (based on one-sixth of one percent of the total U.S. population). As the Commission argued, "in order to advance our national interests . . . American immigration policy should be free from discrimination on the basis of nationality,

race, creed, or color and shall be flexible enough to permit the U.S. to engage fully in such special migration efforts as may be important to the security of the free world."

This view, reflecting the cold-war anti-Communist atmosphere that continued throughout the 1950s, was echoed again in the 1957 message to Congress given by President Eisenhower, in which he stated: ". . . our position of world leadership demands that . . . we (must) be in a position to grant asylum . . ." to Hungarians who had fled their homes ". . . to escape Communist oppression."

Throughout the 1950s and 1960s, the admission of refugees continued to be heavily influenced by such political and ideological—specifically, anti-Communist—motivations. During these two decades, the U.S. has admitted hundreds of thousands of political refugees from Hungary, Cuba, Vietnam, and Cambodia who have fled their countries to avoid living under Communism. As a leader of the democratic world, the U.S. has felt an obligation to make special arrangements to admit thousands of refugees during a number of international crises.

The most recent and dramatic example is the flow of refugees from Indochina following the Communist take-over in South Vietnam and Cambodia. Once again, the U.S. undertook extraordinary initiatives to receive refugees fleeing from the likelihood of living under Communist domination. In 1975, the U.S. Congress approved the Indochina Migration and Refugee Assistance Act, which appropriated $405 million to cover the cost of resettling 140,000 refugees in the United States. An Interagency Task Force was established to coordinate all government activities concerning evacuation, reception, and resettlement of the refugees. It was decided that such resettlement should be made by national voluntary agencies or by state or local governments and that the refugees should have sponsors to provide them with shelter, food, and assistance in locating employment. As part of the resettlement strategy, efforts were designed to encourage the refugees to become self-sufficient economically with the assistance of their sponsors.

The Indochinese refugees will encounter many problems while settling into the American environment, despite these special actions of the U.S. government to aid their resettlement. Like other refugee groups, they face cultural and language barriers; although many had college degrees and good jobs back in Vietnam, they have often had to settle for low-status initial jobs. As with other groups, the process of assimilation will be slow, aided by the personal bonds of family and friends.

These problems are not unique to the Indochinese refugees. They are shared by other ethnic groups who have been admitted to the United States in large numbers as a result of political upheavals. The Vietnamese refugees share, too, the special status of being political refugees, welcome in part because they did not wish to live under Communism.

Some observers would argue that U.S. Foreign policy today has matured beyond the confines of an East-West bipolar mentality. Whether this is true and could provide a broader basis for U.S. policy toward peoples seeking political asylum has not yet been sufficiently tested. In the coming decade, we can expect several parts of the world—particularly southern Africa—will experience political disruption that will provide that test.

However, the thesis that political considerations are an important basis for granting asylum to refugees is, in fact, given support by the recent actions of several African nations as they themselves have selectively admitted refugees from neighboring countries along lines of political compatibility. It may just be that the realist view is correct, that a nation's self-interests will powerfully influence its policy toward political asylum.

Frank Bonilla

These remarks are based on a collective research effort going on at the Centro de Estudios Puertorriqueños at City University of New York. A fuller statement of the present status of this work appears in *Latin American Perspectives* (Vol. III, No. 3, 1976), a journal published at the Riverside campus of the University of California. We start from a general set of premises that have been stated by Ricardo Campos and several others.

1. Direct investment and migration are contemporary modes for the absorption and expulsion of labor reserves from colonized and peripheral areas into metropolitan work forces. Migration may thus be viewed as a criss-crossing movement, often circular and repetitive, of workers in search of low cost labor. In this sense migration has been a pervasive force in the formation, dismantling, and rearrangement of human aggregates in the course of industrialization for more than a hundred years. In broadest terms, then, migration research seeks to clarify ways in which national and class formations are molded, wrenched apart, reassembled, and reproduced by these complex flows of peoples and capitals.

2. The duration and amplitude of the Puerto Rican migration lend a certain transparency to the pertinent movements and their effects on the economy, class structure, and political organization in Puerto Rico and the United States, bringing out possible implications for other countries in which migrations directed toward metropolitan centers are now occurring. There are, nevertheless, great difficulties conceptually and in terms of information to be overcome in forming an integral perspective on this and other migrations. Only recently, for example, has the situation of Puerto Ricans in the U.S. surfaced as a concern at the national level, and it will be much longer before the necessary data on this movement are gathered with sufficient detail and regularity to support the formulation of a viable political economy of migration.

3. Puerto Rico has the particularity of providing migrant settlers, a fluid work force in constant circulation within what is in effect a single labor market, and short-term contract workers to the U.S. This prolonged and massive transfer of people has not only radically altered Puerto Rican society but is having important impact on the work force and social structure of an increasing number of U.S. communities, generating in the process contradictions that project themselves to the national and international level. As migration has become a way of life (we now have, in addition to the above migrant types, commuters as well as persons whose residence is as unstable as their jobs), a complex set of dialectical tensions come visibly into play.

a. On the one hand there is an accenting of differences among Puerto Ricans as the experience of life in non-island settings becomes more diverse and prolonged. At the same time there is an intensification of relations among Puerto Ricans, wherever they are situated, through continuing migration to the U.S., return migration to Puerto Rico, and the accelerating process of dispersal in the U.S., as well as circulation among all these communities. This dialectic of separation and return, differentiation and convergence, rupture and renewal of ties lies at the heart of what is now being discussed among Puerto Ricans as "the national question."

b. At another level the advanced state of integration of the Island and mainland economies reproduces on the Island the class relationships and state apparatus of the dominant, U.S. social formation. Reciprocally, migration reproduces in the U.S. the colonial relationships prevailing on the Island. As a U.S. Commission on Civil Rights report puts it, "It might be said that much of the indifference and insensitivity characterizing United States-Puerto Rico relations has carried over into the relations between the majority group and Puerto Ricans on the mainland." It is important that the report bases this conclusion on an objective assessment of the labor force placement and experience of Puerto Ricans in the U.S.

PUERTO RICANS IN THE UNITED STATES: AN UNCERTAIN FUTURE

1. The reproduction of those colonial contradictions within the U.S. has several implications. On the one hand there are visible cleavages among U.S. hegemonic sectors with respect to the handling of these contradictions and allocating the costs of maintaining these ties for those who profit most directly from them. This can be seen in the instances of the current negotiations of a "new compact" between Puerto Rico and the U.S. and also in some aspects of New York City's fiscal crisis.

2. At the same time, the direct experience within the U.S. of those contradictions brings home in concrete ways for new generations of Puerto Ricans (many of whom have never lived on the Island), the nature of those colonial relations, their economic base, racist content, and persistence over time.

3. As migration to the U.S. continues and diversifies to include a broadening spectrum of colonized peoples, the metropolis introjects and multiplies internally the concrete expressions of formerly external colonial ties and practices. The full gamut of Caribbean and South American expressions of these contradictions as being reconstructed side by side in the U.S. northeast at this time, with political and other consequences that are still hard to assess.

4. A review of the changing patterns and tendencies in migration flows and the occupational configuration of Puerto Ricans in the U.S. reveals long term stagnation and regressiveness in their condition despite a certain amount of occupational diversification, incursions into new areas of employment, and slight but unstable gains in income. This situation has been confirmed by several governmental studies, most recently in the U.S. Commission on Civil Rights report already cited. Thus, work force changes among Puerto Ricans in the U.S. over the last twenty years reflect a diversification of the working class rather than a significant or well consolidated movement into middle sectors. Labor force dynamics reconstruct and perpetuate within the U.S. the migrant's original situation as part of an exploited class and dominated national grouping. There is more persuasive evidence of social deterioration and institutional and individual breakdown through protracted non-use or under-use of people's productive capabilities than of successful assimilation or social mobility.

5. Over the years there have been major readjustments of the political superstructure in Puerto Rico to meet the changing requirement on economic relations with the U.S. Those economic relationships are now more important

than ever to the United States in terms of the magnitude of investment, installed productive capacity, the size of the consumer market profitability, and strategic considerations of long term economic goals in the region and beyond. The status question, which for policy-makers in Puerto Rico and the U.S. reduces to working out the political forms most approrpiate for the advancing economic fusion with the U.S. now in progress, thus becomes as much an internal U.S. issue as an issue in the international sphere. It is no longer likely to be resolved without a major shake-up within the United States itself.

The question of an appropriate superstructure for the Puerto Ricans in the U.S. has not fully emerged as an issue though the community itself has over the years improvised and maintained a variety of organized bases for competition, self-defense, and resistance. This network of ethnic organizations differs from all others in having evolved with the question of PR's unresolved political status as a permanent backdrop. The persistence and renewal in the U.S. setting of colonial practices and relations seems certain to continue to provoke among PR's and others, separatist and corporativist claims difficult to reconcile with the constituted principles and ideology of U.S. federalisms with its assimilationist goals. Ideological and institutional adjustments to these claims in the name of newly defined pluralism can only partially allay these tensions. Some of these tensions, of course, surfaced in the 1960s in the course of the civil rights and anti-war struggles. There is no doubt in my mind that among PR's as a people, a much more informed view and scientifically grounded understanding of our situation exists today than did at that time, I am also sure that we have not been alone in learning.

APPENDIX C

BACKGROUND COMMENTARY[1]

Delores M. Mortimer

"The American Experience" was chosen by the Smithsonian Institution as the theme for its observance of the Bicentennial of the American Revolution. With that in mind, the Office of the Bicentennial Coordinator was established to monitor a number of federally funded projects dealing with the historic peopling of the United States. The one project directed toward examining contemporary, ongoing immigration to this country was carried out by the Research Institute on Immigration and Ethnic Studies. Despite rather limited time, resources, and personnel made available to it, RIIES sought to organize the country's first major national conference on recent immigration into the United States. In so doing it was necessary to engage the assistance of other sections of the Smithsonian Institution and obtain modest financial support from private sources (see Appendix E). Therefore, this publication and the event which it represents are a culmination in the sense that they are the visible capstones to the involvement of the RIIES in Bicentennial related activities.

The RIIES sponsored conference on "The New Immigration: Implications for the United States and the International Community" was held in Washington, D.C., November 15–17, 1976. In combination with its other completed and projected activities, the conference and publication reflect the concern and involvement of RIIES with the study of social phenomena which are not usually within the purview of more conventionally oriented sections of the Smithsonian Institution. Some of the success of the Research Institute in staving off a myopic, regionally insular, and otherwise limited perspective on immigration is due to the counsel and involvement of a wide selection of professionals who agreed to serve, on an ad hoc basis, as advisors, and to the experience gained in carrying out a number of

small preparatory seminars and other ancillary activities in key regions of the U.S.

The small preparatory seminars were titled "Ethnicity, the American Ethos and the New Immigration: Theories and Observations" (held at the Woodrow Wilson International Center for Scholars, Smithsonian Institution, Washington, D.C., on November 7, 1975), and "International Migration as a Policy Issue: The Western Hemisphere" (held at the International Studies Association Convention, Toronto, Canada, February 25–29, 1976). Following its major conference, RIIES sponsored a third small seminar entitled "Evaluating the Asian-American Experience: Themes and Images" as part of the Smithsonian Institution's Sixth International Symposium, "Kin and Communities: The Peopling of America," in Washington, D.C., June 14–17, 1977. The symposium was the Institution's final gesture in observance of the Bicentennial of the American Revolution.

Additionally, the professional staff of the RIIES engaged in site visits or held intensive local workshops in various leading ports of entry of this country, including the Caribbean islands of Puerto Rico and St. Thomas. In some cases the Research Institute also conducted or sponsored short exploratory field studies of special categories of immigrants in these locations, that is, Indochinese refugees and migrant workers in California, alien labor in the Virgin Islands, and so forth. The first workshop held in Washington, D.C., was really a planning activity, and served to lay out the patterns to be followed thereafter. Its participants, though of limited number, represented a wide but pertinent array—policy makers and researchers from government, private consultants, academic scholars and researchers, and delegates from key foreign embassies and international agencies. All these various levels of activities enabled the Institute to establish its ongoing publication series in the areas of bibliographic studies, field research, and methodology, as well as occasional thematic papers (see Appendix E). In addition, the Institute organized and edited a special issue of *Society Magazine,* September/October 1977, entitled "The New Immigrant Wave," which consisted largely of selected papers from the conference as well as contributions of fellows and colleagues in the field.

It was with the cooperation of advisory committee members, and as a result of these preliminary activities, that the RIIES staff was able to design the conference, select themes, organize sessions, and identify participants with expertise on the following issues:

(1) background history of U.S. immigration and related international social movements and the methodology of their study;

(2) conditions, causes, and motives precipitating and determining the characteristics and nature of the "new" movement;

(3) conditions and cultures existing in the source countries;

(4) consequences that flow from linkages maintained by new immigrants with their countries of origin;

(5) implications and problems of economics, governance, and professional or public service that arise as a consequence of new immigration to the U.S. and other host countries;

(6) effects of new immigrants and future citizens upon the racial-ethnic composition of the U.S.;

(7) projections for the future of U.S. society, and development of strategies to anticipate and effectively deal with cultural and institutional change;

(8) implications of the new immigration for U.S. foreign policy, international relations, and their linkages with domestic policy and ethnic politics; and

(9) new directions for the pursuit of research and data preparation, and interdisciplinary international cooperation among students of immigration and its concomittant subject areas.

These were some of the concerns addressed as we

worked toward structuring the conference. And the complexity of issues, coupled with the dynamism of our society, called for incorporation of variety in the final configuration of the conference. Therefore, the conference was ultimately organized to feature a broader range of participants than the traditionally select cluster of U.S.–domestic special interest groups, government consultants, and policy makers. Instead, we tried to provide a fertile atmosphere in which representatives of those three important sectors could interact and exchange ideas and findings with academic specialists on international migration, experts in the field of international studies, and individuals knowledgeable about population planning, demography, and development issues as they pertain to population movement.

Attendance at the conference was largely by invitation and numbered approximately three hundred persons. These included representatives of government, funding foundations, press and public media, publication houses, local and foreign based scholars or researchers and other interested professionals, some special interest and ethnic groups, local students and fellows of the Institute, and the lay public of whom many were Smithsonian Associates (see Supplement).

Without diverging from the substance of the overall theme of the conference, and to encourage interchange, allow choice, and provide opportunity for acquaintance among peers, the program was divided into four pairs of sessions. Each pair was held simultaneously. Additionally, two public panel discussions and a reception were held (see Supplement). The presentations found in the body of the work were largely invited or submitted papers, while the public panels were largely commentaries based in part on observations made at the conference. Additionally, the prepared presentations in each session were buttressed by critical commentaries offered by the presider, discussants, rapporteurs, and audience, of course. The purpose of these arrangements was to assure exposure of a rather ample range and variety of learned opinions or grounded reports on the subject of the new immigration.

So, although the conference was, in general, limited to immigration to the continental United States from the period of 1965 onwards, the program accommodated historical statements as well as comparative discussions of immigration to Europe, Japan, and other geographic areas. It also included foreign migration into and its impact upon the extraterritorial jurisdictions of the United States in the Caribbean: Puerto Rico and the U.S. Virgin Islands.

We very much hope that this volume reflects not only the wealth of ideas expressed and extent of interchange accomplished during the conference, but also that it provides a sense of the complexity of the phenomenon of immigration as process and issue.

Unfortunately, two conference events have received no treatment or representation in this volume beyond our photographic collection (see Appendix F). At this point in our technological development, however, we cannot yet inexpensively mix certain media in our publication. Consequently, certain forms of expression and certain distinctive experiences are lost. It is unfortunate that we are unable to reproduce the marvelous performance-lecture on the steel "piano" (commonly called the steel drum) by Victor Brady of the U.S. Virgin Islands. Neither can we rerun the very informative and exciting bilingual, English-Cantonese film, "From Spikes to Spindles: A History of the Chinese in New York," by Christine Choy of Third World Newsreel. Each activity in its own way provided added dimensions and insight into the realities of the new immigration to the United States: the first was a marvelous display of musical virtuosity, technological innovation, and cultural exportation from the West Indies; the second, a vivid testimony against the commonly held stereotype of oriental complacency, and an insider's explanation of the growing unrest and political activism in Chinatown communities throughout the U.S.

Ignored for a number of years by social scientists, journalists, and public officials, the new immigration has now become a salient public issue in the United States. More news stories, opinionated editorials, public campaigns, research projects, and proposals for public action can be expected to focus on this issue. As these take place we hope that the papers and discussions of this conference will be remembered and consulted for both their contents and their messages. There is substantial need for accurate historical, comparative, and multidisciplinary examinations of the new immigrants, without a contrived emphasis on the so-called clandestine or undocumented immigrants as an isolated issue. One hope of the organizers of the conference, therefore, was to increase awareness to such matters and provide a corrective to the effects of slanted reports which, while disseminated as "objective," are purposefully intended to sway public opinion rather than truly aid in the understanding of what is happening in the United States today. Additionally, the existence of new as well as resurgent social tensions make it imperative for all who live in this country to know more about not only who and how many immigrants enter, but also why they come, what we as a society do to induce the desire to come, and what possible effects the immigrant and citizen communities have upon one another after the immigrants arrive.

Clearly, it was impossible to address as fully as we would have wished all of the important issues affecting our country and the world today. But, we hope that through the cumulative effect of the Research Institute's Bicentennial activities we have contributed to the field of inquiry, and have identified a body of people from widely divergent professional, personal, or political backgrounds who have valuable contributions to make in terms of future dealings with the ramifications of international human migration.

NOTE

1. The author wishes to acknowledge the assistance of her colleagues in the final preparation of this statement, especially R. S. Bryce-Laporte.

CONTRIBUTORS

Franklin Abrams, attorney, Abrams & Abrams, New York City

Lorna Rhodes AmaraSingham, Harvard Medical School

B. William Austin, University of the District of Columbia

Robert L. Bach, Duke University

W.R. Böhning, International Labour Office, Geneva, Switzerland

Edna Bonacich, University of California, Riverside

Frank Bonilla, City University of New York

Aubrey W. Bonnet, Hunter College, City University of New York

Christina Brinkley-Carter, Princeton University

Roy Simón Bryce-Laporte, Research Sociologist and Director, Research Institute on Immigration and Ethnic Studies, Smithsonian Institution

Jorge A. Bustamente, El Colegio de Mexico

Ricardo Campos, Center for Puerto Rican Studies, City University of New York

Phillip Carey, University of Massachusetts

Elsa M. Chaney, Fordham University

Wayne A. Cornelius, Massachusetts Institute of Technology

Stephen R. Couch, Social Science Analyst, Research Institute on Immigration and Ethnic Studies, Smithsonian Institution

Theodore A. Couloumbis, American University

Carmenines Cruz, Corporación Centro Regional de Población, Colombia

Reynaldo A. Cué, Duke University

George A. DeVos, University of California, Berkeley

Mohamed A. El-Khawas, The Federal City College

E. Aracelis Francis, government of the U.S. Virgin Islands

William A. Glaser, Columbia University

Glenn L. Hendricks, University of Minnesota

Frank Hernandez, Instituto de Estudios Aplicado, Santo Domingo, Dominican Republic

Sallie Hicks, American University

John Hucker, government of Canada

Won Moo Hurh, Western Illinois University

Simon Jones-Hendrickson, College of the Virgin Islands

Charles Keely, Fordham University

Hei Chu Kim, Western Illinois University

Kwang Chung Kim, Western Illinois University

Shirley Kolack, University of Lowell, Massachusetts

Gordon K. Lewis, University of Puerto Rico, Río Piedras

Ivan Light, University of California, Los Angeles

Manuel Maldonado-Denis, University of Puerto Rico, Río Piedras

Alemayehu G. Mariam, University of Minnesota

Dawn I. Marshall, Institute for Social and Economic Research, University of the West Indies, Cave Hill Campus, Barbados

Paul Meadows, State University of New York, Albany

Lois Monteiro, Brown University

Dolores Mortimer, Social Science Analyst, Research Institute on Immigration and Ethnic Studies, Smithsonian Institution

Murali Nair, Marywood College

Luis Nieves-Falcón, University of Puerto Rico

Demetrious Papademetriou, West Virginia Wesleyan College

Bradley W. Parlin, Utah State University

Elizabeth McLean Petras, State University of New York, Binghamton

Antonio J.A. Pido, Bradley University

Michael J. Piore, Massachusetts Institute of Technology

Reyes Ramos, University of California at San Diego

Francois Raveau, Centre Charles Richet d'étude des dysfonctions de l'adaptation (CREDA), Paris, France

John A. Rex, University of Warwick, Coventry, England

Anthony H. Richmond, York University

Julius Rivera, University of Texas at El Paso

Eva E. Sandis, Fordham University

Parmatma Saran, Baruch College, City University of New York

Elliot P. Skinner, Columbia University

George J. Stolnitz, Population Division, United Nations

Betty Lee Sung, City University of New York

Frank Wen-hui Tsai, Indiana University, Fort Wayne

Robert Warren, U.S. Bureau of the Census

Charles Choy Wong, University of California, Riverside

Walter P. Zenner, State University of New York, Albany

NAME INDEX*

SUBJECT INDEX*